MICROCOMPUTER SYSTEMS MANAGEMENT AND APPLICATIONS

Other fine titles available from boyd & fraser

Introduction to Computers and Microcomputer Applications
Microcomputer Applications: Using Small Systems Software, Second Edition
Microcomputer Productivity Tools
Microcomputer Applications: A Practical Approach
Microcomputer Systems Management and Applications
Mastering Lotus 1-2-3®
Using Enable®: An Introduction to Integrated Software
PC-DOS®/MS-DOS® Simplified

Computer Information Systems

Database Systems: Management and Design
Microcomputer Database Management Using dBASE III PLUS®
Microcomputer Database Management Using R:BASE System V®
dBASE III PLUS® Programming
A Guide to SQL
Applications Software Programming with Fourth-Generation Languages
Fundamentals of Systems Analysis with Application Design
Office Automation: An Information Systems Approach
Data Communications for Business
Learning Computer Programming: Structured Logic Algorithms, and Flowcharting
COBOL: Structured Programming Techniques for Solving Problems
Comprehensive Structured COBOL
Fundamentals of Structured COBOL
Advanced Structured COBOL: Batch and Interactive
BASIC Fundamentals and Style
Structured BASIC Fundamentals and Style for the IBM® PC and Compatibles
Applesoft BASIC Fundamentals and Style
Complete BASIC for the Short Course
Structuring Programs in Microsoft BASIC

Shelly and Cashman Titles

Computer Concepts with Microcomputer Applications (Lotus 1-2-3®
  and VP-Planner Plus® versions)
Computer Concepts
Learning to Use WordPerfect®, Lotus 1-2-3®, and dBASE III PLUS®
Learning to Use WordPerfect®, VP-Planner Plus®, and dBASE III PLUS®
Learning to Use WordPerfect®
Learning to Use Lotus 1-2-3®
Learning to Use VP-Planner Plus®
Learning to Use dBASE III PLUS®
Computer Fundamentals with Application Software
Learning to Use SuperCalc®3, dBASE III®, and WordStar® 3.3: An Introduction
Learning to Use SuperCalc®3: An Introduction
Learning to Use dBASE III®: An Introduction
Learning to Use WordStar® 3.3: An Introduction
BASIC Programming for the IBM Personal Computer
Structured COBOL: Pseudocode Edition
Structured COBOL: Flowchart Edition

MICROCOMPUTER SYSTEMS MANAGEMENT AND APPLICATIONS

MEHDI KHOSROWPOUR
The Pennsylvania State University
at Harrisburg

COPYRIGHT 1990
BOYD & FRASER PUBLISHING COMPANY
BOSTON

CREDITS

Publisher: Tom Walker
Editor: Sarah Grover
Production Editor: Donna Villanucci
Director of Production: Becky Herrington
Director of Manufacturing: Dean Sherman
Cover Design: Ken Russo/**Book Design:** Becky Herrington
Cover Photography: H. Armstrong Roberts, Inc.
Text Illustration: Tom Schenden
Typesetting: Huntington & Black Typography

REGISTERED TRADEMARKS

Apple®, ProDos®, and Apple DOS® are registered trademarks of Apple Computer, Inc.
CP/M® and CP/M-86® are registered trademarks of Digital Research Corporation
DataEase® is a registered trademark of Software Solutions, Inc.
dBASE®, and Framework® are registered trademarks of Ashton-Tate Corporation
Enable® is a registered trademark of The Software Group
Ethernet® is a registered trademark of Intel Corporation, Digital Equipment Corporation, and Xerox Corporation
Fontrix/Printrix® is a registered trademark of Data Transforms
Harvard Graphics® is a registered trademark of Software Publishing Corporation
IBM®, IBM-PC®, PC-DOS®, Xenix®, IBM-PC Network®, and Display Write® are registered trademarks of International Business Machines Corporation
Lasersoft® is a registered trademark of Business Systems, Int'l
Lotus 1-2-3® is a registered trademark of Lotus Development Corporation
Macintosh® is a trademark licensed to Apple Computer, Inc.
MicroSoft Word®, Multiplan®, MS-DOS®, OS/2®, and Micro Graphics are registered trademarks of Microsoft Corporation
Open Access® is a registered trademark of Software Products
Pagemaker® is a registered trademark of Aldus Corporation
Page Perfect® is a registered trademark of IMSI
Powerform® is a registered trademark of The 'Puter Group
R:BASE® is a registered trademark of Microrim, Inc.
Smart Software System is a registered trademark of Innovative Software, Inc.
Starlan® is a registered trademark of AT&T
SuperCalc® is a registered trademark of Computer Associates International, Inc.
The Newsroom® is a registered trademark of Springboard Software
TRS-80® is a registered trademark of Tandy Corporation
Unix® is a registered trademark of Bell Laboratories
Ventura Publisher® is a registered trademark of Xerox Corproation
Visicalc® is a registered trademark of Visicalc Corporation
VP-Planner® is a registered trademark of Paperback Software, Inc.
WordPerfect® is a registered trademark of WordPerfect Corporation
WordStar® is a registered trademark of MicroPro International Corporation

© 1990 by Boyd & Fraser Publishing Company

All rights reserved. No part of this work may be reproduced or used in any form or by any means—graphic, electronic, or mechanical, including photocopying, recording, taping, or information and retrieval system—without written permission from the publisher.

Manufactured in the United States of America

Library of Congress Cataloging-in-Publication Data

```
Khosrowpour, Mehdi, 1951-
   Microcomputer systems management and applications.

   Includes bibliographies and index.
   1. Microcomputers.  2. PC DOS (Computer operating
system)  3. WordPerfect (Computer program)  4. Lotus
1-2-3 (Computer program)  5. dBASE III PLUS
(Computer program)  I. Title.
QA76.5.K46   1988      005.36             88-19244
ISBN 0-87835-330-5
```

10 9 8 7 6 5 4 3 2 1

Dedication

To my parents and my wife, Rachel, for all their love.

About the Limited-Use Version of WordPerfect 4.2

The Limited-Use introductory version of WordPerfect 4.2 (L-WP) is intended to allow one to learn the features of WordPerfect 4.2; however, the L-WP is not intended to allow one to print usable academic or professional documents[1].

Certain limitations (which should not deter learning WordPerfect through the L-WP) have been encrypted into the L-WP to guard against productive use, and are as follows:

I. One may work with as large a document on screen as desired, but one may only save to a disk a data file no larger than 50,000k (approximately 25–30 regular pages).

   1. A data file created with the L-WP cannot be imported into regular WordPerfect, nor can a file created in regular WordPerfect be imported into L-WP.

II. Data files of any size may be printed through parallel printer port "1" without defining a printer, but font changes and extended ASCII characters are not allowed. Also, "*WPC" will be printed after each paragraph.

III. One will be able to learn all the functions of WordPerfect 4.2's speller and thesaurus by calling up the "readme.wp" file and following the step-by-step directions; however, one cannot use the L-WP speller and thesaurus with any of one's own documents because there are only a limited number of words in the L-WP speller and thesaurus. (The regular speller has 115,000 words, and the regular thesaurus has approximately 150,000 words.)

IV. The help file of L-WP allows the user to retrieve the function-key template, but similar to the speller and the thesaurus described above, space will not allow the full help files on the L-WP disk.

L-WP is designed to be used for introductory word processing courses, and thus far has been well received in these types of environments. Notwithstanding the broad abilities provided in the L-WP, presumably the L-WP will not satisfactorily substitute for regular WordPerfect 4.2, and therefore the full-feature version may be obtained directly from WordPerfect Corporation at a 75% educational discount.

[1] "*WPC" will be automatically printed after each paragraph of text to discourage academic or professional use of the L-WP. See paragraph II above.

TEMPLATES *(CUT ALONG DOTTED LINES)*

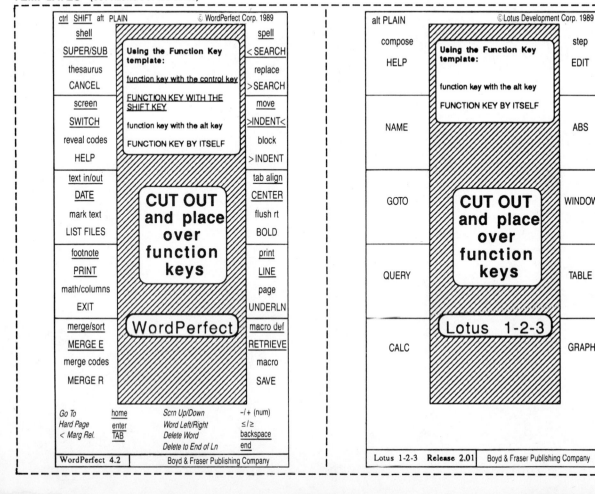

Contents

Preface xxviii
Acknowledgements xxxi

Part 1
DECISIONS AND MICROCOMPUTER RESOURCES

chapter 1
DECISION MAKING AND COMPUTERS

INTRODUCTION 3
TYPES OF DECISIONS 4
THE DECISION MAKING PROCESS 6
   A Business Venture Decision 7
DECISION MAKING AND TYPES OF INFORMATION 8
   Informal and Formal Information 9
INFORMATION PROCESSING SYSTEMS 10
   Manual Systems 10
   Semi-Manual Systems 10
   Automated Systems 11
INFORMATION RESOURCES MANAGEMENT 11
   A Brief History of Information Resource Management 11
      The 1950s 12
      The 1960s 12
      The 1970s 13
      The 1980s 14
THE ROLE OF MICROCOMPUTERS IN INFORMATION PROCESSING 15
MICRO-BASED INFORMATION SYSTEMS 17
SUMMARY 18
KEY TERMS 18
REVIEW QUESTIONS 20
CASE STUDIES 22
SELECTED BIBLIOGRAPHY 24

chapter 2
MICROCOMPUTER HARDWARE

INTRODUCTION 25
A HISTORY OF MICROCOMPUTERS 26
COMPONENTS OF MICROCOMPUTERS 28
    The Central Processing Unit 29
        ROM and RAM 30
        Types of Microprocessors 30
        The System Clock 34
        The Coprocessor 34
        The System Bus 34
        Expansion Slots 34
    Input/Output Devices 36
        The Keyboard 36
        The Monitor 38
        Printers and Plotters 39
STORAGE UNITS AND DEVICES 41
    Secondary Storage Devices and Media 42
        Diskettes and Disk Drives 42
        Hard Disks 44
        Optical Disks 46
COMMUNICATION DEVICES 46
    The Interface Board 47
    The Modem 48
SUMMARY 49
KEY TERMS 50
REVIEW QUESTIONS 52
CASE STUDIES 55
SELECTED BIBLIOGRAPHY 56

chapter 3
MICROCOMPUTER SOFTWARE

INTRODUCTION 57
TYPES OF MICROCOMPUTER SOFTWARE 58
    Systems Software 58
        Control Programs 58
        Operating System 59
    Programming Languages 60
    Application Software 62
        Word Processing Software 64
        Spreadsheet Software 67
        Database Management Software 69
        Graphics Software 71

Communications Software 72
Integrated Software 74
Desktop Publishing Software 76
Miscellaneous Application Software 77
SUMMARY 78
KEY TERMS 78
REVIEW QUESTIONS 80
CASE STUDIES 82
SELECTED BIBLIOGRAPHY 85

Part II
MICROCOMPUTER OPERATING SYSTEMS

Chapter 4
INTRODUCTION TO OPERATING SYSTEMS

INTRODUCTION 89
WHAT IS AN OPERATING SYSTEM? 90
A HISTORICAL PERSPECTIVE 90
COMMON OPERATING SYSTEMS 92
CP/M 92
MS-DOS 92
AppleDOS 93
Macintosh 93
Unix and Xenix 94
OS/2 94
IBM PC-DOS 96
The I/O Handler 97
The Command Processor 97
Utility Programs 97
System Files 97
SUMMARY 98
KEY TERMS 98
REVIEW QUESTIONS 99
CASE STUDIES 100
SELECTED BIBLIOGRAPHY 102

chapter 5
USING IBM PC-DOS

INTRODUCTION 103
BEFORE YOU BEGIN 104
GETTING STARTED 104
   Booting the System 105
      Cold Boot 105
      Warm Boot 107
   Keyboard Arrangement 108
   Screen Adjustments 109
COMMONLY USED PC-DOS COMMANDS 110
   The DIRECTORY (DIR) Command 110
   The VERSION (VER) Command 112
   The DATE Command 112
   The TIME Command 113
   The CLEAR SCREEN (CLS) Command 114
   The FORMAT Command 114
   The SYSTEM (SYS) Command 116
   The VOLUME (VOL) Command 116
   The CHECK DISK (CHKDSK) Command 117
   The COPY Command 119
   The DISKCOPY Command 120
   The DISKETTE COMPARE (DISKCOMP) Command 122
   The COMPARISON (COMP) Command 123
   The RENAME (REN) Command 124
   The DELETE or ERASE (DEL or ERASE) Command 125
   The TYPE Command 126
   Wildcards 126
   The Fragmentation of Data 127
SUMMARY OF DOS COMMANDS 128
KEY TERMS 128
REVIEW QUESTIONS 129
HANDS-ON EXERCISES 131

Part III
ELECTRONIC WORD PROCESSING CONCEPTS AND APPLICATIONS

Chapter 6
MICROCOMPUTER WORD PROCESSING

INTRODUCTION 135
COMPUTERIZED WORD PROCESSING CONCEPTS 136
SOME POPULAR WORD PROCESSING SOFTWARE PACKAGES 138
  WordStar 138
  Microsoft Word 139
  DisplayWrite 141
  WordPerfect 142
    The WordPerfect Diskette 142
    The Printer Diskettes 142
    The Speller Diskette 142
    The Thesaurus Diskette 142
    The Learning Diskette 143
SUMMARY 143
KEY TERMS 144
REVIEW QUESTIONS 144
CASE STUDIES 146
SELECTED BIBLIOGRAPHY 149

Chapter 7
LEARNING WORDPERFECT

INTRODUCTION 151
GETTING STARTED 151
  Booting the System 151
BEFORE YOU BEGIN TO TYPE 153
  Word Wrap 155
  The Insert and Typeover Modes 155
  Responding to a Message on the Screen 156
  Function Keys (F1 through F10) 156
  Keystroke Combinations 156
  A Few Notes and Words of Caution 158

LET'S BEGIN   158
CREATING A BUSINESS LETTER   161
   Create the Heading   162
   Capitalize the Subheading   163
   Add Today's Date   163
   Create the Address   164
   Create the Salutation   164
   Create the Body of the Letter   164
   Create the Closing   166
   Save Your Document   166
   Exit WordPerfect   167
MODIFYING AN EXISTING DOCUMENT   167
   Retrieve a File from a Diskette   168
   Delete a Line   168
   Insert a Line   168
   Insert a New Paragraph   169
   Save Your Corrected Document   170
   Center Your Letter Before Printing   170
   Set Right-Justification Off   171
   Print Your Letter   172
   Exit WordPerfect   172
FILE HANDLING AND FORMATTING A DOCUMENT   173
   List Files   175
   Copy a File into Another File   176
   Delete a File   177
   Retrieve a File   177
   Change Pitch Settings   177
   Change Line Settings   178
   Change Margin Settings   178
   Change Tab Settings   179
   Change Line Spacing   180
   Change Page Length   180
   Page Numbering   181
   Print the Document   182
   Save the Document and Exit WordPerfect   182
BLOCK COMMANDS   182
   Copy and Retrieve a File   183
   Delete a Block of Text   183
   Move a Block of Text   184
   Copy a Block   185
   Format a Block   187
   Print Your Document   188
   Exit WordPerfect   189

SUMMARY OF WORDPERFECT COMMANDS 189
KEY TERMS 190
REVIEW QUESTIONS 190
HANDS-ON EXERCISES 192

Part IV
ELECTRONIC SPREADSHEET CONCEPTS AND APPLICATIONS

chapter 8
ELECTRONIC SPREADSHEETS

INTRODUCTION 199
AN EXAMPLE OF A SPREADSHEET 200
A BRIEF HISTORY OF THE ELECTRONIC SPREADSHEET 202
POPULAR SPREADSHEET SOFTWARE PACKAGES 203
    VisiCalc 203
    Framework 204
    Lotus 1-2-3 204
    The 1-2-3 System Disk 205
    The PrintGraph Disk 205
    The Utility Disk 205
    The Install Library Disk 205
    A View of 1-2-3 205
LOTUS 1-2-3 APPLICATIONS 206
    The Decision Maker 206
    The Microcomputer 206
    Lotus 1-2-3 206
    The Decision Model 207
    Data 207
SUMMARY 207
KEY TERMS 208
REVIEW QUESTIONS 208
CASE STUDIES 210
SELECTED BIBLIOGRAPHY 213

chapter 9
USING LOTUS 1-2-3

INTRODUCTION 215
GETTING STARTED 216
    Booting the System 216
    What Is a Cell? 219
    Mode Indicators 219
    Status Indicators 220
THE KEYBOARD 220
    Function Keys 222
Choosing Menu Structures and Options 222
    The 1-2-3 Command Menu 223
    Correcting Errors While Typing 226
RULES FOR ENTERING DATA 228
    Entering Numbers 228
    Entering Formulas 228
    Entering Labels 229
THE /WORKSHEET COMMAND 231
    Changing the Column Width 233
    Adding and Deleting Columns or Rows 233
THE /COPY COMMAND 234
    A Word on Ranges 234
    Absolute vs. Relative Cell Addressing 235
    Copying Cells 236
THE /FORMAT COMMAND 238
THE /RANGE COMMAND 240
1-2-3'S @ FUNCTIONS 241
THE /MOVE COMMAND 244
THE /PRINT COMMAND 245
    Print Screen 247
THE /FILE COMMAND 247
THE /QUIT COMMAND 249
THE /SYSTEM COMMAND 249
A COMPREHENSIVE WORKSHEET EXAMPLE 250
    Worksheet Specifications 250
    Changing an Assumption 255
SUMMARY OF LOTUS 1-2-3 COMMANDS 257
KEY TERMS 257
REVIEW QUESTIONS 258
HANDS-ON EXERCISES 260

Part V
DATABASE MANAGEMENT CONCEPTS AND APPLICATIONS

chapter 10
MICROCOMPUTER DATABASE MANAGEMENT SYSTEMS

INTRODUCTION 269
FILE PROCESSING 270
WHAT IS A DATABASE? 271
COMPONENTS OF A DATABASE 272
 Data 272
 Database Structures and Organizations 273
  Physical Structure 273
  Logical Structure 273
  Linked List Structure 273
  Hierarchical Structure 275
  Network Structure 275
  Relational Structure 276
 A Database Management System (DBMS) 278
  Creation of a Database 278
  Validation of Data 278
  Addition, Deletion, and Modification of Data 278
  Sorting and Merging 278
  Searching and Indexing Data 279
  Formatting and Reporting Data 279
  Security of Data 279
 Application Programs 280
SOME POPULAR MICROCOMPUTER DBMS SOFTWARE PACKAGES 281
 R:Base 5000 281
 DataEase 282
 dBASE III PLUS 282
  Systems Disks #1 and #2 283
  The Sample Programs and Utilities Disk 283
  The Application Generator 283
  The On-Disk Tutorial 283
SUMMARY 283
KEY TERMS 284
REVIEW QUESTIONS 285
CASE STUDIES 288
SELECTED BIBLIOGRAPHY 291

chapter 11
USING dBASE III PLUS

INTRODUCTION 293
GETTING STARTED 294
    Booting the System 294
    The dBASE III Plus Environment 295
MOVING AROUND IN dBASE III PLUS 298
    Function Keys 299
    Getting Help 299
    Leaving dBASE III Plus 301
    Entering dBASE III Plus Commands 301
    Deciding Which Mode to Use 302
CREATING A DATABASE FILE 303
    Correcting Typing Errors 305
    Setting the Default Drive 305
    Rules for File Names 305
    The CREATE Command 305
    Defining the File Structure 306
        Field Name 306
        Data Type 307
        Width 307
    Entering Data 309
    The DIR Command 311
    The LIST STRUCTURE Command 311
    The LIST Command 312
    The LIST OFF Command 313
    The SET HEADINGS Command 313
    The Pointer Position 313
    The LIST Command with a Condition 314
    The USE Command 315
    The DISPLAY Command 316
MODIFYING THE STRUCTURE OF THE DATABASE 320
    The MODIFY STRUCTURE Command 320
MODIFYING THE CONTENTS OF A DATABASE 322
    The APPEND Command 322
    The INSERT Command 323
    The EDIT Command 325
    The BROWSE Command 326
        Scanning 327
        Editing 327
        Adding 327
        Quitting 328
    The DELETE Command 328
    The RECALL Command   329

The PACK Command 329
GENERATING REPORTS 329
The CREATE REPORT Command 330
Options 331
Groups 332
Columns 332
Locate 334
Exit 334
The REPORT Command 334
The MODIFY REPORT Command 335
SORTING THE DATABASE 335
The SORT Command 336
INDEXING THE DATABASE 339
The INDEX Command 339
Single-Field Indexing 339
Using an Existing Index File 340
Multiple-Field Indexing 341
SEARCHING AND QUERYING THE DATABASE 342
Mathematical Operators 342
Relational Operators 343
SUMMARY OF dBASE III PLUS COMMANDS 347
KEY TERMS 348
REVIEW QUESTIONS 348
HANDS-ON EXERCISES 351

Part VI
MICRO-BASED SYSTEMS DEVELOPMENT

chapter 12
SYSTEMS INVESTIGATION AND ANALYSIS

INTRODUCTION 359
THE SYSTEMS DEVELOPMENT CYCLE 360
SYSTEMS INVESTIGATION AND ANALYSIS 361
Reason: Inefficiency 362
Organizational Growth 362
Management Style 362
Change of Procedure 362
New Information Requirements 363
Reason: Inadequate Control 363
Reason: Improved Productivity 363

Reason: Cost Savings 364
Reason: Improvement in Service 364
ACTIVITIES OF THE SYSTEMS INVESTIGATION PHASE 364
Collecting Background Information 365
Defining the Problem 365
Assessing Information Requirements 366
Available Resources and Constraints 367
Resources 367
Constraints 368
Costs and Benefits Analysis 368
Costs 368
Benefits 369
Documenting Investigation Results 370
Do Nothing 370
Postpone Development 371
Continue the Investigation 371
Develop a System 371
SYSTEM INVESTIGATION REPORT 372
Statement of Problem 372
Information Requirements 372
Costs and Benefits 373
Recommendation 374
SUMMARY 375
KEY TERMS 376
REVIEW QUESTIONS 376
CASE STUDIES 379
SELECTED BIBLIOGRAPHY 381

chapter 13
SYSTEMS SELECTION AND DESIGN

INTRODUCTION 383
ACTIVITIES OF THE SYSTEM SELECTION AND DESIGN PHASE 384
System Security and Maintenance Requirements 384
System Security: Availability of the System 385
System Security: Accuracy of Information Generated 386
System Security: Confidentiality of Information 386
System Maintenance: Programming 386
System Maintenance: Hardware 387
System Maintenance: Software 387
Consultation with Users 387
Software Evaluation 389
Suitability of Software Requirements 390
Security Procedures 390
Software Maintenance 390
Level of Friendliness 391

Quality of Documentation 391
Future Expansion and Updating 391
Degree of Difficulty in Modification 392
Services Provided by the Vendor 392
Language the Package is Developed In 392
Availability of Training Programs 392
Hardware Requirements 393
Reputation of the Vendor 393
Popularity of Package Usage 393
Price of Package 394

Hardware Evaluation 394
Suitability to the Chosen Software 395
Maintenance Options 395
Ease of Operation 395
Quality of Documentation 396
Growth Prospects 396
Industry Standards 396
Installation 396
Networking Capability 397
Programming Languages and Utility Programs 397
Training Programs 397
Reputation of Suppliers 397
Price of Hardware 398

Identifying Alternatives 398
Preparing a System Selection and Design Report 399
Selecting a System 399

SYSTEM SELECTION AND DESIGN REPORT 400
Problems 400
Objectives 400
Alternatives 401
Recommendation 404

SUMMARY 405
KEY TERMS 405
REVIEW QUESTIONS 406
CASE STUDIES 409
SELECTED BIBLIOGRAPHY 412

chapter 14
SYSTEMS IMPLEMENTATION

INTRODUCTION 413
ACTIVITIES OF THE IMPLEMENTATION PHASE 414
System Installation and Testing 415
Developing Application Programs 416
Creating Data Files 418
System Conversion 420
Cold Conversion 421

Parallel Conversion 421
Phased Conversion 421
Developing a User Manual 422
Developing User Training Programs 423
Documenting the System 423
DEFINITION OF APPLICATIONS 424
Inventory Tracking: dBASE III PLUS 424
Mailing Application: dBASE III PLUS 425
Manufacturer Order Maintenance Application: dBASE III PLUS 425
Decision Support System: Lotus 1-2-3 426
Correspondence System: WordPerfect 426
INPUT DATA SOURCES 426
OUTPUT FORMATS 427
SYSTEM PROGRAMMING 427
SYSTEM CONVERSION 428
SUMMARY 428
KEY TERMS 429
REVIEW QUESTIONS 430
CASE STUDIES 432
SELECTED BIBLIOGRAPHY 435

chapter 15
SYSTEMS MAINTENANCE AND MANAGEMENT

INTRODUCTION 437
ACTIVITIES OF THE SYSTEM MAINTENANCE AND MANAGEMENT PHASE 438
Developing a Maintenance and Security Procedure Manual 439
Hardware Maintenance 439
Software Maintenance 439
Programming Maintenance 440
System Security 441
The Post-Implementation Review 441
Cost Analysis 442
Availability of Information 442
Accuracy of Information 443
Personnel 443
Volume of Transactions 443
Satisfaction with Vendors 444
Security and Maintenance Measurements 444
Documenting Post-Implementation Results 444
MAINTENANCE AND SECURITY MANUAL 445
Hardware Maintenance 445
Software Maintenance 446
Program Maintenance 446

Security Procedures 446
POST-IMPLEMENTATION REVIEW RESULTS 447
SUMMARY 448
KEY TERMS 449
REVIEW QUESTIONS 449
CASE STUDIES 451
SELECTED BIBLIOGRPAHY 454

Part VII
ADVANCED TOPICS IN MICROCOMPUTING

chapter 16
MICROCOMPUTER COMMUNICATION AND NETWORKING

INTRODUCTION 457
COMPONENTS OF DATA COMMUNICATION 458
  The Source, or Host, Computer 458
  The Receiving Computer 459
  Data 459
  Communication Protocols 460
  Transmission Components 460
    Communication Channel 460
    Modulation Techniques 461
    Transmission Modes 462
DATA COMMUNICATION APPLICATIONS 464
  Electronic Mail 464
  Electronic Bulletin Boards 465
  Databases 465
  Accessing Other Computers 466
MICROCOMPUTER NETWORKING 466
  LAN Components 467
    Hardware 467
    Software 467
    Transmission Media 467
  Local Area Network Options 469
    Star Topology 469
    Bus Topology 470
    Ring Topology 471
  LAN Applications 472
    Computing Applications 472
    Office Automation 473
    Industrial and Laboratory Automation 473

Choosing a LAN 473
Ethernet 473
IBM-PC Network 474
Starlan 474

MICRO-TO-MAINFRAME LINKS 474

NETWORK PLANNING AND MANAGEMENT 475

SUMMARY 476

KEY TERMS 477

REVIEW QUESTIONS 479

CASE STUDIES 482

SELECTED BIBLIOGRAPHY 485

chapter 17
MICROCOMPUTER CRIME AND FRAUD

INTRODUCTION 487

MICROCOMPUTER CRIME 488
Availability of Microcomputers 488
Improved Communication Capabilities 488
More Knowledgeable Users 488

Types of Microcomputer Crimes 489
Theft of Computer Hardware 489
Theft of Data 489
Destruction of Secondary Storage Media 490
Illegal Copying of Software 490
Unauthorized Program Alteration 490
Unauthorized Accessing of Other Computer Systems 490

Fighting Microcomputer Crime 491

SUMMARY 493

KEY TERMS 494

REVIEW QUESTIONS 494

CASE STUDIES 495

SELECTED BIBLIOGRAPHY 499

chapter 18
DESKTOP PUBLISHING SYSTEMS

INTRODUCTION 501

THE PUBLISHING PROCESS 502
Traditional Approach 502
Desktop Publishing Approach 503

MAJOR USES OF DESKTOP PUBLISHING 506
BENEFITS OF IN-HOUSE PUBLISHING 506
DESKTOP PUBLISHING TERMINOLOGY 508
SYSTEM REQUIREMENTS 510

Hardware 510
The System 511
The Storage 511
Monitors 511
Mouse 511
Printer 511
Scanner 511

Software 512
PageMaker 512
Fontrix/Printix 512
Harvard Professional Publisher 512
Ventura Publisher 513
PagePerfect 513

FUTURE TRENDS AND ISSUES IN DESKTOP PUBLISHING 513
SUMMARY 514
KEY TERMS 514
REVIEW QUESTIONS 515
CASE STUDIES 517
SELECTED BIBLIOGRAPHY 518

Part VIII
APPENDICES

INTRODUCTION TO THE SUNSHINE WINDOW INC., SUPPLIERS CASE

BACKGROUND INFORMATION AND BUSINESS OPERATIONS 521

Manufacturers and Customers 521

Personnel 521
Warehouse Personnel 522
Inventory/Order Clerk 522
Administrative Clerk 523

Management Personnel 524

Appendix B
TEN SAMPLE CASES

INFORMATION PROCESSORS' ASSOCIATION 525
ACCOUNTANTS ANONYMOUS, INC. 526
BETSY'S BASKETS, INC. 528
PEONY AREA COMMUNITY COLLEGE 529
UNITED BRETHREN CHURCH 531
IRON STATE UNIVERSITY 532
ARCHITECTURAL DESIGN ASSOCIATES 534
BORROWER'S UNLIMITED NATIONAL BANK 536
J & E CONCESSION STAND 537
SHANGHAI SURPRISE, INC. 539

Appendix C
ADVANCED DOS COMMANDS

INTRODUCTION 541
   The SORT Command 541
THE DOS EDITOR 543
   The EDLIN Command 544
   The INSERT (I) Command 545
   The LIST LINES (L) Command 546
   The DELETE (D) Command 547
   The END EDIT (E) Command 548
   Applications of EDLIN 548
   Regular Batch Files 548
   Autoexecute Batch (AUTOEXEC.BAT) File 549
HARD DISK DOS COMMAND 550
   Formatting a Hard Disk 550
   The FDISK Program 550
DIRECTORY COMMANDS 551
   The MAKE DIRECTORY (MD) Command 552
   The CHANGE DIRECTORY (CD) Command 552
   Set Search Directory – The PATH Command 552
   The REMOVE DIRECTORY (RD) Command 553
   The TREE Command 553
   The PROMPT Command 554
MISCELLANEOUS DOS COMMANDS 554
   The CONFIGURE SYSTEM (CONFIG. SYS) File 554

    The COPY CONSOLE (COPY CON) Command **555**
        The BACKUP Command **555**
        The RESTORE Command **556**
SUMMARY OF DOS COMMANDS **556**
REVIEW QUESTIONS **557**
HANDS-ON EXERCISES **559**

Appendix D
ADVANCED FEATURES OF WORDPERFECT

INTRODUCTION **560**
WORDPERFECT SPELLER **561**
WORDPERFECT THESAURUS **565**
FILE MERGING **566**
    Combining Files **566**
    Merging Primary and Secondary Files **567**
        Creating the Secondary File **567**
        Creating the Primary File **568**
        Activating the Merge **570**
MAILING LABELS **571**
    Activating the Merge **572**
MACROS **573**
    Activating the Macro **573**
KEY TERMS **573**
REVIEW QUESTIONS **574**
HANDS-ON EXERCISES **575**

Appendix E
ADVANCED FEATURES OF LOTUS 1-2-3

INTRODUCTION **577**
LOTUS 1-2-3 GRAPHICS **577**
    The /GRAPH Command **577**
        Bar Graph **580**
        Selecting Ranges **580**
        View **580**
        Title **581**
        Name **582**
        Save **582**
        Reset **582**
        Side-By-Side Bar Graphs **583**
        Legend **584**

Stacked-Bar Graphs **585**
Line Graph **586**
Multi-Line Charts **587**
Pie Charts **588**

PRINTING THE GRAPH 589

LOTUS 1-2-3 DATABASE MANAGEMENT 591
The /DATA Command **592**
The /DATA SORT Command **594**
The /DATA QUERY Command **595**
The Input Range **595**
The Criterion Range **595**
The Output Range **597**

LOTUS 1-2-3 MACROS 598
Defining a Macro **598**
Entering the Macro **599**
Naming the Macro **599**
Documenting the Macro **599**
Invoking the Macro **600**
Special Keys **600**
A Macro Example **600**

SUMMARY OF LOTUS 1-2-3 COMMANDS AND TERMS 602
REVIEW QUESTIONS 603
HANDS-ON EXERCISES 605

Appendix F
ADVANCED FEATURES OF dBASE III PLUS

INTRODUCTION 610
VIEWS 610
Creating the Database **610**
Inputting Records **611**
Listing the Database **612**
Searching the Database **612**
Indexing **612**
The SELECT Command **613**
The SET RELATION Command **614**
Searching Two Files **614**

LOGICAL OPERATORS 617
CREATING MAILING LABELS 618
FILE MANAGEMENT ACTIVITIES 621
The COPY Command **621**
The COPY FIELD Command **621**
The COPY STRUCTURE Command **622**

The DELETE FILE Command 622
The LIST FILES Command 623
Query Files 623
SUMMARY OF ADVANCED dBASE III PLUS COMMANDS 625
KEY TERMS 625
REVIEW QUESTIONS 625
HANDS-ON EXERCISES 627

Appendix G
ANSWERS TO REVIEW QUESTIONS 629

Glossary 648

Index 657

Summary Commands 669

Preface

In the past decade, the development of reasonably priced, "user-friendly" applications software for microcomputers, and the remarkable increases in computing power and storage capacity, have helped make microcomputers powerful tools for information processing and management. In many ways, the impact of microcomputer technology on productivity in business and industry rivals that of the Industrial Revolution. This increased demand for microcomputers in business has had an equally dramatic impact on education. Today, virtually all two-year and four-year colleges and universities throughout the country offer some type of microcomputer training for their students.

THE NEED FOR ANOTHER TEXTBOOK

One of the most important goals of many microcomputer training courses has been to teach students the fundamentals of using applications software in a "hands-on" environment. The selection of textbooks which support this goal is at least as diverse as the choices of software that could be used in teaching the course.

But equally important, and often ignored by single-minded, "how-to" textbooks, is the significant role today's microcomputer user can and should play in the development, design, implementation, maintenance, and management of an entire microcomputer-based information system.

In addition to knowing how to use commercial software packages, today's student will be called upon to understand the overall role of microcomputers and their capabilities in order to effectively manage the most important product of these systems: information.

LEVEL OF INSTRUCTION

This textbook is primarily designed for use in a one-semester course for business-oriented students enrolled in microcomputer applications and management. The text is particularly well suited for use in programs related to business management.

OBJECTIVES OF THIS TEXTBOOK

This book aspires to making a new generation of microcomputer users informed and self-sufficient. In helping readers become efficient, productive microcomputer users, it emphasizes the value of information and provides insight into effective management of microcomputer information processing system. The primary objectives of this textbook are:

- To provide readers with an appreciation for the role of microcomputers in information processing systems.
- To familiarize readers with microcomputer hardware and software components.
- To assist readers in identifying potential microcomputer uses and applications.
- To instruct readers in using commercial applications software packages in order to solve business problems.
- To provide readers with step-by-step plans for developing microcomputer information systems.
- To instill in readers an appreciation for how microcomputers can be used in effectively managing a business.

DISTINGUISHING FEATURES

Comprehensive/Flexible

We recognize the fact that it may not be possible to cover all of the material presented in this book in a one-semester course. Our intent was to develop a comprehensive, flexible book where instructors could choose the material best suited to meet their course requirements and the needs of their students. The "Recommended Sequence of Coverage" section of this Preface suggests an overall approach for successfully integrating portions of this material into a one-semester course.

Management-Driven Approach

Today, business students at the junior, senior, and graduate levels require knowledge of microcomputers that transcends the basic introduction to software applications. Using a managerial approach, parts Two through Five of this text help business students acquire and use the skills and understanding essential in developing microcomputer applications around the common software packages utilized in this book.

Complete Running Case Study

In this text, every effort has been made to reach beyond the scope of microcomputer manuals and most existing software applications textbooks. Using a systematic approach, most chapters in this text contain applications relating to a comprehensive case study, Sunshine Window Inc., Suppliers (located in Appendix A). This continuing case study is essential in providing students with the opportunity to apply the skills and methodologies presented in the text in a fictional, but realistic, business environment.

Sample Project Cases

Appendix B of this text contains ten microcomputer-related project proposals, similar to the case of Sunshine Window Inc., Suppliers (SWIS). These Sample Project Cases have been developed around realistic business situations and are a valuable tool for students to use through out the semester.

System Development Methodology

Part Six of this textbook introduces readers to the fundamental concepts of microcomputer systems development. These chapters cover the investigation and needs analysis, software and hardware selection, and the design, implementation, maintenance, and management of microcomputer information systems. This material has been tailored to meet the managerial needs of microcomputer system users.

Advanced Topics and Software Applications

Instructors who wish to provide more in-depth coverage of the applications software packages featured in the text are encouraged to choose any of the appendices discussing the advanced features of PC-DOS, WordPerfect, Lotus 1-2-3, and dBASE III PLUS. The text also introduces and discusses advanced microcomputer topics such as Microcomputer Communications and Networking (Chapter 16), Microcomputer Crime and Fraud (Chapter 17), and Desktop Publishing Systems (Chapter 18).

Extensive Actual Screen Illustrations

The instructions for using each software package are fully supported with screen images that exactly reflect what students' screens will look like as they execute each target command. The book includes hundreds of these actual screen illustrations that clarify the detailed impact of each operation students perform.

Software Command Summaries

The last pages of the book contain command summaries for each software package featured in this text. This "command reference guide" appears on colored pages for easy identification. We recommend that students remove this perforated section from the back of the book for use as a handy reference while working at the computer.

Free Educational Software

We are pleased to provide educational versions of WordPerfect 4.2 and dBASE III PLUS to all instructors who adopt this text. We will also provide VP-Planner Plus for optional use with the material featuring Lotus 1-2-3. The educational versions of these software packages support the beginning and intermediate level exercises and projects contained in this text. Some of the more advanced projects, however, would require students to access the commercially available versions.

Boyd & Fraser will supply adopters with master diskettes of any combination of these software packages, along with permission to duplicate the diskette(s) for each student who has purchased a new copy of the text from the publisher for use in class. For information on obtaining this free software please contact Boyd & Fraser Publishing Company, 20 Park Plaza, Boston, MA, 02116, phone 1-(800)-225-3782.

Challenging Self-Test Material

Each chapter in this textbook ends with a list of key terms and their definitions, and review questions pertaining to the material covered in the chapter. Additionally, a selected bibilography for library research and two case studies for class discussion or homework assignments accompany each chapter. The software application chapters are accompanied by practical "hands-on" exercises to be completed in a lab setting.

INSTRUCTOR'S SUPPORT MATERIAL

For use in conjunction with this text, instructors may request from Boyd & Fraser Publishing Company the comprehensive Instructor's Manual featuring:

- Chapter objectives and summaries
- Lecture outlines and suggested approaches
- Test questions
- Transparency masters
- Answers to hands-on exercises

RECOMMENDED SEQUENCE OF COVERAGE

We recommend the following sequence in order to cover the core material in this book during a one-semester course:

Week 1	Chapter 1
Week 2	Chapter 2
Week 3	Chapter 3
Week 4	Chapters 4 & 5 and Appendix A
Weeks 5 & 6	Chapters 6 & 7
Weeks 7 & 8	Chapters 8 & 9
Weeks 9 & 10	Chapters 10 & 11
Weeks 11 & 12	Chapters 12 & 13
Weeks 13 & 14	Chapters 14 & 15
Week 15	Chapter 16

It is a good idea to have students use the Sample Project Cases contained in Appendix B during coverage of Part Six of this text (Chapters 12, 13, 14, and 15). Students will also benefit greatly from reading and using the Sunshine Windows Inc., Suppliers (SWIS) Case contained in Appendix A, toward the beginning of the course. The SWIS Case plays an integral role in helping readers develop basic microcomputer information systems using the concepts of systems development and their knowledge of microcomputer applications.

Instructors interested in providing additional coverage of software applications could choose any of the appendices discussing the advanced features of the software packages. Furthermore, Microcomputer Crime and Fraud (Chapter 17) or Desktop Publishing Systems (Chapter 18) could be added to the recommended schedule or substituted for the chapters suggested above.

ACKNOWLEDGEMENTS

Writing a book of this magnitude is the result of a team's effort, dedication, and determination. I was very fortunate to have the opportunity to work with a group of individuals who were as enthusiastic as I was toward this project. I am indebted to them for their contributions toward enhancing the overall quality of this material.

I gratefully acknowledge the comments and suggested improvements offered by the following individuals: Joyce Abler, Central Michigan University; Bill Bailey, Casper College; Sarah Baker, Miami University of Ohio; John Castek, University of Wisconsin at LaCrosse; Donald Chand, Bentley College; Marilyn Correa, Polk Community College; Eileen Entin, Wentworth Institute of Technology; Henry Etlinger, Rochester Institute of Technology; William Fox, College of DuPage; Dale Hanchey, Oklahoma Baptist University; William Kenney, Mesa College; William Newman, University of Nevada at Reno; R. Waldo Roth, Taylor University; Joseph Szurek, University of Pittsburgh at Greensburg; and Mick Watterson, Drake University.

I would like to credit all the undergraduate and graduate students who took my course and assisted me in examining different parts of this book over the past two years. In particular, I would like to recognize Lori Marchese, Wendy Deimler, Charles Creswell, Catherine Thompson, Carol Kopanoff, John Laporta, Cindy Mignogna, Jack Zogby, Scott Roth, Cordelia Englar, and Jan Springer. Karen Stump deserves special thanks for her valuable assistance in helping me identify errors during the proofreading process. Futhermore, I would like to express my genuine appreciation to my local editor, Sandy Oravec, and my copy editor, Darlyne, for their valuable corrections and suggestions. I am greatful to them for their contributions on my behalf. I would also like to show my appreciation to my division head, Dr. Melvin Blumberg, for all his moral support and guidance. Much gratitude also goes to Louise Smith, Becky Hooven, and Liz Lerch for their assistance and sense of humor.

I am also fortunate to have Boyd & Fraser as my publisher, and to have several talented members of their staff working with me on this project. My sincere thanks to Tom Walker, for all his wisdom, guidance, and moral support. Special recognition and credit are due Sarah Grover, my editor, for her support, assistance, and encouragement. Donna Villanucci, my production editor, merits special thanks for all her well-organized efforts in bringing the pieces together and working on details, and many thanks to Becky Herrington for her endless efforts in directing the production process of this book.

Two more individuals, Sandy Caufman (my admired student), and Linda Zubler (the greatest secretary), are deserving of special recognition. I greatly appreciate all their immeasurable hard work and support. I have been fortunate to have them on my team, and I am thankful for their contributions, patience, intelligence, and thoughtfulness.

Finally, my sincere appreciation and thanks go to my students at Penn State Harrisburg. They believed in my work, and inspired me to write this textbook. I devote this book to my students, and to my profession.

Mehdi Khosrowpour
Information Systems Program
The Pennsylvania State University at Harrisburg
Middletown, PA 17055
January, 1989

Part 1

DECISIONS AND MICROCOMPUTER RESOURCES

chapter 1
DECISION MAKING AND COMPUTERS

- *describe the three types of business decisions.*
- *describe the steps in the decision making process and be able to apply them in personal and business situations.*
- *describe the differences between informal and formal information.*
- *describe the three classifications of formal information systems.*
- *name and discuss the advances made in the past four decades of computer technology.*
- *describe the two basic purposes for microcomputers.*

chapter 2
MICROCOMPUTER HARDWARE

- *list the microcomputer's hardware components.*
- *describe a microprocessor.*
- *describe major input devices.*
- *describe the different types of printers.*
- *describe the difference between ROM and RAM.*
- *describe a floppy disk.*
- *describe a hard disk.*
- *describe a modem.*

chapter 3
MICROCOMPUTER SOFTWARE

- *define a computer program.*
- *name and describe different programming languages.*
- *define systems software.*
- *describe the difference between command-driven and menu-driven software packages.*
- *describe word processing software.*
- *describe spreadsheet software.*
- *describe database management software.*
- *describe graphics software.*
- *describe communications software.*
- *describe integrated software.*
- *describe desktop publishing software.*

chapter 1

DECISION MAKING AND COMPUTERS

After completing this chapter, you should be able to

- describe the three types of business decisions.
- describe the steps in the decision making process and be able to apply them in personal and business situations.
- describe the differences between informal and formal information.
- describe the three classifications of formal information systems.
- name and discuss the advances made in the past four decades of computer technology.
- describe the two basic purposes for microcomputers.

INTRODUCTION

On a personal level, each of us makes decisions every day: which automobile to buy, which college to attend, how much money to spend. Similarly, the core of business management is decision making, an activity common to all levels of management. Business decisions can vary, from decisions dealing with expanding the business, applying for a loan, buying a computer, or merging with another business, to hiring an additional secretary.

In general, **decision making** can be defined as selecting the most appropriate or optimum alternative in order to resolve a problem or achieve a goal. But before someone can select the most appropriate course of action, the situation must be completely defined and analyzed, and alternative solutions assessed. Clearly, information is one of the basic necessities and components of decision making.

The president of a bank may have to make a decision about whether to open a new branch uptown. If the decision is made to open a new branch, then the vice president of human resources will want to make the decision regarding how to staff the new branch. Once the new branch is functioning, a loan officer will have to decide whether to approve or reject a loan request. In all of these managerial decision making situations, the overall quality of the decision is directly related to the information available to the decision maker.

This chapter will first discuss different types and characteristics of business decisions, followed by an outline of the information requirements of different decisions at different levels of organizations. Finally, the chapter will consider the role of computers, particularly microcomputers, in processing and providing information to decision makers.

■ TYPES OF DECISIONS

In general, decisions can be classified as

> strategic decisions.
> tactical decisions.
> operational or technical decisions.

Strategic decisions involve planning at the top management level, where goals and objectives are set for both short-term and long-term periods. Strategic decisions are mainly characterized as future-oriented, and deal with a great degree of uncertainty. For example, in the bank situation discussed above, establishing a new branch is considered to be a strategic decision made by top-level managers and executives of the bank.

Tactical decisions pertain to the allocation of organizational resources and other activities related to attaining the goals or objectives established at the strategic level. Tactical decisions are mainly made by middle-level managers. They involve a certain degree of uncertainty and are mostly oriented toward the immediate. For example, in the bank situation, the decision about how to staff the new branch is considered to be a tactical decision. Another example would be the manager of the bank's maintenance department planning the layout of the building for the new branch.

Operational or **technical decisions** deal with enforcing organizational standards, procedures, and policies to ensure that specific tasks are implemented in an effective and efficient manner. In an organization, operational/technical decisions are made by line, or supervisory managers, those at the lower management level. These decisions deal with a great degree of certainty and are oriented toward the immediate, and often involve frequently repeated situations. In the case of the bank example, the decision for a loan request is classified as an operational decision. Table 1.1 on the following page illustrates different types of decisions and their characteristics.

Decisions made in an organization can be also classified as unstructured, semi-structured, and structured.

TYPES OF DECISIONS	CHARACTERISTICS			
	Degree of Certainty	Decision Making Level	Period Orientation	Frequency of Occurrences
Strategic	Very low	Top Management	Long and Short Term	Very low
Tactical	Medium	Middle Management	Short Term	Medium
Operational/ Technical	Very high	Line or Supervisory Management	Current	Very high

TABLE 1.1 *Types of Business Decisions and Their Characteristics*

In the case of **unstructured decisions,** the decision maker is mainly dealing with probabilistic variables, the performance of which cannot be absolutely determined. Typically, the decision maker will face many "what-if?" type questions, and will make many assumptions in the overall process of decision making. Strategic decisions are classified as unstructured decisions. For example, a car manufacturer who wants to introduce a new model of car will have to try to determine how consumers will react to this new model, what the status of the economy will be when the car is introduced, what gas prices will be like, or if there will be labor disputes. Introducing a new car is an unstructured decision; there are no absolute answers to all the "what-if?" questions that the car manufacturer has to face.

Semi-structured decisions are those in which the decision maker faces a combination of deterministic and probabilistic variables. Tactical decisions are mainly classified as semi-structured decisions, where the decision maker is trying to implement a plan developed at the strategic level. For example, in the case of the car manufacturer, a dealership manager may be interested in starting a new dealer incentive to help sell the new car model.

Structured decisions involve a great degree of certainty and deal mainly with deterministic variables. Operational decisions are classified as structured decisions because the decision maker follows certain rules, procedures, or standards during the decision making process. For example, a salesperson at the car dealership who is selling a new model car to a customer trading an older car will make a structured decision. The salesperson will determine the book value of the traded car, subtract it from the price of the new car, and apply the new car incentive to the total price. This type of decision is very repetitive. Table 1.2 on the following page illustrates unstructured, semi-structured, and structured decisions and their characteristics.

TYPES OF DECISIONS	CHARACTERISTICS			
	Level of Decision Making	Degree of "What-If"	Decision Makers' Level	Variables Status
Unstructured	Strategic	Very high	Top Management	Highly Probabilistics
Semi-Structured	Tactical	Medium	Middle Management	Combination of Probabilistics & Deterministics
Structured	Operational	Very low	Line Management	Highly Deterministics

TABLE 1.2 *Decision Structures and Their Characteristics*

■ THE DECISION MAKING PROCESS

In order to make any decision, a decision maker consciously or unconsciously works through a set of systematic steps known as the **decision making process.** These include

Step 1: Identification of the problem or objective.
Step 2: Analysis of the situation.
Step 3: Identification of alternative solutions.
Step 4: Assessment of alternatives.
Step 5: Selection of the most appropriate solution or course of action.

Regardless of the simplicity of the decision, the decision maker follows these steps. In the case of simple decisions, however, all of the steps may be executed in a few minutes or even seconds; in complex decisions, a more formal approach may be taken. In any case, let's discuss the steps of the decision making process, as illustrated in Figure 1.1 on the following page.

Step 1. At this phase of the decision making process, the decision maker must define the problem or the objective. For example, after driving your old car for a number of years, you begin to think of replacing it. Therefore, your objective would be to purchase a reliable and affordable automobile.

Step 2. During this step, the decision maker tries to analyze the problem or situation as thoroughly as possible. In the case of purchasing a new automobile, you will want to know how much you can afford to spend. What are the other associated costs, such as insurance, maintenance, and gasoline? Do you want an automatic or standard transmission?

Step 3. In this step, the decision maker develops different alternative solutions or approaches for solving the problem. It is possible that you could start with many alternatives, then narrow them down to the few most feasible ones. In the car-buying situation, some of the alternatives could be: (1) purchasing a new car, (2) purchasing a used car, (3) leasing a new car.

Step 4. During this step, the decision maker weighs the advantages and disadvantages of each alternative in view of achieving the initial goal. There is always the possibility that the decision maker may conclude at the end of this stage that no feasible solution exists or that more information is needed. In the car-purchasing example, you could assess the option of buying a new car by examining the financial obligation attached to this option. The option of buying a used car will carry a smaller financial obligation, but there is the possibility of breakdowns and more headaches. The leasing option has the advantage of not requiring any initial investment but, at the same time, you are not contributing any money toward ownership of the car.

Step 5. In this step, the decision maker selects the most appropriate alternative or course of action to solve the problem. In the case of buying an automobile, you will choose the alternative that you are convinced will bring the optimum outcome to the goal of obtaining an affordable and reliable car.

A Business Venture Decision

Imagine that you have recently inherited $100,000 from an uncle. Since you have been studying business for the past several years, you wish to invest the money in a small business venture rather than in the stock market or in bonds. After intensive investigation, you determine that there is a great market for a restaurant close to your campus. It can cater to the many students, faculty, and staff who cannot tolerate the food served at the school cafeteria. Your decision, then, is to invest the money in a restaurant, from which you expect great profit. You have just identified your goal for this business venture.

The next step is to research specific factors affecting the future business, including location, local ordinances and zoning restrictions, and real estate prices. Another factor you will want to investigate is the kind of food your prospective customers might be interested in: American, Chinese, or Mexican, perhaps. You will also need other information about everything from the community and the campus, to interest rates and local government services, to small businesses. Upon completion of this research, you should have all the facts necessary to move to the next step.

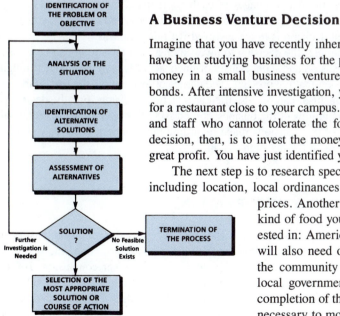

Figure 1.1
The Decision Making Process

The third step is to look at alternative methods of starting and running your business. The available alternatives could include buying a franchised restaurant, starting and running your own unique restaurant, or starting the business and then hiring a manager to handle day-to-day operations.

After you have identified your alternatives, the next step is to assess the feasibility of each of these alternatives. In the case of the franchised business, one advantage would be that the parent company would set up the whole thing, including equipment and decoration, in return for your purchase of the franchise rights and a portion of your profits. A disadvantage might be the significant initial investment required to purchase the franchise; it could be as much as a half-million dollars. Another disadvantage of the franchise might be that you are unable to put your own creativity to work because you must serve whatever is recommended by the franchiser.

In the case of the second alternative (managing the business by yourself), an advantage could be that you could enhance the profitability of the business by devoting your energy and time to it. The biggest disadvantage of this option could be the substantial time investment required, especially if you are still in school.

The third alternative, hiring a manager, likewise has certain advantages and disadvantages. A major advantage of this option might be that you would have more free time. The major disadvantage of this choice might be your concern about the quality of your manager.

Finally, the last step is to make your final decision. After careful evaluation of all of the advantages and disadvantages of each alternative, and with offers of help from a few family members, you decide to start the business and manage it yourself. Therefore, your final decision is to get involved with the business.

In the above example, the decision to invest money in a restaurant can be classified as a strategic decision and, consciously or unconsciously, you have gone through the steps of the decision making process. The choice of location for the restaurant, or the selection of a franchise, can be classified as a tactical decision. Finally, decisions that deal with the operations of the business are classified as operational or technical decisions. For each of the decisions made regarding this business venture, you have gone through the steps of the decision making process.

■ DECISION MAKING AND TYPES OF INFORMATION

Information, a major requirement for decision making, is used by decision makers at different steps of the decision making process. Without information, the decision maker can have little confidence about the validity of his or her conclusion. **Information** is knowledge about an object, phenomenon, environment, issue, or subject. The major function of information is to increase the knowledge of the decision maker about different aspects of the situation under consideration. Another function of information for the decision maker is to reduce the uncertainty related to the choice of various actions or solutions.

Informal and Formal Information

The types of information available to decision makers at all levels of an organization can be classified in two broad categories: informal information and formal information.

Informal information is mainly the product of the human mind, such as a person's experience, education, viewpoint, intuition, judgment, hunches, and opinions. To some extent, informal information will always be needed to complement formal information. Sometimes, in the absence of formal information, the decision maker may rely solely on informal information.

Formal information is the primary product of well-conceived and organized information systems. Examples of formal information could include income statements, balance sheets, inventory status reports, monthly bank statements, absenteeism reports, or payroll listings. An information system can range from a simple manual system, such as a filing system, to a computer-based information system. Generally speaking, formal information is generated through a set of steps systematically executed on data, as shown in Figure 1.2.

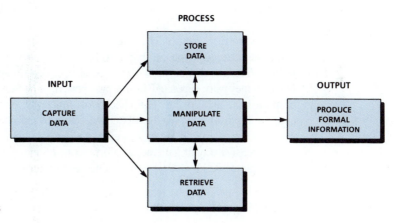

Figure 1.2
Information Processing Steps

While data and information are separate concepts, they are used interchangeably. Information is produced or generated from data. In manufacturing terms, data can be viewed as the raw material that is processed to produce information for the decision maker. An example of raw data is the number "10." By itself, this figure has no meaning. But when this raw data is used in an organization to describe the absenteeism rate during the previous month as "10%," that information allows a decision maker to compare this figure with those of previous periods to determine whether or not this percentage is acceptable. The process of converting raw data to information may be very simple, or may involve a very complex or sophisticated procedure.

The task of a formal information system is to accept raw data, process it, and produce information to be stored for later use, or to be consumed immediately by decision makers, in the form of reports or responses to queries. The human brain is the most sophisticated formal information system, and informal information—such as experience, intuition, and judgment—is, in fact, the result of the steps the human brain takes to capture, process, store, and retrieve information. However, the brain is not classified as a formal information system, *per se,* in this book. Instead, the main focus would be on computer-based information systems, particularly, those which are developed around microcomputers.

INFORMATION PROCESSING SYSTEMS

Formal information can be produced by various formal information systems. These systems can be classified as manual, semi-manual, and automated.

Manual Systems

In **manual systems,** information is organized, produced, and displayed in a traditional office format, such as written documents. The information system is put together in some kind of structure—for example, in filing cabinets that help you capture, process, store, and retrieve data. A checkbook is another example of a typical manual information system because you can record different transactions in the book in an organized fashion. The checkbook user should be able to determine the account's balance, how much money was deposited in the past period, whether a certain check number has been cashed, and so on. The checkbook functions as a provider of information to upgrade the user's knowledge about the status of the checking account. Manual systems have been around for many years, and are still considered the most common and least expensive way of generating information. Many manual information systems have been implemented by all types of businesses to manage information.

Semi-Manual Systems

A **semi-manual system** consists of a collection of manual and semi-manual devices. Semi-manual devices include cash registers, copy machines, calculators, and duplicating devices. In this case, the system is structured so that the user can accomplish certain tasks using manual devices, and others using semi-manual devices. For example, a clerk at a flower shop could record an order for a dozen red roses by entering the data onto a manual device, such as an order form. Next, the clerk makes copies of the order on a semi-manual photocopy machine, and sends them to different parties (e.g., warehouse and billing departments). A bill is generated through the use of a typewriter, a calculator, and a cash register, and one copy is sent to the customer and another retained in the company's file.

Automated Systems

Automated information systems, better known as **computer-based information systems (CIS), business information systems (BIS),** or **management information systems (MIS),** are systems in which computers are the primary component of the information-producing mechanism. Even in a computer-based information system, both manual and semi-manual devices act in conjunction with the computer to capture or accept and process data, and to generate information. However, the majority of the tasks are handled by the computer components. For example, you could use a computer terminal to input data through the information system; a computer storage device, such as a magnetic disk, to store data; and an on-line printer to produce the output.

■ INFORMATION RESOURCES MANAGEMENT

Regardless of their size and type, all organizations have some kind of information system; the main task of management is decision making, and information is a major requirement of the decision making process. In recent years, many organizations have come to realize that information is one of their major resources. This resource must be properly maintained and managed, just like other organizational resources, such as money, personnel, equipment, and material.

Whether an information system consists only of filing cabinets and a few inventory index cards or of a department full of computers, there must be a structure for producing information from raw data. This structure can be compared to that of a shoe factory. In the shoe factory, raw materials—such as rubber, leather, and cotton—are manipulated by various machines in a well-structured fashion to produce the final product: shoes. Besides the mechanical procedures, the operation also includes management supervision to ensure that the whole factory operates in an effective and efficient manner. Along the same lines, a computer-based information system uses raw data, which is processed and manipulated by different computer components under close supervision, to produce the final product: information. Therefore, in general, a computer-based information system can be defined as a collection of electronic devices (hardware) that operate through various instructions (software) provided in a well-defined structure to capture raw data, to process, store, and generate information for decision makers at all levels of an organization.

A Brief History of Information Resource Management

Since the early 1950s, when the first generation of computer systems was introduced for commercial applications, computers have indeed revolutionized the management of information resources. The progress made in computer technology in a little over forty years has been so phenomenal that it cannot be compared with progress in any other industry. To understand the changes that have occurred in computer technology since the early 1950s, it will be useful to review some of the major highlights of computer technology and business applications during the last four decades.

The 1950s.

- Computers were mainly used for scientific and mathematical applications.
- Computers were large and had to be programmed to perform various arithmetic operations.
- Computer use required great technical and mathematical knowledge because computers could only be programmed via the computer's native language (called **machine language**), which consisted of a combination of zeros, ones, and various memory locations.
- Computers were very expensive.

The 1960s.

- Many accounting and financial applications were developed in areas requiring a large number of mathematical operations (addition, subtraction, multiplication, and division).
- Computers became useful tools to accountants, and many organizations developed a computer system either as a part of the accounting department or under the supervision of their accountants.
- These computer systems developed for business applications are better known as **data processing (DP) systems.**
- Computers were viewed as "number-crunching" devices only capable of performing arithmetic operations.
- These computer systems were in the category of **mainframes.** All computing operations were performed by one **centralized system,** as illustrated in Figure 1.3.

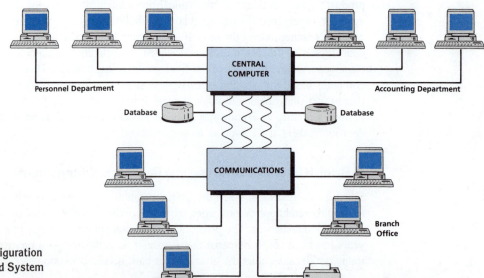

Figure 1.3
A Typical Configuration of a Centralized System

- Many new computer programming languages (known as **high-level,** or **procedural, programming languages**) were introduced. With these languages, which included COBOL, FORTRAN, BASIC, and PL/1, a computer programmer could write a set of instructions in an English-like language, which would be translated into machine language by another set of instructions stored in the computer system.
- Computer systems users had to know at least one computer programming language in order to be able to enjoy the computer's number-crunching power.

The 1970s.

- A new generation of computer hardware, known as **minicomputers,** was introduced. Minicomputers—smaller versions of mainframe systems—were made possible by the shrinking in size of the internal components of computers.
- Many organizations developed computer systems that could assist management by providing timely information in addition to number-crunching. The result was the formation of management information systems (MIS).
- A new concept of managing data files, known as **database management,** was also developed. Now, many users could gain access to information stored in common files (a database). The introduction of this data management concept marked the beginning of the movement from data processing to database processing.
- A new concept of computing—**distributed processing systems**— was introduced. Computing operations could be performed on computer systems at different locations while, at the same time, these systems shared information with each other. See Figure 1.4 on the following page.
- At the mid-point of this decade, developers—most notably Apple Computer—introduced a new generation of devices known as **microcomputers.** This was a mini-revolution unto itself. The basic components of the earlier generations of computers were put together in a single device, to be used by a single user, at a price an individual could afford.
- The development of database management concepts led to the introduction of a new generation of computer programming languages: **non-procedural,** or **fourth-generation, programming languages,** such as Focus. With these languages, the task of writing computer programs was greatly simplified.
- Toward the end of the 1970s, computer systems were developed that could assist decision makers facing semi-structured decisions by allowing them to assess different alternatives and assumptions. This development led to the introduction of **decision support systems (DSS).** These systems comprise of computer programs utilizing various decision models, assigning different probability values to assumptions provided by decision makers, to provide answers to "what-if?" questions.

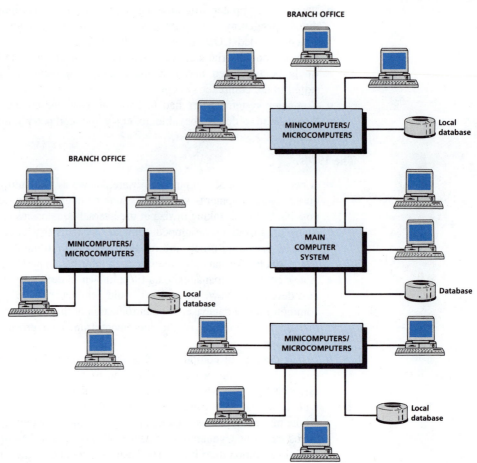

Figure 1.4
A Typical Configuration of a Distributed Processing System

The 1980s.

- Perhaps the most important highlight of this period is the recognition that information is a major corporate resource. Information and information processing tools are considered by many organizations as the "ultimate weapons" for maintaining a competitive edge in the marketplace and, in some cases, for survival in the business world.
- Another important highlight of the 1980s is the recognition of microcomputers as power tools for information processing.
- With the acceptability of the microcomputer as a business tool, many new software packages have been developed for a variety of business applications. You will encounter several of the most common software packages as you read this book.

- The introduction of advanced fourth-generation programming languages, powerful microcomputer hardware, and user-friendly microcomputer software packages has created a new generation of computer users.
- The concept of sharing microcomputer resources has led to the introduction of **local area networks (LANs),** in which a number of microcomputers are linked together to share computing power and information.
- New efforts have been put into the idea of developing a computer-based system that can *think* rather than simply compute. These efforts have led to the introduction of **expert systems,** in which a user can gain access to information stored in the computer memory via expert system software to draw conclusions or to make recommendations to solve a problem. See Table 1.3.

PERIOD	HIGHLIGHTS
1950s	– Computers were used mainly for scientific applications – Large and expensive computers – Difficult to program computers
1960s	– Development of financial and accounting applications – Computer systems known as Data Processing (DP) – Computers were viewed as "number-crunching" devices – Domination by centralized computer systems – Introduction of high-level programming languages (e.g., FORTRAN, COBOL)
1970s	– Introduction of minicomputers – Introduction of Management Information Systems (MIS) – Introduction of database management concepts – Development of distributed processing systems – Introduction of microcomputers – Introduction of Decision Support Systems (DSS) concepts
1980s	– Recognition of information as corporate resource – Acceptance of microcomputers as business tools – Introduction of many powerful software packages for microcomputers

***TABLE 1.3** Summary of the Highlights of the Past Four Decades*

■ THE ROLE OF MICROCOMPUTERS IN INFORMATION PROCESSING

Microcomputers have been identified as the easiest to use, least expensive information processing tools. The relatively low cost of microcomputer hardware and many advancements in software make these devices ideal for those who want computing power so they can access information without going through the rigid and cumbersome process of developing computer programs around mainframe systems. (See Figure 1.5 on the following page.)

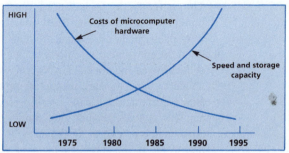

Figure 1.5
Summary Trends of Price vs. Advancement in Performance Capabilities of Microcomputers

In recent years, many organizations have put in place microcomputers to establish information systems or to serve as important integral components of their larger information systems. Microcomputer resources have been classified into two broad categories: hardware and software. The **hardware** of a microcomputer consists of all its mechanical and electronic devices, such as the monitor, the printer, and the keyboard (see Figure 1.6). **Software** includes all the programs and instructions for performing various tasks, such as entering, storing, and retrieving data, as well as producing reports.

Figure 1.6
A Microcomputer Configuration with Monitor, Keyboard and Printer

Chapters 2 and 3 discuss the hardware and software components of microcomputers in great detail.

MICRO-BASED INFORMATION SYSTEMS

With the availability of advanced software packages developed for microcomputer use, many organizations have developed smaller-scaled information systems, known as **micro-based information systems,** for their end users. They have found these computers capable of satisfying their information processing needs without requiring the investment of large sums of money in mainframe or minicomputer hardware and software. The introduction and use of microcomputers in the last decade has thus revolutionized information processing in many organizations.

Microcomputers can be used either as **stand-alone devices** capable of performing all types of computing and information processing, or as part of a **network** of microcomputers linked together for sharing resources, accessing and obtaining information from other larger systems (for instance, mainframes or minicomputers) through the use of communication devices.

In recent years, many end users have had to learn the basics of these systems in order to be able to use them more effectively and efficiently. Furthermore, many users have had to become the primary planners, implementors, and managers of this new generation of information systems without being able to rely on the expertise of a traditional computer system staff or computer programmers. The new generation of microcomputer user might be compared to the average car driver who searches for a car, chooses one based on identified needs, and uses it as a means of transportation, without worrying about automobile technology or how different parts of the car are designed. The main concern of most drivers is the use and operation of the automobile. By the same token, the user of a microcomputer is concerned with applications of the system rather than how to write different programs to manage the system's memory or other components.

Two decades ago, in order to use a computer, an individual had to have technical knowledge of computers, in addition to knowing at least one procedural programming language. But today, with advances achieved in microcomputer technology, a person does not have to be a computer wizard to be able to use a number of applications. In recent years, two groups of computer users have emerged in many organizations as a result of the wide-ranging technological changes: **systems staff** (e.g., system analysts, system designers, and programmers), who are responsible for developing and maintaining computer systems and programs; and **end users** (e.g., managers, administrators, and office workers), who are primarily interested in applying information systems to perform various tasks associated with their jobs.

The material in this book has been developed for microcomputer users rather than systems staff. The following chapters introduce the end user to the fundamentals of microcomputer hardware and software, common software packages for microcomputers, and system development cycle concepts.

■ SUMMARY

This chapter discussed the overall process of decision making, and its several phases: identification of the problem, analysis of the problem, identification of possible alternative solutions, assessment of alternatives, and finally, selection of the most appropriate alternative. The chapter also talked about different types of decisions: strategic, tactical, and operational/technical. We also classified decisions as unstructured, semi-structured, and structured. Decision makers at different levels of organizations utilize two different types of information: informal and formal. Informal information is the type of information produced mainly by the human brain, while formal information is the product of a well-conceived information system.

Formal information systems can be divided into three broad catagories: manual, semi-manual, and automated (or computer-based) information systems. In the last several decades, computer components, particularly microcomputers, have been put to work by many organizations for development of information systems. Microcomputer resources can be divided into two categories: hardware, which consists of the mechanical and electronic parts of the system; and software, which includes all the instructions and programs provided to the hardware components for performing various tasks. The chapter also reviewed some of the major highlights of computer technology and applications in the business world, including the introduction of procedural programming languages during the 1960s, and the later introduction of database management concepts.

Finally, we looked at an overview of the new generation of information systems, known as micro-based information systems, in which the end user is often the major investigator, planner, developer, and user.

■ KEY TERMS

decision making	Selecting the most appropriate or optimum alternative to resolve a problem or achieve a goal.
strategic decision	Involves planning and formulating objectives for the long and short term.
tactical decisions	Allocation of resources to accomplish goals or objectives established at the strategic level.
technical/operational decisions	Enforcing organizational procedures for various tasks.
unstructured decisions	A decision in which the variables are probabilistic.
semi-structured decision	A decision in which the variables are a combination of probabilistic and deterministic.
structured decision	A decision involving a great deal of certainty.
decision making process	A set of systematic steps consciously worked through by a decision maker.
information	Knowledge about an object, phenomenon, environment, issue, or subject.

informal information	Information that is mainly the product of the human mind.
formal information	The primary product of a well-conceived and organized information system.
manual system	A structured accumulation of information.
semi-manual system	A collection of manual and semi-manual devices.
computer-based information system (CIS)	A collection of electronic devices that operate through various instructions provided in a well-defined structure to capture raw data, and process, store, and generate information.
machine language	A computer's native language, usually expressed as a system of zeroes and ones.
data processing (DP) system	Early computer system development for financial and business applications.
mainframes	Large-scale "number-crunching" computers.
centralized system	A mainframe-based computer network, with central computing location for operations of various computing tasks.
high-level (procedural) language	Computer programming language, such as BASIC or COBOL, that allows a user to create instructions in an English-like language.
minicomputers	Smaller versions of mainframes; used mainly in distributed processing systems.
database management	A concept of managing data files by using information stored in common files.
distributed processing system	A new concept in which computing operations can be performed at different locations while, at the same time, sharing computing ability and information with each other.
microcomputers	Compact, affordable, easy-to-use computers.
non-procedural (fourth-generation) language	Language that simplified writing of computer programs.
decision support system (DSS)	Computer systems designed to assist decision makers in dealing with "what-if?" questions.
local area networks (LANs)	A system in which microcomputers can be linked together to share computing power and information.
expert system	A computer-based system with the ability to think rather than simply compute.
hardware	The part of a computer that consists of all its mechanical and electronic devices.
software	The part of the computer that consists of all the programs and instructions for performing various tasks.
micro-based information systems	Scaled-down computer systems that put computing power in the hands of the individual via microcomputers and software application packages.
stand-alone device	A computer used as a single entity.
network	Computers linked by communication programs to share information and computer power.
systems staff	Responsible for developing and maintaining an organization's computer systems.
end users	Those who apply information systems to the real world.

■ Review Questions

1. A decision in regard to allocation of organizational resources for achieving a goal is known as a
   (a) strategic decision.
   (b) operational decision.
   (c) tactical decision.
   (d) none of the above.
2. Which one of the following component(s) is(are) the basic element(s) of the decision making process?
   (a) goal or objective
   (b) formal information
   (c) informal information
   (d) decision maker
   (e) all of the above
3. The following is(are) major function(s) of information for decision makers, EXCEPT
   (a) to reduce uncertainty.
   (b) to clarify doubts.
   (c) to furnish better knowledge.
   (d) to answer unknowns.
   (e) to make decisions for decision makers.
4. Which one of the following would NOT be classified as informal information?
   (a) hunches
   (b) intuition
   (c) balance sheets
   (d) experience
   (e) none of the above
5. A semi-manual device includes the following items, EXCEPT
   (a) a cash register.
   (b) an order form.
   (c) a calculator.
   (d) a duplicating machine.
   (e) a microcomputer.
6. What is(are) the necessary component(s) of a micro-based information system?
   (a) information
   (b) hardware
   (c) software
   (d) raw data
   (e) all of the above
7. Which one of the following descriptions is NOT true for the computers used during the 1950s?
   (a) They needed to be programmed in machine language to perform arithmetic operations.
   (b) They were viewed as "number-crunching" devices.
   (c) They were able to handle scientific areas requiring complicated mathematical applications.
   (d) None of the above.

8. The innovation of computer technology during the 1970s include the following, EXCEPT
   (a) data processing (DP) systems.
   (b) decision support systems (DSS).
   (c) distributed processing systems.
   (d) database management.
9. Which one of the following languages is NOT a high-level (procedural) programming language?
   (a) PL/1
   (b) FORTRAN
   (c) COBOL
   (d) BASIC
   (e) Focus
10. Which of the following is an event of the 1980s
    (a) the introduction of DSS.
    (b) the use of procedural programming languages.
    (c) the introduction of minicomputers.
    (d) the recognition of information as a major corporate resource.
    (e) the introduction of microcomputers.
11. A regional production manager usually makes
    (a) strategic decisions.
    (b) operational decisions.
    (c) tactical decisions.
    (d) none of the above.
12. Explain why the use of computers is more suitable to operational/technical decisions.
13. Briefly describe the systematic steps in the decision making process.
14. Why is informal information also important to a decision maker?
15. A personnel department records on time cards the number of hours worked for each employee each week. Are hours recorded on the time cards data or information? Explain.
16. Is information more valuable to the management of a large company than of a small one? Explain.
17. Why are manual systems still utilized by most businesses?
18. Is it necessary for a firm to have a computer in order to maintain a database?
19. Identify and discuss three ways in which the computer has had an impact on your life.
20. Name some business applications of computer-based information systems.
21. What is the significance of the database management concept?
22. What is the "ultimate weapon" for most organizations? Why is it so important?
23. Describe the components and configuration of a centralized computer system.
24. What is the advantage of a high-level programming language?
25. Describe the configuration of a distributed computer system.
26. Computer technology has made many advances in the last four decades. Name three significant events of each decade.
27. Information management was historically a manual operation. What reasons would a business have for changing to an automated system?
28. In which steps of the decision making process could a computer be helpful? Explain.

Case One
COMPUTERIZED PAST TELLER

It was a nice summer day in Canada. Mike Kingson, an owner of a flower shop located in Harrisburg, Pennsylvania, was vacationing in Canada with his wife Suzanne. On this particular day, they were touring the Canadian National Exhibition (CNE) in Montreal. As they went from one booth to another, they came across a display in which a giant robot toy stood in the middle of a room. People were lined up to tell the operator of the robot their birthdays. In return, the robot told them what happened on the day they were born. In addition, the robot told them their horoscope. The cost of this service was three Canadian dollars and it only took the robot a few seconds to produce an attractive printout for each customer. Mike guessed that the robot was simply a computer with a database containing information about every relevant day in the past. The operator, in this case, the customer, would provide the birthday, then the computer would generate the information for this particular day in history.

As Mike studied the robot, he thought of having a computer in his flower shop and the kind of things he could do with it. Currently, Mike keeps all his customer records, financial records, and other data in hundreds of manila folders maintained in a few filing cabinets. When he started his business ten years ago, this system of maintaining information was very effective. But, in recent years, his business has been doing much better; as a result, sometimes he finds the system incapable of satisfying his information needs.

During the next few days in Canada, Mike kept thinking about a computer system for which he could find dozens of applications in his business. He even discussed the matter with his wife. He told Suzanne that, since he does not know much about computers, perhaps he should hire a new secretary who knows how computer systems work and to help him develop and utilize his own computer system.

Questions

1. What types of decisions does Mike normally make in his business—strategic, tactical, or technical?
2. Do you think that Mike could benefit from a micro-based information system? If yes, explain.
3. What are the typical applications of microcomputers in Mike's business?
4. What is your opinion in regard to hiring a knowledgeable secretary? Is this a wise decision?
5. Use the decision making process discussed in the chapter to analyze Mike's proposal.

Case Two
JETSETTER INVESTMENT CONSULTANTS, INC.

Jay Jetsetter is a 1978 business school graduate. For the last ten years, he has worked in the Department of the Treasury for the Commonwealth of Central State. While working for the state, Jay has been involved in financial analysis in the Treasury Department as well as financial analysis of the Audit Department. As a result of his job, Jay developed duodenal ulcers. He visited his family doctor, who advised him to get into another line of work, preferably one with less stress.

Jay became interested in stock market analysis while in the hospital receiving laser treatment for his ulcers in 1985. Ever since then, he has played the stock market and has become very adept at picking stocks. He made $20,000 on a $5,000 investment on several stocks in a month's time while lying in his hospital bed. This success in picking stocks is the main reason he decided to start his own investment consulting business.

In June of 1987, Jay left the employ of the Treasury Department and started his own consulting and investment firm, which he called Jetsetter Investment Consultants. He initially started the business with $50,000 of his own savings. In July, he took on a partner, Tom Trendsetter, who brought with him an additional $25,000.

The two partners combined their financial resources and became incorporated in August of 1987. The corporation provides many financial services to the public, including financial analysis for individuals as well as for firms and corporations, portfolio analysis, sales of stocks and bonds, and investment analysis, which includes helpful tips for the small investor on where to invest, how much to invest, or what percentage of the investor's income is a safe amount.

As a financial analyst, Jay must constantly monitor the stock market's performance. At present, he must either call his broker every hour or go to a nearby brokerage house to find out how different stock indicators are performing. This can be very time-consuming, especially when ten or more clients need to know at any one time how each of their stocks is performing or is going to perform. As he gets more clients, Jay finds that the way he gets his information is very inefficient. Up-to-the-minute knowledge of stock market performance enhances investment opportunities, which is what Jay and his partner offer to their clients.

The investment services provided by Jetsetter Consultants can be classified as two categories: (1) recommendations for certain investment options, such as common stock, bonds, mutual funds, or limited real estate partnerships; and (2) development and management of investment portfolios for their clients.

In the past two months, Jay and his partner have used a typewriter and several scientific calculators for doing all their typing, calculating, and report preparation. Since Jay and his partner are virtual computer illiterates, all financial services are performed manually. All information processing is also done manually. In the future, Jay's investment business will undoubtedly expand and he will find his present manual system even more inadequate and inefficient.

Last week, Jay attended a seminar for financial analysts in Albuquerque, New Mexico, where he ran into a former finance professor of his, Dr. Timothy Tomasetti. Jay was explaining his new business venture to Dr. Tomasetti and describing how all of the typing, stock-market checking, and calculating that must be done is very inefficient, tedious, and extremely time-consuming. Dr. Tomasetti talked to Jay and enumerated the reasons why he should invest in a computer to facilitate doing all those tasks. Tomasetti explained that Jay's company could access Wall Street with a computer and, with various software packages, could easily handle all the calculations and computations.

Since returning home from his business trip, Jay is extremely anxious to find out more about computers and whether they, in fact, can help him and his partner in their start-up business.

Questions

1. Describe Jetsetter Investment Consultants, Inc.'s information need(s).
2. What are the typical applications of micro-based information systems in this business?
3. In what way would the computer function as an information processor? As a retrieval tool?
4. What are the typical tasks that a computer would perform for this particular corporation?

SELECTED BIBLIOGRAPHY

Berg, T. B., "History of Computers," *Data Management*, October 1981, pp. 40R–40CC.

Bouwman, M. J., "Human Diagnostic Reasoning by Computer: An Illustration from Financial Analysis," *Management Science*, June 1983, pp. 653–72.

Burchett, S., "The Fashion for Modeling [for daily decision-making]," *Euromoney*, October 1985, p. 319.

Caltamaras, P., "The Microcomputer as a Decision-Making Aid," *Byte*, May 1984, p. 122.

Day, C. R., Jr., "High-Tech Tools: A Machine to Help Managers Think [Consensor]," *Industry Week*, January 7, 1985, pp. 62–3.

Day, C. R., Jr., "Information System's New Strategic Role," *EDP Analyzer*, January 1984, pp. 1–12.

_____, "Top Executives Increase Use of Computers in Decision Making [Trinet Exec Info Use Survey]," *Journal of Accountancy*, March 1985, p. 29.

Frieberger, P. and M. Swaine, "Five in the Valley [Microcomputer Revolution; Silicon Valley]," *Marketing Communications*, November 1986, pp. 113–16+.

Gehrt, R. F., "Take a Few Nanoseconds to Explore the Roots of Computers," *Data Management*, April 1983, p. 35.

Hollocks, B., "Simulation and the Micro," *Journal of the Operational Research Society*, April 1983, pp. 331–43.

Hong, R., "What Managers Can Expect from Artificial Intelligence," *Management Review*, December 1983, pp. 14–19.

Kahn, A., "The Chicken and the Computer [Which Came First: The Need or the Computer]," *American Journal of Small Business*, January–March 1983, pp. 10–12.

Mallach, E. G., "Computer Architecture," *Mini-Micro Systems*, December 1982, pp. 246–50+.

Mandell, M., "In the Real World, Managers Do Use Computers," *Computers Decision*, April 1983, p. 10.

Michaelsen, R. and D. Michie, "Expert Systems in Business," *Datamation*, November 1983, pp. 240–4+.

Millar, V. E., "Decision-Oriented Information," *Datamation*, January 1984, pp. 159–62+.

Papageorgiou, J. C., "Decision Making in the Year 2000," *Interfaces*, April 1983, pp. 77–86.

Quigley, J. V., "Effective Decision Making Evolves from Well-Designed Information Systems," *Data Management*, October 1986, p. 12.

Raike, W. M., "A History of Japan's Microcomputer," *Byte*, Summer 1985, pp. 395–6+.

Raymond, L., "Decision-aid for Small Business Computer Selection [French system-selection proc. known as Electre]," *Journal of Systems Management*, September 1983, pp. 19–21.

Seilheimer, S. D., "The Effect of the Evolution of Hardware and Software on Computer Consulting," *Journal of Systems Management*, October 1986, pp. 34–7.

Williams, A. J., "Decisions, Decisions," *Journal of the Operational Research Society*, April 1983, pp. 319–30.

Williams, G. and M. J. Welch, "A Microcomputing Timeline," *Byte*, Summer 1985, pp. 198–207.

chapter 2

MICROCOMPUTER HARDWARE

After completing this chapter, you should be able to

- *list the microcomputer's hardware components.*
- *describe a microprocessor.*
- *describe major input devices.*
- *describe the different types of printers.*
- *describe the difference between ROM and RAM.*
- *describe a floppy disk.*
- *describe a hard disk.*
- *describe a modem.*

INTRODUCTION

Among the first commercial personal computers was the Apple computer, designed and manufactured by Apple Computer Corporation and introduced into the marketplace in late 1975. Shortly after that introduction, Tandy Corporation introduced its first microcomputer, the TRS-80. International Business Machines (IBM) entered the market in 1981 with their version of the microcomputer, the IBM-PC (Personal Computer), and immediately sold more than 200,000 units. Before long, hundreds of companies, including Digital Equipment Corporation, AT&T, ITT, Hewlett-Packard, Univac, and Compaq, were manufacturing computers. Microcomputer products and services are now estimated to be a $20-billion-a-year industry.

During the early days of microcomputers, the field was dominated by the Apple. The founders of Apple Computer Corporation, Steve Jobs and Steve Wozniak, are as highly regarded by some computer enthusiasts as the inventor of the wheel. Jobs and Wozniak developed their first computer as a hobby in a garage. Their idea was that these machines could be used for an enormous range of activities, particularly for educational purposes. Although many consider Jobs as the father of the microcomputer industry, the truth of the matter is that many other people, companies, and government agencies developed the components that eventually went into the microcomputer that these two gifted men developed. They took existing technology and assembled it in a new fashion that has revolutionized the entire business world.

This chapter will primarily discuss the hardware aspects of microcomputers, first by briefly reviewing their history, then by describing the various hardware components for input, output, processing, and communications.

■ A HISTORY OF MICROCOMPUTERS

The development of the semiconductor chip led to the development of microcomputers. Many people believe that semiconductor chip development should be credited to the U. S. space program, which invested a great deal of research during the 1960s into a search for smaller electronic circuitry components that could be installed in spaceship and rocket computers.

A **semiconductor chip** is a collection of thousands of transistors placed on a square of silicon smaller than a postage stamp (see Figure 2.1).

Figure 2.1
A Semiconductor Memory Chip

Prior to the development of the first commercial microcomputer, these chips were used by many hobbyists, who developed their own versions of microcomputers using a simple typewriter keyboard connected to a TV monitor. These homemade devices were primarily considered forms of entertainment, such as video games. At the same time, many enthusiasts used these early microcomputers to learn more about computer functions and how the machines could be programmed to perform various tasks.

The first generation of microcomputers, with the Apple and TRS-80 as the front runners, was used extensively in education. Then, in 1979, the release of a software package called VisiCalc transformed a basic accounting function, spreadsheet analysis, into a microcomputer task (electronic spreadsheets will be discussed in detail in Chapter 8). With the introduction of VisiCalc, it became clear that microcomputers could be applied in numerous business situations to increase productivity at all levels. IBM's introduction of a personal computer line (Figure 2.2) in many ways accelerated the acceptance of microcomputers for business functions. One could argue that the entry of a well-known, established firm like IBM into the microcomputer industry legitimized the use of microcomputers in business.

IBM Personal Computer

IBM Personal Computer XT

IBM Personal Computer AT

IBM Personal System/2 Model 50

COURTESY IBM CORPORATION

Figure 2.2
Four Members of the IBM-PC Family

Soon after its introduction, the IBM-PC became the standard in the young microcomputer industry. So many businesses bought PCs that many computer manufacturers were forced to design their own lines of microcomputers around the PC (Figure 2.3 on the following page). PCs that are built around IBM architectures are referred to as **PC clones, PC compatibles,** or **PC look-alikes** (Figure 2.4 on the following page). The degree of compatibility can vary from one PC clone to another, but the majority are highly compatible with the IBM-PC. This compatibility means that software packages designed for the IBM-PC can be used successfully on the compatible machines. For example, an electronic spreadsheet package such as Lotus 1-2-3 (discussed in Chapters 9 and Appendix D) can be used on almost all PC compatibles on the market. Among the many manufacturers of PC clones are Compaq Corporation, Hewlett-Packard, Kaypro Corporation, Eagle Corporation, Zenith Corporation, Tandy Corporation, Leading Edge, NEC Corporation, and Panasonic.

Figure 2.3
Market Shares of Major Microcomputer Manufacturers for Year 1986

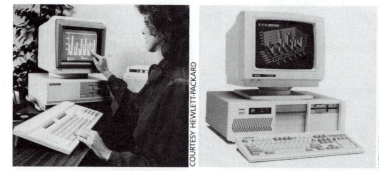

Hewlett-Packard Touchscreen Microcomputer   Kaypro 2861 Microcomputer   NEC APC III Microcomputer

Figure 2.4
Three PC Compatibles

■ COMPONENTS OF A MICROCOMPUTER

A microcomputer is a collection of many electronic components, including a microprocessor, memory chips, mechanical devices such as the keyboard, monitor, and printer, and instructions and programs. As we saw in Chapter 1, the basic components of a microcomputer are divided into two categories: hardware, which includes various physical elements (electronic and non-electronic) of the microcomputer, and software, which includes all the programs and instructions that are used in conjunction with the hardware to perform different functions. This chapter concentrates on the hardware components of the microcomputer; Chapter 3 discusses software components.

Hardware components of microcomputers can be divided into various categories based on the types of task(s) they perform. These components include processing units, input/output units, storage units, and communications units.

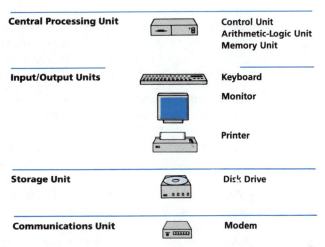

Figure 2.5
The Four Major Hardware Components

The Central Processing Unit

The heart of a microcomputer is the **microprocessor,** a single semiconductor chip containing the necessary circuitry to perform all types of computing tasks, to store data in the memory, and to control input/output operations. The microprocessor in the microcomputer is regarded as the **central processing unit,** or **CPU** (Figure 2.6). The CPU consists of three parts, the control unit, the arithmetic-logic unit (ALU), and the memory unit.

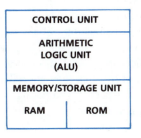

Figure 2.6
Components of the Central Processing Unit (CPU)

The **control unit** comprises all the instructions for performing different functions, such as controlling input and output devices, sending tasks to the ALU, and storing data in the computer memory. In summary, the instructions of the control unit make the "brain" of the microcomputer functional.

The **ALU** is responsible for all types of arithmetic operations, such as addition, subtraction, multiplication, division, and exponentiation. In addition to arithmetic operations, any decision making process—for example, the task of comparing two numbers with each other to find out which one is larger—is handled by the ALU.

The **memory unit** of the CPU is mainly used by the programs of the control unit and the user to store instructions or data. The memory unit is divided into two parts called ROM (Read Only Memory) and RAM (Random Access Memory).

ROM and RAM. **ROM** refers to that part of the memory unit that stores instructions for the use of the system. Generally speaking, what is stored in ROM is available only to the processing unit and its components, not to the user. Read Only Memory is exclusively dedicated to the processing unit. The other unique characteristic of ROM is its ability to hold instructions permanently. The contents of ROM cannot be affected by the absence of a power source or electrical current because these contents normally are stored on a computer at the time of manufacture. The contents of some ROMs can be changed later; these ROMs are referred to as Programmable ROMs, or **PROMs.**

RAM is the part of the memory available to the user of the microcomputer. In many ways, RAM can be viewed as scratch paper for the user. The user stores anything he or she wants in this area. Any program or data needed for processing must be brought into RAM. For example, if the user wants to use a software package to perform a specific task, the first step is to allow the system to bring all of the instructions or programs of the software package into RAM. In addition to storing the programs, RAM also holds the data the software will need to perform its job. The contents of RAM are completely erased whenever the computer's power is turned off. Thus, RAM is also referred to as **volatile memory.**

Types of Microprocessors. Despite the variety of microcomputers available in the marketplace, only a few major microprocessors are components in most of them. In the late 1970s and early 1980s, popular microprocessors in use were Zilog Z80, Motorola 6502, and Intel 8086/8088. The microprocessors most popular in modern microcomputers are Motorola 68000 (Figure 2.7 on the following page), Intel 80286, and Intel 80386. Table 2.1 on the following page illustrates different brands of microcomputers and the types of microprocessors they employ.

Microprocessors differ in their computing power and speed as measured by the number of bits that they normally access during processing. What's a bit? To understand this aspect of computing, you first need to know a little about the inner workings of a computer.

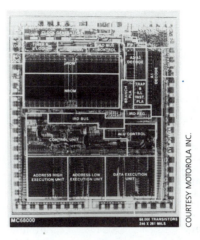

Figure 2.7
Motorola MC 68000 Microprocessor

Apple IIe	Motorola 6502
TRS-80 Model 1	Intel 8080
IBM-PC, PC-XT, PS/2 Model 30, Compaq	Intel 8088/8086
IBM PC-AT, Compaq Deskpro 286, and IBM PS/2 Model 50	Intel 80286
Apple Macintosh	Motorola 68000
Apple IIGs	Motorola 65C816
IBM PS/2 Model 60 and up, Compaq Deskpro 386	Intel 80386

TABLE 2.1 *Popular Microprocessors and Different Microcomputers in Which They are Used*

A microcomputer works internally with a coding system known as **binary code.** In the binary coding system, characters are shown as combinations of 0s (the "off" stage of a circuit) and 1s (the "on" stage of a circuit). Therefore, there are two positions for each circuit, either off (0) or on (1). This representation is known as a **binary digit** or **bit,** which is the smallest unit of computer storage. A collection of bits is called a **byte,** or character. The number of bits per byte, and the representation of different numeric characters (0–9), alphabetic characters (A–Z), and special or notational characters (%, &, ., and so on) are determined by two existing coding systems. The first is **ASCII,** an acronym for American Standard Code for Information Interchange; the second is **EBCDIC,** which stands for Extended Binary-Coded Decimal Interchange Code. In most microcomputers, ASCII represents data, with eight bits per byte. Tables 2.2 and 2.3 on the following page illustrate ASCII and EBCDIC data representation.

DECIMAL VALUE	BINARY REPRESENTATION	ASCII	DECIMAL VALUE	BINARY REPRESENTATION	ASCII	DECIMAL VALUE	BINARY REPRESENTATION	ASCII
48	0011 0000	0	76	0100 1100	L	103	0110 0111	g
49	0011 0001	1	77	0100 1101	M	104	0110 1000	h
50	0011 0010	2	78	0100 1110	N	105	0110 1001	i
51	0011 0011	3	79	0100 1111	O	106	0110 1010	j
52	0011 0100	4	80	0101 0000	P	107	0110 1011	k
53	0011 0101	5	81	0101 0001	Q	108	0110 1100	l
54	0011 0110	6	82	0101 0010	R	109	0110 1101	m
55	0011 0111	7	83	0101 0011	S	110	0110 1110	n
56	0011 1000	8	84	0101 0100	T	111	0110 1111	o
57	0011 1001	9	85	0101 0101	U	112	0111 0000	p
65	0100 0001	A	86	0101 0110	V	113	0111 0001	q
66	0100 0010	B	87	0101 0111	W	114	0111 0010	r
67	0100 0011	C	88	0101 1000	X	115	0111 0011	s
68	0100 0100	D	89	0101 1001	Y	116	0111 0100	t
69	0100 0101	E	90	0101 1010	Z	117	0111 0101	u
70	0100 0110	F	97	0110 0001	a	118	0111 0110	v
71	0100 0111	G	98	0110 0010	b	119	0111 0111	w
72	0100 1000	H	99	0110 0011	c	120	0111 1000	x
73	0100 1001	I	100	0110 0100	d	121	0111 1001	y
74	0100 1010	J	101	0110 0101	e	122	0111 1010	z
75	0100 1011	K	102	0110 0110	f			

TABLE 2.2 Coding Representation of American Standard Coding Information Interchange (ASCII)

DECIMAL VALUE	BINARY REPRESENTATION	EBCDIC	DECIMAL VALUE	BINARY REPRESENTATION	EBCDIC	DECIMAL VALUE	BINARY REPRESENTATION	EBCDIC
129	1000 0001	a	165	1010 0101	v	216	1101 1000	Q
130	1000 0010	b	166	1010 0110	w	217	1101 1001	R
131	1000 0011	c	167	1010 0111	x	226	1110 0010	S
132	1000 0100	d	168	1010 1000	y	227	1110 0011	T
133	1000 0101	e	169	1010 1001	z	228	1110 0100	U
134	1000 0110	f	193	1100 0001	A	229	1110 0101	V
135	1000 0111	g	194	1100 0010	B	230	1110 0110	W
136	1000 1000	h	195	1100 0011	C	231	1110 0111	X
137	1000 1001	i	196	1100 0100	D	232	1110 1000	Y
145	1001 0001	j	197	1100 0101	E	233	1110 1001	Z
146	1001 0010	k	198	1100 0110	F	240	1111 0000	0
147	1001 0011	l	199	1100 0111	G	241	1111 0001	1
148	1001 0100	m	200	1100 1000	H	242	1111 0010	2
149	1001 0101	n	201	1100 1001	I	243	1111 0011	3
150	1001 0110	o	209	1101 0001	J	244	1111 0100	4
151	1001 0111	p	210	1101 0010	K	245	1111 0101	5
152	1001 1000	q	211	1101 0011	L	246	1111 0110	6
153	1001 1001	r	212	1101 0100	M	247	1111 0111	7
162	1010 0010	s	213	1101 0101	N	248	1111 1000	8
163	1010 0011	t	214	1101 0110	O	249	1111 1001	9
164	1010 0100	u	215	1101 0111	P			

TABLE 2.3 Coding Representation of Extended Binary-Coded Decimal Interchange Code (EBCDIC)

The size of the memory (RAM) that a microprocessor manages is normally measured by the capital letter K, which stands for kilobytes (from the Latin "kilo," or 1,000). In computer vocabulary, 1K is precisely equal to 1,024 bytes (2 raised to the 10th power); 1,000K or 1,024K, which is about one million bytes, is known as a megabyte (MB). Similarly, 1,000 MB, or one billion bytes, is known as a gigabyte (GB); and 1,000 GB, or one trillion bytes, is known as a terabyte (TB). Therefore, a computer with a storage capacity of 655,360 bytes (1,024 x 640) will be referred to as having 640K storage capacity. When a user refers to a microcomputer as having an internal memory of 256K, she means that the RAM capacity is about 256,000 bytes or characters, or, to be more precise, exactly 262,144 bytes.

RAM size varies from one machine to another. The earliest microcomputers were equipped with 16K; later, 48K was the standard. When the Apple IIe was introduced in the late '70s with 64K of memory, that amount of memory capacity was considered a luxury. These days, it is common to see microcomputers with 256K, 512K, 640K, or even 1 MB of storage capacity. One major force behind the larger RAM sizes is the increasing amount of memory needed by various programs of many popular, user-friendly software packages. The friendlier the software, the more programs in the software, and eventually, the more memory is needed to use the package.

Microprocessors are known as 8-bit, 16-bit, or 32-bit processors. An 8-bit microprocessor uses one byte (eight bits) at a time for processing, and can access storage capacity of only 65,536 bytes, or 64K. A 16-bit microprocessor uses two bytes (sixteen bits), permitting a maximum addressable storage of one megabyte. A 32-bit microprocessor uses four bytes (thirty-two bits) at a time, and can address storage of 16MB or approximately 16,000,000 bytes. The more bits the microprocessor can access, the faster data can be processed, and the larger the computer's storage capacity. A 32-bit microprocessor is significantly faster than 8-bit and 16-bit microprocessors. A microcomputer equipped with a 16-bit microprocessor runs at 33,000 instructions per second, while a microcomputer equipped with a 32-bit microprocessor runs at approximately four million instructions per second. Table 2.4 lists the common microprocessors and their classifications.

Motorola 6502, Zilog Z80, and Intel 8080	8-bit
Intel 8088, and 80286	16-bit
Motorola 68000	16-bit
Motorola 65C816	16-bit
Intel 80386	32-bit

TABLE 2.4 Bit Classifications of Common Microprocessors

Normally, a processing unit also includes other components. Let's take a look at a few of them.

The System Clock. The **system clock** is a crystal that vibrates at a frequency of several million times per second. Its purpose is to measure the internal operations of the CPU. The clock frequency marks the beginning and ending of each operation that takes place within the computer. This allows different components of the CPU to be activated and deactivated so that all of them can be performing different tasks simultaneously, rather than having some components sitting idle. The clock frequency in millions is rated by MegaHertz, or MHz ("mega" is equal to one million; "hertz" is a unit of frequency measure, one hertz is equal to one cycle per second). The clock rating may vary from 4.77 to more than 20 MHz. The most common clock rates are 4.77 and 8 MHz. The microcomputer with an 8 MHz clock performs operations almost twice as fast as a microcomputer with a clock of 4.77 MHz. The new IBM PS/2 and Compaq Deskpro 386 run at 20 MHz, and experts predict that future machines will operate with even higher clock speeds.

The Coprocessor. Often referred to as a math coprocessor, the **coprocessor** is usally included in the microcomputer to assist with data manipulation—particularly mathematical calculations—and to free the microprocessor for other tasks. Most microcomputers are not equipped with a coprocessor at the time of initial purchase, although having a coprocessor is considered an advantage. Many software packages, particularly those requiring a considerable volume of arithmetic operations, are designed to accommodate the addition of this adjunct to the CPU. A coprocessor that has been installed in a microcomputer is not active during normal processing unless activated by a specific software package.

The System Bus. In order to allow different components of the processing unit to communicate with each other, an electronic pathway, called a **system bus,** is used. In many ways, the tasks performed by this pathway resemble the work done by a shuttle bus working between an airport and its surrounding communities. The bus allows information and instructions to be passed between different components of the processing units. The bus itself is passive, meaning that it does not perform any processing tasks. Its mission is to work as a messenger.

Expansion Slots. Each microcomputer is designed to perform basic computing tasks; any additional tasks can be added by the user. In order to permit this expansion, most microcomputers are equipped with **expansion slots** for optional tasks. Once a system is purchased, the user can obtain devices called boards or cards (such as an interface board, expansion board, or controller board), each of which is placed in one of the expansion slots to perform an additional function. For example, the interface board shown in Figure 2.8 on the following page allows a printer to communicate with the CPU.

Figure 2.8
A Typical Printer Interface Board

Another board might allow the microcomputer to communicate with other computers (a mainframe or mini, or other microcomputers). In the past few years, the idea of allowing microcomputers to communicate with each other or with other types of computer systems—an idea known as **connectivity**—is becoming very popular. Connectivity means sharing data, programs, and hardware resources, both within an organization and outside it. No longer are microcomputers viewed as stand-alone devices; today they are considered part of an organization's information system structure.

The number of expansion slots in a microcomputer can range from one to ten. For example, the IBM-PC is equipped with seven expansion slots. In the new IBM Personal System/2 (PS/2), the number of slots is reduced (three slots in Models 30 and 50, seven slots in Models 60 and 80) because many of the functions that had to be added to the original PC are now built into the PS/2. So that you can plan the expansion of your computer's power, it is important to know how many expansion slots are provided with a microcomputer at the time of purchase.

The CPU's components are connected to a large board, referred to as the **mother board** (Figure 2.9).

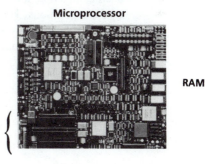

Figure 2.9
Components of the IBM PC Mother Board

Input/Output Devices

The task of entering data into a microcomputer is managed by input devices. Information generated by the system is supplied to the user by the output devices. Collectively called **input/output (I/O) devices,** these units allow users and the microcomputer to communicate with each other (Figure 2.10). The major I/O devices are keyboards, monitors, printers, and plotters. The following sections describe each of these devices and the types of functions they perform.

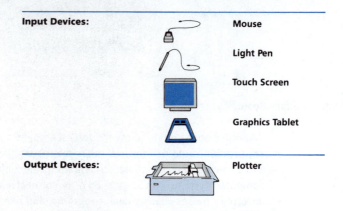

Figure 2.10
Input/Output Devices

The Keyboard. Perhaps the single most common input device on a microcomputer is the **keyboard,** which allows the user to enter data or instructions into the computer. It is similar to a typewriter keyboard, with one major difference. The data or instructions typed on the microcomputer keyboard will be sent to the CPU of the system, in the case of an ordinary typewriter, typed material is printed immediately, without alteration or processing. On most computer keyboards, the main keys are arranged in an identical manner to those of a typical typewriter.

Most computer keyboards also have additional keys to perform specific tasks, such as function keys, an escape key, and some others. We will discuss the purpose of these additional keys in the software chapters of this book. (The availability of these additional keys and their arrangement differ according to the manufacturer.) Figure 2.11 on the following page illustrates the IBM-PC keyboard and its categories of keys.

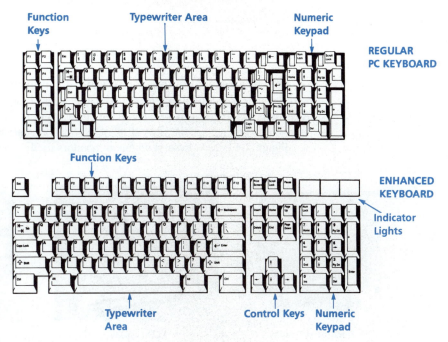

Figure 2.11
Two versions of the IBM PC Keyboard

    The keyboard may be physically attached to the system, or may be what is referred to as a detached keyboard. With a detached keyboard, the user can position the keyboard separately without moving the entire computer. Other microcomputer input devices include mice, light pens, touch screens, line and page readers, and voice recognition devices. A mouse, illustrated in Figure 2.12, allows the user to move a cursor, or pointer, around on the screen by pointing to the appropriate command on the screen.

Figure 2.12
IBM Personal System/2 Model 25 with a Mouse

The Monitor. **Monitors,** or **screens,** are primary output devices in most microcomputers. Monitors perform two major tasks: first, they display data or type instructions so the user can see what he or she actually keyed in and, if mistakes were made, correct them. Second, they display information generated by the system for the user. Figure 2.13 shows several common monitors used with microcomputers.

Monochrome Display

LCD Display

Color Display

Figure 2.13
Three Types of Monitors/Displays Used with Microcomputers

Monitors can be quite different from one another. A monitor may be attached to the system, or detached. A monitor could be a regular TV monitor, or a monitor that is specially designed to be used as a computer monitor. The major difference between a TV monitor and specially made computer monitors is the clarity of the information display, or the resolution. The resolution of a specially designed computer monitor is superior to that of other types of monitors. Monitors can be color or non-color. One type of non-color monitor is the non-monochrome (black-and-white) monitor that uses only one size **pixel.** Pixels (short for picture elements) are dots on the monitor screen that are illuminated to create the image of display characters. The other type of non-color monitor is the **monochrome** monitor which employs many different sizes of pixels to display characters. Monochrome monitors are often preferable to non-monochrome monitors because they are easier to read. On the other hand, color monitors are excellent for graphic presentation. (See Figure 2.14).

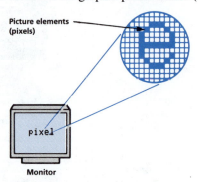

Figure 2.14
Picture Element (Pixel) Structure on the Monitor

Finally, monitors can be based on cathode ray tube (CRT) technology, which utilizes a large tube; on gas plasma; or on the technology of liquid crystal display (LCD), which can create a flat monitor. The LCD technology has been used for many years in electronic watches and calculators, and recently has been incorporated in the flat screens used on laptop microcomputers. The resolution of characters displayed on a LCD monitor is not as good as that of CRTs.

Printers and Plotters. **Printers** provide users with a **hard copy,** or paper printout, of the information generated by the computer system. The printer, the second most common output device, is normally connected to the system through an interface board placed in one of the expansion slots. A printer's performance is measured by the quality and speed of its printing.

Printers use a variety of techniques to print information. The original printer, known as the **dot matrix printer,** is still the most common type, and uses dots (points) to form characters. The speed of printing among dot matrix printers ranges from 80 cps to more than 400 cps (characters per second). Another common type of printer, the **letter-quality printer** (sometimes known as the daisy wheel printer), uses the printing mechanism that is found in most typewriters. The output of letter-quality printers is comparable to that of electronic typewriters. The speed of printing among these printers ranges between 5 and 80 cps (Figure 2.15).

Dot Matrix

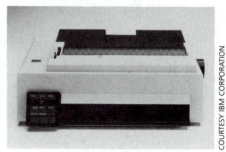
Letter Quality

Figure 2.15
Two Different Types of Printers Used with Microcomputers

In recent years, laser technology has helped in the development of **laser printers,** in which characters are formed by the collection of hundreds of dots. A laser positions dots of magnetically charged ink-like toner on a rotating drum, then transfers the image onto paper by a xerographic process, the same process used in photocopy machines. The quality of laser printing is as good as or better than that of the letter-quality printers. Laser printers' speed is 300 to 400 cps, and they are almost completely quiet, a major advantage in an office situation. The only drawback of these printers is their high cost, normally two times that of a letter-quality printer. The high cost of these printers is due to the relative newness of this technology; experts expect future price reductions. Figure 2.16 shows a laser printer.

Figure 2.16
The Apple LaserWriter Printer

Among other types of printers used with microcomputers are **ink-jet printers,** which use ink cartridges to shoot ink on the paper to print characters. For this reason, ink-jet printers need a special type of paper, and their print speed ranges from 60 to more than 200 cps. **Thermal printers** also use a dot matrix to form characters, except that these dots are generated by burning dots into the paper. Again, a special type of paper is needed for this type of printer; printing speed ranges between 50 and 300 cps.

Printers can also differ in the manner in which data is communicated from the microcomputer to the printer. In this regard, printers are classified as either parallel or serial. In a **parallel printer,** multiple channels are used for transferring data. In **serial printers,** extra bits are added, and only a single channel is used to communicate, making these printers much slower and less attractive than parallel printers. The majority of the printers in use with microcomputers today are parallel printers.

Finally, the last factor that affects the performance of printers is the availability of memory within the printer. This memory is also referred to as a **buffer;** the larger the buffer, the longer the printer can print without asking the computer for more data. A large buffer allows the user to continue working on the microcomputer without having to wait for printing to be completed, thus resulting in higher productivity of the entire system.

Plotters are output devices used mainly in the preparation of graphics and pictures (Figure 2.17 on the following page). They can be equipped with one single color pen, or with multiple pens of different colors. Users have found plotters handy in preparing maps, graphs, and even large-scale blueprints.

Figure 2.17
A Typical Plotter Used with Microcomputers

■ STORAGE UNITS AND DEVICES

Microcomputers use two different types of units for storing data and instructions or programs. One is the **main,** or **primary, memory unit,** which is part of the CPU. The other is referred to as the **secondary,** or **auxiliary, storage,** which stores data and instructions on a permanent basis.

The RAM part of the main memory is used by the processing unit and application software packages to store instructions and data at the time of processing. The microcomputer cannot perform any task unless both the instructions or programs for performing the task and the necessary data are brought into the main memory.

RAM has two major limitations. First, the size of RAM is rather limited. Although great advances have been made in expanding its memory capacity, it is still impossible to store everything in RAM. The other limitation of RAM is that it is incapable of holding data or instructions permanently. As long as a power source is provided to the microcomputer, anything can be stored in RAM, but as soon as the power is gone, everything is completely wiped out. While many people consider this automatic erasure a limitation of main memory, it is also an important part of the computer's architecture. An analogy will make this phenomenon easier to understand. A blackboard in a classroom is written on by different instructors during their various lectures. Now, if every instructor decided to keep his or her material on the board permanently, the size of the blackboard would have to be enormous! That part of the microcomputer's memory available to users is like the blackboard; it holds information only for the duration of each user session. To solve this problem of potential loss of information, secondary storage media are used to store data or instructions permanently.

Secondary Storage Devices and Media

Diskettes and Disk Drives. Early microcomputers used cassette recorders as secondary storage devices, and regular cassette tapes as the secondary storage medium, but this system proved to be very unreliable and difficult to use. The introduction of **disk drives** allowed for storage of data or programs on magnetic disks, better known as **diskettes** or **floppy disks.** The disk drive, which has the task of holding the diskette in place, is connected to the system through an interface board or card located in one of the expansion slots. Normally, one expansion board can handle as many as four disk drives. Figure 2.18 illustrates two types of disk drives: a 5 1/4" and 3 1/2."

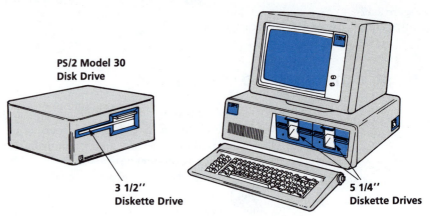

Figure 2.18
Two Common Disk Drives for 3 1/2" and 5 1/4" Diskettes

Soon after their introduction, diskettes became an important secondary storage medium, and, in many ways, contributed to making microcomputers as popular as they are. A diskette is a miniaturized version of the more advanced type of disk used in mainframe and minicomputers. A diskette is a circular piece of mylar plastic, the surface of which has been covered with a ferrous oxide coating capable of holding magnetic markings. Each mark represents a bit of data in the form of either a zero or a one. Like disk drives, diskettes come in different sizes; currently the most common sizes are 5 1/4" and 3 1/2" in diameter, but 8" diskettes are also available. Figures 2.19A and B show the most common diskettes.

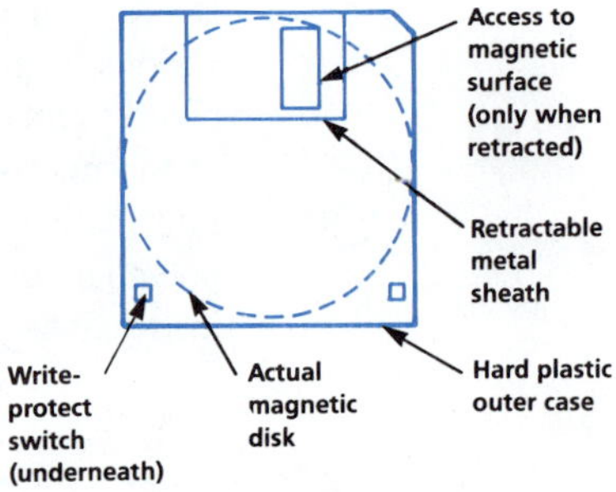

Figure 2.19A
A 3 1/2" Diskette

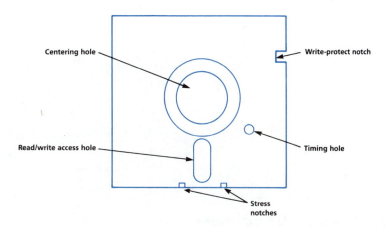

Figure 2.19B
A 5 1/4" Floppy Diskette

In the case of a 5 1/4" diskette, the coated plastic sheet of the diskette is placed in a jacket in order to avoid any direct contact between the disk and another object, including human hands. Each diskette has a large circular hole in the middle, called the **centering hole,** which is used by the disk drive for rotating the diskette in its protective jacket. There is a smaller hole to the right of the centering hole, called the **timing hole**. Under the centering hole, there is a large oval-shaped hole, called the **read/write access hole.** Data is recorded on the surface of the disk or read from it through this hole. On the upper right edge of the diskette is a rectangular-shaped hole, referred to as the **write-protect notch.** The user can cover this notch with a special write-protect tab (usually provided by the manufacturer of the diskette) so that nothing else can be recorded on the diskette. Every time the CPU asks the disk drive to write on the surface of the disk, the disk drive checks this write-protect notch. If the notch is covered, it indicates to the CPU that the user doesn't want anything else to be recorded on the disk. In fact, most diskettes that contain the actual program(s) of a particular software package do not have this notch at all, so that recording on the diskette is blocked permanently. There are two other half-circle holes right below the read/write access hole; they allow the disk jacket to stretch or bend without breaking. These cut-outs are called **stress notches.**

When a **hard-sectored** diskette is manufactured, its surface is divided into many circular rings known as **tracks,** on which data can be stored. Each track is divided into sections called **sectors** (Figure 2.20 on the following page). If a diskette does not contain tracks and sectors on its surface when it is purchased, it is known as a **soft-sectored diskette,** and the microcomputer system user creates the necessary tracks and sectors during a process called **formatting.**

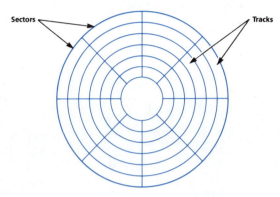

Figure 2.20
Formatted Organization of a 5 1/4" Diskette

A typical IBM formatted diskette contains forty tracks and nine sectors per track, for a total of 360 sectors. Generally, the term *density* is used to describe the number of bytes that can be stored in one sector. In **single-density (SD) diskettes,** only 256 bytes can be stored in each sector, whereas **double-density (DD) diskettes** have the capacity of 512 bytes per sector. By storing as many as 512 bytes or characters in each sector, a diskette's capacity may total 184,320 bytes, or 180K bytes (40 tracks × 9 sectors × 512 bytes), the equivalent of ninety pages of double-spaced, typed text that holds 2,000 characters per page.

Virtually all new disk drives are capable of storing information on both top and bottom surfaces of a disk. Diskettes that can be used with these disk drives are known as **double-sided diskettes.** A double-sided, double density (DS/DD) diskette can store as much as 368,640 bytes, or 360K bytes, of data (2 sides × 40 tracks × 9 sectors × 512 bytes), or the equivalent of 180 pages of double-spaced, typed text. Finally, **high-density diskettes** are a type of disk with storage capacity of up to 1.2 megabytes. Just recently, a 10-megabyte diskette was introduced, but these diskettes are not, as yet, commercially available.

The process of recording data on, or retrieving data from, a diskette is done with the help of the **read/write head,** which is mounted on an arm inside the disk drive that allows the head to move radially as the diskette spins around the middle shaft. The speed of rotation is about 300 revolutions per minute. In the case of double-sided disk drives, there are two read/write heads on two arms.

Hard Disks. The biggest disadvantage of floppy diskettes is their limited capacity for storing data—180K for single-sided, and 360K for double-sided diskettes. This limited capacity is not a problem with many small applications. However, when large data files or multiple applications are involved, a user may need hundreds of diskettes for all the data files and programs involved. In the early 1980s, IBM sought to remedy this problem, by introducing a new device that would allow users to store a significantly greater volume of data on a single disk. These devices are referred to as **hard disks,** or sometimes **Winchester disks.** A hard disk consists of a sealed enclosure containing a rigid metallic platter. This platter spins at a speed of more than 3,000 revolutions per minute. The storage capacity of hard disks can vary from five megabytes (5MB), or 5,000,000 bytes, to 10MB, 20MB, 30MB, 50MB, or more than 200MB. The more common capacities are 20MB or 30MB. A hard disk with a storage capacity of 30MB can store the same volume of data as 166 single-sided diskettes or 83 double-sided diskettes. Data are stored on the platter of the hard disk in the same manner that they are stored on the tracks and sectors of diskettes.

Hard disks come in two forms, fixed hard disks or removable hard disks. **Fixed hard disks** are manufactured as part of the cabinet that houses the microcomputer's CPU. The fixed hard disk is a permanent disk, and once it is mounted in the microcomputer, it cannot be removed except for servicing. Figure 2.21 shows a typical fixed hard disk.

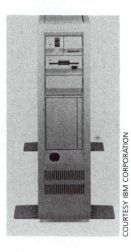

Figure 2.21
An IBM Fixed Hard Disk

Removable hard disks, sometimes called portable hard disks, are designed so that the platter can be taken from one system and used in another.

Due to the speed at which the disk spins and the proximity of the disk to other components of the CPU information can be recorded onto or retrieved from the hard disk much faster than with diskettes.

The major disadvantage of hard disks is the fact that, if the system fails for any reason—either through human error or system error—the entire contents of the disk may be wiped out. In order to prevent this kind of disaster, it is always a good idea to keep backup copies of the contents of a hard disk. In the past, diskettes were used to copy the information stored on the hard disk, but copying 30MB of hard disk data onto eighty or more floppy disks was a tedious task. In recent years, **tape cartridges** have been developed for backup copying. A typical cartridge, which looks something like the audio cassettes you use with your stereo, can store somewhere between ten and sixty megabytes of information, and copying a 30MB hard disk onto a tape cartridge takes only ten to fifteen minutes.

Optical Disks. **Optical disks** employ the same technology used to record sound on compact audio disks (CD) and have a large storage capacity. These disks use a laser to record data on a platter, in a manner similar to the process for recording audio CDs. The optical disks available on the market can record data once, then be used over and over again. However, after the initial recording, nothing more can be written onto the disk. Currently, optical disks are most helpful in applications requiring access to a large volume of data or information, such as the job of storing an encyclopedia. In fact, to get an idea of the storage capacity of an optical disk, consider that a single optical disk can record *all* the information in an encyclopedia set. Experts predict that, in the future, optical disks may be able to accept data additions and deletions just like the other secondary storage media, such as diskettes and hard disks. (See Figure 2.22.)

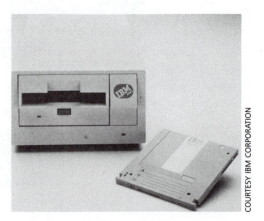

Figure 2.22
An Optical Disk Storage Unit (Cartridge Capacity of 200 Megabytes)

■ COMMUNICATION DEVICES

Microcomputers can either be stand-alone processing devices or work in conjunction with other systems, including other microcomputers, minicomputers, or mainframes. In order to allow a microcomputer to communicate with another system, communication hardware and software are needed. The hardware components needed for communication include an interface board and a modem.

The Interface Board

An **interface board,** or **adaptor,** which is placed in one of the expansion slots, establishes a communication link between one CPU and other computer systems. Without the interface board, data and information cannot be exchanged between any two devices. The interface board may be directly wired to another computer system, or it may utilize a communication device, such as a modem, for long-distance communication. (See Figure 2.23.)

Figure 2.23
A Communication Adapter

The transmission of data between the CPU and other systems can occur in either a parallel or a serial mode. (See Figure 2.24). In a **parallel mode,** the interface board transmits simultaneously all the bits contained in a byte, through at least eight wires, one for each bit. On the other hand, in **serial mode** the bits of a byte are transmitted one at a time. Serial mode, requires at least two wires, one for sending and one for receiving data.

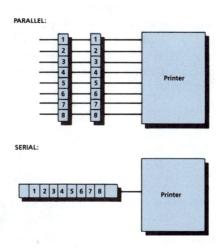

Figure 2.24
Serial vs. Parallel Data Transmission

The parallel mode of transmission is normally used for data transmission with other devices close to the CPU, such as a printer or disk drives. Serial mode is mainly used when the other computer systems are located a greater distance away from the microcomputer. It is common to see serial mode used for data communication between two computers.

The Modem

Traditional communication technology sends data over ordinary telephone lines. Before you can understand this technology, you need to know a little more about how computers and telephones work. Most computers are digital, meaning that data is in the form of a binary code (on and off, or 0 and 1). On the other hand, ordinary telephones are analog systems. In order to transmit digital data over an analog channel or device, the digital data must be converted into an analog signal by the sender, and it must then be converted back to digital by the receiver. This technique, known as modulation, is performed by a device known as a **modem** (MOdulator and DEModulator). (See Figures 2.25 and 2.26.)

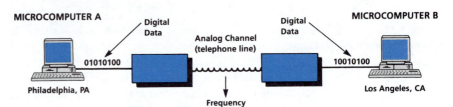

Figure 2.25
A Typical Communication Configuration Between Two Microcomputers

Modems come with a wide range of capabilities. At last count, there were approximately seventy modem vendors and more than 500 different modems. One way to classify modems is by their speed of data transmission. Speed is calculated in bits per second, or **baud**, often abbreviated bps. There are three catagories of speeds: low (up to 300 bps), medium (300 bps to 19,200 bps), and high (19,200 bps and up). Common speeds of data transmission are 300, 1,200, 2,400, 4,800, and 9,600 bps.

Figure 2.26
A Modulation/Demodulation Device (Modem)

Modems can also be classified by their type of communication channel or method of transmission. In **simplex** data transmission, signals move in a single direction. This means that data can be transmitted either from the sender to the receiver, or vice versa, but not both ways. **Half-duplex** refers to data transmission that is bi-directional but not simultaneous. Finally, **full-duplex** data transmission can occur in two directions simultaneously. (Chapter 16 discusses data communication characteristics in more detail.)

In order to allow a microcomputer to communicate with other systems, the specifications—such as baud rate—of the sending system must comply with the receiving system, and vice versa.

■ SUMMARY

The first generation of microcomputers entered the market in the mid-1970s. Steve Jobs and Steve Wozniak have been credited by many for the introduction of the first commercial microcomputer, the Apple. Soon, many vendors began to introduce their own versions of the microcomputer, including the IBM version, known as the IBM Personal Computer, or PC, in 1981. The PC established a standard in the young microcomputer industry; soon afterward, many other vendors began to introduce their own brands of PCs, known as PC compatibles.

Microcomputer components include hardware and software. The hardware encompasses all of the electronic and non-electronic devices, such as the central processing unit, the keyboard, and the screen. The software consists of all instructions and programs we use to perform various tasks with the microcomputer.

There are four catagories of hardware components in microcomputers: processing units, input/output devices, secondary storage devices, and communications devices. The processing unit holds the microprocessor, or Central Processing Unit (CPU), which consists of the control unit, arithmetic-logic unit, and the main memory (RAM and ROM). Other components of the CPU include the system clock, the system bus, the coprocessor, and the expansion slots. Input/Output devices are in charge of capturing raw data and presenting system-generated information to the user. Some of the well-known input/output devices are the keyboard (widely used as an input device), the monitor (which displays information), and the printer (which provides paper documents to the user).

Secondary storage units store data and instructions on a permanent basis. The most common secondary storage device is the floppy diskette. Hard disks are another common type of secondary storage medium in which a large volume of data can be stored. Other less commonly used secondary storage media are tape cartridges and optical disks.

Finally, microcomputer communication units include interface boards and modems. The interface board completes the communication link between the CPU and other computers. Interface boards are classified according to the transmission modes used for data communication. The two possible transmission modes are parallel and serial. A modem converts digital data to analog signals, and analog back to digital. Popular data transmission speeds for modems are 300, 1,200, 2,400, and 4,800 baud.

■ Key Terms

semiconductor chip	A collection of thousands of transistors placed on a square of silicon the size of a postage stamp.
PC clones, lookalikes, or compatibles	Microcomputers built around IBM-PC architectures.
microprocessor	A single semiconductor chip containing the circuitry to perform computing tasks.
central processing unit (CPU)	The heart of the microcomputer; also referred to as the microprocessor.
control unit	Comprises all of the instructions for performing computer functions.
arithmetic-logic unit (ALU)	The unit responsible for all arithmetic operations and decision-making processes.
memory unit	Unit where data and instructions are stored; divided into two parts (ROM and RAM).
ROM (Read Only Memory)	The part of the microcomputer memory that stores system instructions.
PROM	Programmable ROM.
RAM (Random Access Memory)	The memory available to the user of the microcomputer.
volatile memory	RAM.
binary code	A code system consisting of zeros and ones, zero being the "off" stage of a circuit and one the "on" stage.
bit	A single, basic unit of information to be stored.
byte	A collection of bits.
ASCII	Acronym for American Standard Code for Information Interchange.
EBCDIC	Acronym for Extended Binary-Coded Decimal Interchange Code.
system clock	A clock of crystal that vibrates at a frequency of several million times per second and measures the internal operations of the processing unit.
coprocessor	A component that assists with data manipulation, often referred to as a math coprocessor.
system bus	An electronic pathway that allows different components of the CPU to communicate with each other.
expansion slots	Slots that allow for the addition of extra memory cards or boards into the CPU.
connectivity	Sharing data, programs, and hardware resources, both within and outside an organization.

mother board	A large board to which the CPU and all its components are connected.
input/output (I/O) devices	Units that allow the user to communicate with the computer.
keyboard	The most common input device for entering data or instructions into the computer.
monitor	Also called a screen; a primary output device.
pixel	One of the many dots in a screen that form an image when lit.
monochrome	A monitor which uses many dot matrices to display characters.
printer	An output device that provides a hard copy.
hard copy	A paper printout.
dot matrix printer	Most commonly used printer; uses dots to form characters.
letter-quality printer	An impact printer that uses a wheel-shaped element on which the characters are placed.
laser printer	A printer in which a laser positions dots of magnetically charged ink-like toner on a rotating drum, then transfers the image onto paper by a xerographic process.
ink-jet printer	A printer that uses a cartridge to shoot ink onto a page.
thermal printer	A printer that uses a dot matrix to form characters by burning dots into the paper.
parallel printer	One that uses multiple channels.
serial printer	One that uses a single channel.
buffer	The availability of memory within the printer.
plotter	An output device for preparing graphics and pictures.
main, or primary memory unit	Part of the CPU where data or programs are stored while being processed.
secondary, or auxiliary, storage	Devices or media that give users a way to store data on a permanent basis.
disk drive	Hardware component that holds the diskette in place.
diskettes or floppy disks	Storage device of circular mylar plastic.
centering hole	The large circular hole in the middle of the diskette used by the disk drive for rotating the disk in its protective jacket.
timing hole	Small hole to the right of the centering hole.
read/write access hole	An oval-shaped hole under the centering hole through which data is recorded on the surface of the disk or read from the disk.
write-protect notch	A rectangular-shaped hole on the upper right edge of a diskette, which allows material to be recorded on the diskette.
stress notches	Cut-outs on a diskette that allow the jacket to bend without breaking.
hard-sectored diskette	A diskette with tracks and sectors added during manufacture.
tracks	Circular rings on a diskette's surface on which data are stored.
sectors	Sections of a track.
soft-sectored diskette	A diskette that needs tracks and sectors, added through the formatting process.
formatting	Magnetically marking tracks and sectors on a diskette.
single-density (SD) diskette	A diskette on which 256 bytes can be stored on each sector.

double-density (DD) diskette	A diskette on which 512 bytes can be stored on each sector.
double-sided (DS) diskette	A diskette capable of storing data on both its top and bottom surfaces.
high-density (HD) diskette	A diskette with storage capacity of up to 1.2 megabytes.
read/write head	A device mounted on a mobile arm inside the disk drive that writes data on or retrieves data from the diskette.
hard disk or Winchester disk	A storage device consisting of a platter, on which data are recorded, sealed inside an enclosure.
fixed hard disk	A hard disk permanently mounted in a microcomputer.
removable hard disk	A hard disk that can be moved from one microcomputer to another.
tape cartridge	A storage device often used to back up the data stored on a hard disk.
optical disk	A storage device that uses a laser to record data.
interface board or adaptor	An expansion board that helps establish a communication link between one CPU and other devices.
parallel mode	Data transmission (of all the bits contained in a byte) simultaneously through at least eight wires, one for each bit.
serial mode	Data transmission of the bits of a byte, one at a time.
modem	The device that performs the modulating and demodulating of transmitted data.
baud	Baud rate of bits per second (bps); speed of data transmission.
simplex	Data transmission in which signals move in a single direction.
half-duplex	Data transmission that is bi-directional but not simultaneous.
full-duplex	Data transmission in two directions simultaneously.

■ REVIEW QUESTIONS

1. Which of the following companies is/are manufacturer(s) of PC clones?
   (a) Compaq Corporation
   (b) Eagle Corporation
   (c) Leading Edge
   (d) Panasonic
   (e) Kaypro Corporation
   (f) all of the above
2. Which of the following is/are a function(s) of the microprocessor?
   (a) to store data in the memory
   (b) to control input/output operations
   (c) to allow different components of the CPU to communicate with each other
   (d) to perform all types of computing tasks
   (e) all of the above

3. Which one of the following is not a component of the mother board?
   (a) RAM
   (b) ROM
   (c) the expansion slots
   (d) the printer
4. Which one of the following is responsible for comparing two numbers with each other to find out which one is larger?
   (a) the ALU
   (b) ROM
   (c) the math coprocessor
   (d) the system clock
5. ROM stands for _____ .
   RAM stands for _____ .
6. Which one of the following is a data coding system in microcomputers?
   (a) ASCII
   (b) PCPSD
   (c) DRTECID
   (d) ABCDIC
7. Which one of the following is approximately equal to one megabyte (MB)?
   (a) 2,000K
   (b) 1 billion bytes
   (c) 100,000 bytes
   (d) 1,000K
8. Approximately, how much faster does a 32-bit microprocessor run than a 16-bit microprocessor?
   (a) twice as fast
   (b) $e^{32/16} = 7.39$ (7 times)
   (c) 10 times
   (d) $10^{32/16} = $ approximately 100 times
9. In order to obtain hard copy of a program or data, which of the following device(s) is/are required?
   (a) MODEM
   (b) a printer
   (c) a disk drive
   (d) an optical disk
10. Monochrome monitors are preferable to non-monochrome monitors because they
    (a) are easier to read.
    (b) use only one size of pixel to display characters.
    (c) are excellent for graphic presentation.
    (d) are based on cathode ray tube (CRT) technology.
    (e) all of the above.
11. Which one of the following printers require a special type of paper?
    (a) ink-jet printers
    (b) letter-quality printers
    (c) laser printers
    (d) dot matrix printers

12. Which one of the following disks has the capacity of 512 bytes per sector?
    (a) single-density disk
    (b) double-density disk
    (c) high-capacity disk
    (d) all of the above
13. Which one of the followings is *not* a secondary storage device?
    (a) floppy disk
    (b) RAM
    (c) Winchester disk
    (d) optical disk
14. Which one of the following condition(s) is/are required for a microcomputer to communicate with other systems?
    (a) The specifications of the sending system must comply with that of the receiving system, and vice versa.
    (b) Both systems must utilize MODEMs set at the same bits per second (baud rate).
    (c) Both systems must communicate with the same speed of data transmission.
    (d) All of the above.
15. Why are the founders of Apple Computer Corporation regarded as the fathers of the microcomputer industry?
16. Why should the development of the semiconductor chip be credited to the U.S. Space Program?
17. Explain the sequence of the events that led to the acceptance of microcomputers in business use?
18. What is meant by the term "compatibility"? Why is it needed?
19. Which components of microcomputers are more important— hardware or software?
20. What is the CPU? Briefly describe its major units.
21. What are the characteristics of ROM?
22. What are the limitations of RAM?
23. Explain the difference between ROM and RAM.
24. How is a microprocessor's computing power measured?
25. Briefly explain the microcomputer's internal coding system.
26. Distinguish between the arithmetic-logic unit and the math coprocessor.
27. What is connectivity? Why is it important?
28. Describe the factors that affect the performance of printers.
29. Depict how data are recorded on a diskette.
30. What are the advantages and disadvantages of hard disks?
31. Explain the importance of an interface board.
32. A small firm is considering the purchase of a microcomputer system. The company provides literature searches and specialized research to other industries. This requires that they handle large amounts of information and prepare a large number of formal reports. What devices would you recommend for secondary storage and printing?
33. A large company has branches in several cities in the Midwest. Each of these branches uses a microcomputer for information processing. At the end of each month, the branch offices prepare a report of their operations and mail it to the head office, where the reports are consolidated and the information entered into a microcomputer. Could this reporting system be improved? How?

Case One
THE RUMBLING ROLLER RINK

In 1985, Mike Mason decided to buy and operate a roller skating rink. The Rumbling Roller Rink was already in operation, and Mike bought it for $260,000. The building holds 250 lockers, the rink itself, and a large concession area. Thirty people in all are employed by the roller rink.

There are currently three departments: a food service department, an accounting and finance department, and an equipment and maintenance department. The food service department is headed by Mary Mason. She has three people, two cooks and one counter person, working under her.

The accounting and finance department is headed by Mike Mason, manager and owner of the rink. Two accountants work under his supervision.

Steven Sharp heads the equipment and maintenance department. Three people work under his supervision. This department is in charge of all repairs, including electrical, mechanical, and structural repairs. The department is also in charge of all equipment, such as rental roller skates and the costumes that are rented for skating classes and lessons.

The rink is open Monday through Thursday until 10:00 p.m., until 2:00 a.m. Friday and Saturday, and is closed on Sundays. The rink also has a room in which a baby-sitting service is provided.

Various types of skating lessons are offered at the rink by two part-time instructors, and payment for these lessons is required on a monthly basis. Approximately 100 regular customers take advantage of the lessons.

When Mike bought the rink in 1985, the books were not kept up-to-date, and there was a great amount of paperwork that had to be shuffled through before Mike could open the doors for business. Various papers, order forms, supply forms, paychecks—all of these were and still are being handled manually.

Mike, a recent business management graduate, wanted to update all manual forms of recordkeeping to a more efficient, practical method. He wanted to keep paperwork and inventories to a minimum so he could put most of his energy into the management aspect of the skating business.

Recordkeeping, inventories, and paycheck preparation are time-consuming activities, so Mike decided to purchase a few microcomputers to simplify the process. With this idea in mind, Mike consults with an old classmate, John Larotto, a computer salesman at the Rock-Bottom Computer Store in town. John recommends to Mike a microcomputer system that was on sale for $999.99. The system was equipped with 256K RAM, one disk drive, and a monochrome monitor. Mike was told that this machine would suit his needs for the next few years.

Upon purchase of the recommended system, Mike began purchasing various software packages based on recommendations of "expert" friends. It has been now almost six months since he invested several thousand dollars in hardware and software. So far he has not been able to accomplish anything on his computer system, which he thought would solve all his problems.

Questions

1. Define Mike's actual problem.
2. Assess Mike's needs for a microcomputer.
3. What was/were his mistake(s)?
4. What should he have done differently?
5. Suggest or recommend a course of action for Mike.

Case Two
JONES & JONES, P.C.

Sandy Jones works as a financial analyst for the private investment firm of Jones & Jones, P.C. When Sandy and her husband Clifford started the corporation two years ago, they began by doing small investment consulting and have since worked their way into financial management.

Sandy has her bachelor's degree in finance, and Clifford holds a B.A. in business administration, with a major focus in accounting. The couple graduated from Pro Business College in June 1985, married in July, and opened their private corporation in September. Each contributed $25,000 to the corporation, and each is working to bring in more clients and help those clients earn the best possible returns on their investments.

The daily functions of a financial manager include credit management, inventory control, and the receipt and disbursement of funds. Occasionally, a financial manager issues stock or bonds, does capital budgeting, or makes dividend decisions. The major goal for a financial manager is to maximize stockholder wealth.

Jones & Jones has two secretaries on its staff, as well as one salaried office cleaning person. There are three typewriters to aid in the correspondence and report-generation processes.

Two months ago, Sandy and Clifford were attending an accounting convention in El Paso, Texas. There they purchased a microcomputer equipped with a letter-quality printer for the best deal that they could imagine. Upon their return, they purchased a few accounting software packages to use on the new microcomputer. They learned very quickly that the computer they bought does not have sufficient memory for most software packages designed for financial applications. Further, they discovered that the amount of storage capacity that they need to store data on a permanent basis is far more than they originally anticipated. At this stage they do not know what to do.

Questions

1. What is the major problem facing Sandy and Clifford?
2. What was done wrong in the first place?
3. Briefly discuss the types of hardware components needed for their applications.
4. What are their alternatives?
5. What do you recommend they do now?

SELECTED BIBLIOGRAPHY

Hixson, A., "The Mac is Back," *Personal Computing*, April 1987, pp. 102–117.
Honan, P., "The Hidden Power of Your Printer," *Personal Computing*, December 1986, pp. 86–93.
Makrias, S., "High-End Dot Matrix Printers," *Personal Computing*, November 1986, pp. 149–153.
Makrias, S. and P. Honan, "The Complete Guide to IBM Compatibles," *Personal Computing*, April 1987, pp. 141–175.
Mier, E. E., "The Future of Modems: Will it be Boom or Gloom?," *Data Communications*, September 1986, pp. 55–64.
Moskowitz, R., "Rev Up Your PCs," *Datamation*, January 15, 1987, pp. 66–70.
_____, "Computers on the Go," *Modern Office Technology*, February 1987, pp. 43–50.
Pirani, J., "On the Beam with Laser Printing," *Modern Office Technology*, March 1986, pp. 46–54.
Reed, S. and P. Honan, "Hard Questions and Not-So-Easy Answers," *Personal Computing*, March 1987, pp. 63–75.
Taferner, H., "Internal Hard Disks," *Personal Computing*, February 1987, pp. 135–145.

chapter 3

MICROCOMPUTER SOFTWARE

After completing this chapter, you should be able to

- *define a computer program.*
- *name and describe different programming languages.*
- *define systems software.*
- *describe the difference between command-driven and menu-driven software packages.*
- *describe word processing software.*
- *describe spreadsheet software.*
- *describe database management software.*
- *describe graphics software.*
- *describe communications software.*
- *describe integrated software.*
- *describe desktop publishing software.*

INTRODUCTION

Early computers—including the early microcomputers—had to be programmed separately to perform each specific task. First, a system user had to learn how to program in one of the available programming languages. Next, the user would develop a computer program of written instructions governing each step required to accomplish the desired task. A **computer program** is a set of instructions that directs a computer to perform a certain task. The person who develops these instructions is called a **programmer.**

The programs or instructions used in conjunction with the hardware components of a computer are referred to as **computer software.** All types of computers—mainframe, mini, and microcomputers—need both hardware and software in order to perform computing and information processing tasks. Hardware without software is useless and, likewise, software without hardware cannot function at all.

As mentioned, early microcomputers had to be programmed constantly by programmers. Later, the trend moved toward prepackaged programs designed for common tasks such as writing memos, letters, manuscripts, and reports. These prepackaged programs are referred to as microcomputer software packages. Besides task-oriented software packages, many other programs perform a variety of functions, from managing microcomputer hardware resources to allowing users to develop their own computer programs. This chapter will introduce the different types of microcomputer software and their uses and functions.

■ TYPES OF MICROCOMPUTER SOFTWARE

Microcomputer software can be divided into three major categories: systems software, programming languages, and application software (Figure 3.1).

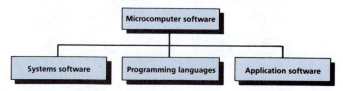

Figure 3.1
The Three Major Categories of Microcomputer Software

Systems Software

Systems software includes those programs that manage all of the resources of the microcomputer and control such things as input/output devices, primary and secondary storage devices, and application software. These programs can be further classified into two categories: control programs and the operating system (Figure 3.2).

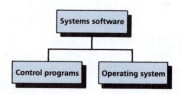

Figure 3.2
The Two Types of Systems Software

Control Programs. **Control programs** are permanent residents of the microcomputer's primary memory, the Read Only Memory (ROM). The control program manages the entire computer system. When a microcomputer is switched on, these programs are executed automatically, one by one, before the user can use the system. These programs examine various components of the computer hardware, such as the memory, keyboard, and secondary storage units. Control programs also are designed to bring other programs from a secondary storage medium, such as a diskette or hard disk, into the main memory of the microcomputer.

Operating System. An **operating system** is a collection of programs designed to manage the *resources* of the microcomputer system. Unlike the control program, which resides in ROM, the programs of the operating system are kept on secondary storage media, such as diskettes or hard disks. Part of the process of getting the system ready to function is bringing the programs of the operating system into the Random Access Memory (RAM). The disk that contains the operating system is called the **system disk.** Once a computer is on, its control program will load some of the operating system programs into RAM and allow the user to communicate with the operating system for many of the functions performed by the control program. The process of loading the operating system into the primary storage area to start the computer is known as **booting the system.**

There are two groups of programs in the operating system: basic command programs and utility programs (Figure 3.3). **Basic command programs,** which are loaded during the booting process, are designed to perform specific tasks essential to the easy operation of the computer. These programs are designed for controlling the cursor on the screen, accepting data from input units, displaying information on the screen, recording data on or retrieving information from the disk, and executing application programs.

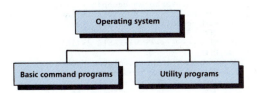

Figure 3.3
The Two Types of Programs in the Operating System

Utility programs are designed to do less routine tasks, such as formatting a blank diskette, copying the contents of one diskette onto another, and making comparisons between the contents of two disks. Utility programs are not loaded into the primary storage area at the time of booting. Instead, they are taken from the operating system disk and brought into the memory for execution as needed.

Despite the existence of hundreds of brands of microcomputers, there are only a handful of operating systems available. Each operating system is designed for a particular type of microprocessor or for a family of microprocessors.

One of the earliest operating systems designed for microcomputers was **CP/M,** an acronym for Control Program for Microcomputers. CP/M was designed to run on Intel's 8080 and Zilog's Z-80 microprocessors. The earliest version of CP/M was referred to as DOS (Disk Operating System). Different versions of CP/M operating systems have been used on a variety of microcomputers.

Today's standard operating system is **MS-DOS** (MicroSoft Corporation Disk Operating System). MS-DOS was designed to be used on Intel's 8088, 8086, or 80286 microprocessors. A version of MS-DOS was developed for use on the IBM-PC. This version is called PC-DOS (Personal Computer Disk Operating System).

Other operating systems available for microcomputers include AppleDOS, TRSDOS, Unix, Xenix, and Microsoft's new Operating System/2, or OS/2, developed for the IBM PS/2 family of microcomputers and compatibles. Chapter 4 discusses in more detail the major differences among microcomputer operating systems, and describes various functions of the IBM-PC operating system, PC-DOS.

Programming Languages

Most microcomputers are equipped with at least one programming language to develop different programs. The programming language used most frequently on microcomputers is **BASIC** (Beginner's All-Purpose Symbolic Instruction Code). A sample program appears in Figure 3.4. Almost every microcomputer is equipped with a BASIC interpreter or compiler. An **interpreter** comprises programs that can accept almost English-like BASIC instructions.

```
100 REM Payroll program
110 REM Developed by M. Khosrowpour
120 REM Date: October 8, 1987
130 REM
140 REM This program accepts employee number
150 REM hours worked, pay rate, and tax rate to
160 REM calculate gross pay, tax, and net pay.
170 REM
180 REM ********* Variable definition *********
190 REM
200 REM        EN = Employee Number
210 REM        HR = Hours Worked
220 REM        RT = Pay Rate
230 REM        ET = Employee Tax Rate
240 REM        GP = Employee Gross Pay
250 REM        TX = Employee Tax
260 REM        NP = Net Pay
270 REM
280 INPUT 'Employee Number'; EN
290 WHILE EN <> 0000
300 INPUT 'Hours Worked'; HR
310 INPUT 'Pay Rate'; RT
320 INPUT 'Employee Tax Rate'; ET
330 REM
340 LET GP = HP * RT
350 LET TX = GP * ET
360 LET NP = GP - TX
370 REM
380 PRINT 'Gross Pay = '; GP
390 PRINT 'Employee Tax = '; TX
400 PRINT 'Net Pay = '; NP
410 PRINT
420 INPUT 'Employee Number'; EN
430 WEND
440 REM
450 END
```

Figure 3.4
A Sample BASIC Program

A programmer develops instructions according to the codes for the spelling, grammar, and syntax required by the language. If the instructions are acceptable, the interpreter will translate them into machine language so the computer can carry out the intended tasks. A **compiler** is a more advanced version of the interpreter, in which additional capabilities speed up the process of execution of the program, such as keeping the translated or compiled version separate from the original program, known as the source program. This allows the programmer to use the compiled version later instead of having to translate the original program again. Figure 3.5 illustrates this process of translation.

Figure 3.5
The Translation Process

In many ways, the whole translation process is similar to that of being an English-speaking person in France who is traveling with an English- and French-speaking interpreter. The English person speaks in English, and the interpreter translates everything into French for the French-speaking people the English-speaker encounters.

In most systems, the user can employ two different versions of BASIC on the microcomputer. In the case of the IBM-PC, there are two different BASIC interpreters: regular BASIC, and BASICA. BASIC is stored in ROM, and BASICA is stored on the operating system disk. As its name implies, BASICA, or Advanced BASIC, is more advanced than regular BASIC. BASICA offers more features and functions than its counterpart. Generally speaking, selecting one version over the other has a lot to do with the programmer's familiarity with BASIC.

Apple II computers are also equipped with two different versions of BASIC: AppleSoft BASIC, stored on ROM, and integer BASIC, kept on the operating system disk.

The process of writing a program in BASIC starts with the programmer defining the task that needs to be programmed, then developing a BASIC program. After development of the program, the programmer will key the program into the computer and then ask the system to run, or execute, the program. At this point, the BASIC interpreter examines the syntax of the program. If the program needs corrections, or if there are mistakes or errors (bugs), the programmer will go back and modify it. The task of correcting errors in a computer program is known as **debugging.** Finally, the error-free program is translated into machine language and immediately executed by the computer. Figure 3.6 on the following page is a diagram of this process.

Another widely used microcomputer programming language is Pascal. Pascal is considered a more advanced programming language than BASIC because it offers many features that most BASIC versions are not equipped with. Pascal requires use of the Pascal compiler, which is rarely stored permanently on ROM. Instead, Pascal compiler programs usually are kept on a diskette or diskettes, separate from the operating system disk. Many noteworthy software packages are also written in Pascal.

Among other programming languages used on microcomputers are COBOL, FORTRAN, Ada (the new programming language adopted by the Department of Defense as a standard language for all their applications), and C.

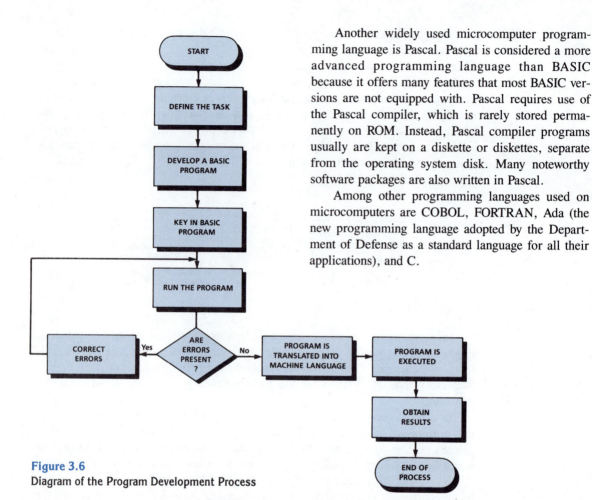

Figure 3.6
Diagram of the Program Development Process

Today, with the availability of many advanced and easy-to-operate software packages for a variety of tasks, a microcomputer user seldom has to develop BASIC programs. Nevertheless, many educators still believe that a good way of learning about the different components of microcomputers is through learning BASIC or some other microcomputer programming language.

Application Software

Application software, commonly known as software packages, have fueled the remarkable growth in the number of microcomputer users. A **software package** is a collection of programs designed to make the computers performance of specific tasks faster, easier, and more efficient. These packages perform functions such as word processing, spreadsheet analysis, and database management, all of which we'll take a look at later in this chapter.

One could argue that the introduction of landmark software packages, such as VisiCalc, paved the way for a new generation of computer applications. In recent years, many popular software packages—such as Lotus 1-2-3 for spreadsheet analysis applications, dBASE III PLUS for database management applications, and WordPerfect for word processing applications—have revolutionized the use of microcomputers in many businesses. These common software packages and their applications will be discussed in detail in later chapters of this book.

The major strength of application software packages is their ease of use. Each piece of software is designed to perform specific tasks. The user can easily take advantage of the package to perform the desired function and leave behind the task of programming.

Early microcomputer software packages were **command-driven.** In order to make the software perform tasks, the user had to use specific instructions, called commands. The commands sometimes consisted of technical terms and were sometimes cryptically abbreviated, such as CLS (CLear the Screen). Often, remembering all the commands and using the right syntax was as tedious to the user as writing programs.

A new generation of software packages have emerged in the market in recent years. These packages offer a different approach, the **menu-driven** approach, in which functions are selected from an on-screen list. For example, in dBASE III PLUS, a well-known software package for database management, the user is presented with a main menu of different functions as shown in Figure 3.7.

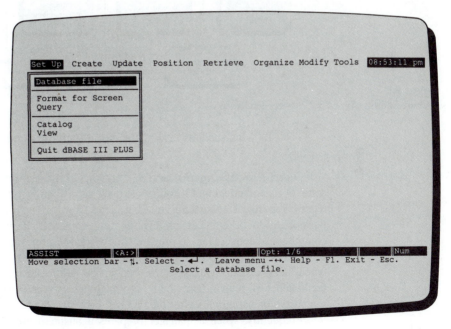

Figure 3.7
The Main Menu of dBASE III PLUS Software Package

The user can choose any available function. Upon selection of the desired function, another menu with another list of options for that function will appear. The process continues until the user defines the desired task.

With menu-driven packages, the user can easily move from one menu to another, select options, and provide necessary information to the system. In most cases, the user does not have to remember hundreds of technical commands or their abbreviations; a few simple commands operate the software and its menus. The subcommands are provided to the user through the different menus, and the user has only to choose the appropriate ones. Software packages with the menu-driven approach are also referred to as user-friendly software packages.

To date, thousands of software packages have been introduced by different vendors, individuals, and even universities for a variety of applications, such as education, business, medicine, the social sciences—even the arts. We can organize software packages into the following categories: word processing packages, spreadsheet packages, database management packages, graphics packages, communications packages, desktop publishing packages, and miscellaneous packages. Figure 3.8 illustrates these categories.

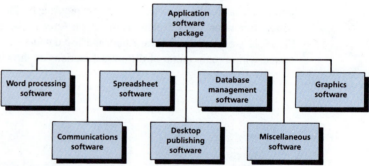

Figure 3.8
A Chart Showing Types of Software Packages

The following sections discuss the overall purpose of each category of software package.

Word Processing Software. A typical business organization must devote some of its personnel and resources to such tasks as preparation of business memos, letters, reports or documents, mailing labels, and so on. Employees often consider these tasks to be a necessary evil of doing business. Before the introduction of computers, managers had to prepare handwritten scratch versions of memos, letters, or reports. Their secretaries prepared final, clean versions of the text using typewriters—usually causing some headaches. Although typewriters in many ways facilitated text preparation, their biggest drawback came while modifying words, sentences, or paragraphs after the text had been prepared.

Frequently, when a manager prepares a business proposal to send to various clients, many revisions are made to the first draft (see Figure 3.9 on the following page). In such a situation in the past, the manager was often left to the mercy of paper pads and pencil, crossing out or adding words or sentences, or playing "cut and paste" games. Or, the manager gave the draft copy of the proposal to a secretary to be typed, so the manager could make corrections and modifications on the typed copy. Then the secretary retyped the marked-up version. Both of these processes can be very time-consuming, as you might imagine.

Another problem occurs when text or figures from a number of corporate reports need to be assimilated into one document. With a typewriter, those parts coming from other documents must be retyped in proper order in the new document. Finally, after completion of the final version of the proposal, different copies must be typed—or photocopied, cut, and pasted—for different clients, so that the documents include the correct names, addresses, and other client-specific information.

Word processing software is an application software program designed to solve these problems of text preparation, manipulation, and management. In the case of the business example illustrated in Figure 3.9, the manager could use a word processing software package on a microcomputer, entering the first draft through the keyboard. The manager—or other colleagues—could easily read the text on the screen of the microcomputer, and could correct it as necessary. Upon completing revisions, the manager could store the text on a secondary storage medium, such as a diskette, for later use or for printing a final hard copy (Figure 3.10 on the following page).

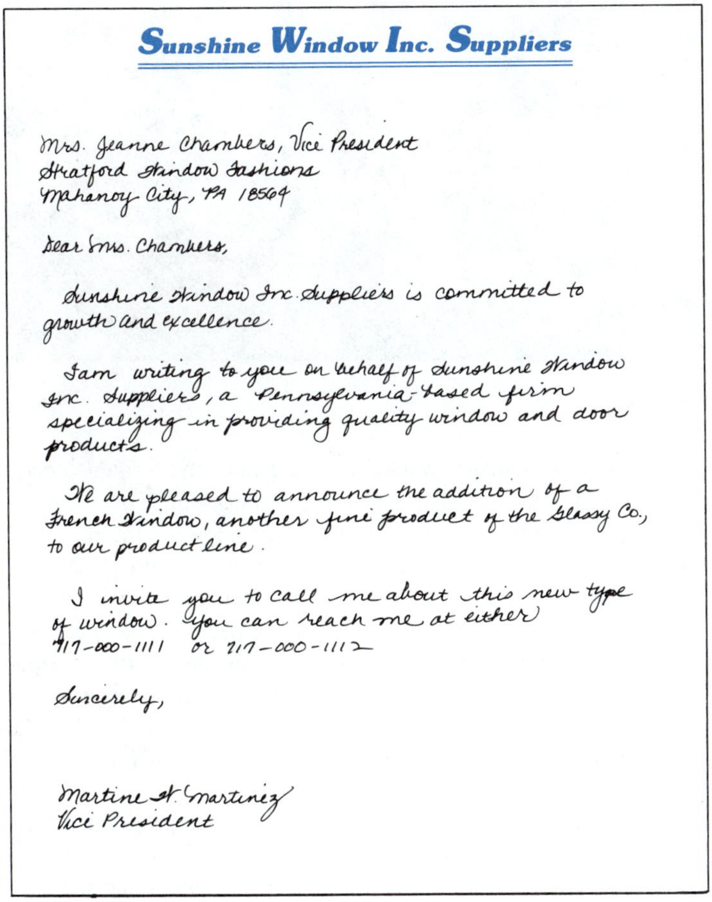

Figure 3.9
A Handwritten Business Promotional Letter

```
                  Sunshine Window Inc. Suppliers


Mrs. Joanne Chambers, Vice President
Stratford Window Fashions
Mahanoy City, Pennsylvania 18564

Dear Mrs. Chambers:

    Sunshine  Window   Inc. Suppliers  is committed   to  growth  and
excellence.
    I am writing to you on behalf of Sunshine Window Inc.  Suppliers, a
Pennsylvania-based firm  specializing in  providing quality  window and
door products.
    We are pleased to announce the addition of a French Window, another
fine product of the Glassy Co., to our product line. Due to the  unique
design of this window, we are confident that it will  become one of our
popular products. The  Glassy Co. has already experienced  a great deal
of success with this product.
    I invite you to call me for more information about this new type of
window. You can reach me at either 717-000-1111 or 717-000-1112.

Sincerely,


Martine W. Martinez
Vice President
```

Figure 3.10
A Microcomputer Configuration for Word Processing

The other alternative for our manager would be to give the hand-written version of the proposal to a secretary who has access to a word processor. The secretary could type the text into the computer memory, print a draft copy for the manager, and store a copy of the document on a diskette. The manager could review the printed copy of the text and make changes. The secretary then could easily access the copy of the text stored on the diskette and incorporate the necessary changes in a short amount of time, without retyping the whole document. Further, if the manager decides to add material from other documents, it could be easily accessed from the stored copies of those documents and added to the current document. Finally, the final version of the document could be printed over and over again for different clients by merging a mailing list file with the document.

In its simplest form, word processing software is a collection of programs which allow the user to create, delete, insert, modify, save, merge and print text.

Many business organizations have benefitted from the word processing software packages that are now on the market. These software packages have assisted managers and secretarial staff to increase their productivity by eliminating some of the time-consuming, tedious tasks of text processing with traditional typewriters.

Already many organizations have replaced their typewriters with microcomputers. With the dramatic drop in the price of microcomputers, many more organizations will be encouraged to do likewise.

Word processing software packages can come with a variety of features. Many of the newer versions are equipped with spelling checkers, an alternative word dictionary or thesaurus, mailing label preparation capability, and other options. Figure 3.11 shows the spelling checker of the WordPerfect software package.

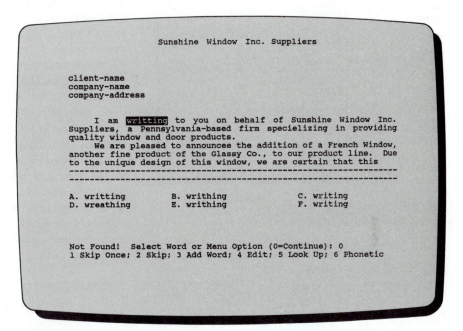

Figure 3.11
WordPerfect's Speller in Action

Some of the best known word processing software packages for microcomputers are WordStar, by MicroPro International Corporation; WordPerfect, from WordPerfect Corporation; Word, by Microsoft Corporation; and DisplayWrite, from IBM. Chapter 6 compares some of these packages; Chapter 7 provides a detailed tutorial for WordPerfect.

Spreadsheet Software. For years, many decision makers used a tool known as a worksheet or spreadsheet, a sheet of accounting paper divided into columns and rows (Figure 3.12 on the following page). Financial figures (e.g., sales, costs, income) were calculated according to different assumptions, such as annual sales growth rate, cost ratios, tax rate, and so on. These decision makers faced many "what-if?" questions that could be answered only by changing their assumptions (such as annual sales growth rate) and recalculating the figures. The task of constantly recalculating a large number of figures was often very tedious.

HOFFMAN DISTRIBUTION COMPANY
BUDGET (DOLLARS IN 000s)

ITEM DESCRIPTION	PERCENT	1ST QTR	2ND QTR	3RD QTR	4TH QTR	TOTAL
SALES		4,200	4,410	4,631	4,862	18,103
Cost of Goods Sold	30%	1,260	1,323	1,389	1,459	5,431
Gross Profit		2,940	3,087	3,242	3,403	12,672
General Administrative Expenses						
Salaries		1,000	1,100	1,100	1,250	4,450
Payroll Taxes	6%	176	185	195	204	760
Commissions	10%	294	309	324	340	1,267
Utilities	5%	147	154	162	170	634
Travel	11%	323	340	357	374	1,394
Entertainment & Promotional	8%	235	247	259	272	1,014
Total G & A		2,175	2,335	2,397	2,610	9,519
Income Before Taxes		765	752	845	793	3,153

Figure 3.12
A Sample Manual Worksheet

A **spreadsheet software** package is a collection of programs which allow the user to create a spreadsheet, perform arithmetic calculations, recalculate, save, and prepare analysis reports. With spreadsheet software packages, the user can type the initial figures of a spreadsheet into the interrelated cells (boxes) provided by the software. Figure 3.13 shows a typical spreadsheet screen for an income projection problem.

Once these figures are entered in the electronic spreadsheet, the user can easily evaluate different alternatives or projections, simply by changing the assumption in the appropriate cell. The change will be reflected throughout the entire spreadsheet as the software recalculates the values of all the dependent cells. For example, the "cost of goods sold" percentage estimate could change from thirty percent to forty percent. Figure 3.14 on the following page shows the new screen with all the recalculated figures.

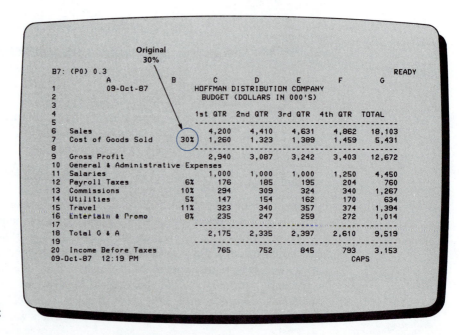

Figure 3.13
A Sample of an Electronic Spreadsheet

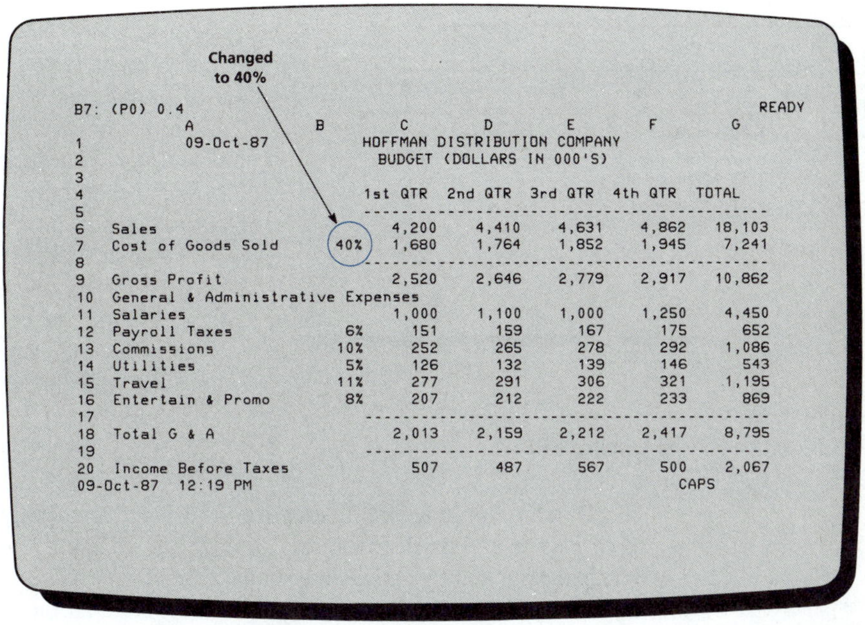

```
                          Changed
                          to 40%
        B7: (P0) 0.4                                                              READY
                A             B         C          D         E         F         G
         1         09-Oct-87            HOFFMAN DISTRIBUTION COMPANY
         2                                BUDGET (DOLLARS IN 000'S)
         3
         4                            1st QTR   2nd QTR   3rd QTR   4th QTR   TOTAL
         5                            ----------------------------------------------
         6   Sales                      4,200     4,410     4,631     4,862   18,103
         7   Cost of Goods Sold   40%   1,680     1,764     1,852     1,945    7,241
         8                            ----------------------------------------------
         9   Gross Profit               2,520     2,646     2,779     2,917   10,862
        10   General & Administrative Expenses
        11   Salaries                   1,000     1,100     1,000     1,250    4,450
        12   Payroll Taxes         6%     151       159       167       175      652
        13   Commissions          10%     252       265       278       292    1,086
        14   Utilities             5%     126       132       139       146      543
        15   Travel               11%     277       291       306       321    1,195
        16   Entertain & Promo     8%     207       212       222       233      869
        17                            ----------------------------------------------
        18   Total G & A                2,013     2,159     2,212     2,417    8,795
        19                            ----------------------------------------------
        20   Income Before Taxes          507       487       567       500    2,067
        09-Oct-87   12:19 PM                                                  CAPS
```

Figure 3.14
The Hoffman Distribution Budget Spreadsheet Example with 40% Change in Cost of Goods Sold

A spreadsheet is a handy tool for decision makers; however, it is definitely not a decision maker itself. A spreadsheet merely helps you assemble and organize all the data and facts about a decision or plan, and then performs calculations that indicate the consequences of specific "what-if?" questions.

Some of the well-known spreadsheet software packages include VisiCalc, from VisiCorp Corporation; Lotus 1-2-3, by Lotus Corporation; Multiplan, by Microsoft Corporation; and SuperCalc, from Computer Associates International Inc. Chapter 8 discusses in detail the major functions of common spreadsheet software packages; Chapter 9 provides a tutorial for Lotus 1-2-3.

Database Management Software. In every business organization, data or information about such entities as customers, inventory, and personnel are constant factors for decision making, report generation, or, simply, obtaining a basic understanding of the organization's status. In an organization with 100 employees, information about personal characteristics—such as age, sex, or number of dependents—could be used by different managers of the organization in making various decisions (Figure 3.15 on the following page). For example, the personnel manager might use the data to prepare a report as part of negotiations with insurance companies for group medical coverage.

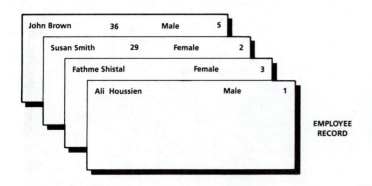

Figure 3.15
A Sample of a Manual Employee File

Traditionally, this data would be kept in a manila folder stored in a filing cabinet labeled, for example, *Employee Files*. A record for each employee would be stored in this cabinet. The process of obtaining data from this file and constantly updating the contents of the file's records is another tedious task. Further, it is possible that there are similar files containing the same employee data in other departments. Managing and coordinating these files and trying to keep them all updated is also very time-consuming.

Database management software is a collection of programs that allow users to keep data in electronic files, and provide the capability for retrieving, updating, manipulating, and reporting data. In the case of the employee file, database management software would allow an organization to store all the data about all employees in a database file. A database can be stored on a secondary storage medium, such as a diskette or hard disk. The database user can easily display the desired information on the microcomputer screen or print a hard copy using a printer.

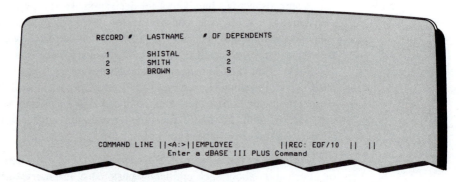

Figure 3.16
dBASE III PLUS Screen for the Retrieval of Employees with Two or More Dependents

The data shown in the sample screen in Figure 3.16 could be utilized, in whole or in part, by different managers of the organization. A significant advantage of database management software packages is in their ability to search through the database for specific data, a task which would normally take hours with traditional methods of filekeeping. Likewise, changes can be easily incorporated into the database.

Among the well-known database management software packages for microcomputers are R:BASE 5000, by Microrim, Inc.; DATAEASE, by Software Solutions, Inc.; and dBASE III PLUS, from Ashton-Tate Corporation. Chapter 10 discusses the major functions of database management software; Chapter 11 is a tutorial for dBASE III PLUS.

Graphics Software. Traditionally, graphic displays of business and financial data, such as the one shown in Figure 3.17, have been prepared by professionals in an art department. While the results were satisfactory, three limitations made this approach unattractive: it is expensive, it is time-consuming, and it takes the production of graphics out of the hands of the end user, which can result in a misinterpretation of the data.

End users and software companies are beginning to realize the tremendous possibilities that presentation graphics hold for them. With **graphics software** packages, users can better analyze data and trends through graphs and charts. With a microcomputer graphics software package, salespeople can communicate the benefits of their products; engineers can rapidly visualize and experiment with a variety of designs; managers can better determine schedules and priorities. (See Figure 3.18).

Figure 3.17
Manpower by Assignment

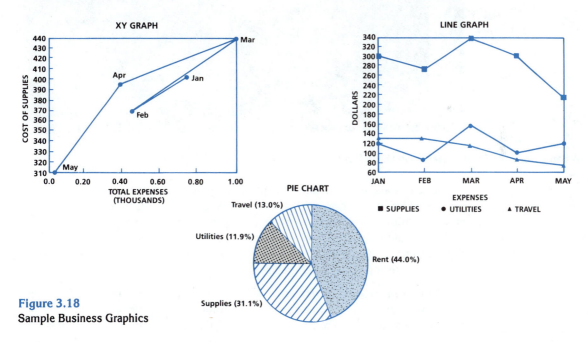

Figure 3.18
Sample Business Graphics

In addition, a visual image or representation of data is often easier to comprehend (and is retained with greater accuracy) than its written equivalent.

In the past several years, many microcomputer graphics software packages have been introduced by numerous vendors. These packages are offered either as stand-alone packages for graphics applications, or as part of another major business software package. The best example of the latter case is the Lotus 1-2-3 spreadsheet software package, which has graphics capabilities. Figure 3.19 illustrates a bar chart prepared with the Lotus 1-2-3 graphics subsystem.

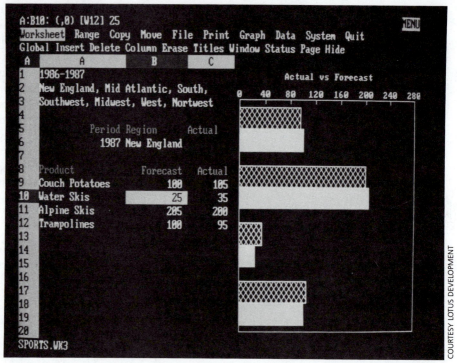

Figure 3.19
A Sample of a Bar Chart Presented in Lotus 1-2-3

Among some of the common stand-alone graphics software packages are Harvard Graphics, by Professional Software, and Micro Graphics, from Microsoft Corporation. Many spreadsheet software packages, such as Microsoft Corporation's Multiplan, and Lotus Corporation's Lotus 1-2-3 are equipped with graphics capabilities. Chapter 8 discusses Lotus 1-2-3 graphics, and Appendix C provides full, detailed lessons on Lotus 1-2-3 graphics.

Communications Software. Most businesses use information generated locally in addition to information obtained from other locations. For example, a decision maker may require certain information that is maintained on the company's mainframe located in San Francisco, or on a minicomputer in the company's East Coast distribution center, or on a microcomputer located in another department within the same building (Figure 3.20).

Early microcomputers were designed to function as stand-alone devices. Later, with advances in the microcomputer and communications industry, ways were developed for microcomputers to be connected to other computers to obtain or exchange information.

A **communication software** package simply allows users of a microcomputer to communicate with other computer systems by establishing the initial connection, transmitting data, receiving data, and monitoring the communication process.

The early generations of communication software packages could only emulate or convert the microcomputer into a "dumb" terminal, thus ignoring its computing capabilities. The new generation of communication software retains the micro's computing ability and, in addition, allows the microcomputer to communicate and share its processing power with other systems.

The main task of a communication package is to set the specifications of the transmitting system to match the specifications of the receiving system. These specifications range from "speed of data transmission," to defining the "type of communications channel," to, in some cases, telephone number selection. In some communication software packages, the task of dialing the telephone number of the receiving computer is done automatically. This feature is referred to as auto-dial capability.

A microcomputer may also be a part of a group of microcomputers connected to each other through communication lines so they can share information, processing power, and hardware resources. This type of communication, referred to as a **Local Area Network (LAN)** is shown in Figure 3.21 on the following page. One of the most important components of any LAN is the communications software.

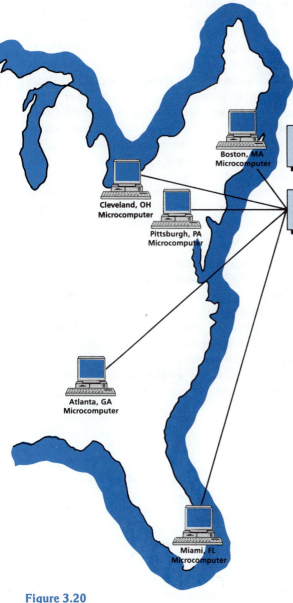

Figure 3.20
Network of Microcomputers and Mainframe Host Computer

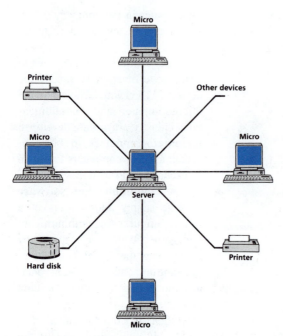

Figure 3.21
A Common Configuration of a Local Area Network (LAN)

Through LANs, an organization can save a significant portion of the costs associated with microcomputer hardware, software, and data by sharing these resources among users. Connectivity—the concept of connecting microcomputers, which we discussed in Chapter 2—is now considered to be a valuable method for maximizing the effectiveness of organizational computer resources. For example, with good connections, a microcomputer in the Order Processing Department can check customer credit data stored on another microcomputer in the Credit Department before shipping an order. Upon completion of shipping, the necessary information can be sent to another department's system for billing. (See Figure 3.22.)

Chapter 16 discusses the communication process and applications in detail, in addition to different LAN techniques and characteristics of available LAN software packages.

Integrated Software. Soon after the separate application software packages we've discussed gained popularity, it became evident that the difficulty of sharing data or information between different software packages was a major problem. Traditionally, text processing would be done with word processing software packages, spreadsheet analysis with spreadsheet packages, data management with database management packages, and graphics with graphics packages.

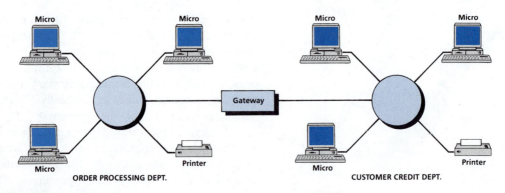

Figure 3.22
Configuration of Two LANs Connected Together

For example, only a few years ago the manager of a small business trying to put together a business loan proposal on a microcomputer could prepare the text part of the proposal on a word processor. Any financial analysis done with a spreadsheet package would have to be either manually added to the proposal or transferred from one package to another using a complicated procedure. Additional data from a database or graphics prepared with a graphics package must be added to the proposal in the same fashion as the financial data.

All that changed with the development of integrated software. An **integrated software** package is a collection of several subsystems capable of providing word processing, spreadsheet, database management, and graphics—all in one software environment as shown in Figure 3.23.

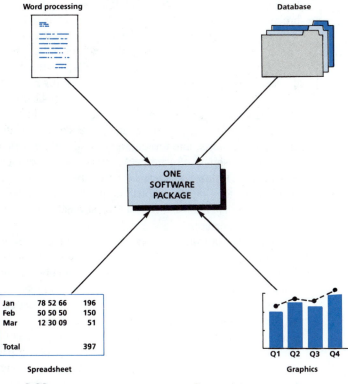

Figure 3.23
Integrated Software Packages

A major strength of integrated software packages is that they allow users to share data or information among subsystems. For example, in the case of our small business manager, one single software package could have solved the dilemma. With an integrated package, the manager could first write the loan proposal utilizing the package's word processing subsystem. Then, to extract some data about customer records, the database subsystem comes into action. After that—without the manager leaving the software environment—the spreadsheet subsystem helps prepare the financial report. Next, the manager could access the financial data of the spreadsheet in the graphics subsystem to create special presentation graphics. Finally, all those newly created data could be moved from different subsystems into the word processing subsystem for inclusion in the final loan proposal.

These software packages have revolutionized the capabilities of many of the earlier application software packages. One of the earliest integrated software packages—Lotus 1-2-3, designed by Lotus Corporation—has three subsystems: spreadsheet, database management, and graphics (Figure 3.24 on the following page).

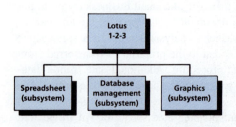

Figure 3.24
Subsystems of the Lotus 1-2-3 Software Package

The latest generation of integrated software packages are also equipped with communication subsystems. An updated version of Lotus 1-2-3, known as Symphony, contains word processing, spreadsheet, database management, graphics, and communication software, all rolled into one package. Other well-known integrated software packages are Framework, by Ashton-Tate; Enable, by the Software Group; Open Access, from Software Products; and Smart Software System, by Innovative Software, Inc.

Desktop Publishing Software. Many business organizations spend a great deal of time and money in producing publications, such as internal office forms, sales brochures, training manuals, reports, and even newsletters.

Traditionally, the original document or sketch of a stationary design was provided by the staff of the organization. A professional printing shop did the typesetting before the final document or form was printed. (See Figure 3.25.) Although this process has worked for years, publishing is still a major expense for many businesses. Today, the whole process of designing, preparing, and professionally printing documents, reports, and forms can be done with the help of desktop publishing software packages available for microcomputers. **Desktop publishing software** integrates personal computers into the publishing production process by allowing users to choose the layout, print fonts, format, and graphical presentations.

Desktop publishing software packages help users prepare and typeset text and graphics. The typesetting performed by desktop publishing software is totally different from traditional typesetting. The user of a desktop software package determines the layout, print fonts, and format right on the microcomputer screen. Then the user can obtain a printed copy of the entire document, and, the document can be saved for later use. Figure 3.26 on the following page demonstrates a business promotional brochure and a business form letter prepared by desktop publishing software.

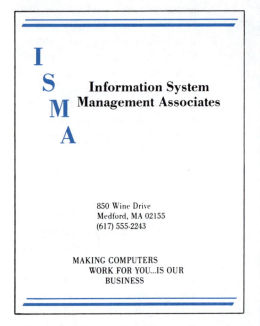

Figure 3.25
A Cover Page of a Promotional Brochure Printed at a Traditional Print Shop

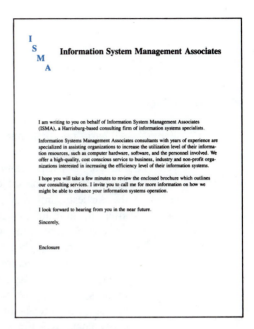

Figure 3.26
A Business Brochure Prepared with a Desktop Publishing Software Package

In addition to desktop publishing software, access to a printer suitable for printing professional documents or forms is essential. Perhaps the most suitable type of printer for this application is the laser printer. Due to the fine quality of printing provided by laser printers, and the dramatic price reduction of these printers, many organizations have established their own publishing centers.

Among some of the well-known desktop publishing software packages are Pagemaker, by Aldus Corp; Lasersoft, from Business Systems International; Powerform, by The 'Puter Group; and The Newsroom, from Springboard Software. Chapter 18 discusses the concepts and applications of desktop publishing software packages in detail.

Miscellaneous Application Software. Although the seven general areas of software packages just discussed represent the majority of the packages available for microcomputer applications in business, a great many other software packages are designed for a variety of specific applications. Some of these applications are statistical, general ledger, payroll, inventory management, and expert systems software packages.

Perhaps the next significant development in microcomputer software for business applications will be the introduction of more advanced expert systems. With these systems, the user will be able to use the power of microcomputers in decision making—not in the traditional sense of decision making, in which computers are used only for manipulation of data and performing quick calculations; rather, by allowing the system to draw its own conclusions and inferences based on the material stored in its database.

■ SUMMARY

All early microcomputers had to be programmed in order to be used, and different computer programs had to be developed by a programmer for various tasks. During the late 1970s, programming became less important for the average computer user because application software packages were developed for all types of tasks. Among the earliest commercial software packages were word processing packages. Soon after the introduction of VisiCalc, designed to be used for spreadsheet analysis, vendors brought to the marketplace thousands of other software packages for a variety of business applications.

There are six major categories of software packages: word processing, spreadsheet, database management, graphics, communications, and desktop publishing. In response to the problem of inability to transfer data among these core software packages, integrated software packages were developed. An integrated package normally contains several major core applications, such as word processing, spreadsheet, database management, graphics, and communications. A user can easily share data and information among these different applications of the integrated package without leaving the integrated software environment.

■ KEY TERMS

computer program	A set of instructions that direct a computer to perform a certain task.
programmer	A person who develops computer programs.
computer software	Programs used in conjunction with the hardware components.
systems software	Programs that manage the microcomputer's resources.
control programs	Programs that manage the entire system; part of ROM.
operating system	A collection of programs designed to manage the resources of the microcomputer system.
system disk	The disk that contains the operating system.
booting the system	Loading the operating system into the primary storage area to start the computer.
basic command programs	Programs loaded during the booting process and designed to perform specific tasks essential to the easy operation of the computer.
utility programs	Programs designed to perform specific tasks.

CP/M (Control Program for Microcomputers)	One of the earliest operating systems designed for microcomputers.
MS-DOS (MicroSoft Corporation Disk Operating System)	Today's standard operating system.
BASIC (Beginner's All-Purpose Symbolic Instruction Code)	The programming language used most frequently on microcomputers.
interpreter	A set of programs that translate instructions from non-machine languages (e.g., BASIC) into machine language.
compiler	A more advanced version of the interpreter.
debugging	The task of correcting errors in a computer program.
application program or software package	Collection of programs designed to make the computer's performance of specific tasks faster, easier, and more efficient.
command-driven	A program that reacts to specific instructions given by the user.
menu-driven	A program that presents screens of function choices, from which the user chooses.
word processing software	A collection of programs that allow the user to create, delete, insert, modify, save, merge, and print text.
spreadsheet software	A collection of programs that allow the user to create a spreadsheet, perform arithmetic calculations, recalculate, save, and prepare financial analysis reports.
database management software	A collection of programs that allow users to keep data in electronic files, and provide the capability for retrieving, updating, data-manipulating, and report-generating.
graphics software	A collection of programs that help users analyze data via creation of graphs and charts.
communications software	A program that allows users of a microcomputer to communicate with other computer systems by establishing the initial connection, transmitting data, receiving data, and monitoring the communication process.
LAN (Local Area Network)	A communications software package that connects locally dispersed PCs with each other allowing them to share both information and processing power.
integrated software	A collection of several subsystems capable of providing word processing, spreadsheet, database management, and graphics, all in one software environment.
desktop publishing software	Integrates personal computers into the publishing production process by allowing users to choose the layout, print fonts, format, and graphical presentations.

■ Review Questions

1. A collection of instructions developed by the user to perform certain tasks is called a/an
   (a) operating system.
   (b) programming language.
   (c) application program.
   (d) control program.
   (e) utility program.
2. _____ is the term used to describe the process of correcting a computer program.
   (a) Fixing
   (b) Programming
   (c) Booting
   (d) Debugging
3. Systems software can be classified into two categories, _____ programs and _____ systems.
   (a) operating; control
   (b) utility; operating
   (c) control; utility
   (d) instructional; computer
   (e) control; operating
4. The diskette that contains the operating system is called the
   (a) system disk.
   (b) operating disk.
   (c) floppy disk.
   (d) basic disk.
   (e) none of the above.
5. The first microcomputer software packages were
   (a) menu-driven.
   (b) command-driven.
   (c) user-friendly.
   (d) none of the above.
6. _____ software is a collection of programs that allow the user to create, delete, insert, modify, save, and print text.
   (a) Database management
   (b) Electronic spreadsheet
   (c) Graphic presentation
   (d) Word processing
   (e) Communications
7. If a large company wanted to manage its employee records in a more efficient manner, which category of software would they use?
   (a) word processing
   (b) spreadsheet
   (c) database management
   (d) graphics

8. _____ still represents the most popular financial management applications for microcomputers.
   (a) Database management
   (b) Electronic spreadsheet
   (c) Graphic presentation
   (d) Word processing
   (e) Desktop publishing
9. _____ software packages combine the capabilities of word processing, spreadsheet, database management, and graphics, all in one software environment.
10. Name the seven categories of microcomputer software.
11. What are the two groups of programs in the operating system?
12. Name several different operating systems available today for microcomputers.
13. Why are menu-driven software packages called user-friendly?
14. The biggest drawback of typewriters is the difficulty of modifying sections of a document after it has been prepared. How has word processing been a tremendous improvement in this area?
15. What is a local area network (LAN)?
16. Name four programming languages.
17. Describe the translation process.
18. What is the difference between spreadsheet software and database management software?
19. The managers of a business are trying to decide what types of software they require. The work they do consists of financial analysis, report generation, and preparation of presentations. They would also like to use their microcomputer to help them create an internal newsletter. What types of software packages would you recommend? Why?
20. Discuss the benefits of graphics software.
21. Discuss the advantages and disadvantages of integrated software packages.
22. How can desktop publishing software help a large business? A small business?
23. What type of printer would you recommend for use with desktop publishing software? Why?
24. What features do communications software packages offer?
25. Describe the function of utility programs.
26. What tasks are performed by control programs?
27. A small business firm has less than twenty employees. Their main product requires a mix of labor, equipment, and raw materials. They intend to use their microcomputer for monitoring their accounting, budget forecasting, and creating financial reports and distribution schedules. Also, they assume that all of their correspondence can be handled by a computer. Because of their capital constraints, should they spend more on a high-quality, reliable printer; a fully integrated software package; or the fastest microcomputer that they can find?
28. Suppose you are the manager of a large firm. Do you think it is better to have the most complete microcomputer network with maximum communication capacity that you can afford, or to separate various operations into several small systems, with each specializing in handling different functions? Which system would be more efficient? More expensive? Require more maintenance?

Case One
THE INFORMATION SERVICES GROUP

PA Utilities Service Company, Inc., a subsidiary of PA Utilities, provides certain accounting, data processing, and management services to the locally operating subsidiaries of PA Utilities. There are fourteen operating subsidiaries throughout Pennsylvania, through which the company provides services. Mr. Prudent is president of Service Company, and vice president of operations for PA Utilities.

The Service Company's data processing services include customer billings, the generation of accounting statements, and payroll. These services are performed on a mainframe computer operated by the Data Processing Department personnel. For security reasons, no terminals access this mainframe in any location other than the Data Processing Department. This security measure has isolated DP from the other functions.

Realizing the need for more efficient information management, Mr. Prudent has begun placing IBM PC-XTs throughout the organization. He is aware of the benefits micros can provide. Over the past two years, PCs have been popping up throughout the organization. At present, there are 42 PCs for 63 users, an average of one PC for every 1.5 users (a ratio of which he is quite proud).

All the PCs are loaded with Lotus 1-2-3. During the past two years, users have been free to use their PCs as they saw fit. However, this freedom did not produce the results that Mr. Prudent intended. Some of the users have produced favorable results with their computers, but, for the most part, the PCs are greatly under-utilized. Mr. Adjutant, Mr. Prudent's assistant, read a magazine article about forming an Information Support group, which he believes to be the solution to their problem. After all, he thinks, the users don't have time to learn the operation of the computers, develop useful applications, and still perform their current job assignments. An Information Support group could also standardize procedures for the entire company. Mr. Adjutant recommended to Mr. Prudent that Service Company form an Information Support group.

Realizing that something must be done, Mr. Prudent authorized the support group, which was formed on January 1, 1988. Sam Byte, the assistant director of DP, with twenty-three years experience in mainframe operation and COBOL programming, was chosen to lead the group. He was assisted by Jane Scholar, a programmer with four years' experience with the company. She also holds a B.S. in Computer Science and a Master's degree in Information Science. Joe Cruncher, an accountant who had developed quite a few helpful Lotus 1-2-3 applications, was also placed in the group.

The three put their minds together to come up with a plan of action. It was unanimously decided that the users needed training with the PCs. Jane suggested the initial training should provide an overview of computers. Sam agreed and said, "Once they are familiar with the computers, then we should teach them some programming."

Because of the company's size and employees' scheduling conflicts, it took three months to get all users through the Introduction to Computers course. The curriculum included a history of computers, a discussion of storage media (cards, tape, and disks), memory and its efficient use, and the basics of bits and bytes. Thus, the course provided a good background on computers.

Sam was pleased with the material covered in the course but was anxious to teach some Pascal programming. Before the programming courses could begin, the company needed to purchase Pascal compiler software. At one point, Joe expressed his discomfort with the decision to provide Pascal training to users, but was shot down by Sam and Jane, who counter-argued that users need to know how to program in order to do computing on their own.

After a few beginning sessions on Pascal, Sam became discouraged with the learning abilities of the users. "They're all just a bunch of accountants. Why do we have to teach them how to use a computer?" he asked. Jane suggested the possibility of teaching BASIC programming first, followed by Pascal. Joe suggested that they start with PC-DOS, then provide instructions on Lotus 1-2-3. Sam told Joe, "Jane and I are the experts here. You're just like the rest of those accountants, thinking Lotus 1-2-3 is the answer to everything. We'll go ahead and teach some BASIC and work our way up to Pascal."

As of January 1, 1989, all users had received two twenty-hour sessions on both BASIC and Pascal programming, as well as the Introduction to Computers course. Mr. Prudent and Mr. Adjutant heard of some difficulties experienced by the users, and brought these to Sam's attention. Sam stated, "This is not simple material and some difficulties can be expected." The two asked for a progress report. Sam said, "It's going to take some time to experience any noticeable results. Programming in BASIC or Pascal is no easy task. These users just learned some basic steps." Mr. Prudent, distressed, responded, "These computers have cost this company a lot of money. I want results. This group was supposed to provide them—now make them happen."

Questions

1. What are the problems?
2. Is Mr. Adjutant's idea of a support group a feasible answer?
3. What steps should have been taken before forming the support group?
4. Would you consider the group a failure?
5. What should be done now?

Case Two
JOB BY VARIETY, INC.

JBV, Inc., is a large manufacturing firm that employs five mainframes for its computer processing. The Computer Department is composed of several divisions, two of which are the Application Support Group (ASG) and Quality Control (QC). ASG is responsible for the design, analysis, and programming for all new systems to be automated. Because ASG is so large, QC was created in order to provide standardization. The corporate structure for these two divisions is displayed in Figure 3.27 on the following page.

Approximately one year ago, Tom Knight, Division Chief of ASG, decided to purchase ten microcomputers so his group could experiment with different software packages. Darryl, the Programming Manager, recommended that Tom purchase a package called Structured Diagramming Tool (SDT). SDT is a tool designed to help systems analysts create better program specifications. (Program "specs" are generalized instructions used by a programmer to write a computer program.)

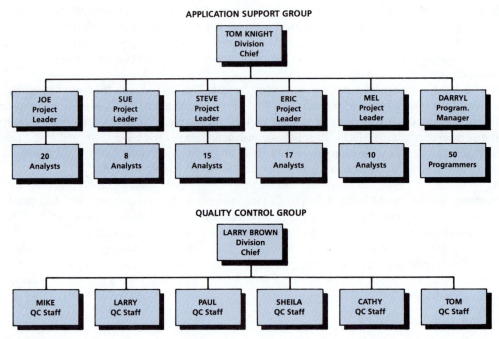

Figure 3.27
Structure of JBV, Inc.'s ASG and QC Groups

After Tom purchased SDT, two programmers, Lee Ann and Brian, were asked to test this package, and formed opposite opinions. However, Larry Brown, Division Chief of Quality Control, and his staff still liked the idea of computer-developed specifications. Therefore, they updated their standards to require that an SDT diagram accompany each program specification. Brian, the programmer who gave SDT a positive rating, was asked to teach all the analysts how to use it. Brian's training classes consisted of an hour lecture supplemented by a ten-page handout (prepared by himself) and limited hands-on experience. Training was complete within a week, after which QC put their new standards into effect. What happened in the following months was a common reaction to computer automation.

First, each analyst faced the problem of finding a microcomputer that was not in use. After that, the analyst had to locate the only copy of the SDT diskette to load into the micro. Once an analyst finally got on a computer, he or she had two major complaints: (1) SDT was too confusing; (2) SDT took too long to use. As a result, most analysts wrote their diagrams by hand. If time allowed, they then used SDT to produce the same diagram on the computer. This created more unrest, because analysts felt they were wasting time doing the same job twice. Larry Brown argued against this point by stressing that SDT was to be used to develop specifications, thereby eliminating the need to first produce the diagram on paper. However, the analysts did not change their methods. Since they were given no extensions on the due dates for their specs, they responded in the only way they considered possible to complete their work on time.

Today, the situation hasn't changed much. There are now twenty microcomputers available, along with two copies of the SDT diskette. Some analysts have accepted SDT and use it regularly, while most still complain and avoid it. To accommodate these analysts, QC has relaxed their requirement for SDT-produced specifications, and is now accepting handwritten ones. Most micros are now used to interface with the mainframe.

Questions

1. Define the many problems experienced by JBV, Inc.
2. Do these problems relate to poor management, the software package, or the analysts' attitudes?
3. Should the SDT package have been purchased?
4. How could Quality Control have introduced a microcomputer tool that would have aided the analysts in their work?
5. What action(s) would you recommend?

SELECTED BIBLIOGRAPHY

Ambrosio, J., "Should Organizations Have One, Two, or More Micro DBMSs?," *Software News*, July 1986, pp. 54–57.

Cashin, J., and J. Desmond, "PC-To-Mainframe Links," *Software News*, May 1986, pp. 58–75.

Cashin, J., "Benefits of Micro CAD/CAM, CAE: Lower Cost, Better Design," *Software News*, July 1986, pp. 64–69.

_____, "Electronic Publishing Taking Computing by Storm," *Software News*, February 1987, pp. 47–49.

_____, "LAN Markets Mandate Multiuser Standards," *Software News*, November 1986, pp. 70–81.

Desmond, J., "Repositioning of DSS Leaders Seen by 1990," *Software News*, September 1986, pp. 39–53.

_____, "Graphics Mass Marketing to Squeeze Small Players?," *Software News*, February 1987, pp. 32–46.

Good, P., "Micro Accounting Migrates to Departmental Computing," *Software News*, October 1986, pp. 55–60.

Horton, L., "Sales Reps Take Computing On the Road," *Software News*, October 1986, pp. 40–54.

Knight, R., "Case Paybacks Perceived, If Not Exactly Measured," *Software News*, February 1987, pp. 56–64.

Layne, R., and A. Leibs, "AI: Approaching the Final Frontier," *Information Week*, March 16, 1987, pp. 20–25.

Leavitt, D., "Evolutionary Tools Also Help Programmer Productivity," *Software News*, June 1986, pp. 54–61.

_____, "Window and Screen Managers: Natural Extension Solutions," *Software News*, May 1986, pp. 84–88.

Lewis, J., "Group Productivity Software," *Datamation*, December 15, 1986, pp. 79–80.

Musgrave, B., "Bulletin Boards and Business," *Datamation*, January 15, 1987, pp. 61–63.

Nelson, R., "Thinking Like a Spreadsheet," *Personal Computing*, December 1986, pp. 79–85.

Spencer, C., "Financial Modeling: Going Beyond Spreadsheets," *Personal Computing*, April 1987, pp. 68–77.

Part II

MICROCOMPUTER OPERATING SYSTEMS

chapter 4
INTRODUCTION TO OPERATING SYSTEMS

- describe the functions of an operating system.
- discuss the history of operating systems.
- discuss the highlights of MS-DOS, CP/M; Apple DOS, Macintosh, Unix, and Xenix operating systems.
- describe PC-DOS and OS/2.
- describe the difference between internal and external programs of PC-DOS.
- describe the three categories of programs in PC-DOS: input/output handler, command processor, and utility programs.

chapter 5
USING IBM PC-DOS

- describe how to care for diskettes, and how to insert a diskette into a disk drive.
- describe the functions of the keyboard keys.
- describe the difference between a cold boot and a warm boot.
- describe how to adjust the contrast, control, and vertical-hold controls on the computer screen.
- discuss the purpose of each PC-DOS command and the procedure for executing each one.
- describe the proper use of wildcards in DOS commands.

chapter 4

Introduction to Operating Systems

After completing this chapter, you should be able to

- describe the functions of an operating system.
- discuss the history of operating systems.
- discuss the highlights of MS-DOS, CP/M, Apple DOS, Macintosh, Unix, and Xenix operating systems.
- describe PC-DOS and OS/2.
- describe the difference between internal and external programs of PC-DOS.
- describe the three categories of programs in PC-DOS: input/output handler, command processor, and utility programs.

INTRODUCTION

Whether you know it or not, the first programs that you access whenever you use a microcomputer belong to the computer's operating system. As mentioned in Chapter 3, operating system programs are one of the two types of programs essential to basic computer operation. Control programs are the other type. Operating system programs which enhance the functionality of the programs of the control units, are designed to perform many tasks and operations among the computer system's components. This chapter discusses the general concepts and functions of an operating system, a few common microcomputer operating systems, and the main characteristics and features of IBM PC-DOS, one of the most popular operating systems. Chapter 5, which serves as a tutorial, introduces you to the different functions and commands of PC-DOS, by providing a hands-on approach to learning how a variety of commands work in the PC-DOS environment.

■ WHAT IS AN OPERATING SYSTEM?

An **operating system** is a collection of programs designed to handle selected microcomputer tasks, such as assisting the execution of application programs, managing input and output devices to enter data or display information, managing data files, storing and retrieving information on storage units, and working with software packages to carry out various functions (Figure 4.1).

> 1. Assisting with the execution of applications programs.
> 2. Managing input/output devices.
> 3. Storing and retrieving information.
> 4. Working with software packages to perform various functions.

Figure 4.1
Functions of an Operating System

The programs of an operating system are either stored on a single floppy diskette or on a hard disk, to be loaded into Random Access Memory (RAM) at the time of start-up, or "booting," of the microcomputer system (see Chapter 3). In many ways, an operating system provides a "bridge" between microcomputer hardware and application software packages. Software packages are not designed to communicate directly with the programs of the control unit; instead, the operating system programs provide the necessary linkage between hardware and application software (Figure 4.2).

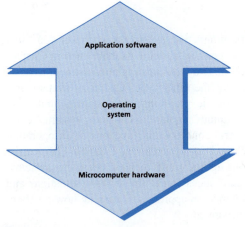

Figure 4.2
Communication Between OS and Application Software

■ A HISTORICAL PERSPECTIVE

In the early days of computers, users performed different functions or tasks by pressing different switches or plugging or unplugging different wires in the computer (Figure 4.3 on the following page). This design was short-lived because it was cumbersome and difficult for human operators to constantly monitor all of the many functions performed by the computer system.

Figure 4.3
An Old Mainframe Computer System

In the next generation of computers, most tasks performed by the computer system were automated, accomplished by programs designed for each specific task. Now, if users wanted the system to perform a task (e.g., copy a program from RAM to a secondary storage medium), they would simply issue a command through an input device, such as a keyboard, instead of physically turning one or more switches on or off. This automation of internal tasks allowed mainframe and minicomputers to become very efficient, performing faster and more accurately.

With the advent of microcomputers, the operating system concepts of larger systems were applied on a smaller scale. The main difference between a mainframe or minicomputer operating system and a microcomputer operating system is the fact that, in the microcomputer, the operating system is not a permanent resident of the Read Only Memory (ROM). (Chapter 2 discusses ROM in more detail.) In most microcomputers, the operating system is kept on a secondary storage medium, such as a diskette or hard disk, and loaded into the system at the time of booting. This flexibility allows the operating system to be moved from one machine to another. Basic knowledge of the microcomputer operating system in use is critical because this software establishes the environment in which the user's program and applications are performed.

During the last few decades, only a handful of popular operating systems have been developed for mainframe, mini, and, particularly, microcomputers. The limited number of operating systems has been of particular advantage to software vendors and developers. Because many computers use the same operating system, software can be developed that runs without modification on all machines using the same operating system.

COMMON OPERATING SYSTEMS

The available operating systems have been developed for different microprocessors, and in fact, the evolution of operating systems development has been directly influenced by the availability of a variety of microprocessors. The following paragraphs discuss the characteristics of some common microcomputer operating systems.

CP/M

One of the pioneers of operating systems development for microcomputers was Digital Research Corporation, which is responsible for **CP/M** (Control Program for Microprocessors) (sometimes referred to as CP/M-80). CP/M, designed around the Intel 8080 and Zilog Z80 8-bit microprocessors, is considered one of the most advanced early operating systems for microcomputers. When it was introduced, CP/M was very popular.

The emergence of 16-bit microprocessors in what were to become the most popular microcomputers, including the IBM-PC and compatibles, required that CP/M be updated. The new version of CP/M, known as CP/M-86, is designed around the Intel 8088/8086 microprocessors. Unlike its earlier version, CP/M-86 has never enjoyed great popularity, mainly due to the fact that IBM did not select CP/M-86 as the operating system on the best-selling IBM family of 16-bit PCs.

MS-DOS

Another early pioneer of microcomputer operating systems was MicroSoft Corporation with its **MS-DOS** (MicroSoft Disk Operating System), designed around the Intel 8088/8086 family of microprocessors. Since its introduction, MS-DOS has become the *de facto* standard operating system on 16-bit microprocessors. Fundamentally, MS-DOS was an outgrowth of CP/M; for this reason there are many similarities between the two. There is, however, one distinct difference: MS-DOS is less difficult for users to understand and learn than its rival, CP/M.

In 1981, IBM selected MS-DOS as the operating system for its family of PCs. The version of MS-DOS used on the IBM-PCs is known as PC-DOS, and differs only slightly from the original MS-DOS. This compatibility allows many software packages developed for an MS-DOS environment to be used in the PC-DOS environment, and *vice versa*, with few or no modifications. Over the last few years, MS-DOS/PC-DOS has become the standard operating system on the IBM-PC and many compatibles, thus fostering the development of thousands of MS-DOS/PC-DOS-compatible software packages.

AppleDOS

The **AppleDOS** operating system was developed by Apple Computer Corporation, manufacturer of Apple computers, around the Motorola 6502 microprocessor. Apple introduced the first version of AppleDOS in conjunction with its Apple II microcomputer. Since then, many software packages have been developed for this operating system. Although AppleDOS was not as sophisticated as its rivals, CP/M or MS-DOS, it became the standard operating system for the Apple family of computers. The more advanced version of AppleDOS, known as **ProDOS,** is used mainly on the Apple IIc and on Apple computers equipped with a hard disk because the original AppleDOS is incapable of handling the large volume of data/information on a hard disk.

Macintosh

The **Macintosh** operating system developed by Apple Corporation for their Macintosh family of microcomputers has little in common with the other operating systems discussed here. This operating system is designed around the Motorola 68000 family of microprocessors. The major distinctive characteristic of this operating system is its use of menus and **icons,** small representative images that the user selects by pointing with a mouse, in addition to a keyboard, for choosing options and issuing commands (Figure 4.4). This "drawing board" for communication between the user and the operating system has made Macintosh one of the most user-friendly and easily operated systems available to the average microcomputer user.

Figure 4.4
A Screen Generated by the Apple Macintosh Operating System

Software packages developed for the Macintosh must use the operating system's interface routines to communicate with the user. Therefore, despite its user-friendliness, this operating system was not greeted with a great degree of enthusiasm at first. In the last few years, however, Apple has successfully established Macintosh as one of the more popular operating systems among microcomputer users.

Unix and Xenix

One of the limitations of all the operating systems discussed so far—CP/M, MS-DOS, and AppleDOS/Macintosh—is the fact that they cannot be used for multiusers or multitasks. Only one user at a time can communicate with each of these operating systems. Furthermore, these operating systems can work on only one task or program at any given time.

Originally, **Unix** was developed at the AT&T research facility known as Bell Labs in the late 1960s for use on Digital Equipment Corporation's PDP-7 and PDP-11 minicomputers. By the early 1970s, Unix was commonly used inside Bell Labs. However, because of government regulations, AT&T—as a telephone communications company—could not market this operating system. In late 1978, the first commercial version of Unix appeared in the marketplace. Since then, Unix has been gaining in popularity and is on its way to becoming the industry standard.

Unix is a powerful operating system with the flexibility to adapt to many different makes and families of microprocessors, including the Intel 8088 and 80286 used by IBM and compatible PCs. This fact makes Unix a "portable" operating system. The Microsoft version of Unix, which is also used on IBM-PCs and IBM-PC compatibles, is referred to as Xenix.

OS/2

Operating System/2, or **OS/2,** was designed jointly by IBM and the Microsoft Corporation for use on the new generation of microcomputers, known as Personal System/2, or PS/2, which IBM introduced in 1987. OS/2 is built around the 32-bit Intel 80386 microprocessor used in PS/2 Model 80 and the Compaq Deskpro 386. OS/2 has the flexibility to run on the Intel 80286 microprocessors, but it will not run on Intel 8088/8086-based machines, such as the IBM-PC, PC-XT, and PS/2 Model 30.

OS/2 is a multi-task operating system, which means it is capable of running several programs simultaneously. For instance, a database program can be sorting a lengthy file, a communication program can be transferring data files from another computer system, a disk can be formatted, and the user can be word processing a memo—all at the same time. OS/2 will run programs under two different modes: the real mode and the protected mode. The **real mode** is the same mode used by many current operating systems; the **protected mode** is the mode that other programs are running under while the user is currently working on something.

The user of OS/2 can easily switch back and forth or view programs running under the protected mode by using the Session Manager feature of OS/2 (Figure 4.5). This feature provides the user with a menu of all the sessions, programs, and jobs available for execution. OS/2 is equipped with many other advanced features, such as Microsoft Windows Presentation Manager and Local Area Network (LAN) manager.

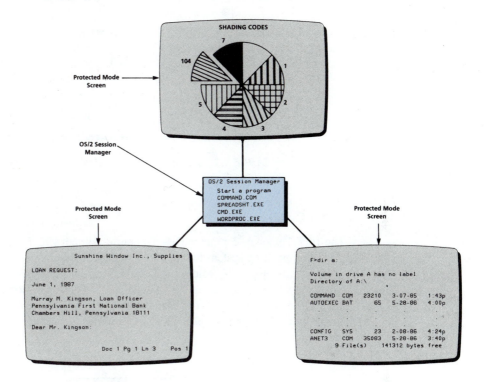

Figure 4.5
OS Session Manager and Protected Modes

Table 4.1 on the following page summarizes the common operating systems discussed in this chapter.

OPERATING SYSTEMS	MICROPROCESSOR	8-BIT	16-BIT	32-BIT	MICROCOMPUTERS	VENDOR
CP/M	Intel 8080 and Z80	X			Radio Shack TRS-80	Digital Research Corp.
CP/M-86	Intel 8088/8086		X			Digital Research Corp.
MS-DOS/PC-DOS	Intel 8088/8086		X		IBM-PC and compatibles	MicroSoft Corp.
AppleDOS	Motorola 6502	X			Apple IIe and Franklin	Apple Computer Corp.
Macintosh	Motorola 68000		X		Macintosh	Apple Computer Corp.
Xenix	Intel 80286		X		PC-AT and compatibles	MicroSoft Corp.
OS/2	Intel 80386			X	PS/2 and compatibles	MicroSoft Corp.

TABLE 4.1 Summary of the Available Operating Systems

IBM PC-DOS

The IBM Personal Computer Disk Operating System (PC-DOS) is the single most common operating system for microcomputers. As mentioned earlier, PC-DOS was originally developed by Microsoft Corporation, in conjunction with IBM, around Microsoft's famous operating system, MS-DOS. For this reason, PC-DOS is almost identical to MS-DOS. The programs of PC-DOS are divided into three categories: input/output (I/O) handler programs, the command processor, and utility programs. (See Figure 4.6.)

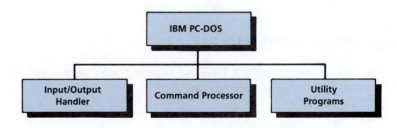

Figure 4.6
PC-DOS and Its Programs

The I/O Handler

The **I/O handler** consists of a group of "hidden files" called IBMBIO.COM and IBMDOS.COM. The basic task of the I/O handler is to manage each character that is entered, displayed, received, or printed in the system. They are responsible for managing data and programs to be stored on secondary media, such as diskettes. In other words, the I/O handler coordinates the microcomputer's communication with the outside world.

The Command Processor

The **command processor** of PC-DOS interprets what the user enters using the keyboard or other input devices. The programs of the command processor can be found in the file called **COMMAND.COM,** which has a number of built-in functions that can handle most basic tasks, such as running programs, copying files, or reviewing the contents of files stored on secondary storage media. Unlike the I/O handler, the COMMAND.COM program appears in the directory of the PC-DOS operating system disk.

Utility Programs

The **utility programs,** also called **external programs,** are those programs stored on the DOS disk as separate files. These programs tend to have special purposes, and thus are less frequently used. Tasks handled by these programs range from formatting a blank disk to comparing the contents of two disks. Table 4.2 illustrates a few PC-DOS utilities and their functions.

COMMAND	FUNCTION
Format	Prepares new diskettes for use
Check Disk	Examines the disk
Disk Compare	Compares two disks
Sort	Sort files of a disk directory
FDISK	Prepares hard disk

TABLE 4.2 A Few DOS Utility Programs

System Files

In DOS vocabulary, the term **system files** refers to those DOS programs needed for booting and basic input/output operations. These programs are transferred from a diskette or a hard disk to the computer memory (RAM) at the time of booting. However, it is possible to direct DOS to store a copy of the system files onto another disk. For example, if a new formatted disk contains system files, then the disk can also be used to boot the PC without the PC-DOS disk. This task is accomplished with the DOS command, SYStem.

Once the system files are stored on a formatted disk, then the disk will be considered a bootable disk. This means that the operating system disk can be used to start the system. It should be remembered that this disk can not substitute for the DOS disk, since only a limited number of DOS programs are stored on it.

■ SUMMARY

Operating systems are used in conjunction with the control programs stored in Read Only Memory (ROM) to enhance the functioning of control programs. In addition, an operating system provides a bridge between the microcomputer and application software packages. Despite the many different microcomputer vendors and models in the market, only a few operating systems have been developed for microcomputers. These systems are designed around different microprocessors.

Among some of the most common operating systems are CP/M 80-86, MS-DOS, AppleDOS, Macintosh, Unix, Xenix, OS/2, and IBM PC-DOS. MS-DOS and PC-DOS are considered the most common operating systems for microcomputers. In the past few years, developers have created many application software packages around PC-DOS and MS-DOS, so these two similar systems have become the standard operating system environment.

The programs of PC-DOS are classified into three categories: the input/output handler, the command processor, and utility programs. The utility programs consist of those programs that are considered special-purpose and are less frequently used. Utility programs are stored on the operating system disk, and are transferred into the main memory as they are needed.

■ KEY TERMS

operating system	A collection of programs designed to handle selected tasks, such as assisting the execution of application programs.
CP/M	An early operating system developed around the 8-bit microprocessor.
MS-DOS	An early operating system designed around the Intel 8088/8086 16-bit microprocessor.
AppleDOS	Operating system developed by Apple Corporation around the Motorola 6502 microprocessor.
ProDOS	The more advanced version of AppleDOS.
Macintosh	Operating system, developed by Apple Corporation, which uses a mouse in addition to a keyboard for selecting options and issuing commands.
Icon	Small representative images the user selects with a pointing device.
Unix	An operating system developed by AT&T Corporation for use on Digital Equipment Corporation's PDP-7 and PDP-11 minicomputers.
Operating System 2 (OS/2)	A multi-task operating system designed jointly by IBM and Microsoft Corporation, capable of running several programs simultaneously.
real mode	Standard mode used by most current operating systems.
protected mode	Allows a user to operate other programs while one is running.
I/O handler	A group of "hidden files" that manage data and programs on the PC-DOS operating system.
command processor	On PC-DOS, the interpreter of data entered.

COMMAND.COM   The command processor program of PC-DOS, responsible for performing many fundamental tasks. This program is loaded into the main memory of the microcomputer at the time of booting.

utility program   Program stored on DOS disk for special tasks, such as sorting.

system files   DOS programs needed for booting and basic input/output operations.

■ REVIEW QUESTIONS

1. The original idea of an operating system was first tried on a
   (a) mainframe.
   (b) minicomputer.
   (c) microcomputer.
   (d) none of the above.
2. MS-DOS was an outgrowth of which of the following operating systems?
   (a) PC-DOS
   (b) AppleDOS
   (c) Unix
   (d) CP/M
   (e) none of the above
3. Which of the following operating systems is a multiuser?
   (a) PC-DOS
   (b) AppleDOS
   (c) Unix
   (d) CP/M
   (e) none of the above
4. Which of the following programs are the same as external programs?
   (a) input/output handler
   (b) utility programs
   (c) command processor
   (d) none of the above
5. With the emergence of 16-bit processors, CP/M-80 was updated to
   (a) CP/M-16.
   (b) OS/2.
   (c) Unix.
   (d) CP/M-86.
   (e) none of the above.
6. Apple's more advanced version of AppleDOS is called
   (a) CP/M.
   (b) Macintosh.
   (c) ProDOS.
   (d) Unix.
   (e) none of the above.

7. The Microsoft version of the Unix operating system is referred to as
   (a) CP/M-86.
   (b) OS/2.
   (c) MS-DOS.
   (d) Xenix.
   (e) none of the above.
8. Why does every microcomputer need an operating system?
9. What is an operating system?
10. What are the differences between single-tasking and multi-tasking operating systems?
11. Describe the unique characteristic of the Macintosh operating system.
12. Name several popular operating systems.
13. Why wasn't CP/M able to maintain its degree of popularity in the early days of microcomputers?
14. What is the meaning of the term "multiuser" when we say that Unix is a multiuser operating system?
15. What are the two major programs of the input/output handler?

Case One:
B&B BOOKSTORE

Barb and Betty Brown were twin sisters who wanted to open their own business. They each read between two and three books per week all through high school and college, and have continued to do so for the last ten years. So it seemed natural when, last summer, the twins opened their own combination book/card/gift shop. Business has been enjoying a steady growth ever since, with Christmas the busiest season and summer the slowest.

The store, called B&B Bookstore, sells magazines, books (both hardback and paperback), candy, greeting cards, stationery, cigarettes, balloons, chewing gum, and various ceramic, wood, and crystal figurines and knickknacks.

Barb and Betty are the co-owners and co-managers of their store, so they alternate their work schedules. Betty works one week of mornings and afternoons while Barb works evenings, and the following week they switch off. There are also three part-time clerks. The store is usually staffed by only one clerk at a time, in addition to one of the managers.

The store does have a steady and somewhat "regular" clientele, and normally grosses between $4,000 and $5,000 per week. Betty and Barb do all of their own bookkeeping and supply ordering. All of their records are kept on one microcomputer. They are also very proud that their spreadsheets, used in bookkeeping, never contain any errors. When these sheets are reviewed by their accountant, their figures come out to the exact amount every time.

Betty and Barb feel they owe part of this exactness to their computer. They own a Compaq 286, which contains a PC-DOS Version 3.2 operating system. The Compaq system utilizes a 30-megabyte fixed hard disk as a secondary storage device.

Betty and Barb have created a database for all books they have in stock (approximately 20,000 volumes). A record is kept of every book by title and by author. So that they can find a book more easily, each book's shelf location is also kept on record. These records are stored on the fixed disk. The only problem is that the fixed disk is almost full. Every month, new books must be added, but few are ever deleted. The hard disk is rapidly becoming obsolete.

When new books are added, the updated file becomes the master list. The old files are never deleted, so there are many old master list versions on the disk. At this point, the disk has room for only five more updates. New shipments of books are received every week, so the sisters must do something soon. Furthermore, during the last Christmas rush, they faced another limitation of this new system: it was incapable of running their spreadsheet and database programs at the same time. Betty became somewhat frustrated when she learned that she had to leave the spreadsheet environment before she could do anything within the database software package.

Betty and Barb feel that, since they spent a considerable amount of money on this computer, it should provide the capability of running multiple applications simultaneously. This morning, Betty called the manufacturer of the fixed disk and explained the problems to the manager in charge, Bob Jones. Mr. Jones told Betty that it is impossible to run out of space on the fixed disk. He told her she must be doing something wrong. He also told her that, in order to accommodate the maximum amount of data, the hard disk must be properly managed. He told her he thought he knew what the problem was, and that there is a solution.

Questions

1. What is the problem?
2. How can these problems be eliminated or corrected?
3. What are the alternative actions to avoid a hard disk problem?
4. What do you recommend to the B&B Bookstore for the better utilization of their microcomputer system?

Case Two:
THE FAMOUS INN RESTAURANT

The Famous Inn is a restaurant located in Baltimore, Maryland. It is owned by Mark Dalton, a Peck State University graduate with a degree in hotel management.

Mark bought the Famous Inn on December 15, 1986, for $575,000. The restaurant has four large dining rooms, one lounge, and two bars. The total seating capacity is 350. Mark functions both as the owner and general manager of the restaurant. There are five cooks at the restaurant, and fifty waitresses/waiters. On a typical evening, the restaurant brings in about $5,000 in combined food and liquor sales.

Mark does all the in-house accounting, recordkeeping, and food and liquor ordering. His greatest aid and most useful tool is his IBM personal computer, which he purchased in November of 1986, one month before opening his restaurant. His IBM-PC is equipped with the PC-DOS operating system. So far, Mark has been very pleased with his choice of personal computer and disk operating system.

His DOS allows him to utilize various software packages, both IBM and IBM-compatible software. The DOS also allows him to format his disks with only a few keyboard strokes, and he is able to make backup copies of each piece of software he owns.

The other day, when Mark was making some final changes to a loan proposal that he was developing with his word processing package, an electrical storm was raging outside. The electrical current was knocked out when lightning struck a utility pole. Mark pressed the Save key, but not soon enough; all of his text was wiped out.

Mark spent a couple hours that day trying to retrieve this lost text file. He was still under the assumption that there must be some key he could press or something that he could do so that his lost data might be retrieved. He reviewed manuals and became very disappointed to find that no satisfactory method to retrieve lost data has been developed. The only thing he could do was retype the lost documents: fifteen, single-spaced pages of text.

Now Mark is still not sure whether he could have recovered his lost proposal. Last week, he consulted with his colleague, Charles, explaining that he had to recreate fifteen pages of text, and that this took him close to five hours. He asked Charles if there was anything he could do to prevent a similar problem in the future. Unfortunately, Charles could not offer any advice.

Mark still wants to know the appropriate procedure for retrieving lost files due to electrical failure, if there is a way to do so. Further, he is anxious to know if there a procedure or routine in his DOS programs or the word processing software that he could use to prevent similar incidents.

Questions

1. Is the inability to retain files lost during a breakdown in electrical current a shortcoming of the existing operating system?
2. Why could or couldn't Mark obtain his data after the storm was over and the electrical system was reinstated?
3. What can be done to prevent data loss during an electrical storm?

SELECTED BIBLIOGRAPHY

Forbes, J., "DOS 3.2 Said to Pave Operating System Path," *Infoworld*, January 20, 1986, p. 5.

Gibsion, M.L. and J.C. Windsor, "PC-DOS: The Next *de facto* Standard for Micro-Computer Operating Systems," *Journal of Systems Management*, July 1986, pp. 6–10+.

Hannaford, S., "The Challenge for Today's Operating System Designer," *Data Communications*, October 1985, pp. 197–8+.

Healey, M., "Toward a Viable OS for the PC," *Datamation*, September 1, 1985, pp. 92–4+.

Lippin, P., "MS-DOS or UNIX – Why Not Both?," *Modern Office Technology*, January 1986, p. 42+.

Mirecki, T., "The Ascent of DOS," *PC Tech Journal*, October 1986, pp. 92–104.

Petzold, C., "DOS Gets Better and More Expensive," *PC Magazine*, July 1986, pp. 110–111.

Sager, I., "Multi-User UNIX Systems: Faster MPUs Boost PC Vendors Efforts," *Electronic News*, January 19, 1987, p. 1+.

Scannell, T., "DOS-UNIX Adds New Mix to OS Market," *Mini-Micro Systems*, February 1987, p. 81+.

Truax, P.G., "Three Levels of Integration and How They Got That Way," (Unix, Pick, and MS-DOS) *The Office*, April 1986, p. 46+.

_____, "Operating Systems," *Mini-Micro Systems*, June 1986, pp. 183–7.

Wolfe, C. and C.E. Wiggins, "Internal Control in the Microcomputer Environment," *Internal Auditor*, December 1986, pp. 54–60.

chapter 5

Using IBM PC-DOS

After completing this chapter, you should be able to

- describe how to care for diskettes, and how to insert a diskette into a disk drive.
- describe the functions of the keyboard keys.
- describe the difference between a cold boot and a warm boot.
- describe how to adjust the contrast, control, and vertical-hold controls on the computer screen.
- discuss the purpose of each PC-DOS command and the procedure for executing each one.
- describe the proper use of wildcards in DOS commands.

INTRODUCTION

As mentioned in Chapter 4, an operating system enhances the functioning of the control programs stored on ROM. In addition, the operating system provides the necessary linkage between hardware, application software packages, and users. Therefore, it is essential for the microcomputer user to have a basic understanding of the many functions of the computer's operating system.

This chapter is designed to introduce the reader to the various functions and commands of IBM PC-DOS. We choose PC-DOS because it is a very popular and easy-to-use operating system. The commands explained in this chapter are also frequently used in MS-DOS, and allow an individual to manage activities, such as formatting disks, copying, and many other functions. We assume that the material explained in this chapter will be practiced on an IBM-PC or IBM compatible.

■ BEFORE YOU BEGIN

It is important to take a minute to recall the proper way to handle the diskettes you will be using with the microcomputer. If they are not handled carefully, damage could result; you might lose part or all of the data that you have taken such time and care to store on the diskettes. Figure 5.1 contrasts proper and improper care of a diskette.

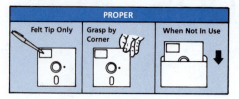
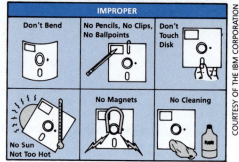

Figure 5.1
Diskette Handling

■ GETTING STARTED

If your microcomputer has only one disk drive, it will always be referred to as Drive A in software manuals and texts. If the computer you are working on has two disk drives, they are either (1) configured horizontally, in which case the left drive is always Drive A and the right drive is always Drive B; or (2) configured vertically, in which case the top drive is Drive A and the bottom one is Drive B. Figure 5.2 shows systems with both arrangements.

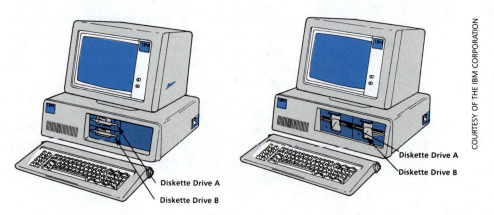

Figure 5.2
Alternative Arrangements of System Disk Drives

Booting the System

As mentioned in Chapter 3, the process of getting the system loaded and ready to use is referred to as booting. There are two ways to boot the system: a cold boot and a warm boot. A **cold boot** is performed when the system is started by turning on the computer's power source. The term **warm boot** refers to the method of restarting the system without having to turn the machine off, then back on. The steps for performing each booting procedure are explained below.

Cold Boot. In order to cold boot the system:

- Place the DOS diskette in Drive A and close the disk drive door. (Figure 5.3 illustrates the proper way of inserting the diskette into the disk drive. Notice the position of the label on the diskette.)
- Turn the microcomputer on. The power switch is located on the right side of the computer toward the back of the machine. The power switch will be in the up position when the computer is on, as in Figure 5.4.

The computer will go through a system check that takes from three to forty-five seconds, depending on the amount of memory or the brand of microcomputer you are working on. During the loading process, the red light at the front of the disk drive will stay on, and you will hear a whirring noise. Wait until the red light goes off, signalling the end of the loading process. The following message will appear on the screen.

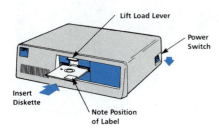

Figure 5.3
Inserting the DOS Diskette into Drive A

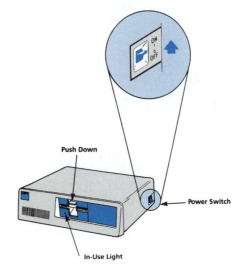

Figure 5.4
The "On" Position of the Power Switch

Figure 5.5
PC-DOS Initial Date Screen

Note: If your microcomputer has a "clock/calendar," the proper date and time will be displayed automatically. If you want to change the current date, enter today's date in the format indicated in the message, otherwise, press the ENTER key (←) to accept the default date. For example, if today is May 13, 1989, you should type 05-13-89 or 05/13/89, then press the **ENTER** key (←).

Next, a similar message will appear, this time displaying the current time.

Figure 5.6
PC-DOS Initial Time Screen

As with the date, if you want to change the current time, enter the new time in the HH:MM:SS.XX format, otherwise, press the ENTER key (←) to accept the default time. For example, if the time is 5:00 P.M., you should type 17:00:00.00, or 17:00, then press the ENTER (←). Notice that "17" was typed instead of "5" because the system clock cannot differentiate A.M. hours from P.M. hours. Therefore, in all computers, the twenty-four hour military time system is used (hours 00:00 through 24:00).

The major advantage of providing the current date and time is that these elements will then be recorded on each file created or modified, allowing the user to know exactly which version of a file is the most current, or when the work was done.

Upon completion of date and time settings, the following information will appear on the screen.

```
The IBM Personal Computer DOS
Version 3.10 (C)Copyright International Business Machines Corp. 1981, 1985
          (C)Copyright Microsoft Corp. 1981, 1985

A>_
```

Figure 5.7
The First PC-DOS Screen after a Successful Booting

Obtaining this screen indicates that you have successfully "booted" the system. All the input/output handler and command processor files have been read from the DOS diskette, and are now stored in the memory of the computer. The **A>** (pronounced A prompt), or **DOS prompt,** signifies that the system is now ready to process any DOS commands or application programs.

Note: DOS commands or program names can be typed with either lowercase characters (a–z) or uppercase characters (A–Z). For example, typing *DIR* will provide the listing of the files on the disk in Drive A, as will *dir*. The blinking underline that appears on the screen is called the **cursor**.

If the microcomputer is equipped with a hard disk, there are two procedures for booting the system. The first procedure assumes that DOS is not stored on the hard disk. In this case, you begin the booting process by placing the DOS program diskette in Drive A and following the procedure discussed above. However, when DOS is stored on the hard disk, there is no need to insert the DOS diskette into Drive A. Instead, you can switch the machine on, and the DOS program will be accessed from the hard disk.

Warm Boot. The difference between a cold and a warm boot is that, in a warm boot, the computer is already on. In the warm boot, the PC user does not have to turn the machine off and then on in order to restart the system. Instead, the user can reboot by pressing three keys simultaneously: **CTRL** (located at the left side of the keyboard next to the "A" character key), **ALT** (located at the left bottom side of the keyboard, below the CTRL key), and **DEL** (located at the right bottom part of the keyboard, below the digits "2" and "3" keys). These keys are not always in the same place; they vary by keyboard manufacturer.

While simultaneously pressing CTRL and ALT, tap the DEL key just once. You may then remove pressure on the CTRL and ALT keys. *Note:* You do not have to press ENTER (←).

Upon releasing the CTRL-ALT-DEL combination, the red disk drive light will go on for a few seconds, and the date prompt will appear at the top of the screen. Type the current date and time in the same way that you did in the cold boot procedure. The warm boot can be performed any time the computer's power is on—but remember, any data you have not specifically "saved" will be lost during a warm boot. Therefore, reboot only when necessary.

Keyboard Arrangement

The PC keyboard layout is in many ways similar to that of a typical typewriter, except that the computer keyboard includes additional keys, such as function keys and numeric keys. Figure 5.8 illustrates two IBM-PC keyboards.

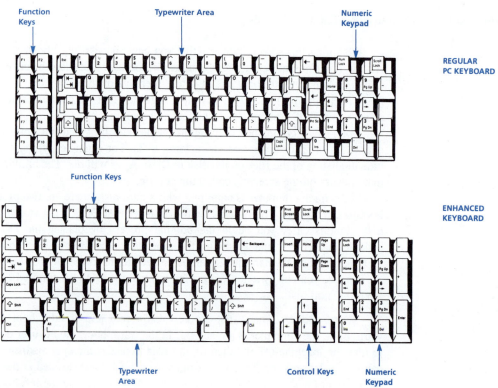

Figure 5.8
Two IBM-PC Keyboard Arrangements

Table 5.1 gives a brief description of some of the keys that you should know and their functions.

KEY	FUNCTION
Caps Lock	When pressed once, this key changes lowercase characters to uppercase or *vice versa*.
↑	When the SHIFT key is held down, functions shown on the upper part of the key will be engaged.
↵	This is the ENTER key, which signals the system to act on whatever was typed on the keyboard before ENTER was pressed.
←	The BACKSPACE key moves the cursor one position to the left, and erases the character in that position.
PrtSc	When the PRINT SCREEN and SHIFT keys are pressed simultaneously, the contents of the screen will be printed on the printer.
⇤ ⇥	These are the TAB keys. The bottom key moves the cursor to the next tab stop. The top key (key + SHIFT) moves the cursor back to the last tab stop.
Num Lock	When the NUMERIC LOCK key is pressed, the numeric pad keys 0 through 9 will be functional.
Ins	Pressing the INSERT key once enables you to insert characters without erasing material you have already entered. Pressed again, this key cancels the "insert" function.
Del	When pressed, the DELETE key deletes the character in the current cursor position.

TABLE 5.1 *Description of Some PC Keys and Their Functions*

Other keys—such as function keys, SCROLL LOCK, BREAK, HOME, END, PGDN, PGUP, and ESC keys—and their functions will be explained as software packages are discussed later in this book.

Screen Adjustments

Before beginning our discussion of the various DOS commands, take a minute to look at the display on your screen. Does the text appear too bright or too dim? Is the contrast suitable? To avoid eyestrain, you should adjust your screen's contrast and brightness. Refer to Figure 5.9 to find the position of these controls on the front of your screen.

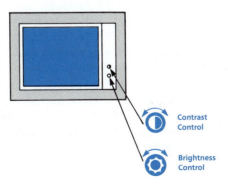

Figure 5.9
The PC's Contrast and Brightness Controls

It may also be important at some point to be able to adjust the vertical hold on the computer if the screen display is not steady, much as you would adjust the vertical hold on your television set. Figure 5.10 illustrates the position of the vertical hold control knob on the back of the computer screen.

■ COMMONLY USED PC-DOS COMMANDS

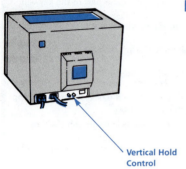

Figure 5.10
The PC's Vertical Hold Control

As mentioned in Chapter 4, the programs of PC-DOS are divided into two groups: internal and external, or utility, programs. The internal programs are loaded into ROM at the time of booting, and they remain in the main memory during the session. The external programs remain on the disk and are transferred automatically as needed. Therefore, it is necessary to maintain the operating system disk in the disk drive.

In this section, we discuss some of the internal and external DOS commands that you can enter from the A> (or the C> if you're using a hard disk). We explain the purpose of each command, then follow with instructions on how to enter the command and a description of command modifications or variations.

To apply a command, the user types in the `highlighted word or character`. In most cases, it is necessary to depress the ENTER key, marked (↵), after you type the command. In these cases, we place the ENTER key in a bracket. Otherwise, you may assume the command does not require the ENTER key.

The DIRECTORY (DIR) Command

Purpose: The **DIRECTORY command,** usually typed as **DIR,** lists the contents (files) of a disk in the specified drive.

How to enter the command: At the DOS prompt, type

A>`dir x:` [ENTER]

where *x* stands for the specified disk drive. DOS will display each data file or program file by listing the file name, its extension, number of bytes used, date of creation, and time of creation, in the format shown in Figure 5.11 on the following page.

File names identify each data or program file. DOS stores each file under a name, such as FORMAT, so that the user can later access that file by referring to its name. Therefore, file names must be unique and can be up to eight characters in length. Following the file name, DOS lists an **extension name,** describing the type of data or instructions stored in the file. The extension name may be up to three characters in length.

```
A>dir a:

Volume in drive A has no label
Directory of A:\
ANSI       SYS      1651    3-07-85    1:43p
ASSIGN     COM      1509    3-07-85    1:43p
ATTRIB     EXE     15091    3-07-85    1:43p
BACKUP     COM      5577    3-07-85    1:43p
  .
  .
  .
AUTOEXEC   BAK         1    1-01-80    1:18a
TEXTFILE   BAK         1    1-01-80   12:52a
TEXT       BAK        25    1-01-80   12:06a
TEXT       TXT        25    1-01-80   12:06a
      45 File(s)       52224 bytes free

A>_
```

Figure 5.11
Directory of a Diskette in Drive A

The extension name is separated from the file name by a period (.). An exception to this format occurs with the use of the DIR command; DOS displays the file name followed by a blank space, followed by the extension name. Some common extensions are EXE and COM, which indicate that the program file is a compiled one; BAT, which indicates some DOS instructions are stored in the file; and AUTOEXEC.BAT, which means the contents of the file will be used during system booting.

File size, which is measured in bytes or characters, also appears in the directory listing. The maximum size of a file, and the maximum number of files, are dependent on the size of the disk. For instance, a 5 1/4" floppy disk can store up to 360K bytes of data.

Modifications: By adding parameters to the basic DIR command, you can perform additional functions. For example

At the DOS prompt, type

A> dir x:/p [ENTER]

Now the contents of the directory will be displayed one page at a time. To see the next page in the directory, strike any key. This feature is especially useful for reading long directories that would otherwise scroll past too quickly for your eyes to follow.

At the DOS prompt, type

A> dir x:/w [ENTER]

The contents of the directory will be listed horizontally on the screen. However, the number of bytes, and date and time of creation are not displayed. This modification is also useful for long directories.

The VERSION (VER) Command

Purpose: The **VERSION command,** usually typed **VER,** is used to find out what version of DOS has been booted. This information is helpful for getting started with some software packages that require a certain version of DOS.

How to enter the command: At the DOS prompt, type

A>ver x: [ENTER]

where *x* stands for the specified disk drive. Upon execution of the VER command, the following information shown in Figure 5.12 will be presented on the screen.

Figure 5.12
Version Screen

The DATE Command

Purpose: The **DATE command** enables the user to change the date currently stored in DOS. Because the date stored in DOS is recorded in the directory along with the names of new or revised files, you should set this parameter to the current date to maintain accurate directory information.

How to enter the command: At the DOS prompt, type

A>date [ENTER]

Upon execution of the DATE command, the message in Figure 5.13 on the following page will appear on the screen.

Figure 5.13
Date Screen

Key in a new date in the format indicated, separating the month, day, and year with either hyphens (-) or slashes (/), then depress the ENTER (↵) key or depress the ENTER (↵) key to accept the default date.

The TIME Command

Purpose: Just as we use the DATE command to change the date, so we use the **TIME command** to change the time of day stored in DOS. DOS records time in hours *(hh)*, minutes *(mm)*, seconds *(ss)*, and hundredths of a second *(xx)*.

How to enter the command: At the DOS prompt, type

A> time [ENTER]

Upon execution of the TIME command, the message in Figure 5.14 will appear on the screen.

Figure 5.14
Time Screen

At this stage, type the current time in the required twenty-four-hour format, using colons (:) to separate hours, minutes, and seconds, and a period (.) to separate hundredths of a second. Now press ENTER. Note that you can also enter partial time information. For example, if you enter only hours and minutes, DOS sets the other parameters to zero by default. Pressing ENTER without typing a time, accepts the default time that is displayed.

The CLEAR SCREEN (CLS) Command

Purpose: The **CLEAR SCREEN command,** or **CLS,** clears the screen and moves the cursor to the top left corner. This command gives the user a clear screen without deleting the information previously displayed on the screen.

How to enter the command: At the DOS prompt, type

A> cls [ENTER]

The FORMAT Command

Purpose: The **FORMAT command** prepares diskettes for the storage of data. (For hard drive preparation, see Appendix C, Advanced DOS Commands.) Formatting a diskette is similar to putting lines on a blank piece of paper to prepare it for writing. When initiated, the FORMAT command first writes to every storage location on the diskette, determines defective areas and segregates them from future use, and sets up the disk directory and file allocation table. This procedure must be carried out on each floppy diskette before it can be used.

Warning: Data or programs that already exist on a diskette will be erased when the diskette is reformatted, so use this command carefully. On the other hand, you can use FORMAT to deliberately erase a diskette and prepare it for reuse.

How to enter the command: At the DOS prompt, type

A> format x: [ENTER]

where *x:* is the drive containing the diskette to be formatted. For example, format b: formats the diskette located in drive B.

Upon depressing the ENTER key, the screen shown in Figure 5.15 will be presented.

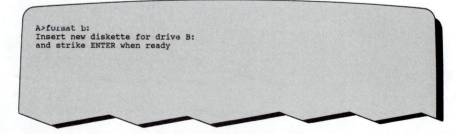

Figure 5.15
Initial Format Screen

At this stage, DOS is asking the user to insert the disk to be formatted in the designated drive, *x*. To carry out our example, you would insert your new disk in Drive B, then press the ENTER key.

It will take twenty to thirty seconds for the diskette to be formatted, depending on its density. During this period, the red light of the disk drive occupied by the formatting disk will stay On, and the message "formatting.." will be displayed at the bottom of the screen. Version 3.3 of MS-DOS/PC-DOS displays the number of the head and cylinder being formatted. While this procedure is being carried out, do not type anything; wait until the red light turns off. Upon execution of the FORMAT command, the screen shown in Figure 5.16 will be presented.

```
A>format b:
Insert new diskette for drive b:
and strike ENTER when ready

Formatting..Format complete

    362496 bytes total disk space
    362496 bytes available on disk

Format another (Y/N)?_
```

Figure 5.16
Format Screen after Formatting a Blank Diskette

When this screen appears, you know that the formatting procedure is completed. The screen will display the diskette's total amount of disk space in bytes, and the total amount of disk space (bytes) available to the user. The message prompt at the bottom of the screen asks whether you want to "format another (Y/N)?" Normally, you would respond *n* for no, then depress the ENTER key. This response terminates the formatting procedure. If you desire to format another diskette, type *y* for yes. DOS will then ask you to insert a new diskette. Upon completion of the formatting process, you will again be asked, "format another (Y/N)?" Once the formatting procedure is terminated, you will see the DOS prompt (A>) at the bottom of your screen.

Modifications: By adding modifiers or parameters to the basic FORMAT command, you can perform additional functions.

A> format x:/s [ENTER]

copies the DOS system files to the formatted diskette in Drive *x*, making it "bootable." The command

A> format x:/v [ENTER]

adds a **volume label** to the diskette formatted in Drive *x*, uniquely identifying each diskette. You may choose a name of up to eleven characters to be entered at the prompt. The command

    A>format x:/s/v [ENTER]

makes the diskette formatted in Drive *x* "bootable," and attaches a volume label.

Let's look at an example of formatting a diskette in Drive B while, at the same time, storing system files on the disk. At the DOS prompt, type

    A>format b:/s [ENTER]

Upon completion of this command, the screen shown in **Figure 5.17** will be displayed.

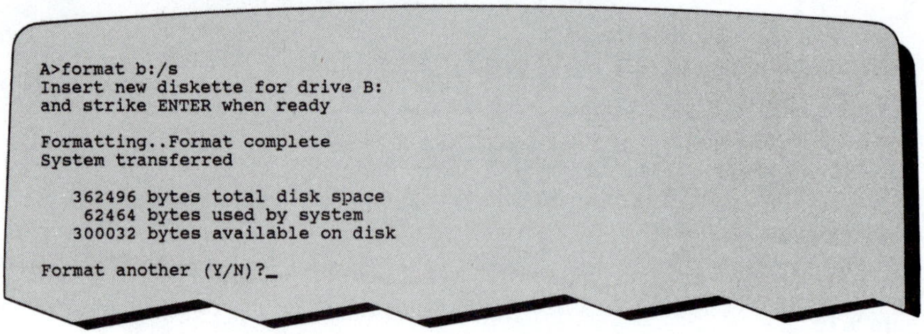

```
A>format b:/s
Insert new diskette for drive B:
and strike ENTER when ready

Formatting..Format complete
System transferred

   362496 bytes total disk space
    62464 bytes used by system
   300032 bytes available on disk

Format another (Y/N)?_
```

Figure 5.17
Format Screen after Formatting a Blank Diskette and Transferring Systems Files to It

The SYSTEM (SYS) Command

Purpose: The **SYSTEM command,** usually typed **SYS,** allows the user to transfer a copy of the system files to a formatted diskette or an application program diskette. This operation allows the new diskette to be used for booting.

How to enter the command: Place the diskette to which you want to transfer system files in Drive *x*. Then, at the DOS prompt, type

    A>sys x: [ENTER]

The VOLUME (VOL) Command

Purpose: The **VOLUME command,** usually typed **VOL,** displays the volume number of the specified diskette. Some diskettes are given volume numbers at the time of formatting. With the VOLUME command, the user can identify that volume number.

How to enter the command: At the DOS prompt, type

    A> vol x: [ENTER]

where *x* is the desired volume. For example, to see the volume number of the disk in Drive B, you would type

    A> vol b: [ENTER]

If the diskette in Drive B was not given a volume number at the time of formatting, the screen shown in Figure 5.18 will be displayed.

Figure 5.18
Volume Screen

The CHECK DISK (CHKDSK) Command

Purpose: The **CHECK DISK command,** usually typed **CHKDSK,** enables the DOS user to produce reports on the status of entire diskettes or individual files to ensure their integrity. CHKDSK also indicates the size of the internal memory, or RAM, of the machine you are using.

How to enter the command: At the DOS prompt, type

    A> chkdsk x: [ENTER]

to check the entire diskette in Drive *x*. The command

    A> chkdsk x:filename [ENTER]

checks only a selected file on diskette *x*.

If several files have the same name but different extensions, you can enter the file name as *filename.ext* to select one file for analysis. Otherwise, all files with the same name will be checked.

Now let's check the diskette that you just formatted. It should be in Drive B. To check your diskette, at the DOS prompt, type

A>chkdsk b: [ENTER]

After entering the CHKDSK command, the data shown in Figure 5.19 will probably appear on the screen.

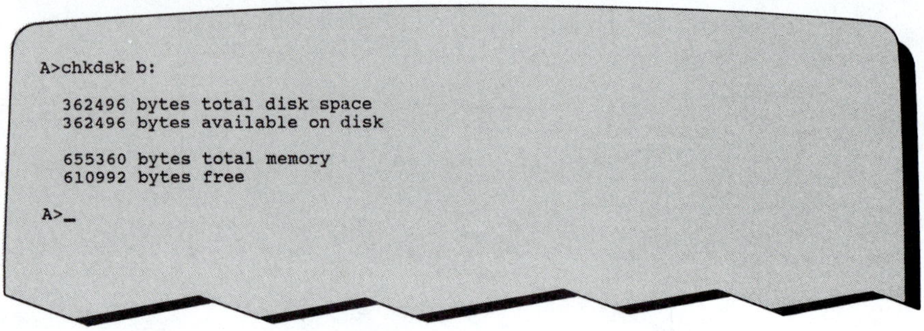

```
A>chkdsk b:

    362496 bytes total disk space
    362496 bytes available on disk

    655360 bytes total memory
    610992 bytes free

A>_
```

Figure 5.19
Screen for CHKDSK Command

This screen provides you with two reports:
1. A disk report containing
   - total disk space in bytes (362,496 bytes).
   - the number of bytes available for use (362,496 bytes).
2. A RAM memory report containing
   - bytes of total memory, or RAM (655,360 bytes).
     In the PC, this is known as 640K of machine memory (640 multiplied by 1,024).
   - bytes of RAM available, or unused (610,992 bytes). Notice that the available memory is less than the RAM size because the DOS system files are now occupying 44,368 bytes of RAM (655,360 minus 44,368 equals 610,992).

Modifications: Two modifiers can be added to CHKDSK. The command

A>chkdsk x:/F [ENTER]

instructs DOS to attempt to correct any errors found in the file allocation table or directory.

Caution: Use this option carefully because it permanently alters the diskette, and you risk the loss of large amounts of data. It is advisable to use CHKDSK without the /F option first, so that effects of attempted repair can be tested without alteration of diskette contents. Then repeat the disk check with the /F option if repair results are satisfactory.

The command option

A>chkdsk x:/v [ENTER]

gives the user a view of files on the diskette and a series of messages concerning the status of each file.

The COPY Command

Purpose: The **COPY command** helps you copy one or more files from one diskette (or hard disk) to another, either retaining the original file name(s) or renaming the copied files as you specify.

How to enter the command: You must supply DOS with the following information: the drive to be copied from (the source, or *s*), the drive to be copied to (the target, or *t*), the file name to be copied, and the file name the copy is to be stored under on the target drive. This operation is carried out at the DOS prompt by entering

A>copy s:filename t:filename [ENTER]

For example, to copy the file BASICA.COM from Drive A to Drive B and retain its name, you would type at the DOS prompt

A>copy a:basica.com b:basica.com [ENTER]

The display shown in Figure 5.20 would appear on the screen.

Figure 5.20
COPY Screen after Copying

Modifications: You can use the COPY command structure noted above as a general model without being concerned which drive is the default drive. This procedure is recommended for novices. As you become more familiar with the COPY command, however, you can modify this structure. DOS will always assume that the source drive (the one to be copied from) is the default drive unless you specify otherwise. Therefore, if Drive A is the default drive, the previous example can be shortened to

A> copy basica.com b:basica.com [ENTER]

Likewise, if the copied file is not to be renamed, there is no need to specify the new file name. In that case, the above example can be shortened to

A> copy basica.com b: [ENTER]

Finally, you can use the COPY command to transfer the entire contents of one diskette to another (or to a hard disk, or *vice versa*) by using the "wildcard" (*) in place of the file name to be copied. (See "wildcards" at the end of this section.)

A> copy a:*.* b: [ENTER]

This wildcard command copies each file on the diskette in drive A, placing them all on the diskette in drive B under their original file names, so that a copy of the entire source diskette is created. It is important to note that this procedure copies each file, one at a time.

Note: The COPY command cannot make workable copies of "copy-protected" diskettes, such as those that house many commercial software programs. On copy-protected software, either the COPY command is unable to perform the copying task or, for legal and ethical reasons, this command should not be used because the program itself is copy-protected. (Chapter 17 discusses these issues at length.)

The DISKCOPY Command

Purpose: The **DISKCOPY command** copies the contents of one diskette to another. The copy is virtually identical to the source diskette.

How to enter the command: As with the COPY command, you must specify both the source and target drives. Using DISKCOPY, the source drive (s) is the first drive specified, while the target drive (t) is the second specified. At the DOS prompt, type

A> diskcopy s: t: [ENTER]

For example, if you typed the DISKCOPY command at the DOS prompt

A> diskcopy a: b: [ENTER]

the display shown in Figure 5.21 would appear on the screen.

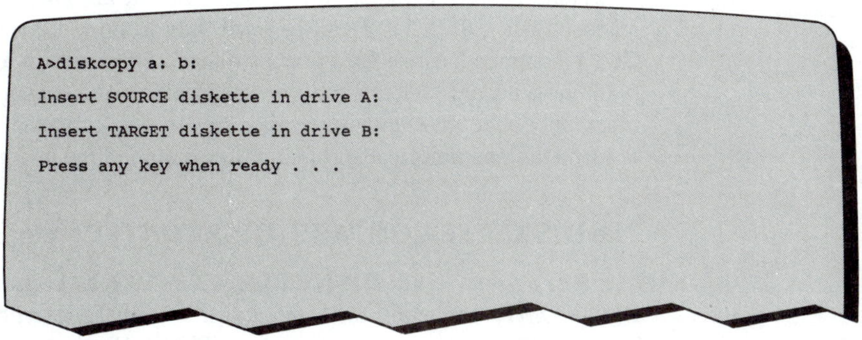

```
A>diskcopy a: b:
Insert SOURCE diskette in drive A:
Insert TARGET diskette in drive B:
Press any key when ready . . .
```

Figure 5.21
DISKCOPY Screen prior to Copying

At this stage, DOS asks you to insert your source diskette in Drive A and the target diskette in Drive B. After so doing, press any key, preferably the ENTER key. DOS then starts copying. The screen shown in Figure 5.22 will appear.

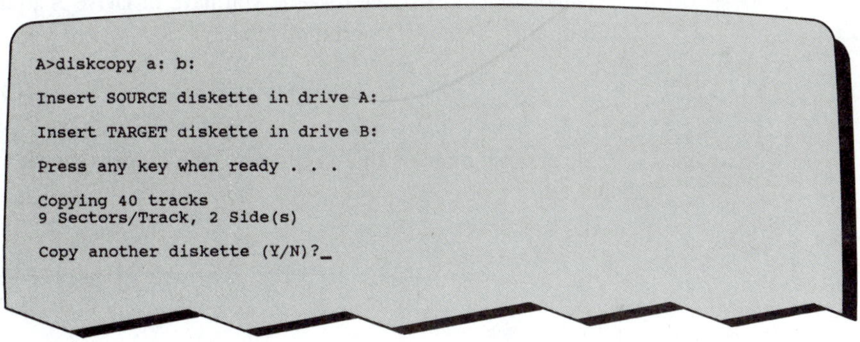

```
A>diskcopy a: b:
Insert SOURCE diskette in drive A:
Insert TARGET diskette in drive B:
Press any key when ready . . .
Copying 40 tracks
9 Sectors/Track, 2 Side(s)
Copy another diskette (Y/N)?_
```

Figure 5.22
DISKCOPY Screen after Copying

At this point, DOS asks you whether you want to make another copy of the source disk. If you have completed your copying, just type *n* (do not press the ENTER key). On the other hand, if you want to make another copy, take the target diskette out, place a new diskette in Drive B, then press *y* (do not press the ENTER key).

Note: To avoid losing data, keep in mind the fact that DISKCOPY erases the contents of the target diskette as the copy is made. Also, you should "write-protect" the source diskette to avoid the possibility of destroying data. Write-protection is easily accomplished by covering the write-protect notch with a write-protect tab.

DISKCOPY cannot be used to make copies of "copy-protected" diskettes, such as those that house many commercial software programs.

There are a few major differences between the DISKCOPY and COPY commands. First, DISKCOPY can be used only to copy the entire diskette, while the COPY command can be used to copy either a single file or all the files on a diskette (with the wildcard '*'). Second, the COPY command cannot format blank diskettes; it can only be used with diskettes that are already formatted. DISKCOPY is capable of formatting an unformatted blank diskette at the time of copying.

The DISKETTE COMPARE (DISKCOMP) Command

Purpose: The **DISKETTE COMPARE command,** usually typed **DISKCOMP,** compares the contents of one diskette with another. After using DISKCOPY, we suggest you employ DISKCOMP as a precautionary procedure to assess the faithfulness of the copy.

How to enter the command: Again the source (*s*) and target (*t*) drives must be specified at the DOS prompt by typing

    A>diskcomp s: t: [ENTER]

Now let's compare the diskette you have in Drive A to the one located in Drive B. To do this, at the DOS prompt, type

    A>diskcomp a: b: [ENTER]

Upon execution of this command, the screen shown in Figure 5.23 will be displayed.

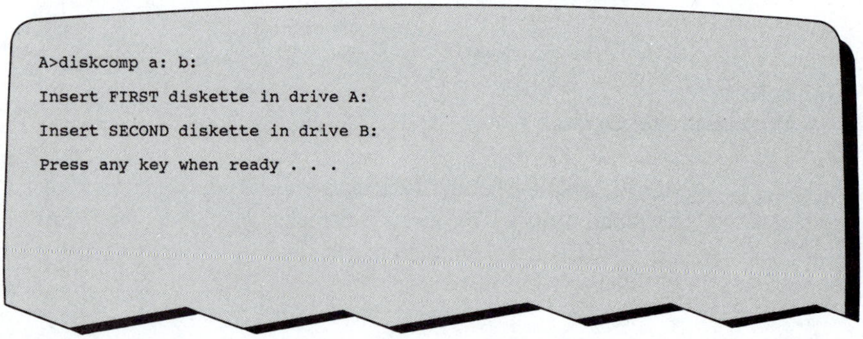

```
A>diskcomp a: b:
Insert FIRST diskette in drive A:
Insert SECOND diskette in drive B:
Press any key when ready . . .
```

Figure 5.23
DISKCOMP Screen prior to Comparing

At this stage you should have the source diskette (FIRST) in Drive A and the target diskette (SECOND) in Drive B. Press any key, preferably the ENTER key.

After the procedure is completed, if the contents of the two diskettes are indeed identical, the screen shown in Figure 5.24 will be displayed.

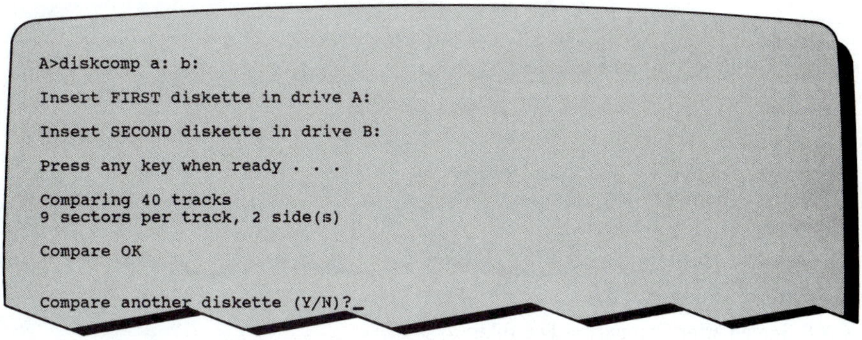

```
A>diskcomp a: b:
Insert FIRST diskette in drive A:
Insert SECOND diskette in drive B:
Press any key when ready . . .
Comparing 40 tracks
9 sectors per track, 2 side(s)
Compare OK

Compare another diskette (Y/N)?_
```

Figure 5.24
DISKCOMP Screen after Comparing

When DISKCOMP asks whether you want to make another comparison, you respond with either *n* for no or *y* for yes. In either case, you do not need to press the ENTER key after you answer the question. A *n* will terminate the disk-comparison session.

Note: DISKCOMP compares all tracks on a track-by-track basis, and displays an error message if the tracks are not equal, giving the track number and side where the mismatch was found. In the case of too many errors among compared files, you can stop the comparing process by holding the CTRL key while pressing the BREAK key.

The COMPARISON (COMP) Command

Purpose: The **COMPARISON command,** usually typed **COMP,** is similar to DISKCOMP, but compares only two specified files rather than all the files on a diskette.

How to enter the command: To use this command, you must provide both the source drive and file name, and the target drive and file name. At the DOS prompt, type

A> comp s:filename.extension t:filename.extension [ENTER]

For example, if you want to compare the file BASICA.COM on the diskette in Drive A to the same file on the Drive B diskette, you should type at the DOS prompt

A> comp a:basica.com b:basica.com [ENTER]

If the file BASIC.COM does not exist on the diskette in Drive B, the screen shown in Figure 5.25 will be displayed.

Figure 5.25
COMP Screen after Comparing Two Files

This indicates that the file BASICA.COM cannot be found on the diskette in Drive B. If BASICA.COM was found on the diskette in Drive B and its contents were identical to the file on the Drive A diskette, then the message "Files compare OK" will appear, indicating that the files are identical.

Modifications: The only variation of the COMP command occurs in its use of wildcards (see the end of this section for an explanation of wildcards). You can use wildcards to compare different file names with identical file extensions, or *vice versa*. For example,

A>comp a:basica.* b:basica.* [ENTER]

or

A>comp a:*.com b:*.com [ENTER]

or

A>comp a:*.* b:*.* [ENTER]

In the last example, all the files on the diskette in Drive A will be compared with the files on the Drive B diskette, regardless of the files names, extensions, or sizes.

The RENAME (REN) Command

Purpose: The **RENAME command,** usually typed **REN,** assigns a new name to a specified file. The command can change both the file name and the extension.

How to enter the command: At the DOS prompt, type

A>ren x:oldname.ext newname.new [ENTER]

For example, if you had a file called SALES.TXT on the diskette in Drive A and you wanted to change its name to FILE1.DAT, at the DOS prompt, you would type

A>ren a:sales.txt file1.dat [ENTER]

No screen message is displayed upon completion of this command. If you wish to see whether the old name has been changed to the new one, use the DIR command to determine if the new name is on the directory listing.

If you made a mistake—for example, if the name you typed is the same as the file name that you were trying to change, or another file already has the new name you are trying to assign—DOS will respond with a "Duplicate file name" or "File not found" message, respectively.

The DELETE or ERASE (DEL or ERASE) Command

Purpose: The **DELETE command** (typed **DEL**), also called the **ERASE command,** removes a file or files from a diskette. When DEL has been used on a file, DOS will deny future access to that file. This command can be used interchangeably with the ERASE command.

How to enter the command: The DELETE command is entered at the DOS prompt by typing

A>del x:filename.ext [ENTER]

For example, to erase a file called *program1.com* from the Drive A diskette, you would enter

A>del A:program1.com [ENTER]

Upon completion of this command, the specified file will be deleted.

Modifications: DOS assumes that the file to be deleted is on the default drive unless you specify otherwise. You can increase the number of files that will be deleted by issuing a "wildcard" (see the end of this section) along with DEL. For example, typing

A>del b:*.com [ENTER]

will delete all files with the *.com* extension, regardless of file name.

Note: The DEL command does not actually erase the data, it just marks it as available to be written over on the diskette. If you accidentally DEL valuable data, you may recover the data through the use of commercially available software.

The TYPE Command

Purpose: The **TYPE command** displays the contents of any file on a diskette, either on the screen or on another output device.

How to enter the command: At the DOS prompt, type

A> `type x:filename` [ENTER]

where *x* is the specified disk drive. For example, if you want to see the contents of the file called PROGRAM2.BAS stored on the diskette in Drive A, at the DOS prompt, enter

A> `type a:program2.bas` [ENTER]

To print the contents on the printer, press the PRTSC key once while pressing CTRL, then issue the TYPE command as described above. Remember, upon completion of printing, you must press the CTRL and PRTSC keys to stop the process.

Wildcards

Purpose: **Wildcards** provide a shortcut for issuing commands involving multiple files whose names have one or more characters in common. The two DOS wildcards, the asterisk (*) and the question mark (?), can be used in conjunction with any DOS command.

How to use: The asterisk (*) wildcard refers to file names and/or extensions. An * indicates that the character in the * position and any further positions can be represented by any character in the original file name. For example, SALES.* would include all files named SALES, regardless of their extensions. The files SALES.TXT, SALES.COM, and SALES.BAT would all be affected by a command issued for SALES.*.

The reverse would also be true. That is, *.COM would include files of any file name with the extension .COM.

Another example, SALES*.* would include all files with the first five letters SALES, any letters in the rest of the file name, and any extension. The files SALES10.WK1, SALES2.REP, and SALESABC.TXT would fall into that category.

A directory of all files on a diskette can be accomplished by using *.*. For example,

    A>dir a:*.* [ENTER]

To delete the contents of a diskette, you can use

    A>del b:*.* [ENTER]

Upon receiving this command, DOS will prompt you with the message, "Are you sure (Y/N)?" Type *y* for yes. There is no need to press the ENTER. The entire contents of the diskette in Drive B will be deleted.

Note: Make sure you check the contents of the diskette that you are erasing before you finalize the DEL b:*.* command.

The question mark (?) wildcard is similar to the asterisk wildcard, except that only one character is variable at the ? position. For example, SALES?.WK1 would reference all files with a six-character file name, the first five of which are SALES, and with any character accepted for the sixth position. The file names SALES1.WK1, SALES3.WK1, and SALESA.WK1 would also be valid. The two wildcards can also be used in combination with each other. For example, SALES?.* would reference files with six-character file names beginning with SALES, and with any extension.

The Fragmentation of Data

Information originally recorded on a diskette is recorded contiguously; that means the data are stored in physically adjacent sectors on the diskette. As old files are deleted and new files added over time, DOS will physically position the new files in sectors where they best fit, but not necessarily contiguously. It therefore becomes likely that some files will be stored in several different physical locations on the diskette (see Figure 5.26). This scattering, called **fragmentation,** can slow down accessing operations, since the drive must move the read/write heads over several areas of the diskette to retrieve an entire file.

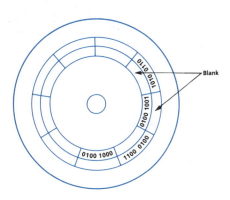

Figure 5.26
Blank Sectors on a Diskette

One way to solve the fragmentation problem is to copy the contents of the diskette onto a new diskette, using the COPY command with the * wildcard. For example, if you want to copy the contents of the diskette in drive A onto the diskette in drive B, at the DOS prompt, type

A> copy a:*.* b: [ENTER]

This task is necessary in situations where a diskette is used frequently for adding and deleting files.

■ Summary of DOS Commands

CHKDSK	Produces a report on the status of files on a diskette to assure their integrity
CLS	Clear the screen
COMP	Compares specified files of one diskette to those of another diskette
COPY	Copy one or more files from one diskette to another diskette
DATE	Change current date
DEL or ERASE	Remove one or more files from a diskette
DIR	Lists the contents of a specified diskette
DISKCOMP	Compares the contents of two diskettes
DISKCOPY	Copies the contents of an entire diskette to another diskette
FORMAT	Prepares new diskettes for data storage
REN	Assign a new name to a specified file
SYS	Transfer system files to a formatted diskette
TIME	Change current time
TYPE	Display contents of any file on a diskette
VER	Determine current DOS version being used
VOL	Display volume number of specified diskette

■ Key Terms

cold boot	Starting the system by turning on the power source.
warm boot	Starting the system without turning the power off, then on.
ENTER	The key marked "Enter" or noted by a bent arrow.
A>, or DOS prompt	The signal that appears on the screen when the system is ready to process commands or an application.
cursor	Blinking underline that tracks the current character position.
CTRL	The CONTROL key, marked "Ctrl," located next to the "A" key.

ALT	The ALTERNATE key immediately beneath the CTRL key.
DEL	The DELETE key, marked "Del", located beneath the "2" and "3" keys.
file name	An identifier for each program or file.
extension name	Accompanies the file name; describes the type of data or instructions stored in the file. Separated from the file name by a period (.).
file size	The number of bytes or characters in a file.
volume label	The name or number assigned to a formatted disk.
fragmentation	Scattering of data over non-contiguous sectors of a diskette.

■ REVIEW QUESTIONS

1. Describe how you use the DOS diskette to start up the system.
2. Which of the following keys enables you to change from the insert mode to the typeover mode?
   (a) CAPS LOCK
   (b) DEL
   (c) HOME
   (d) INS
   (e) none of the above
3. If the A Drive is currently the default drive, the DOS prompt will appear as which of the following?
   (a) A:
   (b) A>
   (c) A<
   (d) :A
   (e) none of the above
4. The _____ command is issued to prepare a new diskette for the storage of data.
   (a) DIRECTORY
   (b) VOLUME
   (c) COPY
   (d) FORMAT
   (e) none of the above
5. What does the CLS command do? Clears screen
6. When would you use the DIR/W command? view wide directories
7. To check the status of a diskette and produce a report on the status, the _____ command would be used.
   (a) CLS
   (b) CHKDSK
   (c) COPYDISK
   (d) DISKCOMP
8. When issuing the COPY command, the _____ drive, the drive copied from, is specified first; the _____ drive, the drive to be copied to, is specified second.
   (a) default, secondary
   (b) origin, destination
   (c) source, target
   (d) primary, default

9. Which of the following is the correct form of the COPY command to copy all files on the diskette in Drive A to the diskette in Drive B?
   (a) copy a:*.* b:
   (b) copy a;*.* b;
   (c) copy b:*.* a:
   (d) copy b;*.* a;
   (e) none of the above
10. To compare the contents of one diskette with the contents of a second diskette, the _____ command would be used.
    (a) CHKDSK
    (b) COMPDISK
    (c) DISKCOPY
    (d) DISKCOMP
11. What is the function of the RENAME command?
12. Where will DOS look for a file that is to be deleted?
13. To display the contents of any diskette file on the screen, the _____ command can be issued, followed by the name of the file.
    (a) DIRECTORY
    (b) VOLUME
    (c) TYPE
    (d) WILDCARD
    (e) none of the above
14. Which of the following is NOT a wildcard character?
    (a) asterisk
    (b) period
    (c) question mark
    (d) all of the above are wildcards
15. How can the screen contents be sent to the printer?
16. Why is it important to handle the diskette carefully?
17. What is the difference between a warm boot and a cold boot?
18. What parameter would you add to the FORMAT command to make the disk "bootable"?
19. What form of the DIRECTORY command would you use if a directory was long and you wanted to see one screen at a time?
20. What parameter would you add to the CHKDSK command to instruct DOS to attempt to repair any errors found in the file allocation table or directory?
21. What is the difference between the COPY command and the DISKCOPY command?
22. What is the difference between the DISKCOMP command and the COMP command?
23. What is the purpose of the SYSTEM (SYS) command?
24. What happens to a file when the DELETE or ERASE command is issued?
25. What is fragmentation? What task should you perform periodically to correct this situation?

□ *chapter* 5

HANDS-ON EXERCISE

For this exercise, insert the DOS diskette in Drive A and a blank diskette in Drive B (once it is formatted, this blank diskette will be referred to as the "exercise" diskette.) Drive A is the default drive.

1. Format the blank diskette in Drive B, making it "bootable."
2. Copy the contents of the diskette in Drive A to the diskette in drive B using the DISKCOPY command.
3. Compare the two diskettes in Drives A and B to verify that the copy process was successful.

Change the default drive to Drive B by typing B: at the DOS prompt so you do not accidentally alter the files on the DOS diskette for the rest of the exercises. The result of this process will look like this:

```
A>  B:
B>  _
```

4. Obtain a directory listing on the exercise diskette in Drive B.
5. Delete the file ANSI.SYS from the diskette in Drive B. Check the directory on Drive B to verify the deletion.
6. Copy the file ANSI.SYS from the DOS diskette in Drive A to the exercise diskette in Drive B.
7. Check the directory on Drive B to verify that the ANSI.SYS file was copied and that it now resides on the diskette in Drive B. If it is not listed, repeat Exercise 5.
8. Using the COMP command, compare the ANSI.SYS file in Drive A to the same file in Drive B.
9. Rename the Drive B ANSI.SYS file as NEWANSI.SYS.
10. Clear the screen.
11. Check the current version of DOS being used by your system.
12. Check the current date being used by your system. If it is incorrect, change it.
13. Obtain a directory listing on Drive B, listing only the files with the .EXE extension. (*Hint*: use a wildcard.)
14. Delete all of the files on the diskette in Drive B.

Part III

ELECTRONIC WORD PROCESSING CONCEPTS AND APPLICATIONS

chapter 6
MICROCOMPUTER WORD PROCESSING

- discuss the development of modern word processors.
- discuss the differences between producing a document on a typewriter and producing a document with a computerized word processor.
- describe the steps involved in producing a document with a computerized word processor.
- discuss the features of the four word processing packages presented.
- describe in detail the six diskettes that make up the WordPerfect software package.

chapter 7
LEARNING WORDPERFECT

- discuss the keyboard keys and their WordPerfect functions.
- describe the function keys and their features.
- discuss how to create a document in WordPerfect.
- discuss how to edit, save, format, and print a document.
- discuss the different ways to retrieve an existing document.
- describe how to copy a file to another file name.
- discuss how to move, copy, and delete a block of text.

chapter 6

MICROCOMPUTER WORD PROCESSING

After completing this chapter, you should be able to

- *discuss the development of modern word processors.*
- *discuss the differences between producing a document on a typewriter and producing a document with a computerized word processor.*
- *describe the steps involved in producing a document with a computerized word processor.*
- *discuss the features of the four word processing packages presented.*
- *describe in detail the six diskettes that make up the WordPerfect software package.*

INTRODUCTION

In any organization, the preparation of documents for internal and external purposes is considered a major function. Documents may include business memos, letters, reports, or mailing labels. For years, office workers labored on typewriters to prepare documents of all types. With the advent of microcomputers, many business organizations began to utilize word processing software packages instead of the traditional typewriter.

This chapter discusses the overall concepts of computerized word processing, and microcomputer word processing software packages in particular. Several common word processing software packages will be introduced. In the last portion of this chapter, the popular word processing program, WordPerfect, introduces the reader to the different functions and capabilities of microcomputer word processing software packages. Chapter 7 is a tutorial in which WordPerfect is applied through a series of hands-on exercises ranging from the basics to advanced concepts.

Figure 6.1
A Typical Word Processing Arrangement

COMPUTERIZED WORD PROCESSING CONCEPTS

Although the terms word processing, text processing, or text management usually refer to computerized word processing, the general definition of word processing covers all methods and all devices for preparing any written communication.

In the nineteenth century, the invention of the typewriter marked the beginning of a new era, especially for businesses and governments. The typewriter became the standard device for written communication. When typewriters were introduced, many employees rejected this new business tool, arguing that writing manually was more effective. This type of resistance did not last long, and soon after the introduction of the typewriter, its opponents came to realize how useful this device could be for document preparation.

The typical cycle in the production of a standard document—a letter, memo, or report—begins with a handwritten draft on paper. When all the corrections and modifications have been made, the manuscript is then typed. Frequently, the document goes through a number of changes, such as adding a word, sentence, or paragraph, moving a sentence or paragraph from one part of the document to another, or deleting part of the document. Changes to the document necessitate retyping it.

It was not until the introduction of microcomputers that electronic word processing became accepted as a powerful tool, available to anyone for improving the overall process of document preparation and text management. With the low cost of microcomputers and their ease of operation, electronic word processing became one of the earliest applications of the microcomputer. As a matter of fact, these applications paved the way for the current popularity of microcomputers. Use of microcomputers for word processing has revolutionized the entire process of text and document preparation and management.

The major difference between using microcomputers and using typewriters is the ease with which a computer user can modify documents before they are produced in final hard copy form.

Suppose you are preparing a term paper for a course. After your library research, you begin to put your thoughts together and write them down. Then you either type those pages or have someone else type them on a typewriter (see Figure 6.2 on the following page).

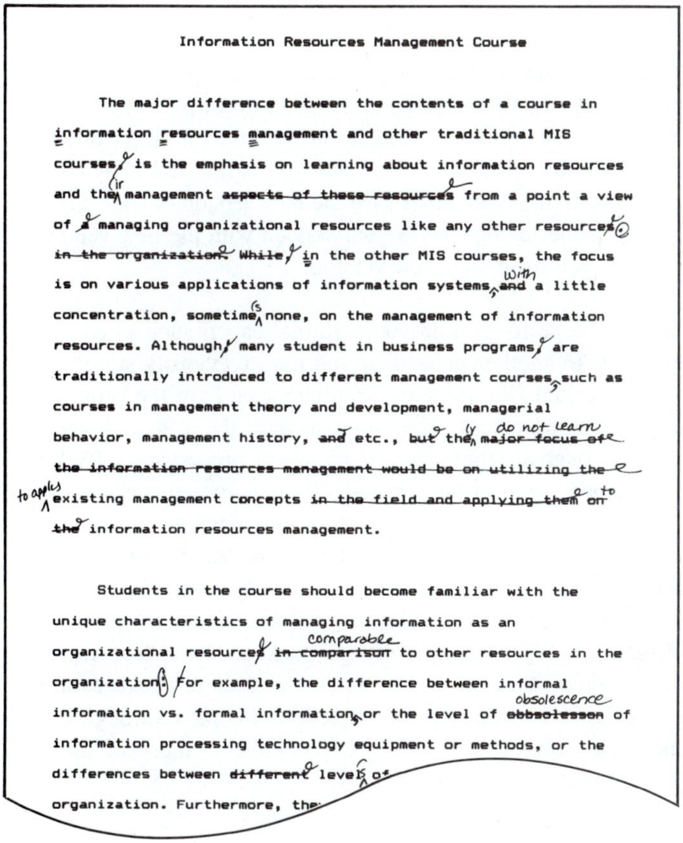
Information Resources Management Course

The major difference between the contents of a course in information resources management and other traditional MIS courses, is the emphasis on learning about information resources and the management aspects of these resources from a point a view of a managing organizational resources like any other resources in the organization. While, in the other MIS courses, the focus is on various applications of information systems, and a little concentration, sometime none, on the management of information resources. Although, many student in business programs, are traditionally introduced to different management courses such as courses in management theory and development, managerial behavior, management history, and etc., but the major focus of the information resources management would be on utilizing the existing management concepts in the field and applying them on the information resources management.

Students in the course should become familiar with the unique characteristics of managing information as an organizational resources in comparison to other resources in the organization. For example, the difference between informal information vs. formal information or the level of obbsolesson of information processing technology equipment or methods, or the differences between different level of organization. Furthermore, the

Figure 6.2
A Typical Page of a Document with Many Changes

After the paper is typed, you may discover some new material that could be added to your paper, or you discover misspelled words, or certain poorly phrased sentences. There is a good chance that any one of these changes would require you to retype the whole paper, or significant parts of it. If you were using a microcomputer and word processing software, you could incorporate these changes within the original version of your paper without retyping the entire paper.

In order to understand how computerized word processing works, let's divide the whole process of text preparation into different discrete steps. These steps assume that you have access to a microcomputer equipped with a keyboard, screen, disk drive, printer, and a word processing software package.

Step 1. You enter your term paper into the computer through the keyboard. Everything you enter is displayed on the screen so that you can easily and immediately correct mistakes. The material you have entered through the keyboard is also kept in the memory (RAM) of the computer. This process of entering data is referred to as **inputting.**

Step 2. Once you have finished inputting your paper, you review the document on the screen to determine if there are any changes to make or errors to correct. When you are satisfied with the paper, you ask the microcomputer to take the final draft of your paper and store it on a diskette as a text file to which you have assigned a name. This process is referred to as **saving** your document.

Step 3. After saving your paper, the next step is to produce a printed copy with the printer. Before printing, you decide how you want your paper to look: how much space should be left at the top of the paper (top margin) before the first line is printed, how much space should be left before a line is started (left margin), where a line should end (right margin), and how much space should be left at the bottom of each page (bottom margin). You also decide to center different titles, print page numbers, and underline certain words or sentences. This process of setting the "look" of your document is referred to as **formatting.**

Step 4. Later, you may want to add new material to the paper you have written. In order to do so, you use the file name you assigned to your paper to call up the text on the screen. You find the location of the addition and insert it. You can also move paragraphs around or rephrase sentences. This function is referred to as **editing.** Upon completion of this updating, you either save the new version of your paper on your diskette under a new name, or replace the old version with the new version under the same name. Finally, you print your new version.

Many advanced tasks can be performed on your original paper, such as adding the entire paper, or parts of it, to another paper that you have previously stored on your diskette. This process is called **file merging.** You can even have the program check your entire paper for spelling errors. You can also have the system suggest other words or expressions through its thesaurus, if the word processing software package you are using is equipped with these features. Your microcomputer can be outfitted with word processing software that features many other functions, such as the ability to prepare a table of contents, a bibliography, footnotes, mailing labels, forms, and even graphics. All of these tasks can be performed by a set of computer programs put together in one word processing software package.

In the last decade, many word processing software packages have been introduced for different microcomputer hardware systems. Some of these packages are only capable of performing basic word processing functions (Steps 1 through 4), while others are equipped with advanced functions comparable to those of more sophisticated mainframe word processing systems.

■ SOME POPULAR WORD PROCESSING SOFTWARE PACKAGES

The following section discusses a few of the more popular word processing software packages and their characteristics.

WordStar

WordStar was introduced in 1979 by MicroPro International. Thanks in large part to its early entry into the market, WordStar became immensely popular. Originally designed for Z80 microprocessor-based microcomputers under the CP/M operating system, WordStar was later redesigned for Intel 8086/8088 microprocessor-based microcomputers (mainly IBM-PCs and compatibles) running under PC-DOS or MS-DOS. The WordStar software package comes in four distinct programs: a word processor (WordStar), a spelling checker (SpellStar), a mail merger feature (MailMerge), and an indexer (IndexStar). Other programs are available, including a thesaurus, a communication program, and a preformatted mailing list program.

Hardware requirements for WordStar include 256K RAM for DOS Version 2.0 or 2.1, and 320K RAM for DOS Version 3.0 or later versions. Furthermore, two disk drives or one floppy disk drive and one hard disk are required. WordStar utilizes the menu structure to its fullest capacity. Most tasks in the software environment are performed through the use of menus. Figure 6.3 illustrates the WordStar opening menu.

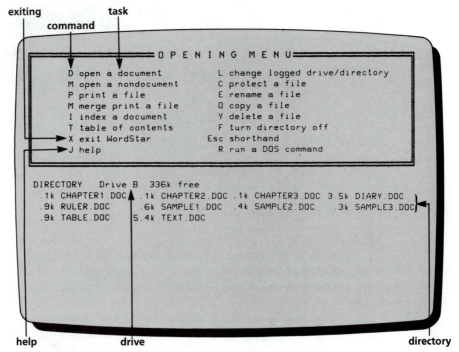

Figure 6.3
WordStar's Opening Menu

Microsoft Word

Microsoft Word was developed by Microsoft Corporation for Intel 8088 microprocessor-based microcomputers using MS-DOS or PC-DOS. Microsoft Word is classified as a menu-driven package, but it also uses keyboard-entered commands. Furthermore, with graphics adapters, a user can communicate with the software and select menu options via a mouse, as shown in Figure 6.4 on the following page. In return, the software package communicates with the user through on-screen graphics.

Figure 6.4
Wordgraphic with a Mouse

Included with Microsoft Word is a spelling checker, a mail merge feature, and an on-screen tutorial. The hardware specifications of this package include 256K RAM and one disk drive. The software runs under DOS Version 2.0 or later. Figure 6.5 shows a sample screen of the Microsoft Word software package.

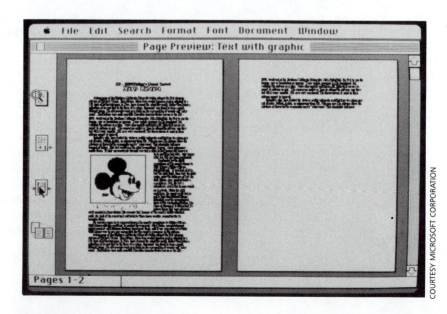

Figure 6.5
A Microsoft Word Screen

DisplayWrite

DisplayWrite was developed by the IBM Corporation for the IBM-PC or compatible machines (the Intel 8086/8088 family of microprocessor-based microcomputers). This word processing software package does just about everything that can be done with electronic word processing. All the programs of DisplayWrite reside on four diskettes. These programs offer a variety of features, such as multiple document editing, split screens, a thesaurus, and the ability to generate a table of contents or an index.

The DisplayWrite software is classified as a completely menu-driven package, and menu commands rely on the use of function keys or the CONTROL key used in conjunction with other keys. Hardware requirements include a minimum of 256K RAM and two disk drives. The main advantage of this package, compared to other available word processing software packages, is its compatibility with a different version of DisplayWrite that runs on IBM mainframe systems. Having a working knowledge of PC-DisplayWrite enables an individual to use the mainframe version of the package as well; it is almost identical to the PC version. Figure 6.6 illustrates a sample screen of DisplayWrite.

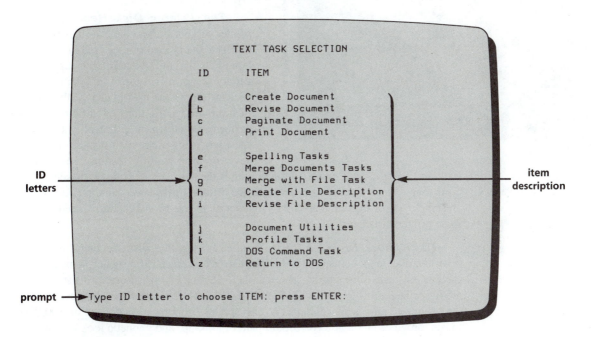

Figure 6.6
A Sample DisplayWrite Screen

WordPerfect

WordPerfect was designed by WordPerfect Corporation for the Intel 8086/8088 microprocessor-based family of microcomputers (the IBM-PC and compatibles) with PC-DOS or MS-DOS. WordPerfect is considered easy to use and offers many helpful features. All the programs of WordPerfect come on six diskettes: WordPerfect, Learning, Speller, Thesaurus, Printer 1, and Printer 2, shown in Figure 6.7.

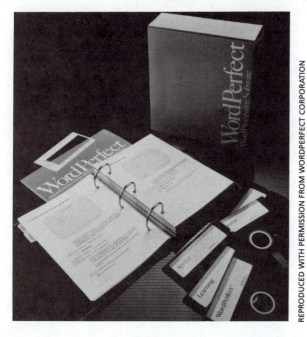

Figure 6.7
The Six WordPerfect Diskettes

The WordPerfect Diskette. The WordPerfect diskette is considered the WordPerfect master diskette, where all the programs necessary for text inputting, saving, editing, and formatting reside. Most WordPerfect functions can be performed by the programs that reside on this diskette, which can be booted either in conjunction with DOS or by itself. In the latter case, it is assumed that you have copied the DOS system files onto the WordPerfect master disk.

The Printer Diskettes. The two printer diskettes allow the WordPerfect user to define the type of printer used in conjunction with the PC. WordPerfect supports a variety of printer types. In addition, the package allows the user to change the specifications and definitions of different tasks performed on the printer. In reality, the average user, using a common printer, does not have to worry about using the printer programs. The default printer defined within the WordPerfect master diskette supports many standard tasks and functions for different brands of printers. Unless you are employing a printer that is very uncommon, you probably won't need to use these printer diskettes.

The Speller Diskette. The WordPerfect **speller diskette** helps the user proof the document created with the WordPerfect package. The speller helps correct spelling mistakes through an on-screen help session, which presents a list of correctly spelled words similar to those that the user is trying to correct. In other words, the speller is an on-line dictionary. The speller supports a dictionary of 100,000 words, provides automatic correction, pattern look-up, and phonetic look-up, checks for double occurrences of a word, permits adding and deleting words from the dictionary, and finally, does a word count.

The Thesaurus Diskette. The WordPerfect **thesaurus diskette** helps users identify words other than the ones they have used over and over again. The thesaurus program displays synonyms and other words that suggest the same idea and meaning as the word in question. This function is similar to that of a traditional thesaurus except that, in WordPerfect, the thesaurus is an on-line dictionary, so the task of searching can be done very quickly. The WordPerfect thesaurus can display up to three words and their references on a single screen.

The Learning Diskette. A **learning diskette** is an on-line tutorial for teaching a program to a first-time user. There are twelve lessons on the WordPerfect learning diskette. Each lesson includes a brief introduction, followed by a series of steps that guide the user through different tasks.

WordPerfect's command structure is tied to the ten function keys on the IBM-PC keyboard. In order to make the most of these keys, each key can be used by itself or in conjunction with the SHIFT, CTRL, or ALT keys. With these combinations, the ten function keys are capable of accomplishing forty separate tasks. WordPerfect utilizes a combination of menu options and commands issued by the user. Since its introduction, many versions of WordPerfect have been released. At the time of this writing, Version 4.2 is the latest version, and its hardware requirements are a minimum of 256K and two disk drives or one floppy drive and a hard disk.

Now compare the programs we have discussed by looking at the information contained in Table 6.1.

WORD PROCESSING SOFTWARE PACKAGE	DEVELOPER	SPELL CHECK	INDEXER	THESAURUS	COMMUNI-CATIONS	GRAPHICS	MAIL MERGE
WordStar	Micropro International	X	X	X	X		X
Microsoft Word	Microsoft Corporation	X		X		X	X
DisplayWrite	IBM Corporation	X	X	X			X
WordPerfect	WordPerfect Corporation	X	X	X			X

TABLE 6.1 Summary of the Featured Packages

■ SUMMARY

The advent of typewriters revolutionized the process of document preparation. Similarly, soon after the advent of computers, it was recognized that electronic devices could be used effectively for document preparations. That led to the development of electronic word processing, one of the earliest applications of microcomputers.

With the help of one of the many word processing packages available for microcomputers, a user can easily create a document (input), store it on a secondary medium for future use (save), correct and modify it later (edit), and obtain a hard copy of the document (print). These are the basic functions of any word processing software package. In addition to these functions, many other tasks can be performed by advanced word processing packages, including merging documents, spell-checking, preparing mailing lists, and many more.

Four common word processing software packages were discussed in this chapter: WordStar, MicroSoft Word, DisplayWrite, and WordPerfect. WordPerfect is the subject of the next chapter, which will provide practical lessons on how to use this popular word processing software package.

■ Key Terms

inputting	Entering data through the keyboard and placing it into the computer's RAM.
saving	Storing data on a diskette as a text file to which you assign a name.
formatting	The process of adjusting your input on the computer until it appears as you want it.
editing	The process of making additions, deletions, and corrections to the input data.
file merging	Adding input data, or parts of it, to another group of data previously stored on your disk.
WordStar	A microcomputer software package that comes in four distinct programs: WordStar, SpellStar, MailMerge, and IndexStar.
Microsoft Word	A software package that is menu-driven but also uses keyboard-entered commands.
DisplayWrite	A software package that does just about everything that can be done with electronic word processing.
WordPerfect	A software package that is considered easy to use and offers many helpful features. All the programs of WordPerfect come on six diskettes: WordPerfect, Learning, Speller, Thesaurus, Printer 1, Printer 2.
speller diskette	Software that allows the user to proof the document created with a software package.
thesaurus diskette	This word processing feature acts as an ordinary thesaurus, suggesting other words or expressions for a particular word or expression.
learning diskette	An on-line tutorial for teaching a program to a new user.

■ Review Questions

1. The process of typing data into the computer's memory is called
    (a) formatting.
    (b) saving.
    (c) inputting.
    (d) editing.
    (e) none of the above.

2. You decide you would like to print your document with page numbers and different margins. This process is referred to as _____ the document.
   (a) editing
   (b) formatting
   (c) merging
   (d) inputting
3. If you decided to add a new paragraph in the middle of an existing document, you would be _____ the document.
   (a) editing
   (b) merging
   (c) formatting
   (d) inputting
4. The process of adding all or part of a document to a second document is called file
   (a) merging.
   (b) combining.
   (c) editing.
   (d) formatting.
5. Describe the functions of a word processing package.
6. Which of the following word processing packages, developed for the IBM-PC, is compatible with a different version that runs on IBM mainframe systems?
   (a) DisplayWrite
   (b) Microsoft Word
   (c) WordPerfect
   (d) WordStar
   (e) none of the above
7. The WordPerfect _____ allows you to proof the document you create with the package.
   (a) learning diskette
   (b) speller diskette
   (c) thesaurus diskette
   (d) master diskette
8. WordPerfect's on-line tutorial diskette is called
   (a) learning diskette.
   (b) master diskette.
   (c) tutoring diskette.
   (d) thesaurus diskette.
9. Which of the following WordPerfect diskettes would help a user identify words other than the one that has already been used?
   (a) printer diskettes
   (b) speller diskette
   (c) thesaurus diskette
   (d) learning diskette
10. Which of the following is *not* one of the keys used in combination with the ten function keys to perform WordPerfect tasks?
    (a) BACKSPACE   (b) SHIFT   (c) ALT   (d) CTRL

11. How is computerized word processing an improvement over a typewriter in the process of modifying a document?
12. How did the introduction of microcomputers help to gain acceptance for electronic word processing?
13. Name the six diskettes included in the WordPerfect word processing package.
14. Under what circumstances would you need to use WordPerfect's printer diskettes?
15. Why is WordPerfect's thesaurus such a useful tool?
16. Explain why WordStar is such a popular package.
17. What is the primary difference between Microsoft Word and the other packages discussed?
18. Judy is an executive secretary for a small firm. Her boss, Director of New Business, writes literally hundreds of letters a week. Most of these letters are form letters seeking new business from a variety of industries. Because of this, he likes to change the basic form of the letter to suit each prospective client. Judy has heard about word processors from her friends in other firms and has often thought that she should speak to her manager about purchasing one for her use. Discuss whether or not Judy would put a word processor to good use.
19. Describe the steps involved in developing a document with a word processor.
20. Bob is an engineering student at a local university. His course work involves the preparation of many reports requiring extensive computations. Because of this, he is thinking about buying a personal computer. However, he does not plan to purchase a word processor because the reports he writes are short—only one or two pages in length—and he thinks it would be a waste of money. What do you think?

Case One:
CENTRAL MEDICAL CENTER VASCULAR LAB

Brenda Murphy is so frustrated with her new IBM PC-AT system that she's ready to throw it out the window and quit. Brenda has worked in the Surgery Department at Central Hospital for the past five years, mainly doing word processing on a Wang microcomputer. Three months ago, she was transferred to a better-paying secretarial position in the Vascular Lab, a new department. Brenda was excited about going into a new job with all new office equipment, and about working for Mrs. Newflyer, the Vascular Lab supervisor, whom she really liked. Her new job would entail essentially the same duties as her old: transcribing dictation, preparing text for scientific publications, preparing correspondence, and other general secretarial duties.

During Brenda's first week on the job, Mrs. Newflyer ordered new word processing equipment for her. Dr. Hacker, who is something of a computer buff, volunteered to help them specify the system. Although he does not work in the department, he does collaborate with them on research projects. Hacker suggested that they purchase an IBM PC-AT system with an enhanced color monitor, and that they use WordPerfect as their word processing software. He has a similar system in his office and another at home and is very pleased, both with the hardware and the application packages that he uses (WordPerfect, Lotus 1-2-3, and dBASE III PLUS). The Vascular Lab had access to a surplus Quietwriter printer, which would work well with the system. Since Dr. Hacker was the expert, Mrs. Newflyer felt this would be the best way to go. Brenda has never used an IBM system, but was sure that she could adapt to the new word processing package with little trouble since she had learned how to use the Wang easily enough.

Dr. Hacker also suggested that they purchase the equipment and software from a local vendor, ComputerEase. An order was placed for an IBM PC-AT with a hard disk. Two weeks later, ComputerEase delivered the AT. The representative set the system up on Brenda's desk, formatted the hard drive, and installed WordPerfect. Before he left, he instructed Brenda to turn the system on and enter "WP" to get started. Since it was late, she didn't try the system until the next day.

When she tried to prepare a document the next day, Brenda was able to get into WordPerfect, but discovered that she couldn't format floppy diskettes (she knew from her Wang experience that this must be done for saving backups), and that the printer wasn't connected for output. She called Dr. Hacker for help. He called ComputerEase to find out what they had loaded and found that DOS hadn't been specified in the original purchase agreement. ComputerEase had only loaded the files necessary to "boot" the machine. This angered Hacker, but he was able to find a copy of the appropriate DOS version and load the remainder of the files. Hacker also found that the printer cable supplied by ComputerEase didn't fit; it was parallel, and the printer was configured as serial. He found out that the printer could be converted to parallel operation by purchasing an interface module, and since this could be done at the same price as a new cable, he bought the new module to get the faster speed of parallel communications.

Hacker also found that Brenda had no knowledge of DOS; her Wang had been configured as a dedicated word processor and required very little file maintenance. He decided that the best approach would be to install a menu system, Fixed Disk Organizer, so that Brenda could use WordPerfect without having to worry too much about directories. He brought the software in from home and set up the menus so that they would load WordPerfect on command. He showed Brenda how to use the menus to enter WordPerfect and told her to read through her WordPerfect manuals and start using it, promising to teach her more about DOS as she went along. Although she wasn't yet an "expert," Brenda was able to prepare and print simple WordPerfect documents by the end of the day.

Although Brenda has learned WordPerfect satisfactorily, she still has problems managing files; she hasn't figured out how to back up onto floppies; she lost several documents because of a mistake in naming her files; and when she enters WordPerfect's "List Files," she gets a whole bunch of program files listed that she doesn't understand. Now, Dr. Hacker is often too busy to help her.

Questions

1. What is the major problem?
2. What mistakes contributed to the problem?
3. Is it necessary to know DOS in order to use WordPerfect?
4. What are the alternative solutions for this case?
5. What would you recommend?

Case Two:
HEALTH-WAY INSURANCE COMPANY

Health-Way is a medium-sized company, employing 750 people, that writes and sells group and individual health insurance. Within the last two years, an Information Center Department (ICD) was established. Consistent with written policy, ICD installed personal computers, both within ICD as a centralized resource and throughout the company. The PCs were set up with a somewhat sophisticated word processing package, Lotus 1-2-3, database software, and other miscellaneous capabilities. This then, in effect, somewhat decentralized the word processing functions.

ICD's manager reports to the vice president of Information Services, John Reason. Also reporting to Reason is the manager of the Word Processing Department, the centralized area that completes the traditional word processing functions of typing, report production, graphics, and copying. One of the purposes of the PCs and the Information Center was to give end users their own capability to produce reports and graphics that previously had been done in the Word Processing Department.

One group of management analysts took quick advantage of this decentralized function. These employees are industrial engineers who analyze the performance of employees and production methods and suggest changes to improve productivity. The employees in this group are college graduates and earn an average of $25,000 per year. They issue monthly reports with a combination of graphics and text, listing and evaluating productivity results of certain areas of the company. The group also routinely issues memos and project reports that analyze the methods of a particular function or area of the company. Both the monthly reports and the project reports had always been sent to the Word Processing unit for completion. Given internal mail delivery schedules and several trips for editing, the final turnaround time was often several days, or even a week. With the availability of the PCs and the Information Center resources, the timeliness of these reports could be greatly improved. The analysts, trained to use the word processing and Lotus software, began producing their own reports with the expected improvement in turnaround. They also viewed this activity as enhancing their jobs, since they were gaining experience with PCs. The manager of the Word Processing Department was equally satisfied with the shift of responsibility because it relieved the department of some of its work.

This reassignment of report production responsibility has been in operation for several months. Reports and memos are produced by the analysts without any use of Word Processing resources. While the analysts are not outstanding typists, the time devoted to reports—five to seven hours per month—is generally considered time well spent.

Recently, in reviewing the analysts' work schedule and monthly activities, the manager of the group, Rufus Gordon, decided that the analysts' time could be better spent on activities for which they are directly responsible: projects and performance analysis. He further reasoned that the analysts should not be doing a job that could be done by the word processing personnel, who were more efficient typists and who were on a lower salary scale with an average income of $17,000 a year. He decided that the work of producing the reports and memos be given back to the Word Processing Department. His decision was supported by his boss, the vice president of Support Services, Vince Jughead, who said, "We should not have a high-grade person doing something that could be done more effectively by someone making less money. The company's money would be better spent this way, and the increased turnaround time is something that we just have to get used to."

When Reason discovered the change in plans, he called Jughead, who restated his position that the jobs were a word processing function and would be completed in a more cost-effective manner in the Word Processing Department. Reason responded that one of the purposes of setting up the Information Center was to distribute and decentralize these types of jobs, and, while there may be direct cost inefficiencies, there was an indirect cost savings from the production of more timely reports and related information.

Questions

1. Whose position do you support?
2. What is the real issue here?
3. Does the proliferation of PCs lead to non-clerical personnel performing clerical activities? If yes, can this diminish the justification of purchasing PCs?
4. How do you resolve the conflict here?

SELECTED BIBLIOGRAPHY

Beck, C.E. and J.A. Stibravy, "The Effect of Word Processors on Writing Quality," *Technical Communications*, 1986, pp. 84–7.

Betts, K.S., "Getting the Word Out," *Modern Office Technology*, June 1986, pp. 80-1 + .

Birmele, R., "WordPerfect 4.1," *Byte*, September 1986, pp. 311–12.

Cole, M., "WordPerfect – A Top Rate Package Worth Every Penny," *Accountancy*, October 1985, pp. 78–9.

Didising, D., "Word Processing: Can It Live Through Integration?," *The Office*, September 1985, p. 170 + .

Dologite, D.G. and D. M. Levine, "Comparative Analysis of Word Processing Packages," *Journal of Systems Management*, September 1985, pp. 8–17.

Edwards, E., "Microbased Writing Tools for Office Professionals," *The Office*, November 1985, p. 130 + .

Fetzer, R., "Word Processors: What Do They Really Cost?," *The Office*, Fall 1986, p. 71.

_____, "5th Annual Guide to Word Processing," (Special Report), *Management World*, April 1985, pp. 13–20.

Fleming, M.V., "Micros and Word Processing in the Automated Office," *The Office*, November 1986, p. 118 + .

Goss, D.R., "WordPerfect 4.1: It Is (Almost) Perfect," *DEC Professional*, May 1986, pp. 136–8.

Grosman, L.H., "Safeguarding Your WP System? It Can Be Done," *The Office*, November 1985, p. 156 +

Hagge, J., "Review Essay (of Word Processors and the Writing Process)," *Journal of Business Communication*, Winter 1986, pp. 63–8.

Hoffberg, A., "It's Never Too Late to Learn How to Use a Computer That Can Prove Invaluable for Everyday Use," *Office Administration and Automation*, July 1985, pp. 82–3.

Kahle, J., "Word Processing's Place in the Offices of Today," *The Office*, June 1985, p. 98 + .

Kapsales, P., "Before and After WP: An Office Automation Productivity Study," *Journal of Systems Management*, April 1986, pp. 7–9.

LeClair, R.T., "On Word Processing," *Journal of the American Society of CLU*, November 1985, pp. 27–8.

_____, "Low-Cost Micro WP Packages Top Test," *Computer Decisions*, January 28, 1986, p. 24.

McKendrick, J.E., "Word Processing: The Dedicated Many," *Management World*, April-May 1986, pp. 48–9.

Meth, C., "The Write Stuff," *Administrative Management*, May 1986, pp. 43–8.

Micossi, A., "Word Processing: From Micros to Mainframes," *Computer Decisions*, August 27, 1985, pp. 17-18.

_____, "New Software, Hardware Products Tackle File Compatibility Problem," (compatibility between word processors and personal computers) *Purchasing*, October 24, 1985, pp. 89-90.

Patterson, W., "Bargain Days for Word Processing," *Industry Week*, September 16, 1985, pp. 59-61.

Paznik, M.J., "WP Compatibility Problem Solved," *Administrative Management*, April 1986, pp. 12-13.

Pile, J., "WordPerfect 4.1 Lives Up to its Name," *PCM*, October 1986, pp. 103-105.

_____, "Polyglot Word Processor," (Multi-Lingual Scribe) *Byte*, March 1986, p. 38.

Rosenbaum, D.J., "New WordPerfect is Highly Rated for Writers and Typists," *PC Week*, June 10, 1986, pp. 77-81.

Shapiro, E., "Turbo Lighting Provides Fast Access," *Byte*, December 1985, p. 37.

_____, "6th Annual Word Processing Guide," (Special Report), *Management World*, April-May 1986, pp. 46-9.

Stermer, N.L., "Coping with Automation: How WP User Groups Help," *The Office*, June 1985, p. 19+.

Sullivan, K.B., "WordPerfect Upgrade to Add More Than 30 New Capabilities," *PC Week*, October 28, 1986, p. 3.

_____, "Two Top Word Processors," *Personal Computing*, June 1986, p. 31+.

Watt, P., "WordPerfect Raising Profile Without Turning Back on Users: Popular Software Has Low-Key Firm Riding High," *Computerworld*, June 9, 1986, pp. 130-132.

_____, "Word Processing for Professionals," *Training*, May 1986, pp. 94-6.

chapter 7

LEARNING WORDPERFECT

After completing this chapter, you should be able to

- *discuss the keyboard keys and their WordPerfect functions.*
- *describe the function keys and their features.*
- *discuss how to create a document in WordPerfect.*
- *discuss how to edit, save, format, and print a document.*
- *discuss the different ways to retrieve an existing document.*
- *describe how to copy a file to another file name.*
- *discuss how to move, copy, and delete a block of text.*

INTRODUCTION

In this chapter you will learn how to use the WordPerfect word processing software package for document preparation and management. The approach used here is strictly hands-on. Therefore, you are advised to practice the material discussed in this chapter on an IBM-PC or compatible with WordPerfect. In order to do so, you will need copies of DOS and WordPerfect that can be used on a PC equipped with a printer.

GETTING STARTED

Booting the System

If the two disk drives of your microcomputer are configured horizontally, then the left one is Drive A and the right one is Drive B. If the two drives are configured vertically, then the one on top is usually Drive A and the bottom one is Drive B. If you have a hard disk system, the single floppy drive is Drive A and the hard disk is Drive C.

The following five steps will allow you to boot the microcomputer and WordPerfect—referred to as "cold booting" because it begins with the power off (see Chapter 5).

Step 1. Insert the DOS diskette, version 2.0 or higher, into Drive A. Close the disk drive door.

Step 2. Turn the computer on. The power switch is usually located on the right side of the computer, toward the back. The computer will take anywhere from three to forty-five seconds to run through a system check.

Step 3. Respond to the date prompt that appears on the screen. Enter the date in the format indicated and press the ENTER key (↵). You will be presented with a similar prompt for the time. Respond by typing the time in the format indicated and press ENTER.

Step 4. When the DOS prompt, A> (pronounced "A prompt"), appears on the screen, remove the DOS diskette from Drive A and insert the WordPerfect diskette in Drive A. (Don't forget to again close the disk drive door.) Insert a blank formatted diskette, onto which you will save your WordPerfect files in Drive B. (For complete instructions on formatting a diskette, see Chapter 5, the FORMAT Command).

Step 5. Type WP (for WordPerfect) and press the ENTER key. You will be presented with a welcome screen such as the one in Figure 7.1.

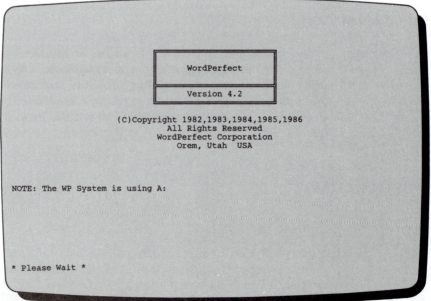

Figure 7.1
WordPerfect's Welcome Screen

The booting process is now complete, and you are in the WordPerfect environment. The screen will look like the one in Figure 7.2.

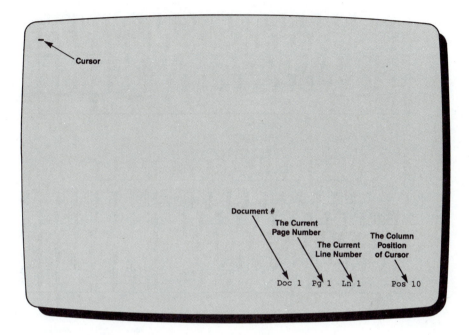

Figure 7.2
A Blank Screen in the WordPerfect Environment

You can think of this screen as a clean sheet of paper on which to type. The **cursor**, the small blinking underline (_), indicates your current column position on the page. The **status line** always indicates your present location in the document, showing you the document number, page number, line number, and column position.

■ BEFORE YOU BEGIN TO TYPE

It is important to familiarize yourself with the various keyboard keys and their functions. All of the keys are divided into three catagories, based on their functions: the function keys (F1 through F10) located on the left-hand side or across the top of the keyboard; the typewriter-like keyboard in the center, and the numeric keypad (numbers 0 through 9 in a calculator-style arrangement) on the right-hand side of the keyboard (see Figure 7.3 on the following page).

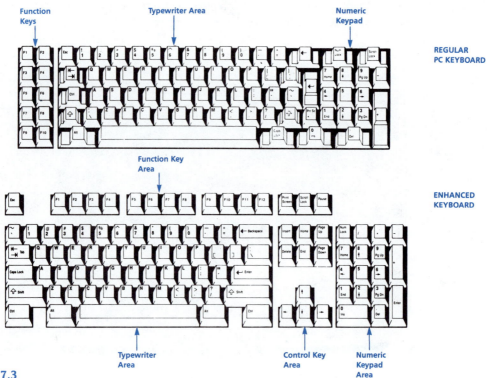

Figure 7.3
Two Types of IBM-PC Keyboards

KEY NAME	FUNCTION
ENTER	Sends a command to the computer or ends a typed line.
INSERT	Toggle key for insert and typeover modes.
SHIFT, ALT, CTRL	Used in combination with function keys to perform some WordPerfect commands.
BACKSPACE	Erases the character immediately to the left of the cursor.
UP ARROW	Moves the cursor one position upward.
DOWN ARROW	Moves the cursor one position downward.
RIGHT ARROW	Moves the cursor one position to the right.
LEFT ARROW	Moves the cursor one position to the left.
DELETE	Erases the character in the current cursor position.
TAB	Indents a line a specified number of columns.
HOME	Pressed twice, followed by UP ARROW or DOWN ARROW, moves to the top or bottom of a document.
CAPS LOCK	Changes the typewriter keys from uppercase to lowercase or *vice versa*.
SPACEBAR	Moves the cursor one space.
PGUP	Moves the cursor to the previous page.
PGDN	Moves the cursor to the next page.

TABLE 7.1 Some Important WordPerfect Keys and Their Functions

Before you begin to type, it is important to know just how to move around in WordPerfect. Therefore, there are some keys on the keyboard with which you need to become familiar. Table 7.1 summarizes the keys you'll be using with WordPerfect.

There are also some other features of WordPerfect that you should be aware of before you begin.

Word Wrap

The **word wrap** feature is one of the major differences between a typewriter and a word processor. When you reach the right margin on a typewriter, you have to return the carriage to the beginning of the next line or run the risk of typing off the page. When you reach the end of a line with a word processing software package (including WordPerfect), the program automatically "wraps" the word around to the beginning of the next line. You do not press ENTER until you get to the end of a paragraph or choose to end a short line. For example, in Figure 7.4 below, when the last character of the word *about* is entered, the cursor wraps the next word around to the beginning of the next line.

Figure 7.4
Automatic Wrap

Try to enter the following paragraph on your screen to see how the word "work" is wrapped around. Do not press ENTER. (Throughout this and other chapters, material you are to type appears in color.) In summary, I would like to express our deep appreciation for the work that you have done for us.

The Insert and Typeover Modes

When you begin typing, WordPerfect is in **Insert mode,** meaning that text will be inserted at the cursor. If you place the cursor into the middle of existing text and begin to type, the new characters will be inserted, and the existing text will be moved to the right and down the page. The words may appear to "run off" the screen, but they will be repositioned on the next line as you continue to type or move the cursor to the right.

What if you find that you have made a typo in the middle of a paragraph? You can position the cursor on the first letter of the word you wish to change and press the INSERT key (often labelled INS) found on the bottom right-hand side of the keyboard. Striking the INSERT key once puts you in **Typeover mode.** The word *Typeover* will appear on the lower left side of the screen. Now any characters you type will replace existing characters. To return to insert mode, strike the INSERT key once.

Responding to a Message on the Screen

While working in WordPerfect, you will be prompted to respond to a message on the screen from time to time. The response could be a simple y (yes) or n (no) as in responding to a message such as "Save document? (Y/N)", or the response could be longer, as in giving the name of the file you want to save. In either case, WordPerfect accepts responses provided in either uppercase or lowercase letters.

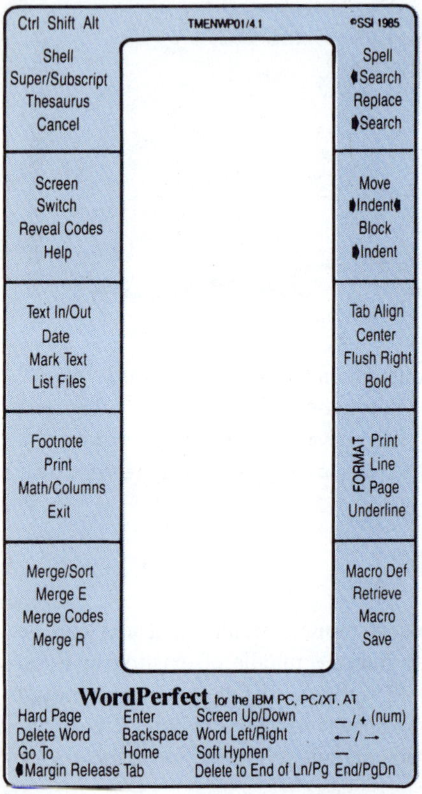

Function Keys (F1 through F10)

The function keys on the left side or across the top of the keyboard are considered the heart of WordPerfect. These keys are designed in such a way that each key is capable of performing four distinct functions. The key can either be used alone by just pressing it, or it can be used in combination with any of three other keys: SHIFT, ALT, or CTRL. The WordPerfect software package comes with a **template**, a guide that fits around the function keys on the left side of the keyboard or across the top (see Figure 7.5).

Each possible WordPerfect function combination is indicated by a color and key combination on the template. The four color possibilities are

Red: Hold down CTRL and press the function key.
Green: Hold down SHIFT and press the function key.
Blue: Hold down ALT and press the function key.
Black: Press the function key alone.

Keystroke Combinations

When you want to use a combination of keys—for example, CTRL-F6—follow these steps.

Step 1. Depress the CTRL key, and hold it down.
Step 2. Without releasing the CTRL key, press down function key F6.
Step 3. Release both the CTRL and F6 keys at the same time.

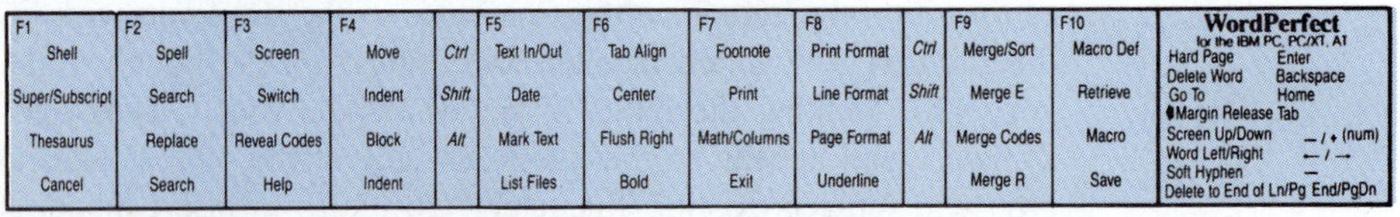

Figure 7.5
WordPerfect Templates for the Regular (top) and Enhanced (bottom) Keyboards

This procedure is the same for any combination of keystrokes you request while working with WordPerfect.

Table 7.2 summarizes the various capabilities of all the WordPerfect function keys. You do not have to memorize these keys or their functions; simply use the chart as a reference. The different functions of the F1 through F10 keys are written in different colors next to the keys on the template. Usually, there are only a few keys that the average user of WordPerfect will put into action. We'll look at more WordPerfect functions as we discuss other WordPerfect features in the remainder of this chapter.

KEY	COMBI-NATION	NAME	FUNCTIONS	KEY	COMBI-NATION	NAME	FUNCTIONS
F1	CTRL	Shell	Gives access to other programs via new copy of DOS	F2	CTRL	Spell	Checks spelling and counts words
F1	SHIFT	Super/Subscript	Inserts superscripts and subscripts	F2	SHIFT	Search	Finds a string of characters above the cursor
F1	ALT	Thesaurus	Provides a list of words with similar meaning	F2	ALT	Replace	Called "global search/replace," replaces a string with another string of characters; allows for verification
F1		Cancel	Cancels other functions in action or backs out of a menu or prompt or stops a macro	F2		Search below	Finds a string of characters below the cursor
F3	CTRL	Screen	Allows for screen appearance functions—change color, line drawings, ruler	F4	CTRL	Move	Cuts or copies text from one part of the document to another location or cuts and copies a part to another document
F3	SHIFT	Switch	Sets up two WP screens to allow editing of two documents at the same time	F4	SHIFT	Indent	Moves both right and left margins in one tab stop
F3	ALT	Reveal codes	Displays the format codes embedded in the text	F4	ALT	Block	Defines a section of text for editing; toggle to begin/end
F3		Help	Activates the help system giving information about WP functions	F4		Indent	Moves left margin in one tab left
F5	CTRL	Text in/out	Converts file to/from DOS text format; locks/unlocks files	F6	CTRL	Tab align	Lines up text on a specific character (such as decimal point)
F5	SHIFT	Date	Inserts current date (or code) into document	F6	SHIFT	Center	Centers text on the current line where the cursor is positioned between margins; toggle on/off
F5	ALT	Mark text	Creates outlines, numbered paragraphs, lists, index; redlines and strikes out text	F6	ALT	Flush right	Aligns text against the right margin; not the same as "right justify"
F5		List files	Directory list of files of the default directory; provides function for file handling (e.g., retrieve, rename, copy ..)	F6		Bold	Highlights text; toggle on/off
F7	CTRL	Footnote	Creates, edits, and formats footnotes	F8	CTRL	Print formats	Sets options to control the printed document
F7	SHIFT	Print	Activates the WP print functions	F8	SHIFT	Line formats	Sets line features—tabs, margins, etc.
F7	ALT	Math/columns	Adds rows and/or columns	F8	ALT	Page formats	Sets page size; controls numbering
F7		Exit	Saves document and leaves WP	F8		Underline	Underlines text; toggle on/off
F9	CTRL	Merge/sort	Activates macros to combine or sort the document contents	F10	CTRL	Macro def	Defines a macro
F9	SHIFT	Merge E	Ends the merge process	F10	SHIFT	Retrieve	Brings document from disk to memory
F9	ALT	Merge codes	Displays the merge code menu	F10	ALT	Macro	Starts the execution of a macro
F9		Merge R	Ends the merge field	F10		Save	Copies document from memory to disk

TABLE 7.2 Summary of WordPerfect Function Keys

A Few Notes and Words of Caution

Before you start using WordPerfect on your PC, carefully review the following advice in order to save yourself some headaches.

Take your time. When using different commands or functions, make sure you don't rush into it. Remember you can correct mistakes before pressing the ENTER key. Also, read instructions carefully before you apply any feature of WordPerfect. Do not type anything while WordPerfect is displaying the message "*Please Wait*." This message indicates that WordPerfect is processing your last function or request.

Remember your default drive. The default drive is the A drive. If you specify no drive change, WordPerfect assumes you are referring to the default drive.

Use the ENTER key properly. Whenever you are asked to press the ENTER key, do so; otherwise, nothing will happen. Do not press the ENTER key automatically. Many WordPerfect features and functions do not require you to press the ENTER key. For example, in many cases, WordPerfect will pose a question and ask for a yes or no answer. In this case, just type *y* or *n*; don't press ENTER.

Cancel a function or command. You can cancel most WordPerfect functions or commands by pressing the F1 key in the top left corner of the function key set. Once this key is pressed by itself (not in combination with any other key), the function or request in progress will be cancelled. Feel free to use this key whenever necessary.

■ LET'S BEGIN

Let's start by putting into practice some of the features we've discussed so far. As an exercise, you will type a paragraph and modify it as you work through this section.

As we begin, the cursor should be in the upper left-hand corner of your screen. If it is not, press F7 (on function keys), in response to "Save Document? (Y/N)Y", type "N" followed by pressing the ENTER key (↵). Type the following paragraph without pressing ENTER until you reach its end. Type the paragraph as you see it, with all the mistakes. Remember, if you make mistakes of your own while typing the paragraph (not the mistakes presented in the paragraph), use the BACKSPACE (←) key to correct them as you type. Use the SHIFT (⇧) key to capitalize the first word of the paragraph.

Type

```
The rapid growth in information technology has
affected the bery fundamentals of organizational
structurees, particulary the decision making pro-
cess.
```

Now let's make the following modifications on the paragraph you just typed.

Insert a Tab: Use the ARROW keys (marked ↑ and ↓ on the numeric keypad) to move the cursor to the *T* in the first word of the paragraph.

Press the TAB (→|) key (located on the left side of the keyboard) once to indent the first line of the paragraph.

Insert a new word: Use the ARROW keys to move the cursor to the letter *t* in the word *technology*.

Type the word `systems`, followed by a blank space.

Correct a word with typeover mode: Move the cursor to the letter *b* in the word *bery*.

Press the INSERT (INS) key once.

Type the letter v.

Press INSERT once again to exit typeover mode.

Move to the bottom of the document: Press the HOME key twice, then press the DOWN ARROW (↓) key once.

Correct a word with DEL: Move the cursor to the second *e* in the word *structurees*.

Press the DELETE (DEL) key once. This key erases the character in the current cursor position.

Insert a character: Move the cursor to the letter *y* in the word *particulary*.

Type the letter l.

Add a centered title: Press the HOME key twice, then the UP ARROW (↑) key once to get to the top of the document.

Press the ENTER key twice to add some space.

Press the UP ARROW key twice to move to the top of the document.

Hold the SHIFT key down and strike F6 once to begin centering.

Press the CAPS LOCK key (located to the right of the space bar) to make the title all capital letters.

Type

COMPUTER UTILIZATION IN STRATEGIC DECISIONS

Press CAPS LOCK again to return to lowercase.

Hold the SHIFT key down and strike F6 once to end centering mode.

Reveal the format codes: If you are not sure you want to center this title, you can delete the centering code. First, reveal the format codes by holding down the ALT key, then pressing F3 to reveal the codes within the document. The Screen will look like the one in Figure 7.6 on the following page.

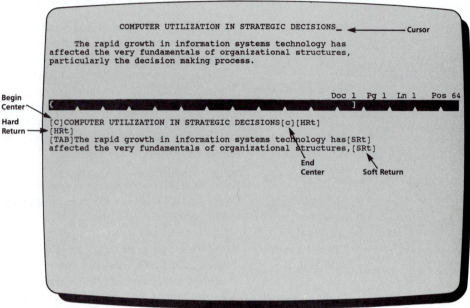

Figure 7.6
WordPerfect Screen with Format Codes Revealed

What you see on the screen in Figure 7.6 is the actual text you entered and all the codes for various functions placed at different locations of the text. For example, when you indicated that you wanted to center, WordPerfect placed a code "C" at the beginning and end of the text part that you centered. Normally, you do not see these codes; the only way you can view them is through the use of the ALT-F3 key combination. The user can always delete any of these codes after implementing the reveal code.

Delete a format code: Use the ARROW keys to move the cursor one space to the right of the "begin center"code [C].
Press the BACKSPACE key to delete the center code.
Press the SPACEBAR to return to the regular screen.
Note: To cancel the centering function, delete either one of the codes; the beginning or ending code.
A **hard return [HRt]** code is inserted into your text when you press the ENTER key. A **soft return [SRt]** code is put into your text at the end of a line when WordPerfect "wraps" the line around to the beginning of the next line.

Exit WordPerfect without saving: Press F7 (Exit).
In response to the message "Save Document? (Y/N)," type "N". (*Note*: you will generally type "Y" for "Yes", but since this is an exercise, it does not have to be saved.) In response to the message "Exit WP? (Y/N)N," Press ENTER to begin a new screen.

By now you should have gained beginning experience with some of the basic WordPerfect keys and their functions. In the following section you will create a business letter with the help of WordPerfect. During this process, you will be introduced to more helpful keys and functions.

■ CREATING A BUSINESS LETTER

Now that you have sampled typing and editing text in WordPerfect, you will want to learn to create a useful document. In this section, you will write a loan request letter to Pennsylvania Finest National Bank, from Sunshine Window Inc., Suppliers (SWIS), a Pennsylvania-based company of which you are vice president (a full description of the SWIS case can be found in Appendix A). The following steps will allow you to create your own letterhead, type the body of the letter, correct mistakes, save the document, and exit WordPerfect. The word processing features we will use are

1. center text
2. boldface text
3. underline text
4. tab
5. save document
6. exit WordPerfect

When completed, your letter will look like the one in Figure 7.7.

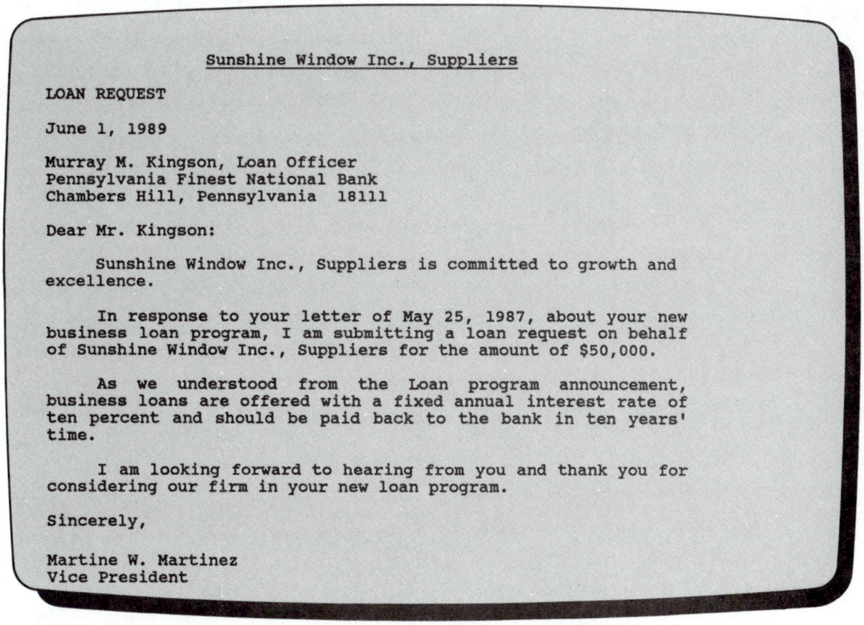

```
                    Sunshine Window Inc., Suppliers
LOAN REQUEST

June 1, 1989

Murray M. Kingson, Loan Officer
Pennsylvania Finest National Bank
Chambers Hill, Pennsylvania  18111

Dear Mr. Kingson:

     Sunshine Window Inc., Suppliers is committed to growth and
excellence.

     In response to your letter of May 25, 1987, about your new
business loan program, I am submitting a loan request on behalf
of Sunshine Window Inc., Suppliers for the amount of $50,000.

     As we understood from the Loan program announcement,
business loans are offered with a fixed annual interest rate of
ten percent and should be paid back to the bank in ten years'
time.

     I am looking forward to hearing from you and thank you for
considering our firm in your new loan program.

Sincerely,

Martine W. Martinez
Vice President
```

Figure 7.7
A Business Letter

This exercise assumes that you will start with a clean screen like the one in Figure 7.2.

Create the Heading

- Press the ENTER key twice without typing anything. This will give you two blank lines at the top of your document.
- Hold the SHIFT key down and press F6 to indicate the beginning of text to be centered. (Centering will end after you press ENTER; if subsequent lines were to be centered, you would need to press SHIFT-F6 at the beginning of each line.)
- Press F6 to begin boldface. (Notice the brightness of the Pos number at the far right bottom of the screen.)
- Press F8 to begin underlining. (Notice the Pos number now is underlined.)
- Type `Sunshine Window Inc., Suppliers`. Use the BACKSPACE key to correct any mistakes you make.
- Hold down SHIFT and press F6 to end centering.
- Press F6 to end boldface.
- Press F8 to end underlining.
- Press ENTER three times to leave a blank space between the lines that you just typed and the next line.

After you have successfully entered the letterhead text and commands, your screen should look the same as the one in Figure 7.8.

Figure 7.8
A Business Letterhead

Capitalize the Subheading

- Press the CAPS LOCK key to type all capital letters (the "Pos" at the bottom of the screen will change to "POS").
- Type LOAN REQUEST.
- Press CAPS LOCK to end capitalization.
- Press ENTER twice to leave two blank lines before you start a new line.

Add Today's Date

- Hold down the SHIFT key and press F5 to enter today's date into the letter; a menu of options will appear at the bottom of the screen as shown in Figure 7.9.

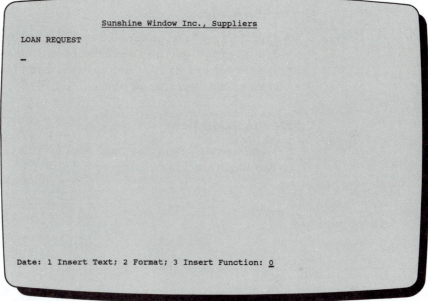

Figure 7.9
A Menu of Options Obtained by Pressing SHIFT-F5

- Press the number 1 to insert the date at the position of the cursor.
  Note: Use the numbers at the top of the keyboard, not on the numeric keypad. If you did not type the current date when you booted the system, WordPerfect will insert the last date that was provided to the system.
- Press ENTER twice to leave blank lines after the date.

Upon inserting the date, your screen should look the same as the one in Figure 7.10 on the following page.

Figure 7.10
Entering the Date

Create the Address

- Type Murray M. Kingson, Loan Officer, and press ENTER.
- Type Pennsylvania Finest National Bank and press ENTER.
- Type Chambers Hill, Pennsylvania 18111 and press ENTER twice to leave blank lines after the address.

Create the Salutation

- Type Dear Mr. Kingson: and press ENTER twice to leave blank lines. Your screen now looks like the one in Figure 7.11.

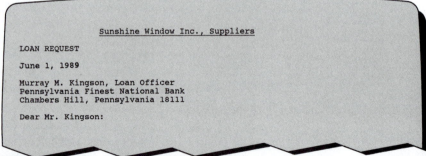

Figure 7.11
Entering the Address and Salutation

Create the Body of the Letter

- Press the TAB key (→|) once to indent the first paragraph.
- Type continuously *without* pressing ENTER

```
            In response to your letter of May 25, 1987, about your new
            business loan program, I am submitting a loan request on
            behalf of Sunshine Window Inc., Suppliers for the amount
            of $50,000.
```

- Press ENTER twice to leave blank lines between paragraphs.
- Press the TAB key to indent the second paragraph.
- Type continuously *without* pressing ENTER

```
            As we understood from the loan program announcement,
            business loans are offered with a fixed annual interest
            rate of ten percent and should be paid back to the bank in
            ten years' time.
```

- Press ENTER twice to leave blank lines.
- Press the TAB key to indent the third paragraph, and type

```
            I am looking forward to hearing from you and thank you for
            considering our firm in your new loan program.
```

- Press ENTER twice to leave blank lines.

At this stage, your screen should look the same as the screen shown in Figure 7.12.

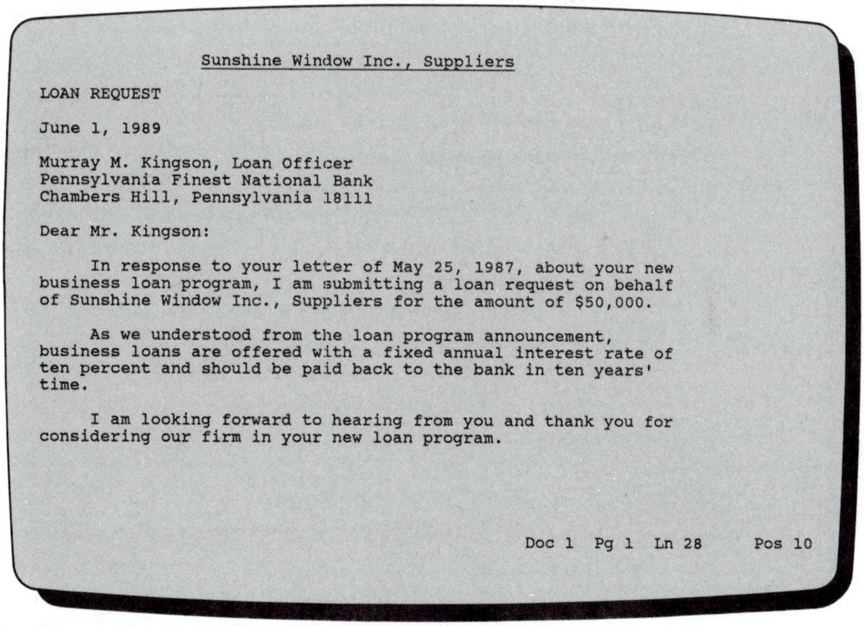

```
                    Sunshine Window Inc., Suppliers
      LOAN REQUEST

      June 1, 1989

      Murray M. Kingson, Loan Officer
      Pennsylvania Finest National Bank
      Chambers Hill, Pennsylvania 18111

      Dear Mr. Kingson:

           In response to your letter of May 25, 1987, about your new
      business loan program, I am submitting a loan request on behalf
      of Sunshine Window Inc., Suppliers for the amount of $50,000.

           As we understood from the loan program announcement,
      business loans are offered with a fixed annual interest rate of
      ten percent and should be paid back to the bank in ten years'
      time.

           I am looking forward to hearing from you and thank you for
      considering our firm in your new loan program.




                                         Doc 1  Pg 1  Ln 28    Pos 10
```

Figure 7.12
Entering the Body of the Letter

Create the Closing

- Type `Sincerely,` and press ENTER four times.
- Type `Martine W. Martinez` and press ENTER.
- Type `Vice President`.

Save Your Document

At this point, you will want to save your letter for future use. The importance of saving your documents cannot be emphasized enough. In fact, it is a good idea to save your documents by pressing F10 at regular intervals while you are working on them. There is the common misconception that every time you save, you are storing another copy of the same document on the diskette. This is not the case. The first time you save your document you give it a name. Then, each time after that, the system saves the document with the additions to the same document in memory, "writing over" the previous copy.

Imagine what could happen if the computer system crashed, or if you became entangled in an error because you mistakenly pressed a key and could not "get out" of a particular environment. Hours and pages of work could be lost if you have to reboot your system or reconstruct files. You'll spend less time, energy, and frustration if frequent saves become a habit.

In WordPerfect, you can give a file a name of up to eight characters, which can be followed by a period and a file extension of up to three characters if desired. Let's save the letter you just created under the name LOAN.LTR on the blank, formatted diskette in your B drive.

- Press F10 to save the letter.
- The message "Document to be saved:" will appear at the bottom of the screen, as shown in Figure 7.13 on the following page.
- Type `B:LOAN.LTR` and press ENTER. (*Note*: The *B:* directs your document to the disk in Drive B. If you forget the B:, WordPerfect will attempt to save the document on the default disk, the A drive.)
- You will see the message "Saving B:\LOAN.LTR". When the save is complete, you will be returned to the text screen and the former cursor position.

Note: If this had not been the first time you were saving the letter, the sequence of events would be

- Press F10 to save the letter.
- The message "Document to be saved: B:\LOAN.LTR" appears.
- Press ENTER.
- The message "Replace B:\LOAN.LTR? (Y/N)N" appears, asking if you wish to write over the previous copy of your letter, thus adding any additions or corrections.

- Type Y if you would like to overlay the old version with the new one.
- The message "Saving B:\LOAN.LTR" will appear; when the save is complete, you will be returned to the text screen and the former cursor position.

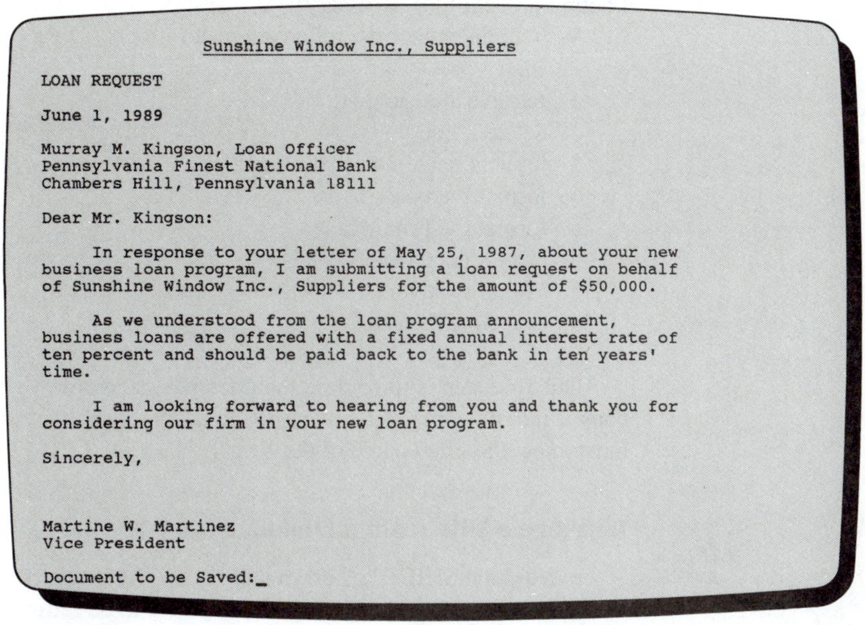

```
              Sunshine Window Inc., Suppliers
LOAN REQUEST

June 1, 1989

Murray M. Kingson, Loan Officer
Pennsylvania Finest National Bank
Chambers Hill, Pennsylvania 18111

Dear Mr. Kingson:

     In response to your letter of May 25, 1987, about your new
business loan program, I am submitting a loan request on behalf
of Sunshine Window Inc., Suppliers for the amount of $50,000.

     As we understood from the loan program announcement,
business loans are offered with a fixed annual interest rate of
ten percent and should be paid back to the bank in ten years'
time.

     I am looking forward to hearing from you and thank you for
considering our firm in your new loan program.

Sincerely,


Martine W. Martinez
Vice President

Document to be Saved:_
```

Figure 7.13
Saving the Document

Exit WordPerfect

- Press F7 to exit WordPerfect.
- In response to the message "Save Document? (Y/N)Y", type N. (If you had not already saved the document, you would have pressed ENTER to accept the "Y" default. In any event, even if you responded with Y, no harm would be done by saving it a second time.)
- In response to "Exit WP? (Y/N)N", press ENTER to accept the N; the entire screen will be erased, ready for a new document. If you do not wish to continue with this exercise at this time, respond with Y, and you will be returned to the DOS environment and the A>. At that point, you can take your diskette out of Drive B and turn off the computer.

■ MODIFYING AN EXISTING DOCUMENT

In this section you will learn to insert, delete, and otherwise modify the text you created. At this point, we assume you have completed the previous section, "CREATING A BUSINESS LETTER," and that you will be working with the document you created. If you are starting fresh, do not forget that you must first boot the system and enter the WordPerfect environment (refer to the instructions on the booting procedure if necessary).

We will encounter the following features:

1. retrieve a document.
2. delete a line.
3. insert a new line or paragraph.
4. format the page.
5. format the printing.
6. print a document.
7. save a document.
8. exit WordPerfect.

Our first step is to retrieve the document stored on your diskette in Drive B and copy it into the computer's memory. To accomplish the retrieval by this method, you must know the exact name of the file.

Retrieve a File from a Diskette

- Hold the SHIFT key down and press F10 to retrieve a file.
- In response to the message "Document to be retrieved:", type B:LOAN.LTR and press ENTER; the letter you stored will appear on the WordPerfect screen.

Delete a Line

This function allows you to delete a complete line in your document.

- Use the DOWN ARROW (↓) to move the cursor to the first letter in *LOAN REQUEST*.
- Hold the CTRL key down and press the END key (located on the bottom right side of the keyboard). Release both keys at the same time. CTRL-END erases everything from the position of the cursor to the end of the line.

Insert a Line

You can reinstate the line just erased while adding one word.

- Press the CAPS LOCK key.
- Type LOAN REQUEST APPLICATION.
- Press the CAPS LOCK key to release.

Insert a New Paragraph

This function allows you to insert a new paragraph within an existing document.

- Use the ARROW keys to move the cursor one position after the colon in the salutation *Dear Mr. Kingson:*.
- Press ENTER twice.
- Press the TAB key once to indent the new paragraph.
- Type

    ```
    Sunshine Window Inc., Suppliers is committed to the
    growth and excellence.
    ```

After you add this paragraph, you realize that you do not need the word *the* before the word *growth*, and you want to delete it.

- Use the ARROW keys to move the cursor to the *t* in the word *the*.
- Press the DEL key (located at the bottom of the numeric pad) four times to delete the word *the*. Or, once the cursor is positioned at the *t*, hold CTRL and press BACKSPACE (←), which deletes a word. Press the DOWN ARROW key once.

At this stage, your screen should look like the one in Figure 7.14.

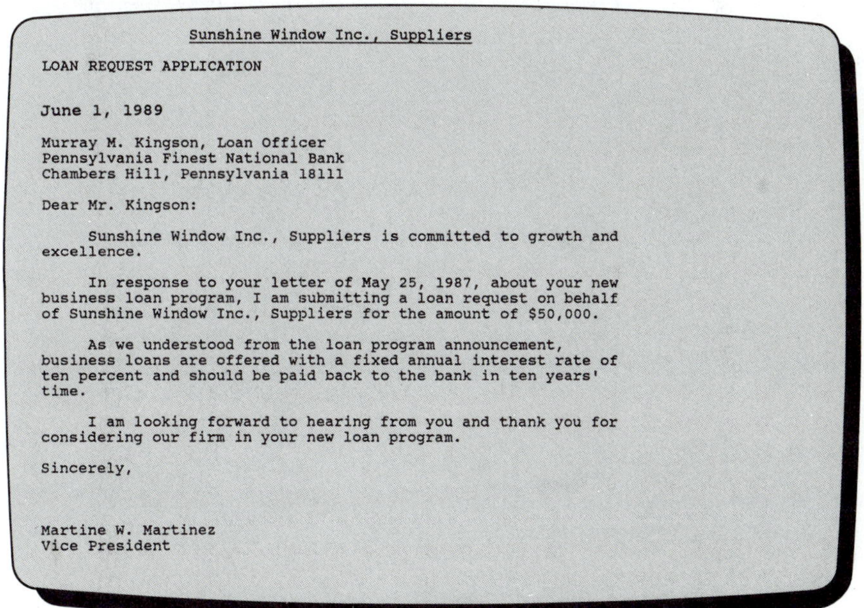

```
              Sunshine Window Inc., Suppliers
LOAN REQUEST APPLICATION

June 1, 1989

Murray M. Kingson, Loan Officer
Pennsylvania Finest National Bank
Chambers Hill, Pennsylvania 18111

Dear Mr. Kingson:

     Sunshine Window Inc., Suppliers is committed to growth and
excellence.

     In response to your letter of May 25, 1987, about your new
business loan program, I am submitting a loan request on behalf
of Sunshine Window Inc., Suppliers for the amount of $50,000.

     As we understood from the loan program announcement,
business loans are offered with a fixed annual interest rate of
ten percent and should be paid back to the bank in ten years'
time.

     I am looking forward to hearing from you and thank you for
considering our firm in your new loan program.

Sincerely,


Martine W. Martinez
Vice President
```

Figure 7.14
Editing Your Document

Save Your Corrected Document

Now let's save the new document under the same file name.

- Press F10 to save the document.
- In response to the message "Document to be Saved: B:\LOAN.LTR," press ENTER to save under the same name.
- In response to the message "Replace B:\LOAN.LTR? (Y/N) N," type Y.

Center Your Letter Before Printing

Before printing the letter, let's adjust the page format to center the letter vertically on the page.

- Press the HOME key twice and then press the UP ARROW to position the cursor at the beginning of the document.
- Hold down the ALT key and press F8 to see the PAGE FORMAT menu, which looks like the menu in Figure 7.15.

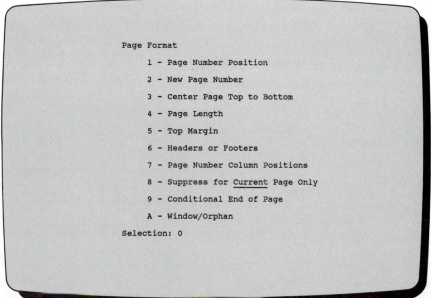

Figure 7.15
WordPerfect's PAGE FORMAT Menu

- Choose the "3 – Center Page Top to Bottom" option by typing the number 3.
    Note: You will hardly see your selected option being displayed at the front of the "selection" prompt. This is because the displaying is done in a fraction of second.

- Press ENTER to exit the PAGE FORMAT MENU.

Note: You can try other options by typing the number of your selection. Look at the specifications, then return to the PAGE FORMAT screen by pressing the ESC key.

Set Right-Justification Off

This final formatting adjustment should be made before you print your letter.

- Hold down the CTRL key and press F8 to view the PRINT FORMAT menu. You'll see a screen like the one in Figure 7.16.

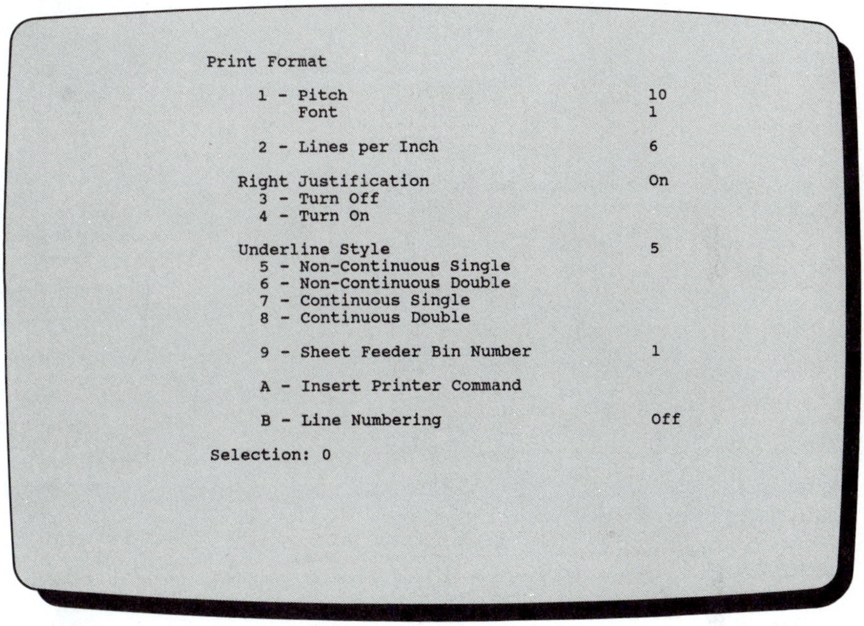

```
Print Format

        1 - Pitch                           10
            Font                            1

        2 - Lines per Inch                  6

        Right Justification                 On
        3 - Turn Off
        4 - Turn On

        Underline Style                     5
        5 - Non-Continuous Single
        6 - Non-Continuous Double
        7 - Continuous Single
        8 - Continuous Double

        9 - Sheet Feeder Bin Number         1

        A - Insert Printer Command

        B - Line Numbering                  Off

Selection: 0
```

Figure 7.16
WordPerfect's PRINT FORMAT Menu

- Choose Option 3 to turn the right-justification off by typing the number 3. Notice the "On" status next to "Right Justification" will be changed to "Off."

Note: When you begin WordPerfect, right-justification is in effect.

- Press ENTER to return to the document.

Print Your Letter

If you want to save your document with these formatting changes before you print it, use the SAVE commands we outlined previously. Otherwise, proceed with printing the letter. *Note:* Make sure that your printer is turned on and the paper is positioned correctly.

- Hold down the SHIFT key and press F7 to activate the print function.
- A list of options will appear at the bottom of the screen, as shown in Figure 7.17.

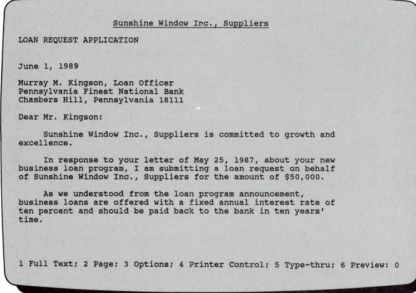

Figure 7.17
WordPerfect's PRINT OPTIONS Menu

- Choose "1 Full Text" to print the entire document by typing number 1.

If you only want to print a certain page of the document, you can choose Option 2 to print the current page. On our single-page document, choosing this option does not make any difference, but it will with larger documents.

After you have made your selection, it will take a few seconds before your letter begins printing on your printer. Your copy should look like the one in Figure 7.7.

Exit WordPerfect

- Press F7 to exit WordPerfect.
- In response to the message "Save Document? (Y/N)Y", press ENTER to accept the "Y" for yes.

- In response to the message "Document to be saved: B:\LOAN.LTR", press ENTER.
- The message "Replace B:\LOAN.LTR? (Y/N)N" will appear, asking if you want to write over the previous copy of your letter, thus adding any additions or corrections. Type Y.
- Wait while the message "Saving B:\LOAN.LTR" appears on the bottom of the screen.
- When the save process is done, the message "Exit WP? (Y/N)N" will be displayed. If you want to continue with this exercise, press ENTER to accept the "N", and a fresh WordPerfect screen will be presented. If you want to end the WordPerfect session at this point, typing Y will place you back in the DOS environment, evidenced by the appearance of the A>.

■ FILE HANDLING AND FORMATTING A DOCUMENT

A word of explanation about the WordPerfect LIST FILES (F5) function is in order before you begin this section. LIST FILES (F5) is one convenient way of doing most of your disk file management in WordPerfect. By pressing function key F5 to access the LIST FILES feature, the names of the current drive and directory will be displayed across the status line of the screen. At this point, you can press the ENTER key to see a list of all files in the directory. An alphabetical list of the files in the directory appears on the screen, along with a header of information and a status line of choices (the menu). An example of the LIST FILES (F5) screen is shown in Figure 7.18 below, and summarized in Table 7.3 on page 175.

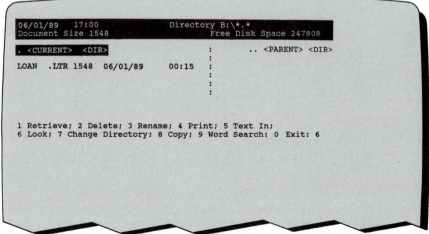

Figure 7.18
WordPerfect's LIST FILES Feature

The header at the top of the screen shows the current date and time, the current directory name, the size of the document currently in memory, and the amount of available disk space.

The alphabetical list of files includes the file size in bytes, along with the date and time each file was last saved. To manipulate a particular file, you must use the ARROW keys to move the highlighted area so that it highlights your chosen file name.

Once the file you want to work with is highlighted, you can choose from nine file-management options from the menu at the bottom of the screen. Let's take a closer look at these options.

The RETRIEVE option allows you to retrieve a copy of an existing file and bring it into RAM and display it on the screen. It is important to note that, if there is already text or a file in memory when you try to retrieve another file, WordPerfect brings the new file into memory and adds to the document that exists in memory. In order to avoid this problem, press F7 (EXIT key) to exit the old file *before* you use the F5 (LIST FILES) function. In response to "Save Document? (Y/N)Y," type N if you have already saved the file; otherwise, type Y to save the file. If your answer is *n*, WordPerfect will prompt you, "Exit WP? (Y/N)." Type N. This action will remove the file or text that you were working on, but you will still be in the Word-Perfect environment. Now you can use the F5 (LIST FILES) function.

The DELETE option allows you to delete an entire file. When you choose DELETE, the message "Delete (filename)? (Y/N) N" is displayed. An answer of *Y* causes the file to be permanently deleted from your disk. Pressing any other key will avoid deleting the file and return you to the menu.

The RENAME option allows you to change the name of an existing file. For example, if a file is saved under the name of OLDFILE.TXT and you want to change the name to NEWFILE.TXT, you can choose the RENAME option and enter the new file name when prompted to do so. The file OLDFILE.TXT will no longer exist after the renaming.

The PRINT option sends a file to the designated printer.

The TEXT IN option brings a copy of a DOS (ASCII) text file to the screen. Do not confuse this option with the RETRIEVE function.

The LOOK option allows you to scroll through the text of a file in a downward direction only, without being able to make any changes to it.

The CHANGE DIRECTORY option allows you to change your default directory simply by typing its name after you make this selection. This function also permits you to create a new directory.

The COPY option allows you to make an additional copy of the current file to another file name, drive, or directory. The same file name can be used for the copy if you are copying the file to another drive or directory. You may want to have an extra copy of an important file saved under another name or in another directory as a backup.

The WORD SEARCH option allows you to select all files that contain one or more specific words or patterns of words somewhere in their text. The list of files satisfying the selection is displayed on the screen. You may use the wildcards * and ? in the selection criteria. The phrase to be searched must be enclosed in quotation marks if it includes a space, semicolon, comma, or quotation marks. Examples of valid selections include:

June
: Lists all the files containing the word *June* in their text. Any combination of uppercase or lowercase letters will be recognized as valid.

"font 1"
: Lists all the files containing the phrase *font 1*. Quotation marks are required because the phrase includes an embedded blank space.

s?t
: Lists all files containing a word that would match the *s?t* pattern (e.g., sit, sat, set).

The EXIT option allows you to leave the LIST FILES menu without choosing any of the options.

1 Retrieve	Retrieves copy of a file to the screen.
2 Delete	Permanently erases a file from the disk.
3 Rename	Changes the name of a file.
4 Print	Sends a file to the printer.
5 Text In	Copies a DOS text file to screen.
6 Look	Scrolls through document.
7 Change Dir	Changes the default directory or creates a new directory.
8 Copy	Copies a current file to another file name, drive, or directory.
9 Word Search	Selects files containing certain pattern of words in their text.
0 Exit	Exits the F5 function with no action taken.

TABLE 7.3 A Summary of LIST FILES (F5) Options

In this section, you will practice some of the LIST FILES options. You will also learn and practice some of the available formatting options, such as changing the pitch and line settings, changing margin and tab settings, and changing the page length. At this point, it is assumed that you have completed the previous two sections, and that you will be working with the document LOAN.LTR that you created and modified in those sections. If you are starting out fresh, remember that you must first boot the system and enter the WordPerfect environment (refer to the booting section for complete instructions, if necessary).

In this section you'll use these features:

1. list files
2. copy a file
3. delete a file
4. retrieve a file
5. set print formats
6. save a document
7. print a document
8. exit WordPerfect

List Files

- Press F5 to list a directory of your files.
- In response to the message "DIR A:*.*" displayed at the status line, type B: [ENTER]

WordPerfect will list a directory of all the files on the diskette in the B drive. Notice the menu at the bottom of the screen. To perform one of these functions on a file, use the ARROW keys to move the highlighted line to the file you want to work with. In this case, highlight LOAN.LTR and type the number of the chosen function.

Copy a File into Another File

You should still be in the LIST FILES (F5) function, and the menu of available file-handling functions should be present at the bottom of the screen. Let's copy the LOAN.LTR file into a temporary file called TEMP.LTR.

- Make sure the LOAN.LTR file is highlighted at the top of the screen.
- Press 8 for the copy option (make sure you press the *8* key at the top of the keyboard, not the *8* on the numerical pad).
- In response to the message "Copy This File To:", type B:TEMP.LTR and press ENTER.
- To see the new directory with TEMP.LTR included, press 7 for the CHANGE DIRECTORY option.
- In response to the message "New Directory = B:\", just press ENTER to acknowledge that the directory of the diskette in Drive B, the same directory you were working with previously, is to be presented.
- In response to the message "DIR B:*.*", press ENTER to see a directory of the files in the B drive.

After copying LOAN.LTR into TEMP.LTR, the screen appearing in Figure 7.19 will be presented.

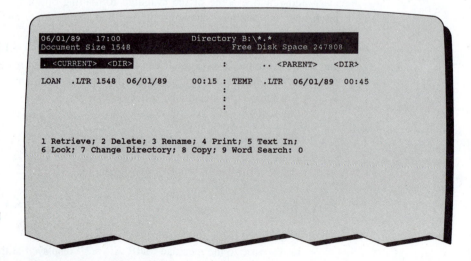

Figure 7.19
The WordPerfect Screen after Copying LOAN.LTR into TEMP.LTR

Delete a File

Now let's delete the TEMP.LTR file that you just created.

- While still in the LIST FILES (F5) function, use the ARROW keys to move the highlighted line to the file TEMP.LTR.
- Choose the DELETE option by typing the number 2.
- In response to the message "Delete B:\TEMP.LTR? (Y/N) N", type Y.
- The file is now deleted from the directory; type 7 to select the CHANGE DIRECTORY option.
- Press the ENTER key twice to view the new directory with the TEMP.LTR file deleted.

Retrieve a File

As you will recall, in the last section you retrieved the file you wanted to work on by using the RETRIEVE (SHIFT-F10) function, which required your having knowledge of the exact name of the file you wanted to retrieve.

You are about to use another method of retrieving a file, this time from within the LIST FILES (F5) function.

- While still in the LIST FILES (F5) function, use the ARROW keys to move the highlighted line to the file called LOAN.LTR.
- To choose the retrieve option, press the number 1. The LOAN.LTR file will appear on the screen.

Now, let's print this document. A number of formatting options can be adjusted to change the appearance of the printed document. The following steps will demonstrate the procedure for selecting formatting options in printing a document.

Change Pitch Settings

When a document is printed, WordPerfect fits ten characters into every inch of a line (ten characters per inch). You can change this setting to any number of characters per inch. The more characters per inch, the smaller the print; the fewer characters per inch, the larger the print.

- Hold down the CTRL key and press F8 for the PRINT FORMAT menu. The PRINT FORMAT menu will be displayed at the bottom of the screen, as you saw in Figure 7.16.
- In response, choose Option 1, "Pitch/Font", by typing the number 1, which will appear after "Selection:".
- The cursor will now be on the "10" next to "Pitch". Type the number 12 to change the pitch/font to twelve characters per inch.
- Press ENTER twice.

Change Line Settings

You may also decide that you would like to change the number of lines per inch while you are still in the PRINT format menu. To do so, follow these instructions.

- To choose the "Lines per inch" option, type the number 2.
- Change the lines per inch to eight by typing the number 8 and pressing ENTER.
- Press ENTER to exit the PRINT FORMAT menu.

Change Margin Settings

Now let's change the left and right margins of your document.

- Hold down the SHIFT key and press F8 to view the LINE FORMAT menu.
- Several options will appear at the bottom of the screen, as shown in Figure 7.20.

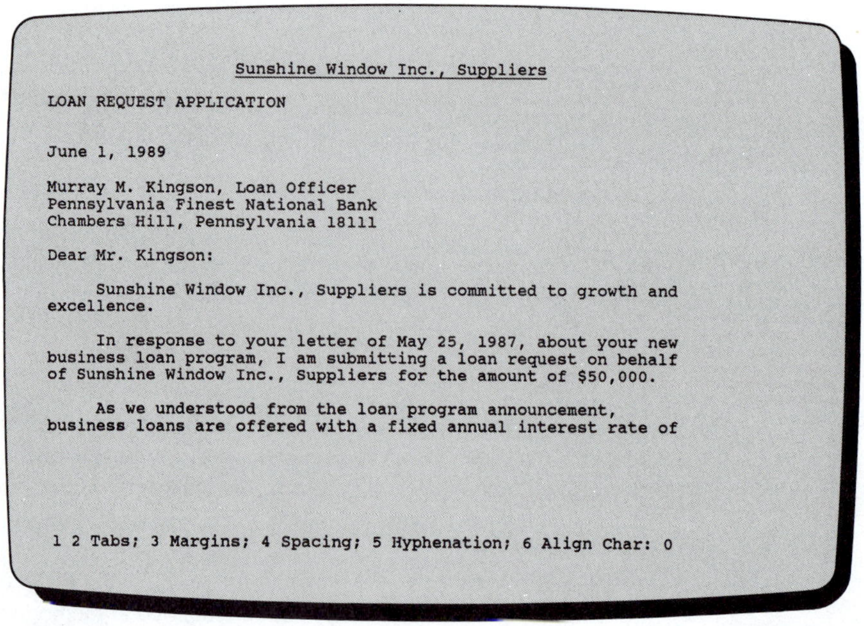

```
                    Sunshine Window Inc., Suppliers
LOAN REQUEST APPLICATION

June 1, 1989

Murray M. Kingson, Loan Officer
Pennsylvania Finest National Bank
Chambers Hill, Pennsylvania 18111

Dear Mr. Kingson:

     Sunshine Window Inc., Suppliers is committed to growth and
excellence.

     In response to your letter of May 25, 1987, about your new
business loan program, I am submitting a loan request on behalf
of Sunshine Window Inc., Suppliers for the amount of $50,000.

     As we understood from the loan program announcement,
business loans are offered with a fixed annual interest rate of




 1 2 Tabs; 3 Margins; 4 Spacing; 5 Hyphenation; 6 Align Char: 0
```

Figure 7.20
WordPerfect's LINE FORMAT Menu

- In response, type the number 3 to choose Option 3, "Margins".
- In response to the message "[Margin Set] 10 74 to Left = ", type the number 12 to set the left margin to column 12.

- Press the SPACEBAR.
- In response to "Right = ", type the number 79 to set the right margin to column 79.
- Press ENTER to exit the LINE FORMAT menu.

Change Tab Settings

You may also want to change the tab settings so that your indentations occur at different character locations. To do so, follow these instructions.

- Hold down the SHIFT key and press F8 to get back to the LINE FORMAT menu once again.
- To change the tab settings, choose Option 1 or 2 by typing the number 1 or 2. One row of tab settings will appear at the bottom of the screen, as shown in Figure 7.21.

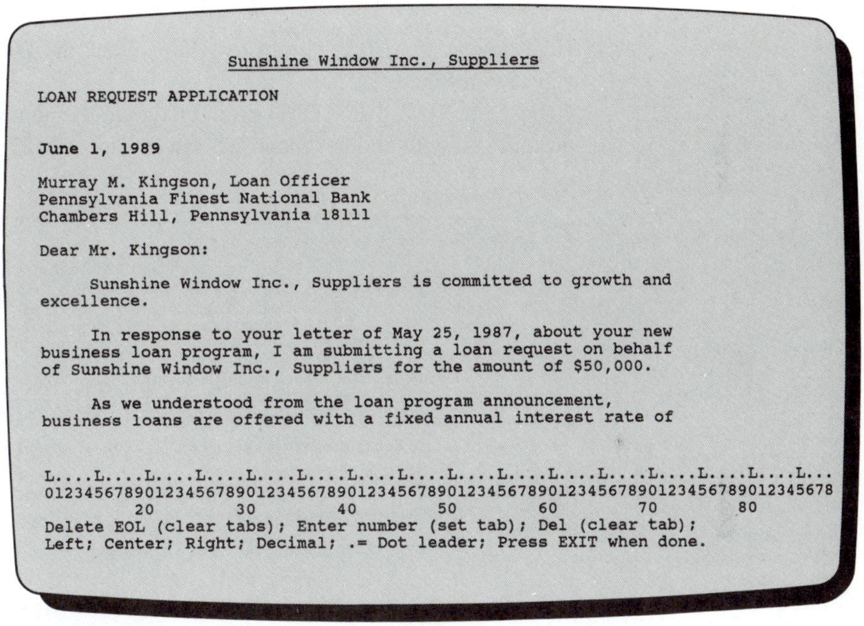

Figure 7.21
WordPerfect's TAB SETTINGS Options

- Hold down the CTRL key and press the END key to erase all the tab settings.
- Type the number 5 to create just one tab setting at Column 5. (You could actually set as many tabs as you like.)
- Press ENTER.
- Press F7 (EXIT) to exit the tab menu.

Change Line Spacing

You may want to change the line spacing from the default (single spacing) to double spacing for a term paper or report.

- Hold down the SHIFT key and press F8 to view the LINE FORMAT options once again.
- Type the number 4 to choose the option "Spacing."
- In response to the message "[Spacing set] 1", type the number 2 for double spacing.
- Press ENTER to exit the LINE FORMAT function.

Change Page Length

You might also want to change the page size by altering the number of lines to be printed on one page. WordPerfect gives three choices of page length: letter size, legal size, and your own specified size. Let's try one on our own document.

- Hold down the ALT key and press F8 to view the PAGE FORMAT menu as you saw in Figure 7.15.
- Choose the PAGE LENGTH option by typing the number 4. WordPerfect will prompt you with another menu, shown in Figure 7.22.

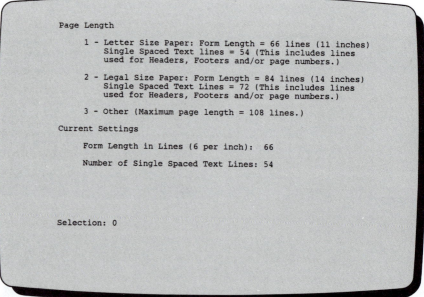

Figure 7.22
WordPerfect's PAGE LENGTH Option

- Press ENTER to accept the current settings shown at the bottom of the screen. Upon completion of your choice, you will be returned to the PAGE FORMAT menu.
- Press ENTER to exit the PAGE FORMAT menu.

Page Numbering

One other useful formatting feature is page numbering. Although it does not apply in the case of our exercise, it is worth discussing at this point. In order to put a page number on each page of your document, WordPerfect asks you to go through two menus. Let's try to place a page number at the top right corner of the LOAN.LTR.

- Hold down the ALT key and then press F8.
- Choose Option 1, PAGE NUMBER POSITION, by typing 1.
- WordPerfect will prompt you with the menu shown in Figure 7.23.

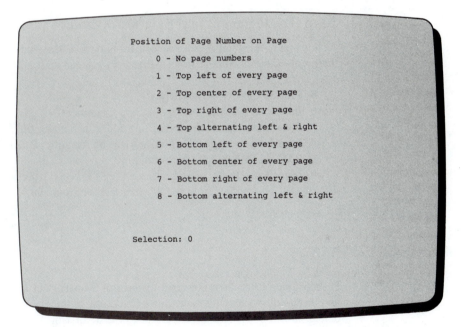

Figure 7.23
WordPerfect's PAGE NUMBER POSITION Option

- Type 3 to select Option 3, which will place a page number at the top right of every page.
- Press ENTER to leave the PAGE FORMAT menu.

Remember, any formatting options you chose will affect only text following that part of the document, unless you place the formatting option at the beginning of the document. For example, if you changed the spacing option from single spacing to double spacing at the beginning of the third paragraph in the text, then only the third paragraph and any text following the third paragraph would be printed with the double-spacing option. The first two paragraphs of the document would be printed with the single-spacing option.

Print the Document

Now let's print the document with the new format specifications.

- Hold down the SHIFT key and press F7.
- Type the number 1 to select "Full Text", which causes the entire document to be printed.

Save the Document and Exit WordPerfect

At this stage, you should save the formatting options that you added to the document, then remove the document from memory so you can start a new one.

- Press F7 to exit WordPerfect.
- In response to the message, "Save Document? (Y/N) Y", type Y to save the document with all the formatting codes in it under different names.
- In response to "Document to be Saved: B:\LOAN.LTR", type B:FORLOAN.LTR, press ENTER.
- In response to the message "Exit WP? (Y/N) N", press ENTER to accept the "N" and to remain in the WordPerfect environment.

BLOCK COMMANDS

Perhaps one of the most powerful features of WordPerfect is the BLOCK command and its combinations with many other functions. In this section you will learn how to delete, move, copy, and format a block of text. In WordPerfect, a **block of text** can be one or more consecutive sentences, a paragraph, or entire pages of a document.

In this section, you will once again be working with the LOAN.LTR file. (We assume that you have worked through the previous sections and have created and modified the LOAN.LTR file. If you are just starting out, remember that you must first boot the system and enter the WordPerfect environment; refer to the booting instructions if necessary.)

In this section, you will use these features:

1. retrieve a file
2. delete a block
3. move a block
4. copy a block
5. format a block
6. save a document
7. print a document
8. exit WordPerfect

Copy and Retrieve a File

The following instructions allow you to copy the LOAN.LTR file into another file called TEMP.LTR so you can practice some BLOCK command functions.

- Press F5 to list a directory of your files.
- In response to the message "DIR A:*.*", type B:.
- Press ENTER.
- Use the ARROW keys to move the highlighted line to the file LOAN.LTR.
- Press the number 8 to choose the COPY option.
- In response to the message "Copy This File To:", type TEMP.LTR, and press ENTER.
- Type the number 7 to see the new directory.
- In response to the message "New Directory = B:\", press ENTER.
- In response to the message "DIR B:*.*", press ENTER.
- Use the ARROW keys to highlight the file TEMP.LTR at the top of the screen.
- Type the number 1 to retrieve the TEMP.LTR file; as a result, the document will appear on the screen.

Delete a Block of Text

Let's try to delete an entire paragraph of our document by using a BLOCK DELETE command.

- Move the cursor to the beginning of the first paragraph, beginning "Sunshine Window Inc., Suppliers is committed...."
- Hold down the ALT key and press the F4 key; the message "Block On" will flash at the bottom left corner of the screen.
- Use the RIGHT ARROW (→) key to highlight the entire paragraph. You can also use the DOWN ARROW (↓) key to highlight an entire line.
- Press either the BACKSPACE or DEL key once.
- Type Y in response to the message "Delete Block? (Y/N) N".
- Press the DEL key twice to delete the extra blank lines. Now the first paragraph is completely removed from the document, and the screen will look like the one in Figure 7.24 on the following page.

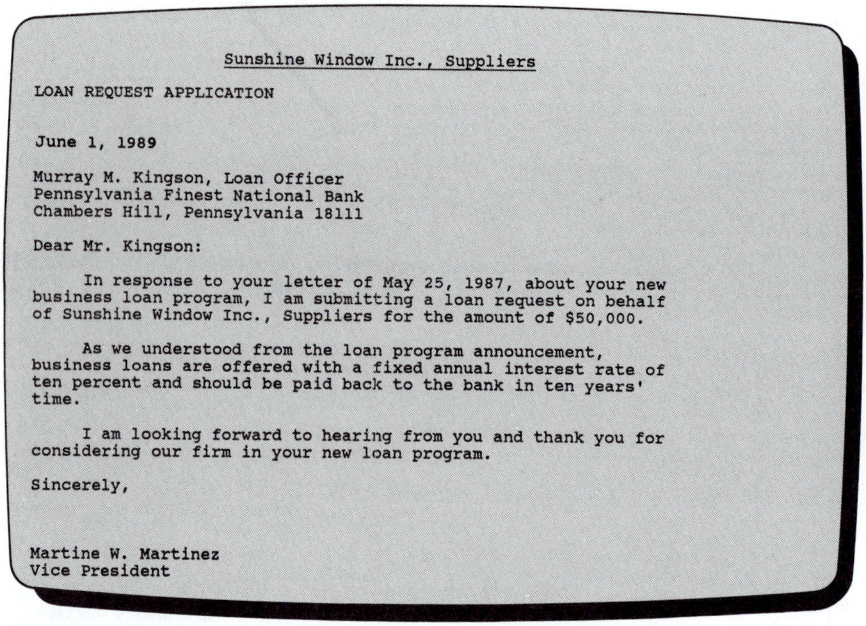

```
                Sunshine Window Inc., Suppliers
LOAN REQUEST APPLICATION

June 1, 1989

Murray M. Kingson, Loan Officer
Pennsylvania Finest National Bank
Chambers Hill, Pennsylvania 18111

Dear Mr. Kingson:

     In response to your letter of May 25, 1987, about your new
business loan program, I am submitting a loan request on behalf
of Sunshine Window Inc., Suppliers for the amount of $50,000.

     As we understood from the loan program announcement,
business loans are offered with a fixed annual interest rate of
ten percent and should be paid back to the bank in ten years'
time.

     I am looking forward to hearing from you and thank you for
considering our firm in your new loan program.

Sincerely,


Martine W. Martinez
Vice President
```

Figure 7.24
Our Document after Deleting a Block of Text

Move a Block of Text

It is often useful to be able to move sentences, paragraphs, or entire pages of text around when creating a document.

- Use the ARROW keys to move the cursor to the beginning of the new first paragraph beginning, "In response to your letter...."
- Hold down the ALT key and press F4 to activate the BLOCK function. Notice that the "Block on" message will start blinking at the bottom of the screen.
- Use the DOWN and RIGHT ARROW keys to highlight the entire paragraph.
- Hold down the CTRL key and press F4 to perform the first step of the BLOCK MOVE command: cutting your block from your document. A menu will be displayed at the bottom of the screen, as shown in Figure 7.25 on the following page.
- Type the number 1 which chooses the first option, "CUT BLOCK". The paragraph has now disappeared from your document.

The CUT option saves text in a temporary file in RAM, and removes the block of text from the screen. The COPY option saves the block of text temporarily in RAM, but leaves it on the screen.

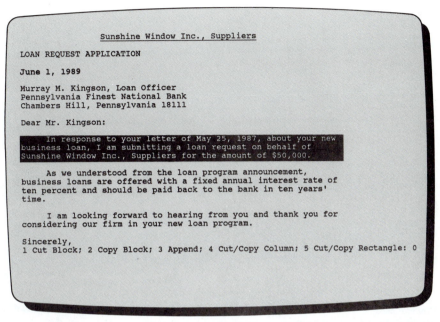

Figure 7.25
Step One of a BLOCK MOVE Command

- Move the cursor to the position where you would like to place the block of retrieved text. Since in this example you simply wish to reinstate the text in its previous position, the cursor does not need to be moved.
- Hold down the CTRL key and press F4 to initiate the second step of the BLOCK MOVE: moving the file from the temporary file back to the cursor position on the screen.
- From the menu on the bottom of the screen, choose Option 5 to retrieve text by typing the number 5; the saved paragraph will be returned to its previous position in the letter. *Caution*: If you don't move (or replace) the cut text immediately (before the very next operation), the cut text may be lost.

Copy a Block

- Move the cursor to the beginning of the paragraph beginning "As we understood from the …."
- Hold down the CTRL key and press F4 to begin the BLOCK COPY command. You'll see a screen like the one in Figure 7.26 on the following page.

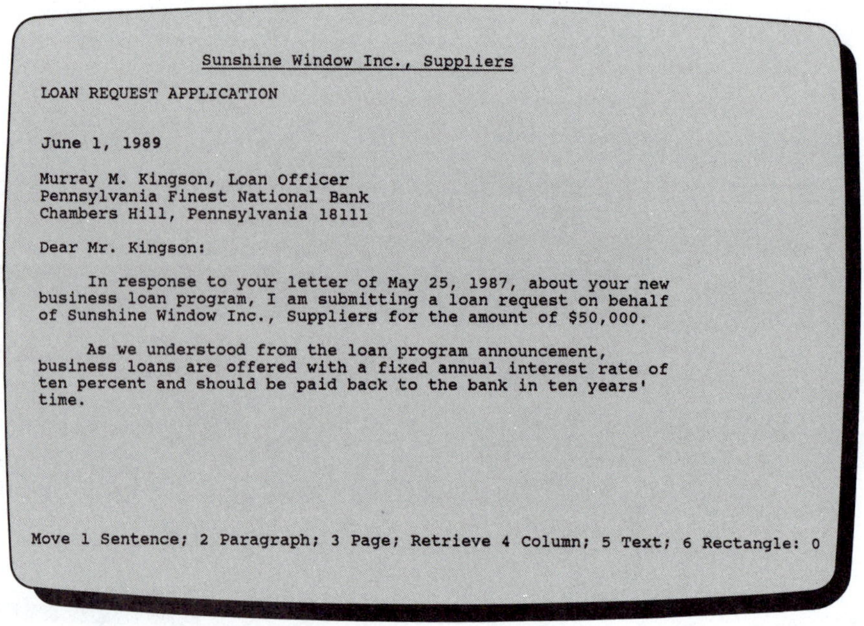

```
              Sunshine Window Inc., Suppliers
LOAN REQUEST APPLICATION

June 1, 1989

Murray M. Kingson, Loan Officer
Pennsylvania Finest National Bank
Chambers Hill, Pennsylvania 18111

Dear Mr. Kingson:

     In response to your letter of May 25, 1987, about your new
business loan program, I am submitting a loan request on behalf
of Sunshine Window Inc., Suppliers for the amount of $50,000.

     As we understood from the loan program announcement,
business loans are offered with a fixed annual interest rate of
ten percent and should be paid back to the bank in ten years'
time.




Move 1 Sentence; 2 Paragraph; 3 Page; Retrieve 4 Column; 5 Text; 6 Rectangle: 0
```

Figure 7.26
Step One of a BLOCK COPY Command

- Choose Option 2, "Paragraph," from the menu at the bottom of the screen by typing the number 2. The menu will change to the one shown in Figure 7.27.

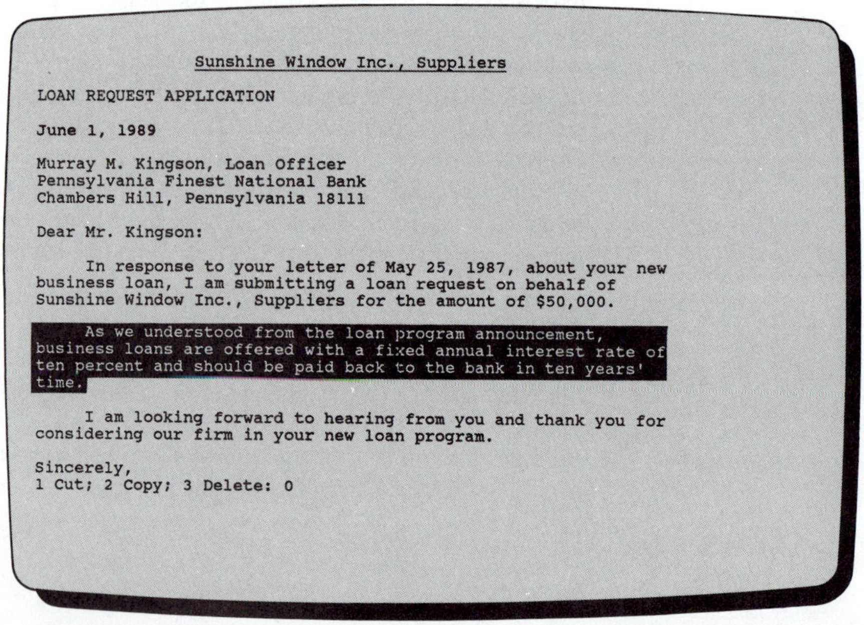

```
              Sunshine Window Inc., Suppliers
LOAN REQUEST APPLICATION

June 1, 1989

Murray M. Kingson, Loan Officer
Pennsylvania Finest National Bank
Chambers Hill, Pennsylvania 18111

Dear Mr. Kingson:

     In response to your letter of May 25, 1987, about your new
business loan, I am submitting a loan request on behalf of
Sunshine Window Inc., Suppliers for the amount of $50,000.

     As we understood from the loan program announcement,
business loans are offered with a fixed annual interest rate of
ten percent and should be paid back to the bank in ten years'
time.

     I am looking forward to hearing from you and thank you for
considering our firm in your new loan program.

Sincerely,
1 Cut; 2 Copy; 3 Delete: 0
```

Figure 7.27
Step Two of a BLOCK COPY Command

- Type the number 2 to choose the copy option.
- Move the cursor to the blank line below the salutation, "Dear Mr. Kingson:".
- Hold down the CTRL key and press F4 once again to use the MOVE function.
- Type the number 5, choosing Option 5 (Retrieve) from the menu. The paragraph has now been copied and appears as both the first and last paragraphs of the letter. Delete the duplicate paragraph by following the instructions for a BLOCK DELETE earlier in this section.

Now let's adjust the text after you have deleted the duplicate paragraph. If there are too many blank lines between paragraphs, you can "drag" the second paragraph up, deleting unwanted blank lines by placing the cursor after the last character of the first paragraph and then pressing the DEL key once for each line you want to delete. Or you can place the cursor at the beginning of any blank line that you want to erase and press the DEL key once, which will cause that line to be deleted.

Format a Block

The last BLOCK command could become useful when you have worked your way through a document and you would like to put a few finishing touches on your work. With the help of the BLOCK FORMAT command, you can boldface or underline a block in a few seconds. Let's see how this feature of the BLOCK command works by bringing a new copy of file TEMP.LTR into memory:

- Press F7 (Exit WordPerfect).
- In response to "Save Document? (Y/N) Y", type N.
- In response to "Exit WordPerfect? (Y/N) N", just press ENTER.
- Press F5 (FILE LIST) to get the directory of your diskette.
- In response to "directory A:*.*", type B: and press ENTER twice.
- Move the highlighted line to the TEMP.LTR file.
- Type 1 to retrieve this file.

Upon completion of the above commands, you should see the TEMP.LTR file on the screen, as shown in Figure 7.28 on the following page.

- Move the cursor to the beginning of the salutation "Dear Mr. Kingson:".
- Hold down the ALT key and press F4 to activate the BLOCK function. As a result, you will see the "Block on" message blinking at the bottom of the screen.
- Use the RIGHT ARROW key to highlight the entire line.
- Once the paragraph is completely highlighted, press F6 (BOLD function). The entire line will be boldfaced.

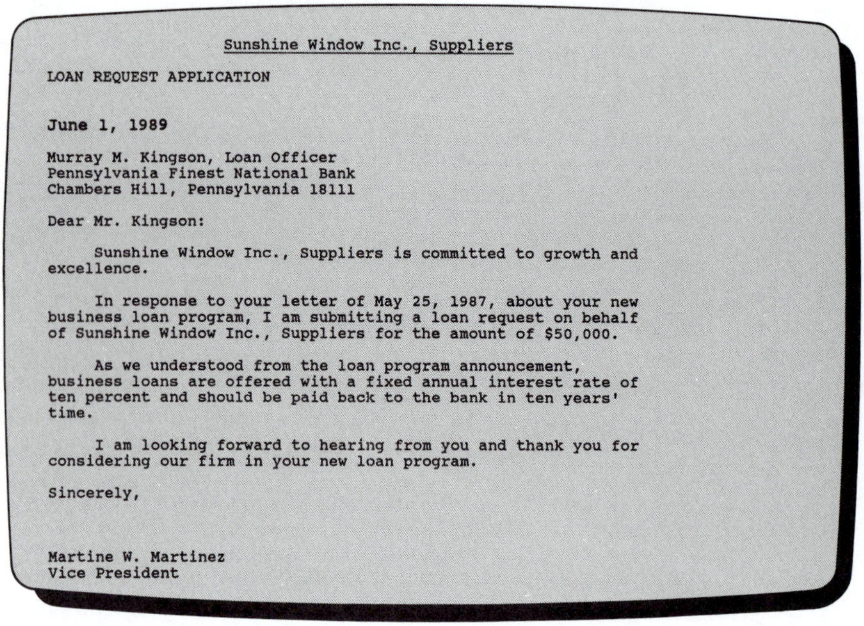

```
            Sunshine Window Inc., Suppliers
LOAN REQUEST APPLICATION

June 1, 1989

Murray M. Kingson, Loan Officer
Pennsylvania Finest National Bank
Chambers Hill, Pennsylvania 18111

Dear Mr. Kingson:

     Sunshine Window Inc., Suppliers is committed to growth and
excellence.

     In response to your letter of May 25, 1987, about your new
business loan program, I am submitting a loan request on behalf
of Sunshine Window Inc., Suppliers for the amount of $50,000.

     As we understood from the loan program announcement,
business loans are offered with a fixed annual interest rate of
ten percent and should be paid back to the bank in ten years'
time.

     I am looking forward to hearing from you and thank you for
considering our firm in your new loan program.

Sincerely,


Martine W. Martinez
Vice President
```

Figure 7.28
A Document Ready for Formatting

Now, let's try the BLOCK function and underline feature of WordPerfect.

- Move the cursor to the beginning of the "LOAN REQUEST" line.
- Hold down the ALT key and press F4.
- Use the RIGHT ARROW key to highlight the line.
- At this stage, press the F8 key (UNDERLINE function). The entire block will be underlined.

Print Your Document

Now let's print a copy of the file TEMP.LTR with all the changes. (Make sure your printer is on.)

- Hold down the SHIFT key and press F7.
- Type 1 to choose the "Full text" option.
- In a few seconds, your document should be printed on your printer.

Your printed document should look the same as the one shown in Figure 7.29 on the following page.

```
                Sunshine Window Inc., Suppliers

LOAN REQUEST APPLICATION

June 1, 1989

Murray M. Kingson, Loan Officer
Pennsylvania Finest National Bank
Chambers Hill, Pennsylvania 18111

Dear Mr. Kingson:

     Sunshine Window Inc., Suppliers is committed to growth and
excellence.

     In response to your letter of May 25, 1987, about your new
business loan program, I am submitting a loan request on behalf
of Sunshine Window Inc., Suppliers for the amount of $50,000.

     As we understood from the loan program announcement,
business loans are offered with a fixed annual interest rate of
ten percent and should be paid back to the bank in ten years'
time.

     I am looking forward to hearing from you and thank you for
considering our firm in your new loan program.

Sincerely,


Martine W. Martinez
Vice President
```

Exit WordPerfect

- Press F7 to exit WordPerfect.
- In response to the message "Save Document? (Y/N) Y", type N.
- When the message "Exit WP? (Y/N) N" is displayed, type Y to exit WordPerfect; you are now back in the DOS environment as evidenced by the appearance of the A>.

  Note: You cannot exit until printing is complete.

Figure 7.29
A Document with All Changes in Place

■ SUMMARY OF WORDPERFECT COMMANDS

SAVE	Stores a file on a diskette.
EXIT	Leaves a file or WordPerfect.
RETRIEVE	Retrieves a file from a diskette.
DELETE	Deletes a file from a diskette.
INSERT	Inserts text within the existing text.
PRINT	Provides a hardcopy of a document.
RIGHT-JUSTIFY	Aligns the right-end of lines in a document.
LIST FILES	Handles file management in WordPerfect by pressing F5.
LIST FILES: RETRIEVE	Obtains a copy of a file from a diskette.
LIST FILES: DELETE	Erases a file from your diskette.
LIST FILES: RENAME	Changes a file name.
LIST FILES: PRINT	Sends a file to a designated printer.
LIST FILES: TEXT IN	Brings a DOS (ASCII) file to the screen.
LIST FILES: LOOK	Scrolls through a document without allowing changes.
LIST FILES: CHANGE DIR	Changes the default directory or makes a new directory.

LIST FILES: COPY	Copies the current file to another file, drive, or directory.
LIST FILE: WORD SEARCH	Selects all files that contain one or more specific words.
LIST FILES: EXIT	Leaves the LIST FILES menu.
BLOCK DELETE	Erases a specified block of text.
BLOCK MOVE	Moves a specified block of text.
BLOCK COPY	Makes a copy of a specified block of text in a specified location.
BLOCK FORMAT	Changes the format of a specified block of text.

■ Key Terms

cursor	The small blinking underline that indicates your current position on the screen.
status line	Indicates your current location in the document.
word wrap	When the end of a line of text is reached, WordPerfect automatically "wraps" the next word around to the beginning of the next line.
insert mode	Characters are inserted at the current cursor position. In WordPerfect, insert is the default mode.
typeover mode	Activated by pressing the INSERT key; characters typed replace existing characters. Toggle on/off by pressing INSERT again.
template	A guide that fits over the function keys on the keyboard; function key combinations are color-coded on it.
hard return (HRt)	A return the user inserts into the text by pressing ENTER.
soft return (SRt)	A return the program inserts into the text at the end of a line when wrapping the text around.
block of text	One or more consecutive sentences, paragraphs, or pages of a document.

■ Review Questions

1. The _____ key moves the cursor to the left and erases the previous character entered in that position.
   (a) DEL
   (b) BACKSPACE
   (c) ENTER
   (d) RETURN
2. The _____ keys (F1 through F10) are located on the left side or top of the keyboard and are used to invoke WordPerfect's various features.
   (a) feature
   (b) function
   (c) ARROW
   (d) TAB

3. Which of the following keys is *not* used in conjunction with a function key?
   (a) CTRL
   (b) SHIFT
   (c) DEL
   (d) ALT
4. To reposition the cursor at the bottom of the document, the HOME key is pressed twice, followed by pressing the _____ once.
   (a) PGDN
   (b) RETURN
   (c) DOWN ARROW
   (d) TAB
5. What is the difference between retrieving a file with the LIST FILES command and using the RETRIEVE command?
6. Depressing the _____ key will indent a paragraph a specified number of columns.
   (a) TAB
   (b) RIGHT ARROW
   (c) DEL
   (d) RETURN
7. What is the most important command that should be used while working with WordPerfect to ensure that you won't lose a document?
8. The _____ key is pressed to change from the insert to the typeover mode.
   (a) TYP
   (b) PGUP
   (c) TAB
   (d) INS
9. Which of the following keys moves the cursor to the previous page?
   (a) HOME
   (b) PGDN
   (c) PGUP
   (d) END
10. The keystroke combination _____ will delete text from the current cursor position to the end of a line.
    (a) DEL-RIGHT ARROW
    (b) ALT-DEL
    (c) CTRL-END
    (d) CTRL-ENTER
11. How is a document saved?
12. Which of the following is *not* one of the file-handling options of the LIST FILES (F5) feature?
    (a) SAVE
    (b) PRINT
    (c) RENAME
    (d) LOOK

13. The _____ key is used to erase the character on which the cursor is currently positioned.
    (a) DEL   (c) INS
    (b) BACKSPACE   (d) CTRL
14. What is meant by the term *pitch?*
15. Which of the following keystroke combinations erases all of the tab settings?
    (a) SHIFT-F5   (c) HOME-↑
    (b) CTRL-END   (d) ALT-F6
16. Explain the term *word wrap.*
17. Explain the procedure to reposition the cursor back to the beginning of the document.
18. What is the difference between a hard return code and a soft return code?
19. What is a block of text?
20. What is the difference between the CUT option and the COPY option when moving a block of text?
21. Is LETTER.HOME a valid document name? Explain.
22. What is a *keystroke combination?* Give some examples.
23. How can a command be cancelled?
24. What keystroke combination allows you to view the format codes within a document?
25. Describe the steps involved in saving a document.
26. How can a line of text be deleted?
27. Which of the following keystrokes will access the PRINT FORMAT menu?
    (a) ALT-F8   (c) SHIFT-F8
    (b) CTRL-F6   (d) CTRL-F8
28. How would you send a document to the printer? List the steps.
29. What is the difference between PAGE FORMAT and PRINT FORMAT?
30. What happens to a file in memory if another file is retrieved?

☐ *chapter* 7

HANDS-ON EXERCISES

1. Type the following paragraph as it appears with all the errors. Type continuously without pressing ENTER (↵). (You will correct the paragraph in the steps below.)

   ```
   Word processing has revoltionized the way documents are produced,
   increasing the speed with which documentss can be created, edited, and
   stored for future use.
   ```

a. Indent the paragraph.
b. Correct the misspelling of *revoltionized* in the first line, making it *revolutionized*.
c. In the second line after the word *speed*, add the phrase `and efficiency` so the line reads ...*the speed and efficiency with which* ....
d. Correct the misspelling of *documentss* in the third line.
e. Center the title *THE AGE OF WORD PROCESSING* at the top of the page. Underline and capitalize the title.
f. Exit WordPerfect without saving this document.

2. Type the following paragraph as it appears with all the errors. Type continuously without pressing ENTER. (You will correct the paragraph in the steps below.)

   ```
   All guests will be requested to register in the lounge before procead-
   ing to their assigned rooms. Breakfast will be served at 7:30 A.M.
   tomorrow morning in the Fantasy Tea Room.
   ```

   a. Indent the paragraph.
   b. Delete the words *will be* in the first line and replace them with the word *are*.
   c. Use typeover mode to change the *a* in the word *proceading* to the letter *e*, making the spelling of the word *proceeding*.
   d. At the beginning of the third line, add the word `promptly` and underline it.
   e. Center the title *NOTICE TO GUESTS* at the top of the page. Use the boldface feature to make it noticeable.

3. Create a sample resume and then edit it. Start a new WordPerfect file, and type the resume as it appears in Figure 7.30, paying close attention to spacing and underlining. Center the heading and capitalize where indicated.

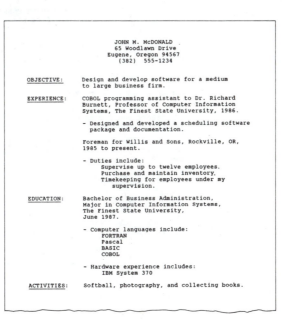

Figure 7.30
A Sample Resume

Now edit the resume, following the instructions below: (*Note:* You should obtain a hardcopy of this resume at this stage before changes are incorporated.)

a. John McDonald has moved across town since he last edited his resume. Delete the street address *65 Woodlawn Drive*.
b. Insert the new street address where you deleted the old by typing `42 E. Main Street`.
c. Move the block of text under the heading of *EDUCATION* to come before the topic of *EXPERIENCE*. Adjust the spacing between lines if necessary. The block to be highlighted and moved includes
   EDUCATION: Bachelor of Business Administration
   .
   .
   .
                  IBM System 370
   When the move is completed, the order of topics should read OBJECTIVES, EDUCATION, EXPERIENCE, and ACTIVITIES.
d. Insert a new line after *Supervise up to twelve employees* under the *Duties include* heading. Add the line
      `Prepare job layout.`
e. Save the document under the name of B:RESUME.1.
f. Exit this file, but do not exit WordPerfect. You should now have a clean screen with which to work.
g. Use the LIST FILES function to retrieve the file you saved as B:RESUME.1.
h. Change the margins to: Left margin = 12, Right margin = 80.
i. Save the document under the same file name.
j. Print the resume.
k. Exit WordPerfect.

4. Create an interoffice memorandum, then edit your final draft. Begin with a new WordPerfect file, and type the memo exactly as it appears in Figure 7.31.

```
                          ENGLANDER COMPANY
                         Interoffice Memorandum

        TO:        Nathan Sebastian, Manager

        FROM:      Patrice Grove, Committee Chairman

        DATE:      March 21, 1989

        SUBJECT:   MEETING ON MARCH 23


              Thank you for agreeing to talk with our Committee on Human
        Resource Management on March 23.
              After reviewing the various topics you mentioned in your
        recent memo, the committee has decided that it would like you to
        address the following issues:

              1.  Strategies for improving employer/employee
                  relationships.

              2.  Ways for improving employee satisfaction and
                  productivity.

              The committee will meet at 4:00 P.M. in the conference room.
        We look forward to your discussion.
```

Figure 7.31
A Sample Memorandum

Now edit the memo, following the instructions below.

a. Use the BLOCK feature to format a block of text. Block the heading *ENGLANDER COMPANY* to change it to boldface letters. Repeat the steps to underline the subject *MEETING ON MARCH 23*.
b. At the end of the first paragraph, insert the line
   `I have put you second on the agenda for that day's meeting.`
c. The time and place of the meeting has now been changed. Use the BLOCK feature to highlight and delete the words *4:00 P.M. in the conference room*. Insert in its place
   `3:30 P.M. in the second floor lounge.`
d. Save the memo using the file name B:memo.1.
e. Exit this file, but do not exit WordPerfect.
f. Use the RETRIEVE function (SHIFT-F10) to retrieve the file you saved as B:memo.1.
g. Center the memo vertically on the page using the PAGE FORMAT option (Alt-F8).
h. Save the memo under the same file name.
i. Print the memo.
j. Exit WordPerfect.

5. You have been asked to submit a proposal to teach a seminar in Lotus 1-2-3. The letter of transmittal that you have written to accompany your proposal appears in Figure 7.32. Type the letter as it appears including any spelling errors you may find; you will make some revisions later. Obtain a hardcopy after you are done typing this letter.

```
Computer Management, Inc.
400 Vine Street
Middletown, PA  17057
June 7, 1989


Joanne Smith, President
Woodward Lumber Company
801 Front Street
Harrisburg, PA  17101

Dear Mrs. Smith:

     In response to your recent interest in the seminars I have
been conducting for Computer Management, Inc., I am submitting the
enclosed proposal to teach a seminar in Lotus 1-2-3 to your
company's accounting and management staff.

     As you mentioned, this seminar could benefit your company at
this time by getting your employeees working with the new
microcomputers and software as quickly as possible.

     The accounting department staff, who have been performing
their functions manually, will discover the surprising ease with
which these same jobs can be performed with Lotus 1-2-3.  The
management team will find Lotus 1-2-3's applications vital in the
area of decision support.

     I appreciate your interest in my seminars and hope to be
able to serve your company in the near future.  Please give me a
call if you have any questions concerning the proposed seminar.

Sincerely,


(your name)

Encl:   Proposal
        Resume
```

Figure 7.32
A Sample Proposal

Now edit the letter of transmittal.
- a. In the first paragraph, correct the misspelling of the word *submiting* by adding a *t* to make it *submitting*.
- b. In the second paragraph, delete one e in the word *employeees* so it is spelled correctly (*employees*).
- c. It would be helpful if Mrs. Smith was given a phone number in case she has any questions. In the fourth paragraph, add
    `at 717-555-5515`
    so the sentence will read *Please give me a call at 717-555-5515* ....
- d. Move the second paragraph, beginning *As you mentioned* ..., so that it follows the third paragraph beginning *The accounting department*.... In other words, switch the second and third paragraphs, adjusting the spacing if necessary.
- e. Boldface your company's name:
    `Computer Management, Inc.`
- f. Save the letter using the file name B:PROPOSAL.LTR.
- g. Exit this file, but do not exit WordPerfect.
- h. Use the LIST FILES function to view the directory of files. Highlight the file you just saved as B:PROPOSAL.LTR and rename the file as B:SEMINAR.LTR.
- i. While still in the LIST FILES directory, retrieve the file you just renamed as B:SEMINAR.LTR.
- j. Print the letter.
- k. Save the letter under the same name.
- l. Exit WordPerfect.

Part IV

ELECTRONIC SPREADSHEET CONCEPTS AND APPLICATIONS

chapter 8
ELECTRONIC SPREADSHEETS

- describe and work through a manual spreadsheet analysis problem.
- discuss the three generations of spreadsheet software packages.
- discuss the history of electronic spreadsheet packages.
- discuss the features of the VisiCalc and Framework spreadsheet software packages.
- discuss the features and application capabilities of the Lotus 1-2-3 spreadsheet software package.
- describe in detail the five diskettes that make up the Lotus 1-2-3 spreadsheet software package.

chapter 9
USING LOTUS 1-2-3

- describe the features of a Lotus 1-2-3 worksheet.
- discuss how to use the keyboard keys to move around in a worksheet.
- discuss the rules for entering data into a worksheet.
- discuss in detail the 1-2-3 commands and their sublevels.
- describe the difference between absolute and relative cell addressing.
- describe how to create and format a worksheet.
- describe how to copy formulas or move data from one area of the worksheet to another.
- describe the use of 1-2-3 @ functions.
- discuss the procedure to print a worksheet.
- describe the process of saving and retrieving files with the /FILE command.

chapter 8

ELECTRONIC SPREADSHEETS

After completing this chapter, you should be able to

- *describe and work through a manual spreadsheet analysis problem.*
- *discuss the three generations of spreadsheet software packages.*
- *discuss the history of electronic spreadsheet packages.*
- *discuss the features of the VisiCalc and Framework spreadsheet software packages.*
- *discuss the features and application capabilities of the Lotus 1-2-3 spreadsheet software package.*
- *describe in detail the five diskettes that make up the Lotus 1-2-3 spreadsheet software package.*

INTRODUCTION

Contrary to common belief, the use of spreadsheets in business is not a new concept. For years, accountants and financial analysts used a tool known as a **worksheet** or **spreadsheet**—a sheet of paper divided into columns of figures representing different entities. These figures could be recalculated or modified whenever changes occurred in the assumptions used to generate the original figures. This recalculation had to be done with a calculator, which was tedious and time consuming, particularly when the user had to deal with a worksheet with many columns and numerous items within each column.

A few years after the introduction of microcomputers, business people discovered that the entire process of spreadsheet analysis could be performed more easily on microcomputers. This discovery led to the advent of the electronic spreadsheet software package, which many experts believe has been the backbone of modern microcomputer use in the business community.

This chapter provides an overview of spreadsheet analysis, including the concept of electronic spreadsheets, a brief history of spreadsheet software packages, a survey of popular spreadsheet software packages, and finally, an introduction to the Lotus 1-2-3 software package and its components. Chapter 9 describes in detail some of the Lotus 1-2-3 features.

■ AN EXAMPLE OF A SPREADSHEET

Before we get into a discussion of electronic spreadsheets and how different microcomputer spreadsheet software packages work, you should learn how to use a manual spreadsheet. Let's assume that you have been assigned to make a two-year income projection for Sunshine Window Inc., Suppliers (SWIS), where you are working as a financial analyst. Here are the figures you will need for this projection:

	1989
Sales	460,000
Commission	– ?
Net Sales	?
Cost of Goods Sold (COGS)	– ?
Gross Profit	?
Tax	– ?
Net Profit	?

In this case, all you have been given is the 1989 sales total and the following assumptions to calculate the other missing figures.

1. Sales will grow annually on a ten percent basis.
2. Five percent of the total sales goes to commission.
3. Net sales equal total sales minus commission.
4. Fifty percent of the total sales cover the company's cost of goods sold.
5. Gross profit is cost of goods sold minus gross sales.
6. Forty percent of the gross profits is paid as taxes.
7. Net profit is taxes minus taxable profit.

Let's further assume that, for ease of calculating, you have devised a table of columns and rows, separated from each other by vertical and horizontal lines. As a result, you ended up with many little boxes, which you have numbered according to row and column position (rows are numbered 1 through 17, columns are lettered A through D). You read these columns and rows as A1, B1, C1, D1, A2, B2, and so on. Figure 8.1 illustrates such a worksheet.

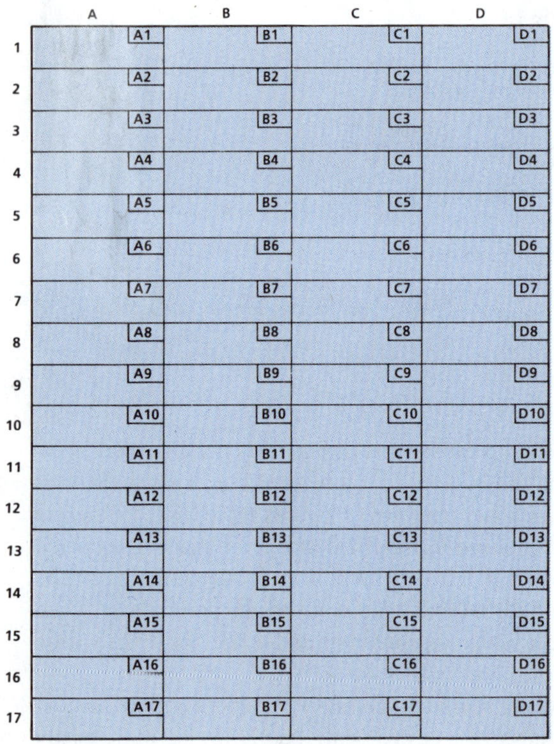

Figure 8.1
A Blank Worksheet

	A	B	C	D
1	A1 ITEM	B1	C1	D1
2	A2	B2	C2	D2
3	A3 ANNUAL GROWTH RATE	B3 .10	C3	D3
4	A4 COMMISSION RATE	B4 .05	C4	D4
5	A5 COST OF GOODS SOLD RATE	B5 .50	C5	D5
6	A6 TAX RATE	B6 .40	C6	D6
7	A7	B7	C7	D7
8	A8	B8 1987	C8 1988	D8 1989
9	A9	B9	C9	D9
10	A10 SALES	B10 460,000	C10 ?	D10 ?
11	A11 COMMISSION	B11 ?	C11 ?	D11 ?
12	A12 NET SALES	B12 ?	C12 ?	D12 ?
13	A13 COST OF GOODS SOLD RATE	B13 ?	C13 ?	D13 ?
14	A14 GROSS PROFIT	B14 ?	C14 ?	D14 ?
15	A15 TAX	B15 ?	C15 ?	D15 ?
16	A16 NET PROFIT	B16 ?	C16 ?	D16 ?
17	A17	B17	C17	D17

Figure 8.2
A Worksheet with Labels and Figures

Let's say that you have arranged all the labels and figures for this sales projection project in the different boxes of your worksheet as shown in Figure 8.2. Now, to calculate the missing values, all you have to do is use the assumptions given. (In the remainder of our discussion, we will refer to each figure by its position in the worksheet.) For example, to calculate commissions, we take the sales figure in box B10 and multiply it by the commissions rate in box B3. Then, we could calculate net sales by subtracting B11 (commissions) from B10 (sales). Once we have calculated all the figures for 1989, we can calculate the 1990 sales, which are expected to be ten percent over 1989 sales (1989 sales [$460,000] times annual growth rate [.10], added to 1989 sales [$460,000], or [B10 times B3] plus B10). The rest of the figures for 1990 can be calculated using the given rates. Finally, 1991 sales and all other 1991 figures can be calculated in the same fashion as those for 1990. Figure 8.3 illustrates these calculations.

So far the task does not appear to be tedious but rather very straight forward. However, if one assumption changes—say, the annual growth rate prediction becomes fifteen percent instead of ten percent—we have to recalculate all the items again, as shown in Figure 8.4 on the following page.

What if the company decides to increase its commission rate to seven percent? We need to recalculate all the figures again! As you can see, the task of recalculating every time there is a change could be very time consuming and tedious, particularly if you are dealing with many items and figures.

	A	B	C	D
1	A1 ITEM	B1	C1	D1
2	A2	B2	C2	D2
3	A3 ANNUAL GROWTH RATE	B3 .10	C3	D3
4	A4 COMMISSION RATE	B4 .05	C4	D4
5	A5 COST OF GOODS SOLD RATE	B5 .50	C5	D5
6	A6 TAX RATE	B6 .40	C6	D6
7	A7	B7	C7	D7
8	A8	B8 1987	C8 1988	D8 1989
9	A9	B9	C9	D9
10	A10 SALES	B10 460,000	C10 506,000 (B10 × B3) + B10	D10 556,600 (C10 × B3) + C10
11	A11 COMMISSION	B11 23,000 B10 × B4	C11 25,300 C10 × B4	D11 27,830 D10 × B4
12	A12 NET SALES	B12 437,000 B10–B11	C12 480,700 C10–C11	D12 528,770 D10–D11
13	A13 COST OF GOODS SOLD (COGS)	B13 230,000 B10 × B5	C13 253,000 C10 × B5	D13 278,300 D10 × B5
14	A14 GROSS PROFIT	B14 207,000 B12–B13	C14 227,700 C12–C13	D14 250,470 D12–D13
15	A15 TAX	B15 82,800 B14 × B6	C15 91,080 C14 × B6	D15 100,188 D14 × B6
16	A16 NET PROFIT	B16 124,200 B14–B15	C16 136,620 C14–C15	D16 150,282 D14–D15
17	A17	B17	C17	D17

Figure 8.3
A Worksheet with Formulas

	A	B	C	D
1	ITEM [A1]	[B1]	[C1]	[D1]
2	[A2]	[B2]	[C2]	[D2]
3	ANNUAL GROWTH RATE [A3]	.15 [B3]	[C3]	[D3]
4	COMMISSION RATE [A4]	.05 [B4]	[C4]	[D4]
5	COST OF GOODS SOLD RATE [A5]	.50 [B5]	[C5]	[D5]
6	TAX RATE [A6]	.40 [B6]	[C6]	[D6]
7	[A7]	[B7]	[C7]	[D7]
8	[A8]	1987 [B8]	1988 [C8]	1989 [D8]
9	[A9]	[B9]	[C9]	[D9]
10	SALES [A10]	460,000 [B10]	529,000 (B10 × B3) + B10 [C10]	608,350 (C10 × B3) + C10 [D10]
11	COMMISSION [A11]	23,000 B10 × B4 [B11]	26,450 C10 × B4 [C11]	30,417.50 D10 × B4 [D11]
12	NET SALES [A12]	437,000 B10–B11 [B12]	502,550 C10–C11 [C12]	577,932.50 D10–D11 [D12]
13	COST OF GOODS SOLD (COGS) [A13]	230,000 B10 × B5 [B13]	264,500 C10 × B5 [C13]	304,175 D10 × B5 [D13]
14	GROSS PROFIT [A14]	207,000 B12–B13 [B14]	238,050 C12–C13 [C14]	273,757.50 D12–D13 [D14]
15	TAX [A15]	82,800 B14 × B6 [B15]	95,220 C14 × B6 [C15]	109,503 D14 × B6 [D15]
16	NET PROFIT [A16]	124,200 B14–B15 [B16]	142,830 C14–C15 [C16]	164,254.50 D14–D15 [D16]
17	[A17]	[B17]	[C17]	[D17]

Figure 8.4
The New Calculation for a Fifteen Percent Sales Growth

The use of spreadsheets can be greatly facilitated by microcomputers and spreadsheet analysis software packages. Spreadsheet software packages allow the user to create a worksheet on the screen of a microcomputer and to enter all the figures and relationships between boxes in the form of equations, the same way we worked out Sunshine Window Inc., Suppliers' two-year income projection. The difference between an electronic spreadsheet and a manual spreadsheet is that, with an electronic spreadsheet, changes can be incorporated in a matter of a few seconds. For example, in our SWIS case, recalculating all the figures for a fifteen percent sales growth rate instead of ten percent would only require changing the initial sales growth rate in box B3 from '.10' to '.15'. This change would cause the computer to recalculate all the figures because all the relationships between boxes have already been established.

An **electronic spreadsheet** is a collection of interrelated boxes, better known as **cells**, for different figures, labels, or equations and formulas. In electronic spreadsheets, the computer's memory is put to work, replacing the traditional worksheet paper and calculator. Since the introduction of the first spreadsheet software package, thousands of applications have been developed: business planning, project planning, and investment analysis. Furthermore, these packages have been used in payroll calculations, accounts receivable, accounts payable, and inventory management.

■ A BRIEF HISTORY OF THE ELECTRONIC SPREADSHEET

The first electronic spreadsheet software package, called **VisiCalc** was designed for the Apple II computer by a Harvard University student named Dan Bricklin in 1978. Soon after its introduction, VisiCalc began to be called a landmark in the history of microcomputers. As a matter of fact, this package can be considered the father of modern microcomputer software packages. In the late 1970s, when many business people were skeptical of the applicability of microcomputers for business tasks and decisions, VisiCalc became the first practical microcomputer business application.

From 1978 through the early 1980s, VisiCalc—one of the few spreadsheet software packages available for microcomputers—was the best-selling package worldwide. Soon, users demanded more power and additional features that the program was not capable of delivering. Shortly thereafter, many VisiCalc-based software packages with more advanced capabilities—SuperCalc, Microplan, Multiplan, PC-Calc, Lotus 1-2-3, Framework, and Symphony—began to enter the market.

All spreadsheet software packages available today can be divided into three generations, based on their capabilities and features. **First-generation spreadsheet packages,** which include VisiCalc and PC-Calc, were mainly limited to spreadsheet analysis. Later, the market began to demand spreadsheet software packages that could perform other spreadsheet-oriented functions, such as graphics and database management. Eventually, this demand led to the creation of **semi-integrated,** or **second-generation, spreadsheet packages** such as SuperCalc-3 and Lotus 1-2-3. These integrated packages included three different groups of programs in one software package that could be used for spreadsheet analysis, graphics, and database management. The various applications could communicate easily with each other without requiring the user to get into and out of different software environments.

The popularity of these early integrated software packages led to the introduction of a **third-generation** (also called **integrated** or **full-skilled**), **software packages,** such as Framework and Symphony. This last generation offers programs that can be used for word processing, spreadsheets, graphics, database management—even communications. The characteristics of the three generations of spreadsheet software packages are summarized in Table 8.1.

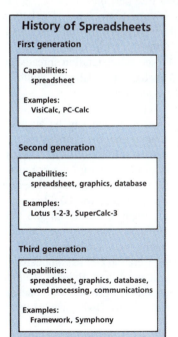

■ POPULAR SPREADSHEET SOFTWARE PACKAGES

Let's look at some examples of a first generation spreadsheet package (VisiCalc), Lotus 1-2-3, and a full-skilled software package (Framework). Afterwards, we'll concentrate on our major spreadsheet package, Lotus 1-2-3.

VisiCalc

As mentioned earlier, VisiCalc is considered the first practical business application software package developed for microcomputers. VisiCalc, designed by Dan Bricklin, who eventually formed VisiCalc Corporation, was intended for use on the family of Apple II computers developed around the 8-bit 6502 microprocessor. Different versions of VisiCalc were later developed for other machines, such as the Commodore PET and Radio Shack TRS-80, but not for the IBM-PC and clones, which are

TABLE 8.1 Characteristics of Three Generations of Spreadsheet Software Packages

based on the 16-bit microprocessor. The unavailability of VisiCalc for the PC was perhaps the major contributing factor in this spreadsheet software package's decline. Furthermore, the original package was only capable of providing a spreadsheet with a maximum of 63 columns and 254 rows. VisiCalc's hardware requirements include 64K RAM and a single disk drive, and the package runs under AppleDOS or TRS-DOS.

Framework

The original spreadsheet software package was designed solely for spreadsheet analysis. **Framework** is considered one of the best-known third-generation integrated software packages. Designed by Ashton-Tate, it is capable of handling the diverse applications of word processing, spreadsheets, graphics, database management, and communications—all in one single package. Framework allows the user to switch easily from one application to another without switching programs or diskettes. The package is designed for 16-bit microprocessor-based machines, mainly the IBM-PC and compatibles. It runs under MS-DOS/PC-DOS operating systems. Hardware requirements include 640K RAM and two disk drives, or a hard disk and a single drive. The software package is completely menu-driven.

Lotus 1-2-3

Lotus 1-2-3 is undoubtedly the single most widely used software package ever developed for microcomputers. Although it is not considered a full-skilled integrated package, Lotus 1-2-3 is still the most popular of all integrated packages. The program's popularity can be credited in part to the IBM-PC, but, one could argue that the IBM-PC would have not been as popular as it is without Lotus 1-2-3. The bottom line here is that the IBM-PC and Lotus 1-2-3 together have been the major forces in making microcomputers useful for business applications.

As mentioned earlier, Lotus 1-2-3 is considered a second-generation spreadsheet software package. The applications of Lotus 1-2-3 include spreadsheets, graphics, and database management. Figure 8.5 illustrates these applications.

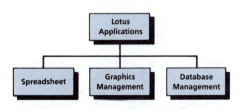

Figure 8.5
Lotus 1-2-3 Applications Chart

All three Lotus 1-2-3 applications reside on a single main program known as 1-2-3, which can be accessed either from the main menu at the time of booting or directly from the master disk of the Lotus 1-2-3 software package. Once the user is in this program environment, all the functions of the three applications can be easily accessed via the menus. For example, you could create a spreadsheet, then develop graphics based on the data stored in the spreadsheet. Finally, you could use the same information to create and manipulate databases.

Since its introduction, Lotus 1-2-3 has appeared in two different versions: Release 1 and Release 2. (The material in Chapter 9 is based on Release 2 of Lotus 1-2-3.) The software package comes in five diskettes: 1-2-3 System Disk, PrintGraph, Utility Disk, Install Library Disk, and A View of 1-2-3.

The 1-2-3 System Disk

The 1-2-3 System Disk contains the entire 1-2-3 program for spreadsheets, graphics, and database management. In addition, an on-line help facility is included on this diskette. The diskette also contains a program called LOTUS.COM, which allows the user to switch from the 1-2-3 System Disk to companion programs on other diskettes without returning to the operating system.

The PrintGraph Disk

You can develop graphics applications through the 1-2-3 System Disk, but they cannot be printed directly from that diskette. Instead, users must save graphics as graphics files on another diskette. Graphics files are printed with the PrintGraph Disk, which contains a separate program designed for printing graphs created under the 1-2-3 System Disk. PrintGraph allows the user to choose a variety of colors and layouts for printed graphs.

The Utility Disk

The programs on the Utility Disk are mainly designed for installing Lotus 1-2-3 on a particular microcomputer. In other words, before a user can operate Lotus 1-2-3, he or she must use the Utility Disk to identify particular characteristics of the hardware in use, such as printer type (e.g., dot matrix or letter-quality) or monitor type (e.g., monochrome or color). The Utility Disk asks the user about different components of the hardware system through the use of menus. You need to perform the installation process only once before using the package for the first time; after that, there is no need to install the program again unless hardware components are changed. In addition to the installation program, the translating program also resides on the Utility Disk, allowing the user to transfer data between 1-2-3 and other software packages.

The Install Library Disk

The Install Library Disk contains a library of programs that can be utilized by the Utility Disk for installation purposes. Therefore, the user will be required to use this disk during the installation process.

A View of 1-2-3

The diskette called A View of 1-2-3 contains an on-line overview of many common 1-2-3 features, which are introduced to the user through tutorial sessions. In addition, many commonly used business applications of Lotus 1-2-3 are demonstrated on this diskette.

■ LOTUS 1-2-3 APPLICATIONS

Lotus 1-2-3 can be used in straightforward, computational applications, such as payroll, accounts receivable, and accounts payable, where the process is known to be structured. In other words, a **structured process** is one in which all the steps are well-defined and no human intervention is necessary during their execution. On the other hand, Lotus 1-2-3 can also be used as a support tool in the decision-making process for those problems in which not all the parameters or assumptions are predefined. This latter category of problems, categorized as **semi-structured processes,** are problems that deal with "what-if?" questions. In this class of problems, Lotus 1-2-3 can play the role of a **Decision Support System (DSS),** where a decision maker provides all the values of the known parameters in the form of a **decision model,** a set of instructions or procedures necessary to solve a problem. The decision maker then tests the model by changing the assumptions and assessing the impact of these changes on the model's overall outcomes. Generally speaking, when Lotus 1-2-3 is used as a decision support tool, there are five distinct components involved in the process, as shown in Figure 8.6.

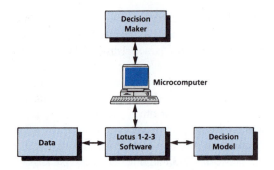

Figure 8.6
Elements of Decision Support Systems with Lotus 1-2-3

The Decision Maker

A **decision maker** is a person who utilizes a program such as Lotus 1-2-3 as a Decision Support System. For example, in the case of Sunshine Window Inc., Suppliers discussed earlier in this chapter, we used a spreadsheet to predict the next two years' profits. Upon entering all the data, the decision maker interacts with the system by changing assumptions and assessing the impact of different changes. The process can continue to the point where the decision maker is satisfied with the overall outcome.

The Microcomputer

The decision maker interacts with Lotus 1-2-3 through a microcomputer. The decision maker enters the model through the keyboard, then enters changes, which are incorporated into the model by Lotus 1-2-3. The results are immediately displayed on the screen for the decision maker's evaluation.

Lotus 1-2-3

This software package is used in conjunction with the microcomputer to provide the necessary communication and computational capabilities to the decision maker. The decision maker interacts with a model established within the 1-2-3 environment. Therefore, the software package can be viewed as a Decision Support System.

The Decision Model

In order to be able to use Lotus 1-2-3 as a DSS, it is essential that you first provide the computer with a decision model. For example, if you as a decision maker wanted to use Lotus 1-2-3 to solve Sunshine Window Inc., Suppliers' two-year profit projection problem, you would enter all the necessary instructions for calculating the figures in the proper cells of a Lotus 1-2-3 spreadsheet. In addition, you would provide all the parameters or assumptions, such as sales growth rate or tax rate. Upon entering the basic instructions, the decision maker could use 1-2-3's capabilities to change any of the assumptions, and have the program recalculate all the figures affected by the changes.

Data

Data for the model you create in the Lotus 1-2-3 environment could be obtained from different sources: from the decision maker through the keyboard, or from a computer data file. It is also possible to provide a portion of the data through the keyboard, and the rest from data file(s). In the case of Sunshine Window Inc., Suppliers, all the data were provided through the keyboard.

SUMMARY

The idea of using worksheets or spreadsheets for accounting and financial applications is an old concept, but it has been only in recent years that microcomputers were recognized as useful tools for spreadsheet analysis. An electronic spreadsheet applies the same concept as a manual worksheet except that the computer's memory is used instead of paper and a calculator.

Generally speaking, a spreadsheet is a collection of interrelated cells used to store data, labels, or formulas and equations. In the past decade, many spreadsheet software packages have been introduced for microcomputer use, beginning with VisiCalc. These packages can be divided into three categories: first-generation packages suitable only for spreadsheet analysis; second-generation packages that could provide other, related applications, such as graphics and database management; and third-generation packages, which provide multiple applications: word processing, spreadsheets, graphics, database management, and communications.

Lotus 1-2-3 falls into the category of second-generation spreadsheet software packages. In the past few years, this package has been used for a variety of applications, ranging from accounts receivable to those problems that deal with "what-if?" questions.

■ Key Terms

spreadsheet or worksheet A sheet of paper divided into columns of figures representing different entities.

electronic spreadsheets Software packages developed for spreadsheet analysis on microcomputers.

cells Interrelated boxes for different figures, labels, or equations and formulas on the electronic spreadsheet.

VisiCalc The first electronic spreadsheet software package; the first microcomputer business application.

first-generation, spreadsheet packages Spreadsheet packages limited to spreadsheet analysis (VisiCalc and PC-Calc).

second-generation, or semi-integrated software packages Integrated software packages capable of performing three different groups of programs in one software package (spreadsheet analysis, graphics, and database management).

third-generation, or full-skilled software packages Software packages that can be used for word processing, spreadsheets, graphics, database management and communications.

Framework One of the best-known third-generation, or full-skilled, integrated software packages.

Lotus 1-2-3 A second-generation spreadsheet software package; the most popular of all microcomputer software packages.

structured process A procedure in which all steps are well-defined and no human intervention is necessary during their execution.

semi-structured process A procedure in which all parameters or assumptions are not predefined; answers "what-if?" questions.

Decision Support System (DSS) A system assisting the decision maker in solving semi-structured problems.

decision model A set of instructions or procedures necessary to solve a problem.

decision maker A person who uses a spreadsheet as a Decision Support System.

■ Review Questions

1. An electronic spreadsheet is a collection of interrelated boxes known as
   (a) cells.
   (b) blocks.
   (c) data.
   (d) blanks.
2. The first electronic spreadsheet software package, VisiCalc, was designed in
   (a) 1960.
   (b) 1975.
   (c) 1978.
   (d) 1980.

3. First-generation spreadsheet packages were
   (a) semi-integrated.
   (b) integrated.
   (c) limited to spreadsheet analysis.
   (d) full-skilled.
4. Second-generation spreadsheet packages were
   (a) user-friendly.
   (b) semi-integrated.
   (c) menu-driven.
   (d) command-driven.
5. Symphony is a _____ , or full-skilled, spreadsheet package.
   (a) third-generation
   (b) second-generation
   (c) semi-integrated
   (d) command-driven
6. Which of the following statements about VisiCalc is false?
   (a) It was originally designed for the Apple II.
   (b) It was designed for the 8-bit microprocessor.
   (c) It was available for the IBM-PC and PC clones.
   (d) It required 64K of RAM.
7. Lotus 1-2-3 is considered a _____ spreadsheet software package.
   (a) third-generation
   (b) second-generation
   (c) first-generation
   (d) command-driven
8. Which of the following Lotus 1-2-3 diskettes allows you to access an on-line help facility?
   (a) The 1-2-3 System Disk
   (b) PrintGraph
   (c) The Utility Disk
   (d) A View of 1-2-3
9. Which of the following Lotus 1-2-3 diskettes is mainly used during installation of Lotus on a particular microcomputer?
   (a) The 1-2-3 System Disk
   (b) PrintGraph
   (c) The Utility Disk
   (d) A View of 1-2-3
10. Which of the following Lotus 1-2-3 diskettes offers tutorial sessions?
    (a) The 1-2-3 System Disk
    (b) PrintGraph
    (c) The Utility Disk
    (d) A View of 1-2-3
11. Which of the following Lotus 1-2-3 diskettes allows the printing of Lotus 1-2-3 graphs?
    (a) The 1-2-3 System Disk
    (b) PrintGraph
    (c) The Utility Disk
    (d) A View of 1-2-3

12. When using Lotus as a Decision Support System, it is essential to first supply the set of instructions or procedures for solving the problem. This is known as a
    (a) decision maker.
    (b) instruction set.
    (c) decision model.
    (d) support model.
13. What applications is Framework capable of handling?
14. What are the application capabilities of Lotus 1-2-3?
15. What diskettes are included in the Lotus 1-2-3 software package?
16. In Lotus 1-2-3, what are "what-if?" questions?
17. When Lotus 1-2-3 is used as a DSS, what are the five components in the process?
18. What are the characteristics of a second-generation spreadsheet program?
19. Lotus 1-2-3 was introduced at about the same time as the IBM-PC, and has been very popular for that reason. Is there any argument that the IBM-PC owes its popularity to Lotus?
20. What is the primary difference between a first-generation spreadsheet software package and second- and third-generation spreadsheets?
21. Lotus 1-2-3 can be used to analyze which of the following types of problems?
    (a) semi-structured
    (b) unstructured
    (c) structured
    (d) (a) and (c)
    (e) (a) and (b)
22. Why did the development of micro-based systems lead naturally to the introduction of electronic spreadsheets?
23. What are some typical business applications of electronic spreadsheets?
24. VisiCalc was originally designed to operate on the _____ microcomputer system.
    (a) TRS-80
    (b) Apple II
    (c) IBM PC-XT
    (d) PET
    (e) WANG
25. A manager is attempting to determine his purchasing requirements to support a manufacturing line. He knows the line's capacity, he has the company's policies for inventory levels (both raw materials and finished goods), and he has a series of projected sales figures from his marketing department. Since he has access to an IBM-PC, he wants to stuff all of this information into the computer and let it figure out what to do. What must this manager do to achieve this goal?

Case One:
FELICIA'S FITNESS SPA

Felicia Ferguson is a health fanatic. She keeps her body in excellent physical condition by running five miles a day and doing exercises and aerobics. During her high school days, Felicia was twenty pounds overweight. She was always conscious of her weight problem but had trouble keeping the extra pounds off.

After graduating from high school, Felicia went on to Finest State University, where she majored in physical education. She lost the twenty pounds and learned to use fitness equipment and exercise to the greatest advantage.

After graduating from college, Felicia opened her own health and fitness center, called Felicia's Fitness Spa. She offered aerobic classes for women and men, and a special one for senior citizens. She had Nautilus equipment, weights, a sauna, a swimming pool, and various other equipment for toning and trimming the human body.

Felicia opened her business with $70,000 inherited from her uncle, and now grosses approximately $12,000 per month in aerobic class tuition, club memberships, and equipment fees. About 200 people use the pool and sauna on a regular basis, and approximately 150 members renew their memberships each month.

Felicia employs five aerobics instructors, two of whom are on the premises at any one time during the spa's operating hours, 8:00 a.m. to 9:00 p.m., Monday through Saturday. The spa is open on Sundays from 12:00 p.m. until 8:00 p.m., but there are no aerobics classes.

Felicia is the owner and manager of the health spa and has two people working in the general office. One does mostly secretarial-type work and the other functions as an office manager, scheduling employee hours and doing some light accounting/bookkeeping work. The office has one computer, which the office manager uses for bookkeeping entries, payroll, and monthly balance sheets.

The computer is an IBM PC-XT with 640K of memory. Susan Blasto, the office manager, uses Lotus 1-2-3 software for all of her accounting functions. The spreadsheets have done away with the traditional analysis tools—the accountant's pad, pencil and calculator—thereby cutting down on tedious and time-consuming manual data and numerical manipulations.

But Susan Blasto finds that payroll processing is still a time-consuming and tedious part of her job. She used to work as a manager in a clothing store, where the payroll was done with the use of a special compiler in a new programming language called "C" to develop tailored programs for payroll processing. She has suggested to Felicia that she would like to utilize this compiler, which Felicia would have to buy, in order to develop a similar payroll program for the spa. Felicia likes the idea of less time being spent on payroll functions with the aid of this compiler.

One day last week, while Felicia was attending a conference, she ran into a colleague, Brenda Brenneman, who manages a department store. Felicia explained to Brenda the proposal of a compiler and the "C" language for payroll processing. Brenneman explained to Felicia that there was a better solution than using a compiler. Brenneman said she uses a program called Lotus 1-2-3, which does not need a special compiler, to do payroll processing. This suggestion by Brenneman prompted Felicia to inquire further into the Lotus 1-2-3 software package.

Felicia, in her investigation, found out that Lotus 1-2-3 is a spreadsheet package and is useful for accounting functions. She still does not know whether 1-2-3 will help in payroll processing.

Questions

1. What is the problem?
2. Is it possible to use Lotus 1-2-3 for other applications besides accounting?
3. What is your recommendation to help solve Susan Blasto's problem?

Case Two: MARCEL & MARGOSIAK

Mary Smith recently graduated from Kans State College with a Master's degree in business. Her undergraduate degree is in accounting. After graduating from Kans, Smith was hired to work with a major accounting firm. She had to move from her small hometown of Elizabethtown to the much larger city of Boston, Massachusetts.

Mary accepted this job with the firm of Marcel & Margosiak during her last month of school and had been eager to get started with her new life in the big city. She moved to Massachusetts two years ago and started her junior accounting position at $35,000 per year. She is now a senior accountant making $60,000 per year. The next promotion will be to junior partner, which she doesn't expect to happen for another five to eight years. Usually, becoming a partner in an accounting firm takes approximately ten years, after which time the partner shares in any partnership monetary benefits above and beyond salary. The profits of the firm are divided—according to seniority and various other means—between the partners.

Marcel & Margosiak is an accounting firm that still utilizes the old-fashioned pencil and paper method of financial analysis and recordkeeping. All records, financial reports, balance sheets, and income statements, are done manually. Since Mary Smith was hired two years ago, she has been trying to talk some of the partners into using an electronic spreadsheet for accounting applications. She has explained the benefits, especially the potential time-saving. She has explained that doing things by hand is a slower and more time-consuming accounting method than using a computerized system in an integrated approach. Melvin Marcel, senior partner and co-owner, is unimpressed. He went to college in the 1950s and is very happy with—and somewhat stubbornly attached to—the pencil and paper method.

On the other hand, Marvin Margosiak, the other co-owner, who also went to college in the '50s, likes the idea of a computerized system because the final output will be much neater than a handwritten page, and the final printout will be available in one-tenth the time it would take to do it in longhand.

Marvin Margosiak wants Mary Smith to attend next month's board meeting to present the advantages of an electronic spreadsheet package. Mary wants to be well-prepared and to be able to talk about one of the best and most widely used spreadsheet software packages.

Questions

1. Imagine that you are Mary and you are at the board meeting. Discuss spreadsheet software packages and how they will benefit this accounting firm.
2. Outline the advantages and disadvantages of electronic spreadsheet packages over manual systems.
3. Among the electronic spreadsheet packages discussed in this chapter, which one is most appropriate for Marcel & Margosiak?

SELECTED BIBLIOGRAPHY

Bissell, J.L., "Spreadsheet Planning and Design," *Journal of Accountancy*, May 1986, p. 110+.
Bodily, S.E., "Spreadsheet Modeling as a Stepping Stone," *Interfaces*, September-October 1986, pp. 34-52.
Brock, T.L., "Cash Flow Statements on Lotus 1-2-3," *Journal of Accountancy*, April 1986, pp. 111-113.
Buell, B. and A.R. Field, "Will Lotus Ever Learn to Count Past 1-2-3," *Business Week*, February 10, 1986, p. 34.
Burke, R.W., "Ten Tips for Getting Started with Electronic Spreadsheets," *The Practical Accountant*, May 1986, pp. 75-8+.
Chew, R.L. and R. Goel, "Transaction Processing Using Lotus 1-2-3," *Journal of Systems Management*, January 1987, pp. 30-4.
Haynes, J.L., "Circuit Design with Lotus 1-2-3," Byte, Fall 1985, pp. 143-6+.
_____, "How Do Spreadsheet Programs Compare?" *Journal of Accountancy*, December 1985, p. 142+.
Klahr, C., "Using Expert Spreadsheets on a Personal Computer Can Help Save You on Long-Distance Circuit Costs," *Communications News*, April 1986, p. 28.
_____, "Lotus 1-2-3 Still Tops," *Computer Decisions*, June 3, 1986, p. 30.
Ludlow, W.J., "Entering the Micro Age Using the PC to Improve Personal Productivity," *Credit and Financial Management*, January 1987, pp. 25-6.
McCartney, L., "The Spreadsheet Clones Put Pressure on Lotus," *Business Month*, March 1987, pp. 77-8.
Malloch, H., "Manpower Modeling with Computer Spreadsheets," *Personnel Management*, May 1986, pp. 44-6.
Micossi, A., "Lotus Links: Not as Easy as 1-2-3," *Computer Decisions*, June 4, 1985, p. 16+.
_____, "Microcomputer Spreadsheets: Their Use and Abuses," *Journal of Accountancy*, June 1985, pp. 90-3.
Patterson, W., "Does 1-2-3 Still Add Up?" *Industry Week*, December 9 1985, pp. 64-5+.
Peterson, D.J., "Maximizing the Power of an Electronic Spreadsheet," *Online*, November 1986, pp. 102-4.
_____, "Setting Sights on 1-2-3," *Sales and Marketing Management*, January 13, 1986, p. 34.
_____, "Spreadsheets: Lotus Standard," *Banker*, September 1985, p. 116.
Szandrowski, R.A., "Electronic Spreadsheet Modeling: The Microcomputer Financial Tool of the Century," *Credit and Financial Management*, May 1986, pp. 25-6+.

chapter 9

Using Lotus 1-2-3

After completing this chapter, you should be able to

- describe the features of a Lotus 1-2-3 worksheet.
- discuss how to use the keyboard keys to move around in a worksheet.
- discuss the rules for entering data into a worksheet.
- discuss in detail the 1-2-3 commands and their sublevels.
- describe the difference between absolute and relative cell addressing.
- describe how to create and format a worksheet.
- describe how to copy formulas or move data from one area of the worksheet to another.
- describe the use of 1-2-3 @ functions.
- discuss the procedure to print a worksheet.
- describe the process of saving and retrieving files with the /FILE command.

INTRODUCTION

In this chapter, you will learn how to use the Lotus 1-2-3 spreadsheet software package. The chapter starts with an introduction to 1-2-3 and its components, followed by a simple spreadsheet example that will allow you to become acquainted with different features of the Lotus 1-2-3 software package. (Appendix E explains the graphics capabilities of Lotus 1-2-3 in addition to database management and other advanced features.)

CHAPTER NINE   USING LOTUS 1-2-3

■ GETTING STARTED

Booting the System

If the microcomputer you are working on has only one disk drive, we will refer to it as Drive A. If you have two disk drives, and they are configured horizontally, then the left one is Drive A and the right one is Drive B. If the two drives are configured vertically, then the one on top will be Drive A and the bottom one will be referred to as Drive B.

Now follow these five easy steps to start up the microcomputer—referred to as a cold boot when you begin with the power off—and enter the Lotus 1-2-3 environment.

Step 1.   Insert the DOS diskette into Drive A and close the disk drive door.

Step 2.   Turn the computer on. The power switch is located on the rear right side of the computer. The computer will take from three to forty-five seconds to run through a system check.

Step 3.   Respond to the date prompt that appears on the screen. To change the current date, enter today's date in the format indicated and press the ENTER (↵) key. If you want to accept the date as it appears, simply press ENTER. You will be presented with a similar message for the current time. Respond by pressing the ENTER key to accept, or type the current time in the format indicated, and press ENTER.

Step 4.   When the DOS prompt, A> (pronounced "A prompt"), appears on the screen, remove the DOS diskette from Drive A and insert the Lotus 1-2-3 system diskette in Drive A. (Don't forget to close the disk drive door again.) Insert a blank formatted diskette on which to save your LOTUS spreadsheet files in Drive B. (For complete instructions on formatting a diskette, see Chapter 5, FORMAT command.)

Step 5.   Type LOTUS, and press the ENTER key. After several seconds, the Lotus Access System Command Menu will appear as shown in Figure 9.1 on the following page.

The menu items are listed on the top row of the display. Use the LEFT (←) and RIGHT ARROW keys (→) to move the menu pointer (the highlighted area) to highlight the item you would like to select. Use the ARROW keys to highlight "1-2-3" if the menu pointer is not already there. Now press the ENTER key to make your selection.

When an empty Lotus 1-2-3 worksheet appears on the screen, your screen will look like the one in Figure 9.2 on the following page.

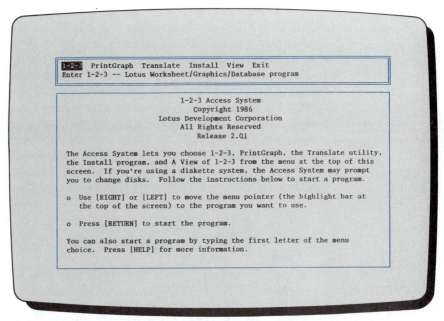

Figure 9.1
The Lotus 1-2-3 Welcome Screen

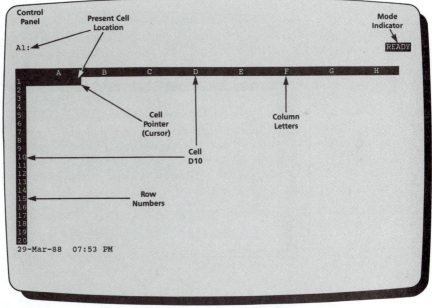

Figure 9.2
A Lotus 1-2-3 Worksheet

The letters A through H across the top of the worksheet label the columns, and the numbers 1 through 20 down the left side of the worksheet label the rows; together they constitute the worksheet border. Although you are only able to see eight columns and twenty rows on the screen, there are actually 256 columns and 8,192 rows available to you. The columns are lettered A through Z followed by AA through AZ and so forth, with the last column being IV.

The box formed by the meeting of a column and a row is called a **cell.** The **cell pointer,** or **cursor,** as it is often called, is the rectangular highlighted area positioned in the upper left corner of the worksheet under the letter A and beside the number 1. The terms *pointer* and *cursor* will be used interchangeably throughout this chapter.

At this time, you should have a clean worksheet on the screen in front of you. You can see for yourself the maximum number of columns (IV) and rows (8,192) available by following these steps.

- Locate the UP (↑), DOWN (↓), LEFT (←), and RIGHT (→) ARROW keys on the right side of the keyboard (on the 2, 4, 6, and 8 keys of the numerical pad).
- Press the END key located on the lower right-hand side of the keyboard, then press the RIGHT ARROW key once. These actions move the pointer to the extreme right edge of the worksheet.
- Press the END key once again, then press the DOWN ARROW key once. These keystrokes move the pointer to the lower right corner of the worksheet. The worksheet's border of columns and rows should look like those in Figure 9.3.

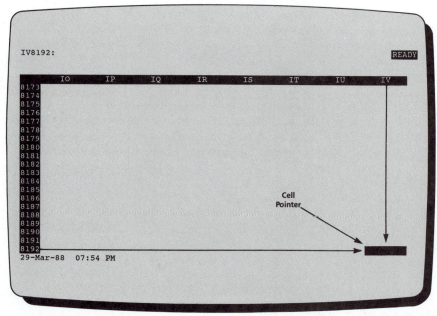

Figure 9.3
The Farthest Reaches of a 1-2-3 Worksheet

- To return to the upper left corner of the worksheet where you began, press the HOME key, which is located on the upper right-hand side of the numerical pad of the keyboard.

What is a Cell?

The worksheet is made up of cells. A cell is a unique address that distinguishes each location in the worksheet from all others. A particular cell address is located by finding the intersection of a particular row with a particular column. For example, to find cell D10 (refer to the worksheet in Figure 9.2 on page 217), you would follow column D down until you reached the point where it intersected (crossed) row 10; that particular location would be called cell D10.

Let's try to locate cell D10.

- The pointer should be in the upper left corner of the worksheet (if it is not there, press the HOME key).
- Press the DOWN (↓) ARROW key nine times.
- Press the RIGHT ARROW key three times. The pointer is now situated in the cell labeled D10.
- To return to the upper left corner of the worksheet, press the HOME key once.

Mode Indicators

Notice the word "READY" in the upper right-hand corner of the worksheet. This is the **mode indicator** area that lets you know the current status of your 1-2-3 worksheet. Table 9.1 lists some of the more common mode indicators that will be displayed at different times while you are working in 1-2-3.

MODE INDICATOR	DESCRIPTION
READY	Lotus 1-2-3 is waiting for you to enter a command.
LABEL	Tells you the entry you are making is a label.
VALUE	Tells you the entry you are making is a number or a formula.
EDIT	You are currently editing, or changing, a cell's contents with 1-2-3's EDIT feature.
ERROR	You have tried to enter something that 1-2-3 could not accept; press the ESC or ENTER key to clear it.
HELP	You are currently in the HELP feature.
POINT	You are using the pointer method of pointing to a cell or a range of cells.
WAIT	A command is being processed and 1-2-3 cannot accept another command at this time.
MENU	A menu is currently being displayed and you are to make a selection.
FIND	You are in the database management feature and a query is being processed.

TABLE 9.1 *Some 1-2-3 Mode Indicators*

Status Indicators

There are several **status indicators** that may appear at the bottom right-hand corner of your 1-2-3 screen. These indicators tell you when the CAPS LOCK, NUM LOCK, END, insert (OVR), or SCROLL LOCK keys have been pressed. In addition, the status indicators tell you when formulas in your worksheet need to be recalculated by displaying *CALC*, or when a macro is being executed by displaying *CMD*.

■ THE KEYBOARD

The keyboard layout for the IBM-PC is shown in Figure 9.4.

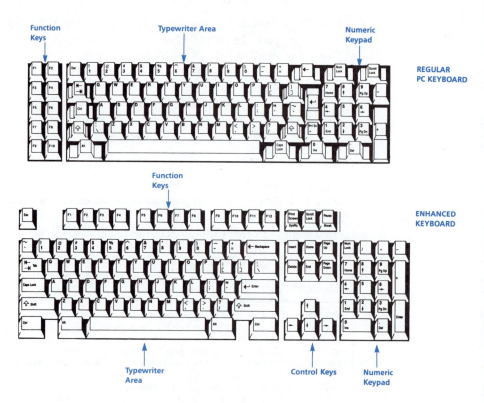

Figure 9.4
Two Versions of the IBM-PC Keyboard

The keyboard can be divided into three sections. The left side of the keyboard contains the ten function keys (F1 through F10), which perform special tasks in 1-2-3. The center of the keyboard closely resembles a typewriter keyboard, with the exception of a few keys (ESC, CTRL, ALT, PrtSc) that are explained below. The numeric keypad is located on the right side of the keyboard. These keys control pointer movement. When the NUM LOCK key (located at the top of this section) is pressed, the keys on the right side function as a numeric keypad. When the NUM LOCK key is pressed a second time, this feature is released.

The keys in the center and on the right side of the keyboard are listed in Table 9.2 along with the function each performs.

KEY	DESCRIPTION
ESC	The ESCAPE key allows you to "back out" of the current command; the current entry is cancelled.
TAB ⊢ ⊣	Moves the pointer one screen to the right. When used in conjunction with the SHIFT key, it moves the pointer one screen to the left.
CTRL	The CONTROL key, when used in conjunction with the SCROLL LOCK key (located in the top right corner), will cancel the present command and return you to READY mode. When used in combination with either the LEFT or RIGHT ARROW keys, the pointer is moved one whole screen to the left or right.
SHIFT	Used to change the center section of the keyboard to uppercase letters and characters.
ALT	Changes the meaning of the letter keys. ALT can also be used to begin a keyboard macro.
BACKSPACE ←	Erases the last character you typed, the character to the left of the cursor.
ENTER ↵	Sends the present command or information to 1-2-3.
PRTSC	The PRINT SCREEN command, when used with the SHIFT key, sends a copy of the present screen to the printer.
CAPS LOCK	When pressed, all the letters are typed as uppercase; when pressed again, returns letters to lowercase.
INS	In the edit mode, the INSERT key allows switching back and forth between inserting characters in existing text and typing over existing text.
NUM LOCK	When pressed, changes the keys on the right side of the keyboard to a numeric keypad; when pressed a second time, the feature is released.
SCROLL LOCK	Used in conjunction with the CTRL key (see CTRL key above).
HOME	Returns the pointer to the upper left corner of the worksheet.
PGUP	Moves the pointer up one full screen.
PGDN	Moves the pointer down one full screen.
↑	(UP ARROW) Moves the pointer up one cell.
↓	(DOWN ARROW) Moves the pointer down one cell.
→	(RIGHT ARROW) Moves the pointer one cell to the right.
←	(LEFT ARROW) Moves the pointer one cell to the left.
END	When used in combination with HOME, moves the pointer to the lower right-hand corner of the worksheet; when used in conjunction with one of the ARROW keys, moves the pointer to the next non-blank cell in that direction.
DEL	The DELETE key erases the character under the cursor.
/	The SLASH activates the menu of commands.
.	The PERIOD is used to anchor down the beginning of a range.
\	The BACKSLASH is used to copy the character that follows into the cell. For example, \- would fill the current cell with dashes (-). Handy for creating lines between sections of the spreadsheet.

TABLE 9.2 Summary of 1-2-3 Keys Function

Several of these keys are used frequently. Follow the exercises below to familiarize yourself with these keys and their functions.

- Press the HOME key to move the pointer to cell A1.
- Press the TAB key (→|) to move the pointer one screen to the right.

- Hold down the SHIFT key and press the TAB key (|←) to move the pointer one screen to the left.
- Locate the PGDN key and press it once. The pointer is moved down one full "page."
- Locate the PGUP key and press it once to move the pointer back up to the first screen of the worksheet.

Function Keys

The ten **function keys** (F1 through F10), which are located on the left side of the keyboard, are listed and described in Table 9.3.

FUNCTION KEY		DESCRIPTION
F1	HELP	This function can be used whenever you need help with your current operation or with the current menu options. A HELP screen will be displayed with a menu of additional information. Press the ESC key to return to your worksheet when you are finished.
F2	EDIT	Activates the EDIT mode so the contents of a cell can be modified; eliminates the need for having to retype the entire cell. Use BACKSPACE and DEL keys to erase unneeded characters, arrow keys to move along the edit line, and insert a character by typing the character at the cursor.
F3	NAME	Displays a list of range names being used in the current worksheet. If F3 is pressed a second time, a full screen display of range names will appear.
F4	ABS	Used to define a cell as an absolute value.
F5	GOTO	Used to quickly move the pointer to any cell in the worksheet. After pressing the function key, type the cell location to move to and press ENTER (↵).
F6	WINDOW	When the window is split, F6 moves the pointer to the other side of the window.
F7	QUERY	Allows you to repeat the most recent query operation when using the Database feature.
F8	TABLE	Allows you to repeat the most recent data table operation.
F9	CALC	Recalculates the worksheet formulas when the worksheet is not set to do recalculations automatically.
F10	GRAPH	Redraws the graph most recently defined.

TABLE 9.3   Summary of 1-2-3 Function Keys

Choosing Menu Structures and Options

All the functions and commands of 1-2-3 are selected from a wide range of available menus. You can access the main menu easily by pressing the SLASH (/) key located at the right side of the keyboard below the '?'. Once you are in the main menu, you can choose an option by using the RIGHT and LEFT ARROW keys to move the highlighted cursor over the desired option. There is a good chance that the option you choose will provide you with a menu of its own, and you can again choose an option in the new menu by using the ARROW keys. The other method of choosing an option is by pressing the first letter of the option name. For example, if you want to save a worksheet, you would type / (to obtain the menu) *F* (FILE option) and *S* (SAVE a file), /FS. As you go through the sessions of this chapter, you will be introduced to different levels of menus and their options.

The 1-2-3 Command Menu

The main command menu of 1-2-3 is activated by pressing the SLASH (/) key. When the SLASH is pressed, the main menu is displayed on the control panel at the top of the worksheet, as illustrated in Figure 9.5.

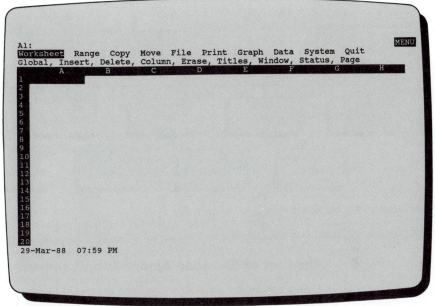

Figure 9.5
Lotus 1-2-3's Main Command Menu

To make a selection from the main command menu, use the LEFT and RIGHT ARROW keys to highlight your choice; then press ENTER or simply type the first letter of the command you choose. For example, if you want to select the WORKSHEET option by the latter method, you would type /W.

- Press the / key once.
- Use the LEFT and RIGHT ARROW keys to move back and forth across the menu line.

As you move across the main menu on the first line of the control panel, notice what is displayed on the panel's second line. For each command highlighted by the pointer on the first line, a menu of subcommands is presented on the second line.

To back out of the main menu or any of its sublevels, simply use the ESCAPE (ESC) key.

- Try choosing one of the main menu options on the first line of the control panel by typing the first letter of the command for example, *W* for Worksheet.

- Choose any of the options from the next sublevel of the command you chose by typing that command's first letter.
- To back out of the command menu and return to the worksheet, press the ESC key three times.

The complete hierarchy of 1-2-3 commands is presented in Figure 9.6. A detailed description of the subcommands will be presented as each command is introduced.

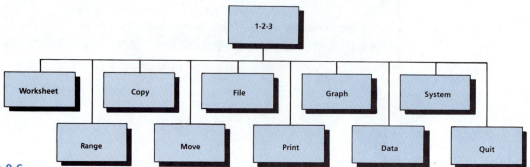

Figure 9.6
The Hierarchy of 1-2-3 Commands

The Case of Sunshine Window Inc., Suppliers

In this part of the chapter, you will be instructed to set up your own spreadsheet in Lotus 1-2-3. You will create a spreadsheet for Sunshine Window Inc., Suppliers (SWIS). The company currently represents five major manufacturing firms and their products. Sales for the past four quarters have been generated and broken down according to their respective firms. At this point, management is interested in assessing the performance of the different firms in different quarters. Carefully follow the instructions given below. *Note*: Throughout this chapter, we use this case to teach you how to use Lotus 1-2-3 to solve real-life problems. Make sure you apply the instructions for this case *only* where you are told to refer *Back to the Case of SWIS*.

- Begin with the pointer at cell A1 (press the HOME key if the pointer is not in cell A1). "READY" appears as the current mode indicator, telling you that 1-2-3 is ready to accept a command.
- Press the SLASH (/) key to invoke the main menu of commands. (Do not worry about the actual commands; they will be explained later.)
- The mode indicator now reads "MENU," as illustrated in Figure 9.7 on the following page.
- Press the ESC key, (located on the upper left side of the keyboard), to exit the main menu. The mode indicator has now returned to "READY."
- Press the CAPS LOCK key, located on the bottom of the keyboard to the right of the spacebar, to allow the typing of all uppercase letters throughout the

worksheet. Notice the status indicator "CAPS" is displayed in the lower right corner of the worksheet.

- Use the RIGHT ARROW key to move the cursor to cell B1.
- You will give the worksheet the title of *SUNSHINE WINDOW INC., SUPPLIERS.*

Type the first letter: S

Observe the mode indicator. 1-2-3 interprets a cell entry beginning with a letter as a label. The mode indicator has now changed to "LABEL," as shown in Figure 9.8.

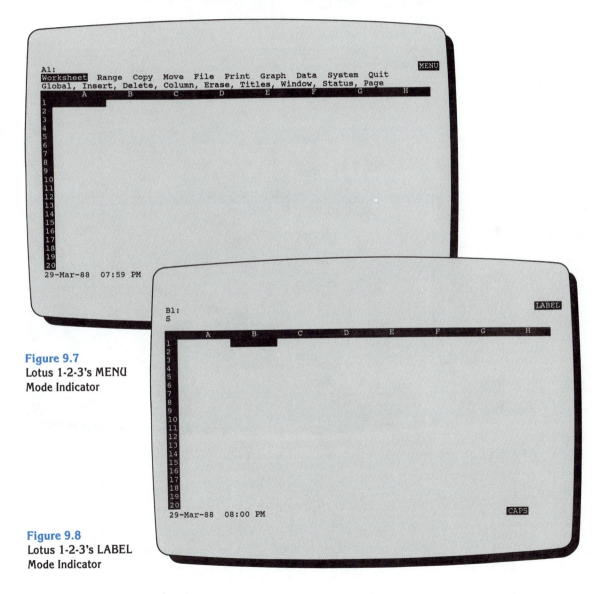

Figure 9.7
Lotus 1-2-3's MENU Mode Indicator

Figure 9.8
Lotus 1-2-3's LABEL Mode Indicator

- Finish typing the complete heading SUNSHINE WINDOW INC., SUPPLIERS and press ENTER. The mode indicator is once again "READY" to accept the next entry.

Note: If you make a mistake while typing the title, use the BACKSPACE key (←), found on the top row of the keyboard above the ENTER key to erase the characters to the left of the cursor. Then continue typing. Look at your entry carefully to make sure it is correct before you press the ENTER key.

- Press the F5 (GOTO) key.
- Type B2 as the cell you wish to GOTO, and press ENTER. The pointer is now in the B2 cell.
- Type the second line of the heading for the worksheet, SALES BY FIRMS - 1986. Press ENTER.

Your worksheet will now look like the one in Figure 9.9.

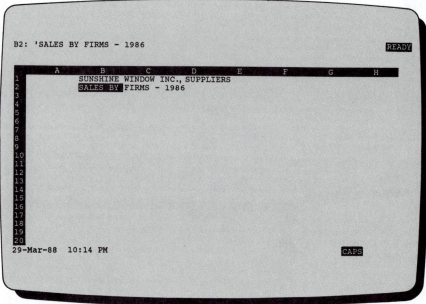

Figure 9.9
The Worksheet with Headings

Correcting Errors while Typing

As mentioned earlier, while you are typing a cell entry and *before* you have pressed the ENTER key, you can use the BACKSPACE key to erase the character to the left of the cursor. Once you have finished a cell entry and press ENTER, there are two methods of making corrections.

- 1-2-3 makes it quite simple to change the contents of a cell. If you decide to change the cell entry, you can simply move the pointer to the cell to be corrected and retype the entry. The new information will replace the old information. If you decide that a cell's contents should be cleared, move the pointer to that particular cell and press the SPACEBAR once. 1-2-3 will interpret this as a new entry, and the cell will be changed to a blank cell.
- If a cell entry is quite long or involved and only one or two characters are in error, you might not want to retype the entire entry. In this case, the EDIT mode can be invoked by pressing the F2 function key. When F2 is pressed, a copy of the cell's contents is displayed on the second line of the control panel. You will see a blinking cursor just after the data displayed. You may now begin editing the information using the following keys.

HOME	Moves cursor to beginning of line
END	Moves cursor to end of line
ARROW keys	Move cursor left and right along the line
BACKSPACE	Erases character to the left of cursor
DEL	Erases character under cursor
ESC	Cancels EDIT mode and returns to worksheet without any changes

Back to the Case of SWIS

You realize that you have inadvertently typed the wrong year in the second line of the heading—1986, when you meant to type 1989. It would seem senseless to retype the entire entry for the sake of changing one character, so you decide to correct the cell by using the EDIT mode.

- While the cursor is positioned at cell B2, press the function key F2 to activate the EDIT mode. (Notice the mode indicator now reads EDIT.)
- Use the LEFT ARROW key to position the cursor on the number 6 in *1986*.
- Press DEL once to erase the number *6*.
- Type the number 9. (See Figure 9.10 on the following page for the worksheet display during the EDIT process.)
- When you are certain the line is correct, press ENTER to return to the worksheet.

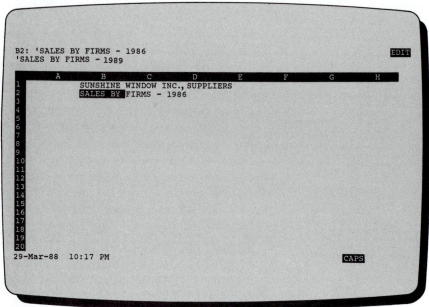

Figure 9.10
The Worksheet in EDIT Mode

■ RULES FOR ENTERING DATA

There are three types of information that can be entered into a cell: numbers or values, formulas, or labels.

Entering Numbers

1. Numbers can only begin with: 0 1 2 3 4 5 6 7 8 9 . $.
2. Numbers can end with a % sign, which tells 1-2-3 to divide by 100.
3. Numbers may have only one decimal point (.).
4. Numbers may be entered in scientific notation.

Entering Formulas

1. If 1-2-3 is to recognize a formula, the entry must begin with one of the following characters:
   + − (@ # $
2. To enter a formula, you may type in the formula directly. To do so, you will place the pointer in the cell where the formula is to be entered and type the formula. The alternative method is called the **pointing method,** where you

use the ARROW keys to move the pointer to the cell locations involved in the operation.
3. The valid operators for formulas include:
   - ^   exponentiation
   - *, /   multiplication and division
   - +, -   addition and subtraction

The order in which the operations in a formula are performed is important. The precedence of the operations is explained below.

1. Parentheses ( ) have first precedence and can override the order of operations.
2. All exponentiation (^) is performed second, in left-to-right order.
3. Multiplication (*) and division (/) are evaluated third, in left-to-right order.
4. Finally, addition (+) and subtraction (–) are performed in left-to-right order.

For example, the formula 5/5*(3+2)–4 would be evaluated as
1. Add 3+2.
2. Divide 5 by 5 and multiply the result times the result of 3+2.
3. Subtract 4.

Entering Labels

1. Labels are usually used for headings. They can be as long as 240 characters and contain any alphabetic or numeric characters.
2. When typing an entry into a cell, if the entry does not contain any of the beginning characters for a number or formula, 1-2-3 reads the entry as a label. The indicator mode will change to LABEL.
3. You can right-justify, left-justify, center, or repeat characters by beginning the label with one of the following characters.
   - '   left-justify
   - "   right-justify
   - ^   center
   - \   repeats a character across the entire cell

The default setting is left-justification. When 1-2-3 recognizes a label, it automatically places a single quote (') in front of the label for left-justification unless you indicate otherwise.

4. You might have a problem if you want to use a number as a label—for instance, placing the year 1988 in a heading as the first word in your worksheet. To solve this problem, simply precede the figure with a single quote (') so 1-2-3 will recognize it as a label. For example, the date could be entered as '1988 to left-justify the label, or "1988 to right-justify the label in the cell.

Back to the Case of SWIS

Now let's finish typing the labels in our worksheet example.

- Use the ARROW keys to move the pointer to cell B4.
- Type "1ST QTR and press the RIGHT ARROW key once to move to cell C4. The label will be right-justified in the cell. Notice that the first character is " because the first character of *1ST QTR* is a numerical character or digit.
- In cell C4, type "2ND QTR and press RIGHT ARROW once.
- In cell D4, type "3RD QTR and press RIGHT ARROW once.
- In cell E4, type "4TH QTR and press the ENTER key once.
- Press F5 and type A6 as the cell to GOTO and press ENTER.
- In cell A6, type BOB & SON and press the DOWN ARROW key once.
- In cell A7, type DAYLIGHT and press DOWN ARROW once.
- In cell A8, type GLASSY and press DOWN ARROW once.
- In cell A9, type PROTECT and press DOWN ARROW once.
- In cell A10, type SKYLIGHT and press DOWN ARROW three times.
- In cell A13, type TOTAL SALES and press ENTER once.

You have now finished inserting all of the necessary labels into the worksheet; it should look like the one in Figure 9.11.

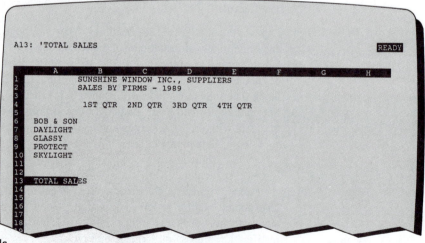

Figure 9.11
Our Worksheet with Labels

Using the conventions for entering numbers into a worksheet, let's insert the values for each division.

- Type the values in the cells as follows. Type the numbers as they appear. *Do not* insert commas; that will be taken care of later. After typing each number, use the ARROW keys to move to the next cell.

In cell:	Type:	In cell:	Type:
B6	16490	D6	19645
B7	11500	D7	12666
B8	27900	D8	31697
B9	20233	D9	20942
B10	60500	D10	54000
C6	16570	E6	18999
C7	11895	E7	12850
C8	26112	E8	33520
C9	18500	E9	21577
C10	40943	E10	46520

Press ENTER after typing the final number. Your worksheet will now look like the one in Figure 9.12.

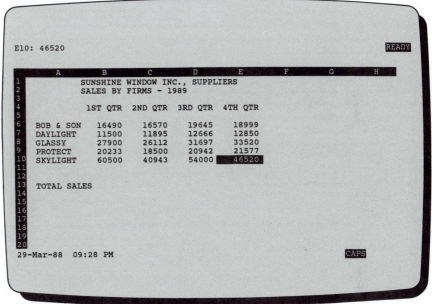

Figure 9.12
Our Worksheet with Values

■ THE /WORKSHEET COMMAND

The WORKSHEET option of the main menu has many choices of its own that can be selected by the 1-2-3 user. Figure 9.13 on the following page illustrates the WORK-SHEET menu and all its sublevel menus and options.

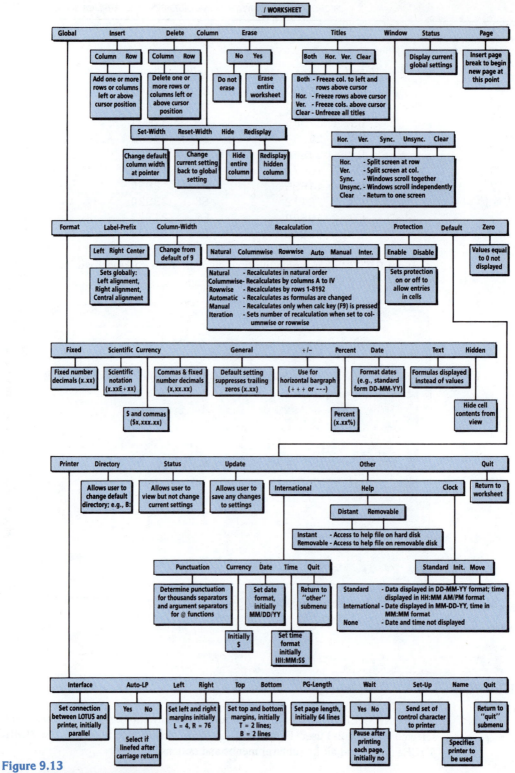

Figure 9.13
Lotus 1-2-3's WORKSHEET Menu and Options

Changing the Column Width

The /WORKSHEET command and several subcommands can be used to change the column width. You can change the column width for just one column or for the entire worksheet. Let's change the column default width of nine to a column width of twelve for the entire worksheet.

Back to the Case of SWIS

- Press / to invoke the main menu.
- Press the letter W to select the Worksheet option.
- Press the letter G to select the GLOBAL option (the term *global* means that the action being performed will be applied to the entire worksheet).
- Press the letter C to select COLUMN-WIDTH.
- Type the number 12 to set the column width to twelve, and press ENTER.

Your worksheet should now look like the one in Figure 9.14.

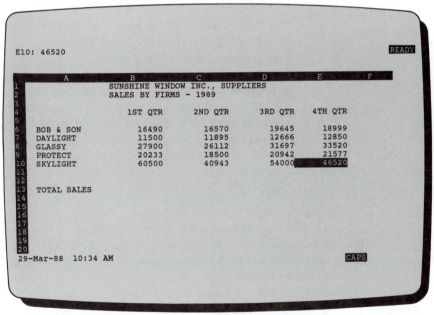

Figure 9.14
Our Worksheet after Setting Column-Width to Twelve

Adding and Deleting Columns or Rows

You will often find it convenient to be able to insert a blank row or column into the worksheet, or to be able to delete an unnecessary row or column. Two options under the /WORKSHEET command make these tasks possible.

Back to the Case of SWIS

To see how to add a column or row, let's insert a blank row before the current row 6 in our SWIS worksheet. Remember, the blank row is always added *before* the current pointer position.

- Place the pointer at cell A6.
- Press / to invoke the main menu.
- Type W to select the WORKSHEET option.
- Type I to select the INSERT option.
- Type R to select ROW.
- In response to the message: "Enter row insert range: A6..A6", press ENTER. In this example, you only want to insert one row; however, to insert more than one row, you would enter a range or rectangular grouping of cells, at this point. Row 6 is now a new blank row, and all subsequent rows have been moved downward.

Now you decide that you do not care for the look of the worksheet with the extra blank row added. Let's practice deleting a row by getting rid of this blank row.

- With the pointer in cell A6, press / to invoke the main menu.
- Type W to select the WORKSHEET option.
- Type D to select the DELETE option.
- Type R to select ROW.
- In response to the message: "Enter range of row to delete: A6..A6", press ENTER. The worksheet is now back in its original state. Again, if you had wanted to delete more than one row, you would have entered the appropriate range of row.

■ THE /COPY COMMAND

The /COPY command is one of the most useful and time-saving commands in Lotus 1-2-3. It allows you to copy labels, values, and formulas from one cell or a range of cells into one or more other cells, saving both time and typing when you are creating a large worksheet.

A Word on Ranges

Before we continue with our discussion of the COPY command, it is important that you understand the concept of ranges since you'll often want to copy a range, or block, of cells at once.

As we said earlier, a **range** of cells is a rectangular grouping of cells. The largest possible range would be the entire worksheet, and the smallest possible range would be one cell. Specifying a range allows you to process blocks of cells at one time in commands and formulas. Examples of valid and invalid ranges are shown in Figure 9.15.

Figure 9.15
Valid and Invalid Ranges

In specifying a range of cells to be copied to another location, all four corners of the range need not be defined. It is only necessary to identify any two opposite corners of the range; for example, points A and D of the valid range labeled A B C D in Figure 9.15. We'll look at the procedure for copying a range of cells and how to specify a range in detail in the step-by-step example later in this section.

Absolute vs. Relative Cell Addressing

It is important to understand the manner in which 1-2-3 interprets the formulas you want to copy. Take, for instance, the following example:

	Column A	Column B	Column C
Row 15	+A11+A12 ----->	+B11+B12 ----->	+C11+C12

This is an example of **relative,** or **variable addressing.** The copying of the formula in cell A15 to cells B15 and C15 can be thought of as forming a relationship. The variables are "relative" to the cells that they are copied into. In other words, the formula +A11+A12, when copied to cell B15, becomes +B11+B12, making it relative to the cell B15.

There are times, however, when you will want one or more of the variables in a formula to stay constant. This will require **absolute** addressing, or **permanent addressing,** which you indicate by placing a $ in front of the column and row in the cell address. Consider the following example:

	Column A	Column B	Column C	Column D
Row 5		Interest Rate:	.05	
.				
.				
.				
Row 15	+A6*C5 ----->	+B6*C5 ----->	+C6*C5	

Suppose you wanted to multiply a value in cell A6 by the interest rate of 5% in cell C5, then store the result in cell A15. This formula is then to be copied to cell

B15 and C15. If cell C5 was not designated as absolute, the formula would have been incorrectly copied as +B6*D5, and a zero would have been entered in cell B15 because cell D5 is blank and therefore considered to be zero. Likewise, the formula would have been incorrectly copied to cell C15 as +C6*E6.

Copying Cells

Now let's return to the /COPY command. The two most common ways of specifying a range are

1. pointing to cells.
2. entering cell addresses through the keyboard.

Each of these methods will be demonstrated in the SWIS case example, which follows. Figure 9.16 shows the two ranges that must be specified in the COPY operation.

First, we will use the pointing method to draw a line of dashes to divide the worksheet.

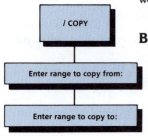

Figure 9.16
The Ranges that must be Specified in the /COPY Command

Back to the Case of SWIS

- Move the pointer to cell A5.
- Press the \ key. (Do not confuse the BACKSLASH (\) key with the SLASH (/) key.)
- Type a dash (-) once, and press ENTER to fill the A5 cell with dashes.

The line of dashes in cell A5 will now be copied throughout the worksheet, from cells B5 to E5.

- Press the / key to invoke the main menu.
- Type C to select the COPY command.
- In response to the message "Enter range to copy FROM: A5..A5", press ENTER to accept cell A5 as the location to copy from.
- The message "Enter range to copy TO: A5" will now be displayed.
- Press the RIGHT ARROW key once to move the pointer to cell B5.
- Type a period (.) to anchor the B5 cell as the beginning of the range to copy to.
- Press the RIGHT ARROW key three times so that the pointer is now located in cell E5.
- Press ENTER to signal E5 as the end of the range to copy to.

Row 5 is now filled with a line of dashes and should look like the worksheet in Figure 9.17 on the following page.

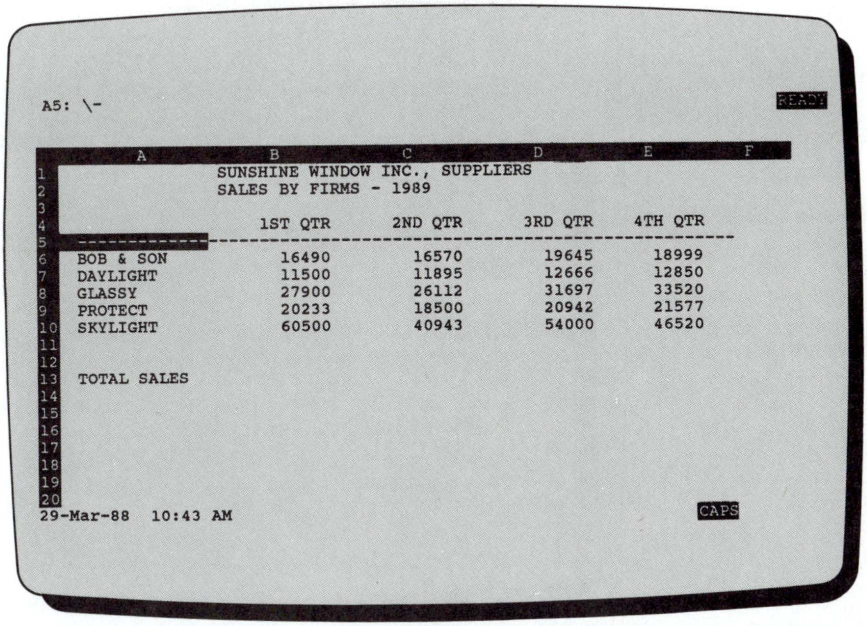

```
A5: \-                                                                    READY

          A              B              C              D              E         F
                     SUNSHINE WINDOW INC., SUPPLIERS
 1
 2                   SALES BY FIRMS - 1989
 3
 4                     1ST QTR        2ND QTR        3RD QTR        4TH QTR
 5   ------------------------------------------------------------------------
 6   BOB & SON         16490          16570          19645          18999
 7   DAYLIGHT          11500          11895          12666          12850
 8   GLASSY            27900          26112          31697          33520
 9   PROTECT           20233          18500          20942          21577
10   SKYLIGHT          60500          40943          54000          46520
11
12
13   TOTAL SALES
14
...
20
29-Mar-88   10:43 AM                                                      CAPS
```

Figure 9.17
Our Worksheet with a Second Range of Copied Cells

Now let's use the method of entering cell addresses from the keyboard to make a second line of dashes.

- Move the pointer to cell A11.
- Press the \ key, then type a dash (-).
- Press ENTER.

The line of dashes in cell A11 will be copied to cells B11 through E11.

- Press the / key to invoke the main menu.
- Type C to select the Copy command.
- In response to the message "Enter range to copy FROM: A11..A11", press ENTER.
- In response to the message "ENTER range to copy TO: A11", type B11.E11 and press ENTER.

Row 11 is now filled with dashes, and the worksheet should look like the one in Figure 9.18 on the following page.

```
                  SUNSHINE WINDOW INC., SUPPLIERS
                  SALES BY FIRMS - 1989

                       1ST QTR    2ND QTR    3RD QTR    4TH QTR
         ----------------------------------------------------------
         BOB & SON      16490      16570      19645      18999
         DAYLIGHT       11500      11895      12666      12850
         GLASSY         27900      26112      31697      33520
         PROTECT        20233      18500      20942      21577
         SKYLIGHT       60500      40943      54000      46520
         ----------------------------------------------------------

         TOTAL SALES
```

Figure 9.18
Our Worksheet with a Second Range of Copied Cells

THE /FORMAT COMMAND

We have two options for formatting our worksheet. The /WORKSHEET GLOBAL FORMAT option allows you to format the entire worksheet, while the /RANGE FORMAT option allows you to format a particular part of the worksheet. The /RANGE FORMAT option has precedence over the /WORKSHEET GLOBAL FORMAT option; in other words, the latter option will format only those cells not already defined by the /RANGE FORMAT option. Regardless of which of the two commands you choose, the FORMAT submenu will present the choices shown in Figure 9.19 and in Table 9.4 on the following page.

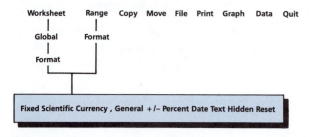

Figure 9.19
Lotus 1-2-3's FORMAT Structure

FORMAT	EXPLANATION AND EXAMPLES
Fixed	Defines a fixed number of decimal places (0 to 15). Example: 15.34, –42.1.
Scientific	Displays data in scientific notation format. Example: 4.32E +12, –15.3E –17.
Currency	A dollar sign ($) is displayed before each cell entry, commas (,) are placed after thousands, and negative numbers are placed in parentheses ( ). Example: $14.95, $1,278.00.
, (Comma)	This option is the same as the Currency format except the dollar sign is suppressed. Example: 1,774, 14.95.
General	This is the initial default setting; trailing zeros are suppressed after the decimal point. Example: –2.6, 235.76.
+/–	A horizontal bar graph is displayed representing the integer part of the number; + signs for positive numbers and – signs for negative values. Example: + + + + + for +5, ——— for –3.
Percent	Cell entry is shown in percentage (%) format with specified number of decimal places. 1-2-3 multiplies the value entered in the cell by 100. Example: 13.8%, –42%.
Date	When a date is entered in a cell, it appears as an integer value (the number of days since Dec. 31, 1986). Choose one of the three formats available: Day-Month-Year Example: 13-Jun-87 Day-Month Example: 13-Jun Month-Year Example: Jun-87
Text	Displays the underlying formula as entered, instead of the actual value of the cell. Example: +B1*G3.
Hidden	Hide cell contents from view.
Reset	This command changes any cell(s) defined in a range back to the global format.

TABLE 9.4 Options of the FORMAT Structure

The number values in your worksheet are in the general default setting, so are not easily read and recognized as dollar figures. Let's use the FORMAT command to change the format of all numbers in the worksheet to a setting of currency (dollars and cents). Since the entire worksheet will be formatted with the same setting, we'll use the /WORKSHEET GLOBAL option instead of the /RANGE option.

Back to the Case of SWIS

- From any position in the worksheet, press the / key to invoke the main menu.
- Type W to select Worksheet.
- Type G to select Global.
- Type F to select Format.
- Type C to select Currency.
- Press the ENTER key to accept 2 as the number of decimal places desired.

All the number values in the worksheet are now in a dollar-and-cents format, and are thus easier to read. Your worksheet should now look like the one in Figure 9.20 on the following page.

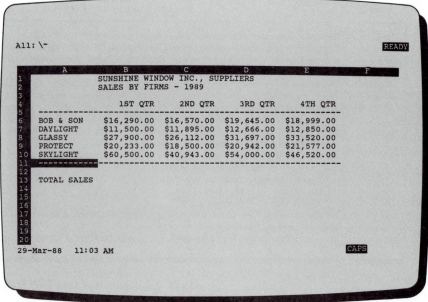

Figure 9.20
Our Worksheet in Currency Format

■ THE /RANGE COMMAND

As mentioned in the last section, instead of formatting the entire worksheet with the /WORKSHEET GLOBAL FORMAT command, we could have formatted one or more cells using the /RANGE FORMAT command. It is often necessary to format or in some way manipulate only part of the worksheet.

As illustrated in Figure 9.21 on the following page, we can use the /RANGE command to align labels in a range of cells, erase a range of cells, create a range name, adjust the width of a column of cells containing labels, specify a range of cells as protected or unprotected, convert a range of formulas to their values, or transpose a range of cells by switching the rows and columns.

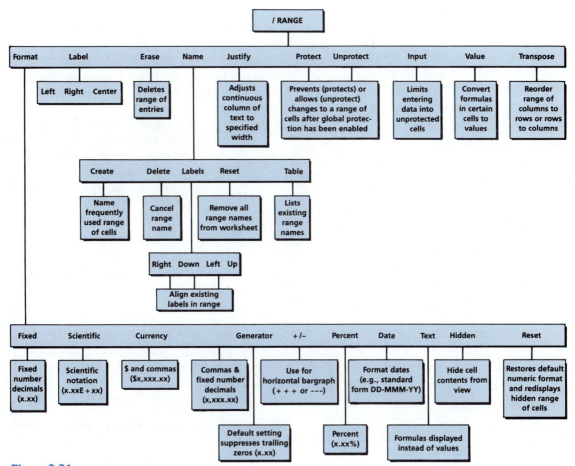

Figure 9.21
Lotus 1-2-3's /RANGE Command Options

■ 1-2-3's @ FUNCTIONS

Lotus 1-2-3's **@ functions** (pronounced at-functions) are pre-programmed sets of instructions that perform mathematical tasks that would otherwise take the user a number of keystrokes and calculations to accomplish. For instance, using our SWIS worksheet example, if you wanted to find the average sales for the year in the PROTECT firm by using the quarterly sales figures, you would use the formula

+(B9+C9+D9+E9)/4

Using the @ function AVG to perform the same task, you would type

@AVG(B9.E9)

Just as a number you enter into a cell tells 1-2-3 to expect a value, the @ sign signals the beginning of a function. The structure of an @ function is as follows:

@*functionname(argument1..argument2.....argumentx)*

Enter the entire @ function as one continuous string, as indicated in the above example. Do not leave any blank spaces between the function name and the arguments, and always enclose the arguments in parentheses. The arguments indicate which cells will be evaluated by the @ function.

Some of the more commonly used @ functions are listed in Table 9.5 with a brief description of each. (Refer to the *Lotus 1-2-3 Reference Manual* for a comprehensive list of @ functions.)

MATHEMATICAL FUNCTIONS:

FUNCTION	DESCRIPTION
@ABS(x)	Finds the absolute value of the number *x*.
@INT(x)	Finds the integer portion of the number *x*.
@MOD(x,y)	Finds the remainder of *x* divided by *y*; for example, @MOD(6,4) would divide 6 by 4 yielding a remainder of 2; note that this function does not concern itself with the quotient of the division, but returns only the remainder; @MOD is often used when determining whether a year is a leap year—a remainder of 0 would indicate a leap year.
@ROUND(x,n)	Rounds the number of cell location *x* to *n* places.
@SQRT(x)	Finds the square root of *x*.

STATISTICAL FUNCTIONS:

FUNCTION	DESCRIPTION
@AVG(list)	Averages the values of the cells in the range.
@COUNT(list)	Counts all the non-blank cells in the range specified.
@MAX(list)	Finds the largest number in the range of cells.
@MIN(list)	Finds the smallest number in the range of cells.
@STD(list)	Finds the population standard deviation of the values in the range.
@SUM(list)	Finds the sum of the values in the range.
@VAR(list)	Finds the population variance of the values in the range.

Note: The argument "list" in each of the following functions refers to a range of cells; for example, @AVG(B6.B9).

FINANCIAL FUNCTIONS:

FUNCTION	DESCRIPTION
@FV(pmt,int,term)	Finds the future value of an annuity, based on a given payment amount, interest rate per period, and the term (number of payment periods).
@PMT(prin,int,term)	Finds the mortgage payment, given the principal amount, the interest rate, and the term (number of payment periods).
@PV(pmt,int,term)	Finds the present value of an annuity, based on a given payment amount, interest rate per period, and the term (number of payment periods).

DATE FUNCTIONS:

FUNCTION	DESCRIPTION
@DATE(year, month,day)	Finds the number of days between the date specified in the argument and the date January 1, 1900.
@NOW	Finds the number of days between today's date and January 1, 1900.
@DAY(date)	Returns the day of the month from a date stored in a particular cell; for example, if the date 13-June-87 is stored in cell B4, the function @DAY(B4) will return a value of 13.
@MONTH(date)	Returns the month number for a date stored in a particular cell.
@YEAR(date)	Returns the last two digits of the year for a date stored in a particular cell.

Note: The date numbers yielded by the functions below can be formatted with the /Range Format Date command.

TABLE 9.5
Lotus 1-2-3's @ Functions

Using the function @SUM, let's finish inserting the values in our SWIS worksheet example, totaling each column for the four quarters, and showing total sales for each quarter.

Back to the Case of SWIS

- Move the pointer to cell B13.
- Type `@SUM(B6.B10)` and press ENTER. The total sales figure for the first quarter now resides in cell B13, as shown in Figure 9.22.

Rather than typing this same formula for each of the other three quarters, we will use the /COPY command to copy the formula in cell B13 to cells C13 through E13.

- Type `/C` to invoke the main menu and select the COPY command.
- Press ENTER in response to the message "ENTER range to copy FROM: B13..B13".
- Type `C13.E13` in response to the message "ENTER range to copy TO: B13", and press ENTER.

The sales totals are now displayed for all four quarters. These figures are automatically formatted because we formatted the entire worksheet for currency. Your completed worksheet should look like the one in Figure 9.23.

B13: @SUM(B6..B10) READY

	A	B	C	D	E
1		SUNSHINE WINDOW INC., SUPPLIERS			
2		SALES BY FIRMS - 1989			
3					
4		1ST QTR	2ND QTR	3RD QTR	4TH QTR
5	-----	-----	-----	-----	-----
6	BOB & SON	$16,290.00	$16,570.00	$19,645.00	$18,999.00
7	DAYLIGHT	$11,500.00	$11,895.00	$12,666.00	$12,850.00
8	GLASSY	$27,900.00	$26,112.00	$31,697.00	$33,520.00
9	PROTECT	$20,233.00	$18,500.00	$20,942.00	$21,577.00
10	SKYLIGHT	$60,500.00	$40,943.00	$54,000.00	$46,520.00
11	-----	-----	-----	-----	-----
12					
13	TOTAL SALES	$136,423.00			

Figure 9.22
Adding the Total Sales Formula to Our Worksheet

B13: @SUM(B6..B10) READY

	A	B	C	D	E
1		SUNSHINE WINDOW INC., SUPPLIERS			
2		SALES BY FIRMS - 1989			
3					
4		1ST QTR	2ND QTR	3RD QTR	4TH QTR
5	-----	-----	-----	-----	-----
6	BOB & SON	$16,290.00	$16,570.00	$19,645.00	$18,999.00
7	DAYLIGHT	$11,500.00	$11,895.00	$12,666.00	$12,850.00
8	GLASSY	$27,900.00	$26,112.00	$31,697.00	$33,520.00
9	PROTECT	$20,233.00	$18,500.00	$20,942.00	$21,577.00
10	SKYLIGHT	$60,500.00	$40,943.00	$54,000.00	$46,520.00
11	-----	-----	-----	-----	-----
12					
13	TOTAL SALES	$136,423.00	$114,020.00	$138,950.00	$133,466.00

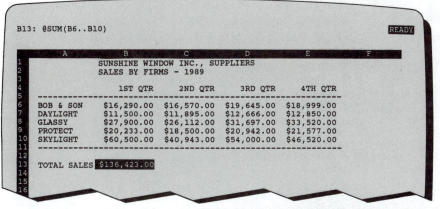

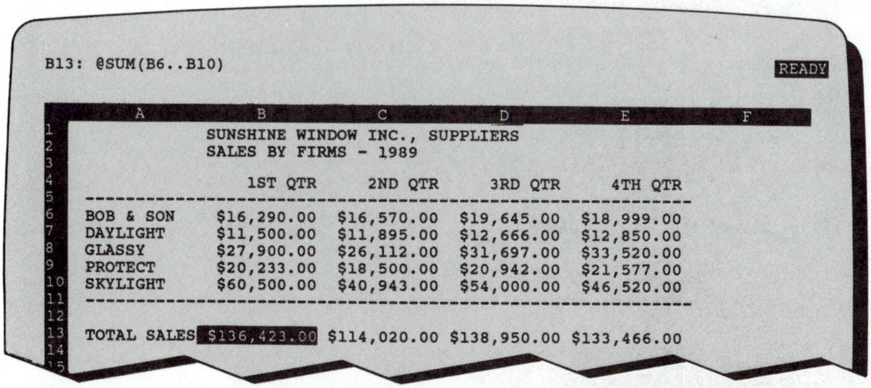

Figure 9.23

Copying the Total Sales Formula in Our Worksheet

■ THE /MOVE COMMAND

As you use 1-2-3, you will sometimes want to move the contents of one cell or a range of cells from one part of the worksheet to another, automatically retaining the functional relationships among the cells that are transferred. You can accomplish these goals using the /MOVE command.

The /MOVE command, although similar in the way it is executed, is not to be confused with the /COPY command. The /COPY command transfers an exact copy of the range to the receiving area, while leaving the original sending area intact. In contrast, the /MOVE command transfers a range of cells to another part of the worksheet, destroying the contents of the original sending area. The two steps involved in the /MOVE command are shown in Figure 9.24.

To practice the /MOVE command, suppose you decided to move the contents of row 13 (Total Sales) to row 16. You would proceed as in our SWIS example below.

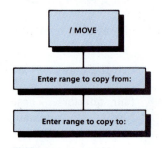

Figure 9.24
The Steps Involved in the /MOVE Command

Back to the Case of SWIS

Type /M to invoke the main menu and select the MOVE option.
In response to the prompt "ENTER range to move
FROM: B13..B13", type A13.E13 and press ENTER.
In response to the prompt "ENTER range to move
TO: B13 ", type A16.E16 and press ENTER.

The contents of row 13 have been moved, intact, to row 16, as illustrated in Figure 9.25.

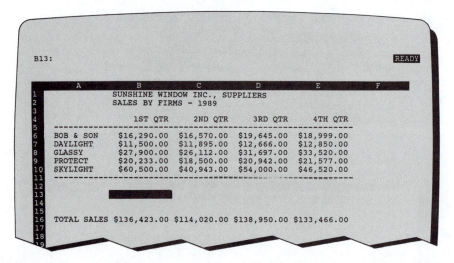

Figure 9.25
Moving the Contents of Row 13 to Row 16

To move the Total Sales row back to its original position, follow these steps.

- Type /M to invoke the main menu and select the MOVE option.
- In response to the prompt "ENTER range to move FROM: B13..B13", type A16.E16 and press ENTER.
- In response to the prompt "ENTER range to move TO: B13", type A13.E13 and press ENTER.

The Total Sales row has safely been moved back to its original position in row 13.

THE /PRINT COMMAND

After finalizing your worksheet, you will probably want to get a hard copy of it or send it to an ASCII file to be printed or processed at a later time. Using the /PRINT command, shown in Figure 9.26 on the following page, you may choose to print the entire worksheet or any part of it.

To initiate the /PRINT command, first invoke the main menu and choose the printer options by typing */PP* (for /Print Printer). The following menu will then be displayed.

Range   Line   Page   Options   Clear   Align   Go   Quit

Here is a brief explanation of each of these submenu options:

Range	Selects the row and columns to be printed.
Line	Advances the page one line.
Page	Advances the paper to the top of the next page.
Options	Invokes submenu to place headings or footers, set margins, place borders, and so forth.
Clear	Returns any print options that have been reset to their default settings.
Align	Informs 1-2-3 that the printer is at the top of a new page.
Go	Sends the output to the printer.
Quit	Exits the print option and returns you to the worksheet in READY mode.

The designated range and any of the print options that are changed will be saved with the worksheet.

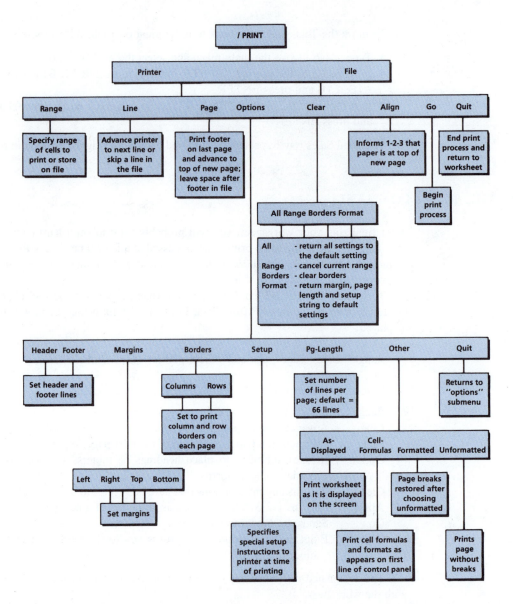

Figure 9.26
Lotus 1-2-3's /PRINT Command Options

Back to the Case of SWIS

Let's print the completed Sunshine Window Inc., Suppliers worksheet.

- Type **/** to invoke the main menu.

- Choose the PRINT option by typing P.
- Press ENTER to select the PRINTER option.
- Type R to set the RANGE setting.
- In response to the message "ENTER Print range: B13", type A1.E13 and press ENTER.
- We will not change any of the default settings, so type A for ALIGN. This command tells 1-2-3 that it is at the top of a new page.
- Type G to select GO; the output will now be sent to the printer.
- After the print operation is complete, type P to advance the printer to the top of the next page.
- Press ESC three times to exit menu mode.

Print Screen

You may, at some point, want to have a printed copy of the worksheet as it appears on the screen. For example, it may be desirable to have a record of the worksheet at different stages of its development. When you depress the SHIFT and PRTSC keys at the same time, an exact copy of the screen you are presently viewing will be sent to the printer.

THE /FILE COMMAND

Now that you have created a worksheet, you will want to save it on your diskette for later use. (If you exit 1-2-3 without saving your worksheet, all the information you typed would be lost.) We'll now look at some commands that will help us save and retrieve 1-2-3 worksheets.

Commands that help us save and retrieve worksheets fall into the category of /FILE commands, as summarized in Figure 9.27 on the following page. The /FILE SAVE command prompts the user to enter the name of the file to be saved. A file name can be up to eight characters long and can be made up of the letters A–Z, numbers 0–9, and the underline (_) character. 1-2-3 automatically adds an extension of .WK1 to all worksheet files.

Back to the Case of SWIS

Let's use the /FILE SAVE command to save the completed SWIS worksheet. To save the file, you'll need to place a blank, formatted diskette in the B drive.

- Type /F to invoke the main menu and select the FILE option.
- Type S to select the SAVE option.
- In response to the prompt "ENTER save file name: A:\", Press ESC to clear A:\ and type B:EXAMPLE1.

The entire SWIS worksheet has now been safely stored on your diskette.

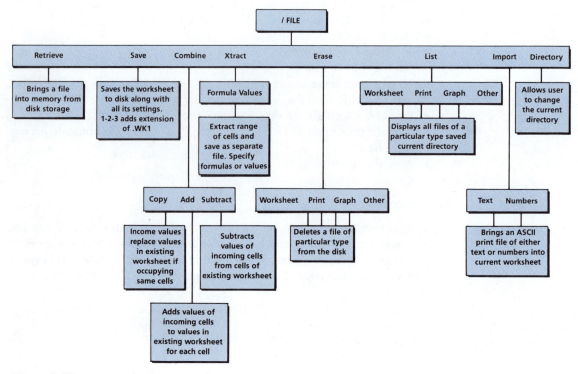

Figure 9.27
Lotus 1-2-3's /FILE Command Options

The next time you want to work on this or any other worksheet you have saved, you will need to know how to retrieve the file from the diskette you saved it on. Once again, the /FILE command takes care of the file handling. Once you are in the 1-2-3 environment (refer to the complete start-up instructions at the beginning of this chapter) and a clean worksheet is displayed on the screen, you can follow these steps to retrieve your file. We will assume you want to retrieve the B:EXAMPLE1 file, but first let's erase the worksheet on your screen.

Back to the Case of SWIS

- Type /W to invoke the main menu and WORKSHEET option.
- Type E to erase the worksheet.
- Type Y to erase the entire worksheet.
- Type /F to invoke the main menu and select the FILE option.
- Type R to select the RETRIEVE option.
- In response to the message "Name of the file to retrieve: A:*.WK?", press ESC twice. You can now either (1) type B:EXAMPLE1 and press ENTER, or

(2) type B:, press ENTER and then use the RIGHT ARROW key to move the highlighted area to the file you want to work with and press ENTER.

After you complete the above steps, the EXAMPLE1 file will be displayed on your screen, ready to work with. When you are finished with the session, do not forget to save the worksheet before exiting so that any modifications to the worksheet are stored on your diskette.

■ THE /QUIT COMMAND

Once you are finished with a worksheet session and want to exit 1-2-3, you can use the /QUIT command, summarized in Figure 9.28. (Be sure you have saved your worksheet before exiting.)

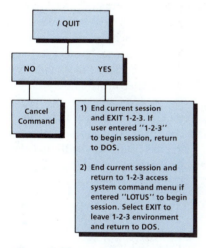

Figure 9.28
Lotus 1-2-3's /QUIT Command Options

Back to the Case of SWIS

- Type /Q to invoke the main menu and select the option to QUIT.
- Type Y to end the session.

At this point, you will be presented with the Lotus Access System command menu. Type E for Exit. After a few seconds, you will be out of the Lotus 1-2-3 environment and back in the DOS environment, evidenced by the DOS prompt (A>).

■ THE /SYSTEM COMMAND

The /SYSTEM command, shown in Figure 9.29, is a convenient way of switching back and forth from 1-2-3 to DOS without having to restart 1-2-3 and retrieve the file you were working on.

When you execute the command by typing /S, 1-2-3 is temporarily exited and control is returned to the computer's operating system. Once you are in the DOS environment, you can, for example, format a diskette, create a new directory, or change the current system's date. When you have completed the task in DOS, you can return to your 1-2-3 worksheet by typing the word Exit at the A> and press ENTER.

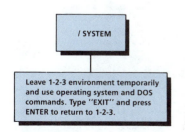

Figure 9.29
Lotus 1-2-3's /SYSTEM Command

■ A COMPREHENSIVE WORKSHEET EXAMPLE

At this point, let's utilize 1-2-3 in the example that we first discussed in Chapter 8: the Sunshine Window Inc., Suppliers sales projection, with more detailed data. This example is designed as a comprehensive review of the worksheet concepts presented in this chapter.

SWIS is interested in estimating its potential sales and profits for the next two years, assuming an annual growth rate of ten percent.

Worksheet Specifications

For simplicity, since all labels will be entered in uppercase letters, make sure the CAPS LOCK is depressed throughout this exercise. The year labels, 1989 through 1991, should be centered in the cells. The values in the table at the top of the worksheet will be formatted as Percent, the date in column E1 will be formatted as Date, and the remainder of the worksheet will be globally formatted as Currency. The global column width will be changed from nine to fourteen (to accommodate the large dollar figures) with the exception of column A, which will be individually set to a width of ten. Remember, individual settings take precedence over global settings. You should note that the completed worksheet will consume more than one "page;" therefore, you won't be able to view the worksheet in its entirety on the screen.

You should have a clean worksheet on the screen in front of you and a blank diskette in Drive B to store your worksheet data. Figure 9.30 is an illustration of what your finished worksheet will look like. Don't be daunted; you'll find that entering all this information is easy if you follow our instructions.

```
              SUNSHINE WINDOW INC., SUPPLIERS                29-Mar-88
              PROJECTED INCOME FOR 1989-1991

              ANNUAL GROWTH RATE                 10.0%
              COMMISSION RATE                     5.0%
              COGS (% OF SALES)                  50.0%
              TAX RATE                           40.0%

                            1989           1990           1991

   SALES                $460,000.00    $506,000.00    $556,600.00
   COMMISSION            $23,000.00     $25,300.00     $27,830.00
                       -------------  -------------  -------------
   NET SALES            $437,000.00    $480,700.00    $528,770.00
   COGS                 $230,000.00    $253,000.00    $278,300.00
                       -------------  -------------  -------------
   GROSS PROFIT         $207,000.00    $227,700.00    $250,470.00
   OPERATING EXPENSES    $50,000.00     $50,000.00     $50,000.00
                       -------------  -------------  -------------
   OPERATING PROFIT     $157,000.00    $177,700.00    $200,470.00
   DEPRECIATION          $10,000.00     $10,000.00     $10,000.00
                       -------------  -------------  -------------
   EBIT                 $147,000.00    $167,700.00    $190,470.00
   INTEREST              $30,000.00     $30,000.00     $30,000.00
                       -------------  -------------  -------------
   TAXABLE INCOME       $117,000.00    $137,700.00    $160,470.00
   TAX                   $46,800.00     $55,080.00     $64,188.00
                       -------------  -------------  -------------
   NET PROFIT            $70,200.00     $82,620.00     $96,282.00
                       =============  =============  =============
```

Figure 9.30
The Completed SWIS Worksheet

The complete instructions for building the worksheet follow, with an illustration of the cell that the command affects, the command or key to be pressed, and an explanation of the operation that the command performs.

In Cell	Type/Press	Explanation
A1	/W G C 14[ENTER]	Set the global column width to 14.
A1	/W C S 10 [ENTER]	Change the global setting for column A to a column width of 10.
B1	SUNSHINE WINDOW INC., SUPPLIERS [↓]	Type the first line of the worksheet title.
B2	PROJECTED INCOME FOR 1989-1991 [↓] [↓]	Type the second line of the worksheet title.
B4	ANNUAL GROWTH RATE [↓]	Type the first label in the table of percentages.
B5	COMMISSION RATE [↓]	Type the second label in the table of percentages.
B6	COGS (% OF SALES) [↓]	Type the third label in the table of percentages.
B7	TAX RATE [ENTER]	Type the fourth label in the table of percentages.
D4	.10 [↓]	ENTER an annual growth rate of ten percent.
D5	.05 [↓]	ENTER the commission rate of five percent.
D6	.50 [↓]	ENTER the percentage of cost of goods sold as fifty percent of sales.
D7	.40 [ENTER]	ENTER the tax rate as forty percent.
D4	/R F P 1 [ENTER] [↓] [↓] [↓] [ENTER]	Format the range D4..D7 as percent with one decimal place. Highlight the entire range by pressing the DOWN ARROW key three times in response to the message "ENTER range to format:".
C9	^1989 [→]	Type the label for the year 1989, specifying with the ^ symbol that it be centered in the cell.
D9	^ 1990 [→]	Type the label for the year 1990, specifying with the ^ symbol that it be centered in the cell.
E9	^1991 [ENTER]	Type the label for the year 1991, specifying with the ^ symbol that it be centered in the cell.

A11	SALES [↓]	Type the label.
A12	COMMISSION [↓] [↓]	Type the label.
A14	NET SALES [↓]	Type the label.
A15	COGS [↓] [↓]	Type the label.
A17	GROSS PROFIT [↓]	Type the label.
A18	OPERATING EXPENSES [↓] [↓]	Type the label.
A20	OPERATING PROFIT [↓]	Type the label.
A21	DEPRECIATION [↓] [↓]	Type the label.
A23	EBIT [↓]	Type the label for Earnings Before Interest and Taxes.
A24	INTEREST [↓] [↓]	Type the label.
A26	TAXABLE INCOME [↓]	Type the label.
A27	TAX [↓] [↓]	Type the label.
A29	NET PROFIT [ENTER]	Type the label.

The table of percentages and all the labels are now inserted into the worksheet. Check your worksheet against the one in Figure 9.31 before continuing.

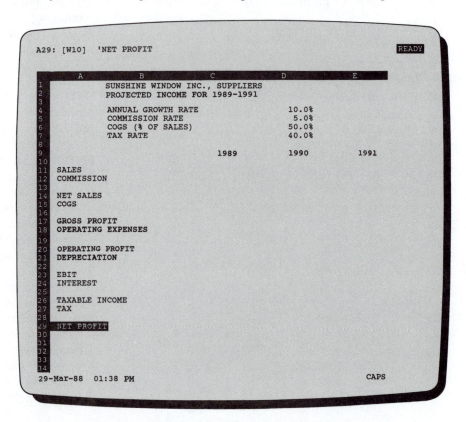

Figure 9.31
The SWIS Worksheet with Labels

In Cell	Type/Press	Explanation
C11	460000 [↓]	Type the 1989 sales figure as it appears. Do not add a $, commas, or decimal points. That will be taken care of when you format the rest of the worksheet.
C12	+C11*D5 [↓] [↓]	Multiply the sales figure by the commission rate to arrive at the commission. Notice the $ before the column and row of the commission rate. We need to make this an absolute address so that when it is copied to other cells in the worksheet, the correct calculations will be made.
C14	+C11-C12 [↓]	Sales minus commissions equals the net sales.
C15	+C11*D6 [↓] [↓]	Cost of goods sold is figured as a percentage of sales (Sales * 50%).
C17	+C14-C15 [↓]	Net sales minus COGS equals gross profit.
C18	50000 [↓] [↓]	Operating expenses are entered at a fixed rate.
C20	+C17-C18 [↓]	Gross profit minus operating expenses equals operating profit.
C21	10000 [↓] [↓]	Depreciation is entered at a fixed rate.
C23	+C20-C21 [↓]	Operating profit minus depreciation equals earnings before interest and taxes.
C24	30000 [↓] [↓]	Interest is entered at a fixed rate.
C26	+C23-C24 [↓]	EBIT minus interest equals taxable income.
C27	+C26*D7 [↓] [↓]	Tax is figured by taking the taxable income times the tax rate.
C29	+C26-C27 [ENTER]	Taxable income minus taxes equals net profit.
D11	+C11*D4+C11 [ENTER]	Multiplies the 1989 sales by the expected annual growth rate of 1.10% to arrive at the 1990 sales figure.
D11	/C [ENTER] [→] [ENTER]	Copies the formula in cells D11 to E11.
C13	\- [ENTER]	Type as shown to insert dashes in the worksheet at cells C13, C16, C19, C22, C25, C28, and a double line in cell C30.
C16	\- [ENTER]	
C19	\- [ENTER]	
C22	\- [ENTER]	
C25	\- [ENTER]	
C28	\- [ENTER]	
C30	\= [ENTER]	
C12	/C C12.C30 [ENTER] D12.E30 [ENTER]	Copies the contents of cells C12 to C30 to cells D12.E30.

All the values are now entered into the worksheet. Once again, compare your worksheet to the one shown in Figure 9.32 before continuing.

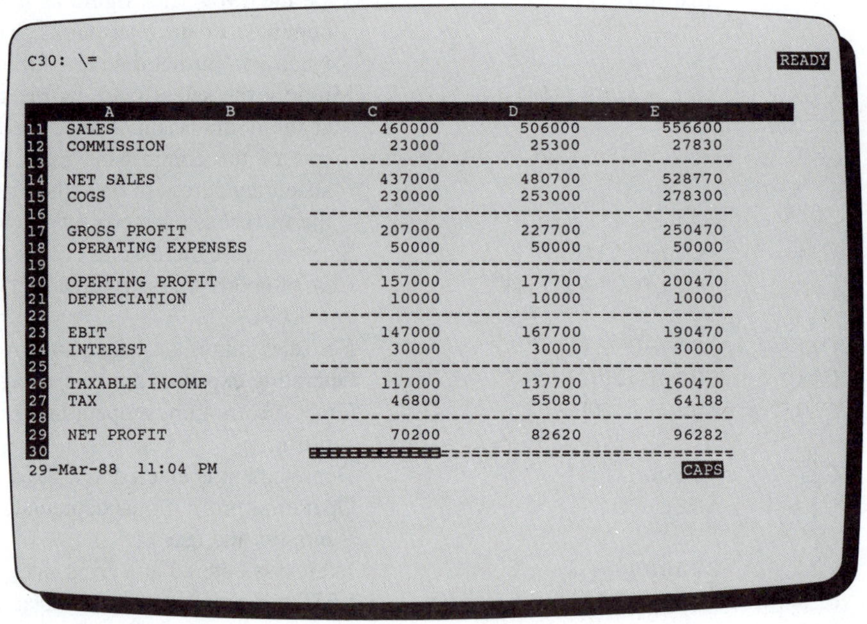

```
C30: \=                                                              READY

              A         B              C              D              E
11   SALES                          460000         506000         556600
12   COMMISSION                      23000          25300          27830
13                              ------------------------------------------
14   NET SALES                      437000         480700         528770
15   COGS                           230000         253000         278300
16                              ------------------------------------------
17   GROSS PROFIT                   207000         227700         250470
18   OPERATING EXPENSES              50000          50000          50000
19                              ------------------------------------------
20   OPERTING PROFIT                157000         177700         200470
21   DEPRECIATION                    10000          10000          10000
22                              ------------------------------------------
23   EBIT                           147000         167700         190470
24   INTEREST                        30000          30000          30000
25                              ------------------------------------------
26   TAXABLE INCOME                 117000         137700         160470
27   TAX                             46800          55080          64188
28                              ------------------------------------------
29   NET PROFIT                      70200          82620          96282
30   ==========================================================
29-Mar-88   11:04 PM                                                  CAPS
```

Figure 9.32
The SWIS Worksheet with Values

In Cell	Type/Press	Explanation
A1	/W G F C [ENTER]	The final touch: formatting the worksheet to make your profits easily readable in dollars and cents. Note that the table of percentages was left unchanged because the individual formatting took precedence over the global format setting.

E1	@Now [ENTER]	Date your worksheet with today's date.
E1	/R F D 1 [ENTER]	Format cell E1 as a date in the format (dd-mm-yy).

The Sunshine Window Inc., Suppliers worksheet is finished, and should look like the completed example shown in Figure 9.30 at the beginning of this exercise. Now let's save the worksheet and print a hardcopy.

In Cell	Type/Press	Explanation
A1	/F S ESC: EXAMPLE2 [ENTER]	Now that you have completed the worksheet, it is important that you save it. The worksheet is being saved on the disk in Drive B as EXAMPLE2.WK1 (1-2-3 will attach the extension of .WK1 automatically).
A1	/P P R A1.E30 [ENTER] A G P	This series of commands sends the worksheet, range A1 through E30, to the printer, aligns the paper at the top of a new page, executes the print process, and advances the paper to the top of the next page.
A1	ESC three times	Exits the menu.

Changing an Assumption

At this point, you can easily change any of the assumptions you made in your worksheet, such as annual growth rate or tax rate, and see the impact of it on the rest of the worksheet values. Follow the instructions below to change the sales growth rate from ten percent to fifteen percent, and the tax rate from forty percent to thirty-five percent.

In Cell	Type/Press	Explanation
D4	.15 [ENTER]	Changes the annual growth rate to fifteen percent and immediately recalculates all other values in the worksheet.

```
            SUNSHINE WINDOW INC., SUPPLIERS              29-Mar-88
            PROJECTED INCOME FOR 1989-1991

            ANNUAL GROWTH RATE              15.0%
            COMMISSION RATE                  5.0%
            COGS (% OF SALES)               50.0%
            TAX RATE                        35.0%

                                 1989          1990          1991

    SALES                   $460,000.00   $529,000.00   $608,350.00
    COMMISSION               $23,000.00    $26,450.00    $30,417.50
                            -----------------------------------------
    NET SALES               $437,000.00   $502,550.00   $577,932.50
    COGS                    $230,000.00   $264,500.00   $304,175.00
                            -----------------------------------------
    GROSS PROFIT            $207,000.00   $238,050.00   $273,757.50
    OPERATING EXPENSES       $50,000.00    $50,000.00    $50,000.00
                            -----------------------------------------
    OPERATING PROFIT        $157,000.00   $188,050.00   $223,757.50
    DEPRECIATION             $10,000.00    $10,000.00    $10,000.00
                            -----------------------------------------
    EBIT                    $147,000.00   $178,050.00   $213,757.50
    INTEREST                 $30,000.00    $30,000.00    $30,000.00
                            -----------------------------------------
    TAXABLE INCOME          $117,000.00   $148,050.00   $183,757.50
    TAX                      $40,950.00    $51,817.50    $64,315.13
                            -----------------------------------------
    NET PROFIT               $76,050.00    $96,232.50   $119,442.38
                            =========================================
```

Figure 9.33
The SWIS Worksheet after Changing the Sales Growth Rate and Tax Rate

Notice how the net profit has increased due to the change in annual growth rate.

In Cell	Type/Press	Explanation
D7	.35 [ENTER]	Changes the tax rate to thirty-five percent. All other values within the worksheet will be automatically recalculated.

Again, the 1990 and 1991 net profits will be increased due to the reduction in tax rate. Your worksheet should now look like the one in Figure 9.33.

As you can see, a decision maker at Sunshine Window Inc., Suppliers can easily use this model of profit projections and make as many changes in the assumptions as needed to assess the overall impact of changes. In this regard, Lotus 1-2-3 is a powerful tool in business situations where the decision maker needs to evaluate different assumptions in order to make decisions that will maximize net profits.

Now follow the procedure you learned earlier to exit 1-2-3.

■ Summary of LOTUS 1-2-3 Commands

/WORKSHEET	Subcommands perform functions such as formatting, set column width, add or delete rows and columns, or erase the worksheet.
/RANGE	Subcommands perform functions such as the formatting, naming, or protecting of a specified portion of the worksheet.
/COPY	Copies a cell or range of cells to another location in the worksheet.
/MOVE	Allows you to move the contents of a cell or range of cells to another area of the worksheet.
/FILE	Subcommands perform file handling functions such as retrieving, saving, listing, or combining files.
/PRINT	Allows you to get a hardcopy of your worksheet or send your work to an ASCII file.
/SYSTEM	Allows you to switch back and forth from your 1-2-3 worksheet to DOS.
/QUIT	Used to exit the 1-2-3 environment at the end of a session.

■ Key Terms

cell	Unique address that distinguishes each location in the worksheet from all others; found by the intersection of a worksheet column and a worksheet row.
cell pointer or cursor	Rectangular highlighted area—the cursor.
mode indicator	Displays the present status of the worksheet.
status indicator	Displays when special keys have been pressed (CAPS LOCK, NUM LOCK, and so forth.).
function keys	(F1–F10) Perform predefined tasks (HELP feature, EDIT, and so forth).
pointing method	Method of entering a formula by using the ARROW keys to move the pointer to the cell locations involved in the operation.
range	A rectangular grouping of cells.
relative, or variable, addressing	Variables in a formula are relative to the cells they are copied into.
absolute, or permanent, addressing	The variable in a formula stays constant.
@ functions	Preprogrammed sets of instructions that perform mathematical tasks.

■ Review Questions

1. The _____ , or cursor, is the rectangular highlighted area that shows the present position in the worksheet.
   (a) cell pointer
   (b) mode indicator
   (c) status indicator
   (d) block indicator
2. A _____ is a unique address that distinguishes each location in the worksheet from all others.
   (a) block
   (b) range
   (c) cell
   (d) cursor.
3. Which of the following keys, when pressed, returns the cell pointer to the upper left-hand corner of the worksheet?
   (a) END
   (b) HOME
   (c) ESC
   (d) TAB
4. Which of the following is *not* a status indicator?
   (a) CAPS
   (b) NUM
   (c) END
   (d) READY
   (e) CMD
5. The _____ (GOTO) function key allows you to quickly move the pointer to any cell in the worksheet.
   (a) F2
   (b) F4
   (c) F5
   (d) F7
6. Which of the following keys, when pressed, invokes the main menu?
   (a) \ (BACKSLASH)
   (b) ESC
   (c) / (SLASH)
   (d) HOME
7. Which of the following keys, when pressed, allows you to "back out" of the main menu?
   (a) \ (BACKSLASH)
   (b) ESC
   (c) / (SLASH)
   (d) HOME

8. If an entry begins with a + sign, 1-2-3 will recognize it as a
   (a) formula.
   (b) range.
   (c) quantity.
   (d) value.
9. Which of the following is *not* one of the characters that distinguishes an entry as a 1-2-3 label?
   (a) '
   (b) ^
   (c) "
   (d) ;
10. When using the /WORKSHEET _____ command, a new row will always be added before the current pointer position.
    (a) INSERT COLUMN
    (b) INSERT ROW
    (c) ROW INSERT
    (d) COLUMN DELETE
11. A _____ of cells is a rectangular grouping of cells.
    (a) block
    (b) range
    (c) field
    (d) view
12. Which FORMAT option will format a value with dollar signs, commas, and negative numbers placed in parentheses?
    (a) , (comma)
    (b) Fixed
    (c) Currency
    (d) General
13. Lotus 1-2-3 _____ are preprogrammed sets of instructions that perform mathematical tasks.
    (a) formulas
    (b) macros
    (c) ranges
    (d) functions
14. Is it possible to print only a part of a 1-2-3 worksheet? Explain.
15. Files can be saved or retrieved by using the _____ command.
    (a) /WORKSHEET
    (b) /DISK
    (c) /FILE
    (d) /SAVE/RESTORE
16. The _____ command allows you to switch back and forth from 1-2-3 to DOS without having to restart 1-2-3.
    (a) /DISK
    (b) /QUERY
    (c) /HELP
    (d) /SYSTEM

17. Once the ENTER key has been pressed, what are the two methods of making a correction to a cell entry?
18. What is the difference between absolute and relative cell addressing?
19. What are the two methods of entering cell formulas? Explain each method.
20. What is the difference between the /MOVE command and the /COPY command?
21. What are the two options for formatting a worksheet?
22. What is meant by the "pointing method?"
23. When would the /RANGE FORMAT command be used? Give examples.
24. Which of the following is a mode indicator?
    (a) EDIT
    (b) CAPS
    (c) NUM
    (d) RANGE
25. Which of the following tells 1-2-3 to center a label?
    (a) '
    (b) "
    (c) ^
    (d) \
26. _____ justification is the default for all 1-2-3 labels.
    (a) Right-
    (b) Left-
    (c) Center-
    (d) None of the above
27. What is the maximum number of characters that can be used in a label?
28. Is it possible to have a number as a label? Explain.
29. You are setting up a large worksheet that will show the same information for each of several years. Rather than enter the formulas for each year's information, what would you do?
30. How can the current screen be sent to the printer?

☐ chapter 9

HANDS-ON EXERCISES

1. The managers at SWIS have changed their minds and feel that a four-year sales and profits projection would be more beneficial than the three-year projections calculated in the comprehensive exercise. You are to add a column for the year 1992 to the worksheet you created in this chapter.

    a. Retrieve the EXAMPLE2.WK1 file from your disk.
    b. Use the EDIT function to change the title to read *PROJECTED INCOME FOR 1989-1992*.

c. In cell F9, enter the label ^1992.
d. Copy all of the formulas from column E to column F in order to calculate the figures for 1992.
e. Change the date in cell E1 to the current date, only if date displayed is wrong.
f. Print the updated worksheet. It should look like the one in Figure 9.34.
g. Save the worksheet as B:LOTEX1; the file will be saved with the .WK1 extension.
h. Change the annual growth rate from ten percent to five percent. Note the impact on company sales and profits. Do not save these changes.
i. Exit this worksheet to get a clean worksheet for the next exercise, or exit the 1-2-3 environment if you want to end this session.

```
           SUNSHINE WINDOW INC., SUPPLIERS              29-Mar-88
           PROJECTED INCOME FOR 1989-1992

           ANNUAL GROWTH RATE              10.0%
           COMMISSION RATE                  5.0%
           COGS (% OF SALES)               50.0%
           TAX RATE                        40.0%

                             1989          1990          1991          1992

SALES                    $460,000.00   $506,000.00   $556,600.00   $612,260.00
COMMISSION                $23,000.00    $25,300.00    $27,830.00    $30,613.00
                         -----------   -----------   -----------   -----------
NET SALES                $437,000.00   $480,700.00   $528,770.00   $581,647.00
COGS                     $230,000.00   $253,000.00   $278,300.00   $306,130.00
                         -----------   -----------   -----------   -----------
GROSS PROFIT             $207,000.00   $227,700.00   $250,470.00   $275,517.00
OPERATING EXPENSES        $50,000.00    $50,000.00    $50,000.00    $50,000.00
                         -----------   -----------   -----------   -----------
OPERATING PROFIT         $157,000.00   $177,700.00   $200,470.00   $225,517.00
DEPRECIATION              $10,000.00    $10,000.00    $10,000.00    $10,000.00
                         -----------   -----------   -----------   -----------
EBIT                     $147,000.00   $167,700.00   $190,470.00   $215,517.00
INTEREST                  $30,000.00    $30,000.00    $30,000.00    $30,000.00
                         -----------   -----------   -----------   -----------
TAXABLE INCOME           $117,000.00   $137,700.00   $160,470.00   $185,517.00
TAX                       $46,800.00    $55,080.00    $64,188.00    $74,206.80
                         -----------   -----------   -----------   -----------
NET PROFIT                $70,200.00    $82,620.00    $96,282.00   $111,310.20
                         ===========   ===========   ===========   ===========
```

Figure 9.34
Completed Worksheet for LOTEX1

2. This exercise is designed to allow you to practice some of the @functions presented in this chapter. Start with a clean worksheet and follow the instructions below to create a worksheet of student grades. The average for each student will be calculated along with the average, standard deviation, variance, highest grade, and lowest grade for the class as a whole. The worksheet, when completed, will look like the one in Figure 9.35 on the following page.

```
                                    ENGLISH 101
22-Apr-88
STUDENT NAME      EXAM 1      EXAM 2      EXAM 3      FINAL EXAM      AVERAGE
JOE                   85          94          95          83              89
LUCY                  60          78          84          78              75
KEVIN                 76          72          80          81              77
ROY                   91          96          88          85              93
JONI                  78          85          81          77              80
SANDY                 86          82          90          92              88
PAT                   82          66          75          84              77
KATHY                 68          79          78          80              76
KEITH                 70          76          69          73              72
JOHN                  90          88          85          81              86

AVERAGE               79          82          83          82
STANDARD DEV.        9.6         8.9         7.2         6.3
VARIANCE            93.0        80.0        51.9        40.0
HIGEST GRADE          91          96          95          95
LOWEST GRADE          60          66          69          73
```

Figure 9.35
Completed Worksheet for CLASSEX2

a. Globally change the column width to thirteen.
b. ENTER today's date in cell A1 using the @NOW function. Format the cell as "date" in the format DD-MMM-YY.
c. ENTER the worksheet title, "ENGLISH 101," in cell C3 and the headings in cells A5 through F5. Left-justify the label in cell A5, and right-justify the remaining headings in cells B5 through F5. ENTER the remaining labels in cells A7 through A22.
d. ENTER all values into the proper cells, rows 7 through 16 (refer to the worksheet above).
e. Insert rows of dashes (-) in rows 6 and 17.
f. ENTER the formula to calculate an individual's average in cell F7. The average is to be rounded to the nearest percentage point (e.g., 89.25 rounds to 89). *Hint*: Use the @ROUND function and the @AVG function in the same formula. In this case, in cell F7, enter @ROUND ((@AVG(B7.E7)),0). Copy the formula to cells F8 through F16.
g. ENTER the formulas to calculate the class average (rounded to the nearest percentage point), the standard deviation, the variance, the highest grade, and the lowest grade in cells B18 through B22. Format the standard deviation and the variance as "fixed" format with one decimal place. Refer to page 242.
h. Copy the formulas in cells B18 through B22 to the range C18.E22.
i. Save the exercise as B:CLASSEX2.
j. Print the worksheet.
k. Exit the worksheet.

3. Glenn's Sporting Goods has prospered since its inception in 1965 and now has four stores in the San Francisco area. The owner would like to see a report of the stores' quarterly sales figures for 1989. You are to create the report for the current year. Start with a clean worksheet. The completed worksheet is shown in Figure 9.36 on the following page.

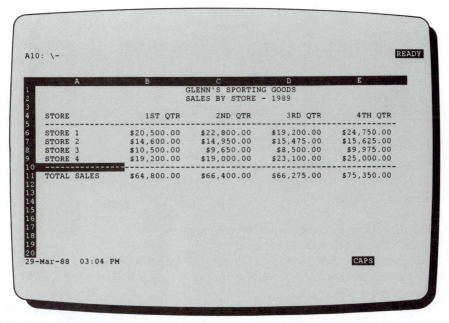

Figure 9.36
Completed Worksheet for STOREEX3

   a. Globally format the worksheet to a column width of fourteen.
   b. ENTER the worksheet title in cells C1 and C2.
   c. Left-justify the label in cell A4. Right-justify the labels in cells B4 through E4.
   d. Left-justify the remaining labels in cells A6 through A11.
   e. ENTER the values into the worksheet without dollar signs or commas.
   f. Format the entire worksheet as "currency" with two decimal places.
   g. ENTER the formula in cell B11 to calculate the total sales. Copy the formula in cell B11 to cells C11, D11, and E11.
   h. Insert a line of dashes (-) in rows 5 and 10.
   i. Save the file as B:STOREEX3.
   j. Use SHIFT-PRTSC to obtain an exact copy of the worksheet as it appears on the screen.
   k. Exit the 1-2-3 environment.

4. You are the treasurer for your university's business club. The club is selling t-shirts at $5.00 each as a fund raiser. You decide to create a worksheet to keep track of the t-shirts each member has taken to sell, the money turned in, and the money still outstanding. The completed worksheet is shown in Figure 9.37 on the following page.

```
             23-Apr-88 BUSINESS CLUB FUND RAISER
      NAME           NO. T-SHIRTS     $ RECEIVED     BALANCE DUE
      ==========================================================
      SUE SMITH            12            $60.00           $0.00
      JUDY KOCH            15            $50.00          $25.00
      DEBBIE CLINE          6            $20.00          $10.00
      DOUG CLOUGH          25            $45.00          $80.00
      JERRY WEISE          35           $110.00          $65.00
      LARRY MASO           10            $50.00           $0.00
      LINDA MARROW          8            $25.00          $15.00
      MARK SMELTZ          20            $35.00          $65.00
      ----------------------------------------------------------
      TOTALS              131           $395.00         $260.00
```

Figure 9.37
Completed Worksheet for CLUBEX4

    a. Globally set the column width of the worksheet to fourteen.
    b. ENTER today's date in cell A1 and format it.
    c. ENTER the worksheet title *BUSINESS CLUB FUND RAISER* in cell B1.
    d. Left-justify the first label in cell A3, and right-justify the labels in cells B3, C3, and D3.
    e. Insert a double line (=) in row 4.
    f. ENTER the names in cells A5 through A12. ENTER the number of t-shirts in cells B5 through B12. ENTER the money received in cells C5 through C12 as whole numbers (e.g., enter *$60.00* as *60*).
    g. ENTER the formula to calculate the balance due in cell D5 (e.g., for the case of Sue Smith, $(12 \times 5 - 60 = 0)$. Copy the formula to the range D6..D12.
    h. Insert a row of dashes (-) in row 13.
    i. ENTER the word "TOTAL" in cell A14. ENTER a formula in cell B14 to SUM the figures in column B. Copy the formula to cells C14 and D14.
    j. Format the range C5.D14 as "currency" with two decimal places.
    k. Save the file as B:CLUBEX4.
    l. Print the worksheet.
    m. Exit the 1-2-3 environment.

5. The financial analyst for Kings Construction Co., Inc. would like you to prepare a *pro forma* income statement for a three-year period. The base year of 1989 is to be projected two years into the future. Here is some basic information to help you complete this worksheet.

        1988 Sales   = $195,000
        Commission = 2% of Sales
        Net Sales   = Sales – Commissions
        COGS   = 60% of Sales
        Gross Profit = Net Sales – COGS
        Tax   = 46% of Gross Profit
        Net Profit = Gross Profit – Tax

    a. Globally set the column width to fourteen.
    b. ENTER the two lines of headings in cells B1 and B2.

c. ENTER the labels in cells B4 through B7. Refer to Figure 9.38.
d. ENTER the percentages in cells C4 through C7 as .05, .02, .60 and .46; they will be formatted.
e. Format the range C4..C7 as "percent" with zero decimal places.
f. Right-justify the labels in cells B9 through D9.
g. ENTER the labels in column A in the cells indicated.
h. ENTER the sales figure of 195000 in cell B10.
i. ENTER the formula in cell C10 to increase the 1989 sales level by five percent. Copy that formula to cell D10.
j. Calculate the formulas in cells B11 through B19.
k. Insert dashes (-) in cells B12, B15, and B18.
l. Copy cells B11 through B19 to the range C11..D19.
m. Globally format the worksheet as "currency."
n. Save the file as B:KINGEX5.

The completed worksheet is shown in Figure 9.38.

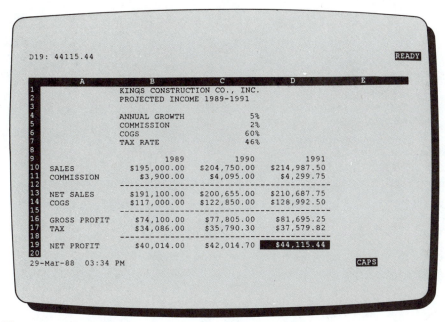

Figure 9.38
Completed Worksheet for KINGEX5

o. Use SHIFT-PRTSC to get an exact copy of the worksheet as it appears on the screen.
p. Change the annual growth rate to seven percent. Notice the change in net profits for the three years. Do not save these changes.
q. Exit the 1-2-3 environment.

Part V

DATABASE MANAGEMENT CONCEPTS AND APPLICATIONS

chapter 10

MICROCOMPUTER DATABASE MANAGEMENT SYSTEMS

- discuss the traditional manual and electronic methods of file processing.
- define a database.
- describe the data component of a database.
- discuss the difference between physical and logical database structures.
- discuss the four major types of logical organization used for structuring a database.
- describe a database management system and its functions.
- discuss two methods of accessing and manipulating the database.
- discuss R:Base and DataEase, two common DBMS software packages.
- discuss dBASE III PLUS, a popular database software package, and the contents of the diskettes included in the package.

chapter 11

USING dBASE III PLUS

- describe the features of the assist menu.
- discuss how to use the keyboard keys to move around in dBASE III PLUS.
- describe the syntax of a command in the command mode.
- describe the procedure for creating a database: defining the structure and inputting data.
- describe the procedure for modifying the structure and contents of a database.
- describe the procedure for generating reports.
- describe the procedure for sorting a database.
- describe the procedure for indexing a database.
- describe the process of searching, or querying, a database for a specific record.

chapter 10

MICROCOMPUTER DATABASE MANAGEMENT SYSTEMS

After completing this chapter, you should be able to

- discuss the traditional manual and electronic methods of file processing.
- define a database.
- describe the data component of a database.
- discuss the difference between physical and logical database structures.
- discuss the four major types of logical organization used for structuring a database.
- describe a database management system and its functions.
- discuss two methods of accessing and manipulating the database.
- discuss R:Base and DataEase, two common DBMS software packages.
- discuss dBASE III PLUS, a popular database software package, and the contents of the diskettes included in the package.

INTRODUCTION

Contrary to common belief, the concept of database management is not a new one. It has been used over the last several centuries for managing information representing specific entities. What is new is the concept of using microcomputers to store data in electronic files and to manipulate the stored data. For years, data or information about an organization's customers, employees, inventory, and other aspects of business life were kept in manual files: file cabinets, index cards, manila folders, even sometimes on blackboards. When it became necessary to update the files, all additions, deletions, or changes had to be done manually. As organizations became larger and more complex, the old method of managing information proved incapable of providing timely and accurate information to decision makers. The microcomputer revolution has helped many organizations to manage their data in a more effective way by storing them in electronic data files that are easy to create and manipulate.

This chapter discusses the overall characteristics of traditional computer data file processing, database processing (particularly with microcomputer-based software packages), and common microcomputer database software packages, in particular dBASE III PLUS. Chapter 11 covers dBASE III PLUS in hands-on computer sessions. Furthermore, Appendix F discusses the advanced features of dBASE III PLUS.

■ FILE PROCESSING

A **data file** is a collection of records, each of which contains information about an item, person, or situation, organized into a form of specified fields. Data files can be kept in manual systems (such as file cabinets) or stored in computers. For example, Figure 10.1 illustrates a typical customer file for a business.

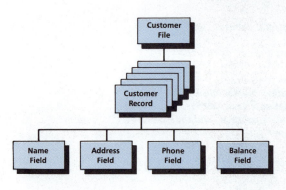

Figure 10.1
Customer File Organization

When it was discovered that computers could be used for storing information in electronic files, many organizations made huge financial investments in converting their traditional manual files to computer files. The tasks of creating, manipulating, and updating files were performed in the numerous high-level computer programming languages that had been invented since the early 1950s. As a matter of fact, a new profession—known today as **data processing** (DP)—evolved to carry out the task of managing files and other computer functions. It should be mentioned here that the single most important component of a computer-based information system, regardless of whether it is mainframe-based, mini-based, or micro-based, is *data*. In most systems, data files constitute a great proportion of the system, and the way the files are managed is very important.

Traditionally, in a typical computer-based information system, there were multiple files containing information about different entities of the organization. At the same time, there were computer programs to use the file data to produce information for decision makers. Figure 10.2 on the following page illustrates a typical data file and the application program for generating reports.

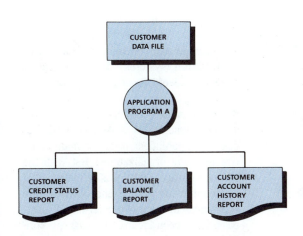

Figure 10.2
Data File, Application Program, and Reports

Two major problems arose with this approach. First, data files are not independent; rather, they are considered part of a computer program or programs. Second, duplication and inconsistency arises because data representing the same entities are located in different files. For example, in an organization with many departments, a customer file in the accounting office might be used with application programs developed for manipulating that department's data. At the same time, another file for the same customer might exist in the marketing department, where it is used with application programs developed around marketing needs. It is possible that, at any time, one of these files could be more accurate than the other one. In any case, a considerable amount of duplication exists among the files.

These problems of traditional file processing eventually led to the development of another method for file or data management, known today as **database management.**

By the early 1970s, businesses began to see the concept of the database and its applications as a solution to traditional file-processing problems. Three factors contributed to the formation of database concepts and applications. One, the volume of data that had to be managed grew dramatically. Two, direct-access media, such as magnetic disks, became increasingly available at low cost. Three, business recognized data as an important organizational asset that should be properly managed and made available to decision makers at all levels in a timely fashion.

■ WHAT IS A DATABASE?

A **database** is a collection of interrelated data files stored to serve the community of users in an optimal fashion. The stored data in a database are independent of the application programs that use the data.

One major database could serve all the users in an organization, or there could be multiple databases designed and developed for different communities of users. The latter case normally applies to larger organizations where the vast volume of data requires a number of smaller databases for the sake of efficiency. Figure 10.3 on the following page illustrates a common configuration of a database environment.

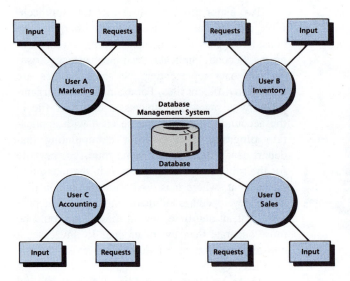

Figure 10.3
The Configuration of a Database

The applications of database management were initially designed around mainframe-based or minicomputer-based information systems. Microcomputers were considered inadequate for database processing during the 1970s. The fact that the early microcomputers had a limited storage capacity and only low-speed processing capabilities made them unattractive to many organizations. But with the recent significant advances in the areas of microcomputer storage and power, more sophisticated microcomputer-based databases have been created. Experts are confident that the trend toward the use of microcomputers in database management will continue.

■ COMPONENTS OF A DATABASE

Typically, the components of a micro-based database environment consist of

- data
- database structures or organizations
- a database management system (DBMS)
- application programs

Let's look at each of the above components at length.

Data

The most important component of any database is data. These data represent different characteristics and the overall status of an entity. The entity could be information related to a business's customers, products, markets, or employees. Within the database are files consisting of records. A **record** is all of the necessary information about one member of the overall file. For example, in an accounts file, information regarding the customer named Hank Williams makes up one record.

The information stored in the database initially is taken from different resources and files, either manual or computer files. A database can store all types of data, including numeric, alphabetic, alphanumeric, chronological, Boolean, and other special forms.

Database Structures and Organizations

The way that records are organized and related to each other in a database is known as the **database structure** or **organization.** There are two distinct types of data structures within a database: physical and logical.

Physical Structure. **Physical structure** of a database refers to how the records are organized on the computer media or within the internal memory of the computer. The physical structure of a database is similar to the storage of books, articles, documents, and other material on rows of shelves in a library. Each book is numbered according to its title, subject material, and author(s). The shelves are also numbered according to different categories, such as early eighteenth-century literature. The row of shelves is also numbered according to broader catagories, such as literature. Even a room or floor of a building could be organized for one category of material, such as government publications. In the same fashion, a database can hold files representing different entities, such as customer files and employee files. The records in these files contain a group of items related to an individual member of the file, such as one particular customer or one particular employee. Finally, the **fields** in each record represent particular characteristics of the member, such as customer age. In reality, the users of a database are not concerned with how fields, records, or files are organized on the computer media. Rather, this task is performed by a series of computer programs in your database management software. We'll look at these programs, known as database management systems, later in this chapter.

Logical Structure. The **logical structure** of a database deals mainly with the way files, records, and fields within that database are related to each other. In other words, the logical structure/organization represents the overall relationship environment of the database and its data components. This is very similar to the way that books and other materials in the library are organized on index cards. A user of the library can easily identify a book by knowing either the author's name or the title of the book. Therefore, the user needs very little information to find what he or she is looking for. Furthermore, the user does not have to go through hundreds of shelves or books to find the desired book, but can browse through the logical organization of the library catalog system, locate the book, and go directly to it. The logical structure used in databases is very similar to the logical structure of libraries.

Over the last two decades, different types of logical structures have been developed for organizing data within databases. We'll now take a look at the four major types of logical organization: linked list, network, hierarchical, and relational.

Linked List Structure. Normally, one field within each record contains a unique type of data used as identification for that record. That field, called the **primary key,** could be a customer number in a customer file, a student number in a student file, an employee number in an employee file, or an item number in an inventory file. In addition to the primary key, there may be many other fields that contain either unique or non-unique data that identify a record or assist in searching the records. These fields are known as **secondary keys.**

In a **linked list structure,** records are logically connected to each other based on these different keys. In this structure, **pointers** are placed within each record to establish the relationship. Pointers can be viewed as connectors between records that allow the user to go from one record to the next, based on the direction that the pointer provides. For example, in an inventory file, records could be connected to each other through the item number, a pointer that contains unique values and is considered the primary key. On the other hand, records could also be connected to each other through the use of a secondary key, such as the supplier's name, which can be retrieved in alphabetical order. In the latter case, a pointer would be placed at the end of each record, identifying the position of the next record. Figure 10.4 illustrates the linked list structure of such a file.

Figure 10.4
Inventory File with Linked List Structure

Number pointers in a linked list file can be either single or multiple. In other words, there could be either a single logical structure or many logical organizations among the members of a file. A final point: in the linked list structure, the pointer may also provide direction to the records of other files. In other words, records of different files could be logically organized with the help of a linked list structure.

Hierarchical Structure. This type of organization is very similar to many business organizational structures in which there is a president who has subordinate vice presidents who have subordinate department heads. Assuming that each subordinate reports to a superior, we have what is known as a **hierarchical,** or **tree structure.**

The logical structure of a data system can be based on this same concept of organizational structure. For example, an inventory database could have many files designed to hold information about an item, supplier, quantity, and price. In a hierarchical structure, if you wanted to find out about the quantity of an item on hand, you would be directed to the level of the tree that contains data about account balance and reordering of this particular item. From this level, the account balance would direct the computer to go to the next level of structure, which would have information for on-hand and on-order inventory status. Figure 10.5 graphically illustrates this situation.

Network Structure. The **network structure** is very similar to the hierarchical structure. The major difference between a network structure and a tree structure is that the network has multiple superiors to each subordinate. In other words, a record could be under one upper-level record and at the same time be connected to a record on the same level and yet another record at the upper level. In the previous inventory example, an ITEM DESCRIPTION in a network structure could be under both ITEM and QUANTITY. At the same time, the status ON HAND could be under both ITEM # and QUANTITY. Figure 10.6 illustrates a network structure for an inventory database.

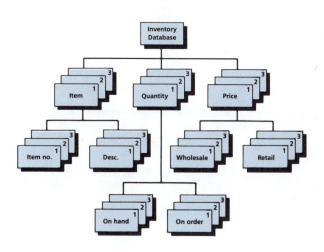

Figure 10.5
The Hierarchical Structure of an Inventory Database

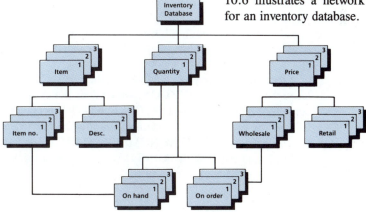

Figure 10.6
The Network Structure for an Inventory Database

Relational Structure. In a **relational structure,** data are stored in the form of **tables,** sometimes referred to as **flat files,** in which each row represents a record. Relationships are not predefined in this structure; rather, the user of the database decides how to relate the tables and their rows when using the database. Perhaps because of this capability, relational structures are known for their flexibility in allowing users to change relationships as it becomes necessary. Once the relationships between data are defined in the three structures we have discussed up to this point, they are almost impossible to change. In a relational-based database, our inventory example would feature several tables or files of data for different characteristics of the database, such as an ITEM table, a QUANTITY table, a PRICE table, and a SUPPLIER table. Figure 10.7 illustrates these tables.

ITEM TABLE

ITEM NO.	ITEM DESCRIPTION
111	Bow window #12
112	Octagon window
113	Double window
114	Single window

QUANTITY TABLE

ITEM NO.	ON HAND	ON ORDER	REORDER POINT
111	112	10	24
112	54	5	35
113	75	0	50
114	35	25	45

PRICE TABLE

ITEM NO.	COST PER UNIT	RESALE PRICE
111	69.95	83.94
112	220.00	264.00
113	180.00	216.00
114	120.00	144.00

SUPPLIER TABLE

ITEM NO.	SUPPLIER NO.	SUPPLIER NAME	SUPPLIER ADDRESS
111	221	Bob & Son	Boston
112	222	Daylight	New York
113	223	Protect	Miami
114	224	Skylight	Mobile

Figure 10.7
Inventory Database with the Relational Structure

In order to obtain information from a relational database, the user either searches a particular table or merges two tables on a column common to the two tables. For example, in the above case, in order to find the on-hand inventory status of a particular item, you could search the QUANTITY table. Or, if you needed to know the ITEM DESCRIPTION, which does not exist in the QUANTITY table, you could first merge the two tables (ITEM and QUANTITY) by using the ITEM NUMBER as the common field. The result of this merger would be a more detailed table with information on ITEM NUMBER, ITEM DESCRIPTION, ON HAND, ON ORDER, and REORDER POINT. Upon completion of the merger, you could search the new table which is temporary.

One major feature of relational databases is the ability to compile an **index**. The index is a limited version of a table, which contains only one or a small number of key fields. You could think of this table as similar to the index you find at the end of a book. A book index is a guide for quick location of a particular term, name, or concept in the book. A book might include several indices—one for terms, one for people's names, and one for concepts. The number of indices in a book will not change the physical arrangements of the contents of the book. Applying this concept to the case of our inventory database, the SUPPLIER table could have an index connected to it that contains the SUPPLIER NUMBER in numerical order, with the appropriate ITEM for each item of the table. Once this index is established, the user could later check the SUPPLIER table by using this index as the structure instead of using the original SUPPLIER table structure based on the SUPPLIER NUMBER as the key field. Figure 10.8 illustrates the index created for the SUPPLIER table.

SUPPLIER INDEX

ITEM NO.	SUPPLIER NO.
111	221
112	222
113	223
114	224

SUPPLIER TABLE

ITEM NO.	SUPPLIER NO.	SUPPLIER NAME	SUPPLIER ADDRESS
111	221	Bob & Son	Boston
112	222	Daylight	New York
113	223	Protect	Miami
114	224	Skylight	Mobile

Figure 10.8
The Supplier Index for the Inventory Database

A table can have as many indices as needed. These indices do not change the physical or logical structure of the initial tables. Rather, the indices are separate tables stored within the database environment at the time of processing. The major difference between the linked list structure and the index structure is that, in the linked list structure, a pointer or pointers are added to the records of a file to create additional logical relationships. In the case of the index structure, no pointer is added. Separate files are created instead to contain the necessary data.

The first three logical structures we have discussed—linked list, hierarchical, and network—are mainly used by database software packages designed for mainframes or minicomputers. The relational structure is employed by most software packages for microcomputer database processing.

A Database Management System (DBMS)

A **DBMS** is a software package that is a collection of programs that manage database-related activities. These activities might include the creation of new files, the addition or insertion of new data, deletion of old records, and retrieval of information for users. In many ways, DBMS resembles the operating system, with one difference: the operating system manages the activity of the microcomputer, while a DBMS manages a database environment. The main objectives of a DBMS are to

- increase data independence
- reduce data redundancy
- provide interaction and communication between users and the database.

Creation of a Database. A DBMS allows the user to create the necessary structure for a database. As mentioned earlier, you could design databases around any one of the data structures we've already discussed, but it is a given fact that the majority of microcomputer databases are designed around the relational model. Upon creating the structure—a process that consists of defining the record, the fields within each record and their size, and the type of data that will be stored in them—the raw data is loaded into the structure. The data will be stored on the diskette in the space allocated by the DBMS, with the defined structure attached to it. Whenever the user wants to access the data file, the DBMS will use the structure of the file to send the information from the file to the user.

Validation of Data. Another function of a DBMS is to validate incoming data with regard to its type and size. For example, if you define a field to store a social security number, which is all in numeric form, and you then attempt to enter non-numeric data either by accident or deliberately, the DBMS will not allow the data to be entered into the file.

Addition, Deletion, and Modification of Data. Once your database is created, you will occasionally need to add new data, delete old data, and modify existing data within the database. All these functions are performed with the help of the DBMS. Data can either be added to the end of a file, a process referred to as **appending,** or inserted into any part of the data file. Furthermore, the DBMS allows the user to modify old structures as it becomes necessary.

Sorting and Merging. Sometimes you'll need to rearrange the records of a file in a specific order. For instance, in a student file, you'll probably want to arrange the records in order of age, perhaps from youngest to oldest. The task of rearranging data within a file is referred to as **sorting.** Sorting can be done according to any field of a record, regardless of the type of data it holds. For example, you could sort records of the student file alphabetically by student name. If the sorting is based on increasing sequential factors, it is referred to as **ascending** order; if it is arranged according to decreasing sequential factors, it is called **descending** order. In addition, sorting can be done by using as the sorting key a single key or multiple keys. In the case of multiple keys, one key is considered the primary key and the rest are classified as secondary keys.

On the other hand, it is sometimes necessary to combine files or to update the contents of one file based on the contents of another file. This process is known as **merging.** The functions of both sorting and merging are performed by the DBMS.

Searching and Indexing Data. One of the most common activities performed in a database is the task of searching. Most DBMSs offer a variety of searching options and methods. **Searching** is the process of finding a particular record, field, or piece of data. The need for searching can arise for one of two basic reasons. First, the user might require a list of a particular group of records. For example, in an inventory file, a user might be interested in obtaining a list of all those items whose current quantity balance is less than that designated at the reordering point. In this case, the DBMS would search the entire inventory file and pull out those records that satisfy the *condition* that is set by the user. Second, the user might need an answer to a particular question. For example, a user of the inventory file might be interested in knowing the most expensive item in the inventory file. The searching process could be based on a single condition or multiple conditions. In order to facilitate the search process, most microcomputer DBMSs allow the user to create index files.

Formatting and Reporting Data. One of the most important features of most DBMSs is the function of formatting and reporting. The user of a database requires the formatting function for two purposes. First is screen formatting, so that the screen of the microcomputer will be formatted in such a way that the information is clear and usable. Second is formatting for hard-copy output. In the latter situation, most DBMSs offer a report-generating option that allows the user to specify the format of the report that must be generated. Report generation is a common function of most databases and, because of this, most software packages offer this capability.

Security of Data. Sometimes a portion of a database, or particular files, or the entire database should not be available to certain users for reasons of confidentiality. Most DBMSs allow an organization to establish security measures to protect the information stored in the database from unauthorized users. This task is normally performed by assigning a password to a file or to the entire database. Any user who wants to access the data has to know the password in order to get into the database; otherwise, the user will be stopped at the point of entry. Another type of security measure could be developed for those situations where a user or a group of users may retrieve data from the database but are not authorized to delete, add, or modify any information.

Figure 10.9 on the following page summarizes the DBMS functions we have just examined.

> **FUNCTIONS OF A DBMS**
>
> Creation of the database
>
> Data validation
>
> Addition, deletion, modification of data
>
> Sorting and merging
>
> Searching and indexing
>
> Formatting and reporting
>
> Security

Figure 10.9
Summary of DBMS Functions

Application Programs

A database can be accessed in two ways: by query access or via application programs. If it does not provide both options, a DBMS will most likely provide the query access option. In the case of **query access,** the process can be performed either on a menu-driven mechanism or through a sequence of commands issued by the user. For example, in order to sort an inventory under ITEM NUMBER (in ascending order), the user might key in a command such as SORT ON ITEM NUMBER TO SORTFILE. In this case, the sorted version of the inventory file would be stored in a file called SORTFILE. Another method of accessing and manipulating the contents of a database is to develop computer **application programs.** These programs, similar in many ways to ordinary computer programming languages, are coded by someone who is familiar with the syntax of the language. Upon completion of coding, the programs are compiled and executed. The average user of a database does not have to write the application programs; rather, these programs are developed by those people in an organization who are in charge of managing the activity of the database.

In recent years, most DBMSs were designed to provide query-based interactions between users and the database. The user-friendliness of a DBMS is considered to be an important factor in selection. The following paragraphs will discuss a few popular microcomputer DBMS software packages that are known for their high level of friendliness.

SOME POPULAR MICROCOMPUTER DBMS SOFTWARE PACKAGES

In the last decade, many DBMSs have been introduced by different vendors for microcomputer database applications. Three of the most commonly used software packages are R:Base 5000, DataEase, and dBASE III PLUS.

R:Base 5000

R:Base 5000, a relational DBMS designed by Microrim, Inc., is an advanced version of the earlier Microrim package known as R:Base 4000. This software package is designed for the family of IBM-PCs or 100 percent compatible clones. R:Base 5000 is known for its level of friendliness. It offers a menu-driven option for database processing in addition to a natural language query option and application programming development capability. Hardware requirements of R:Base 5000 are a minimum of 256K (preferably 640K) of memory, and two disk drives or a hard disk. The software package runs under PC-DOS version 2.0 or higher. Some of the storage capabilities of the software are: maximum fields per database, 4,000; maximum record size, 1,530 characters; maximum number of files in the database, 40. This software package is also known for its report-generation subsystems, called EXPRESS. Furthermore, the package utilizes some of the most advanced relational database concepts and applications which, until a few years ago, could be applied only on mainframe-based and mini-based systems. Figure 10.10 shows a sample R:Base 5000 screen.

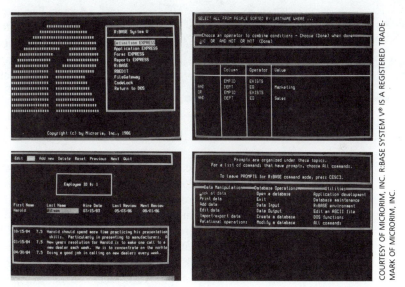

Figure 10.10
Screen of the R:Base 5000 DBMS

DataEase

DataEase, designed by Software Solutions, Inc., is another relational database management software package. It is designed for the family of IBM-PCs and compatibles, Wang, and other selected machines running MS-DOS or PC-DOS. DataEase provides a powerful data query language for data manipulation. The hardware requirements include minimum memory of 320K (preferably 640K) and two disk drives or a hard disk. Maximum data storage and handling capabilities of the database management system are 255 characters per field; 255 fields per record; 4,000 characters per record; and 65,535 records per file. The software offers password security both at the database level and at the field level. This system also offers query-by-example and comprehensive reporting functions, in which the user can either choose a predefined report format or create a custom-made format. Figure 10.11 shows a sample DataEase screen.

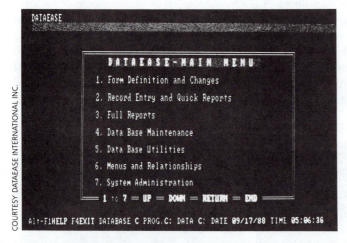

Figure 10.11
Screen of the DataEase DBMS

dBASE III PLUS

Perhaps the most commonly used microcomputer relational database management system in recent years is **dBASE III PLUS,** developed by Ashton-Tate, Inc. The first version of this package was introduced in the early 1980s as dBASE II, designed mainly for the IBM-PC and compatibles running MS-DOS or PC-DOS. Later, Ashton-Tate introduced a different version of the package that could be used under the CP/M operating system with Apple computers. Subsequently, two additional versions of the software package have been introduced: dBASE III and dBASE III PLUS.

Hardware specifications of the dBASE III PLUS version are minimum RAM storage capacity of 256K, preferably 640K; one disk drive, but preferably two drives; and a monochrome or color monitor. A dBASE III PLUS record can include up to 128 fields and up to 4,000 characters total data values. A file may have as many as a billion records. The actual limit to dBASE III PLUS database size comes from the availability of disk space. The entire software package comes in several diskettes: System Disk #1, System Disk #2, Sample Programs and Utilities Disk, dBASE Administrator #1, dBASE Administrator #2, Application Generator, and On-Disk Tutorial. The following paragraphs will discuss the contents of these disks.

System Disks #1 and #2. All the main programs of dBASE III PLUS are stored on these two diskettes. In order to start the software package, a user begins with System Disk #1, where the main program, "dBASE" is stored. Upon execution of this program, the system will ask the user to insert System Disk #2, which consists of more programs needed to complete the booting process and display the assist menu of the software package. Once in the dBASE environment, the user is provided with a menu.

The Sample Programs and Utilities Disk. This diskette contains all the sample data files used with the lessons of the On-Disk Tutorial (see below). In addition to these test data files, there are programs that can be used for database-related activities, such as converting data files developed by other systems to the dBASE III PLUS environment.

The Applications Generator. The programs on this diskette, written in the dBASE programming language, help users to create other dBASE programs and provide menu-driven assistance to the user who is interested in developing an application program. The application programs developed with the help of this application-generator program would be common, routine ones, such as showing information or printing.

The On-Disk Tutorial. Ashton-Tate, the designer of dBASE III PLUS, offers an on-line tutorial program that allows a user to become familiar with the overall capabilities of the software package. Many lessons are provided as part of the program of this diskette, which includes a few sample data files. The approach that is used in these lessons is based on an "assist" menu.

Chapter 11 provides a hands-on approach to the study of dBASE III PLUS and its programs.

■ SUMMARY

Over the past few decades, computers have been used in incorporating database concepts into computerized databases. Many database management systems (DBMSs) have been developed for mainframe and minicomputer systems. With the popularity of microcomputers, more DBMSs have been designed for use on microcomputers. A typical database environment consists of data, a database structure or organization, a DBMS, and application programs.

Data are a major substance of a database, which is used for information retrieval and manipulation. Database structures consists of physical and logical structures with four common logical structures: linked list, network, hierarchical, and relational structures. The third element of a database is the DBMS, which consists of a group of computer programs designed to manage the activity of a database. These activities include creating data files, validating incoming data, adding new information, deleting old data, modifying existing data, sorting and rearranging records, merging files, searching for information, generating reports, and providing security facilities. A database can be accessed, be manipulated, or retrieve information by using either a query-type language or the assistance of computer programs written in the procedural language of the package.

In the past decade, several microcomputer database management software packages have become known for their level of power and popularity. Three of these packages are R:Base 5000, DataEase, and dBASE III PLUS. The last package has been the most popular DBMS package with microcomputer users. The package, designed around the relational model and runs on the family of IBM-PCs and compatibles, offers a variety of database facilities, including application generators that allow users to develop application programs.

■ Key Terms

data file	A collection of records, each of which contains information about an item, person, or situation, organized into a form of specified fields.
data processing	The profession that evolved to carry out the task of managing files and other computer functions.
database management	A method of file or data management.
database	A collection of interrelated data files stored to serve the community of users in an optimal fashion.
record	Information related to one member of a file.
database structure or organization	The way that records are organized and related to each other in a database.
physical structure	The way records are organized on the computer media or within the internal memory of the computer.
field	Information related to one characteristic of a record.
logical structure	The way files, records, and fields within the database are related to each other; the overall relationship environment of the database and its data components.
primary key	A field within a record that contains a unique type of data used as identification for that record.
secondary key	Fields which contain either unique or non-unique data that identify a record or assist in searching the records.
linked list structure	One of the four major types of logical structure that uses fields known as primary and secondary keys to logically connect records.
pointers	The connectors between records in a linked list system that allow the user to go from one record to the next.
hierarchical, or tree, structure	A type of organization, very similar to many business organizational structures, defining the position of various elements, which assumes each subordinate reports to one superior.

network structure	A structure with multiple superiors to each subordinate.
relational structure	A structure that stores data in the form of tables, referred to as "flat files," in which each row represents a record.
tables, or flat files	Data stored in a form such that each row represents a record.
index	A limited version of a table, which contains only one or a small number of key fields.
database management system (DBMS)	A software package that is a collection of programs that manage database related activities.
appending	Adding data to the end of a database file.
sorting	The task of rearranging data within a file.
ascending	A sorting method based on increasing sequential factors.
descending	A sorting method based on decreasing sequential factors.
merging	To combine files.
searching	The process of finding a particular record, field, or piece of data.
query access	The process of accessing files performed either by a menu-driven mechanism or through a sequence of user-issued commands.
application programs	A method of accessing files in which the programs are coded by someone who is familiar with the syntax of the language.
R:Base 5000	A relational DBMS designed by Microrim, Inc.
DataEase	A relational DBMS software package designed by Software Solutions, Inc.
dBASE III PLUS	The most commonly used microcomputer relational database management system, which was developed by Ashton-Tate, Inc.

■ Review Questions

1. A _____ is a collection of records, each of which contains information about an item, person, or situation, organized into a form of specified fields.
   (a) file system
   (b) data file
   (c) database
   (d) filing cabinet
2. A data file is a new concept referring only to _____ files.
   (a) manual
   (b) electronic
   (c) traditional
   (d) all of the above
3. The profession known as _____ was created to carry out the task of managing files and other computer functions.
   (a) database management
   (b) data processing
   (c) electronic processing
   (d) data manager

4. The most important component of a computer-based information system is
   (a) the file structure.
   (b) data.
   (c) the records.
   (d) none of the above.
5. A _____ is a collection of interrelated data files stored to serve the community of users in an optimal fashion.
   (a) file
   (b) system
   (c) database
   (d) structure
6. How many databases are required for an organization?
7. Why were microcomputers considered inadequate for database processing during the 1970s?
8. Which type of data can be stored in a database?
   (a) numeric
   (b) alphanumeric
   (c) Boolean
   (d) all of the above
9. The way that records are organized and related to each other in a database is known as its
   (a) structure.
   (b) organization.
   (c) status.
   (d) (a) and (b).
   (e) (b) and (c).
10. The _____ structure of a database refers to the way files, records, and fields within the database are related to each other.
    (a) organizational
    (b) logical
    (c) physical
    (d) chronological
11. The _____ structure of a database refers to how the records are actually organized on the computer media or within internal memory.
    (a) physical
    (b) organizational
    (c) logical
    (d) actual
12. A field that contains a unique type of data used as identification for that particular record is called the _____ field.
    (a) linked list
    (b) primary key
    (c) pointing type
    (d) secondary key

13. A relational structure stores data in _____ , sometimes referred to as flat files.
    (a) blocks
    (b) tables
    (c) groups
    (d) arrays
14. In which of the following types of logical organization would it be easiest to alter a relationship between data once it has been established?
    (a) linked list
    (b) network
    (c) hierarchical
    (d) relational
15. A DBMS
    (a) is hardware associated with database technology.
    (b) takes the place of the operating system.
    (c) is a software package that manages database activities.
    (d) none of the above.
16. The functions of a DBMS include all of the following *except*
    (a) creation of the database.
    (b) formatting and reporting.
    (c) allow for security measures.
    (d) choose the appropriate logical structure for an application.
17. How can data be entered into an existing database?
18. _____ , a relational database management system produced by Microrim, Inc., offers menu-driven and natural language query options, and application programming capabilities.
    (a) REFLEX
    (b) R:Base 5000
    (c) R:LATION
    (d) DATABASE
19. _____ is designed by Software Solutions, Inc., and offers query-by-example and comprehensive reporting functions.
    (a) dBASE III PLUS
    (b) DATA:BASE
    (c) DataEase
    (d) R:Base 5000
20. _____ has been the most popular database management system used on microcomputers in recent years.
    (a) DataEase
    (b) R:Base 5000
    (c) DATA:BASE
    (d) dBASE III PLUS
21. What is the disadvantage to having multiple files containing information about different entities of the organization, while at the same time having computer programs that use the data in those files?
22. What factors led to the development of database concepts?
23. Name the components of a micro-based database system.

24. What are the two types of data structures within a database? Define each one.
25. What are the four types of logical structures for a database?
26. What are the main objectives of a DBMS?
27. Name two ways of accessing a database.
28. List the diskettes that comprise the dBASE III PLUS database software package.

Case One:
KEY STATES MANUFACTURING, INC.

Key States Manufacturing, Inc. is a medium-sized concern that produces rubber balls, tires, and a variety of other rubber items. Key States has been located in Pittsburgh, Pennsylvania since 1950.

Key States distributes its products throughout the United States and Germany. Twenty manufacturing plants are subsidiaries of Key States, all located in Pennsylvania.

The Pittsburgh office is the home office. All accounting, payroll, financial, and marketing functions are carried out here (see Figure 10.12). Key States has a multi-million dollar inventory and spends $5 million per year in advertising its best-selling product: automobile tires. Most American adults own a car, and every one of them uses tires. And who knows more about tires than Key States? This is part of the Key States slogan.

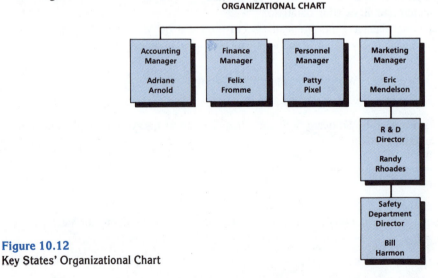

Figure 10.12
Key States' Organizational Chart

Key States is so successful that forty-seven percent of all the rubber products made in the U.S. are made by Key States. The company utilizes the most up-to-date, state-of-the-art equipment, both in manufacturing and in the support functions provided by the office staff. Key States realizes that information and data are a company's most valuable tools, so it is of the utmost importance that these data are processed, used, and manipulated in the most effective ways. Key States, therefore, uses the latest mainframe computer system on the market.

The safety department is one of the most important departments in the company. Laws are constantly being made more rigid to protect the consumer, and Key States prides itself on the innovative features and safety of its manufactured products.

Data for the safety department are currently maintained on the mainframe, but there are many problems with the mainframe system. Sometimes access to the computer by key personnel is not a simple task. Often, breakdowns and overloads occur. There is also a concern that the mainframe is not all secure, and safety data is theoretically available to everyone in the company. Trade secrets could easily leak out and create havoc.

The director of the safety department, Bill Harmon, discussed these problems of the mainframe with his boss, the director of research and development, Randy Rhoades. Bill told Randy that the safety department recently purchased an IBM Personal System/2 Model 50, which is equipped with one 20MB fixed disk.

Randy reviewed the mainframe problem in his spare time. He acquired some valuable information and called Bill on the telephone to tell him about it. Randy told Bill about database management and suggested it was time for Bill to set up his own database.

There is only one problem. Bill does not know where to start in developing this management system. He will be meeting with his superior next Wednesday and needs to bring up this matter of a database management system for the safety department at that meeting.

Questions

1. You are Bill, and you must get your facts together for the Wednesday meeting with your superiors. What would you bring up at the meeting?
2. What are the advantages of a local database system? Are you convinced that the company needs a local database? If you answered yes, explain.
3. Name a few appropriate database software packages suitable to their needs.
4. Give your recommendations.

Case Two:
STONEY INSURANCE AGENCY

The Stoney Insurance Agency is a rather small agency, with a main office located in Ft. Lauderdale, Florida, and a second office in Tampa. The Ft. Lauderdale office employs twenty-seven people, and all accounting, payroll, and financial functions are carried out there through the use of five IBM-compatible computers. These PCs are also used by the secretaries for word processing applications. Each PC is equipped with two disk drives and 640K of memory. In addition to these five PCs, there are two NEC 3550 letter-quality printers.

Stoney Insurance's organizational chart appears in Figure 10.13 on the following page.

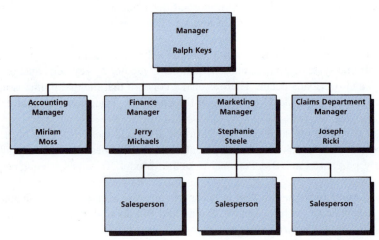

Figure 10.13
Stoney Insurance's Organizational Chart

The accounting department has a manager and three staff members. The finance department has a manager and four staff members; the marketing department, a manager and three salespersons; the claims department, a manager and three staff members; the secretarial pool, five members. The rest of the employees are salespeople, agents, underwriters and, last but not least, the cleaning staff.

Ralph Keyes has been Stoney's manager for the past ten years. While in his role as manager, the company has grown by fifteen percent every year. When he started out, the business was grossing close to $400,000 per quarter. Ralph has had several courses in economics and knows that, sooner or later, the firm will reach a point of diminishing marginal returns.

Ralph wants to upgrade his firm in every possible way, from management to computer applications. He knows that by operating in the most efficient manner, the firm will achieve the highest percentage of profit.

Currently, clients' files are kept on floppy diskettes. Each diskette contains records of many clients. These files are kept in alphabetical order, but it is still difficult to locate a specific customer file when information must be updated or when a claim is made.

Ralph believes that, in the insurance business, the most important person is the customer. Quick and easy access to customer records is vital. Ralph wants to start a client database where he could have all the information about his clients managed, but is not sure where to begin. He doesn't know what hardware or software he needs in addition to the existing five PCs and printers.

Questions

1. What is the problem?
2. Describe Ralph's information requirements.
3. Will a micro-based database solve Ralph's problems?
4. What are the available alternatives for Ralph, in regard to the client database system?
5. What would you recommend?

SELECTED BIBLIOGRAPHY

_____, "Ashton-Tate Recalls Some dBase III PLUS Software Packages," *Electronic News*, January 20, 1986, p. 25.

Bottom, J. et al, "The Art of Modeling," (microcomputer database manager prototyping tool), *Datamation*, November 15, 1985, pp. 140-2+.

Browning, D., "A Data Manager: The Evolving Standard," *PC Tech Journal*, May 1986, pp. 166-188.

Church, W.C., "Database Management Can Ease Your Job," *Security Management*, September 1985, pp. 77-8.

_____, "dBase III: The Right Stuff?" M. Nesary, *Computer Decisions*, July 15, 1985, pp. 49-50+.

Eisenberg, R., "A Plus for dBase III," *PC World*, October 1986, pp. 252-259.

Gold, J., "Micro DBMS to Suit," *Computer Decisions*, September 24, 1985, pp. 74-7+.

Hart, G., "dBase III PLUS," *PC Magazine*, June 24, 1986, pp. 125-126.

Krause, A., "Ashton-Tate's dBase III Plus Offers Better Performance, Features," *Computer Reseller News*, October 27, 1986, pp. 68-70.

Kull, D., "Good Things in Small Packages," *Computer Decisions*, September 24, 1985, p. 34+.

Liskin, M., "dBase III PLUS," *Personal Computing*, May 1986, pp. 201-208.

Liskin, M., "Which dBase is Right for You?" *Personal Computing*, June 1986, pp. 113-121.

Miller, M.J., "Database Management Software: Corporate Buyers Weight Ease of Use vs. Power: IBM PC Programs Become Easier," *Infoworld*, May 5, 1986, pp. 39-42.

Morgan, J.P., "Sizing Up Software: Databases - Filing and Retrieving Information," *Purchasing*, April 24, 1986, pp. 79-80.

Myers, E., "No DBMS is an Island," *Datamation*, June 1, 1986, p. 32+.

Myers, E.D., "Distributed DBMSs: In Search of Wonder Glue (distributed relational databases)," *Datamation*, February 1, 1987, pp. 41-2+.

Neumann, B.R. and L.A. Friedman, "Database Management Systems Extend Computer Use," *Healthcare Financial Management*, June 1986, pp. 50-3+.

Porter, K., "dBase III PLUS: A Programmer's Perspective," *Business Software*, May 1986, pp. 60-66.

Snyders, J., "Past Tense, Future Perfect?" (IBM's activity in database management area), *Infosystems*, January 1987, p. 26+.

Warren, C., "Databases Manage Network Environments," *Mini-Micro Systems*, May 1986, pp. 95-6+.

chapter 11

Using dBASE III Plus

After completing this chapter, you should be able to

- *describe the features of the assist menu.*
- *discuss how to use the keyboard keys to move around in dBASE III PLUS.*
- *describe the syntax of a command in the command mode.*
- *describe the procedure for creating a database: defining the structure and inputting data.*
- *describe the procedure for modifying the structure and contents of a database.*
- *describe the procedure for generating reports.*
- *describe the procedure for sorting a database.*
- *describe the procedure for indexing a database.*
- *describe the process of searching, or querying, a database for a specific record.*

INTRODUCTION

This chapter provides a hands-on approach to the basic features of dBASE III PLUS, the most popular database management software package used on microcomputers. The chapter highlights different aspects and features of the software package through a series of examples based on our on-going case of Sunshine Window Inc., Suppliers. (Appendix F discusses some of the more advanced features of dBASE III PLUS.)

■ GETTING STARTED

Booting the System

If the microcomputer you are working on has only one disk drive, it will be referred to as Drive A. If you have two disk drives, configured horizontally, then the left one is Drive A and the right one is Drive B. If the two drives are configured vertically, then the one on top is Drive A and the bottom one is Drive B.

Follow these steps—referred to as a "cold boot" because it begins with the computer turned off—to start up the microcomputer and begin dBASE III PLUS.

Step 1. Insert the DOS disk into Drive A and close the disk drive door.

Step 2. Turn the computer on. It will take from three to forty-five seconds for your computer to run through a system check.

Step 3. Respond to the date prompt that appears on the screen by typing the current date in the format indicated, then pressing the ENTER (↵) key. You will be presented with a similar message for the current time. Respond either by pressing ENTER to accept the current time, or by typing the time you desire in the format indicated, and pressing ENTER.

Step 4. When the DOS prompt, A> (pronounced *A prompt*), appears on the screen, take the DOS disk out of Drive A and insert dBASE III PLUS Disk #1 in Drive A.

Step 5. Type DBASE and press ENTER. You will see a copyright notice displayed on the screen as shown in Figure 11.1.

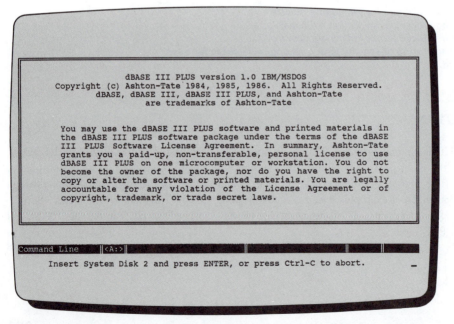

Figure 11.1
The dBASE III PLUS Copyright Screen

Notice that at the bottom of the screen a message appears that instructs you to "Insert System Disk 2 and press ENTER, or press Ctrl-C to abort."

Step 6. Remove System Disk #1 from Drive A and insert the dBASE III PLUS System Disk #2. Close the disk drive door and press ENTER. The booting process is complete, and you are now in the dBASE environment. The screen will look like the one pictured in Figure 11.2.

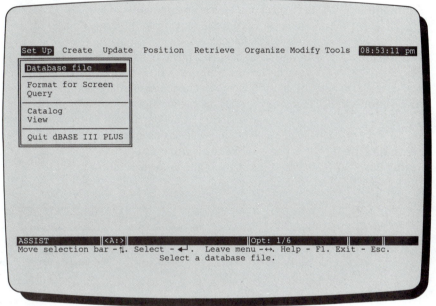

Figure 11.2
The dBASE III PLUS Assist Menu

The dBASE III PLUS Environment

The dBASE III PLUS database management software has the distinction of being both a menu-driven and a command-driven package. The command-driven portion of the package is called the **dot prompt command mode.** The initial mode, which is menu-driven, is called the **Assistant,** or simply the **assist menu.** At any point, you can easily quit the assist menu and get into the dot prompt command mode by simply pressing the ESC key. To get back into the assist menu from the command line, type ASSIST at the dot prompt position. Figure 11.2 shows you what the assist menu looks like.

Figure 11.3 details some of its functions. See Figure 11.4 on the following page for a diagram of the dBASE III PLUS menu and submenu options, and a brief description of each of their functions.

Screen Feature	Explanation
Menu Bar	The menu bar, located at the top of the screen, contains the menu selections and a clock.
Submenu	Each menu option has an associated submenu of options. Each menu option can, in turn, call up another submenu.
Action Line	As you select the assist menu options to build a command, the directions are written on this line as they would be entered in command mode syntax.
Navigation Line	This area provides instructions for moving around the screen and selecting an option, as well as error messages in case a mistake has been made by the user.
Message Line	This line explains the active menu.
Status Bar	Indicates the status of the following categories of information:

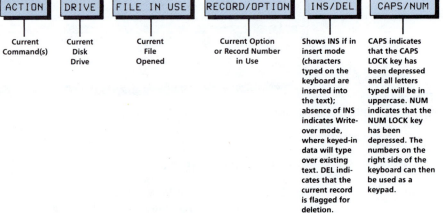

Figure 11.3
The Assist Menu Functions

MICROCOMPUTER SYSTEMS MANAGEMENT AND APPLICATIONS 297

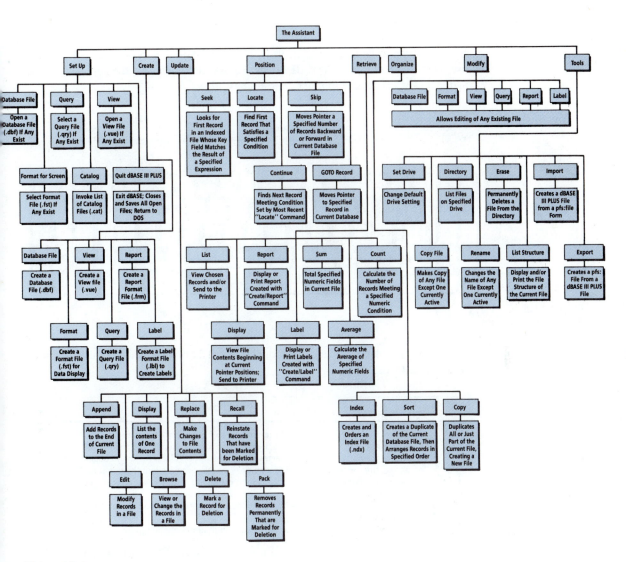

Figure 11.4
The dBASE III PLUS Menu Options

■ MOVING AROUND IN dBASE III PLUS

It is important to familiarize yourself with the keyboard and those keys that you will use most frequently in dBASE III PLUS. Figure 11.5 illustrates the keyboard layout and labels of the most important dBASE keys.

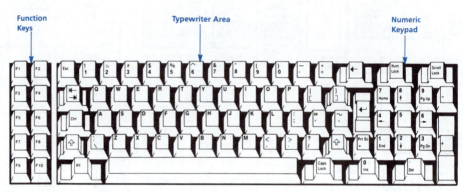

Figure 11.5
A Standard Keyboard

Table 11.1 describes the function keyboard keys that you will use to move around in dBASE.

KEY	FUNCTION
↑	Moves the cursor up one line or up one menu option in the submenus.
↓	Moves the cursor down one line or down one menu option in the submenus.
←	Moves the cursor left one character or left one option along the menu bar.
→	Moves the cursor right one character or right one option along the menu bar.
END	Moves the cursor to the next word in the command or to the last option on the right of the menu bar.
HOME	Moves the cursor to the previous word in a command or to the first option on the left of the menu bar.
↵	The ENTER key must be pressed to select a highlighted menu option or after a command is typed.
ESC	Used to back out of submenus or to leave the assist menu and enter the dot prompt command mode

***TABLE 11.1** A Summary of dBASE III PLUS Keys*

At this point, you should have the initial dBASE III PLUS menu on your screen. Using the LEFT (←) and RIGHT (→) ARROW keys, move back and forth along the menu options. The pull-down menus reveal the available options under each of the eight main menu options.

Function Keys

The function keys (F1 through F10) are located on the left side or the top of the keyboard. You can invoke a pre-set command by pressing each function key instead of typing the command at the dot prompt. The keys and their functions are listed in Table 11.2.

KEY	FUNCTION
F1	Invokes the HELP menu.
F2	Returns you to the assist menu from the dot prompt.
F3	Invokes the LIST command.
F4	Invokes the DIRECTORY command.
F5	Invokes the DISPLAY STRUCTURE command.
F6	Invokes the DISPLAY STATUS command.
F7	Invokes the DISPLAY MEMORY command.
F8	Invokes the DISPLAY command.
F9	Invokes the APPEND command.
F10	Invokes the EDIT command.

TABLE 11.2 A Summary of dBASE III PLUS Function Keys

Getting Help

dBASE III PLUS has a convenient built-in help system that you can access when you have a question about a specific command or menu option. Also, when you are entering a command in the dot prompt mode and make a mistake, dBASE asks you "Do you want some help? (Y/N)". If you answer by typing a *Y* for *YES*, a message screen explaining the command's correct syntax will be displayed. The help feature can be accessed from the dot prompt by typing the word Help. You can also ask for help at any time either from the assist menu or while in dot prompt mode, by pressing the HELP function key, F1. You can exit the help menu and return to the dot prompt at any point by pressing the ESC key.

Let's try out the help feature.

- Press ESC to enter the dot prompt mode.
- Press the F1 key.

The main help screen will be displayed as shown in Figure 11.6 on the following page.

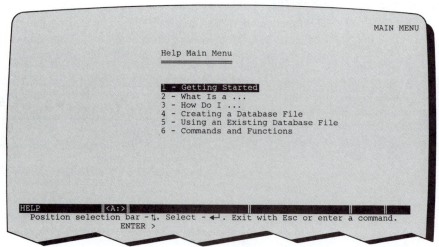

Figure 11.6
The dBASE III PLUS Main Help Screen

- Use the DOWN ARROW (↓) key to highlight option number six, Commands and Functions, and press ENTER.
- Press ENTER to select option number one, Commands (Starter Set).
- Let's look at the menu for the list command; type LIST and press ENTER. The screen in Figure 11.7 shows the help menu for the LIST command.

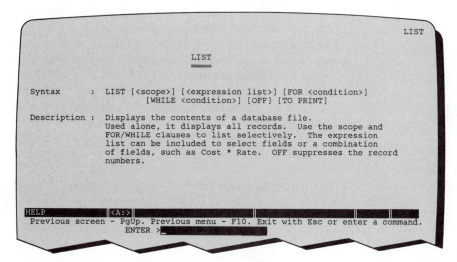

Figure 11.7
Help Menu for the LIST Command

- To exit the help feature and return to the dot prompt mode, press ESC.
- Type ASSIST and press ENTER to return to the assist menu.

Leaving dBASE III PLUS

When you have finished your session in dBASE III PLUS, you can exit the program by typing *QUIT* at the dot prompt or by selecting the *QUIT dBASE III PLUS* option under the assist menu's *SET UP* option. It is important to remember to leave the dBASE environment via the QUIT command. If you exit by simply turning off the computer or by some other means, you could lose data records. When the QUIT command is issued, dBASE saves and closes all open files. The message that appears in Figure 11.8 is then displayed on your screen.

Figure 11.8
The dBASE III PLUS End-of-Session Screen

Entering dBASE III PLUS Commands

In any computer program, the structure of a command is called its **syntax.** Each command line begins with a verb, which is the basic command. Many commands also have one or more parameters that tailor the command to meet a particular need. The general syntax of a dBASE command is:

COMMAND [<scope>] [<expression>] [FOR <condition>]

The COMMAND portion tells dBASE III PLUS exactly what action to perform. The scope portion defines the range of the commands, determining whether all or only part of the file will be processed by the command. The expression list is usually the object—a file or a field—on which the command acts. Many times, the expression is a list of fields that will be displayed. The condition portion usually specifies some criterion on which the command will act.

The items enclosed in square brackets ([ ]) are optional. They may be entered in any order. Capitalized items are entered exactly as shown. Items enclosed by angle brackets (< >) are selected by the user. Do not type the square brackets or angle brackets when entering a command. Commands may be typed in either lowercase or uppercase. Here is an illustration of a dBASE command:

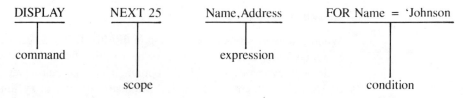

Deciding Which Mode to Use

As mentioned earlier, there are two ways to use dBASE III PLUS. First, you can enter the dBASE commands directly in the COMMAND mode. Second, you can use the menu-driven package known as the Assistant.

The assist menu is a convenient, user-friendly way of becoming acquainted with the dBASE III PLUS package. As you select menu options, dBASE builds the command on the action line as it would appear in the dot prompt mode. In this way, you can become familiar with the syntax of dBASE commands. On the other hand, it can be quite a time-consuming way of accomplishing tasks in dBASE by using the assist menu. For this reason, the command-driven mode is usually preferred as the quick, easy, and direct approach to entering dBASE commands.

To illustrate this point, let's compare the number of steps needed to accomplish two simple tasks in dBASE III PLUS. (Don't worry about using them at this time.)

The following steps set the default drive to Drive B and select an existing database file as the active file.

In Assist Menu Mode

1. Move the cursor to the "tools" option.
2. Select "Set drive" by pressing ENTER.
3. Move the cursor to B: and press ENTER.
4. Move the cursor along the menu bar to "Set up".
5. Select "Database file" by pressing ENTER.
6. Move the cursor to B: and press ENTER.
7. Move the cursor to the desired file name and press ENTER.
8. Type *n* in response to the prompt: "Is the file indexed (Y/N)?" and press ENTER.

In Dot Prompt Mode

1. Type SET DEFAULT TO B: and press ENTER (↵).
2. Type USE <*filename*> and press ENTER.

As you can see, it is a considerably longer task to issue these two commands in the assist menu. To allow you to begin using the dot prompt mode sooner, the commands presented in the remainder of this chapter will be issued at the dot prompt.

■ CREATING A DATABASE FILE

Many different types of files can be created in dBASE, based on the contents and function of the file. We specify the type of file by the extension name assigned to it. Table 11.3 lists the types of files that can be created in dBASE III PLUS, and a brief description of each.

EXTENSION	FILE TYPE	DESCRIPTION
.dbf	Database	Stores data in records and fields. Created with the CREATE command and changed with the MODIFY STRUCTURE command.
.dbt	Database Memo	Auxiliary file to database (.dbf) file, when memo field is specified as a field in the data structure.
.ndx	Index	Used with a database (.dbf) file to work with the database as if its records were sorted.
.prg	Program (or Command)	Contains sets of dBASE instructions that have been stored as programs.
.lbl	Label	Contains the information needed by the LABEL FORM command to format labels.
.qry	Query	Contains a condition that restricts the records displayed in commands.
.vue	View	Contains information relating different database files to each other.
.frm	Report Form	Contains information used by the REPORT command to generate reports.
.fmt	Format	Contains custom screen forms for data entry and report generation.

TABLE 11.3 Types of Files Created in dBASE III PLUS

The Case of Sunshine Window Inc., Suppliers

Sunshine Window Inc., Suppliers (SWIS) would like to use the dBASE III PLUS software they have purchased to convert their manual inventory system to a computerized one. The owners, Martine Martinez and Chico Gonzales, have decided on the relevant inventory data that they would like to see stored in the database. They think the database should include the product number, a description of the product, the cost to SWIS to purchase the product from the manufacturer, the retail price of the product, the balance on hand, the reorder point, and, finally, the manufacturer's name. The completed database, as it will appear after you have created it, is shown in Figure 11.9 on the following page. Throughout this chapter we use this case to teach you how to use dBASE III PLUS to solve real-life problems.

```
PRODNUM PRODDESC          COST   PRICE  BALANCE LIMIT MANUFACTUR
   111  Bow Window #12    69.95  83.94     112    24  Bob & Son Co.
   112  Octagon Window   220.00 264.00      54    35  Bob & Son Co.
   113  Double Window    180.00 216.00      75    50  Bob & Son Co.
   114  Single Window    120.00 140.00      35    45  Bob & Son Co.
   211  Patio Size #2    450.00 540.00      12    10  DayLight Co.
   212  Patio Door #2    210.00 254.00      25    15  DayLight Co.
   213  Patio Window     175.00 210.00      12    20  DayLight Co.
   214  Patio Shade      120.00 144.00      15    10  DayLight Co.
   311  Single Door      160.00 192.00      25    20  Glassy Co.
   312  Sliding Glass    285.00 342.00      10    15  Glassy Co.
   313  French Door      300.00 360.00      12    10  Glassy Co.
   314  Split Door       180.00 216.00      15    20  Glassy Co.
   411  Storm Window     210.00 254.00      25    35  Protect Co.
   412  Storm Door       350.00 420.00      12    10  Protect Co.
   413  Safe Window      220.00 264.00      19    15  Protect Co.
   414  Barn Window      250.00 300.00      14    12  Protect Co.
   511  Roof Window      175.00 210.00      25    20  SkyLight Co.
   512  Side Window      125.00 150.00      55    60  SkyLight Co.
   513  Sunshine Door    260.00 312.00      22    20  SkyLight Co.
```

Figure 11.9
A Complete Database for the SWIS Case

Before we begin to create a database file, insert a blank formatted diskette in Drive B in order to save the data you create. To build this database, carefully follow the instructions given below.

- Press the ESC key to leave the assist menu and begin working in the dot prompt mode (if you are still in the assist menu mode). The dot prompt (.) will appear on the screen with the flashing cursor next to it. You will enter the dBASE III PLUS commands at this location. Your screen should look like Figure 11.10:

Figure 11.10
A Blank Screen of the Dot Prompt Mode

Note: Remember to always press the ENTER (↵) key after you type a command. The status bar and the message line will appear at the bottom of the screen.

Correcting Typing Errors

If you make a mistake after you enter a dBASE command but before you press the ENTER key, simply press the BACKSPACE (←) key to delete the character(s) to the left of the cursor. You can also use the ARROW keys (←, →) to move the cursor to the mistake, then simply type over the character or characters in error. If you would like to insert characters into the existing line of the command, use the INS key located on the bottom right of the keyboard to switch from writeover to insert mode. When you activate the INS key, the letters *Ins* will appear on the status bar. Press the INS key again to toggle back to writeover mode.

Setting the Default Drive

The initial default drive is Drive A. In order to direct any files to be saved or retrieved onto your blank diskette in Drive B, you must use the SET DEFAULT command to change the current setting as follows:

- Type SET DEFAULT TO B: at the dot prompt and press ENTER.

Note: All dBASE commands can be entered in either lowercase or uppercase letters.

Rules for File Names

A dBASE file name can be up to eight characters long and must begin with a letter. The rest of the file name can consist of letters, numbers, or the underscore (_). For example, *clients1*, *emp_recs* and *db155* would all be valid file names. If no extension name is specified, dBASE automatically adds the *.dbf* extension to all your database files.

The CREATE Command

The general form of the CREATE command is

CREATE <*newfile*>

You will now use the CREATE command and the rules you have learned for naming files to create a database file called INVENTRY.

Note: The word *INVENTRY* is not misspelled; we have shortened it to eight characters to satisfy the eight-character limit for a file name.

- At the dot prompt, type CREATE INVENTRY and press ENTER.

Defining the File Structure

To create a data file in dBASE, the first step is to define the structure of the file with regard to the number of fields, types of data that will be stored in the fields, and the size of the fields. After you have issued the command CREATE, which indicates that a new data file is in the creation process, dBASE will display the field definition form as shown in Figure 11.11.

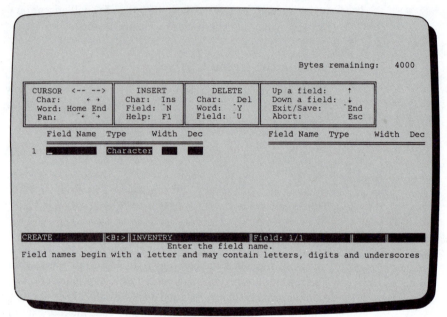

Figure 11.11
A Screen Showing a Blank Field Description

The display at the top of the screen lists all the valid combinations of keystrokes available. The ^ character signifies the CTRL key. For example, to exit and save the file structure when you are done, you press the CTRL key and the END key simultaneously (^END).

Three items must be defined for each field of the file—the field name, the type, and the field width. The number of decimal places must be entered if the field is designed for numeric decimal values.

Field Name. The field name can be up to ten characters long. It must begin with a letter, and contain only letters, numbers, or the underscore(_). If the field name you enter is a full ten characters, you will hear a beep, and the cursor will move automatically to the beginning of the *Type* area. If the field name is less than ten characters long, you will have to press the ENTER key to move the cursor to the *Type* area.

Now begin to enter the field information.

- With the cursor in the first "Field Name" area, type PRODNUM (for product number). Press ENTER to jump to the *Type* area.

Data Type. There are five data types available in dBASE.

- Character
- Numeric
- Date
- Logical
- Memo

In order to define a field, you can type the first letter of the data type (*C* for character, *N* for numeric, *D* for date, *L* for logical, or *M* for memo). Or, by pressing SPACEBAR, you can view all data types; when the desired data type is shown on the display, press ENTER to accept it.

- Press SPACEBAR until you have viewed all the possible data types.
- Continue to press SPACEBAR until the data type *Numeric* appears. Press ENTER to accept it and move the cursor to define the width.

Width. The field width is the maximum number of characters that will be allowed in the field. The width of two of the data types is automatically set by dBASE. The date data type is always set to eight (mm/dd/yy)—six characters for the numeric date and two characters for the slashes. The logical data type evaluates whether a statement is true or false, and is always one character in length (T or F).

- In the *width* area, type the number 3 and press ENTER.

Note: Whenever a numeric data type is selected, the cursor will move to the *Dec* (for decimal place) area. If the field was to contain a decimal, it would be entered now.

- In *Dec*, press ENTER to jump to the next field definition, since our product number is an integer and does not require a decimal.

Now follow the same procedure for the product description.

- In *Field Name*, type PRODDESC and press ENTER to jump to the beginning of *Type*.
- In *Type*, press ENTER to accept the data type character for this field.
- In *Width*, type 15 and press ENTER for the field size. Upon completion of this step, the cursor will jump to the beginning of a new field definition.
- In *Field Name*, type COST and press ENTER.
- In *Type*, press SPACEBAR once to change the character type of numeric, and press ENTER.

- In *Width*, type 6 and press ENTER.
- In *Dec*, type 2 and press ENTER.
- In *Field Name*, type PRICE and press ENTER.
- In *Type*, press SPACEBAR once to change the character type of numeric, and press ENTER.
- In *Width*, type 6 and press ENTER.
- In *Dec*, type 2 and press ENTER.
- In *Field Name*, type BALANCE and press ENTER.
- In *Type*, press SPACEBAR once and press ENTER.
- In *Width*, type 4 and press ENTER.
- In *Dec*, press ENTER.
- In *Field Name*, type LIMIT and press ENTER.
- In *Type*, press SPACEBAR once, followed by ENTER.
- In *Width*, type 4 and press ENTER.
- In *Dec*, press ENTER.
- In *Field Name*, type MANUFACTUR.

Note: The word *Manufactur* is not misspelled; rather, it has been shortened to satisfy the ten-character limit for a field name.

- In *Type*, press ENTER.
- In *Width*, type 15 and press ENTER.

You have just defined all of the fields of the database INVENTRY. The next step is to enter the data, but before you can do that, you must end the structure definition form. The finished field definition form should look like the one in Figure 11.12.

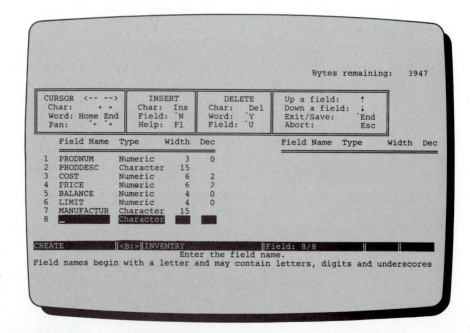

Figure 11.12
A Screen Showing a Completed Field Description

Now end the field definition form.

- In *Field Name*, press the CTRL and END keys simultaneously. The message "Press ENTER to confirm, any other key to resume" will appear below the status line.
- Press ENTER.
- The message "Input data records now?(Y/N)" will appear at the bottom of the screen.
- Type Y for "Yes."

Entering Data

It is now time to enter data into our INVENTRY database. While you are entering records, a beep will sound and the cursor will automatically advance to the next field when you enter data in the last position of the current field. Otherwise, you must press the ENTER key to advance to the next field. The first blank data entry form should look like the one in Figure 11.13.

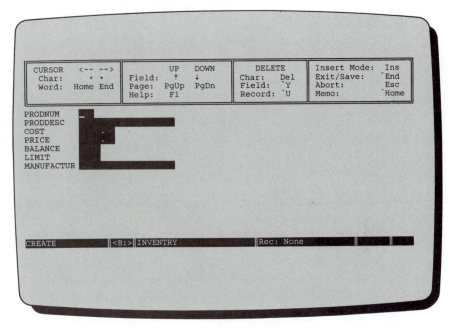

Figure 11.13
A Screen Showing a Blank Data Entry Form

ENTER the data for the first record.

- Type 111 in the *ProdNum* field.
- Type Bow Window # 12 in the *ProdDesc* field.
- Type 69.95 in the *Cost* field. Do not type a dollar sign.
- Type 83.94 in the *Price* field.
- Type 112 in the *Balance* field and press ENTER.
- Type 24 in the *Limit* field and press ENTER.
- Type Bob & Son Co. in the *Manufactur* field, and press ENTER or PGDN to advance to the next record.

Note: If at any time you want to see a previously entered record, use the PGUP key. To move back to a field in which you have already entered data, use the BACKSPACE key. Further, if the cursor does not move to the beginning of the next field, press ENTER.

Enter the following records in the same manner as you entered the first one.

ProdNum	ProdDesc	Cost	Price	Balance	Limit	Manufactur
112	Octagon Window	220.00	264.00	54	35	Bob & Son Co.
113	Double Window	180.00	216.00	75	50	Bob & Son Co.
114	Single Window	120.00	144.00	35	45	Bob & Son Co.
211	Patio Size # 2	450.00	540.00	12	10	DayLight Co.
212	Patio Door # 2	210.00	254.00	25	15	DayLight Co.
213	Patio Window	175.00	210.00	12	20	DayLight Co.
214	Patio Shade	120.00	144.00	15	10	DayLight Co.
311	Single Door	160.00	192.00	25	20	Glassy Co.
312	Sliding Glass	285.00	342.00	10	15	Glassy Co.
313	French Door	300.00	360.00	12	10	Glassy Co.
314	Split Door	180.00	216.00	15	20	Glassy Co.
411	Storm Window	210.00	254.00	25	35	Protect Co.
412	Storm Door	350.00	420.00	12	10	Protect Co.
413	Safe Window	220.00	264.00	19	15	Protect Co.
414	Barn Window	250.00	300.00	14	12	Protect Co.
511	Roof Window	175.00	210.00	25	20	SkyLight Co.
512	Side Window	125.00	150.00	55	60	SkyLight Co.
513	Sunshine Door	260.00	312.00	22	20	SkyLight Co.

Upon typing the last field of the last record (*SkyLight Co.*), *do not press* ENTER. To save the data that you just entered into the INVENTORY database,

- In the *Manufactur* field, press the CTRL and END key simultaneously to exit the data-entry process and return to the dot prompt.

Look at the status bar at the bottom of the screen. The message "Rec: 19/19" indicates that the file contains nineteen records.

The DIR Command

The DIR (directory) command allows you to see the list of database files of all types on your Drive B diskette. In order to make sure that the file INVENTRY has been created on the diskette,

- At the dot prompt, type `dir` and press ENTER. A message like the one in Figure 11.14 will be displayed.

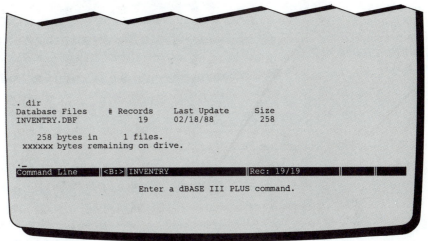

Figure 11.14
A Listing of All Files on a Drive B Diskette

The LIST STRUCTURE Command

The general form of the LIST STRUCTURE command is

LIST STRUCTURE [TO PRINT]

The LIST STRUCTURE command displays the file structure of the current .dbf file (the data you entered in the field definition form). It provides the following information: the file name, the number of data records, the last date that any database item was changed, the complete definition of each field, and the total number of bytes in each record.

- At the dot prompt, type `clear` and press ENTER.
- Type `LIST STRUCTURE` and press ENTER. A display like the one in Figure 11.15 on the following page will appear.

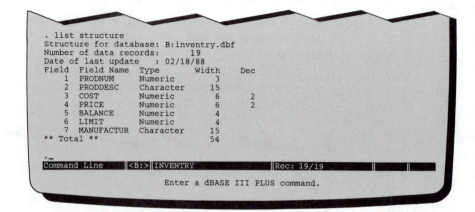

Figure 11.15
A Screen Showing the Result of the LIST STRUCTURE Command

The LIST Command

The general form of the LIST command is

LIST [<scope>] [<expression list>] [WHILE <condition>]
[FOR <condition>] [TO PRINT]

The LIST command displays the records in a file. The record pointer is automatically positioned at the beginning of the file so the entire file's contents are displayed.

Type LIST and press ENTER.

The output to the screen will look like Figure 11.16.

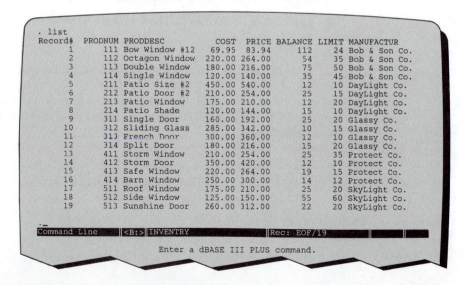

Figure 11.16
A List of Information in the INVENTRY Database

Output can also be sent to the printer by adding a TO PRINT command to the LIST command. (Before issuing this command, make sure your printer is on.)

- At the dot prompt, type LIST TO PRINT, and press ENTER. At this time, your output should print on the printer.

The LIST OFF Command

The general form of the LIST OFF command is

LIST [OFF] [<scope>] [<expression list>]
   [WHILE <condition>] [FOR <condition>] [TO PRINT]

This command lists specified records without their record numbers.

- Type list off and press ENTER to obtain a list of the records within the INVENTRY database without their record numbers.

The SET HEADINGS Command

The general form of the SET HEADINGS command is

SET HEADING ON/OFF

This command turns the column and field headings on or off.

- Type set headings off and press ENTER.
- Type list and press ENTER. Notice the column headings are not displayed.
- Type set headings on and press ENTER.
- Type list and press ENTER.

The Pointer Position

At any given point in a file, one record is considered to be the **current record**—the record that was last created or accessed. Facing this current record is a marker that is not seen by the user of the database. This marker is called the **current record pointer**. To know what record is the current record or what record the pointer is facing, all you have to do is to look at the command line at the bottom of your screen. On that line you'll see the message "Rec: EOF/19." The first item (EOF) indicates that the current line is the end of file; in other words, the pointer is facing the end of the file. Many commands can move the pointer around or make a specific record the current record. Table 11.4 on the following page illustrates these commands and their roles. As you learn about them, try them on the file that you have just created, making sure that you check the record indicator on the status line.

COMMAND	DESCRIPTION
GOTO n	This command can send the pointer anywhere in the file. n is an integer number. For example, type GOTO 12 and press ENTER.
GOTO TOP	This command makes the first record of the file the current record. For example, type GOTO TOP and press ENTER.
GOTO BOTTOM	This command directs the pointer to the bottom of the file. For example, type GOTO BOTTOM and press ENTER.
SKIP –/+ n	This command moves the pointer backward (when the minus sign is used with n) or forward (when the plus sign is used). Example (1): Type SKIP –19 and press ENTER to place the pointer at the front of the first record. With the SKIP command, dBASE will notify you which record is the current record. Example (2): Type SKIP and press ENTER to go to the next record. Example (3): Type SKIP + 10 and press ENTER to move the pointer ten records down.
?RECNO()	This command allows you to find the position of the pointer at any time. For example, type ?recno() and press ENTER to find the position of the current record.

TABLE 11.4   *Pointer Commands*

The LIST Command with a Condition

At times, you will not need to see all of the information in the database, but only selected material. At those times, the LIST command, with certain criteria added, can be very useful. For example, to list only the INVENTRY records that pertain to the DayLight Co.,

- At the dot prompt, type `clear` and press Enter.
- Type `list for manufactur = 'DayLight Co.'` and press ENTER. The list in Figure 11.17 will be displayed on the screen.

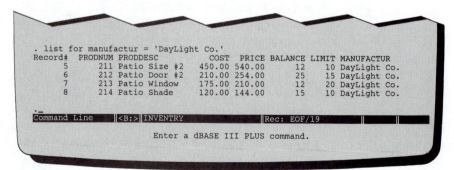

Figure 11.17
A List of Records for the DayLight Co.

Note: Because the name *DayLight Co.* is a character string, it must be enclosed in single or double quotes. If it had been a numeric value, the quotes could have been left off.

You may still feel that more information is displayed than you actually need. You can limit the amount of information even further by specifying that certain fields be displayed. For example, perhaps you are only interested in the retail price of Day-Light Co. products. You can list the company's name, the product description, and its price, as follows:

- At the dot prompt, type `clear` and press ENTER.
- Type `LIST MANUFACTUR, PRODDESC, PRICE FOR MANUFACTUR = 'DayLight Co.'` and press ENTER.
- Notice that you do not need to request the selected fields in the same order that they are stored in the database. The display for this version of the LIST command will look like Figure 11.18.

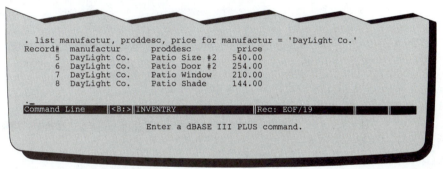

Figure 11.18
A List of Records with Selected Fields for the DayLight Co.

The USE Command

The general form of the USE command is

USE <*filename*> [INDEX <*index file list*>]

Whenever you try to access a database, dBASE will bring the file or files of the database into a temporary file area in RAM. This area is referred to as the current **active file area.** In the INVENTRY example, since we just created the database, the file is already in the active file area. However, if we tried to access this file later on, we would have to first bring it back into the active file area. This task is performed by the command USE, which signals dBASE to activate a file.

Now, in order to see how this command works, let's try the following instructions.

- At the dot prompt, type `clear` and press ENTER.
- Type `USE INVENTRY` and press ENTER.

- Type LIST and press ENTER. Your screen should look like Figure 11.19.

```
. list
Record#   PRODNUM PRODDESC         COST   PRICE  BALANCE LIMIT MANUFACTUR
     1      111  Bow Window #12    69.95   83.94    112    24  Bob & Son Co.
     2      112  Octagon Window   220.00  264.00     54    35  Bob & Son Co.
     3      113  Double Window    180.00  216.00     75    50  Bob & Son Co.
     4      114  Single Window    120.00  140.00     35    45  Bob & Son Co.
     5      211  Patio Size #2    450.00  540.00     12    10  DayLight Co.
     6      212  Patio Door #2    210.00  254.00     25    15  DayLight Co.
     7      213  Patio Window     175.00  210.00     12    20  DayLight Co.
     8      214  Patio Shade      120.00  144.00     15    10  DayLight Co.
     9      311  Single Door      160.00  192.00     25    20  Glassy Co.
    10      312  Sliding Glass    285.00  342.00     10    15  Glassy Co.
    11      313  French Door      300.00  360.00     12    10  Glassy Co.
    12      314  Split Door       180.00  216.00     15    20  Glassy Co.
    13      411  Storm Window     210.00  254.00     25    35  Protect Co.
    14      412  Storm Door       350.00  420.00     12    10  Protect Co.
    15      413  Safe Window      220.00  264.00     19    15  Protect Co.
    16      414  Barn Window      250.00  300.00     14    12  Protect Co.
    17      511  Roof Window      175.00  210.00     25    20  SkyLight Co.
    18      512  Side Window      125.00  150.00     55    60  SkyLight Co.
    19      513  Sunshine Door    260.00  312.00     22    20  SkyLight Co.

Command Line    <B:> INVENTRY                Rec: EOF/19
                Enter a dBASE III PLUS command.
```

Figure 11.19
A List of Records in the INVENTRY Database

If you were finished with the INVENTRY file, for example, and wanted to change the current active file, the USE command would accomplish this by saving and closing INVENTRY and opening the next file to be activated. If the INVENTRY is not replaced by a new file, it will be saved when you issue the QUIT command at the end of your dBASE session.

The DISPLAY Command

The general form of the DISPLAY command is

DISPLAY [<scope>] [<expression list>] [WHILE <condition>] [FOR <condition>] [TO PRINT]

The DISPLAY command is similar to the LIST command in that its purpose is to reveal the contents of the active file. The difference is that the DISPLAY command, when used by itself, will only display the record to which the pointer is currently pointing. For example, if the pointer is at the end of a file and you issue the DISPLAY command, the only output would be the field names, as shown in Figure 11.20 on the following page.

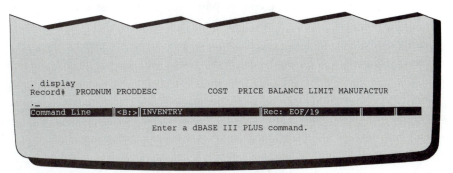

Figure 11.20
DISPLAY Screen with Pointer at EOF

However, you can specify which record is to be displayed.

- Type `clear` and press ENTER.
- Type `goto 12` and press ENTER.
- Type `display` and press ENTER to display the contents of record number twelve. Now the output will look like Figure 11.21.

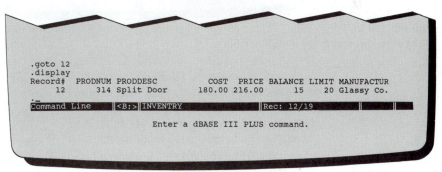

Figure 11.21
Displaying the Record Number 12

In order to display on the screen all the records in the file, as we did with the LIST command, you must specify the ALL parameter. With DISPLAY ALL, you don't have to use GOTO to position the pointer to the beginning of the file; rather, dBASE will display everything in the file. Note that, if you had a long file with several hundred records in it, DISPLAY ALL would only show you twenty lines at a time on the screen. You could press any key to see the next page of records. Let's try DISPLAY ALL.

- Type `clear` and press ENTER.
- Type `display all` and press ENTER.

The output on your screen should look like Figure 11.22.

```
. display all
Record #   PRODNUM PRODDESC         COST    PRICE  BALANCE LIMIT MANUFACTUR
     1       111   Bow Window #12    69.95   83.94     112    24 Bob & Son Co.
     2       112   Octagon Window   220.00  264.00      54    35 Bob & Son Co.
     3       113   Double Window    180.00  216.00      75    50 Bob & Son Co.
     4       114   Single Window    120.00  140.00      35    45 Bob & Son Co.
     5       211   Patio Size #2    450.00  540.00      12    10 DayLight Co.
     6       212   Patio Door #2    210.00  254.00      25    15 DayLight Co.
     7       213   Patio Window     175.00  210.00      12    20 DayLight Co.
     8       214   Patio Shade      120.00  144.00      15    10 DayLight Co.
     9       311   Single Door      160.00  192.00      25    20 Glassy Co.
    10       312   Sliding Glass    285.00  342.00      10    15 Glassy Co.
    11       313   French Door      300.00  360.00      12    10 Glassy Co.
    12       314   Split Door       180.00  216.00      15    20 Glassy Co.
    13       411   Storm Window     210.00  254.00      25    35 Protect Co.
    14       412   Storm Door       350.00  420.00      12    10 Protect Co.
    15       413   Safe Window      220.00  264.00      19    15 Protect Co.
    16       414   Barn Window      250.00  300.00      14    12 Protect Co.
    17       511   Roof Window      175.00  210.00      25    20 SkyLight Co.
    18       512   Side Window      125.00  150.00      55    60 SkyLight Co.
    19       513   Sunshine Door    260.00  312.00      22    20 SkyLight Co.
.
Command Line       <B:> INVENTRY                     Rec: EOF/19
               Enter a dBASE III PLUS command.
```

Figure 11.22
A List of the Records in the INVENTRY File

You can also use the DISPLAY command to list a limited number of records in the database. For example, if you want to print the first ten records of the database,

- Type clear and press ENTER.
- Type goto top and press ENTER.
- Type display next 10 and press ENTER.

The output on your screen should look like Figure 11.23 on the following page.

Further, the DISPLAY command, like the LIST command, can display selected fields of the database. For example,

- Type clear and press ENTER.
- Type goto top and press ENTER.
- Type display next 10 prodnum, proddesc, manufactur and press ENTER.

The output on your screen should look like Figure 11.24 on the following page.

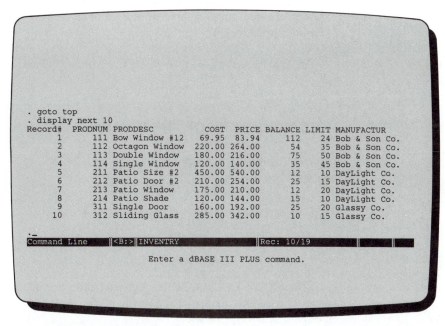

Figure 11.23
A List of the First Ten Records in the INVENTRY Database

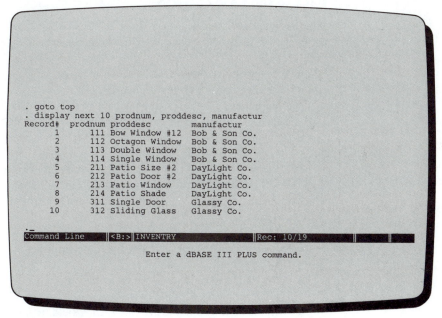

Figure 11.24
The First Ten Records with Selected Fields

You can execute the DISPLAY command in conjunction with the print parameter. For example, if you want to print a list of all items in the database (first making sure your printer is on);

- Type `display all to print` and press ENTER.

MODIFYING THE STRUCTURE OF THE DATABASE

You can update the structure of the database, as well as its contents, as the need arises.

The MODIFY STRUCTURE Command

The general form of the MODIFY STRUCTURE command is

MODIFY STRUCTURE [<*filename*>]

The MODIFY STRUCTURE command alters the record structure of an existing database file. This command allows you to add new fields, delete existing fields, or change a field's type or width.

Back to the Case of SWIS

Let's assume that, after you created the INVENTRY database, you realized that the width of two fields, COST and PRICE, should be expanded by one more position.

- Type `clear` and press ENTER.
- Type `use inventry` and press ENTER.
- Type `modify structure` and press ENTER. The structure of the active database will be displayed on the screen as shown in Figure 11.25 on the following page.

The record structure is now presented for you to make any necessary alterations. The menu at the top of the screen displays the cursor movement keys, the keys with which to make insertions or deletions, and the keystrokes to save or abort your changes to the file.

- Press the DOWN ARROW key two times to bring the highlighted line to the *COST* field.
- Press END key twice to move the cursor to *Width*.
- Type 7 and press ENTER twice.
- With the highlighted line over the *PRICE* field, press the END key twice to go to *Width*.

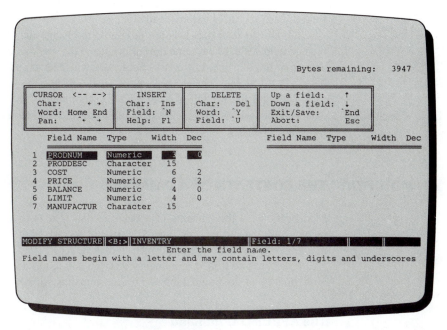

Figure 11.25
A Screen Showing the List Structure of the Active INVENTRY Database

- Type 7 and press ENTER twice.
- Press the DOWN ARROW key twice.
- Press CTRL and END simultaneously.
- In response to the message "Press ENTER to confirm. Any other key to resume", press ENTER. At this stage the changes that you made will be saved onto the diskette.

To double-check whether the width of the two fields *COST* and *PRICE* has indeed been expanded,

- At the dot prompt, type `use inventry` and press ENTER.
- Type `modify structure` and press ENTER. Make sure that the *COST* and *PRICE* width is seven.
- Press the ESC key to abort the modify session.
- In response to the message "Are you sure you want to abandon operation? [Y/N]", type Y.

In MODIFY STRUCTURE, you can also insert a new field by positioning the cursor at the desired location in the file and pressing the CTRL and *n* keys simultaneously. To delete a field that you no longer need, position the cursor at that field and press the CTRL and *u* keys simultaneously. The data that were contained in that field of each record is automatically deleted.

You should note that it is not advisable to change the field name and the data type or field width at the same time. Because of the way that dBASE III PLUS moves data from the old field to the new field, data will be lost and your new field will be blank. Perform each change separately. First, change the field name and save the file. Then use the MODIFY STRUCTURE command a second time to change the data type or field width. To avoid losing data, you also should not insert or delete fields and change a field's name at the same time.

■ MODIFYING THE CONTENTS OF A DATABASE

Modifications to the contents of a database fall into three categories: adding new records, editing old records, and deleting old records. Let's look at how these file manipulation activities are performed in dBASE III PLUS.

There are two dBASE commands that you can use to add a new record or group of records to an existing database. These commands are APPEND and INSERT.

The APPEND Command

The general form of the APPEND command is

APPEND [*blank*]

The APPEND command adds records to the end of an existing database file.

- Type `use inventry` and press ENTER.
- Type `append` at the dot prompt and press ENTER. A blank data entry form will be displayed on the screen.
- Press the PGUP key once to see the last record that you entered into the file.
- Press the PGDN key and enter the following new record into the blank data entry form.

Field	*Record 20*
ProdNum	514
ProdDesc	Sunshine Window
Cost	140.00
Price	168.00
Balance	30 [ENTER]
Limit	20 [ENTER]
Manufactur	SkyLight Co.

- Press the CTRL and END keys simultaneously to save the record and return to the dot prompt.
- Use the LIST command to confirm that the twentieth record now resides in the database. Your screen should resemble Figure 11.26.

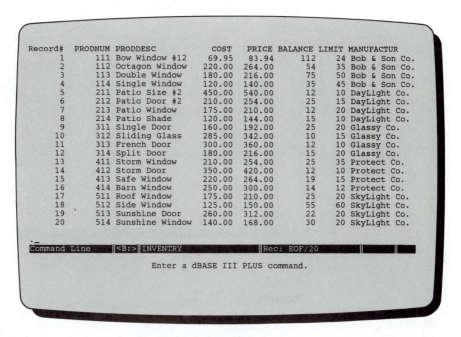

Figure 11.26
A List of Records in the INVENTRY Database Including the Record Added at the End

The INSERT Command

The general form of the INSERT command is

INSERT [*blank*]

The INSERT command allows new records to be inserted into the database at any position. The INSERT command adds the new record after the record that the pointer is facing; its new position is shown in the record position information in the status line.

Back to the Case of SWIS

In order to see how this dBASE command works, let's assume that SWIS recently added a new item manufactured by the Glassy Company. To add this item to the database, follow these instructions.

- At the dot prompt, type `goto 12` and press ENTER.
- Type `insert`, and press ENTER. A blank data entry form like the one in Figure 11.27 will be displayed.

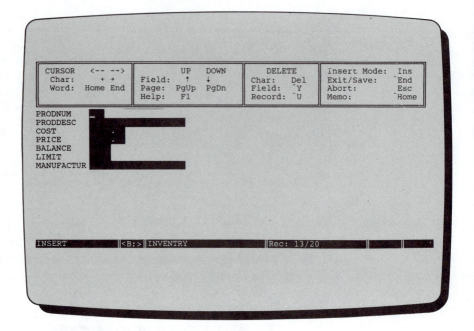

Figure 11.27
A Blank Entry Form

- Type the following data for this new item, which will become the new Record 13.

Field	*Record # 13*
ProdNum	315
ProdDesc	French Window [ENTER]
Cost	185.00
Price	222.00
Balance	29 [ENTER]
Limit	30 [ENTER]
Manufactur	Glassy Co. [ENTER]

Upon completion of your entry in the last field, dBASE will add the new record to the existing INVENTRY file, as you see in Figure 11.28 on the following page.

- At the dot prompt, type l i s t and press ENTER.

```
 1     111 Bow Window # 12     69.95    83.94    112   24 Bob & Son Co.
 2     112 Octogon Window     220.00   264.00     54   35 Bob & Son Co.
 3     113 Double Window      180.00   216.00     75   50 Bob & Son Co.
 4     114 Single Window      120.00   144.00     35   45 Bob & Son Co.
 5     211 Patio Size #2      450.00   540.00     12   10 DayLight Co.
 6     212 Patio Size #2      210.00   254.00     25   15 DayLight Co.
 7     213 Patio Window #2    175.00   210.00     12   20 DayLight Co.
 8     214 Patio Shade        120.00   144.00     15   10 DayLight Co.
 9     311 Single DoorPati    160.00   192.00     25   20 Glassy Co.
10     312 Sliding Glass      285.00   342.00     10   15 Glassy Co.
11     313 French Door        300.00   360.00     12   10 Glassy Co.
12     314 Split Door         180.00   216.00     15   20 Glassy Co.
13     315 French Window      185.00   222.00     29   30 Glassy Co.
14     411 Storm Window       210.00   254.00     25   35 Protect Co.
15     412 Storm Door         350.00   420.00     12   10 Protect Co.
16     413 Safe Window        220.00   264.00     19   15 Protect Co.
17     414 Barn Window        250.00   300.00     14   12 Protect Co.
18     511 Roof Window        175.00   210.00     25   20 SkyLight Co.
19     512 Side Window        125.00   150.00     55   60 SkyLight Co.
20     513 Sunshine Door      260.00   312.00     22   20 SkyLight Co.
21     514 Sunshine Window    140.00   168.00     30   20 SkyLight Co.
```

```
Command Line    ||<B:>||INVENTRY          ||Rec: EOF/21     ||      ||
                    Enter a dBASE III PLUS command.
```

Figure 11.28
A List of Records in the INVENTRY Database, Including the Inserted Record

The EDIT Command

The general form of the EDIT command is

EDIT [<scope>] [FIELDS <list>] [FOR <condition>]

The EDIT command alters the contents of a record or records in an active database file. When you activate the EDIT command, the current record is displayed and ready for changes. If the record at the current record pointer is not the one you want to alter, you can use the PGUP or PGDN keys to move to the desired record. Another alternative is to specify the desired record at the time you issue the EDIT command.

Back to the Case of SWIS

For example, Record 12 in the INVENTRY database has been found to contain an error. This particular item is suppose to be a split window instead of a split door. The database must be updated to reflect this change.

- Type `edit 12` and press ENTER. Record 12 is displayed on the screen for editing.
- Use the ARROW keys to position the cursor under the word *Door*.
- Type the word `Window`.
- To exit and save the change, press CTRL-END.
- Type `list` and press ENTER to verify the change.

The BROWSE Command

The general form of the BROWSE command is

BROWSE [FIELDS <*field list*>] [LOCK <*expN*>]

Using the BROWSE command, you can scan, edit, and append records to the database. Therefore, you can use the BROWSE command as an alternative to the DISPLAY command for viewing a record, the EDIT command for updating a record, and the APPEND command for adding records to a file.

- Type `goto 1` and press ENTER.
- Type `BROWSE` at the dot prompt and press ENTER. The screen shown in Figure 11.29 will be displayed.

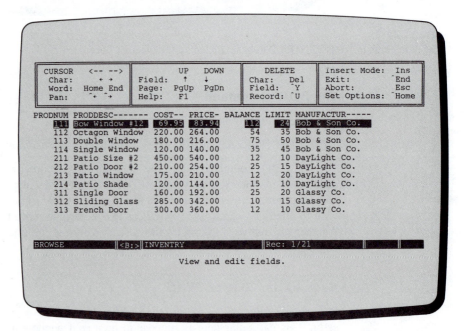

Figure 11.29
A List of Records in the INVENTRY Database, with the BROWSE Menu at the Top

The menu at the top of the screen displays all the cursor control and editing keys. Let's examine more closely some of the functions of the BROWSE command.

Scanning. Upon activating the BROWSE command, you can easily move through the database, simply by pressing a few keys.

- Use the LEFT and RIGHT ARROW keys to move across Record 1.
- Use the DOWN ARROW key to move to the next record.

The BROWSE command contains a menu bar, which is not displayed on the screen unless you press the F10 key.

- Press the F10 function key to display the menu. The following options appear at the top of the screen.

    Bottom   Top   Lock   Record No.   Freeze

The *Bottom* option moves the record pointer to last record in the file, making it the current record. The *Top* option moves the record pointer to the first record in the file, making it the current record. The *Lock* option prompts you for the number of contiguous fields on the left of the screen that you do not want to lose when you view fields that are off the screen to the right. The *Record No.* option allows you to choose a specific record by its number. You are prompted to enter a record number, and this record then becomes the current record. The *Freeze* option allows you to edit only one field until you reissue the BROWSE command.

Now let's put some of these BROWSE options to work.

- Move the cursor to the *Bottom* option and press ENTER. Notice the pointer status is changed to "Rec: 21/21".
- Press F10 again.
- Move the cursor to the *Top* option and press ENTER. The pointer is positioned at the first record in the file.

Editing. The BROWSE command can also help you edit records. Use the cursor keys displayed in the menu at the top of the screen to move the cursor to the desired record and field. Errors can be corrected simply by typing over the mistake or by pressing the INSERT key to insert characters into the desired field. Press the CTRL and END keys simultaneously to end the editing session, save the corrections, and return to the dot prompt.

Adding. You can append new records to the end of the file by moving the cursor to the last record in the file, then pressing the DOWN ARROW key one more time. A message will appear at the bottom of the screen that asks "Add new records? (Y/N)". If you type *Y*, a blank, reverse-video record will appear directly beneath the last record in the file. Type in the new record. Press the CTRL and END keys simultaneously to save the file changes and return to the dot prompt.

Quitting. There are two ways to quit the BROWSE session. First, you can press CTRL and END after you have made changes to the database. Or, you can simply press the ESC key. Remember, if you use the ESC key after you make changes to a file, all of your modifications will be ignored.

- Press CTRL-END to exit the browse.

The last category of file modification is the deletion of old record(s). The dBASE program offers three commands related to the deletion process. These are DELETE, RECALL, and PACK.

The DELETE Command

The general form of the DELETE command is

DELETE [<scope>] [WHILE <condition>] [FOR <condition>]

The DELETE command marks a record in the active database for deletion but does not actually remove it from the file.

Back to the Case of SWIS

SWIS has been notified that the Glassy Co. will no longer be manufacturing their french window. Therefore, product number 315 (Record 13) is to be deleted from the INVENTRY database.

- Type `goto 13` and press ENTER to make Record 13 current.
- Type `delete` and press ENTER to mark the record for deletion. It is a good idea to display the record to make sure that the correct record has been marked for deletion.
- Type `display next 5` and press ENTER. You will see a display like the one in Figure 11.30. Notice the asterisk (*) next to record #13. This symbol indicates that the record has been marked for deletion.

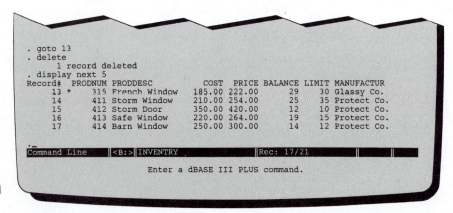

Figure 11.30
A List of Five Records with Record 13 Marked for Deletion

The RECALL Command

The general form of the RECALL command is

    RECALL [<scope>] [WHILE <condition>] [FOR <condition>]

The RECALL command may be used to reinstate all records that you have marked for deletion. If for some reason you changed your mind and did not want Record 13 to be deleted, you could reinstate the record with the RECALL command (as long as the record has not yet been physically deleted from the file).

- Type `goto 13` and press ENTER to make Record 13 current.
- Type `recall` and press ENTER to reinstate Record 13.
- Type `display next 5` to verify that the record has been reinstated. The asterisk has been removed from the front of Record 13, showing that it is no longer marked for deletion.

The PACK Command

The general form of the PACK command is

    PACK [*blank*]

The PACK command permanently removes records that have been marked for deletion. You decide that Record 13 does, in fact, need to be deleted. Once again, mark the record for deletion.

- Type `goto 13` and press ENTER.
- Type `delete` and press ENTER.
- Type `display next 5` and press ENTER. Make sure you are about to delete the correct record.

Now let's permanently erase the record with the PACK command.

- Type `pack` and press ENTER.
- Type `LIST` to view the entire file. Product number 315 has been deleted from the file.

GENERATING REPORTS

The purpose of storing and updating data in a database is to provide decision makers with accurate, timely reports. Therefore, being able to generate these reports from your database is an important task in dBASE III PLUS.

The CREATE REPORT Command

The general form of the CREATE REPORT command is

CREATE REPORT <.frm filename>

In the same fashion that we used the CREATE command to create the INVENTRY database, we can also use it to create a report file consisting of all necessary information, such as titles and formatting codes, for preparing a report.

Back to the Case of SWIS

Chico and Martine want to see a report based on your INVENTRY file so that they can begin making some decisions about SWIS's product inventory. To begin creating the report,

- Type create report Inventry and press ENTER. A screen like the one in Figure 11.31 will appear.

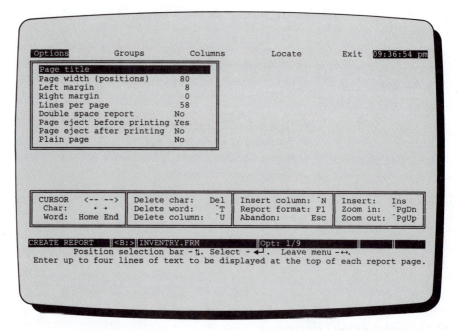

Figure 11.31
The Main Menu of the dBASE III PLUS Report Generator

Because dBASE III PLUS automatically gives report files an extension of *.frm*, there will be one INVENTRY.DBF for the actual database and INVENTRY.FRM for the report file.

The menu at the top of the screen has the options:

Options   Groups   Columns   Locate   Exit

Options. The first item of the options menu is *Page Title*. This option allows you to enter up to four lines to appear as headings in the report.

- With the highlighted line on *Page Title*, press ENTER. The menu shown in Figure 11.32 will be displayed.

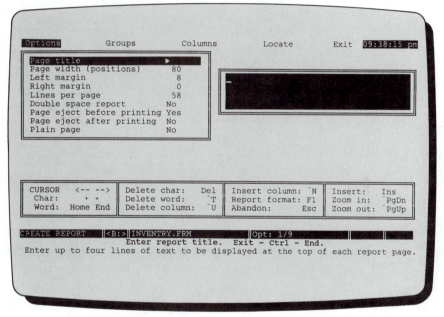

Figure 11.32
The Main Menu for the Page Title Option

- Type Sunshine Window Inc., Suppliers and press ENTER.
- Type Complete Inventory Report and press ENTER.
- Type By July 12, 1988 and press ENTER.
- Press ENTER once to skip the fourth line.

Don't worry about trying to center the headings; dBASE will do that for you. However, you can change any of the other settings in the options menu. For our example, we will use the default settings.

- Press CTRL-END to save the page titles.

Groups. The next step is to choose the *Groups* option, which tells dBASE to group records by a particular key data field in the report.

- Use the RIGHT ARROW to go to the *Groups* option. The screen shown in Figure 11.33 will be displayed.

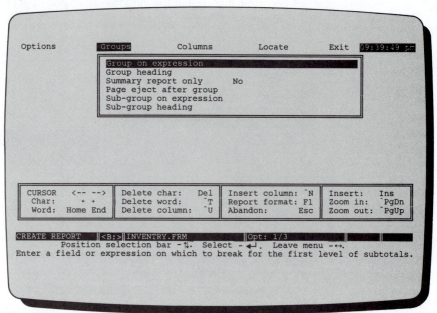

Figure 11.33
The Main Menu for the Groups Option

We will not be using the grouping feature, since our report will be based on the entire database. If we were, we would press F10 to display the field submenu and select the field to use for grouping. After selecting the grouping settings, you would press CTRL-END to save the settings.

Columns. The next option is *Columns*, which allows you to select fields, place them in columns in the report, and provide the appropriate.

- Use the RIGHT ARROW to go to the *Columns* option.
- Press ENTER once while the highlighted line is on the first option, *Contents*. An arrow will be placed to the right of the *Contents* option.
- Press F10 to display the field submenu. The screen in Figure 11.34 on the following page will be displayed.

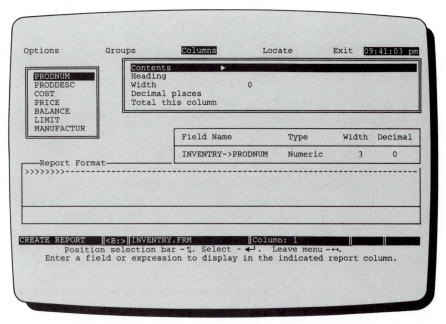

Figure 11.34
A Menu Showing the Group and the Field

- Use the DOWN ARROW to move the highlighted line in the field menu displayed on the left side of screen to *PRODDESC*, and press ENTER twice. *PRODDESC* will be placed to the right of *CONTENTS*.
- Use the DOWN ARROW to move to the *Heading* option of the *Columns* menu, and press ENTER. A little screen will appear on the right side of your screen for you to type the column headings.
- Type `;;Product;Description` and press ENTER four times. Semicolons indicate that two blank lines are to be skipped, and that the word *Product* starts at the beginning of the third line and the word *Description* on the next line.
- Press PGDN. You will end up with a clean form for the *Columns* menu. Look at the bottom of your screen. In the *Report Format* area, you should be able to see the first column heading.
- Press ENTER, then press F10.
- Press DOWN ARROW twice to go to *COST*.
- Press ENTER twice.
- Press DOWN ARROW once to go to *Heading*, and press ENTER.
- Type `;;Cost per;Unit` and press ENTER four times.
- Press PGDN.
- Press ENTER, then press F10.

- Press DOWN ARROW four times to go to *BALANCE*.
- Press ENTER twice, then press DOWN ARROW.
- With the highlighted line over *Heading*, press ENTER.
- Type `; ;Balance on;Hand` and press ENTER four times.
- Press PGDN.
- Press ENTER, then press F10.
- Press DOWN ARROW six times to go to *MANUFACTUR*.
- Press ENTER twice, and press DOWN ARROW.
- With the highlighted line over *Heading*, press ENTER.
- Type `; ;Product;Manufacturer` and press ENTER four times.

Note: You might hear a beep sound (if the bell is not turned off) and a message displayed at the bottom of your screen indicating that you exceeded the print position. If you get this message, press ENTER key.

- Press the CTRL and END keys simultaneously to close the area and return to the menu.

Locate. This option of the report menu will let you find out what fields you selected to be included in the report.

Exit. When the report form is completed, you can exit the menu in two ways.

- Use the RIGHT ARROW to move the highlighted line to the menu option *Exit*. You will see two options: *Save* or *Abandon*.
- With the highlighted line over the *Save* option, press ENTER. At this stage, your report format will be saved on your diskette and you should end up with a clean screen. The *Abandon* option would discard the report form file without saving it.

The REPORT Command

The general form of the REPORT command is

REPORT FORM *<filename>* [TO PRINT]

Once you have created a report form file (*.frm*), you can use it over and over again. The REPORT command takes data from the active database file and uses the specified report form file to print a report. If the TO PRINT parameter is included, the report is sent to the printer. If TO PRINT is not included, the output will be displayed on the screen.

- Type `report form inventry to print` and press ENTER. Your printout should look like Figure 11.35 on the following page.

```
                    Page No.    1
                    05/29/88
                                     Sunshine Window Inc., Suppliers
                                         Complete Inventory Report
                                              By July 12, 1987

                    Product                    Cost per          Balance on  Product
                    Description                  Unit              Hand     Manufacturer

                    Bow Window #12               69.95              112  Bob & Son Co.
                    Octogon Window              220.00               54  Bob & Son Co.
                    Double Window               180.00               75  Bob & Son Co.
                    Single Window               120.00               35  Bob & Son Co.
                    Patio Size #2               450.00               12  DayLight Co.
                    Patio Size #2               210.00               25  DayLight Co.
                    Patio Window #2             175.00               12  DayLight Co.
                    Patio Shade                 120.00               15  DayLight Co.
                    Single Door                 160.00               25  Glassy Co.
                    Sliding Glass               285.00               10  Glassy Co.
                    French Door                 300.00               12  Glassy Co.
                    Split Window                180.00               15  Glassy Co.
                    Storm Window                210.00               25  Protect Co.
                    Storm Door                  350.00               12  Protect Co.
                    Safe Window                 220.00               19  Protect Co.
                    Barn Window                 250.00               14  Protect Co.
                    Roof Window                 175.00               25  SkyLight Co.
                    Side Window                 125.00               55  SkyLight Co.
                    Sunshine Door               260.00               22  SkyLight Co.
                    Sunshine Window             140.00               30  SkyLight Co.
                    *** Total ***
                                               4199.95              604
```

Figure 11.35
A Sample Report Output

The MODIFY REPORT Command

The general form of the MODIFY REPORT command is

    MODIFY REPORT <*filename*>

Once you have created a report form, it is a simple matter to make changes to it at any time via the MODIFY REPORT command, followed by the name of the report form file you wish to alter.

The menu for the MODIFY REPORT command is identical to the CREATE REPORT menu, except that the data has already been entered. Make any corrections that are needed, and exit to save your changes when you are finished.

■ SORTING THE DATABASE

The data in database files is stored in the same order that it was originally entered into the file. As the file changes, with additional data being added and outdated data being deleted, the database becomes unorganized. dBASE III PLUS offers a solution to this problem—the SORT command.

The SORT Command

The general form of the SORT command is

SORT TO <*newfile*> ON <*field*> [/A] [/C] [/D]
[, <*field2*> [/A] [/C] [/D]...] [WHILE <*condition*>]
[FOR <*condition*>]

With the SORT command, you tell dBASE which database file to use and the field(s) that you want to use as the sort basis. The dBASE program will automatically rewrite your data file based on your sort requirements.

The database file cannot be sorted to itself. The original file stays intact, while the sorted records are stored under a new file name.

The file can be sorted in either ascending order (the default setting) or descending order. The /A parameter causes the file to be sorted in ascending order. The /D parameter causes the file to be sorted in descending order. The /C parameter causes the sort to treat uppercase and lowercase letters the same way. If the /C parameter is used in combination with one of the others, the slash (/) is only entered once (e.g., /CD, /CA).

Back to the Case of SWIS

The INVENTRY database is to be sorted by *Product Description* and stored under the name INVSORT1.

- At the dot prompt, type `clear` and press ENTER.
- Type `use inventry` and press ENTER.
- Type `sort to invsort1 on proddesc` and press ENTER. The message below will be displayed.
    100% Sorted   20 Records sorted
- Type `use invsort1` and press ENTER.
- Type `list` and press ENTER to see the contents of the sorted data file. The screen in Figure 11.36 on the following page will be displayed.

Next, let's sort the INVENTRY database under two fields: product description (the secondary key), within the manufacturer's name (the primary key). In other words, the manufacturers' names will be sorted first; then, within each manufacturer's name, the product descriptions will be sorted. The new file name will be INVSORT2.

- Type `use inventry` and press ENTER.

- Type sort to invsort2 on manufactur, proddesc and press ENTER.
- Type use invsort2 and press ENTER.
- Type list and press ENTER. The new sorted file will look like the display in Figure 11.37.

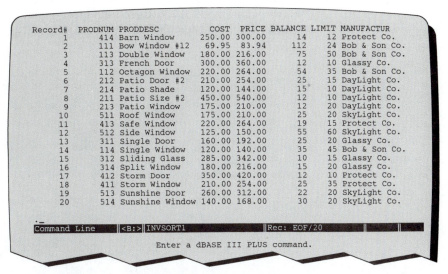

Figure 11.36
A List of Sorted Records with PRODDESC as the Sorting Field

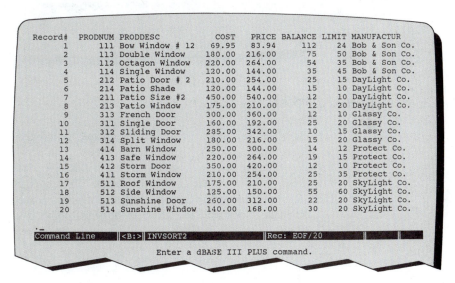

Figure 11.37
A List of Sorted Records with MANUFACTUR as the Sorting Field

Let's sort the INVENTRY file one more time. This time, the file will be sorted by *COST* in descending order, from most expensive item to least expensive item, and stored in a file called INVSORT3.

- Type use inventry and press ENTER.
- Type sort to invsort3 on cost /d and press ENTER.
- Type use invsort3, and press ENTER.
- Type list and press ENTER. The sorted file will appear as shown in Figure 11.38.

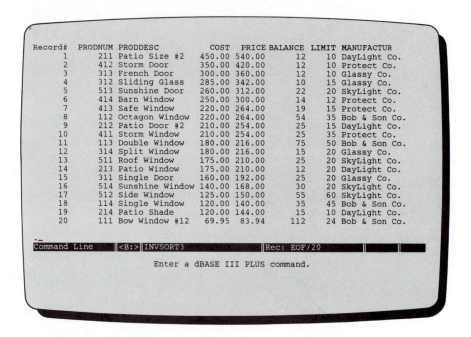

Figure 11.38
A List of Sorted Records with COST as the Sorting Field

There are drawbacks to the SORT command. To maintain order, a data file must be sorted every time data is added or deleted. For a data file that experiences frequent changes, this would not be an acceptable procedure. Also, sorting a large file takes a lot of computer time, and since the SORT command generates a new file each time the command is executed, valuable memory space would be consumed.

Let's take a look at an alternative to the SORT command, the INDEX command.

INDEXING THE DATABASE

Another way of keeping your database file organized is through indexing using the INDEX command.

The INDEX Command

The general form of the INDEX command is

INDEX ON <*key expression*> TO <*filename*>

The INDEX command sets up an index file (*.ndx*) that contains the key field entries in ascending order, and each record number as ordered in the original file. Once a database file is indexed, dBASE III PLUS automatically updates the index file as additions and deletions take place. So, with the INDEX command, you do not need to sort after every operation to keep your file in the proper order. An index file also operates much faster in searches and consumes less memory space.

You can build as many index files as you want for each database. Each of your index files use a different key field.

Single-Field Indexing

A **single-field index** is one that is indexed on only one key field. Using the INVENTRY database, let's index the file on the *PRODDESC* field.

- Type `use inventry` and press ENTER.
- Type `index on proddesc to product` and press ENTER. This command will set up an index file called "product" and order it by product description. The dBASE III PLUS program will automatically attach an extension of *.ndx* to the product file. The status of the indexing will appear on the screen as

    .index on proddesc to product
    100% indexed   20 Records indexed

To see the sorted file,

- Type `list` and press ENTER. The database, ordered by product description, will be displayed as in Figure 11.39 on the following page.

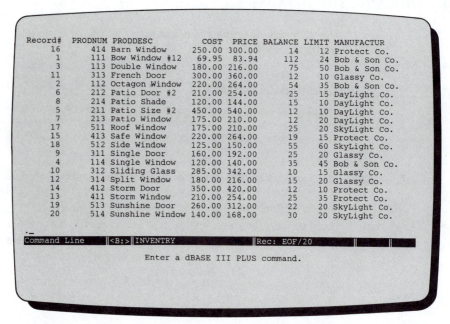

Figure 11.39
An Index Listing of the INVENTRY Database Ordered under PRODDESC

To prove that the original database has not been altered, use the following commands.

- Type use inventry and press ENTER.
- Type list and press ENTER. The original database will be listed as shown in Figure 11.40 on the following page.

Using an Existing Index File

To re-index the existing INVENTRY database file,

- Type use inventry and press ENTER.
- Type set index to product and press ENTER.

Issuing the LIST command now would show the ordered database file once again.

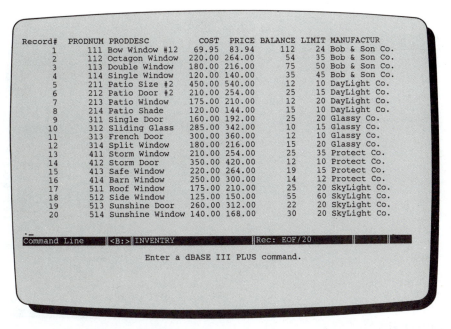

Figure 11.40
A List of the Original Records in the INVENTRY Database

Multiple-Field Indexing

The general form for multiple-field indexing is

INDEX ON <*field1*> + <*field2*> +...TO <*filename*>

Often it is desirable to sort a database file on more than one field. Such a file is called a **multiple-field index.** As can be seen from the structure above, the command to accomplish multiple-field indexing is similar to that for single-field indexing, except that the key fields are separated with a plus sign (+). To index the INVENTRY file by manufacturer's name and product description, you would issue the following commands.

- Type use inventry and press ENTER.
- Type index on manufactur + proddesc to multiple and press ENTER.

To view the sorted file:

- Type list and press ENTER. The indexed database will appear as shown in Figure 11.41 on the following page.

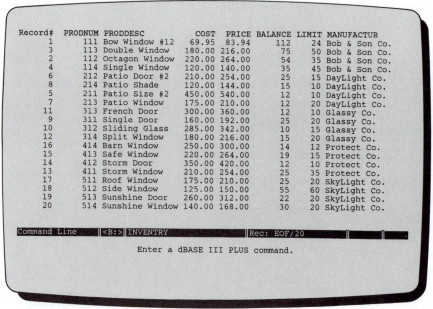

Figure 11.41
A List of Records Indexed under MANUFACTUR and PRODDESC

■ SEARCHING AND QUERYING THE DATABASE

You saw some simple examples of searching, or querying, a database for a specific record or records during our discussion of the LIST and DISPLAY commands. In this section, we will expand on those examples and introduce some of the operators that are available to search a database for selected records.

Mathematical Operators

The mathematical operators are listed here in order of precedence when more than one operator is used in the same arithmetic expression. Note that multiplication and division both hold third priority, and addition and subtraction both hold fourth priority.

1. ( )   Parentheses are used for grouping
2. ^ or **   Exponentiation
3. *   Multiplication
   /   Division
4. +   Addition
   –   Subtraction

Relational Operators

Relational operators evaluate an expression to be true or false. Relational operators can be used with either numeric or character data, as long as the expressions on either side of the operator are of the same type.

<	Less than
>	Greater than
=	Equal to
< > or #	Not equal to
< =	Less than or equal to
> =	Greater than or equal to

Back to the Case of SWIS

Try the following simple queries on the INVENTRY database, using the dBASE III PLUS commands you have already learned.

Query 1. List the manufacturer's name and product description for product number 212.

Procedure:

- Type `clear` and press ENTER.
- Type `use inventry` and press ENTER.
- Type `list manufactur, proddesc for prodnum = 212` and press ENTER.

Display:

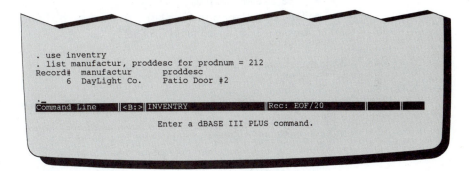

Figure 11.42
Displaying Record for PRODNUM 212

Query 2. List the product numbers and product descriptions for the manufacturer named SkyLight Co.

Procedure:

- Type `clear` and press ENTER.
- Type `list prodnum, proddesc for manufactur = 'SkyLight Co.'` and press ENTER.

Display:

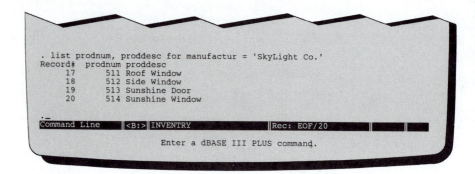

Figure 11.43
Displaying the Four Products of Skylight Co.

Query 3. Display the manufacturer's name, product number, balance on hand, and reorder point (limit) for every product with a balance on hand less than its reorder point.

Procedure:

- Type `clear` and press ENTER.
- Type `display manufactur, prodnum, balance, limit for balance < limit` and press ENTER.

Display:

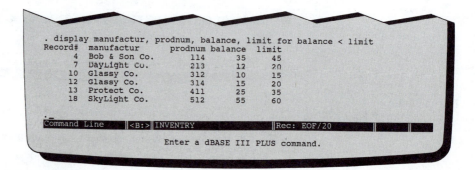

Figure 11.44
INVENTRY Items with their Balances Less than their Ordering Limits

Query 4. Display all the product numbers and the product descriptions for any products with more than a forty-dollar markup between price and cost.

Procedure:

- Type `clear` and press ENTER.
- Type `display prodnum, proddesc for price - cost > 40.00` and press ENTER.

Display:

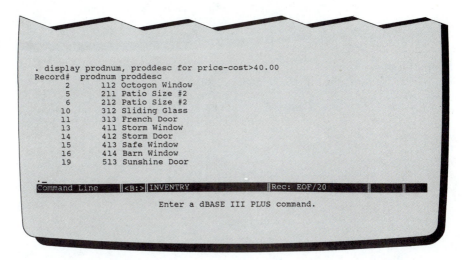

Figure 11.45
INVENTRY Items with Price Greater than 40

Query 5. List the manufacturer's name, product number, and cost of all products that cost SWIS $300 or more.

Procedure:

- Type `clear` and press ENTER.
- Type `list manufactur, prodnum, cost for cost >= 300` and press ENTER.

Display:

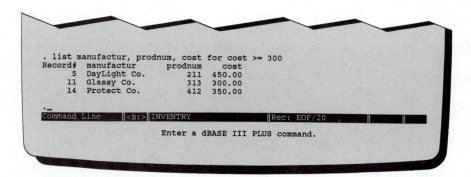

Figure 11.46
INVENTRY Items with Cost Greater or Equal to 300

Query 6. Use the indexed file MULTIPLE.NDX to perform this query. List the manufacturer's name and product description for the Glassy Co.

Procedure:

- Type `clear` and press ENTER.
- Type `use inventry index multiple` and press ENTER.
- Type `list manufactur, proddesc for manufactur = 'Glassy Co.'` and press ENTER.

Display:

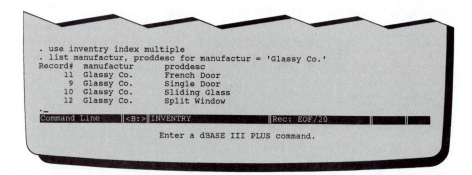

Figure 11.47
INVENTRY Items Manufactured by the Glassy Co.

■ Summary of dBASE III Commands

SET DEFAULT	Used to change the current disk drive setting.
CREATE	Creates a new data file.
DIR	Lists all database files on the diskette in the current disk drive.
LIST STRUCTURE	Displays the file structure of the active .dbf file.
LIST	Displays all records in the active file.
LIST OFF	Displays specified records from the active file without their record numbers.
SET HEADINGS	Allows the setting of field or column headings on or off.
USE	Signals dBASE to activate a specified file.
DISPLAY	Displays the record to which the pointer is currently pointing.
MODIFY STRUCTURE	Used to alter the record structure of an existing database file.
APPEND	Allows the addition of records to the end of an existing database file.
INSERT	Allows the addition of records at any position in an existing database.
EDIT	Alters the contents of a record(s) in an active database file.
BROWSE	Used to scan, edit, and append records to the active database file.
DELETE	Marks a record in the active database for deletion but does not actually remove it from the file.
RECALL	Reinstates all records that have been marked for deletion.
PACK	Permanently erases records that have been marked for deletion.
CREATE REPORT	Creates a report file (*.frm*).
REPORT	Takes data from the active database file and uses a specified report form file (*.frm*) to print a report.
MODIFY REPORT	Used to make changes to an existing report form.
SORT	Allows the active database to be arranged in a specified order and stored under a new file name.
INDEX	Sets up an index file (*.ndx*).

■ Key Terms

dot prompt command mode The command-driven portion of the dBASE III PLUS software package.

assist menu (the Assistant) The menu-driven mode of the dBASE III PLUS software package.

syntax The structure of a command.

current record The last record created or accessed.

current record pointer An unseen marker which marks the current record.

active file area A temporary file area in RAM.

single-field index An index based on one key field.

multiple-field index An index based on more than one key field.

■ Review Questions

1. The command-driven feature of dBASE III PLUS is called the _____ command mode.
   - (a) Assistant
   - (b) dot prompt
   - (c) menu
   - (d) assist menu
2. The menu-driven feature of dBASE III PLUS is called the _____ .
   - (a) command menu
   - (b) Assistant
   - (c) dot prompt
   - (d) assist menu
   - (e) (b) and (d)
3. Which of the following is *not* a valid dBASE file name?
   - (a) cs250
   - (b) student1
   - (c) 2student
   - (d) stud_num
4. To save and exit the field definition form, you would press _____ .
   - (a) ESC
   - (b) FS
   - (c) CTRL-END
   - (d) ESC-END
5. The dBASE program allows _____ characters for file names.
   - (a) eight
   - (b) ten
   - (c) six
   - (d) twelve
   - (e) none of the above

6. Which of the following is *not* a data type available in dBASE?
    (a) date
    (b) character
    (c) integer
    (d) logical
7. The _____ command allows you to see the list of database files of all types on your diskette.
    (a) LIST
    (b) DIR
    (c) DEF
    (d) FIL
8. Which of the following commands could be used with the LIST command to direct the output to the printer?
    (a) PRINT
    (b) TO PRINT
    (c) PRINT OFF
    (d) Any of the above will work.
9. To bring an existing file into the active file area, you would use the command _____ .
    (a) FIL
    (b) INV
    (c) DIR
    (d) ACT
    (e) USE
10. The BROWSE command can be used for all of the following *except*
    (a) creating a file.
    (b) adding records.
    (c) scanning a file.
    (d) editing a file.
11. The _____ command permanently removes a record from the file.
    (a) DELETE
    (b) RECALL
    (c) PACK
    (d) ERASE
12. The _____ option of the CREATE REPORT command allows the user to group records by a particular key data field in the report.
    (a) columns
    (b) group
    (c) locate
    (d) options
13. A report is easily altered by using the _____ command.
    (a) REPORT FORM
    (b) CREATE REPORT
    (c) CHANGE CREATE
    (d) MODIFY REPORT

14. To sort a file in descending order, the _____ parameter is added to the sort command.
    (a) /D
    (b) /A
    (c) /C
    (d) /B
15. When a file is indexed on more than one field, it is called _____ indexing.
    (a) group
    (b) multi-file
    (c) multiple-field
    (d) field
16. Which of the following is *not* a relational operator?
    (a) < >
    (b) < =
    (c) **
    (d) #
17. Which of the following is the correct syntax to display the name and overdue fields of a file called LIBRARY, in which the days overdue are greater than ten?
    (a) display name overdue for overdue > 10
    (b) display name, overdue for library > 10
    (c) display name, overdue for overdue > 10
    (d) display name overdue, for overdue > 10
18. What is the difference between the LIST command and the DISPLAY command?
19. What is the purpose of the MODIFY STRUCTURE command? What functions does it allow you to perform?
20. What is the difference between the APPEND command and the INSERT command?
21. What is the function of the PACK command?
22. What is the difference between the SORT and INDEX commands?
23. Which of the following is *not* an arithmetic operator?
    (a) ^
    (b) /
    (c) **
    (d) =
24. What is the difference between the DELETE and PACK commands?
25. The _____ exit option discards a report without saving it.
    (a) save
    (b) delete
    (c) pack
    (d) abandon

□ chapter 11

HANDS-ON EXERCISES

Note: To save database files that you create, insert a blank formatted diskette in Drive B. These exercises assume that you have booted up the system and are ready to begin in dot prompt mode.

1. Rachel's Fashions, with three boutiques in the Phoenix, Arizona area, would like to have its employee records stored in a database on its newly acquired computer system using dBASE III PLUS. You are to create a database for their employee records.
   a. Set the default to Drive B.
   b. Create a database file with the name EMPLOYEE.
   c. Define the fields using the following structure.

Field	Type	Width	Dec
EMPID	Numeric	4	
LASTNAME	Character	10	
FIRSTNAME	Character	8	
SALARY	Numeric	8	2
DATEHIRE	Date	8	
STORENUM	Numeric	1	

   d. Save the field definition form.

2. Input the following ten records into the EMPLOYEE database you created in Exercise 1.

EMPID	LASTNAME	FIRSTNAME	SALARY	DATEHIRE	STORENUM
001	Hart	Lorraine	22115.00	08/16/80	1
002	Tell	Sue	23800.00	02/01/81	1
003	Royer	Ruth	17500.00	06/13/81	2
004	Rupp	Bess	23000.00	03/31/82	3
005	Sheipe	Grace	19500.00	08/05/82	2
008	DePew	Sharon	15400.00	09/10/83	3
009	Smith	Joan	16200.00	10/15/84	2
011	Staz	William	23400.00	11/20/85	1
013	Williams	Joe	19200.00	12/05/85	3
014	Mobley	Nancy	22900.00	10/26/86	2

   a. Save and exit the data entry form.
   b. List the database that you just created.

The completed database will look like the one pictured in Figure 11.48 on the following page.

```
Record#  EMPID  LASTNAME  FIRSTNAME  SALARY    DATEHIRE  STORENUM
      1      1  Hart      Lorraine   22115.00  08/16/80         1
      2      2  Tell      Sue        23800.00  02/01/81         1
      3      3  Royer     Ruth       17500.00  06/13/81         2
      4      4  Rupp      Bess       23000.00  03/31/82         3
      5      5  Sheipe    Grace      19500.00  08/05/82         2
      6      8  DePew     Sharon     15400.00  08/10/83         3
      7      9  Smith     Joan       16200.00  10/15/84         2
      8     11  Staz      William    23400.00  11/20/85         1
      9     13  Williams  Joe        19200.00  12/05/86         2
```

Figure 11.48
Rachel's Fashions Employee Database

3. Perform the following operations on the EMPLOYEE database.
   a. List the entire file on your printer.
   b. List only the data for employee Bess Rupp.
   c. Insert the following record after the current record 8 (in other words, the new record will become the new record 9).

Field	Data
EMPID	012
LASTNAME	Klein
FIRSTNAME	Debra
SALARY	18850.00
DATEHIRE	11/21/86
STORENUM	2

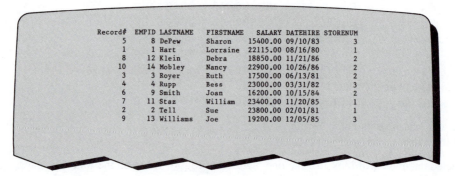

```
Record#  EMPID  LASTNAME  FIRSTNAME  SALARY    DATEHIRE  STORENUM
      5      8  DePew     Sharon     15400.00  09/10/83         3
      1      1  Hart      Lorraine   22115.00  08/16/80         1
      8     12  Klein     Debra      18850.00  11/21/86         2
     10     14  Mobley    Nancy      22900.00  10/26/86         2
      3      3  Royer     Ruth       17500.00  06/13/81         2
      4      4  Rupp      Bess       23000.00  03/31/82         3
      6      9  Smith     Joan       16200.00  10/15/84         2
      7     11  Staz      William    23400.00  11/20/85         1
      2      2  Tell      Sue        23800.00  02/01/81         1
      9     13  Williams  Joe        19200.00  12/05/85         3
```

Figure 11.49
Sorted Employee File

d. Delete Employee 5 (Grace Sheipe has terminated her employment) and remove the record permanently from the database.
   e. List the updated database and send the listing to the printer.
4. Sort the EMPLOYEE database file using a single-field index.
   a. Make sure that the EMPLOYEE file is the active file.
   b. Set up an index file called EMPSORT and sort the EMPLOYEE file on the LASTNAME field.
   c. List the EMPSORT file on your printer. The sorted file will look like Figure 11.49 on the opposite page.
5. Using the indexed file EMPSORT, create and print a report. Figure 11.50 is an example of the finished report.

```
Page No.      1
04/26/88
                        RACHAL'S FASHIONS
                         EMPLOYEE LISTING
                          JULY 1, 1988


        EMPLOYEE        EMPLOYEE                YEARLY  DATE
        LAST NAME       FIRST NAME              SALARY  HIRED




        DePew           Sharon                  15400.00 09/10/83
        Hart            Lorraine                22115.00 08/16/80
        Klein           Debra                   18850.00 11/21/86
        Mobley          Nancy                   22900.00 10/26/86
        Royer           Ruth                    17500.00 06/13/81
        Rupp            Bess                    23000.00 03/31/82
        Smith           Joan                    16200.00 10/15/84
        Staz            William                 23400.00 11/20/85
        Tell            Sue                     23800.00 02/01/81
        Williams        Joe                     19200.00 12/05/85
        *** Total ***
```

Figure 11.50
Rachel's Fashions Employee Listing Report

   a. Create the report form called EMPFILE.
   b. Enter the following page title.

   ```
   RACHEL'S FASHIONS
   EMPLOYEE LISTING
   JULY 1, 1988
   ```

   c. Create the following column headings from the fields as indicated.

Field	Column heading
LASTNAME	;;EMPLOYEE;LAST NAME
FIRSTNAME	;;EMPLOYEE;FIRST NAME
SALARY	;;YEARLY;SALARY (for salary heading also change 'Total this column' option to 'no' by pressing ENTER)
DATEHIRE	;;DATE;HIRED

d. Print the report to the screen for viewing. If satisfactory, send a copy of the report to the printer.
6. Perform the following queries on the EMPLOYEE database file.
   a. Make the EMPLOYEE file the active file.
   b. List the last name, first name, and salary for Employee 4.
   c. Display all employees who make at least $20,000 per year on your printer.
   d. List the last name, first name, salary, and date hired for all employees working at Store 1 on your printer.
7. The Westover Swim and Fitness Club, located in a suburb of San Diego, has purchased a microcomputer system. As the club's membership has grown, it has become a cumbersome and time-consuming task to maintain the records. Marcy Ulsh, the club's director, recommended automating the membership file using dBASE III PLUS. One database in the system is to contain the names of all persons in the different swim programs. You have been given the job of creating the SWIM database file.
   a. Set the default to Drive B.
   b. Create the database file with the name SWIM.
   c. Define the fields using the following structure.

Field	Type	Width	Dec
LAST_NAME	Character	10	
FIRST_NAME	Character	8	
MALE	Logical	1	
PROGRAM	Character	8	
DATE	Date	8	
BALANCE	Numeric	6	2

   d. Save the field definition form.
8. Input the following records in the database SWIM that you created in Exercise 7.

LAST NAME	FIRST NAME	MALE	PROGRAM	DATE	BALANCE
Wallace	Susan	F	Aquacise	01/10/88	0.00
Shearer	Fred	T	Beginner	11/14/87	14.00
Wirt	Pam	F	LifeSave	11/25/87	30.00
Able	Sally	F	Aquacise	04/04/88	5.00
Krauser	David	T	Adult	04/10/88	0.00
Jones	George	T	Beginner	05/16/88	15.00
Binkley	Ben	T	Intermed	06/17/88	25.00
Berkheimer	Cindy	F	Aquacise	08/08/88	0.00
Young	Danny	T	LifeSave	10/10/87	10.00
Shaeffer	Larry	T	Adult	07/30/88	0.00

   a. Save and exit the data entry form.
   b. List the structure on your printer to confirm that it was entered correctly and saved.
   c. List the entire file on your printer.

The completed database will appear as shown in Figure 11.51.

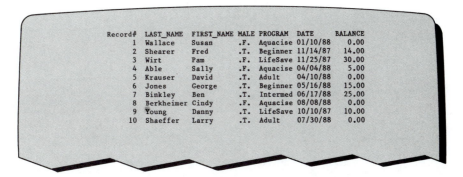

Figure 11.51
Westover Swim and Fitness Club Database

9. Perform the following operations and queries on the SWIM database file.
   a. Record 7 contains an error. Ben Binkley should be listed as having taken the Beginner course, not the Intermediate course. Edit the file and change the *PROGRAM* field from Intermed to Beginner.
   b. One record was missed when the data was entered. APPEND the following record to the SWIM database file.

Field	*Date*
LAST_NAME	Bosso
FIRST_NAME	Nick
MALE	T
PROGRAM	LifeSave
DATE	02/07/88
BALANCE	13.00

   c. DISPLAY the entire updated database and send the display to the printer.
   d. Mark Record 1 for deletion. List the database to make sure it has been marked. You then learn that the record was marked for deletion by mistake; reinstate Record 1 with the RECALL command. List the file to verify the reinstatement.
   e. List the LAST_NAME, FIRST_NAME, and DATE for all persons who have ever been enrolled in the Aquacise program on your printer.
   f. List the LAST_NAME, FIRST_NAME, and BALANCE for those persons with an outstanding balance on your printer.
   g. There is a special program being offered for all females. List the LAST_NAME, FIRST_NAME, and DATE last enrolled for all females in the SWIM file and send it to your printer.
   h. Index the file by *PROGRAM* and *LAST_NAME* (the file will be indexed by last name within each program) to a file called SWIMSORT.
   i. List the sorted file to the printer.

Part VI

MICRO-BASED SYSTEMS DEVELOPMENT

chapter 12

SYSTEMS INVESTIGATION AND ANALYSIS
- define a micro-based information system.
- name the stages in the systems development cycle.
- describe the reasons that could prompt a systems investigation.
- describe the steps taken to conduct a systems investigation.
- describe possible alternatives.
- outline possible recommendations as a result of an investigation.

chapter 13

SYSTEMS SELECTION AND DESIGN
- name the activities that constitute the selection and design phase.
- discuss maintenance concerns for a micro-based information system.
- discuss the security concerns of a micro-based information system.
- discuss the importance of working closely with users during this phase.
- describe the criteria for evaluating software packages.
- describe the criteria for evaluating hardware components.
- describe the formulation and use of a system selection and development report.

chapter 14

SYSTEMS IMPLEMENTATION
- name the activities that constitute the implementation phase.
- describe a company's considerations during system installation and the importance of testing system components.
- describe the alternatives and procedures for developing application programs.
- describe the task of creating data files for the system.
- describe the alternative methods of converting an old manual system to a new micro-based information system.
- describe the task of developing a user's manual.
- describe the importance of training sessions for users of the system.
- describe the importance of documenting all steps in the implementation phase.

chapter 15

SYSTEMS MAINTENANCE AND MANAGEMENT
- explain the procedures to be included in the maintenance manual for maintaining hardware components.
- explain the procedures to be included in the maintenance manual for maintaining system software.
- explain the procedures to be included in the maintenance manual for maintaining application programs.
- describe the means of providing system security to avoid misuse of the system.
- describe the process of assessing the system's status in the post-implementation stage.
- name and describe the areas for review in the post-implementation stage.
- describe the benefits of thoroughly documenting the review results and all modifications to the system.

chapter 12

Systems Investigation and Analysis

After completing this chapter, you should be able to

- *define a micro-based information system.*
- *name the stages in the systems development cycle.*
- *describe the reasons that could prompt a systems investigation.*
- *describe the steps taken to conduct a systems investigation.*
- *describe possible alternatives.*
- *outline possible recommendations as a result of an investigation.*

INTRODUCTION

An **information system** is an entity designed and developed by an individual or individuals for an organization in order to manage, process, and produce information for decision makers. This information may be used in various ways: to inform the user about the status of different functions within an organization, to provide assistance to decision makers in the decision making process, or to give the user better control over part or all of an organization.

In the last four decades, many organizations have devoted billions of dollars and other significant resources to the development of sophisticated information systems. Today, **information resources** are numbered among the six major corporate resources, along with money, materials, equipment, personnel, and management. This means that effective management and processing of information resources is more vital than ever to the well-being of an organization.

Mainframe computers and minicomputers predominated in most early computerized information systems. However, in recent years, the lower cost of microcomputers and the ease of use of these systems have led to the business community's recognition of microcomputers as acceptable tools for information processing.

This chapter first discusses microcomputer systems development, followed by a discussion of different aspects of the systems investigation and analysis phase. We will apply this material to the case of Sunshine Window Inc., Suppliers (SWIS) at the end of the chapter.

■ THE SYSTEMS DEVELOPMENT CYCLE

Companies of all types and sizes are establishing a new generation of computer information systems, known as **microcomputer information systems,** or **micro-based information systems.** Although these new systems are not as powerful and sophisticated as mainframe- and minicomputer-based information systems, they can serve a user's local needs, provide vital assistance in information management, and give the user full control over the information system and its processes. It is this last feature, perhaps, that makes these systems so popular and so appealing to many users. Unlike larger information systems, most micro-based information systems can be developed directly by the systems' users, who know their own needs and functions better than anybody else.

The task of developing a microcomputer information system can be complex and costly if it is not carried out in well-defined stages. For many people, the process of establishing a micro-based information system is little more than purchasing hardware and software. However, effective systems development is much more complex.

In the same way that building a house or establishing a business deserves careful analysis, planning, and management, the process of developing an effective, efficient, micro-based information system also requires and deserves attention and commitment on the part of the users.

There are distinct stages that occur in systems development. The whole process, with all of its stages, is referred to as the **systems development cycle,** illustrated in Figure 12.1. In this chapter, we discuss the first phase, known as **systems investigation and analysis.** (In subsequent chapters, we cover the rest of these stages: systems selection and design, systems implementation, and systems maintenance and management. It should be mentioned here that the term *systems* is used frequently in this chapter and the following chapters as an alternate term for *micro-based information systems.*)

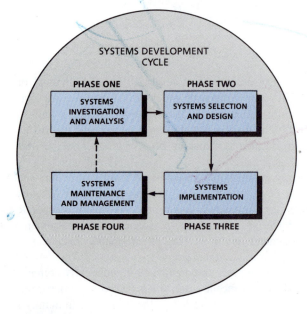

Figure 12.1
Phases of the Systems Development Cycle

SYSTEMS INVESTIGATION AND ANALYSIS

The investigation and analysis task is simply the process of assessing the problems, causes, information needs, and available resources related to the development of a micro-based information system. During the course of this process, the investigator or analyst will try to collect background information, define the specific problem(s), assess information requirements, identify available resources, constraints and limitations, estimate the associated costs and benefits, and prepare a report of the results and a recommendation. Figure 12.2 is a diagram illustrating these activities.

A systems investigation can be prompted by any of a number of reasons. Some of these are described below and summarized in Figure 12.3.

- Inefficiency in the existing methods of processing and managing information systems
- Inadequate control or supervision over some organizational functions and related information
- The need to improve the productivity of different functions and/or individuals performing them
- The need to reduce the costs of processing information
- The need to improve services provided by the organization

We discuss these reasons in full detail in the following sections.

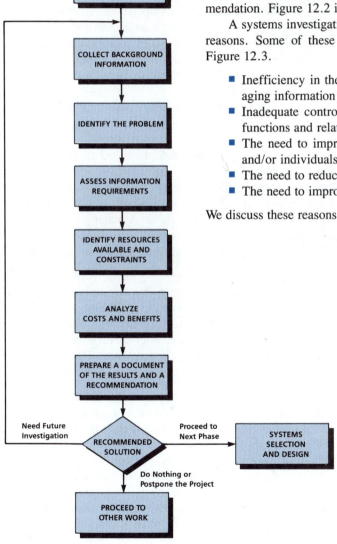

Figure 12.2
A Diagram of Investigation Activities

1. Lack of efficiency
2. Inadequate control
3. To improve productivity
4. Cost savings
5. To improve services

Figure 12.3
Five Factors that could Prompt a Systems Investigation

Reason: Inefficiency

Inefficiency in existing information processing and management methods or mechanisms can be a major reason to begin a systems investigation. Numerous factors can cause inefficiency, including organizational growth, management team structure or style, change in procedures for performing tasks or functions, or new information requirements. These factors are summarized in Figure 12.4.

1. Growth of the organization
2. Management style
3. Change of procedure
4. New information requirements

Figure 12.4
Factors Affecting Organization Efficiency

Organizational Growth. Many companies start as small operations. As businesses prosper, they must expand the resources needed to manage their operations. In other cases, a department or functional area within an organization may expand its operations or the services it provides, either to customers or to other functional units within the firm. As a result, management must think of new ways to accomplish the additional tasks and resources of the unit.

One particular area of concern to many managers is the efficient and effective processing, management, and dissemination of information. Because of the enormous costs of large computer systems, many small organizations have had to either rely on information processing services provided by outside firms, or stick to their old, inefficient, manual systems.

In the case of a large organization with an expanding unit, it was necessary in the past to rely on central computer information systems. A major problem was the fact that, in most cases, the users could not obtain timely and precise information. Today, the micro-based information system is an alternative that can be considered by both small and large organizations.

Management Style. Different managers have different styles. Some managers prefer to oversee all business activities, reviewing every decision made in their areas of responsibility. Other managers prefer to delegate authority, allowing subordinates to make decisions. In either case, micro-based information systems can serve as decision support tools, capable of providing timely assistance. The utilization of micro-based information systems can do a great deal to serve the needs of managers.

Change of Procedure. It is common for organizations to change procedures as functions change. For example, moving from a manual to a computerized information system is a common type of change. In addition, it is often necessary to make periodic changes within existing computerized systems. In other cases, change in procedure may be mandated by environmental factors. For example, changes in the tax laws or other government regulations require changes in procedures related to these laws and regulations. In all of these cases, individuals and organizations can look to the creation and utilization of micro-based information systems as a way of incorporating changes into the existing systems or formulating new ways of performing a task.

New Information Requirements. Information required by various decision makers or organizations can vary significantly. New or additional information requirements may be caused by expansion of the business, changes within the organization, or new ways of conducting business. The information required by the government is subject to constant change. Information demanded by a parent organization can also change significantly. In many cases, existing methods of generating information may be incapable of producing the new information requirements. As a result, an organization may initiate an investigation into the possibility of creating a micro-based information system or of modifying an existing one.

Reason: Inadequate Control

Sometimes it is necessary for an organization to establish more control over an organization, or a particular function, and the corresponding information. For example, a department manager may wish to have more control over the departmental budget. The manager might hesitate to store budgetary data in the central computer information system of the firm, fearing that the confidentiality of the data could be jeopardized. In a case such as this, one alternative the manager might consider is that of a micro-based information system, which could be totally controlled by the department manager and staff at their own location.

In another case, a department or branch office of a large organization might want information representing different entities—such as customers, inventory, or personnel—to be stored in a system that is managed by the department's staff, rather than controlled by a central office. One major benefit of this approach is that, if the central system is malfunctioning or damaged or its security is violated, then the local office or department will be protected. As a matter of fact, many managers prefer having local control over their operations to being controlled by forces thousands of miles away. One could say the desire for local control over information processing resources has been satisfied in part by the introduction of minicomputers.

These days, with the vast computing power available from inexpensive microcomputers, many organizations are moving one step further: to establish micro-based information systems within individual departments of a division or branch office. These systems can function either as stand-alone units or as part of a larger network system, and can provide greater local control in the management of information processing.

Reason: Improved Productivity

Throughout the history of business, increased productivity has been a primary goal. Higher productivity results from performing a task more quickly, more accurately, more effectively, and more efficiently.

Many tools and techniques have been implemented to increase productivity levels. Perhaps computers, more than any other tool, have been most instrumental in achieving this goal. In the last several decades, computers and their applications have been cited as the ultimate productivity tools. As discussed in Chapter 1, information is the main ingredient of the decision making process. Therefore, it is important for an organization to be able to manage information in the most effective and efficient ways. The timeliness and accuracy of information provided by formal information systems to information users eventually could become the major factor in an increase in productivity. Over the last few years, many organizations have established microcomputer information systems for improving the productivity of their managers and staff, and this concern could prompt others to investigate the feasibility of such an alternative.

Reason: Cost Savings

The use of microcomputers to generate information for management has resulted in dramatic cost savings for many organizations. No longer are small organizations at the mercy of outside data-processing firms to meet their needs. These days, a firm can establish a micro-based system for several thousand dollars; even further reduction in the cost of these systems is expected in the not-too-distant future. But despite the potential cost savings of microcomputers, an investigator must be aware of the hidden costs of creating and operating a micro-based information system. Unfortunately, in some cases, because of a lack of careful assessment and evaluation of all associated costs and benefits, these systems have proved very inefficient tools for some organizations. Later in this chapter we will examine the costs and related advantages and disadvantages of these systems.

Reason: Improvement in Service

A major criterion in assessing the effectiveness of a business is the quality of goods and services offered by the organization to its customers. Computer information systems have helped many organizations expand the range of products and services they provide, and, in many ways, to improve the quality of their products and services.

Information generated by microcomputer systems can keep consumers informed about all aspects of their involvement with a firm. For example, a computer in a doctor's office could easily provide timely information to patients with regard to their financial obligations, appointments, special notices, and educational programs. The manager of an insurance agency could provide customers with all types of computer-generated information about their policy status, alternatives, and other services offered by the firm.

■ ACTIVITIES OF THE SYSTEMS INVESTIGATION PHASE

The investigation process, then, could be prompted by one, or in some cases, all of the reasons just discussed. Regardless of the cause, the task of investigating the creation of a micro-based computer system requires full commitment on behalf of an individual and an organization. The importance of the investigation process and its final results should not be downplayed because it is during this process that the strategy for the creation of a system is formulated. It is also critical to remember that the organization may determine that the need for a system does not exist, or that a micro-based system will not satisfy the organization's actual needs. Let's take a closer look at the activities involved in the systems investigation phase (see Figure 12.5).

Collecting Background Information

1. Collect background information
2. Define the problem
3. Assess information requirements
4. Identify resources and constraints
5. Estimate costs and benefits
6. Prepare documentation of results

Figure 12.5
Activities of the Systems Investigation Phase

Before an investigator can define an organization's problem, it is necessary to collect information about the situation, company, environment, and people involved. Background information may include information about the nature of a business, its functions, or terminologies used in the field. For example, if the situation under investigation is in an accounting department, and the investigator is not familiar with the nature of the tasks performed and with accounting terminology, the first step would be to learn as much as possible about the department's function. Looking at past and current methods of performing a job would be part of a background investigation. An investigator should also carefully study the people. In other words, the investigator has to achieve a clear understanding of the overall business, the tasks performed in the area under investigation, and the people involved—their functions, level of decision making, and needs.

The more the investigator knows about the situation, the better prepared he or she will be to define the problem. There is no standard procedure that can be followed to collect background information. Instead, the investigator must use every available means to collect information. Some commonly used methods include reviewing the company's files and related documents, conducting surveys, or interviewing individuals. The investigator should remember that the best source of background information will come from *people.*

Defining the Problem

Upon completion of the information collection process, the investigator should be able to clearly define the specific problem to be addressed. The investigator should avoid ambiguous assumptions; instead, the definition should be clearly based on the collected facts. Ideally, the investigator should be able to define the main problem in a small paragraph, followed by a list of related problems or secondary issues. In defining the specific problem, the investigator should also identify general organizational shortcomings and associated costs. In addition, the investigator should make a list of the causes of the problem and contributing factors. These clear definitions should enable the investigator to proceed to the next step.

Assessing Information Requirements

The main product of any information system is the information that is generated. Therefore, it is very important to determine the organizational and individual needs related to an information system. For example, a warehouse manager may want to see an inventory status report on a weekly basis, or a branch manager may need to report certain periodic budgetary data to the company's main office. Assessing information requirements can be achieved through two channels: formal and informal.

Formal channels consist of company files and documents generated by the existing system, such as personnel or inventory files. **Informal channels** include employee interviews, needs analysis surveys, and finally, personal judgment and intuition. It should be remembered that, in many cases, the investigator is the person who will also be the primary user of the micro-based system, if it proves to be warranted. While this makes the task of collecting information and identifying information requirements much easier than it would be for an outside investigator, the inside investigator should not rely primarily or exclusively on personal experience. This breadth of analysis will minimize the possibility that some of the assumptions made by the investigator are influenced by personal judgments, leading to an incorrect conclusion and recommendation.

How much data will be handled?

What type of data will be handled?

How often is the information needed?

How large are the output documents?

What is the output format?

How repetitive is the processing?

Figure 12.6
Information Characteristics

The investigator must also determine different characteristics of the required information, such as its volume, timeframe, and presentation. First, it is very important at this stage to determine the volume of data that will be handled by the system. For example, if creation of a customer database is one required function, then what is the average record size (e.g., number of characters) and maximum number of records in this database? If word processing is another required function, then it is important to know the average size of the documents generated and the length of the largest document created to date.

With regard to timeframe, the investigator should determine how often information outputs are needed: daily, weekly, monthly, or quarterly. Or does the users want to receive the information on an on-line or interactive basis?

The presentation of the generated information is also very important. For example, some accounting managers like to see detailed financial reports, while others prefer to see summarized reports. Many managers prefer graphical presentations of financial information. The investigator should constantly remember that the ultimate users of the system will be people, and it is important to determine their needs and preferences. See Figure 12.6 for a summarized list of information characteristics.

The other determination that must be made at this stage is whether the task under consideration is repetitive or occasional. For example, the task of preparing payroll listings is considered to be repetitive, performed on a weekly or monthly basis, while an annual report is occasional.

Another question that must be considered during the investigation is whether the required information is qualitative or quantitative. Computer systems use only quantitative data; therefore, if the data involved cannot be quantified, a computer system cannot be a suitable solution to the problem. For example, at this stage of computer development, it is unlikely that a system would be identified as the solution to a decision making problem in which judgment calls or intuition are involved. There is hope that, in the foreseeable future, expert computer systems will be capable of drawing inferences, making judgments, and even offering recommendations between various acceptable options.

Finally, during the assessment phase, the investigator should be concerned not only with immediate information requirements or needs, but also with future needs as the company grows or expands.

Available Resources and Constraints

During the course of the investigation, an investigator must examine organizational resources and possible constraints to the development of a micro-based information system. Let's consider some of these resources and constraints, which are summarized in Figure 12.7.

Resources:
- Existing computer hardware
- Existing computer software
- Skill level of personnel

Constraints:
- Limited financial resources
- Unavailability of skilled personnel

Figure 12.7
Organizational Resources and Constraints

Resources. Two major company resources must be carefully assessed during the course of the investigation before the investigator can determine that a micro-based information system is needed. These resources fall into two categories: computer hardware and software resources and human resources.

In the area of computer hardware and software resources, the investigator must first determine if there is an existing computer system within the firm. Second, is it a mainframe system or is it minicomputer-based? Furthermore, the investigator should make a list of all available software, if any, that is relevant to the problem under consideration. The best source for this information would be the staff of the company's information processing center. Often, what are perceived to be new or unusual information needs can be satisfied very inexpensively by a firm's existing computer system. Full knowledge of what is and what is not available will allow the investigator to accurately judge the company's actual needs.

In many situations, a larger computer information system will be a far more suitable solution to the problem under consideration than a micro-based information system. The investigator should not allow the technical language used by some computer systems staff to discourage identifying the available computer resources within the firm.

In the area of human resources, the investigator must identify personnel who might be affected by a micro-based solution, and their level of skill and attitude toward computers and computer applications. It is important to know which employees are familiar with specific software packages or programming languages, particularly those languages used on microcomputers. Knowing about personnel computer skills can assist the investigator in determining the level of training that would be needed if a micro-based information system were recommended.

Constraints. Potential constraints to the development of a computer system could range from limited financial resources to limited human resources. The investigator should be aware of the maximum amount of money that the company would be willing to spend on a micro-based information system. If the investigator is unaware of the organization's fiscal realities, he or she might make a recommendation that could not be funded because of budget limitations. The investigator also should determine the sources of funds, whether they are short-term or long-term, and the willingness of the company to invest in a possible micro-based information system.

Another potential constraint to the development of a system might be the shortage of personnel with skills to use the proposed system. For example, the firm might not be able to assign any individual to maintenance, programming, and other related activities of a micro-based information system, even on a part-time basis. It is very important at this stage—before any commitments are made—to determine who will be responsible for management of the system.

Costs and Benefits Analysis

The next step of the system investigation phase is the assessment of the associated costs and the possible benefits of developing and operating a micro-based information system.

Costs. The cost of the entire system is very important to the systems development process. As a matter of fact, in some cases, cost is the single most important factor. During the cost determination process, the investigator will try to estimate the overall costs, direct and indirect, of the systems that may be recommended.

Direct costs include the costs of hardware, software, and personnel. One of the first steps taken by an investigator in estimating the overall cost of a system is to identify some of its common applications. Next, the investigator must identify some software packages that could carry out these applications, and the price range of these packages. Then, the investigator needs to determine which hardware is compatible with the identified software, and how much the hardware costs. This information can be obtained from various sources, such as hardware and software vendors or library publications, colleagues who are using the same applications, computer stores, computer interest groups, or trade or professional associations.

Another direct cost is personnel. If the system requires a skilled individual to operate it, then estimated personnel costs must reflect the number of hours, pay rate, and even the costs of fringe benefits for that employee.

There are many indirect costs that may at first go unnoticed but must not be overlooked. Some of these costs summarized in Figure 12.8 and discussed here, will vary according to circumstances. Perhaps the most important are the personnel costs of the individual who will design, develop, and implement the system. In most cases, the individual will be a manager whose time is very valuable to the company. For example, if a manager whose annual salary is $35,000 needs to spend approximately 200 hours in the system development cycle, then the cost to the company will be at least $3,500.

Other indirect costs include the cost of maintaining the system once it is in operation; the cost of training staff to use the system; the cost of furniture; the conversion cost for transforming the old manual system to the new micro-based system; the cost of insurance, if needed; the cost of expanding the system to keep pace with company growth; communication costs, if the system needs to be connected to other systems; and, finally, the cost of supplies. At this stage, the investigator can at least estimate most of these costs, keeping in mind lack of attention to these costs could be very damaging to the system's overall success.

Benefits. The investigator should identify some potential benefits of the system, and try to place some dollar amounts on these benefits. The investigator should not underestimate the fact that many managers understand dollar figures better than any other type of information. The many potential benefits of a micro-based information system include reduction in staff requirements, increase in productivity of staff, increase in accuracy and precision of information generated, increase in quality of services provided to customers, increase in assistance provided to decision makers, improvement in security procedures for the firm's information, and reduction in the amount of time needed to generate information (see Figure 12.9 on the following page).

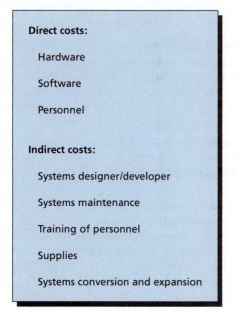

Figure 12.8
Summary of Direct and Indirect Costs

Figure 12.9
Summary of Potential Benefits

1. Reduction in staff
2. Increase in productivity
3. Increase in accuracy
4. Increase in quality of services
5. Assistance to decision makers
6. Improvement in generating information

Of course, not all of these benefits can be estimated in terms of direct dollar savings. However, you can estimate the possible monthly savings that could result from staff reduction, or the amount of time saved due to computerizing manual systems. Eventually, all of these benefits will help the firm reduce costs and increase the profitability of the organization.

Documenting Investigation Results

The single most important product of the systems investigation and analysis is the report that outlines the study's findings and offers recommendations. In this report, called the **investigation report,** or the proposal to develop a micro-based information system, the investigator states the main problem, followed by a list of secondary problems. Further, the document includes the organization's and individual's information requirements, as well as statements explaining the status of available computer resources (if any) and the major constraints involved. Finally, a recommendation must be made (see Figure 12.10). Perhaps the investigator suggests that the firm do nothing, or that the firm postpone the development process. Perhaps the investigator wants to conduct further investigation. Or he may recommend that the firm proceed to the next phase of the systems development cycle: systems selection and design. Let's look at possible reasons for each recommended action.

Do Nothing. In many cases, there is no real need for a new system to be developed. In the majority of these cases, the user is not aware of the firm's available computer resources. The investigator's responsibility would then be to direct users to the proper channels or to assist them in satisfying their needs.

During the investigation stage, the analyst must try to remain neutral toward the possible outcome. The analyst should not assume that a micro-based information system is the answer for every problem. The proper approach is to find the most suitable solution to the problem, whether it involves a microcomputer or not.

Other reasons for the "do nothing" recommendation could be that the function in question is not a repetitive task by nature; that the information involved cannot be quantified for use in the system; or that the financial resources of the firm cannot support the project. Given this recommendation, the project will end at the completion of the investigation phase, and the investigator will return to his or her work on other activities.

1. Statement of the main problem
2. Information requirements
3. Costs and benefits
4. Recommendation

    Do nothing
    Postpone development
    Continue the investigation
    Develop a system

Figure 12.10
The Format of the Investigation Report

Postpone Development. Another possible recommendation would be to postpone the development of a system. There could be several reasons for such a recommendation. First, it is possible that more important projects are waiting to be completed, and that the solution of the problem under consideration is a low priority. Second, funds necessary for the development of a system may not be budgeted, but may become available in the near future. Another reason to recommend postponement could be that current technology is unable to carry out the applications considered necessary for the proposed system. Finally, there may be a lack of support from the firm's management. Without management commitment, the completion and success of a system would be highly questionable.

Continue the Investigation. The investigator could decide that further investigation is necessary. The investigator may not have had sufficient time to gather all the necessary information, or may not have had access to the information needed to formulate a recommendation. For example, some of the information required during the investigation process might be confidential, and the investigator did not have the proper authorization to access it.

Yet another reason could be lack of cooperation on the part of the staff who would be affected by the system. It is still common for some employees to fear for their jobs when they hear rumors of computerization. Unfortunately, some might even attempt to sabotage the investigation by not cooperating in the fact-collecting process. The investigator must be alert to this danger, examining a variety of sources to obtain the needed information and cross-checking the facts collected to confirm their validity.

A final reason to continue the investigation could be that new developments occurred within the investigation area after the information was collected. For example, let's say that, after an investigator has gone through relevant files and conducted extensive interviews, the firm experiences some major changes, such as diversifying their services or markets. In this case, the investigator may not feel confident in recommending a solution based on old data and, instead, calls for further investigation.

Develop a System. The fourth alternative is to recommend the development of a micro-based system. With this recommendation, the investigator demonstrates a conviction that, based on the collected data, a new micro-based information system is needed. It is very important to know exactly what is expected of the proposed system. The main objectives of the proposed system must be clearly identified before the investigator can proceed to the next phase of systems development. Lack of clear identification of applications, physical location, and primary users could later result in confusion and major problems. If the investigator is not completely satisfied that all relevant factors have been considered, it would be wise to go back and attempt to gather more information to ensure that all aspects of the situation have been examined.

Back to the Case of SWIS

Sandy Cofman has conducted a complete investigation of the SWIS company's information needs. During the course of her investigation, she talked to both the partners and their employees about their information requirements, examined the firm's resources and constraints, and estimated the costs and benefits of a possible micro-based information system. The results of her findings have been documented in this investigation report.

■ SYSTEM INVESTIGATION REPORT

Statement of Problem

The main problem in the SWIS organization is the lack of a structured means of storing, obtaining, processing, and managing information in a timely fashion by managers and staff. The lack of a structured information processing system has been the cause of the following more specific problems:

- Poor management control over information processing procedures
- Inefficient use of information by decision makers
- Lack of information needed by decision makers for planning and forecasting
- Unavailability of a decision support system to assist in a decision making process
- Inefficient use of administrative time
- Decreased productivity of administrative personnel
- Poor space allocation for information storage
- Inadequate response to customer needs
- Inability to provide proper inventory control
- Inefficient correspondence capabilities to both current and potential customers as well as to other organizations.

Other related problems are a high degree of frustration in finding information when it is needed, duplication of information in many files, and the inability to handle the workload properly.

Information Requirements

During the preliminary investigation of the situation, it became clear that SWIS needs many mechanisms for processing information. The following list describes those mechanisms.

- *Inventory tracking information mechanism:* to gather and organize information about products ordered and the current inventory levels of those products; to produce reports about the product line, and product availability; to trigger the ordering of more inventory.

- *Order information mechanism:* to compile and present reports on manufacturer suppliers. The reports should be organized by product, manufacturers, and product order dates.
- *Text processing mechanism:* to compile and process information for preparation of form letters, mailing labels or lists; to produce memos, reports, and other written communications for the firm; to provide a means to organize and retain correspondence.
- *Decision Support System:* to develop a more efficient means of preparing standard and specific reporting and analyses; to provide a means to evaluate future financial and human resource needs under various assumptions of company growth.

Costs and Benefits

The estimated cost of a possible micro-based information system could be divided into three areas: (1) start-up costs, which include the cost of hardware and software, training, developer's time and conversion from the manual system to the new system; (2) operation costs, which include the cost of supplies and stationery, as well as clerical time; (3) maintenance costs, which include the cost of maintenance contracts on hardware, software updating, and insurance.

Apart from the start-up costs, most of these costs are already being accrued within the firm to operate the existing manual system. Table 12.1 illustrates the cost breakdown over the next five years of a possible micro-based information system. The ongoing costs are based upon yearly ten-percent increases.

TABLE 12.1 Estimated Cost of a Micro-based Information System

COST ITEM	FIVE-YEAR COST					
	1	2	3	4	5	Total
START-UP COSTS						
Hardware	$ 3,000	$ 0	$ 0	$ 0	$ 0	$ 3,000
Software	600	0	0	0	0	600
Training	500	0	0	0	0	500
Conversion	500	0	0	0	0	500
Developer Time	2,000	0	0	0	0	2,000
Misc. Cost	500	0	0	0	0	500
OPERATING COSTS						
Stationary (paper, ribbons, disks, etc.)	$ 600	660	726	799	879	3,664
Admin Clerk	6,240	6,864	7,550	8,305	9,136	38,095
MAINTENANCE COSTS						
Hardware	$ 0	500	550	605	666	2,321
Software	0	200	220	242	266	928
Expansion	0	300	330	363	399	1,392
Total	$13,940	$8,524	$9,376	$10,314	$11,346	$53,500

Some of the possible benefits of a micro-based system for SWIS are: to improve management effectiveness in obtaining necessary information for planning and day-to-day operations; to increase the productivity of the staff in performing office functions; to improve customer service; to provide a method of inventory control; to expand the business market; and to bring harmony to the operations of the firm. Eventually, these improvements will bring substantial savings and additional revenue to the firm. Table 12.2 demonstrates the potential dollar saving—and possible additional revenue—generated through the use of an effective information system. The ongoing savings are based upon yearly ten percent increases.

BENEFIT ITEM	FIVE-YEAR BENEFIT					
	1	2	3	4	5	Total
Secretarial time saving (10 hrs. saving, $10 per hour a week for 52 weeks, or 10 × 10 × 52)	$ 5,200	$ 5,720	$ 6,292	$ 6,921	$ 7,613	$ 31,746
Managerial time saving (10 hrs. saving, $50 per week in management time, or for 52 weeks 10 × 50 × 52)	26,000	28,600	31,460	34,606	38,066	158,732
Net Profit from Sales Generated in Response to Better Customer Service	0	10,000	11,000	12,100	13,310	46,410
Net Profit from Sales Generated in Market Areas	0	20,000	22,000	24,200	26,620	92,820
Total	$31,200	$64,320	$70,752	$77,827	$85,609	$329,708

TABLE 12.2   Estimated Benefits of a Micro-based Information System

The benefits of an information system in terms of cost savings will overwhelmingly surpass the cost of developing the system. In other words, the benefits definitely justify the costs of the system. The total savings ratio is more than six to one ($329,708 [benefits]/$53,500 [costs]). Although most figures in the cost benefit analysis are estimates, the benefits by far outweigh the costs.

Recommendation

After her evaluation and consultation with the owners of the firm, Sandy Cofman is convinced the best solution to the problem of information processing at SWIS is a micro-based information system. Through the use of a system, inventory, product, and manufacturer data could be stored on interrelated databases that could be accessed easily by all involved personnel. A database management system could store, retrieve, and process these databases. Moreover, a word processing software package could help employees manipulate the data and text for supporting management decisions and written communication capabilities. Repetitive typing tasks could be reduced, thereby increasing administrative productivity. Word processing provides greater flexibility in the preparation of written reports and will be helpful to the personnel developing such documents.

With a spreadsheet package, employees can prepare special reports and analyses. The package would serve as a decision support system for management, improving their ability to evaluate alternatives in the decision making process. Eventually, clerical tasks requiring frequent mathematical calculations could be automated.

This system—consisting of a database management system, word processing package, and spreadsheet package—should solve the immediate problems of SWIS information handling. At the same time, it will allow growth in the computer system as SWIS grows. Management will be able to forecast and plan for the future growth of the company. The costs of such a system can be met easily from the substantial savings realized from utilizing the system.

■ SUMMARY

Over the last few decades, many firms have established information systems to help them manage their resources, increase their productivity, and improve the services they provide. Until recently, centralized mainframe and minicomputers have dominated the environment of computer information systems. Today, with the availability of inexpensive and powerful microcomputers, many organizations, large and small, are creating individualized micro-based information systems.

The process of developing a micro-based information system involves more than buying hardware and software. A series of systematic tasks should be completed in order to create an effective micro-based information system. The whole process of developing a system, known as the systems development cycle, includes the phases of investigation and analysis, selection and design, implementation, and maintenance and management.

The investigative phase may be prompted by any of a number of reasons; lack of efficiency, the need to improve company services, a demand for higher productivity, or the desire to establish more control over certain functions. Among the activities of the investigation phase are collecting background information, defining the specific problem, assessing information requirements, identifying available resources and constraints, estimating associated costs and benefits, and preparing a document of findings and recommendations. By the end of this investigation phase, the investigator should be able to make a recommendation based on the research. Some of the possible recommendations made by the investigator could include: do nothing, postpone system development, continue with further investigation, or develop a micro-based information system. If the last action is recommended by the investigator, then the analyst will proceed to the next phase of the system development cycle.

■ Key Terms

information system	A system designed to manage, process, and produce information for an organization's decision makers.
information resources	One of the six major corporate resources, along with money, materials, equipment, personnel, and management.
microcomputer information systems	Also known as micro-based information systems.
systems development cycle	The process of developing a system, which includes system investigation and analysis, selection and design, implementation, and maintenance and management.
systems investigation and analysis	First phase of the systems development cycle.
formal channels	Company files, documents, and so on generated by the existing system.
informal channels	Employee interviews, needs analysis surveys, personal judgment and intuition.
investigation report	A report made after the systems investigation and analysis, which states the main problem, gives information requirements, states the costs and benefits, and provides recommendations.

■ Review Questions

1. What is *not* one of the functions of an information system?
   (a) manage information
   (b) manipulate information
   (c) process information
   (d) delegate authority
   (e) produce information
2. Which feature makes micro-based information systems most popular to many users?
   (a) They serve the user's local needs.
   (b) They provide vital assistance in information management.
   (c) They give the user full control over the information system.
   (d) The lower cost of a microcomputer.
   (e) The ease of use of a microcomputer.
   (f) All of the above.
3. Which process is *not* part of the microcomputer information systems development cycle?
   (a) systems investigation and analysis
   (b) systems selection and design

(c) systems customizing and modification
   (d) systems implementation
   (e) systems maintenance and management
4. Which one of the following factors is *not* the cause of inefficiency in existing information processing?
   (a) procedural changes
   (b) growth of the organization
   (c) change in salaries
   (d) change in management style
   (e) new information requirements
5. What is the most important problem associated with an external central computer information system?
   (a) privacy and security of information
   (b) can only be used by a large organization
   (c) users cannot always obtain timely and precise information
   (d) the costs are prohibitive
   (e) all of the above
6. Which is a potential cause of change in information required?
   (a) the need to generate more detailed analysis
   (b) re-organization within the firm
   (c) new methods and techniques
   (d) expansion of the business
   (e) changes in demand by the government
   (f) all of the above
7. Which is a valid reason for more local control over information?
   (a) information can be obtained on a more timely basis
   (b) confidentiality of budgetary data
   (c) data to be monitored by local staff
   (d) privileged information to be obtained by the selected individual
   (e) critical or protected information should not be changed
   (f) all of the above
8. What kind of background information is *most* essential to the investigation process?
   (a) the people involved
   (b) financial status of the organization
   (c) nature of the business
   (d) tasks performed in the area under investigation
   (e) none of the above
9. Which is the *least* important element for an investigator in defining the problem?
   (a) summarizing the main problem to be defined in a small paragraph
   (b) approximating the desired alternatives
   (c) listing the causes of problem and contributing factors
   (d) listing the related issues
   (e) identifying limitations and constraints
   (f) identifying the brand of the microcomputer that will be selected

10. Which resources are important for consideration during the systems investigation process?
    (a) computer hardware resources
    (b) computer software resources
    (c) human resources
    (d) existing computer resources
    (e) financial resources
    (f) all of the above
11. Which is the *least* important constraint in selecting a micro-based information system?
    (a) corporate image
    (b) capital resources
    (c) fiscal realities
    (d) skilled personnel
    (e) none of the above
12. Which is a potential cost benefit in using a micro-based information system?
    (a) decrease in time needed to record data
    (b) decrease in time needed to prepare reports
    (c) reduction in staff requirements
    (d) increase in quality of products and services provided
    (e) increase in quantity of products and services provided
    (f) improvement in security procedures of firm's information
    (g) all of the above
13. What is *not* a possible recommendation after the proposal to develop a micro-based information system has been prepared?
    (a) Do nothing.
    (b) Require more time and resources to conduct further investigation.
    (c) Select a complete hardware system.
    (d) Postpone the development process.
    (e) None of the above.
14. Identify the six major corporate resources. Which is the most important? Explain.
15. What are the steps of the systems investigation and analysis phase?
16. List four reasons why a system investigation may need to be carried out further.
17. Briefly describe the benefits in information processing offered by a micro-based information system for small firms. For large firms.
18. Why is it necessary for an organization to change procedures periodically?
19. Explain how a micro-based information system can aid in increasing productivity.
20. How can better services be provided by using a microcomputer information system?
21. Is it preferable to have an inside or outside investigator assess the information requirements in a company? Explain.
22. What are the critical characteristics of the required information during the assessing process? Which one is the most important?
23. Identify the potentially overlooked indirect costs of developing a micro-based information system.
24. Why would an investigator want to postpone the development of a computer system?

25. What advantages does computer-based information processing have over human information processing?
26. What are the benefits of end-user computing?
27. Identify and discuss the reasons that an investigator concludes at the end of the systems investigation and analysis that further analysis is needed.

Case One:
BOBBI'S BAKERY

Bobbi Benjamin began her bakery in 1974 in a small building she rented for $250 a month. The building previously had housed a bake shop, so she did not need to install baking ovens, counter space, or cupboards. Mixing bowls, blenders, and all the other necessary baking equipment stayed in the building when Bobbi purchased it for $57,900.

Bobbi initially had three assistants to help her bake and sell her goods. In the first five years, Bobbi grossed $400,000. At the end of the fifth year, Bobbi decided to build a larger bake shop. She hired three additional people and established two departments: a sales department, headed by Tom Tsung, and a baking department, headed by Betty Book. Betty made all the decisions about what was to be baked when, and how much of each item was to be made. The sales department managed to market the bakery's products. Further, they kept inventory records on baking ingredients, equipment for the bakery, and basic accounting tasks such as billing, payroll, and budgeting.

Bobbi no longer helps out in the baking process. She is involved only in the management of the bakery. She has the sales department do profit-and-loss statements and break-even analyses. This department also takes care of the income statements and balance sheets. All of the sales department's work is done manually, a process frequently referred to as the pencil-and-paper or pen-and-paper method.

Since the business keeps growing by twenty percent a year, the manual method is becoming more and more cumbersome and time-consuming. The existing methods of keeping records, processing, and managing information is becoming less and less efficient.

The company has inadequate control and supervision over some organizational functions and related information, and management needs to improve the productivity of different functions and of the individuals performing them. Also, Bobbi wants the company to be more cost efficient, if at all possible. Bobbi also wants to make any improvements in service—both to the bakery and to its customers—that she can.

Questions

1. What is the problem?
2. Would the bakery benefit from a systems investigation? Why? Why not?
3. What background information would you collect?
4. What are the information requirements?
5. Are there available resources to warrant the installation of a computer system? What are the constraints, if any?
6. What is your recommendation?

Case Two:
ST. PAUL'S DAY CARE CENTER

In September, 1983, a non-profit Day Care Center opened at St. Paul's Church. The initial enrollment was thirty-five students, with four adult leaders and one director. The director's duties were to schedule the adult leaders, based upon the number of children scheduled for each day; to figure each child's bill each week; to show any prospective student's parents through the center; to procure the children's snack food for each week; to help take care of the children; and to sit on the Board to help direct the center's course.

The Center separates the children into five groups based upon age. Each group is guided by one leader, with an assistant assigned to any group that has a large number of children that day. The number of children in each group varies each day and each week due to an increasing number of "part-time" students that have been added to the program.

The billing rate varies with the number of hours that a child is scheduled, either full-time (over forty scheduled hours) or part-time (twenty to forty scheduled hours). There is also an added charge for disposable diapers for children that need them. The rates also vary according to a child's age, with younger children paying a higher charge. There is a discount for siblings.

Every Friday, the director plots out the coming week's attendance in each age group to schedule the adult leaders for the coming work week. She must also calculate the coming week's billing for each child because payment is due on the first day of child care for each week. The director calculates the billing for each child on index cards, and must take into account the proper billing rate figured by age and enrollment (full- or part-time) and scheduled hours, half-day credit for each sick day from the previous week, any diaper charges, and any held-over balance due. In addition, some of the parents are paying for a full month in advance, with all sick-day and vacation-day credits being carried to the next month's bill.

Over the years, the billing procedure became a "black art" rather than a scientific system, with only the director really knowing who pays monthly, who is receiving discounts from multiple children enrolled, and who receives credit for non-monetary payments (some parents donate needed food, diapers, or furniture in lieu of payment). When the director is not there to administer the billing charges, the billings are never correct.

By 1988, attendance at the day care center was approaching 225 children, and the director was spending more and more "wasted" time doing the scheduling and the billing. At this time, the Board approached the director about methods of reducing the paperwork that was absorbing so much of her time so that she could be better utilized in expanding the programs offered at the day care center.

Questions

1. What are the problems?
2. Would the center benefit from a systems investigations? If yes, explain.
3. What are the possible alternatives for eliminating the problems?
4. What the possible constraints in developing a micro-based information system?
5. What are the monetary benefits of a micro-based system for the center?
6. What is your recommendation?

SELECTED BIBLIOGRAPHY

Camillus, J.C., and A.L. Lederer, "Corporate Strategy and the Design of Computerized Information Systems," *Sloan Management Review*, Spring 1985, pp. 35-42.

Copenhauer, S., "Involving Users in Systems Design," *Magazine of Bank Administration*, April 1986, p. 42+.

Goyette, R., "Fourth Generation Systems Soothe End User Unrest," *Data Management*, January 1986, pp. 30-2.

Mann, L.E., "User Profiles for System Planning and Development," *Journal of Systems Management*, April 1984, pp. 38-40.

Martin, M.P., "The Human Connection in Systems Design," *Journal of Systems Management*, October 1986, pp. 6-29.

Mendus, S.L., "Computer Systems Development: Why Not Let Auditors Help?," *Journal of Systems Management*, May 1986, pp. 36-40.

Nicholas, J.M., "User Involvement: What Kind, How Much, and When?," *Journal of Systems Management*, March 1985, pp. 23-7.

Sandburg, D., "Avoiding OA Project Design Pitfalls," *Office Administration and Automation*, June 1985, p. 75.

Sharpe, J., "Getting the User Involved in Systems Design," *National Underwriter* (Life Health Insurance Ed.), February 22, 1986, pp. 28-9.

Tanner, R.F., "Systems Planning and Selection," *Trusts and Estates*, April 1985, pp. 41-6.

Tozer, J., "Making the Systems Match the Users," *Management Today*, October 1985, p. 41+.

_____, "Planning for a New System — A User's Viewpoint," *Personnel Management*, October 1985, p. 69.

chapter 13

Systems Selection and Design

After completing this chapter, you should be able to

- *name the activities that constitute the selection and design phase.*
- *discuss maintenance concerns for a micro-based information system.*
- *discuss the security concerns of a micro-based information system.*
- *discuss the importance of working closely with users during this phase.*
- *describe the criteria for evaluating software packages.*
- *describe the criteria for evaluating hardware components.*
- *describe the formulation and use of a system selection and design report.*

INTRODUCTION

Most people conduct extensive research for some major personal investment. For example, a woman in the market for a car will first determine the type of car she wants to buy. This decision will probably be the result of a lengthy process in which she collects information from different sources: talking to friends about different cars, reading advertisements in newspapers, using a consumer guide such as *Consumer Reports*, and recalling past personal experience with a certain type or model of car.

Just as a major personal decision requires research, developing a micro-based information system similarly requires a great deal of consideration.

Through the investigation and analysis phase described in the previous chapter, the investigator has determined whether an organization needs a micro-based information system, whether the benefits of a micro-based information system will substantiate its cost, and whether the firm can afford the initial costs of developing such a system. If the answer to all of these questions is "yes," then the investigator will recommend the development of such a system.

During the investigation phase, the investigator examined many sources of information before making the final recommendation. Even more information will be needed as the selection process progresses. The tasks of identifying necessary features of the system, identifying different alternatives, and choosing and obtaining actual system components comprise the **system selection and design phase** (Figure 13.1). The **system developer**—the person who carries out the tasks of this phase—usually is the same person who did the investigation. However, in some cases, a different person may assume these duties.

This chapter discusses different activities of the system selection and design phase in detail. We'll then apply the material to the continuing case of Sunshine Window Inc., Suppliers (SWIS) at the end of this chapter.

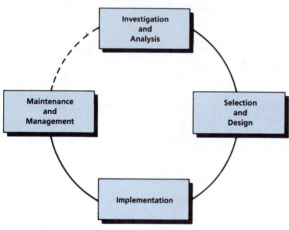

Figure 13.1
The System Selection and Design Phase

1. Identify security and maintenance requirements
2. Consult with users
3. Evaluate software
4. Evaluate hardware
5. Identify alternatives
6. Prepare a selection and development report
7. Select the most appropriate system

Figure 13.2
A Summary of System Selection and Design

■ ACTIVITIES OF THE SYSTEM SELECTION AND DESIGN PHASE

The system selection and design phase is the process of selecting components of a micro-based system based on the requirements identified in the investigation phase. Among the activities that constitute this process are identifying system security and maintenance requirements; consulting with users; software evaluation; hardware evaluation; identifying different alternatives; preparing a system selection and development report; and selecting the most appropriate system. Figure 13.2 illustrates these activities in the order that they must be executed. Let's take a more detailed look at these steps.

System Security and Maintenance Requirements

Many individuals do not consider the security and maintenance requirements of micro-based information systems an important issue at the time of development. Rather, they consider it an issue that must be dealt with after the entire system is selected, implemented, and in operation. Unfortunately, in most of these cases, organizations discover too late that the system they developed is not capable of meeting their security and maintenance requirements.

Once the security and maintenance requirements and procedures of the system under consideration have been identified (see Figure 13.3), then the developer can incorporate these requirements into an evaluation of the software, hardware, and any applications developed for the system.

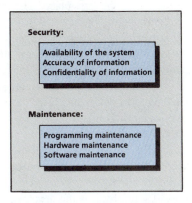

Figure 13.3
Security and Maintenance Requirements

There are three major types of **system security** concerns in a typical micro-based information system environment: availability of the entire system, accuracy of information generated by the system, and the confidentiality of certain information stored in the system. With regard to maintenance of the system, the developer must also determine at the development stage how the system will be maintained once it is in operation. There are three types of maintenance: programming maintenance, hardware maintenance, and software maintenance.

System Security: Availability of the System. It may be desirable for an organization to limit access to different hardware and/or software components of a micro-based information system to certain users. For example, the system might be restricted to some employees after business hours so that personal use is eliminated. The system could be limited to certain employees because of the confidentiality of data stored in the system. If data regarding employee salaries and raises, for instance, were stored onto a hard disk that can be accessed by all employees, the organization would be jeopardizing the privacy of the individuals working for the firm.

The system developer must consider restrictions on the availability of the system if there is an immediate concern, or if such a concern might develop in the future. Knowing about this issue in advance will allow the developer to look for ways to satisfy this requirement. For example, some microcomputers, are equipped with a lock which protects the system from unauthorized users.

On the other hand, many software packages also include security procedures, such as a password to stop unauthorized individuals from accessing either the software or certain data.

System Security: Accuracy of Information Generated. This requirement concerns the validity and accuracy of the information generated by the software. Of course, a micro-based information system, like any other information system, will generate wrong information if incomplete or erroneous data is provided to the system in the first place. The common expression to describe this phenomenon is "garbage in, garbage out."

However, a software package may be able to identify incorrect data entering into the system. Some software packages that allow data validation can examine the type of data entered against the types specified by the system designer (e.g., entering alphabetic characters for dollar figures), test the sign of the data (e.g., the algebraic sign of numeric data), or check the data range (e.g., the maximum or minimum range of numeric data).

It should be noted here that a software package will not provide these options automatically. Rather, the system user has to specify the option that is needed, and where. This can be accomplished only when a software package is equipped with validation features. There are many software packages that do not contain these features. Therefore, it is the developer's responsibility to consider the availability of these features in software selection if they are needed.

System Security: Confidentiality of Information. As you know, information is a valuable resource of any corporation. Unfortunately, information can be accessed easily by unauthorized users if it is not protected. As a company becomes more involved with microcomputer-based information systems, the issue of protecting the information used by and stored in these systems becomes a matter of increasing importance. In the same way that most mainframe-based information systems offer a full range of security, a micro-based system must be able to provide some kind of security for all resources of the system, particularly information. The system developer must determine the level of security needed by the firm as a whole, and by the different individuals using the system applications, before any software or hardware is selected.

If security of information is considered an important issue, the developer must make sure that appropriate features are available to provide that security. Furthermore, it is the developer's responsibility to discuss the security issue with potential users of the system before the actual system is in place. Most people incorrectly think that they don't need to worry about security until the system is developed, and many are under the false impression that full security protection is always available.

System Maintenance: Programming. The task of modifying and expanding programs developed as a part of an information system is referred to as **programming maintenance.** In most micro-based information systems, specific applications are developed through the use of software packages or the programming language of the system. In either case, as the organization grows or as user requirements change, the programs must be updated, corrected, or modified. The developer's concern at this stage is to anticipate how and by whom, this task will be accomplished. For example, there might be an individual(s) within the firm who is familiar with programming concepts and willing to accept the responsibility of doing maintenance programming. Or, it might be necessary to train an individual to do this task. If neither of these two options is possible, then the developer may have to consider developing the system in such a way that the task of programming will be minimized.

System Maintenance: Hardware. **Hardware maintenance** refers to the procedures required to keep the hardware components of the system in working order. The issue of how the system will be fixed if it breaks down must be dealt with before the hardware components of the system are selected. Just like stereo and television makers, some computer manufacturers and vendors offer limited hardware maintenance, while others offer long-term maintenance, either as part of the initial price of the system or for a fixed monthly or annual payment. Hardware components of a system can fail or may need constant service to prevent breakdown. The question that the developer must confront at this stage is how hardware maintenance will be handled once the system is in operation.

System Maintenance: Software. **Software maintenance** deals primarily with problems, or "bugs," encountered during use of software packages. For example, some software vendors offer a free debugging service if any errors are discovered within a software package.

Software maintenance also includes modifications to software packages, either to have the package perform additional tasks or perform a task differently. For example, it might be necessary to modify a software package in order to generate a summary report from various separate reports. The task of modifying a software package to suit the needs of an organization is referred to as **customizing.** Some vendors do not allow modification of the original programs of the software package. Therefore, the developer must examine the need for future modifications before selecting a restricted software package.

The other issue that arises concerns how the software package will be updated, if necessary. For instance, if the software company puts on the market an updated version of the same software package, will they update their older versions automatically? Confronting these various security and maintenance issues during the selection and design phase will allow the developer to make a more knowledgeable decision about the kind of system that should be selected and developed.

Consultation with Users

Information systems are not normally developed for machines. They are developed for people. It is very important to ensure that the users of these systems have been thoroughly consulted in advance about their needs. Otherwise, the probability of success of the system in achieving its stated goals will be very slim, regardless of the size of the investment in the information system.

Since a micro-based system may be used by a small group of users—in some cases, two or three—it should not be too difficult for the developer of a system to establish effective channels of communication with them. In many cases, the developer will be one of the major potential users of the system, and should be careful not to make assumptions about what other users want to see out of the system. The system developer must constantly consult with others about their needs.

Another advantage of communicating with users of the system at this early stage is that the users can be a great source of ideas for the developer. In most cases, once the users feel that they are part of the development team, they will be willing to perform different tasks and cooperate more fully. The developer must constantly keep in mind that people are the best sources of information and are the ultimate users of the system; therefore, at no time should their importance be underestimated.

During the consultation part of the system development phase, the developer should try to collect more information about the needs of potential users (see Figure 13.4). These needs can be identified in terms of short and long term. The developer must encourage users to think of their future requirements as well as their immediate needs. In addition, the developer should try to learn more about the volume of data that will be processed. How often will data need to be processed? Would the user prefer to see the generated information displayed on a screen or a printer, or both? What will be the size of the average document that must be printed? How often will the user use the system? Does the user need to have the system connected to other information systems? The answers to most of these questions should come from the users, rather than the developer.

If the system is a project of significant magnitude, the developer might consider collecting the users' needs and specified system requirements in report form, which then could be distributed to different system vendors, soliciting their proposals for the system they think would satisfy the firm's requirements. This form, referred to as a **Request for Proposal (RFP),** consists of objectives of the systems, user requirements—both immediate and future—and other relevant information about company needs.

In the past, many micro-based information systems were developed to meet the immediate needs of users, ignoring future needs. The majority of these systems became obsolete after a few short months. The developer must remember that, as users become acquainted with the system, their horizons will expand and they will discover further utilization and applications for the system. Therefore, it is the developer's responsibility to recommend a system that can accommodate future needs and applications.

The developer also should estimate the impact of a micro-based information system on individual employees. Over the last few decades, many researchers have studied the overall impact of computer technology on organizations and their

1. Short- and long-term needs
2. Volume of data
3. Frequency of processing
4. Desired format
5. How frequently the system will be used
6. Communications concerns

Figure 13.4
Information that must be Collected from Users

employees. The fact is that many employees still consider this technology as, ultimately, a replacement for themselves. The majority of these employees have false perceptions of computer technology due to a lack of understanding of computers and their role in overall organizational functions.

The developer must emphasize to potential users the idea that the system is only a support tool, similar to other support tools, such as typewriters. Typewriters did not replace secretaries; instead, when typewriters were introduced, secretaries simply learned how to use them to perform their jobs more efficiently. It has been proven that informed employees will have more positive attitudes toward a new micro-based system than uninformed ones. The developer should remember that resistance to change is part of human nature. The important issue is to manage that resistance. The developer must try to work with resistant individuals, to make sure that they are aware of the real intention of the system and how the system ultimately will help them do their jobs better.

During the entire system development cycle, potential users of the system must be constantly informed about the status of the system. In many cases, changes in the initial requirements will be needed, and it is a lot easier to incorporate changes during the early stages of the system development cycle than to incorporate them after the system is in operation. Finally, the developer must carefully consider user reaction to the results of different phases of the development cycle.

Software Evaluation

When selecting the components of a micro-based information system, too many people start by selecting hardware rather than software. This approach is the same as first buying a house and then choosing a location for the house. A smart house buyer will first identify a desirable location, based on the available school systems, proximity to shopping, and other factors, and then try to buy a house in that location. The same thing is also true in the case of software selection versus hardware selection.

After identifying the needs of the users and the requirements of the system under development, the developer will try to evaluate the various software packages designed for these applications. The developer starts first by identifying the different software packages available in the market, then evaluating each to find out which will best satisfy the needs of the firm. As mentioned in the previous chapter, many sources could help identify suitable packages, such as asking colleagues in the field, checking various publications in the library, checking with different vendors, and consulting with professional organizations. If the developer submits an RFP to different hardware vendors, each vendor will recommend a software package that he or she thinks is the most suitable for the firm's applications. This is, perhaps, the best source of free, relevant information. In evaluating software packages, the developer must consider many factors. The following sections discuss some of these factors, in order of priority. Figure 13.5 on the following page summarizes the factors.

Suitability of package requirements	How closely will the software package satisfy the information requirements?
Security procedures	What types of security procedures are offered?
Software maintenance	How will the package be maintained, by who, and at what cost?
Level of friendliness	What is the level of ease of operation of the system by non-computer users?
Quality of documentation	How well-written is the software package documentation?
Future expansion and updating	What is the future expansion capability of the system, and how can it be updated?
Degree of difficulty in modification	How difficult is it to modify certain procedures or programs of the system?
Services provided by the vendor	Does the vendor offer an 800 toll-free telephone number support for problems that the user may encounter?
Language the package developed in	Is the language used in development of the system popular and easy to use?
Availability of training programs	How easily can training programs be found for the software package?
Hardware requirements	What are the specifications of the needed hardware?
Reputation of the vendor	How well does the vendor serve the clients?
Popularity of package usage	What is the magnitude of this package use in the field?
Price of the package	What is the initial cost, and what might be some future costs?

Figure 13.5
Summary of Software Evaluation Criteria

Suitability of Software Requirements. The foremost consideration in choosing a software package is how closely the package conforms to the stated requirements of the system. Regardless of the package's degree of sophistication, if it cannot satisfy the user's requirements, it must be classified as unsuitable.

The specifications of the work to be performed by the software package must be clearly understood by the system developer. The developer must beware of confusing sales talk sprinkled with computer jargon. If the information about certain functions is ambiguous, the developer must request a complete explanation. The developer should never be embarrassed to ask questions about confusing aspects of the software package.

Security Procedures. If security has been identified as an important issue, then the developer must carefully evaluate the type of security built into the package. Security features could range from the simple assignment of a password to possible **encryption** of data stored on the secondary storage devices (**encryption** involves converting data to an unrecognized format). Information about system security can be obtained from either the system documentation or the vendor.

Software Maintenance. As software is employed by users, it gets worn out, bugs are discovered, and damage to the original diskettes may occur. A vendor's willingness to assist the user in dealing with software maintenance problems should be ascertained during the software evaluation process. For example, would it be the purchaser's responsibility to correct errors discovered during use of the software? If the vendor is willing to solve the problem, how long would it take them to do so? If a software diskette is damaged, will the vendor provide another copy? If yes, how much will it cost? And how long will it take to replace the diskette? These are the types of questions that should be posed to a vendor during the evaluation period.

Level of Friendliness. Ease of operation of the software must be the second criterion for software selection. In the last few years, a new generation of microcomputer software packages, known as **user-friendly** software, has emerged in the market. The idea behind these software packages is that a user should not have to memorize commands or instructions in order to operate the software; instead, the software should allow a user to interact with its programs in the simplest possible way.

It has been demonstrated that the use of menus for selection of options is the easiest method of software operation. As a result, most software developers have incorporated menus in their software. They are known as **menu-driven** packages.

Another factor that the developer must consider is the availability of help menus within the software. Many software packages are equipped with numerous help sessions built into different menus to assist users who have problems or questions. It should be remembered that ease of operation is a key factor for system users, and may be instrumental in getting computer non-enthusiasts involved.

Quality of Documentation. The quality of the documentation accompanying a software package is another important factor in evaluation. **Documentation** normally consists of a tutorial guide or training manual, a reference manual, and possibly a programming manual. The most important factor in judging the quality of documentation is the simplicity of the language used for explanations. Use of computer jargon, technical terms, or buzzwords is a clear indication of poor-quality software.

The documentation of a software package—particularly the user training manual— must be written in such a way that anyone, regardless of the person's computer background, can follow the instructions and operate the software. This is the same basic idea behind the manuals that accompany new cars. Car manufacturers are not concerned with how much the average car driver knows about the mechanics of the car; they are interested in conveying operating information to car users. Similarly, the average microcomputer user should not have to know about bits and bytes in order to operate a software package.

In recent years, many major software vendors have been providing users with tutorial diskettes in addition to a printed user manual. Tutorial diskettes consist of lessons in how to use the software through hands-on experience rather than by reading the manuals. This method of training has been considered very effective. Furthermore, the simplicity of tutorial instructions minimizes the potential for error.

Interaction of the software package with other packages, and the required hardware for this task, must also be carefully evaluated.

Future Expansion and Updating. It is possible to expand most software packages. Some software packages can be expanded by allowing additional application programs to be added to the software; others offer enhancement of the original package by allowing it to work with other software packages. It also has become common for software vendors to allow buyers to exchange the original software package for an updated version, for a modest fee. This option is very useful because it means that the buyer does not have to dispose of the original version whenever an updated version is issued. It also allows a firm's software applications to expand as more sophisticated versions of the software are introduced. It would be very costly to a firm to discover, after a year of use, that a piece of software is not capable of handling a growing volume of data or tasks.

Degree of Difficulty in Modification. Many of the software packages purchased for micro-based systems have to be modified in order to match the specifications and requirements of an individual firm's applications. Therefore, it is important to know whether the software can be modified easily if it is necessary to do so. It should be remembered that some software vendors do not allow modification of their software packages. This restriction makes the software very inflexible for users. The documentation of a software package must provide a clear explanation of the programs within the package in case modifications are necessary.

Services Provided by the Vendor. The dependence of the user upon services provided by the vendor during initial use of the software package, and even later on, should not be underestimated. Unlike many mainframe computer information systems, which are operated by large computer departments with knowledgeable staff who are available to help end users, microcomputer users normally have few expert resources within the firm. They must obtain most of their assistance from the vendor of the software package. Many vendors provide toll-free telephone numbers that customers can call to get help or instruction. Do not allow the sales representative of a local computer store to sell you the idea that any help you need will be provided to you at the local store. The truth of the matter is that the majority of local salespeople know little about individual software packages apart from a few basic commands and functions. Make sure that the vendor will back you up with the software company whenever you are confused by a software problem.

Language the Package is Developed In. It is important to know what programming language was used to develop the software. The main reason for this concern is the fact that, if it becomes necessary to modify the system, it will be easier and less expensive to work with a package that is written in a programming language that either the user or some of the firm's programmers are familiar with. Imagine what would happen if the package's programs were written in a rare language that nobody except the package's developer knows anything about! In a situation such as this, you would need to either send someone to get special training for this language, or hire a (possibly expensive) consultant. Make sure that you know which programming language was used in developing the system, and also find out if the language is a common one.

Availability of Training Programs. Some software vendors offer training programs for their software packages, either free of charge or for a moderate fee. If the software package happens to be a popular one in the field, users can easily identify other available training programs at a local college or training center. One major problem with less common or less popular software packages is the lack of availability of training programs through sources other than the vendor. In recent years, many major software vendors have been offering training programs in more cities and locations to satisfy the needs of their current users and to promote their products to potential buyers. Determine if the software company you are considering offers such training programs, and, if they do, how often and where. Furthermore, before selecting the software, check local college or university continuing education programs to find out if they offer training seminars or workshops for the software package under consideration.

Hardware Requirements. At this stage of the software evaluation process, the developer should determine the hardware requirements of the software package. The information should allow the developer to find out what types of hardware components are needed. For example, the software may require a minimum internal memory of 640K or a hard disk with a 30MB storage capacity. It may require a color monitor instead of a monochrome monitor, or it may run only in the IBM PC-DOS environment, or on some special equipment.

Having full knowledge of the hardware requirements of the package allows the developer to evaluate the software with respect to the availability and cost of the required hardware components. Imagine the problems that could occur if the hardware had been selected first, and it was then discovered that the preferred software required totally different hardware.

Reputation of the Vendor. It is important to know the reputations of the vendor and the local supplier of the package. The best sources of information about both the vendor and the local supplier are previous users of the software package. Ask the supplier or vendor to provide you with a list of users of the software package (not two or three, but *many* previous users). Call some of them and ascertain what kind of service they have received from the vendor or the local supplier. Make sure that the seller of the software is concerned not only with selling you the package, but also with providing you with a full range of support services whenever you need them.

Popularity of Package Usage. The extent of use of the software package among professionals in the field is very important because a great deal of information about the package's features comes by word of mouth. Therefore, if the software package is not a popular one, the user's choices are limited. For example, if the software was originally developed in another country and nobody in your country has used it, the user might have difficulty in obtaining help, training, or information from other users. Another benefit of using a popular software package is that you can talk to other people in the field about its capabilities, of which you may not be aware.

The software vendor can answer technical questions, but when it comes to those questions that relate to the software's applications, sometimes your best source of information will be your colleagues who are using the same software package.

Price of Package. For reasons you can see, the price of a software package is the last factor to be considered in software evaluation. There is no value to saving a few hundred dollars by buying an inexpensive software package if it does not satisfy your more important criteria. The developer must remember that price should not be considered a major criterion for software selection. Given how inexpensive most common software packages are, most users would be better off spending a few dollars more and obtaining a package that will satisfy the needs of the firm. For purposes of comparison, hiring a computer consultant to do twenty hours of maintenance programming for a less expensive software package for which the vendor does not provide maintenance services would cost approximately $600 to $1,400.

It is very common to evaluate software packages for different categories of applications, and in the end, choose one for each category. In other words, for a typical micro-based information system, you could choose a software package for word processing, one for database management, one for spreadsheet, one for graphics, and one for telecommunications. However, all of these capabilities could be included in a single package, such as Lotus Corporation's Symphony. Therefore, the developer should concentrate on finding one or a few packages that can satisfy all of the applications identified during the investigation phase.

Hardware Evaluation

Upon completion of the software evaluation process, the developer must select the required hardware. Hardware evaluation is as important as software evaluation. Microcomputer technology is rapidly evolving around more powerful and sophisticated hardware components, and a firm does not want to spend several thousand dollars for hardware that may become obsolete in a short time. Another reason for the importance of hardware evaluation is the availability of a variety of brands of microcomputers with different capabilities. The following sections discuss, in order of their importance, some of the criteria that should be considered during hardware evaluation. These factors are summarized in Figure 13.6.

Figure 13.6
Summary of Hardware Evaluation Criteria

Suitability to the chosen software	How close does it match the software requirements?
Maintenance options	How will the system be serviced and maintained?
Ease of operation	How easily can an average person operate the hardware?
Quality of documentation	How difficult is it to follow the explanations given in the documentation?
Growth prospects	What are the prospects of family growth and future expansion?
Industry standards	How close is the system to the industry standard?
Installation	How will the system be delivered and installed?
Networking capability	What are the capabilities of the system in data communications and networking?
Programming languages and utility programs	Is the system's program language(s) a common one? How many utility programs come with the system?
Training programs	Are training programs available through either the vendor or other sources?
Reputation of suppliers	How has the supplier served previous customers?
Price of hardware	What is the initial price, and what are other future associated costs of the system?

Suitability to the Chosen Software. Perhaps the most important factor in selecting the hardware components of the system under development is the suitability of the hardware with regard to the selected software. The first criterion for hardware evaluation is whether the software can, in fact, be used on the hardware. Many business application software packages can be used only on the IBM-PC or compatibles.

A number of other cases show the critical importance of selecting the right hardware. For example, Lotus 1-2-3 cannot be used on Apple computers. If the identified software happens to be 1-2-3, it would be very unwise to buy an Apple computer, even if the local dealer is offering an excellent bargain on the machine. Another consideration should be whether the hardware can match the specifications or requirements of the software.

Maintenance Options. The second most important factor to be considered is the availability of different maintenance options. Normally, the components of a system have at least a ninety-day warranty, but some computer manufacturers do offer a one-year warranty. In some cases, the local supplier offers additional warranty coverage for service and maintenance. It is important to know at this stage how the system will be serviced and maintained. In addition to the initial warranty, many manufacturers offer extended maintenance programs for a modest monthly or annual fee. The developer should note that the cost of fixing a system that is not under warranty could be prohibitive.

Another consideration for the developer is how long it takes for a system under warranty to be repaired. Is there a local shop that the system could be taken to? Would the manufacturer have the system repaired on-site? What would be the cost of an extended maintenance program, if one is available? It is important to address questions about repairs and maintenance so that future problems can be anticipated without needless anxiety. Also, the developer should be aware that, while it will probably not be too difficult to have a system sent out for repairs during the first few weeks after purchase (before the system is fully utilized), it will be very tedious and costly to shut the system down after it is in full operation.

Ease of Operation. Some of the early microcomputers were very difficult to operate. They required many floppy diskettes to be exchanged in and out of the machine before the system could be operational. As you now know, the new generation of microcomputers are much easier to operate. Nevertheless, the developer should be concerned with how easily the average person can start the system. Does the user have to enter many technical commands in order to get the computer system started, or is there an automatic start-up program? Is the keyboard comparable to a standard typewriter keyboard? Is the color of the display monitor easy on the eyes? Does the keyboard offer additional numerical keys for arithmetic operations, or function keys for special tasks? The developer should be concerned not only with his or her own reaction toward the system's ease of operation, but should closely consult those employees, such as secretaries, who will be the main users of the system.

Quality of Documentation. The documentation of the system is as important as its ease of operation. As a matter of fact, these two factors are closely related because operating instructions are provided as a part of the system documentation. Therefore, it would be very difficult to learn how to operate a system from a poorly documented user manual. The documentation of the system should be written in simple language, contain illustrations of different parts of the system that clearly explain the components and their functions, and provide examples of how different functions would be carried out by the system. The system reference manual should not contain technical jargon or buzzwords. It should have explanations of possible errors within the system, and information about other devices that can be added to the system, with their precise specifications.

Growth Prospects. Normally, after a micro-based information system is installed and utilized, the need for more memory, power, and other functions will grow. The pertinent question is, can the system be expanded? As a part of the hardware evaluation, the developer must determine the prospects of family growth of the system. Unfortunately, in the past, many micro-based information systems were developed without enough consideration given to growth prospects. As a result, many of them were incapable of dealing with new requirements. Normally, the number of users of a micro-based information system is small at the system's inception, but, as more users become aware of applications, the number will grow.

Also at the beginning, user applications are normally few and limited. As users learn more about different system capabilities, applications will become larger and more sophisticated. The possibility of system expansion should be almost unlimited. The developer should also be concerned whether additional devices can be added to the system. Are there enough—or any—expansion slots within the system? Would the vendor help in upgrading the system if this is necessary?

Industry Standards. Since the birth of the first IBM-PC in 1981, a kind of standard, known as the **PC standard** has evolved. Perhaps the main reason for this evolution is the fact that so many IBM-PC look-alikes use architecture and design similar to IBM-PCs. As a result, many software vendors have designed application software for the most common business microcomputers: the IBM-PC and compatibles. Furthermore, numerous expansion devices have been developed for these machines by different vendors, making the task of expansion easier and less costly. In summary, the main advantage of buying hardware designed around the industry PC standard is the availability of all kinds of software, expansion options, and services by vendors other than the manufacturer.

Installation. The task of installing a system can be a tedious one. Many microcomputer manufacturers or suppliers offer delivery and installation for free or for a very modest fee. It is important to decide in advance how the system will be installed. Some microcomputers are easier to install than others, but the key point is that neither the developer nor any other individual in the company needs to be an expert in hardware installation procedures. Rather, the developer should consider the issue of system installation as a hardware evaluation factor. Many microcomputers come with a variety of components, and it makes evaluating hardware easier if the developer knows that the manufacturer or supplier will provide free installation as a part of the purchase.

Networking Capability. A decade ago, microcomputers were viewed as stand-alone computing devices capable of serving only one user at a time. But with the recent advancements achieved in microcomputer and telecommunications technologies, a microcomputer can now be linked to a mainframe, a minicomputer, or other microcomputers via communication devices. Therefore, it is important to know the **networking capabilities** of the system under consideration. Even if there is no concern for communication with other systems at the time of development, the developer must keep in mind that this need may arise in the future as users become better educated about the capabilities of the system and its applications. Therefore, the developer must examine the networking capability of the system during system selection. Many newer microcomputers come with built-in communication capabilities.

Programming Languages and Utility Programs. It is important to know what programming language or languages and utility programs are supplied with the hardware. The most common programming language for microcomputers is **BASIC**. In fact, this language has become the standard language for microcomputers. Many manufacturers now supply other popular languages in addition to BASIC, such as Pascal and C. If a system is equipped with a programming language that is common and easy to use, system users have the option of developing in-house programs and applications. However, if the system is equipped with an obscure language that nobody knows, the option of developing in-house applications may be eliminated.

Almost every microcomputer comes with a collection of utility programs. These programs are developed for a variety of standard system-related tasks, such as making backup copies, diagnosing flaws in diskettes or hard disks, formatting the screen, reprogramming function keys, matching files, or merging files. The availability of different utility programs is essential to maintenance and management of the system.

Training Programs. The availability of training programs offered by the manufacturer, the local supplier, or local educational institutions is an important factor in evaluating the hardware. If the system is not a common one, it will be much more difficult to obtain the necessary training. In particular, if the system was designed overseas and is not popular in the United States, do not count on the existence of training programs. Check a few local educational institutions about the availability of seminars or workshops for the system under consideration. Many vendors offer on-site training programs, either free or for a modest fee. This option is considered the most effective way of obtaining the necessary training about operations and features of the system. In any event, the developer must determine in advance how training will be obtained.

Reputation of Suppliers. In some cases, a microcomputer is not purchased directly from the manufacturer, but from a local supplier. In the past, many suppliers or their salespersons made empty promises about services they would provide after a system was purchased. Unfortunately, because many of these promises were never fulfilled, it is important to find out something about the supplier's reputation and history with previous customers. The best sources of information are previous buyers. Another source of information, the local Better Business Bureau or Chamber of Commerce, could help you find out whether complaints have been filed by previous customers. Finally, the last source of information would be friends and colleagues who have either dealt with the supplier themselves or who know others who have been involved with the supplier.

Price of Hardware. The last factor in the consideration of the hardware evaluation, just as in software evaluation, is the price. One could argue, that since every firm is in business to generate revenue, how can price be the least important factor during the hardware evaluation process? The answer is very simple. One way to generate business revenue is to minimize the costs of conducting business. One should not be fooled by the illusion that one is saving money by purchasing a microcomputer that does not satisfy the criteria discussed here, or one that temporarily satisfies a few of the criteria but, after a few months, reaches its maximum capacity and cannot be expanded. A system may be priced very inexpensively by a computer company that just entered the microcomputer market six months ago and is already on its way out. The developer should not compromise other criteria over a few hundred dollars in initial savings.

Identifying Alternatives

Upon completing the software and hardware evaluation, the developer must be able to identify various alternatives or options for the system under development. Each alternative should include descriptions of software and hardware, possible benefits, additional comments, and the overall cost of the particular alternative. There may be many possible alternatives, but the developer should limit the choices to the most pertinent few. It is also possible that, after extensive investigation, the developer may realize that no suitable software package can be found for the information requirements of the proposed micro-based information system. Therefore, the developer might recommend that in-house programs be developed, or a consultant be hired to develop necessary programs for the system. Furthermore, if someone within the organization will be assigned to install the system, write programs, test the system, and provide training programs, then all the associated costs of that individual's time must be estimated. One other alternative for obtaining programs and developing different procedures for the system is to contact local colleges to see whether they have qualified students who are willing to provide the necessary assistance.

In many cases, the developer presents the identified alternatives to the owner of the firm, members of a committee, or a supervisor for further evaluation and selection. In these cases, the developer should try to provide precise information about each alternative and remain unbiased. Normally at this stage, the developer will prepare a report on the overall status of the system evaluation and alternatives for consideration by other people involved in the selection process. This report sometimes is referred to as the **system selection and design report.** Now let's examine the recommended content of this report.

Preparing a System Selection and Design Report

The report should begin by restating the main problems and all the associated problems that prompted the system investigation, followed by a list of the objectives of the system under consideration. The alternatives should be outlined, with specifications, benefits, and comments for each. The overall cost of each alternative must be clearly stated. In some cases, the developer must make a recommendation in addition to listing alternatives identified for the system. In this case, the developer will recommend the alternative that he or she is convinced would satisfy the information requirements of the firm. If the developer is making a recommendation, it is important to include some justification for this decision. Figure 13.7 summarizes the format of the system selection and design report.

1. Restatement of original problem

2. List of system objectives

3. Description of systems being considered

    Specifications
    Benefits
    Comments

4. Cost of each alternative system

5. Recommendation

Figure 13.7
Format of the System Selection and Design Report

Selecting a System

Upon careful evaluation and consideration of all available alternatives, the most suitable alternative will be selected by the developer, a committee, or the owner of the firm. At the end of this stage, it is again possible that the feasibility of developing a micro-based information system could be questioned, and a recommendation be made to "do nothing." One possible reason for such a recommendation might be the cost of the system. Although we estimated the overall cost of a system during the investigation stage, the developer may come up with figures that are far higher than the estimated costs after conducting a thorough cost analysis. Therefore, management might decide to take no action, or to postpone any further action until funds are available for system development.

Back to the Case of SWIS

After careful examination of all the requirements of the system and evaluation of software packages and hardware for the proposed micro-based information system for SWIS, Sandy Cofman prepared the following system selection and design report.

SYSTEM SELECTION AND DESIGN REPORT

A system selection and design study of the information problems at Sunshine Window Inc., Suppliers has been completed. This report outlines the current problems, objectives of the new system, user requirements, and alternative courses of action, as well as an evaluation of each alternative. A recommendation as to the best alternative is included at the end of this report.

Problems

As outlined in the investigation report submitted earlier, the problems at SWIS stem from the lack of means to store, process, and report on various information. Specific problems to be addressed are:

- Management has not been able to make informed strategic decisions about SWIS because of a lack of organized and concise information. Forecasts and planning reports are nonexistent, and currently the information is not available to develop them.
- The managers' decision making process is hindered by the lack of resources available to them. Information is not accessible in organized formats; managers lack the tools to sufficiently evaluate alternative strategies.
- Mailings have not been reaching the intended customers or manufacturers on a timely basis. The result has been a decline in service, and subsequently, a loss of orders.
- Information concerning product inventory has not been processed efficiently. No periodic or query-generated reports can be produced at this time. Current procedures lead to inventory shortages. Important customers are not receiving products by the requested delivery times.
- The current filing system for storing and maintaining manufacturer information is inadequate. At present, there are great inconsistencies in the records.
- The ways in which data records are maintained in the manual system are slow, inefficient, and redundant.
- Administrative tasks involving letter preparation, memos, and reports are duplicated unnecessarily.

Objectives

The loss of orders and other costs associated with the above problems are unacceptable to the management of SWIS, which would like to reap the benefits of the extra orders that could be generated by quality customer service with a new system. Management has identified its requirements and objectives for a new system. These are:

- The new system should provide detailed and concise periodic reports on information needed to make strategic decisions and daily decisions about customers and orders.

- The new system should provide the necessary information for planning and forecasting the long-term profitability of the firm.
- The system should enhance and improve the managerial decision-making process.
- The new system should lessen the time it takes to determine inventory levels and general product information.
- The new system should lessen the time required to enter, store, and maintain product, order, and manufacturer data.
- The new system should use already compiled customer and manufacturer supplier information to produce specific and mass mailings according to the immediate needs of the company.
- The new system should allow administrative staff to prepare documents in a more timely fashion while permitting greater flexibility in report preparation.

Alternatives

After extensive research conducted by talking to friends and colleagues, checking computer stores, reading various computer publications, and consulting with professors, the following three alternatives have been identified for the system under consideration.

Alternative One: Design the system around the dBASE III PLUS database management system (DBMS) software package, using the DBMS as a foundation for other packages. This package offers a variety of database features, including mailing list and report generation options. In addition, we could purchase the Lotus 1-2-3 spreadsheet package for preparation of profitability analysis and forecasting reports. Lotus 1-2-3 provides a decision support system capability for management. We could purchase the WordPerfect word processing package for external and internal written communications. All three software packages—dBASE III PLUS, Lotus 1-2-3, and WordPerfect—run on an IBM-PC and on many IBM compatible PCs. The software packages will operate with 256K (640K recommended) RAM, two disk drives (recommended hard disk) secondary storage, monochrome (preferably color) monitor, and 2.0 or later version of DOS. With regard to these requirements, an IBM PS/2 Model 60 with One MB RAM, 44MB of hard disk, DOS 3.3, and a color monitor has been identified as the best hardware match. In addition, we could consider purchasing an Epson LQ-1000 letter-quality printer that prints 300 characters per minute (cpm) and has a form feeder.

Benefits: The following benefits could be gained by utilizing this alternative.

- All three packages offer security procedures.
- The packages are popular ones, with a variety of features and applications.
- The software packages run on the standard PC.
- The hardware is an advanced system, with future expansion options.
- Both the software and hardware vendors have good reputations for service and continued support of their customers.

Comments: The software packages dBASE III PLUS and Lotus 1-2-3 offer menu-assistance features, which allow non-programmers the capability of putting various options into play without distress. WordPerfect commands are quite easy to use; the command structure is activated from ten function keys on the keyboard. In addition, the DBMS package offers a programming language that we can eventually use to develop in-house applications. Lotus 1-2-3 offers spreadsheet, graphics, and database capabilities. SWIS's word processing needs could be fulfilled by WordPerfect. The hardware carries a one-year warranty; an extended warranty could be purchased from a third party.

Costs: The following costs have been identified for Alternative One.

software packages		$ 1,300
dBASE III PLUS	$500	
Lotus 1-2-3	400	
WordPerfect	400	
hardware		5,000
printer		700
training		200
implementation and conversion		1,000
hardware maintenance program		800
miscellaneous cost		300
(furniture, paper, etc.)		
TOTAL COST		$ 9,300

Alternative Two: This alternative calls for a micro-based information system to be developed incorporating the R:BASE 5000 database management system software package. The package is known for its advanced options, and offers a variety of database management features, mailing list preparation, and report generation. SuperCalc will be purchased for spreadsheet applications and forecasting, while WordStar will be purchased as a word processing system. The three software packages run on the IBM-PC and many IBM compatible PCs. The combined hardware requirements of these software packages are 256K (640K recommended) RAM, two disk drives (hard disk recommended) secondary storage, a monochrome (preferably color) monitor, and a later version of MS-DOS. In response to the software requirements, a PC-compatible Compaq 286, with 640K RAM, 30MB hard disk, and a color monitor has been identified as a suitable machine. In addition, we have found a NEC Spinwriter 3550 printer that can print 350 cpm and has a form feeder.

Benefits: The following benefits could be gained by choosing Alternative Two.

- The software offers adequate security procedures.
- The software runs on standard PCs.
- The hardware offers many advanced features of existing PC technology.

- The prospect for future expansion is very good.
- Both software and hardware vendors have good reputations for the services provided to their customers.

Comments: These software packages offer many advanced features for database management, spreadsheets and text editing. Like dBASE, the R:BASE 5000 package is a menu-driven software package. In addition, the package offers a programming language for in-house applications development. The only drawback in the case of this software package is that the package is relatively new in comparison to dBASE, and it is not as widely used. SuperCalc offers spreadsheet analysis and other spreadsheet-oriented functions; however, it is not as popular as Lotus 1-2-3. Therefore, more literature is available for the Lotus software package. WordStar and WordPerfect are very similar word processing packages. Both are easy to use, yet WordPerfect has an advantage due to its stronger presence in the marketplace. With regard to the hardware, the manufacturer has been around for some time, and it is a strong contender in the PC market.

Costs: The following costs have been identified for Alternative Two.

software packages		$ 1,900
R:BASE 5000	$900	
SuperCalc	500	
WordStar	500	
hardware		4,500
printer		900
training costs		200
implementation and conversion		1,200
hardware maintenance program		1,000
miscellaneous costs		300
(furniture, paper, etc.)		
TOTAL COST		$10,000

Alternative Three: The third alternative is a combination of purchasing software and hiring a consultant to develop programs for the firm's database management requirements. A consultant could be hired to design and code all the programs necessary to handle the database information needs. The programs could be written either in the BASIC or Pascal programming language. Lotus 1-2-3 spreadsheet applications would be developed and documented by the consultant. Furthermore, the consultant could instruct the WordStar users. Suitable hardware for this alternative is an IBM PS/2 Model 60 with One MB RAM, 44MB hard disk, and a color monitor. Furthermore, a Turbo Pascal compiler and a NEC quality-printer with 300 cpm and form feeder will be required.

Benefits: The following benefits could be gained by utilizing Alternative Three.

- The system will be developed totally around the needs of the firm.
- The software will be customized.
- Changes in the system could be incorporated.
- The hardware vendor has a good reputation.
- The hardware can be easily expanded.

Comments: The idea of developing an in-house system sounds very exciting, except for the costs of developing such a system. Furthermore, the firm would need a skilled programmer to constantly maintain the system. Therefore, the cost of this alternative is its major drawback. Lotus 1-2-3 and WordStar are designed with the user in mind and, although a consultant is desirable, one is not necessary.

Costs: The following costs have been identified for Alternative Three.

Pascal compiler	$ 250
hardware	5,000
printer	900
training	500
system design and programming	3,000
implementation and conversion	5,000
maintenance programming (per year)	1,000
Lotus 1-2-3	400
WordStar	500
hardware maintenance	800
TOTAL COST	$17,350

Recommendation

In view of the company's needs, and after careful consideration and consultation with future users of the proposed microcomputer information system, Alternative One is recommended as the most suitable alternative for this company for the following reasons.

- This alternative satisfies all the requirements.
- Both software and hardware offer adequate security and maintenance procedures.
- Future family growth prospects for the hardware are very bright.
- The programs dBASE, Lotus 1-2-3, and WordPerfect are very powerful and popular software packages.
- Many training programs are available for both the software and hardware.
- Finally, this alternative is the least costly.

■ SUMMARY

The task of identifying the initial needs and information requirements of a firm is performed during the system investigation phase. If it is decided that the firm is in need of a micro-based information system, the second phase of the system development cycle begins. The activities of this phase include identifying system security and maintenance requirements; consulting with users of the system; software and hardware evaluation; identifying alternatives; preparing the system selection and design report; and, finally, selecting the most appropriate alternative.

It is important to know in advance how the system as a whole and the information stored in it will be protected from unauthorized users. It is also important to know how the system will be maintained once it is in full operation. Security and maintenance procedures should be carefully studied before any software or hardware is selected. Furthermore, it is essential to consult with end users to learn their specific requirements for the system.

The software for a micro-based information system must be carefully evaluated first, before any hardware can be evaluated. Many criteria, such as suitability of the software package to the firm's requirements, security options, software maintenance, level of friendliness, quality of documentation, future expansion and updating possibilities, degree of difficulty in modification, vendor services, availability of training programs, hardware requirements, reputation of the vendor, popularity of the package, and the price of the package, must be considered.

In the area of hardware evaluation, among the criteria that must be considered are suitability to the software package, maintenance options, ease of operation, quality of documentation, growth prospects, industry standard conformity, installation services, networking capability, programming languages and utility programs provided, availability of training programs, the reputation of the supplier, and price of the hardware.

Upon completion of the software and hardware evaluation, a report on the possible alternatives must be prepared. This report is called the system selection and design report. The final step of this phase is selection of the most appropriate option for the system under consideration.

■ KEY TERMS

system selection and design phase
The tasks of identifying necessary features of the computer system, identifying different alternatives, and choosing and obtaining actual system components.

system developer
The person who carries out the tasks of the systems selection and design phase.

system security
Availability of the entire system, accuracy of information generated by the system, and the confidentiality of certain information stored in the system.

programming maintenance	The task of modifying and expanding programs developed as a part of an information system.
hardware maintenance	The procedures required to keep the hardware components of the system in working order.
software maintenance	Handling problems encountered during the use of software packages; including modifications to software packages, either in having the package perform additional tasks or perform a task differently.
customizing	The task of modifying a software package to suit the needs of an organization.
Request for Proposal (RFP)	A request provided to various vendors specifying requirements of the system under development.
encryption	Converting data/information to an unrecognized format.
user-friendly	The software that allows a user to interact with its programs in the simplest possible way.
menu-driven	Software packages that incorporate menus for selection of options.
documentation	Consists of a tutorial guide or training manual, a reference manual, and programming manual.
PC standard	An industry standard in which IBM-PC look-alikes use architecture and design similar to IBM-PCs.
networking capability	The ability of a microcomputer to communicate with other systems in which a microcomputer is linked to a mainframe, a minicomputer, or other microcomputer through the use of communication devices.
BASIC	Beginners' All-Purpose Symbolic Instruction Code, the most common programming language for microcomputers.
system selection and design report	A report on the possible alternatives of software and hardware options.

■ Review Questions

1. The first consideration in developing a micro-based information system should be
   (a) hardware requirements.
   (b) security and maintenance requirements.
   (c) software packages.
   (d) user needs.
2. For security purposes, some microcomputers are equipped with a _____, which is used to protect the system from unauthorized users.
   (a) password
   (b) combination
   (c) lock
   (d) none of the above
   (e) both (a) and (c)

3. The task of maintaining computer programs developed as a part of the system must be dealt with during the _____ phase of the selection process.
   (a) maintenance
   (b) security
   (c) user interview
   (d) software evaluation
   (e) hardware evaluation
4. Information systems should be developed to meet the needs of
   (a) people.
   (b) equipment.
   (c) software.
   (d) none of the above.
5. During the design stage, the developer should
   (a) try to collect more information about the needs of users of the system.
   (b) recommend a system that can accommodate immediate needs.
   (c) avoid individuals who are resistant to the new system.
   (d) all of the above.
6 When selecting components of a micro-based information system, _____ selection should be made after _____ selection.
   (a) hardware, software
   (b) software, hardware
   (c) software, operating system
   (d) both (b) and (c)
7. In evaluating a software package, the foremost consideration should be
   (a) level of friendliness.
   (b) security procedures.
   (c) suitability of package to requirements.
   (d) software maintenance.
8. The task of modifying a software package to suit the needs of the user is referred to as _____ a package.
   (a) debugging
   (b) documenting
   (c) updating
   (d) modifying
   (e) customizing
9. Which of the following statements concerning software packages is false?
   (a) Microcomputer users must normally rely on the vendor for assistance with software packages.
   (b) It is important to know which programming language was used to develop the software.
   (c) Many vendors allow an exchange of software for an updated version at no cost.
   (d) Some vendors offer training for their software packages.

10. _____ is the least important factor when selecting software.
    (a) User-friendliness
    (b) User requirements
    (c) Security
    (d) Price
    (e) Maintenance
11. _____ diskettes consist of lessons in how to use the software through hands-on experience.
    (a) Update
    (b) Turning
    (c) Tutorial
    (d) Encrypted
12. Which of the following statements concerning hardware evaluation is false?
    (a) The most important factor is the suitability of hardware with regard to selected software.
    (b) It is important to know before the purchase how a system will be serviced and maintained.
    (c) Future growth of the system should be an important consideration.
    (d) Unlike software evaluation, price is a major consideration.
13. Which is more important, software evaluation or hardware evaluation? Why?
14. A large amount of software documentation is filled with computer jargon and technical buzzwords. Is this an indication of the quality of the documentation? Explain.
15. Should the area of networking be considered during system selection even if communication with other systems is not a concern at the time of development? Explain.
16. What are the activities that constitute the design phase?
17. What are the three types of security concerns in a typical micro-based information system environment?
18. Name the three types of system maintenance.
19. The developer, in his consultation with the user, should learn more about the volume of data that will be processed and whether output should be sent to the screen or a printer. What are some other considerations in this area?
20. What is an RFP?
21. What questions concerning software maintenance should be asked of vendors during the software evaluation process?
22. What is the main advantage of buying hardware that is designed around the industry PC standard?
23. After completion of the software and hardware evaluation, what areas should be included in each of the proposed alternatives?
24. What is a system selection and design report?
25. A medium-sized business has been using their mainframe computer for all of their information requirements. However, this has caused them to spend a large amount of time and effort preparing special reports, generated by secretaries on typewriters. The accounting department also spends a lot of time manually evaluating production reports generated by the mainframe. The controller has determined that they can save a significant amount of time by the use of a micro-based information system. She has decided to go to the local computer store and buy what they recommend. What do you think of this idea?

Case One:
CRUNCH-E COMPANY

Crunch-E Company, a large firm headquartered in a rural Midwestern community, produces snack and other foods for consumer sale. It has an international distribution network for its products, which include a full range of potato- and corn-based snacks. Crunch-E is a totally integrated company involved in the processing, packaging, and distributing of its products in wholesale and retail centers around the U.S. Crunch-E has risen to a dominant position in its market in the U.S. with sales presently at the $2 billion level and employees numbering 30,000.

The engineering management in this company recently evaluated the advantages and disadvantages of dedicating a microcomputer to each of the engineers in the group. The department is responsible for developing technologies to improve existing manufacturing processes at the various plant locations. Engineers also develop processes to manufacture the new products being developed by food scientists in the company. Both the product development and process engineering groups are part of the R&D department.

The engineering group is divided into two separate subgroups—one for new products and the other for improved processes. These are organized as shown in Figure 13.8.

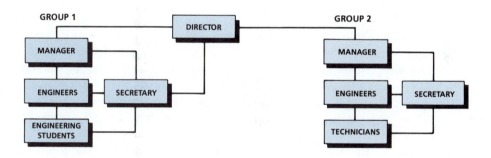

Figure 13.8
Crunch-E Company's Engineering Group

The company also has in place an Information Resources Management (IRM) group that is very sparsely staffed. This group handles corporate activities in the area of mainframe applications, but recently has made a transition into the microcomputing area, mainly prompted by the interest of many other groups within the corporation. Current company policy dictates that all microcomputer purchases be approved by the IRM group. Communication with the IRM group in the past has been sketchy, at best. Most employees feel that all the IRM group does is make policy because it is not properly staffed to maintain and support the microcomputer efforts of other groups. In fact, IRM is not able to maintain the microcomputer systems that are currently in place throughout the company.

The engineering managers were not certain whether the engineering staff would benefit from micros. Past exposure of the engineers to microcomputing ranged from ownership of a home computer to negligible experience. In the office, a micro has been transported from office to office in a portable cabinet for the last two years, with a recent substantial increase in demand. Applications include word processing for technical reports, mass calculations around process systems, graphing test data, and so on.

There is a mainframe system within the engineers' technical facility. Local workstations are located at the computer lab, but are not available at each of the engineer's desks. There doesn't appear to be much activity in the computer lab, although the resources for assisting the engineers with their tasks—such as plotting and graphing of data and statistical analyses—are available. Various engineers have told management they would like a micro or workstation right on their own desk top.

During the recent evaluation of microcomputer use by engineering management, the director, John Ranko, felt that increased productivity would justify the expenditure. However, he was concerned that an appropriate level of productivity be returned from his investment. There was even some consideration given to purchasing only one or two micros to justify the investment in the hardware. John felt this would be the more conservative approach. The question was, which of the engineers would get the new system for his or her office?

Quite a bit of time was spent discussing the hardware and associated costs of the proposed purchase. The IRM group was not involved in this part of the decision making process; they only had to O.K. the final purchase. Little time was spent discussing the other components of the total microcomputer system (people, software, documentation, procedures) with each of the engineers.

The managers, Harry Cranshaw and Tony Biddle, felt that purchasing computers without any preliminary involvement by the engineering personnel might result in a lack of acceptance. The engineers divide their time between "office-related activities," for which micros would be beneficial, and "pilot plant or plant site activities," in which there would be limited micro use. Harry and Tony were both also concerned with their budgetary constraints. Consideration of PC-clones and even a local area network (LAN) within the engineering group were discussed. However, company policy, developed by the Information Resources Management group, dictated that all PCs be either IBM or Hewlett-Packard types for use within the corporation. There were only a few cases of other PC types being accepted, and only when all IBM or Hewlett-Packard options were exhausted for a given application. Harry and Tony did inform John that other groups in the company were also looking at clones as a lower-cost alternative.

The inevitable occurred after the decision was made for all the engineers to be supplied with IBM or Hewlett-Packard microcomputer systems, as per IRM specifications. One year later, only fifty percent of the engineers were applying microcomputer applications to their work. The other systems were dormant. John Ranko met with his managers to determine what had gone wrong and why there wasn't an adequate return on the investment the group had made.

Questions

1. What problems did this company have in applying the microcomputer as a productivity tool?
2. Who should have dictated policy on microcomputer software and hardware issues?
3. What steps should the director and managers have taken to investigate the potential for PCs to increase engineers' productivity?
4. Do you feel the less expensive clones would have increased the director's return on investment?
5. Would there have been any advantage to a LAN?

Case Two:
RADIOLOGIST SUPPORT SYSTEMS, INC.

Radiologists Support Systems (RSS) is a firm located in Lebanon, Pennsylvania, which serves thirty-five groups of radiologists throughout the state. RSS contracts with hospitals and independent radiologists to process their insurance claims. Their work entails all administrative and clerical duties associated with claims processing to ensure that the hospitals and doctors are paid for services rendered.

RSS began operations back in July of 1982. Tom Rosman, president of the firm, had worked in several large insurance claim departments for fifteen years prior to starting his own business. During those years, he logged many hours on microcomputers and appreciated the efficient manner in which they helped process insurance claims. To enjoy the same efficiencies at RSS, Tom decided to use an IBM PC-AT with a 30MB hard disk to support and act as a server to fifteen other IBM-PC clones. Eight of these PCs have multi-color CRTs, while the remaining seven have black and white. Other hardware attached to the network includes two Epson LQ-1500 desktop printers, a high-speed laser printer, and a communication modem that links the entire network to an MIS located in Albuquerque, New Mexico.

Tom's microcomputer network is well suited for RSS. He is very pleased with his decision to purchase this equipment and would not have gone with anything else. However, because of the type of work RSS does on its automated system, Tom's employees spend the majority of their working day on the computer. They are staring at CRTs continuously, sitting in the same seats, processing data on microcomputers. The only working time spent away from the computer is during their breaks or their short jaunts to the printers, which are few and far apart.

This presents a concern for Tom, a concern for the protection of his employees' physical health and mental well-being. Tom has spent the majority of his working career sitting in front of CRTs, processing data on microcomputers. Because of long hours working in poorly designed workstations with hand-me-down furniture, Tom has developed severe neck and lower back problems. He attributes his poor back to all of those hours spent sitting in awkward positions to reach the keyboard while hunched over to view a CRT. His eyesight has also been deteriorating over the past few years, and even though he cannot prove his bad eyesight is a result of overexposure to CRTs, he personally feels that it was a contributing factor. Tom's real concern, from his own experience, is to help prevent these same types of physical problems from affecting his employees who are exposed to long hours on the computer.

Questions

1. What are the problems?
2. Are there other physical or mental stresses that may be associated with long periods of exposure to CRTs?
3. What are the alternatives available to Tom?
4. What do you recommend at this stage?

SELECTED BIBLIOGRAPHY

Brady, P., "Avoiding the Pitfalls of New Computer Systems," *CPA Journal*, November 1986, pp. 120-1.

Burch, J., "Designing Information Systems for People," *Journal of Systems Management*, October 1986, pp. 30-33.

_____, "Solving Logistics at a Page a Minute," *Infosystems*, September 1984, p. 37+.

Cerullo, M.J., "Designing Accounting Information Systems," *Management Accounting*, June 1985, pp. 37-42.

Hughes, J.R., "Moving Out of the Middle Ages," *Infosystems*, October 1986, pp. 76-7+.

Khosrowpour, M. "Are MIS Capable to Set Goals?," *Journal of Systems Management*, October 1983, pp. 25-28.

Laszlo, G., "Ten Steps to Successful Systems Design," *Administrative Management*, October 1986, pp. 23-6.

Martin, J., "From Analysis to Design," *Datamation*, September 15, 1985, pp. 129-30+.

Meredith, D.C., "Don't Gamble When Choosing a System Development Methodology," *Data Management*, July 1986, pp. 36-9.

Quigley, J.V., "Effective Decision Making Evolves from Well-Designed Information Systems," *Data Management*, October 1986, p. 12.

Santos, B.L.Pos, "A Management Approach to Systems Development Projects," *Journal of Systems Management*, August 1986, pp. 35-41.

Spock, R.E., "Break with Tradition," *Datamation*, May 1, 1985, pp. 111-12+.

Summer, M. and J. Sitek, "Are Structured Methods for Systems Analysis and Design Being Used?," *Journal of Systems Management*, June 1986, pp. 18-23.

_____, "Developing High Quality Systems Faster," *EDP Analyzer*, June 1986, pp. 1-16.

Vincent, D., "Corporate Culture," *Computerworld*, November 5, 1984, p. ID21+.

Windsor, J.C., "Are Automated Tools Changing Systems Analysis and Design?," *Journal of Systems Management*, November 1986, pp. 28-32.

chapter 14

Systems Implementation

After completing this chapter, you should be able to

- name the activities that constitute the implementation phase.
- describe a company's considerations during system installation and the importance of testing system components.
- describe the alternatives and procedures for developing application programs.
- describe the task of creating data files for the system.
- describe the alternative methods of converting an old manual system to a new micro-based information system.
- describe the task of developing a user's manual.
- describe the importance of training sessions for users of the system.
- describe the importance of documenting all steps in the implementation phase.

■ INTRODUCTION

When a company decides to develop a micro-based information system instead of a mainframe system, the procedures are, in many ways, similar to those of a personal decision, such as buying a vacation home. A person may want a vacation home in a shore area, but cannot afford—or may not want to invest in—a luxury villa. For purposes of our comparison, let's say the person chooses a mobile home instead. The process of buying a mobile home normally starts by selecting a site, then selecting a particular model home. Finally, the mobile home is delivered and installed on the selected site.

There are many similarities, then, between choosing a mobile home over an expensive vacation home, and developing a micro-based information system instead of a sophisticated mainframe computer information system. A microcomputer information system, like a mobile home, is an alternative that can satisfy certain needs on a small budget. In many ways, installing a mobile home and making it liveable is similar to installing the hardware and software components of a micro-based information system and making them operational. This process is known as the **system implementation phase** of the system development cycle. It is the process of bringing the selected system into operational use and turning it over to the user (see Figure 14.1).

This chapter discusses various activities of the system implementation phase. We will then apply these concepts to the case of Sunshine Window Inc., Suppliers (SWIS).

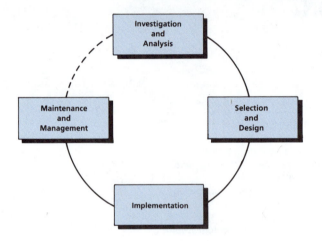

Figure 14.1
The Implementation Phase of the System Development Cycle

■ ACTIVITIES OF THE IMPLEMENTATION PHASE

During the system implementation process, the selected system is delivered, installed, tested, and made completely operational. The tasks of this phase are sometimes carried out by the same individual who performed the investigation and selection and development phases. In either case, in this book we refer to the person who conducts the activities of system implementation as the **system implementor**.

Generally speaking, it is during the implementation phase that the actual existence of the system will be noticed by end-users. The hallmarks of this phase are numerous inconveniences and interruptions to the normal flow of work in the organization. Therefore, the implementor should be aware of the possible discomforts that can occur during this phase to those who will eventually use the system.

Furthermore, the implementor may notice some individual resistance to the system during this period. The implementor must be prepared to deal with some possible resistance and should try to manage it by informing the users about the actual intended goals of implementing the system. Finally, the implementor should be careful to notify those individuals who will be using the system, or those who will be affected by the system, about the implementation schedule and some of the inconveniences that might be caused by the activities of this phase.

The activities of the system implementation phase are installation and testing, applications program development, data file creation, system conversion, development of the user manual, development of the users' training programs, and documenting the system. Figure 14.2 on the following page lists these activities and the order in which they must be performed.

System Installation and Testing

During this step, the selected system is installed in the appropriate location within the firm. As mentioned earlier, some microcomputer vendors or suppliers offer free delivery and installation. If the system you purchased has this option, make sure the system is properly delivered and installed at your company site. If the system does not come with free installation, make sure in advance that someone in the organization is capable of installing the system. In some cases, it would be better to pay a skilled person to install the system than to expect someone within the organization with no expertise to handle the installation.

The implementor must carefully consider a number of things during the installation process. First, if new furniture has been purchased for the system, the furniture should be assembled before the system arrives. Second, the implementor should make sure that all the components that are delivered match the ordered system's specifications. If there are any inconsistencies, the implementor should clarify them with the vendor or supplier. Third, the implementor should carefully examine the system documentation to make sure that everything has been delivered and is in good condition. Finally, the implementor should see that all software is properly installed.

Normally, software installation involves three separate steps. First, the configuration of the system—such as the number of disk drives, type of monitor, type of printer, and RAM capacity—must be communicated to the software. The software documentation should include a section for installing the software package. Second, some software requires that a part of the operating system in use be copied to the main application software diskette. This allows the user to boot the system with the application software, eliminating the additional step of installing the operating system diskette. Third, if the system is equipped with a hard disk, the software packages must be copied onto the hard disk within appropriate directories or subdirectories. Appendix C discusses hard disk directories in more detail.

Related issues that the implementor might consider during the installation process are the convenience of the system location and the comfort of computer-related furniture. For example, if the system will be used by a secretary for eight hours a day, would he or she like to see adjustments in chair or table height, lighting, or noise levels? In recent years, many companies have been subjected to multi-million-dollar lawsuits by employees who argued that certain elements or conditions of the workplace have caused them physical or mental harm.

Another concern that the system implementor should have about the system environment involves productivity. If the system environment is poorly designed and the user is not comfortable with it, that person's productivity could be significantly reduced. Therefore, for reasons involving both legal and productivity issues, it is a good idea to give adequate consideration to the user's environment.

1. Install and test the system
2. Develop the application programs
3. Create the data files
4. Convert the system
5. Develop a user manual
6. Develop a training program
7. Document the system

Figure 14.2
The System Implementation Phase

An entire field of study, known as **ergonomics,** examines different techniques, elements, arrangements of furniture, and other factors affecting the physical aspects of the workplace and their impact on employees and productivity. It would be helpful for the implementor to check the local library and read a few articles in the field of ergonomics to make sure that the furniture and arrangements are adequate.

Once the system is properly installed, the next step is to test the hardware components and the software programs. In the area of hardware, for example, the implementor should check the internal memory, the disk drives, the printer, the keyboard, and the monitor.

Most microcomputer systems come with programs known as **system diagnostics programs.** These programs conduct status tests on each component of the system. If the selected system is equipped with such programs, the implementor must make sure they are utilized.

The operating system itself is another tool the implementor can use to test different components of the system. For example, the formatting program of the operating system can format blank floppy diskettes or a hard disk to make sure that the disk drives are working properly. The copying program can make backup copies, with the operating system diskette in one disk drive and a blank diskette in the second drive, to make sure that the two disk drives can interact with each other.

If your microcomputer system is an IBM-PC or compatible, you are encouraged to work through Chapter 5 on PC-DOS, and to practice some of the PC-DOS functions on the system. Hands-on experience is the key to learning about the different functions of PC-DOS or any other software.

The implementor also needs to test the software package's different programs. At this stage of system implementation, the features of the software must be examined rather than actually tested. For example, if Lotus 1-2-3 is one of the chosen software packages, the implementor will need to run Lotus and view the screen contents after properly installing the software. The implementor must ask questions like "If the system has a color monitor, is Lotus displaying in color or not? Is the printer properly installed to get a hard copy of something created in Lotus?"

Generally speaking, most common software user manuals contain short, sample applications that a first-time user can employ to test the software package and its basic functions or features. More detailed testing of the software programs and their results should be conducted during the application programs development stage, which we'll examine next.

Developing Application Programs

Some software packages require proper installation of only the particular package used in the system. For example, with some word processing packages, once the package is installed, it is up to the package's users to create, modify, save, and retrieve text.

Another good example is one of the many statistical software packages developed for microcomputers, such as Mini Tab. With these packages, the user goes through a series of pre-defined menus to choose the desired function. Once the user selects a function, the software package asks for the necessary data through an interactive process. There is no need to develop special in-house programs or applications for end-users; the package is ready to be used.

On the other hand, some software packages require that application programs be developed for end-users before the particular system can be totally utilized. For example, with database management software packages, the implementor must develop application programs, create data files, and devise menus for users of the system. With user-friendly software packages, the development of application programs is much easier than with those packages that are not classified as user-friendly.

For example, dBASE III PLUS, a well-known database management software package for microcomputers, offers two possible tools for application program development. One is the **assistance menu** of the package, a tool that allows the user to create data files, routines, menus, and reports without writing one single line of a computer program. The second tool is the dBASE programming language, which can be used to develop in-house application programs and routines, and to perform other tasks that cannot be accomplished through the use of the menu assistance feature of the package. Of course, the first feature is much easier to use, but it is also very limited in comparison to the system's programming capabilities.

As programs are developed through either a menu package or a program language, each must be individually tested with factual data containing both correct and incorrect entries. Testing application programs must be done in a realistic environment as possible. For this reason, it is wise to test programs with incorrect data (e.g., provide alphabetic data to a field that is assigned only to numeric data). The testing data can be drawn from the firm's files, or created by the user of the system.

In some cases, software and all the application programs can be developed in-house. The task of developing a program requires full knowledge of the relevant programming language and program development concepts. The programs are developed by first identifying the user requirements, the incoming data and information that must be generated by the system. Then the programmer develops the logical structures of the programs by utilizing many tools available for this task, such as flow charts, pseudocodes, and hierarchy charts.

After the logical structure is developed, the programmer begins coding the logical solutions in the programming language. The next step is to input the program codes into the system and begin testing them to find out whether the generated results are the same as the predicted results. In this step, the programmer can encounter two types of errors: logical errors, caused by incorrect program logic, and syntax errors, caused by incorrect use of the syntax or grammar of the coding language. Once the programmer is satisfied with the outcome of the program and has confirmed that it is error-free, the program's documentation takes place. This last step is crucial for future updating and modification of the programs.

It should be mentioned here that the task of programming is a skilled one, and not as fast or as easy as this summary might suggest. If in-house programs must be developed from scratch, the implementor must obtain the necessary knowledge of programming development concepts and the appropriate language. The other alternative is to hire a computer programmer to develop the necessary programs.

Application programs must be developed through close consultation with system users rather than in a closed-door laboratory. User involvement is essential at this stage of system development. First, each program must be developed around the specifications of the user. Second, as each program is developed, the user must be able to test the application program and the outcomes, and make suggestions and recommendations. Do not forget that, in most cases, the application programs will be used mainly by people other than the system implementor. Therefore, lack of user participation means that there will be a good chance of failure in the system goals.

If the users are a bit slow in getting acquainted with the system and its applications, the implementor should make sure they are not rushed into it. The implementor should be as patient as possible, and ensure that the end-users understand each step of the implementation process. It is generally unwise to leave end-users on their own during the initial period of system testing and use. The implementor should remember that many users suffer from a high degree of anxiety in their early experience with computers. Providing proper assistance and complete explanations are the most effective ways of getting users started on a new system.

The amount of program testing to be done depends on several factors. The first factor is the sensitivity of the information generated by the system. For example, if the system will be used to prepare customer billing or creditor statements, then the implementor must make sure that accurate information is generated by the system. Second, the cost of testing applications is a factor and is heavily dependent on the availability of the financial and human resources of the company.

The last factor that determines the degree of testing required is the complexity of the applications. Some software packages contain only a few uncomplicated application programs that can be easily tested. On the other hand, if the system consists of many interrelated complex programs, these will require extensive testing to assure the accuracy of the generated information. The bottom-line product of any information system is accurate and precise information. If accurate information cannot be generated, then—regardless of the sophistication of the hardware, software, and all the application programs—the system is not worth a penny.

Finally, the implementor must carefully document all the testing procedures, types of data, and degree of testing for future reference. Figure 14.3 summarizes the steps in the program development process.

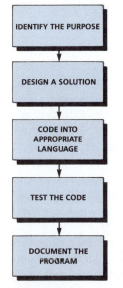

Figure 14.3
The Program Development Process

Creating Data Files

Frequently, an information processing system requires the creation of data files or databases in addition to application programs. In most information systems, there are many data files or databases representing different entities. These files or databases are as essential as the application programs. Without data files or databases, application programs are worthless.

In its simplest form, a data file or a database is a collection of records representing an entity. For example, a customer file or customer database might contain one record for each customer of the firm. This record would contain information categorized in different fields, with each field representing a certain characteristic or identity of the customer. For example, a customer record could consist of a customer name field, where the contact or owner's name is kept, as well as fields representing customer age, credit limit, current balance, address, or sex. Therefore, a **record** can be defined as a collection of fields. A **field** is a collection of characters (e.g., alphabetic characters A–Z, numeric characters 0–9, or special characters %, &, !, #, or $) put together to name an object or to represent an attribute. In computer terminology, the characters of a field are also referred to as **bytes,** which are the smallest pieces of information that can be recorded in the memory of the system. The number of fields and their types would be the same in each of the records of a file; the only difference between records of the same file is their contents. Figure 14.4 illustrates the organization of a customer file.

A typical microcomputer information system could contain a customer, employee, inventory, or sales file, and many others. In most cases, these files are established as part of a database. Normally, the actual data for these computer files are collected from manual files, if any exist. These manual files could be such things as sales invoices, personnel books, bank statements, inventory cards, or customer bills.

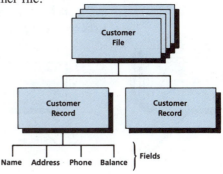

Figure 14.4
A Sample File Organization Structure

Data collection often presents many difficulties. Sometimes, no documented manual data source exists. In this case, the implementor must try to collect the necessary data by examining different sources and interviewing the users. Another possible difficulty might arise when there are multiple sources for the data of a single entity, with many variations in the data. For example, a customer credit limit in a sales file could be $2,000, while the customer file shows the limit as $1,200. In such cases, the implementor must cross-reference as many sources as possible to make sure the data obtained is accurate. The implementor also must verify the data collected from multiple sources with the users.

The last possible obstacle in the data collection process is the conversion of qualitative data to quantitative data. For example, a customer credit limit in a manual file could be ranked as poor, fair, or good, with each ranking indicating a certain level of credit or status. One way to convert this ranking system to a quantitative form is to find out how much money each rank actually represents, then put the numerical amount in the files as the credit limit. Sometimes, of course, the numerical figure for each rank cannot be determined easily, since different people in the firm define the ranking differently. Another related problem is the fact that a great deal of informal information, such as personal judgments, experiences, and intuition, is very difficult to convert to numerical form for storage in the information system.

The permanent data files in a microcomputer information system are sometimes called **master files.** Normally, these files are kept on secondary storage media, such as floppy diskettes or a hard disk. Files created on a temporary basis are known as **transaction files.** These files usually contain all the data changes that must be incorporated into the master file. Usually, they are created on a periodic basis and then run against the master file. This process, known as **updating a file,** is illustrated in Figure 14.5.

Finally, the implementor should remember that data stored in these files determine the credibility of the information system and its generated information. Normally, during the first few weeks or months after a system is implemented, many doubtful eyes are watching the system for performance deficiencies in order to substantiate their claims that a computer-based information system is not effective. Establishing the system's credibility right from the beginning is very important.

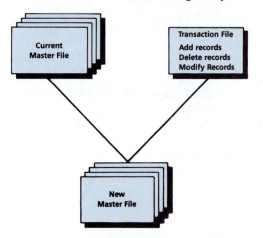

Figure 14.5
The File Updating Process

System Conversion

Once the micro-based information system is tested, the application programs are developed, and master data files or databases are created, it is time to transfer the tasks performed by the manual system to the computerized system. This **system conversion** process, which can be a tedious one, may create a great degree of discomfort and confusion for the people involved if it is not properly planned and supervised.

Prior to converting the manual system to an automated one, the system implementor should consult users of the system about different methods, degrees, and schedule of the actual conversion. Unplanned conversion procedures can create many problems for a firm, such as interruption in the work flow, user dissatisfaction, and damage to the credibility of the system. Many successful techniques may be employed for the changeover process. Let's take a look at three common conversion techniques, which are summarized in Figure 14.6 on the following page.

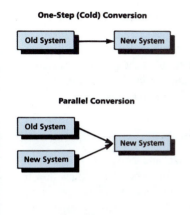

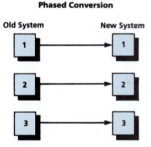

Figure 14.6
Three System Conversion Techniques

Cold Conversion. The first method is the obvious one: simply stopping the old system and starting the new one. If you choose this method, sometimes known as **cold conversion,** or **one-step conversion,** it is a good idea to select a time schedule when the changeover process can take place with minimum interruption to normal work routines—for example, a holiday or weekend.

Cold conversion is the simplest and cheapest conversion method, but at the same time the riskiest method of changeover. The biggest risk is that, if the new system is not performing exactly as was expected, many new problems could be created. As a matter of fact, this technique is not suitable to many situations, especially those where the flow of information is critical and where many tasks must be converted from the old manual system to the new system. Finally, the system implementor must be realistic about the possibility of unexpected human or system errors, or malfunctioning of certain system components. Therefore, the implementor must devise a contingency plan. Lack of an alternative method can create chaos if the cold changeover process is not successful.

Parallel Conversion. The second method of conversion, called **parallel conversion,** allows the old system to be changed over to the new system with some overlap. Instead of turning everything over to the new system in one step and eliminating the old system, the old system is immediately converted to the new system, then both systems operate side-by-side for a specified period of time. During this period, the results of both systems can be compared for possible errors. The parallel conversion method is considered to be an almost risk-free technique for converting an old system to a new one. With this method, the firm or people using the system will have sufficient time to monitor the performance of the new system. Errors and deficiencies can be corrected and the system's performance fine-tuned to the firm's precise information requirements. The major drawback of this method is that significant resources, particularly human resources, must be invested in the process. Also, the costs of operating the two systems side-by-side may be very high.

Phased Conversion. The third method of changeover, **phased conversion,** calls for the conversion process to be done in phases or modules. With this technique, the old system is converted to the new system in different pre-planned phases at specified times. Once one phase is successfully completed, the next phase begins. Obviously, the success of a subsequent phase is completely dependent upon the success of the previous phase.

The major difference between this method and the parallel method is that, in the phased method, all tasks to be converted are broken down into different catagories or related groups, then each group is converted from the old system to the new system in one step. In many ways, this method is similar to cold conversion, except that the conversion task is divided into several phases instead of one phase, thus reducing the degree of risk.

The main advantage of the phased conversion method is that it allows the conversion process to take place in several steps, so that some of the problems solved in the early phases can allow other phases to proceed more smoothly. Also this method costs less than the parallel method and does not require as many resources.

Developing a User Manual

Regardless of a micro-based information system's size and complexity, a user or operation manual must be developed in order to assist users who do not know how to operate the system. In some cases, the manual consists only of instructions about how to turn the system on, how to run different software, how to save documents on the secondary storage media, and how to use the printer. In other cases, the manual might provide additional information, such as specific instructions about the different features of each piece of software, how these features can be utilized, and the different results and outputs that may be obtained.

Simplicity of explanation and validity of assumptions should be the key elements of a useful user manual. In preparing the manual, the implementor should avoid vague language or assumptions that users have any degree of knowledge of the system. The implementor should remember that most new users suffer from a high degree of anxiety about getting used to a system. If the user manual does not explain procedures clearly, the user's fear may be reinforced by lack of success in using the system. It has been suggested that the best author of a user manual is an average user of the system, not a computer programmer or systems analyst. The main argument in favor of this approach is the fact that the average user will not use technical terms; since the author is also a user, the manual's language will be related to actual use of the system, rather than to an analysis of the system as a whole.

In the user manual, the implementor must provide a brief introduction to the system and its main features, a list of hardware and software components of the system, a description of procedures, and instructions on running the appropriate software. Any explanation of features, functions, or routines of a software package should be done in a straightforward manner, illustrated by sample screens or descriptions of how the screen should look, and followed by sample outputs. In this way, the user can simply compare what is on the screen at any given moment with what is explained in the manual. The implementor is encouraged to include a list of potential operator errors and the steps that can be taken to correct them at the end of the manual. Furthermore, the manual should be designed with the idea that it will provide basic instructions for system use; the user can be directed to the appropriate hardware or software manuals for detailed information.

Developing User Training Programs

In addition to the user manual, appropriate training programs should be developed for system users. Training programs might consist simply of a few hours of hands-on experience in which users are taught about the different system components, how to boot the system, how to use different applications, and how to use the printer or secondary storage devices. Bringing in an outside instructor for staff training is one alternative. Another alternative is to encourage users to sign up for courses or classes in software applications offered by local educational institutions. The best place to get information about the availability, cost, and schedule of these courses is the continuing education department of local colleges or universities. As another alternative, determine whether the vendor of the software package offers training programs.

As mentioned in Chapter 13, the availability of training programs is a factor that should be carefully considered during the software evaluation process. Some vendors offer training programs as part of the price of the software package, and some offer discounts on training to their users. It is important for a user to obtain the necessary training for the chosen software packages. In many cases, users will need only the instructions provided in the user manual. Others will start by following the manual; then, as they become more familiar with the system and some of its applications, they may want to obtain more advanced training. The implementor or company officials should encourage users to further develop their skills.

Finally, the last alternative in providing training programs is the use of training videos. Many companies specialize in producing these videos for the most popular software packages. Some videos cost only a few hundred dollars, or may be leased for a specific period of time.

Documenting the System

The last step in the implementation phase is the process of documenting all the phase's previous steps, particularly if in-house application programs have been developed. Obviously, the implementor will not be around forever; the whole process should be documented in such a way that almost anyone could follow the documentation and understand the entire system.

Very often, a system will be updated during its lifespan. As relevant state or federal laws change, new procedures or techniques develop, and the firm's information requirements are modified. The system needs to be updated in order to accommodate these changes. The lack of proper documentation may make it absolutely impossible for a new person to understand the system and make necessary changes.

Unfortunately, many systems have suffered because one person implements the entire system, then leaves the firm or is transferred to another branch, and a new person is assigned to the system to make necessary changes. If the system has been completely documented, the new person can easily learn the system and make changes within its boundaries. In most cases, without proper documentation of the system, a new person will need to develop entirely new programs or applications in order to incorporate the necessary changes.

System documentation provides guidelines mainly in the area of application programs. It must consist of a list of all the computer programs that have been developed, and should include sample outputs of these programs. The sources of input data must also be clearly specified.

Now let's examine the steps taken during the system implementation phase at Sunshine Window Inc., Suppliers.

Back to the Case of SWIS

In our system selection phase (see Chapter 13), we selected a system that consisted of an IBM PS/2 Model 60 with a 44MB hard drive and a single diskette drive, one MB of RAM, a color monitor, and an Epson LQ-1000 letter quality printer. On the software side, we selected dBASE III PLUS as the most appropriate database management system, Lotus 1-2-3 as the best spreadsheet system, and WordPerfect for word processing capabilities. Since we purchased both hardware and software from a single vendor, the vendor agreed to provide free delivery and on-site installation and testing. Immediately following the system installation and testing, we began the process of developing application programs.

In the area of database creation and program development, Sandy Cofman was lucky. She had already taken a microcomputer course that covered the dBASE III and Lotus 1-2-3 software. The administrative clerk was familiar with WordPerfect word processing from a previous job. After careful evaluation, Sandy prioritized the application programs needed for SWIS's information system. She first listed the various applications needed and the primary software used in each application. Later, she defined each application carefully and determined its relationship with other applications. Here is the implementation report Sandy prepared.

■ DEFINITION OF APPLICATIONS

The SWIS information system is composed of several applications and databases. Each fulfills a specific purpose. The descriptions of the applications and the primary software used are presented in this report.

Inventory Tracking: dBASE III PLUS

This application processes information on products and inventory levels. Data on product numbers, product descriptions, and manufacturers will be keyed into the computer. Data on the cost of products, the current selling price, and available inventory are included in this database. The inventory balance on hand and the reorder point will be detailed according to specific products. From this database, the inventory clerk can produce queried and monthly reports on inventory levels. A comparison between the balance on hand and the limit data will trigger the clerk to reorder more products. An example listing from the database is displayed in Figure 14.7.

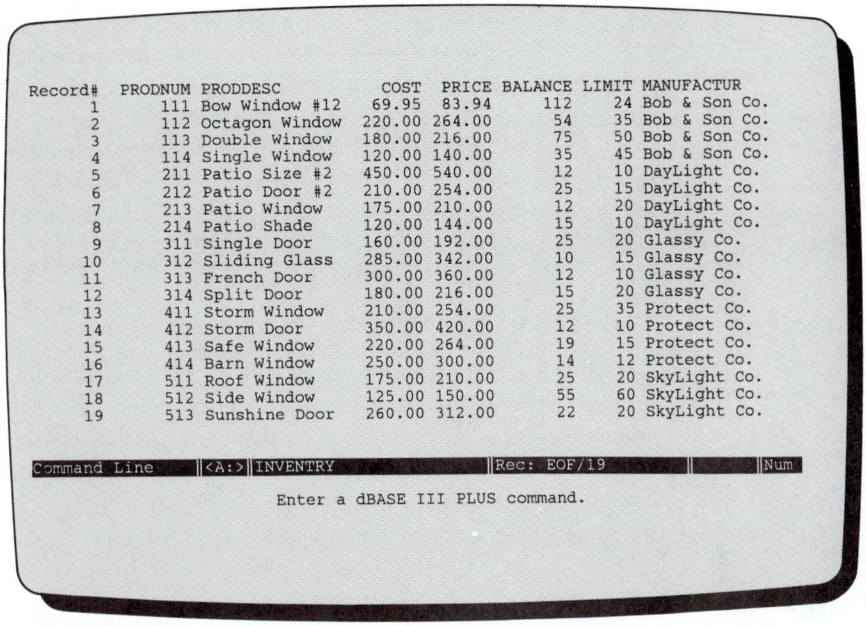

```
Record# PRODNUM PRODDESC         COST   PRICE  BALANCE LIMIT MANUFACTUR
      1    111 Bow Window #12    69.95  83.94     112    24  Bob & Son Co.
      2    112 Octagon Window   220.00 264.00      54    35  Bob & Son Co.
      3    113 Double Window    180.00 216.00      75    50  Bob & Son Co.
      4    114 Single Window    120.00 140.00      35    45  Bob & Son Co.
      5    211 Patio Size #2    450.00 540.00      12    10  DayLight Co.
      6    212 Patio Door #2    210.00 254.00      25    15  DayLight Co.
      7    213 Patio Window     175.00 210.00      12    20  DayLight Co.
      8    214 Patio Shade      120.00 144.00      15    10  DayLight Co.
      9    311 Single Door      160.00 192.00      25    20  Glassy Co.
     10    312 Sliding Glass    285.00 342.00      10    15  Glassy Co.
     11    313 French Door      300.00 360.00      12    10  Glassy Co.
     12    314 Split Door       180.00 216.00      15    20  Glassy Co.
     13    411 Storm Window     210.00 254.00      25    35  Protect Co.
     14    412 Storm Door       350.00 420.00      12    10  Protect Co.
     15    413 Safe Window      220.00 264.00      19    15  Protect Co.
     16    414 Barn Window      250.00 300.00      14    12  Protect Co.
     17    511 Roof Window      175.00 210.00      25    20  SkyLight Co.
     18    512 Side Window      125.00 150.00      55    60  SkyLight Co.
     19    513 Sunshine Door    260.00 312.00      22    20  SkyLight Co.

Command Line    <A:> INVENTRY              Rec: EOF/19              Num
                 Enter a dBASE III PLUS command.
```

Figure 14.7
A Sample Inventory Database Listing

Mailing Application: dBASE III PLUS

We will use this application for distributing standard form letters to customers and manufacturers who receive certain mailings. The user will be presented with a query screen that gathers information needed to create the file. Mailing labels can then be created from the manufacturer order maintenance database. The application will be integrated with the WordPerfect package for form letter generation.

Manufacturer Order Maintenance Application: dBASE III PLUS

This application will allow the user to maintain a database containing all current manufacturer orders. The user can add, change, delete, transfer, view, and search for orders in a database. Orders may be entered directly into this subsystem, or may flow from the inventory tracking application. Screens and reports will use information from both the order and inventory databases. The user may obtain a variety of reports about current orders by product number, or by manufacturer.

Decision Support System: Lotus 1-2-3

The system will consist of various spreadsheet applications developed with Lotus 1-2-3 software. The applications will vary in structure, but all will enhance and improve the managerial decision making process. Lotus 1-2-3 spreadsheets permit the user to view the results of a problem when given varied assumptions. The "what-if?" analysis is useful when evaluating alternative strategies in a problem solving situation. The spreadsheet applications can be developed to project future sales revenue and calculate the long-term profitability of the company. Assumptions on the rate of company growth, cost of goods sold, and administrative expenses can be evaluated to determine their impact on long-term financial solvency. Over time, we will be able to develop more Lotus 1-2-3 applications to automate any mathematical or analytical calculations frequently performed.

Correspondence System: WordPerfect

The WordPerfect software package will provide us with the means to compile and process information for preparation of form letters, lists, reports, and other written communication. The correspondence system will give us a method of organizing and retaining correspondence, thereby reducing repeat typing and enhancing report preparation, and increasing administrative productivity.

■ INPUT DATA SOURCES

Data will enter SWIS's databases at various points. The greatest amount of information will be entered into the inventory tracking system. The inventory data will originate from records generated from the warehouse on product deliveries and from purchase orders written by Emily, the inventory clerk. The manufacturer order maintenance database will share some data with the inventory tracking system. The two databases could be used together in report preparation. Data about manufacturer products in which SWIS may be interested are collected from the following sources.

1. *Promotional material*: Periodic letters and announcements from manufacturers informing SWIS about new products available.
2. *Phone calls*: Calls from manufacturers and customers. Orders resulting from customer requests for products will supply the majority of inventory data.
3. *Industry Publications*: Periodicals, newsletters, and advertisements concerning products.

The source data for the Lotus 1-2-3 spreadsheet applications will vary with the specific problem being analyzed. Lotus 1-2-3 spreadsheets handle mathematical and financial problems most easily. The source data for a profitability projection could come from historical accounting records and company sales estimates.

The correspondence system will handle data from a variety of sources. The information may come from a person writing a letter, or the data could originate from the addresses in the manufacturer order maintenance database. The correspondence system can be used for any form of written communication.

OUTPUT FORMATS

Output from SWIS's microcomputer information system is generally in the form of reports to management. A list of sample reports and their respective applications is presented below.

1. *Mailing application reports*: Monthly reports listing customers or manufacturers who received specific mailings; labels that can be used in distributing mass mailings.
2. *Inventory tracking reports*: Biweekly reports on current inventory levels and projected reorder points, a copy of which will be sent to sales representatives and warehouse personnel; queried reports on products by product number, manufacturer, cost, or price levels.
3. *Order maintenance reports*: Weekly reports on all orders currently being processed; monthly reports on orders requested from the manufacturer broken down according to product and manufacturer; queried reports on all orders currently being processed, broken down according to order dates, manufacturer, or product; reports on items that have reached their reorder point or limit.
4. *Decision Support System*: Quarterly, monthly, and annual reports on projected sales levels; by request, report analysis on specific problems; monthly reports evaluating projected sales and expenses, determining continued financial solvency.
5. *Correspondence application*: Any letter, form, report, or document previously prepared on a manual typewriter; form letters used in mass mailings to customers and manufacturers.

SYSTEM PROGRAMMING

For the next few months, Sandy Cofman used the various software packages to develop each of the applications of SWIS's microcomputer information system through close consultation with future users of the system.

Once all the programs developed by Sandy Cofman were tested, she prepared complete documentation of the system and all of its databases. Furthermore, Sandy taught Alice Freeman, the administrative clerk, how to use the system. Alice suggested that Sandy should develop a user manual for other employees. Alice thought a manual that employees could read before getting on the system would help alleviate anxiety problems caused by changing to a new automated system.

During the next few weeks, Sandy Cofman set up all the databases and practiced different features of SWIS's system until she was convinced that she had mastered it. She then developed a user manual for other individuals who will use the system. Finally, Sandy provided hands-on training to other system users. She contacted her local college and found out that they offer three-day workshops and seminars on microcomputer applications. Sandy recommended that both SWIS owners, Gonzales and Martinez, sign up for one of these workshops in order to obtain additional understanding of the capabilities of their micro-based information system.

■ SYSTEM CONVERSION

With regard to the changeover process, Sandy consulted with Gonzales and Martinez. All three determined the best conversion alternative for this system was the phased technique. They developed the following schedule, which estimates the time needed to convert the SWIS operations to the system over the next three months.

Application	Conversion Time
Inventory tracking	Three weeks
Manufacturer Order Maintenance	Three weeks
Mailing system	One week
Correspondence system	Two weeks
Decision Support System	Three weeks

■ SUMMARY

Upon selection and purchase of the hardware and software components of the system, the implementation phase begins. The implementation process makes the system operational and turns it over to users. The activities of this phase include system installation and testing, application programs development, creation of data files or databases, converting the old system to the new system, developing a user manual, and developing appropriate user training programs.

System installation and testing may be provided by software and hardware vendors as part of the sales package, or may be performed by knowledgeable staff of the firm. The testing procedures include testing both hardware components, such as disk drive functions and internal memory, and different features of the chosen software packages.

Once the system has been completely tested, the application programs are developed, as necessary. These programs can be developed either by the implementor or by a professional computer programmer. In either case, the programs must be developed in close consultation with system users.

Normally, in order to develop the necessary programs, the programmer first divides the entire system into subsystems. Next, each subsystem is clearly defined. Then, the sources of input data are identified. As programs for each subsystem are developed, they must be carefully tested. The last step in application program development is the documentation of all steps and procedures. Following the development of application programs, the necessary data files or databases are created.

The process of converting from the old system to the new system should be carefully evaluated and planned. The three possible changeover techniques are cold conversion, in which the old system is stopped and the new one started; parallel conversion, in which the old system is converted to the new system and both systems operate side by side for a specific period of time; and phased conversion, in which the changeover process is completed in stages.

The development of a user manual is the next step in the system implementation phase. A user manual should be developed in such a way that it will be easy for users to follow and understand. Avoid vague language and technical terms. Upon completion of the user manual, users should be provided with training programs, either in-house or at other locations outside of the company—perhaps a local college or university. Complete documentation of the entire implementation process is also very important because it allows people other than the implementor to make necessary modifications within the system without encountering major difficulties or problems.

■ Key Terms

system implementation phase	The process of bringing the selected system into operational use and turning it over to the user.
system implementor	The person who conducts the activities of system implementation.
erogonomics	The field of study that examines the physical aspects of the workplace and their effect on productivity.
system diagnostics programs	Programs that conduct status tests on each component of the system.
assistance menu	A tool that allows the user to create data files, routines, menus, and reports without writing one single line of a computer program.
record	A collection of fields.
field	A collection of characters.
bytes	The characters of a field.
master files	The permanent data files in a microcomputer information system.
transaction files	Files created on a periodic basis and then run against the master file.
updating a file	Process of applying transaction files to the master file.

system conversion	Transferring the tasks performed by the old system to the new system.
cold or one-step conversion	Simply stopping the old system and starting the new one.
parallel conversion	Both old and new systems operate side-by-side for a specified period.
phased conversion	Converting to the new system in phases.

■ REVIEW QUESTIONS

1. The _____ phase of the system development cycle involves the process of bringing a selected system into operational use and turning it over to the user.
   (a) selection
   (b) development
   (c) implementation
   (d) investigation
2. The field of study that examines the physical aspects of the work place and their impact on employees and productivity is known as
   (a) economics.
   (b) ergonomics.
   (c) agronomics.
   (d) electronics.
3. Most microcomputer systems come with _____ programs to conduct status tests of each component of the system.
   (a) system control
   (b) system diagnostics
   (c) operating system
   (d) none of the above
4. Why should software packages be thoroughly tested during the implementation stage?
5. When inputting and testing program codes into the system, the programmer can encounter _____ and _____ errors.
   (a) language, system
   (b) syntax, control
   (c) logical, system
   (d) logic, syntax
6. Which of the following statements concerning the development of application programs is true?
   (a) Program documentation is crucial for future updating and modification of programs.
   (b) User involvement is essential.
   (c) Development of these programs requires full knowledge of the programming language.
   (d) All of the above.

7. A _____ is a collection of records representing an entity.
   (a) data file
   (b) database
   (c) customer file
   (d) master file
   (e) both (a) and (b)
8. Permanent data files in a microcomputer information system are called _____ files.
   (a) master
   (b) transaction
   (c) data
   (d) conversion
9. The _____ technique of conversion allows the process to be done in stages.
   (a) cold
   (b) parallel
   (c) phased
   (d) system
10. What are the key elements of a useful user manual?
11. "The best approach to developing the user manual for the system is to have it written by a computer programmer or a systems analyst." Do you agree with this statement? Why or why not?
12. The last step in the implementation phase is the process of _____ all the steps taken during this phase.
    (a) converting
    (b) implementing
    (c) documenting
    (d) evaluating
13. What are the activities of the implementation phase?
14. How can the operating system act as a tool for testing during installation?
15. Name three tools that a programmer can use to develop the logical structure of a program.
16. What are the factors that determine the extent of program testing?
17. What kinds of problems can result from poor planning of the conversion procedure?
18. Name the three common methods of converting from an old manual system to a new computerized system.
19. What alternatives are available for training the new users of a system?
20. What are the advantages of the cold conversion process?
21. What are the disadvantages of the phased conversion process?
22. Which of the three conversion processes would you recommend to a small company that has been in business for six months? A large company formed twenty-five years ago? Explain your answers.

Case One:
COMPUTERIZED MEDICAL SYSTEMS

Computerized Medical Systems, better known as CMS, is in the business of providing microcomputer-based billing systems to the medical profession. The company sells an entire turnkey package consisting of its own software package (which can be tailored easily to accommodate individual needs) in conjunction with appropriate hardware. On-site training is included in the purchase price of the system.

The basic function of the system is to automate the process of billing patients and their insurance companies. Information about patient services is keyed into the system by office personnel. While introduction of the system into an office greatly eases the monumental task of sending out bills, it also changes the daily office routine by requiring employees to take the time to enter information into the computer during normal office hours.

CMS has installed this system in many offices, ranging in size from a one-doctor specialist to a hospital environment with many doctors and several physical locations. When the system was originally marketed, implementation was done entirely by CMS personnel (specifically, all initial data files were keyed in before conversion). At that time, users were trained only in very basic day-to-day use of the system, leaving more intricate functions until questions arose about them. With a growth in sales and customer base, however, a more intensive training program has been established so that maintenance and "help" calls are kept to a minimum and users are more self-sufficient. A user manual is provided with the system, although most users still prefer to pick up the phone when they have a question. The establishment of initial data files is now done by the purchaser after training on the system. System conversion has always been done in one step after the initial files are established, a method that has always been successful.

This system recently has been sold to a medical practice of two doctors who employ five office workers. The sale included a clause giving a six-month money-back guarantee if the doctors are not completely satisfied with the system. After the system was physically installed in their office, a three-day training session was held there. It consisted of one general group session for the five employees, and hands-on sessions with individuals. At the end of the last day of training, one of the doctors appeared and demanded to be trained on the system. The trainer obliged by staying late to train the doctor to use the system. During this session, the doctor mentioned that his colleague needed to be trained, too, and that he had also noticed that one of his employees had not received her hands-on session. He and the trainer also discussed what method would be used to convert their system. The trainer explained the three possible implementation methods and the pitfalls and benefits of each. The doctor decided that they would use the one-step approach. They set a date for the conversion to take place the following week.

The day before the confirmed conversion date, the CMS trainer, Sally Peach, received a call from the doctors' office manager, Mary Able. Able said that she had had a problem getting her personnel to key in the initial data files, and that instead of doing a full one-step conversion as the doctors had decided, she preferred to run the manual and computer systems in parallel until the manual system could be closed out. Peach explained that the matter had been discussed with the doctors and that they had decided that a one-step conversion would be done. Able replied that she, not the doctors, was in charge of all decisions relating to the office.

Questions

1. What are some of the problems here?
2. If you were Sally Peach, what would you communicate to Mary Able about her decision regarding the conversion (if anything)? Would you try to have her change her decision?
3. Peach's boss has hinted to her that he feels that the company's training expenses are becoming too high. How important is user training? How much training can users reasonably expect? What recommendations could Peach make to her boss about improving training or decreasing its expense to the company?
4. What can be learned from this situation that could be avoided in the future?
5. Could some procedures be implemented that would circumvent any of the problems?

Case Two:
CUMBERLAND PRESS

Cumberland Press of Harrisburg is one of the fifteen subsidiaries of Tyler Corporation, a multi-product printing firm with corporate headquarters in Chicago. Cumberland Press prints commercial orders (letterheads, business cards, announcements) for over 2,000 dealers who place orders on request from businesses. The firm also provides direct service to 100 major corporate accounts in a sales territory that covers all states east of the Mississippi River. Cumberland Press's size (volume of business and number of employees) has doubled in the past year to its current level of 123 employees who process an average of 4,000 orders per week.

Previously, all processing of order forms and invoices, maintenance of inventory and production control records, and calculation of time cards was done manually. When a dealer's order (containing several orders) came into the plant, one copy of each order was sent to production, and one copy was kept in the office, where an invoice was typed by one of ten typists. That two-part invoice was sent to the shipping department, where it was matched, by dealer number, to the completed orders. The product and one copy of the dealer invoice were shipped to the dealer. The second invoice was returned to the office, where the information was entered manually into the daily Sales Journal. Not only was the order-control process time-consuming, it did not provide for an accurate accounting of the status of each order in the production process. If a dealer called regarding the status of a specific order, the only way to determine the order status was to locate the order form by checking through all of the invoices located throughout the plant.

Supervisors determined the production efficiency of their employees and the cost of each of the steps in the production process by manually calculating information recorded on production cards. Time cards were handled in the same way. One person used a calculator to determine the hours worked by each employee. For inventory control, the inventory control clerk took a physical inventory each week and recorded that information in an Inventory Journal. He calculated and recorded the number and dollar value of each stock item in the current inventory.

In an effort to improve efficiency and accuracy and to gain control of the flow of the orders through the production process, the management staff at the corporate office decided to install a computer and implement a computer package that they developed and had in operation at two other subsidiary plants.

The company installed three microcomputers, which were networked to a central unit. The computer software package included a program which, when orders were entered, would print invoices, including specifics of the order and total charges. One of the programs in the package provided a system for maintaining a dealer-accounts receivable file and for issuing monthly statements. Any of the staff requiring information on specific orders would be able to determine the status of an order immediately. The computer would be able to print a list of rush orders that had to be completed within a specified time. In addition, an expansion program to the basic package would calculate the information input from production records and maintain inventory control records.

The plant manager, Steve Bumpkin, was receptive to the idea of installing a computer and implementing the program. Unfortunately, only one staff member had any computer experience. Since the corporate office handled all accounting and payroll records, there previously had been no perceived need for a computer. With a limited computer background, Keith Jackson, office manager, went to the corporate office for training on the use of the computer and the computer package.

When Jackson returned from the two-day training session, he began to set up a master file of dealers-accounts receivables, and a product-pricing list. He gave a short training session on input procedures to two secretaries. With so many dealers having similar names, he found it difficult to accurately code the information without causing a mix-up in the identity of the dealer. Compounding that problem was the volume of items in the product line, with prices dependent on a variety of factors. He soon became overwhelmed by the enormity of the task of input. Despite working fourteen hours a day developing the master file while still fulfilling his previous responsibilities, he was not able to complete the master file.

He met with his supervisor, Jack Alf, the production manager, and requested additional staff and two additional computers. Alf discussed this request with his supervisor, Mr. Bumpkin, who stated that the funds for staff and office equipment were already over-budgeted, and suggested that Mr. Jackson continue with the implementation as time allowed.

Finally, after a six-week delay, Jackson started the process of transferring the manual operation to a computerized operation. He began by processing only incoming orders, leaving those already in the production process to be handled by the old system. A backlog of incoming orders soon developed. Three days into the conversion process, Jackson developed bronchial pneumonia and was hospitalized to recuperate from exhaustion.

Processing of the orders soon became chaotic. No one knew how to work with the computer or with the computer package. Some orders were in the system. No one knew how to call up those orders. The production manager pulled out the unprocessed rush orders and had those processed using the old system. He retrieved the production cards, which were to have been calculated by the program, and distributed them to the department supervisors for manual calculation. The original backlog of orders had grown to a sizeable amount. Dealers and corporate representatives complained to customer service representatives about not receiving their orders. Customer service representatives often were unable to determine where individual orders were in the production process.

Finally, in desperation, Mr. Bumpkin, frustrated by his inability to learn (over the phone) the operation of the computer and the computer package, asked the corporate staff to send a computer specialist to straighten out the backlog. Two computer operators arrived, and, within two days, reduced the backlog to an acceptable minimum.

The next day, Jackson returned to continue the conversion process. After a month, despite continuous input on the three computers, a backlog still existed. He also found that, while the computer was printing invoices, it could not generate any other data. This caused delays for all departments. The customer service representatives were unable to access information in order to answer the questions that dealers had about the status of their orders. The lag time between receiving and shipping the orders increased by twenty percent. Since there was not sufficient time to input the production cards, supervisors returned to the old system of calculating the information.

The corporate management requested that Bumpkin write an evaluation of the implementation of the program and submit a proposal for other system needs that he felt might improve the efficiency of the production process.

Questions

1. What is the problem here?
2. What could have been done differently to ensure a smoother conversion from the old system to the new system?
3. What would you recommend that Bumpkin include in his evaluation?
4. What other areas of production could be considered as targets of a new system or a system modification? What should the corporate staff or Bumpkin keep in mind when developing another system?

SELECTED BIBLIOGRAPHY

Bandes, H., "Defining and Controlling Documentation Quality," *Technical Communications*, 1986, pp. 6–9.

Beaver, J.E., "Breaking Down Old Barriers," *Computer Decisions*, April 22, 1986, pp. 74–7.

Bryant, S.F., "Corporate Micro Users Speak Out," *Computer Decisions*, July 2, 1985, p. 30+.

Checkland, P., "Achieving Desirable and Feasible Change: An Application of Soft Systems Methodology," *Journal of the Operational Research Society*, Spring 1985, pp. 82–31.

Dekle, J.C., "The Corporate Integration of Data Processing," *Business*, April, May, June 1986, pp. 9–14.

Dmytrow, E.D. and P. Kirsch, "Basic Data Capture Techniques Reduce New Technology Risks," *Data Management*, May 1985, pp. 38–9+.

Heuser, D., "Maximizing Data Center Efficiency," *Infosystems*, April 1985, pp. 70–1.

Hofmeister, S., "User-Friendly Documentation," *Venture*, January 1986, p. 74+.

Mandell, M., "Is Near Quality Enough?" *Computer Decisions*, July 30, 1985, p. 11.

Mansfield, M.D., "Covering the Bases: Documenting Your Micro Programs," *Managerial Accounting*, May 1985, pp. 44–7.

Martin, R., "Data Center Survival Techniques: Change Control and Problem Tracking," *Infosystems*, December 1985, pp. 54–5.

Potter, G.D., "Software Maker Creates Manuals In-House," *Mini-Micro Systems*, January 1986, pp. 51–2+.

Saunders, C.S., "Impact of Information Technology on the Information Systems Department," *Journal of Systems Management*, April 1986, pp. 18–24.

_____, "Keeping Data Centers on Track," *Computer Decisions*, April 9, 1985, p. 38+.

Snyder, J., "Documentation Software: Blueprinting Systems for Better Productivity," *Infosystems*, December 1985, pp. 40–2.

Whieldom, D., "Consolidating the Micro Revolution," *Computer Decisions*, November 5, 1985, p. 86+.

chapter **15**

Systems Maintenance and Management

After completing this chapter, you should be able to

- *explain the procedures to be included in the maintenance manual for maintaining hardware components.*
- *explain the procedures to be included in the maintenance manual for maintaining system software.*
- *explain the procedures to be included in the maintenance manual for maintaining application programs.*
- *describe the means of providing system security to avoid misuse of the system.*
- *describe the process of assessing the system's status in the post-implementation stage.*
- *name and describe the areas for review in the post-implementation stage.*
- *describe the benefits of thoroughly documenting the review results and all modifications to the system.*

INTRODUCTION

Recall our Chapter 14 example of the mobile home in a shore resort. Let's say the owner would like to rent the home to other vacationers when she is not using it. In order to rent the unit to anyone, the owner must develop a complete set of operation, maintenance, and security procedures so renters will maintain the home in good shape. Further, the security of the renters themselves must be protected.

In the areas of maintenance and security, the owner could specify a list of steps to be taken by the tenants to keep the unit in good condition. The owner could also provide a list of local persons or businesses to be contacted if the tenant encounters a more serious problem. For example, if there is a problem with the electricity, the tenant might first be directed to examine the fuse box to determine if one of the fuses is out. If the problem is not in the fuse box, then the tenant is directed to call the local power company. The telephone number of the power company could be included in the maintenance manual. The owner could also indicate where a flashlight is kept, and specify some security precautions for the tenants' safety.

There are many similarities between the maintenance, security, and management of the vacation home and of a micro-based information system. Unfortunately, many firms invest large amounts of money in microcomputer resources without pre-planning for on-going maintenance and operations. If proper care is not taken, costs and problems in these areas could far exceed the benefits. Earlier, in Chapter 13, we discussed how we should carefully study the maintenance and security concerns of the system before making any investment. Furthermore, we outlined a few maintenance considerations with regard to hardware, software, and program maintenance and security.

In this chapter, we discuss how maintenance and security procedures should be developed and carried out. In addition, this chapter discusses the process of post-implementation review, normally conducted by system management to identify current problems and plan for the future. Finally, at the end of this chapter, we'll apply these concepts to the case of Sunshine Window Inc., Suppliers.

ACTIVITIES OF THE SYSTEM MAINTENANCE AND MANAGEMENT PHASE

The activities of the system maintenance and management phase can be summarized as development of a maintenance and security procedure manual, post-implmentation review, and documentation of post-implementation results (see Figure 15.2).

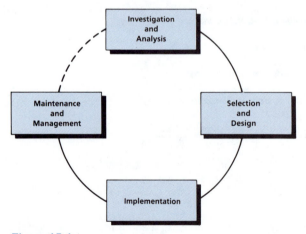

Figure 15.1
The Maintenance and Management Phase of the System Development Cycle

1. Develop a maintenance and security procedure manual
2. Conduct a post-implementation review
3. Document the post-implementation results

Figure 15.2
System Maintenance and Management Activities

Developing a Maintenance and Security Procedure Manual

One of the important tasks of this stage is the preparation of the **maintenance and security procedure manual.** This manual must cover four areas: hardware maintenance, software maintenance, programming maintenance, and system security (see Figure 15.3). Let's take a closer look at the different aspects of each area.

Contents:
- Hardware maintenance
- Software maintenance
- Programming maintenance
- System security

Figure 15.3
The Contents of the Procedure Manual

Hardware Maintenance. The **hardware maintenance** portion of the manual should clearly identify the procedures for keeping the hardware components in working order. The manual should identify the source to be contacted for repair or routine maintenance on the system, and some possible steps that could be taken to solve unexpected problems.

In many ways, a microcomputer is similar to a car; when it is not maintained properly, it can break down and cause problems. Cars are serviced periodically to prevent major mechanical problems. In the same fashion, the hardware components of a microcomputer information system should be checked and serviced periodically.

Certain preventive measures can be taken by the users of the system. For example, many systems come with diagnostics programs that test the status of different components, such as the tracks of a floppy diskette, a hard disk, or RAM. If the vendor does not provide such programs, a similar package may be purchased from other sources. Good day-to-day care of the system, such as covering the hardware to protect it from dust, the most harmful environmental element, will help to prevent system breakdown.

The user can easily solve some problems that occur. For example, if the printer is not working, the user can take certain steps—such as checking to make sure that paper is being fed properly through the printer, that the electrical cable is plugged in, and that the cable between the computer and the printer is connected before contacting maintenance people. If none of these steps works, then the proper individual should be contacted. Steps such as these are the kind of thing that should be explained in the hardware maintenance manual.

The manual should also clearly and precisely specify the terms of each maintenance contract: for example, that during the first year, the system is totally covered for parts, labor, and delivery costs. If, after the first year, the system is covered under another maintenance contract, the terms of the new program should also be clearly specified.

Software Maintenance. In the same way that hardware maintenance must be conducted to ensure that the system remains in good operational condition, the importance of software maintenance should not be underestimated. The procedures for software maintenance are different from the ones for hardware components. **Software maintenance** deals primarily with the software programs themselves and the information kept on secondary storage media. If software programs and data stored on secondary media are not well maintained, the firm could suffer serious problems. The software portion of the maintenance manual should clearly specify the steps necessary to maintain everything in good working condition. These steps can be classified into two categories: preventive measures and corrective measures.

With regard to preventive measures, the manual should make the user aware of some of the procedures needed to prevent losses or disasters. These steps could range from proper handling of floppy diskettes, to how to make backup copies of data files and application programs.

Many times, floppy diskettes are left on the top of a printer or monitor, both of which emit electrical impulses that could cause serious damage to the contents of a diskette. In other cases, diskettes are left on dusty tables, sometimes even on wet ones, which could also cause damage. Making the user aware of basic preventive procedures for handling diskettes could save the user a great deal time and protect the firm from wasted work hours and money.

The manual should also discuss the importance of making backup copies of the contents of each diskette and any hard disks within the system so that, in case of loss or damage to the originals, the user can restore important files. Many software vendors provide at least one backup copy of their software package diskette. The software section of the manual should make the user aware that the backup copies must be kept in a safe place and should be used only if the original is damaged. If backup copies are not provided, the manual should include directions on how to make the necessary backup copies.

The manual also must include information on making backup copies of all the data diskettes, particularly the contents of the hard disk. A well-defined procedure should be developed for copying everything from the hard disk to other media at the end of each transaction day.

In the case of lost software programs, the user can be directed to take corrective steps by using the backup copy or, if no backup copy exists, to contact the software vendor. In most cases, a vendor will sell another copy of the package for ten to twenty dollars to legitimate owners of the original package. In the case of data loss without backup copies, the best sources of information are the printouts previously generated by the system. Make the user well aware of the consequences of not keeping backup copies of programs and data diskettes. Reinforce the user's appreciation of the fact that loss of valuable data or programs that have taken months of time and significant company resources is both wasteful and potentially damaging. Investing a few minutes of time in making a backup could save hours of frustration.

Programming Maintenance. **Programming maintenance** involves making sure that programs are working properly and that necessary adjustments are made as needed. The system's users or managers should constantly monitor the performance of the application programs developed for the micro-based information system. These procedures must be outlined in the maintenance manual.

For example, it is possible that, due to lack of sufficient capacity on the secondary storage media, additions or updates to a data file have not occurred, and that the user is unaware of the problem. Or, information may be assigned to a field that was not large enough to house that figure; as a result, the program displays or prints only a portion of the figure. The latter case is a very common problem in programs developed for a small operation.

As a firm grows and money transactions occur, the programs may not be able to handle the additional volume. Unfortunately, sometimes a system provides no warning of this problem to the user, but simply initiates its own default steps. The manual should make users aware of these system characteristics in advance to avoid the possibility of loss to the firm.

In larger computer information systems, programming maintenance is considered an ongoing process and constitutes a major portion of the system development process. On the other hand, a microcomputer information system does not require the same level of programming maintenance as do mainframe computer information systems. Nevertheless, procedures outlining periodic program checking and testing can help a firm prevent major losses.

System Security. In the area of **system security,** the manual can define certain measures for the system's users. As stated earlier, information is a valuable asset for an organization. Like other organizational assets, information and data must be protected against theft and misuse. Unauthorized use, by employees or others, of the micro-based information system's hardware, software, and files must be prohibited.

The user can take certain basic steps to reduce the risk of information system misuse. These steps can range from properly locking the system components in a safe place, to posting the company's policy regarding the unauthorized system use.

In many firms, file cabinets containing confidential information about customers, employees, or other entities of the firm are locked or secured during regular hours or after hours. At the same time, within the same firm, it is possible to find floppy diskettes containing valuable information lying around in the workplace without any protection whatsoever. Perhaps the average user still does not realize that the information stored on a diskette can be misused in the same way as, perhaps even more easily then, information stored in a file cabinet. Therefore, it would be helpful if the maintenance manual raises the user's awareness of potential misuse of the system in general, and particularly of the information stored in the system. Chapter 17 discusses the issue of microcomputer crime and misuse at more length.

The Post-Implementation Review

Regardless of its size or complexity, any system requires a certain amount of finetuning and modification after it has been in operation, and micro-based information systems are no exception. The process of assessing the current status of the system and comparing it to past performance and future needs is known as the **post-implementation review.** During this process, the person conducting the review examines a variety of factors to assess the system's degree of success and effectiveness as well as its weaknesses and strengths. This information will allow the firm to take steps to correct existing problems and apply the lessons of the past to future system development.

Many times, during the last few steps of the system implementation stage, some issues or tasks are not properly assessed and performed. There are two kinds of reasons for this behavior. Sometimes a firm is too eager for a system to begin operation because it wants to see the results of its considerable investment during the development process. Obviously, this eagerness can lead to haste in starting up the system, so that procedures are simplified or too many assumptions are made. The second problem, of a more uncontrollable nature, concerns the fact that a company simply cannot know all of the issues and tasks that should be addressed before a system begins operation.

It is common to see users change their requirements for the information sought from the system or ask for more information than planned for initially. It is not unusual to discover that, as users become familiar with the system and its services, their needs also will grow. Therefore, the only way a system can be corrected for deficiencies or to meet additional needs is through a post-implementation review after the system has been in operation for a quarter, for six months, or for a year. Now let's examine some of the areas with which the post-implementation review is concerned (see Figure 15.4).

Cost analysis

Availability of information

Accuracy of information

Personnel requirements

Volume of transactions

Satisfaction with vendor

Security and maintenance measurements

Figure 15.4
Areas of Post-Implementation Review

Cost Analysis. After the system has been in operation for some time, the overall cost of the project should be assessed to determine how actual costs compare to projected costs. In addition, some hidden costs may be discovered and can be projected for future system development. The fact is that almost every system runs over its projected budget, and the concern should be how to minimize that overrun. Also, by this time, the firm has a better understanding of other factors, such as actual operating and maintenance costs of the system.

Availability of Information. The most important question for any business manager or business owner who has spent financial and human resources in development of a micro-based information system is how closely the system is satisfying the information needs of its users. The most important product of a micro-based system is the information to be used by decision makers in making better decisions. The availability and timeliness of this information can only be assessed after the system has been in operation for some time. This assessment can be done either by conducting interviews or by doing a survey of the system. Valuable suggestions can be made by system users after they have acquired some experience with its capabilities and failings. Some of these ideas could later be incorporated into adjustments or modifications of the system. For example, it might be discovered that certain additional information could be very beneficial to the user, or that some supplemental reports should be generated by the system.

Accuracy of Information. The accuracy of the information generated is the major factor in establishing the credibility of the micro-based information system. As mentioned in the last chapter, extensive testing of hardware, software, and all the application programs must be conducted to ensure the accuracy of the information generated by the system. During the post-implementation review process, this accuracy should be closely examined. The difference between the tests conducted at this stage and the tests conducted earlier is the fact that, after the system has been in operation for some time, its pattern of performance and the quality of information generated can be greatly affected by the volume of processed data. At this stage, random testing would be the most appropriate way of examining the accuracy of the generated information.

Personnel. The clerical and operational staff of the system should also be carefully reviewed at this time. It is possible that, during the initial planning stage of system development, it was decided that there was no need to designate an employee for management and operation of the system. During the post-implementation review, it may be discovered that, due to the volume of data processed and unexpectedly heavy use of the system, it is now necessary to assign someone, either on a full-time or part-time basis, to manage system operations. Furthermore, it might be discovered that, because of the lack of a system operations person, maintenance and other associated costs have soared. Other staff-related factors to be assessed during a post-implementation review might be the degree of satisfaction among system users and the availability of a staff person who can assist users in solving problems or implementing ideas. Finally, the security of the system may also be affected by the status of the systems personnel; this factor should also be part of the post-implementation review.

Volume of Transactions. As mentioned earlier, a system can and does grow in its use and in the volume of data processed. When an information system is designed, the designer normally does not select and design the system according to the volume of data processed at the time of system investigation. Rather, the system is normally designed to anticipate and accommodate future needs.

The initial system should have a reserve capability that could be utilized as the system grows larger and the volume of data increases. At the same time, it is possible that—despite careful planning—system growth is more dramatic than projected initially, and system reserve capabilities are not sufficient to accommodate new needs or unexpected growth. Therefore, the post-implementation review may discover that certain actions must be taken to bring the system in line with the new demands.

Another related factor that should be reviewed is the speed of information processing. System speed can be affected by two factors: the volume of data and the speed of the operating system. As discussed in Chapter 3, different microcomputer operating systems are designed around different microprocessors with different processing capabilities. Some are known as 8-bit processors, and some are known as 16-bit processors. The post-implementation review may uncover needs that should be addressed in this area of processing speed.

Satisfaction with Vendors. After the system has been in operation, the degree of the firm's satisfaction with the services received from both hardware and software vendors should be carefully assessed. The benefits of this review are twofold. First, it allows the firm to determine how many of the original promises made by vendors at the time of purchasing were honored. This could be valuable information for future system selection. Second, this review gives the firm the opportunity to satisfy any outstanding claims against the vendor. For example, if software diskettes were destroyed, the vendor may never have provided replacements.

Security and Maintenance Measurements. The maintenance and security status of the system must be constantly assessed. During the post-implementation review, past maintenance procedures should be carefully assessed to pinpoint the major problem areas. Next, the projected maintenance plan should be compared with actual maintenance to discover the deficiencies and strengths of the original plan and how future maintenance issues could be handled in more effective and efficient ways. Furthermore, the status of existing maintenance programs should be examined to make sure that policies and procedures are still valid. If no maintenance policy exists, one might be considered at this time. Of course, this decision will be made only after careful consideration of costs and related factors.

In the area of security, the post-implementation review allows the firm to reassess current security procedures in effect, and if there are weaknesses, to revise the plan. There is also a good possibility that new security concerns will be discovered during the post-implementation review that were non-existent in the initial security planning process.

Documenting Post-Implementation Results

One item often neglected during the post-implementation review is documentation of the review results and any updating or modifications to the system. There is no value to the post-implementation review if its results are not fully documented. The documentation of these results—as important as the documentation of system implementation—allows the firm to compare results with other post-implementation reviews previously conducted on the system. Further, documentation of the results will enable the firm to correct deficiencies, either immediately or in the future. The documentation should include the findings in all areas included in the post-implementation review process.

Back to the Case of SWIS

Upon completion of the system implementation phase, a maintenance and security manual was prepared for SWIS's microcomputer information system. This manual consisted of four parts: hardware maintenance, software maintenance, application program maintenance, and security procedures.

MAINTENANCE AND SECURITY MANUAL

The care and security of the system are tasks that must be performed by every user of the SWIS micro-based information system. The following suggestions will facilitate these tasks.

Hardware Maintenance

You should remember that a microcomputer is a delicate device, capable of breaking because of a minor problem. Therefore, you should follow the steps below to avoid any inconvenient down-time.

- Make sure that the electrical plug is not near your feet or somewhere it could be jarred loose. A two-second breakdown in the electrical current could bring the system down and cause a lot of headaches.
- In rebooting the system, try not to turn the machine "off" and then "on" (known as cold booting). Instead, simultaneously press the CTRL-ALT-DEL keys to boot the system (warm booting). This procedure will allow the system to last longer.
- Handle your floppy diskettes with care by following these steps:
    - Never leave a diskette on top of the printer, the monitor, or any other electronic or electrical device.
    - Keep the diskette in its appropriate jacket.
    - Do not touch the surface of the diskette on the parts that are not covered.
    - Keep diskettes from direct heat and sunshine. Any form of heat can severely damage the diskette.
- Make sure the hard disk drive rests on a very secure spot. Even a slight shake when the system is in use could cause the disk drive head to crash.
- Keep the equipment completely covered when not in use.

In the case of breakdown of any hardware, consult the appropriate equipment manual for suggested corrective steps. If the problem cannot be solved, call 111-999-0001 and refer to the maintenance contract number B00009.

Software Maintenance

Generally speaking, the software packages come with a few floppy diskettes which contain the programs of the software. These diskettes do not last forever, and sometimes the contents of the diskettes can be damaged. The following preventive measures should be taken to avoid problems.

- Make sure that you make backup copies of the software disks and keep them in a secure place; the backup procedure applies to dBASE III PLUS, Lotus 1-2-3, WordPerfect, and any packages subsequently purchased. Lotus Corporation will supply backup copies of Lotus 1-2-3 diskettes.
- When you make backup copies, make sure the contents of the backup diskettes are the same as the contents of the original diskettes.
- Periodically examine the contents of backup copies to make sure that they are in good shape.

In the case of software problems, consult the appropriate software package manual for solutions. If the problem cannot be solved, call the software company.

Program Maintenance

The application programs developed for SWIS require maintenance as much as the system software and hardware. In addition, all the data stored in the system needs constant maintenance. Follow these steps:

- Keep sufficient backup copies of all the application programs in a safe place.
- Keep backup copies of all data files and databases, either on floppy diskettes or hard disk. Files located on the hard disk should be backed up onto floppy diskettes.
- Periodically examine the contents of the backup copies against current data to make sure the backup copies have been updated.
- Keep an extra copy of all the application program documentation in a safe place, and make sure that the extra copy is updated whenever any updating or modifications are made in the originals.

In the event of a problem, please consult the application program documentation for possible answers. If you still have questions, contact Sandy Cofman.

Security Procedures

Certain security practices are needed to ensure the integrity and safety of the system and of the information stored in it. The following security procedures will help prevent many security-related problems, such as loss of information.

- Lock the room where the system is housed whenever the system is not in use.
- Make sure that the software company's copyrights are not being violated.

- Do not let the system run during off-hours. This will prevent an unauthorized user from accessing the system and its information.
- Keep your software, programs, and data file disks in a safe place.
- Keep a log of all users of the system.

Through each user's awareness of security issues and attention to the security measures discussed here, the system and its components, particularly the information stored in it, will be protected.

POST-IMPLEMENTATION REVIEW RESULTS

Six months after the SWIS microcomputer information system became operational, an extensive post-implementation review process was conducted by Sandy Cofman, the principal coordinator of the system. At the end of the process, the following findings were compiled and submitted to the owners of the company.

Cost: The overall costs of the system exceeded the projected budget by about ten percent. It was discovered that the projected budget for the next two years must be increased by twenty percent in order to keep the system in good operating condition. Other review findings will clarify the need for a twenty percent increase in the next two years' budget.

Availability of Information: Through interviews of system users, it was learned that some minor changes in some of the application programs will make some of the reports generated by the system more meaningful and usable. Furthermore, it was discovered that the system could be used for other applications, such as applying the spreadsheet packages to budgeting and accounting functions, payroll, accounts receivable and billing.

Accuracy of Information: Random tests of the information generated by the system revealed that the accuracy of the system has been maintained at its highest level.

Personnel: SWIS now is a company with $525,000 in sales; the company had $500,000 in sales at the prior year end. The company currently employs four sales representatives, one office manager, three full-time office personnel, and three warehouse personnel. The company's micro-based information system needs have increased dramatically in the last six months. Because the system is heavily used by more people, it is now necessary to have a part-time staff person, responsible only for managing system operations and updating, in order to coordinate system functions efficiently.

Volume of Transactions: Due to the growth of the company, the volume of data stored in the system has doubled. Despite the increase in volume of data, current processing and storage capabilities are considered to be sufficient. However, if growth continues at the same rate, additional components will be needed. Therefore, it is suggested that another review process be conducted in six months to assess the need for expanding the system's processing and storage capabilities.

Satisfaction with Vendors: The hardware and software were all purchased from a local computer supplier, and the services provided by the supplier's staff have been extremely helpful and beneficial. In addition, both the hardware and software manufacturers have offered very constructive suggestions and have always assisted SWIS in finding answers to the problems that occurred during the last six months, particularly during the initial utilization of the system. Therefore, all parties are recommended for future business.

Security and Maintenance: In the area of hardware, the only deficiency discovered was the fact that the procedure used to make a backup of the hard disk is very tedious and impractical. Therefore, the SWIS system needs a cartridge tape drive that could be used at the end of each transaction day for copying everything from hard disk to tape. The information would be copied back the next day. The hardware and software maintenance procedures for the SWIS micro-based information system have been followed carefully in the last six months. No major problems have occurred. The system has been in operation for only six months, so the full one-year warranty is still in effect. With regard to program maintenance, databases and their growth in the next cycle (six months) should be carefully monitored. To date, we have not fully enforced the system's security procedures. Cases of illegal copying of the software package have been noted. Therefore, it would be wise for the firm to communicate to its employees its policy with regard to software pirating. We recommend that the policy be posted on the wall beside the system components. Overall, the SWIS information system has been fulfilling its initial objectives to manage the firm's information and provide timely information to the managers. However, since initial system development, the firm has grown dramatically. Therefore, it will be necessary to monitor system performance carefully to make sure the system capability is not exceeded. Finally, during the post-implementation review, we learned that both owners of the firm now are thinking of ordering additional microcomputers for the administrative staff use. Due to this new direction in thinking, it would be feasible to evaluate the possibility of establishing a local area network (LAN) around the existing information system.

■ SUMMARY

Once a micro-based information system is in operation, the system must be maintained properly and the security of the system must be carefully planned and executed. The activities of the system maintenance and management phase include developing system maintenance and security procedures, conducting a post-implementation review, and documenting post-implementation review results.

The maintenance and security procedure manual should cover four areas: hardware maintenance, software maintenance, programming maintenance, and system security. The hardware maintenance section should outline the steps that can be taken to keep the hardware components of the system in good working condition. These steps include normal check-up procedures, what to do in the case of unexpected problems, sources who should be contacted for help, and information about any maintenance programs. In the area of software maintenance, certain preventive measures, such as keeping backup copies of the disks of the software packages, and checking the backup copies periodically, could be specified. The application programs developed for the system also require constant updating and modification. Finally, some security steps should be specified, such as locking up the area where the system is housed and keeping software and data file diskettes in a safe place.

After the system has been in operation for some time, a post-implementation review must be conducted. This review should include the areas of cost analysis, availability of information, accuracy of information, personnel concerns, volume of transactions, satisfaction with vendors, and security and maintenance measurements. Each of these areas should be carefully assessed with regard to its shortcomings, current status, and future needs. The results of the post-implementation review must be carefully and precisely documented for future reference.

■ KEY TERMS

maintenance and security procedure manual The manual that covers hardware maintenance, software maintenance, programming maintenance, and system security.
hardware maintenance The procedures for keeping the hardware components in working order.
software maintenance The procedures for maintenance of the software and information kept on secondary storage media.
programming maintenance Making sure that programs are working properly and necessary adjustments are made as needed.
system security Protecting information and data against theft and misuse.
post-implementation review The process of assessing the current status of the system and comparing it to past performance and future needs.

■ REVIEW QUESTIONS

1. The hardware maintenance manual should include
    (a) steps a user can take to correct a problem.
    (b) maintenance contract information.
    (c) diagnostic information.
    (d) all of the above.

2. The printer is not working. The first thing the average user should do is
   (a) call a maintenance person.
   (b) consult the maintenance manual for self-help tips.
   (c) take the printer apart and see if it can be fixed.
   (d) leave it for someone else to fix.
3. The procedures for software maintenance are _____ those for hardware components.
   (a) the same as
   (b) different than
   (c) similar to
   (d) none of the above
4. _____ and _____ measures are the two areas that should be covered in the software portion of the maintenance manual.
   (a) Maintenance, repair
   (b) Preventative, corrective
   (c) Backup, restore
   (d) Replacement, purchase
5. A microcomputer information system requires _____ level of programming maintenance as mainframe computer information systems.
   (a) the same
   (b) a higher
   (c) a lower
   (d) none of the above
6. Assessing the current status of the system and comparing it to past performance and future needs is known as the _____ review process.
   (a) system
   (b) implementation
   (c) post-implementation
   (d) pre-implementation
7. Which one of the following statements concerning the areas involved in the post-implementation review is false?
   (a) The availability and timeliness of the information produced by the system should be assessed to see if it is meeting requirements.
   (b) The accuracy of the information produced should be closely examined.
   (c) Only the operational staff of the system need to be reviewed.
   (d) The volume of data processed should be reviewed to determine if it is within expected system reserve capabilities.
8. Are all security concerns identified during the selection phase of system development? Explain.
9. It is important to _____ the results of the post-implementation review for future reference.
   (a) remember
   (b) document
   (c) ignore
   (d) forget

10. What are the activities of the system maintenance and management phase?
11. What areas should a maintenance manual cover?
12. Discuss some security measures that can be taken to guard against misuse of the system.
13. What are some preventive measures for maintaining software?
14. With what areas is the post-implementation review concerned?
15. What should the hardware maintenance manual contain? The software maintenance manual?
16. What should be done if a software program is lost or damaged?
17. What are some problems that can result from a lack of programming maintenance?
18. Are the security procedures for micro-based information any different than for other types of information?
19. A company is expanding its micro-based system; unfortunately, the individual that coordinated the original installation has left the firm. Since no one else was involved in the implementation, the company will have to duplicate much of the work performed before. What could have prevented this problem?

Case One:
RUMFORD COMMUNITY POISON CONTROL CENTER

The Rumford Community Poison Control Center (RCPC), located in Rumford, Maine, has been in operation just over five years. RCPC's mission is to provide information to the public and to health care providers about exposure to poisonous substances or chemicals. Located in an office adjacent to the Rumford Community Hospital Emergency Room, RCPC can draw upon the resources of the medical and nursing staff for any cases involving serious poisonings or overdoses. RCPC has experienced a steady growth in calls in the past five years. The volume of calls—approximately 7,700 per year—is still low enough to be handled by a single person manning the phone lines. Most of the staff are part-time workers who take calls about exposures to potentially toxic drugs or chemicals, and who provide information about treatment or hospital referral.

The main source of information the staff uses is the Poisindex, a microfilm-based database containing information about thousands of chemical and drug products and their toxicities. It has always been cumbersome for part-time staff to use the microfilm system efficiently, especially when handling more than one call at a time.

Two years ago, the Poisindex database became available on a CD-ROM disk. This is a digitally encoded disk that is read by a laser-equipped disk drive and processed by a microcomputer. The information on the disk is updated quarterly. The computerized Poisindex is designed to be a single-user system. If a busy poison control center were to require two or more staff members working at the same time, they would each have to have a microcomputer and CD-ROM drive.

The microcomputer system was tested for a month, and found to be easy to use and much quicker at data retrieval than the microfilm system. RCPC's manager felt that this would allow the part-time poison center staff to handle sudden increases in call volume, and would improve their ability to provide information quickly and reliably. The system was purchased primarily for these reasons. The cost of the system included $4,000 for the microcomputer, $500 for a printer, and $2,000 for the CD-ROM drive. The annual subscription to the computerized Poisindex is $2,000. This compares with a previous annual subscription of $1,000 for the microfilm system. The managers felt that the system might eventually pay for itself, both in improved efficiency and in cost savings through use of the microcomputer for other purposes.

A source of significant ongoing costs to RCPC is the analysis and reporting that needs to be performed on all calls received. A contract existed with an outside firm to perform this statistical analysis and data reporting. Each call had to be documented on a form, which has a tear-off section that must be coded with special pencils. These sections of the forms were then sent to the data analysis firm at the end of the year and fed into a computer for report generation. The cost of the forms and of the data analysis services were approximately $600 per year. It was felt that, with the new microcomputer, this task could now be done "in-house," thus saving a substantial yearly expenditure. A micro-based database program was purchased for $400 and was programmed to accept the required data from each call received.

Now RCPC's staff is required to enter large amounts of data into the microcomputer; previously, they were only required to pencil-in forms. Most of the staff have little or no typing skills, and the process of entering data into the database is very time-consuming. There is already a two-month backlog of data that needs to be entered into the database. The backlog continues to grow because most of the staff's time is spent fielding calls and using the microcomputer for its original purpose: Poisindex information retrieval. The pressure to catch up with this backlog has forced some of the staff to keep the database on-line during the day for data entry, while reverting to the backup microfilm system for Poisindex information retrieval. The level of dissatisfaction with this arrangement has steadily increased.

Another problem has to do with system maintenance. When the system was originally purchased, the vendor made little or no reference to the need for an equipment maintenance contract. RCPC's management had no experience with acquiring this type of equipment, and therefore did not budget for repairs and maintenance. Two years later, the CD-ROM drive had to be repaired twice, and the computer monitor had to be replaced once. Each repair involved a one- or two-week period of "down time" during which the backup microfilm system had to be used. The equipment is kept running on a continuous twenty-four-hour basis, and management is now wondering whether additional money should be spent to purchase an equipment maintenance contract at a cost of twenty-five percent of the annual cost of the system itself.

The poison control center staff unanimously feel that the computerized information retrieval system has greatly improved their ability to handle calls more efficiently and effectively, and they feel more at ease handling several calls simultaneously. However, there is some disenchantment with their new data-entry job, especially when it interferes with the use of the Poisindex information system. The level of frustration also increases significantly whenever system repairs are required.

Questions

1. What are the problems?
2. What are the apparent benefits of the new system?
3. What are the actual costs of this system?
4. What should been done differently?
5. What recommendations would you make to solve the problems?

Case Two:
HEMPFIELD TOWNSHIP GOVERNMENT OFFICES

Hempfield Township is a suburban township with a population of about 25,000 people located outside of Lancaster City. The township offices include the township manager, the sewer authority, and the police department, all located in the same building. Each office operates independently of the other.

Sam Patton, the sewer authority manager, has been considering the purchase of an office computer system to handle customer billing for 10,000 sewer rental and water usage customers. He is currently utilizing the computer facilities of Crafco Computing Company to print the township's quarterly sewer bills. All changes to the computer files are made by his office personnel via handwritten changes on a computer printout.

Mr. Patton approached John Goldfarb, the township manager, about the possibility of jointly computerizing both offices. A committee consisting of two township commissions—Mr. Goldfarb, two sewer authority members, Mr. Patton, and an independent computer consultant—was formed to study the township's needs. The committee wanted to find the least costly and most viable method of computerizing the offices. Using a previous proposal for computer hardware and software for the township, the consultant prepared RFPs (request for proposals) for a turnkey solution to the township and authority offices' hardware and software needs.

Three companies proposed systems for the township. The microcomputer solution bid by AJAX Computer Systems of Palmyra was selected by the committee because it was the lowest-cost bid that could do the job. Mr. Thomas, president of AJAX, and his staff met with Mr. Patton and Mr. Goldfarb to review the software that had been used by other similar installations. They found it to be adequate and agreed that employee training would commence with installation of the hardware in four weeks.

The sewer authority office personnel were very excited about the arrival of the new computer. They had been told by Mr. Patton that this computer was going to save them a lot of time, and that it was quite likely that one of their positions may soon become part-time.

When the hardware was delivered, a computer terminal was installed on the desk of each person in the authority office. The employees were introduced to the new computer system by Sue Allen, a training representative for AJAX Computer Systems. One high-speed printer would be shared by both the offices. Two more computer terminals were placed in the township office, with a letter-quality printer for their word processing functions. The sewer authority office was given the responsibility of making backups of the system each night for their office and the township office.

The following day the authority employees were instructed on the use of the program that would create their customer master file. They were left with program documentation and hardware manuals and a phone number to call in Palmyra if they had any problems. Mr. Patton proudly looked at the new office equipment and returned to his office to attend to his regular duties.

After one day, the authority personnel had accumulated many questions about the system. Much of the documentation consisted of computer manuals that came with the hardware. The office employees had not been trained to look up their problems in these manuals. They went to Mr. Patton right away with their concerns. They were told that other townships were using this system, so he had confidence that they could, too.

After several weeks of adding customers to the new computer system and performing all the other routine office functions, employees had completed about ten percent of the conversion process. Mr. Patton was very unhappy with the lack of progress and accused his employees of deliberately slowing down the job. In order to speed things up, he hired Telly Girls for assistance. He contracted to hire the fastest keypunch operator Telly Girls could supply. The first person from Telly Girls left in a huff when Mr. Patton observed the production rate was not what he had contracted for and then called Telly Girls to complain in front of the entire office.

The authority personnel volunteered to work overtime for additional pay, which Mr. Patton promptly refused. This computer was supposed to save the office time and money, and it certainly hadn't yet.

Questions

1. What are the problems?
2. What has Mr. Patton done incorrectly?
3. How can the system be accepted by the office personnel?
4. What can Mr. Patton do at this point to solve the problem?

SELECTED BIBLIOGRAPHY

_____, "Bloomingdale's Avoids EDP Panic Calls," *Chain Store Age Executive*, May 1985, pp. 13–14.

Burkhardt, M.E., "Applying a System Development Cycle to Information Security," *Security Management*, July 1985, pp. 32–4+.

Carliner, S., "Help on a Shelf: Developing a Customer Service Manual," *Technical Communications*, 1985, pp. 8–11.

Chamberlain, M.B., "Taking the Sting Out of Computer Repair," *Office Administration and Automation*, July 1985, pp. 48–50+.

_____, "Facing the Foe: Third-Party versus First-Party," *Electronic Business*, March 15, 1986, p. 76.

Homer, L.C. and T.S. Spencer, "What are the Vendor's Responsibilities in the Purchase Agreement," *Healthcare Financial Management*, June 1985, pp. 50–2+.

_____, "IBM's Services: Not Merely Super," *Data Communications*, April 1985, p. 84.

Kapsales, P., "Before and After WP: An Office Automation Productivity Study," *Journal of Systems Management*, April 1986, pp. 7–9.

Lacob, M., "Coddling Your Computers," *Computer Decisions*, June 18, 1985, pp. 76–8+.

Landgarten, H., "Beware of Security Risks When Implementing Micro-Mainframe Links," *Data Management*, April 1985, pp. 16–18.

Meyer, B.D., "The Hardware Conspiracy," *Technical Communications*, 1985, pp. 12–14.

Micossi, A., "Keeping Downtime Down," *Computer Decisions*, April 23, 1985, p. 16+.

Miller, J.E., "Avoiding Security Blunders," *Infosystems*, May 1985, p. 60+.

Nieman, W., "Performance Contracts: You Can Negotiate Them and Win," *The Office*, November 1985, p. 144+.

O'Reilly, B., "Making Computers Snoop-Proof," *Fortune*, March 17, 1986, p. 65.

Quinn, T., "When Good Can Go Bad: The Need for Preventive Maintenance," *Management World*, March 1986, pp. 38–9.

Whitaker, L.A., "Maintenance: The Simple Cure for Computer Woes," *The Office*, May 1985, pp. 106–8.

Part VII

ADVANCED TOPICS IN MICROCOMPUTING

chapter 16

MICROCOMPUTER COMMUNICATION AND NETWORKING

- describe the components of a data communication system.
- describe the difference between serial and parallel data transmission.
- explain the distinction between synchronous and asynchronous serial data transmission.
- describe the data communication applications of electronic mail, bulletin boards, and databases.
- describe a local area network (LAN).
- describe the components of a LAN.
- describe the concept of network topology.
- describe star, bus, and ring topology.
- list some applications of LANs.
- describe some common commercial LANs available.
- describe the reason for establishing micro-to-mainframe links.
- discuss the planning, management, and maintenance of a LAN.

chapter 17

MICROCOMPUTER CRIME AND FRAUD

- discuss the changes over the past decade that have contributed to the sharp increase in computer crime.
- discuss the different types of computer crime and misuse.
- describe how each type of computer crime affects the company.
- discuss why preventive measures, as well as controlling measures, are a must in dealing with computer crime.
- describe the ten security measures for protecting a company's microcomputer resources against computer crime and misuse.

chapter 18

DESKTOP PUBLISHING SYSTEMS

- describe the steps involved in the traditional method of preparing a publication.
- describe the streamlined method of preparing a publication utilizing desktop publishing.
- discuss three major business applications for desktop publishing.
- discuss the benefits of in-house publishing.
- define the specialized terminology associated with desktop publishing.
- describe the hardware requirements for desktop publishing.
- discuss six popular desktop publishing software packages.
- identify some future trends in desktop publishing.

chapter 16

MICROCOMPUTER COMMUNICATION AND NETWORKING

After completing this chapter, you should be able to

- describe the components of a data communication system.
- describe the difference between serial and parallel data transmission.
- explain the distinction between synchronous and asynchronous serial data transmission.
- describe the data communication applications of electronic mail, bulletin boards, and databases.
- describe a local area network (LAN).
- describe the components of a LAN.
- describe the concept of network topology.
- describe star, bus, and ring topology.
- list some applications of LANs.
- describe some common commercial LANs available.
- describe the reason for establishing micro-to-mainframe links.
- discuss the planning, management, and maintenance of a LAN.

INTRODUCTION

As we've discussed in earlier chapters, the first microcomputers were designed to serve as stand-alone devices, used by one person at a time. Then, creators developed ways that microcomputers could communicate with other systems, particularly mainframe computers. In the early mainframe systems, the micro served only as a dumb terminal, accepting information from another source or transmitting information to that source. Nevertheless, this discovery affected users' perceptions of the microcomputer's status and applicability. Soon after, techniques were developed that allowed microcomputers to communicate with each other, and, furthermore, to share information, programs—even computing capability. Today, microcomputers are not regarded as devices of limited use or simply as substitutes for typewriters. Rather, they are seen as major components of most information systems.

The communication industry has come a long way—from telephone lines to advanced telecommunication options, techniques, and devices. Today it is almost impossible to find an information system that is not somehow connected to other remote sites or other information systems. Information generated in one organization no longer has to be confined to that organization.

■ COMPONENTS OF DATA COMMUNICATION

In a typical data communication configuration, the following components will exist:

- the source, or host, computer
- the receiving computer
- data
- communication protocols
- transmission components

Figure 16.1 illustrates a common configuration of these components. The characteristics of these components and their individual roles in the overall communication process are discussed in detail in this section.

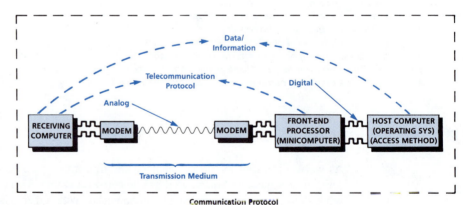

Figure 16.1
A Basic Communications Configuration

The Source, or Host, Computer

A **source computer,** also called a **host,** is that part of the communication configuration from which information is transmitted to other devices. The source, which may be a mainframe information system, a minicomputer, or a microcomputer, can provide two types of services: *computing capability* or *information retrieval*. In larger computer information systems, the components of a data source normally consist of both hardware and software. Among the hardware components might be a **front-end processor,** a programmable minicomputer that handles the data communication network for a host mainframe computer. Other hardware components, called the **ports,** connect the source to another computer or front-end processor. In the area of software, the **host operating system** is the main software that coordinates the data communication process. Another software component of the host computer, the **telecommunication access method (TCAM)** or **virtual telecommunication access method (VTAM),** allows the data management facilities of the host operating system to support data communication.

The Receiving Computer

The **receiving computer** may be a "dumb" terminal or a microcomputer temporarily converted into a dumb terminal for purposes of communication. A microcomputer is called a dumb terminal whenever its computing capability is ignored by the source computer during the communication period. In either case, the receiving device is the means through which the user accesses the computing capability or information of the host computer. The receiving device must match the specifications of the host computer in such areas as speed of transmission and the data coding system (EBCDIC, Extended Binary-Coded Interchange Code, or ASCII, American Standard Coding Information Interchange). In order to use a micro as a dumb terminal to communicate with a host computer, communication software and an interface board are needed. The board provides the necessary link between incoming and outgoing data and the CPU. The main objective of communication software is to allow a microcomputer to **emulate** a dumb terminal. Emulation refers to the process of preparing a microcomputer's internal environment to work with a transmitter. Furthermore, the software package allows the user to set the specifications of the receiving device to match those of the host computer.

Communication interface boards vary in their capabilities. The simplest board provides only the basic link between the CPU and the host computer. This type of board requires a device known as a **modem** (MOdulator/DEModulator) and a telephone for dialing. More advanced boards include a modem in addition to the basic linkage, so the only additional thing you need is the telephone. An advanced board is the type in which the basic board, the modem, and the telephone all are packaged in one single interface unit. With this board, the only thing you need is the telephone line. In any case, a communication software package is always required.

Data

The most important element of a communication system is data. The only reason for establishing a communication link between two computers is to be able to share data or information. Therefore, a communication system is incomplete if data cannot be shared or accessed. In other words, all other components of a communication system set the stage for data communication.

Data can be communicated between two systems in either digital or analog form. In digital form, data are represented as a combination of 0s and 1s. In analog form, data are represented by a continuous flow with different frequencies. Coding systems that represent digital data are either EBCDIC or ASCII. EBCDIC is mainly used in IBM computer systems; ASCII is most popular on non-IBM computers.

Communication Protocols

A **communication protocol** is a set of rules outlining how data should be exchanged within a communication network. There are many communication protocols for establishing connections between various devices. The most common is the device control protocol, which specifies codes transmitted to devices for performing tasks such as new page, scroll, carriage return, linefeed, and tab codes. The data link control protocol regulates the process of initiation, verification, and retransmission of data between any two points in a communication network. Finally, the data format control protocol specifies the format and content of data and control messages to be communicated.

Transmission Components

In order to transmit information from the source computer to the receiver and *vice versa*, different **transmission components** and specifications are required. These include a communication channel, a modem, and a transmission mode.

Communication Channel. A **communication channel** may range from an ordinary telephone line to a satellite. In some cases, only a single channel is used; in other cases, a combination of channels is put together to establish the necessary communication link between two or more computers. For example, say you want to use your micro-based information system, located on the East Coast, to communicate with a host mainframe, minicomputer, or microcomputer on the West Coast. Digital data will be converted to analog signals via a modem (see next section), then sent through your local telephone lines to the nearest satellite earth station. There, the data will be transmitted to a communication satellite in orbit approximately 22,000 miles above the earth. The communication satellite will bounce the data back to earth to the satellite station nearest the host computer on the West Coast. From that earth station, data will be transmitted through local telephone lines to another modem, where the analog signals will be converted to digital signals and sent to the host computer. The same process will be followed in reverse when the host computer transmits data to the receiving computer. Figure 16.2 on the following page illustrates this communication link.

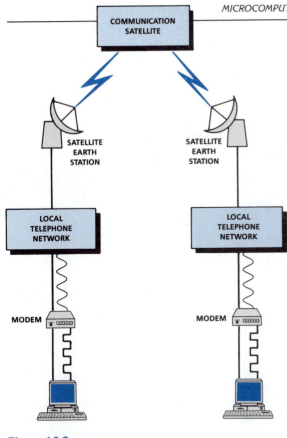

Figure 16.2
A Common Communications Link

Modulation Techniques. Transmission of digital data over communication channels that accept only analog signals requires a conversion process referred to as **modulation.** The most common device used for conversion is the modem. Modems can be classified into many catagories and types. One way to classify modems is according to the speed at which they transmit data from one computer to another. The speed of data transmission is measured in number of bits transmitted in a second (bps). Low-speed modems transmit at up to 300 bps; average-speed modems, between 300 and 19,200 bps; and super-speed modems, 19,200 bps or more.

Another way of classifying modems is according to their method of transmission: simplex, half-duplex, or full-duplex. With a **simplex modem**, data transmission is unidirectional. In other words, a simplex transmission is like a one-way street, where cars can travel only in one direction. A **half-duplex modem** allows data to be transmitted in both directions, from host to receiving computer and *vice versa*, but not simultaneously. Data transmission via half-duplex can be compared to a one-lane tunnel, in which cars going in one direction must stop from time to time in order to allow cars to travel in the opposite direction. **Full-duplex modems** allow data transmission in both directions simultaneously, as on a normal two-way street. Figure 16.3 illustrates the three data transmission types.

Finally, we can classify modems as **internal** (or **smart**) **modems,** which have a dialing capacity, or **external modems,** which are separate entities located outside of a microcomputer. External modems require a communication link between the modem and the interface board and must conform to a set of interface specifications to ensure compatibility. This modem-computer interface is accomplished through use of a standard communication link known as an **RS-232 interface,** which

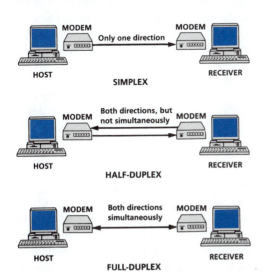

Figure 16.3
An Illustration of Simplex, Half-Duplex, and Full-Duplex Transmissions

is an electrical circuit for inputting and outputting data to and from the microcomputer. Figure 16.4 depicts a RS-232 electrical circuit.

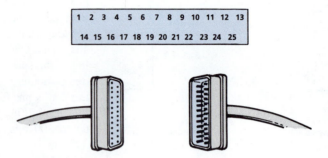

Figure 16.4
An RS-232 Connector

Transmission Modes. Data can be transmitted from one computer to another over a communication channel in one of two possible modes: serial or parallel. Let's examine each of these transmission modes in more detail.

In **serial transmission,** bits of a byte or character are transmitted one at a time, and only a single communication channel is required. In simple terms, all bits of a byte are transmitted in a straight, single line. Upon data arrival at the receiver site, the incoming bit stream is translated back into bytes. This translation process is known as **bit and character synchronization.** Bit synchronization ensures that both the receiver and transmitter are operating at the same rate of data transmission. For example, if the transmitter is operating at 1200 bps, then the receiver must be operating at the same rate. On the other hand, character synchronization ensures that the receiver is correctly interpreting the bit formation generated by the host device. In other words, the receiver must use the same number of bits that were used by the transmitter for forming a byte. Figure 16.5 illustrates the serial data transmission mode.

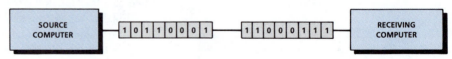

Figure 16.5
An Illustration of Serial Transmission

There are two types of serial data transmission: asynchronous and synchronous. **Asynchronous transmission** occurs when different signals are sent to represent the status of data transmission. In the example shown in Figure 16.6 on the following page, '1' represents **mark status,** indicating that data transmission is beginning. The '0' represents **space,** which indicates that data transmission is not occurring. To transmit four bytes, a single bit ('1') is transmitted by the sender to the receiver, indicating the start of the first bit of the first byte. This bit is called the **start bit.**

After the start bit, the bits of the character are transmitted. These are followed by a **stop bit** indicating the end of that group of bits. The same pattern is used for the other three bytes. Therefore, in order to transmit an eight-bit byte, ten bits will actually be transmitted: one start bit, seven ASCII bits for forming a byte, a **parity bit** to examine and validate the accuracy of the seven bits, and one stop bit. It is generally assumed that, in asynchronous serial data transmission, twenty percent of the transmission time is used strictly for signaling the stop and start of data formation. It is very common for microcomputers to use the asynchronous serial transmission mode for data communication.

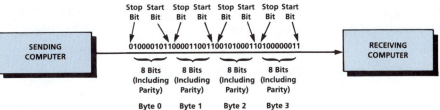

Figure 16.6
An Illustration of Asynchronous Transmission

In **synchronous transmission,** start and stop bits are not required for each byte. Instead, bits for a large number of bytes are sent in block form. Prior to each block, certain bytes, known as **synchronization bytes** or **characters,** are transmitted to signal the characteristics and arrival of a block of bits. The task of forming the bytes into their original form requires measuring the time needed to transmit bits of a byte. This calculation is normally performed by a modem, which provides clock information for the modulation process that returns the data to their original form. Synchronous serial data transmission is usually used for high-speed transmission of a large volume of data. Figure 16.7 illustrates synchronous transmission.

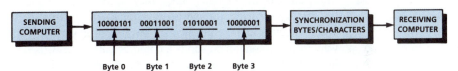

Figure 16.7
An Illustration of Synchronous Transmission

In **parallel transmission,** the second type of way to send data over a communication channel, all the bits of a byte are transmitted simultaneously. In other words, one communication channel is assigned to each bit of data transmission. To transmit an 8-bit byte, for example, eight communication channels will be utilized. Parallel transmission, has no need for synchronization because, as bits of a byte arrive at the point of destination, they form the original byte. Figure 16.8 on the following page illustrates the parallel mode of data transmission.

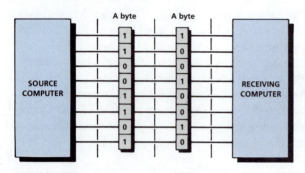

Figure 16.8
An Illustration of Parallel Data Transmission

The availability of multi-communications channels and elimination of the need for synchronization makes the parallel mode of data transmission ideal for high-speed data communication. On the other hand, the cost of parallel data transmission is very high. For this reason, use of the parallel mode for long-distance data transmission is very impractical and rarely done. The parallel mode is mainly used to transmit data within a computer, or between a computer and its nearby input/output and secondary storage devices, such as a printer or a disk drive.

DATA COMMUNICATION APPLICATIONS

Through the use of data communication devices and techniques, a stand-alone microcomputer can be connected to a world of information. The system can utilize many publicly and commercially owned information sources, in addition to accessing the power of other computer systems or sharing information with other systems. The following sections discuss some of the common data communication applications.

Electronic Mail

Electronic mail, sometimes known as **E-Mail,** is a way of exchanging information electronically. In the same manner that we use the postal system for paper correspondence, we can use E-Mail to send a message from one computer user to another. The location of the users may be a few buildings or thousands of miles apart. E-Mail allows users to store information or messages on a temporary or permanent basis. E-Mail concepts are not new; rather, they are based on similar concepts used earlier in the century for telegram and telex systems. Today, with the availability of inexpensive computers and communication devices, it is very easy for two individuals who want to correspond to do so via a communication network. There are many networks in operation, such as BITNET, a consortium of college and university computers with the ability to communicate with each other.

For example, a student at Pennsylvania State University-Harrisburg, who has access to the university's mainframe computer through a PC equipped with a modem, wants to send a message to a fellow student at Temple University in Philadelphia, who also has access to Temple's mainframe through a PC and modem. Both universities are part of BITNET, a well known electronic mail network. In this case, the Penn State student needs to know the Temple student's system ID, which you can think of as a mailbox number. Once the first student has finished writing her message, she can direct it to the Temple student's "mailbox."

Generally speaking, there are two types of message-sending techniques. One is the type that requires the receiver of the message to be logged-on (using a computer at the time of message transmission). This means that the message will be received and displayed on the receiver's screen as soon as it has been sent, unless the receiver has his message-receiving option deactivated (turned off). This type of communication, which can be conducted between two or more people "talking" to each other, is referred to as **computer conferencing.** In the second type of message handling, the receiver does not have to be using his computer at the time of message transmission. Instead, the transmitted message will be placed in the user's file, or "mailbox," for later review. This technique works in exactly the same fashion as ordinary mail, except that it is handled electronically.

Electronic Bulletin Boards

An **electronic bulletin board (EBB)** is in many ways similar to a newspaper that a reader can browse through for items of interest. Today, there are many EBBs in operation, owned and managed either publicly or by private corporations or firms. Public EBBs are mainly used by special interest groups for sharing information and ideas. Many of these public EBBs offer their members free software packages developed by other members of the EBB.

Accessing these bulletin boards is as easy as placing a long-distance call on your telephone. With the majority of EBBs, all the user has to know is the telephone number of the bulletin board. When the EBB computer answers the call, it will ask the caller to identify the type of terminal or micro in use. Once the connection is made, the user can go through a variety of menus for choosing among the EBB's options and features.

Commercial EBBs offer the same kind of services, in a more organized and sophisticated way. The user of the commercial EBB must hold a membership, which is available for a monthly or annual fee. The services of these EBBs range from a library of information to E-Mail. Among many commercially available bulletin boards is The Source, a Texas-based company with members all around the United States.

Databases

The number of public and commercial databases has dramatically increased in the past several years. Many databases are supported by federal, state, and local government agencies; they contain information ranging from census data to health care programs, research findings, and legislation. The majority of these databases can be accessed free of charge and are available to everyone. Many commercial databases are available only to member users. These contain valuable data about many aspects of business, including investments, insurance, and real estate.

One of the most popular commercial financial databases is the Dow Jones database, owned and managed by the Dow Jones Corporation. Individuals interested in information about stock markets, bonds, commodities, or precious metals can join this database for an annual fee. Dow Jones users can constantly monitor stock market behavior, the prime interest rate, and many of their financial indicators. In addition, this database offers its users financial information about different markets, industries, and corporations.

Accessing Other Computers

As we mentioned earlier, a microcomputer equipped with a modem can easily access other computers. In many firms, a microcomputer user can dial the firm's main computer to use its processing power or retrieve information stored there. A basic connection can be made in which the micro emulates a dumb terminal. In this case, the micro's computing power is ignored. Instead, the host computer provides controlling and processing capabilities to the micro in use. (A micro can also retain its processing power and at the same time share the information and processing power of the host computer. Some of the characteristics of this type of communication will be discussed later in this chapter.) A micro also can talk to other micros through communication networks for sharing information, software, application programs, and even E-Mail functions. The next section of this chapter discusses microcomputer networking and different characteristics of common networking options.

■ MICROCOMPUTER NETWORKING

During the early growth period of their use, microcomputers were placed in different offices or rooms of the same building and used as stand-alone devices. Generally speaking, each micro was viewed as a complete system, sometimes equipped with a printer, plotter, modem, and other auxiliary devices. Each of these micros had to have its own copy of the various software packages in use. Furthermore, the only way that two micro users could share data or application programs was to store everything on floppy diskettes and pass the diskettes to each other.

After micros and their applications became recognized as valuable tools for carrying out different business functions, many users began to think of other ways of sharing resources. Let's look at an example that shows the real magnitude of the problems caused by individual use of microcomputers.

Suppose that ABC Company has its administrative offices in a single building on different floors. Various decision makers, administrators, and support staff have micros in their offices. Each micro is equipped with a printer and several common software packages (e.g., DOS, WordPerfect, Lotus 1-2-3, and dBase III PLUS). Furthermore, let's assume that there are twenty micros altogether in the building; therefore, there would also be twenty printers and twenty copies of the software packages in use. It is common for one micro user in this company to use the same data or information used by others. In this case, the users have two alternatives. One is to keep multiple copies of diskettes containing the necessary information. The other is to allow each person to share the use of a single information diskette. In addition to all the problems of sharing data, consider the expense of having twenty printers and hundreds of diskettes containing copies of software packages!

The solution for situations such as this is **networking.** Networking means that the micros are connected to each other so they can share programs and data. Since all the micros are located in the same building (assuming it is a small building), there is no need to use modems or other communication devices for the micros to communicate with each other. Instead, they can easily be hard-wired together. This concept of connecting locally dispersed micros with each other is called a **local area network,** better known as a **LAN.** Communication networks that involve connection to a distant mainframe computer are referred to as **wide area networks (WANs).**

A local area network can be defined as a private, high-speed communication network that connects microcomputers and other supporting electronic equipment, such as input/output, storage, or communication devices, dispersed within a limited geographic area, such as an office, a building, or a college campus. A LAN is intra-company, privately owned and managed, and not subject to regulation by the Federal Communication Commission (FCC). A local area network could also be part of a WAN, or could be connected to other LANs.

With a LAN there is no need for keeping multiple copies of different software packages for different users. Instead, a copy of each software package is installed on the network where all users can access it. At the same time, each user of the network can have separate data files for individual use, or information can be shared by other users of the network.

LAN Components

LAN components can be divided into three major categories: hardware, software, and transmission media. The following discussion describes the different characteristics of these components.

Hardware. The main hardware component of a LAN is the interface board that allows communication between a micro and other network devices. In order to connect a micro to a LAN, an interface board must be placed in one of the micro's expansion slots. This board establishes the necessary links between the micro's CPU and the network's software. Without the board, no connections can be made.

Software. The software components of a LAN consist of two parts. The first part is a communication program that controls the overall functions of networking, allowing users to share software packages, information, application programs, security procedures, accessing privileges, and devices connected to the network. The second part consists of communication programs used on individual micros in order to make the initial connections and prepare the micros for communication.

Transmission Media. The **transmission medium** provides the necessary connection between the LAN devices. The choice of transmission medium will have a direct impact on the LAN's networking alternatives, capabilities, installation, and maintenance. The three common transmission media in use in LANs are twisted-pair wiring, coaxial cable, and fiber optics.

Twisted-pair wiring, sometimes known as copper wire, is a popular transmission medium for LAN links (see Figure 16.9). Much of its popularity is linked to its traditional use for telephone wiring. This medium is known for its ease of installation, mobility, and inexpensive cost. One of the limitations of twisted-pair is its inefficiency in transmitting data over long distances. The longer the distance, the longer it takes to transmit the data. For example, if the distance between microcomputer A and microcomputer B within a network is about a mile, then approximately 1.5 megabytes of data per second will be transmitted. If the distance is reduced to a quarter-mile, the speed of data transmission increases to 6 megabytes per second. Another limitation of the twisted-pair medium is its susceptibility to noise. But despite these shortcomings, twisted-pair wire is a common transmission medium in many local area networks.

Figure 16.9
A Strand of Twisted-Pair Wire

Coaxial cable (see Figure 16.10) is another popular transmission medium used by many LANs. Coaxial cable is known for its traditional use in the cable television industry. Among its many advantages are its high-speed data transmission; its lower susceptibility to noise; its greater transmission capacity; and its ease of maintenance due to a lesser amount of cable. The shortcomings of coaxial cable are that it is more expensive than twisted-pair wiring, and more difficult to install because of its stiffness or lack of flexibility.

There are two types of coaxial cable generally in use: baseband and broadband. **Baseband coax,** commonly known as coaxial cable, provides a single channel with data rates typically between 10 to 15 megabytes per second in the half-duplex mode. Baseband is suitable for transmission for up to about 1.5 miles. On the other hand, **broadband coax,** better known as cable TV (CATV) cable, provides hundreds of low-speed channels, and uses radio frequency transmission to divide a much broader frequency range into a number of channels.

In recent years, another transmission medium is rapidly becoming a major factor in the LAN industry. **Fiber optics** technology (see Figure 16.11 on the following page) uses laser technology for data transmission. With the dramatic price reduction of this medium, it has been estimated that, in a few years, this medium will become the most popular for data transmission in LAN environments. The fiber optics medium has all the advantages of both twisted-pair and coaxial cable without their

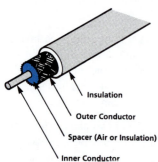

Figure 16.10
A Coaxial Cable

shortcomings. The carrying capacity for size and weight is far greater than that of twisted-pair and coaxial cables. Fiber optics are virtually immune to noise interference and provide a more secure environment for data transmission. The current use of fiber optics by various telephone companies is paving the way for greater use of this transmission medium in local area networks.

Figure 16.11
Fiber Optics

Local Area Network Options

The geometric arrangement pattern in which the transmission media and devices of a LAN are linked together is referred to as the **network topology,** or structure. Among the many topologies in use, three basic ones are worth a closer look.

Star Topology. In **star topology,** all the individual network units have direct point-to-point communication links with a central unit known as a **server** or **controller.** The architecture of star topology is the same as that of a local telephone system, in which each telephone is cabled directly to the central switch. The server is normally a microcomputer equipped with a hard disk, on which the network software or communication programs and all the other software packages, application programs, and data files are kept. In star topology, all functions must go through the server. The server acts as the central administration point of the network. Figure 16.12 illustrates a star topology.

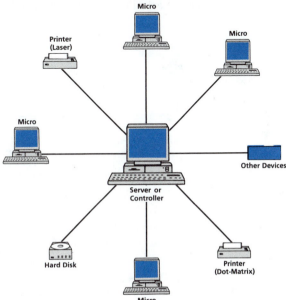

Figure 16.12
A Star Topology

The main advantage of a star topology is its security. Because all devices are connected to the server, strict security can be maintained. However, the dependence of the units on the server, which is sometimes referred to as **total connectivity,** makes star topology vulnerable to complete breakdown of the entire network, since all the units depend on the central unit. Another disadvantage is the high cost of wiring between individual devices and the controller. Yet, another shortcoming of star topology is increasingly noticed as more devices are added to the network. Because each device must have a direct connection to the server, the many cables and switches required to make the connections can become a major headache.

Bus Topology. In **bus topology,** all devices are attached to a common transmission medium, called the **bus,** that allows software, application programs, and data to be transferred among the participating units of the network, independent of any central server or controlling unit. Bus network architecture is the same as that used by the CPU for sharing information and instructions among different components of the motherboard. Data transmission among the units of a LAN with bus topology requires that each transmission carry origination and destination IDs, and that each device within the network carefully monitor these IDs to determine which is the unit to receive a particular communication. This task is normally performed through a communication interface unit (CIU), and each device is connected to the transmission medium through a CIU.

In a bus network, the transmission medium is most often passive, meaning that the bus does not control any functions. Rather, the units of the network handle the communication. Unlike the star network, where the server is the critical resource, the bus is the critical resource in the bus network. At each end of the bus, transmission signals are absorbed to make sure that they travel through the network only one time. Figure 16.13 illustrates the bus topology structure.

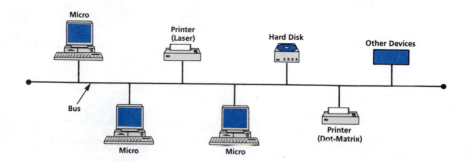

Figure 16.13
A Bus Topology

One of the major disadvantages of the bus structure is its lack of security; all devices could easily access all information as it passes through the transmission medium. However, this problem can be solved by means of encryption, a process by which confidential information is encoded at the time of transmission. Advantages of bus topology include the fact that failure of one unit will not stop the flow of information among other members of the network. It is also very simple to add new units or to modify the network.

An extended version of the bus structure is **tree topology,** in which multiple buses are connected together on a single bus, as though they were units of a bus network. Figure 16.14 shows a tree structure.

Ring Topology. **Ring topology** is the same as that of the bus structure, except that the two ends of the bus are connected. Data transmission is performed in one direction only because there are no ends to absorb transmitting signals. In ring topology, as in the bus structure, there is no central device or server; instead, data transmitted by one device travels through the transmission medium until it reaches its destination, where it is absorbed by the receiving unit. If data transmission makes a complete circuit through the transmission medium and no destination is found, it will be absorbed by the originating unit. Devices in this network are connected to the ring through **repeaters,** devices that form point-to-point links. Figure 16.15 illustrates the structure of ring topology.

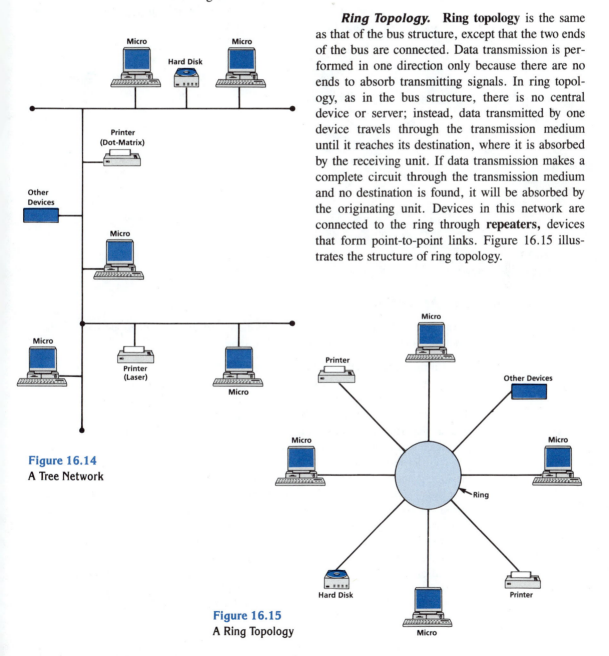

Figure 16.14
A Tree Network

Figure 16.15
A Ring Topology

In the past, a combination of ring and star topologies, known as a **star-shaped ring topology,** has been used. In this architecture, the devices of the network are connected to a central wiring system sometimes called a **wiring closet.** The main advantage of this version of the ring structure is that it protects the interfaces from damage at different network locations. What's more, this approach provides far greater control over security and maintenance than the normal ring structure. Figure 16.16 shows a star-shaped ring network.

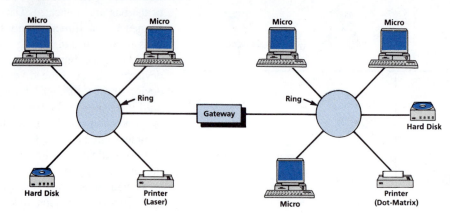

Figure 16.16
A Star-Shaped Ring Network

LAN Applications

In the last few years, LAN applications have expanded in all aspects of business functions. Let's look at some major LAN applications.

Computing Applications. During the 1960s and 1970s, mainframes and minicomputers helped establish centralized data processing networks so users could take advantage of computing power to perform a variety of functions, and at the same time, share information. With the advent of microcomputers, many smaller firms or smaller departments of larger firms had access to computing power without large investments in mainframes or minicomputers. Opponents of microcomputers argued that their stand-alone characteristics prevented them from being practical for multiple users wanting to share information and computing power.

Today, with the availability of many software packages for LANs and with various topology options for their construction, these powerful, inexpensive information processing devices can no longer be ignored. A LAN easily allows for the centralization and sharing of a firm's microcomputing resources. Through a LAN, a firm's management can also ensure that all of a firm's decisions are based on the same data and not on each user's collection of data. A LAN can be either an alternative to mainframe or mini systems, relieving these systems of less sophisticated computing projects, or as a substitute for mainframe or mini systems that are too expensive for a company to consider.

Office Automation. In a typical office, a LAN can provide users with fast and efficient access to common information files or databases such as customer files, employees files, and sales files. It allows a firm to establish standard formats for data file and document creation, and to minimize deviation from these standards. The LAN also allows an office to share expensive resources, such as printers and storage media. Furthermore, a LAN can facilitate the paper and document flow within an office, eliminating the circulation of paper documents by replacing them with electronic communication. Ultimately, a LAN can provide either one-to-one communication or computer conferencing through the use of E-Mail. At the same time, the PCs of a LAN can still be used as typewriters, duplicators, and computers. The LAN also offers a firm's management a more direct direct way to monitor employees' performance and to control the process of information handling throughout the entire office.

Industrial and Laboratory Automation. In many industrial or laboratory settings, the efficient processing of different tasks requires rapid feedback from monitoring units to a central hub. An automated factory, with collections of electronic devices such as robots, sensor devices, measuring instruments, and processing units, is a perfect environment for a LAN. The use of LANs in an automated factory can greatly improve productivity of both workers and mechanical devices due to rapid sharing of performance information. In the past, the only way to automate a manufacturing process was through the use of mainframe systems. Today, LAN applications are rapidly becoming popular for automating various manufacturing functions and for communication between people and equipment.

Choosing a LAN

Today there are many LAN alternatives available in the marketplace. This section briefly describes a few of the most well-known systems.

Ethernet. Ethernet, one of the first commercial LANs, has become one of the most commonly used LAN alternatives in the past few years. Ethernet is jointly developed by Intel Corporation, Digital Equipment Corporation, and Xerox Corporation. It is a bus LAN that employs baseband coaxial cable as a transmission medium, referred to as **ether,** a designation for a passive medium. Devices are connected to the ether through a controller and a transceiver.

The controller is an integrated circuit chip that allows different types of devices to be connected to the ether, regardless of their manufacturer. The transceiver enters and extracts information or messages sent along the ether. In Ethernet vocabulary, the term **station** refers to that point where a device, the controller, and the transceiver are connected to the ether. Approximately 1,000 devices can be connected to the Ethernet, on the condition that no two stations are more than 1.5 miles apart. An Ethernet can be connected to other communication networks through special transceivers called gateways.

IBM-PC Network. This LAN, which is an IBM product for the networking of PCs, uses CATV cable and broadband transmission. It transmits data at a rate of 2 megabytes per second, and is designed around a bus topology that connects up to seventy-two PCs dispersed no more than 1,000 feet apart. Expansion units allow close to 1,000 devices to be interconnected. Each device is connected to the bus through a translator, which allows the device to communicate with other devices in the network.

Starlan. This LAN, developed by AT&T Corporation for interconnection of common microcomputers, is based on bus topology using twisted-pair wires. It is capable of transmitting up to 1 megabyte per second. Its advantage over other commercial LANs is that Starlan is designed to utilize existing telephone wires. Many office buildings have telephones wired with hubs containing twenty-five pairs of twisted-pairs, where all the wires come together. These hubs, or closets, house the LAN wire and bus.

■ MICRO-TO-MAINFRAME LINKS

Both mainframes and microcomputers have many features that make one or the other the better choice for specific applications. On one hand, mainframes possess processing speed and power, mass storage capacity for managing large data files or databases, and greater communication capacity. On the other hand, microcomputers are easy to use, less expensive, and have the greatest number and least expensive software packages for analyzing business, technical, and scientific data.

Despite its advantages, however, a stand-alone microcomputer can become counterproductive, particularly when required applications demand excessive computing power and access to data sources stored on a mainframe system. In this case, productivity and decision making can be improved when important data in mainframe files or databases is available to microcomputer users. This connection is referred to as the **micro-mainframe link.** Both the stand-alone microcomputer and the mainframe must be equipped with the necessary communication hardware and software to allow them to communicate with each other.

A common application is that of a microcomputer user accessing information stored on a mainframe, transferring the data from the mainframe to the microcomputer (a process known as **downloading**), manipulating the data, and perhaps transferring data back to the mainframe (**uploading**).

There are many reasons why a firm would want to develop micro-to-mainframe linkage. Let's look at a few.

- ■ Many decision makers feel that they could use mainframe data, but waiting for the data-processing department to produce the desired information or reports takes too long, so they would prefer to access the data themselves. A micro-to-mainframe link could improve decision makers' productivity if it is used correctly.

- Departments originally bought microcomputers mainly for secretarial workstations. Now microcomputer access to the mainframe would add to the versatility and functioning of the system.

The level of micro-mainframe linkage can vary significantly. In brief, there are three levels of connections. The first level, which is also considered to be the lowest level of communication, is based on the process of having a micro emulate a dumb terminal. In this case, the micro functions as a terminal with no computing power of its own. Earlier in this chapter, we talked about different components of this level of communication between a micro and a mainframe computer.

In the next level of linkage, the microcomputer retains the information passed to it by the mainframe and stores it in files for local processing at a later time. In other words, the micro emulates an intelligent terminal. This option allows the micro to utilize its limited local processing capabilities. For example, screen formatting and other functions that display information are left to the communication software of the microcomputer.

The highest level of micro-to-mainframe linkage, which is also the most sophisticated and expensive level of communication, requires a communication board and communication software to be installed in the microcomputer as well as in the mainframe. This process allows the micro to sort through data retrieved from the mainframe, translate it into a form that is readily usable by the microcomputer's own software package, then store it in a file for local processing.

NETWORK PLANNING AND MANAGEMENT

Establishing communication networks, like developing a microcomputer information system, requires a great deal of investigation and analysis before actual development and financial investment. The question of how the network will improve overall information processing should be the first concern of the investigator. The concerns for security and maintenance should also be carefully assessed during the investigation stage. Generally speaking, the best sources of information about requirements of the proposed network are the end users of the system, their managers, and top management.

Some of the questions that could be asked during the investigation are: What kind of network applications (e.g., information sharing, E-Mail, software sharing) will be needed? What type of control and security does management require? How many sites will the LAN support? What is the distance between devices? What is the initial number of units or devices (e.g., printers, storage units, communication unit) and the number of future units? What type of transmission is required now, and what will be required in the future? How will the network be maintained? What is the total initial cost and future related costs? Answers to these questions will help provide sufficient information about the current and future demands on the proposed LAN.

Upon determination of requirements or needs and their order of priority, a request for proposal (RFP) must be developed and sent to various vendors. This process allows the firm to consider different proposals for the LAN. To evaluate the hardware and software needed for the LAN, the same criteria discussed in Chapter 13 for software and hardware selection for a micro-based system should be carefully followed.

Once a LAN is installed and in operation, it requires a great deal of maintenance and management. LAN management should provide reliable and effective service to its users. Installing software packages, application programs, data files or databases, allowing users to join the network, and allocating resources requires effective coordination and monitoring. In a well-managed LAN, overall system performance is constantly monitored through examination of delay statistics, information flow, and system speed. There are many LAN software support utility programs that can be utilized to obtain this data. The growth rate of the LAN must be continuously assessed to anticipate the need for rearrangement or expansion. Finally, as a LAN becomes more sophisticated and utilized in an organization, it might be necessary to have a specific person designated with management responsibility and authority to administer the LAN properly.

■ SUMMARY

Microcomputers can be stand-alone devices or may be part of a network of micros, mainframes, or minicomputers. With recent advances in telecommunication technology, microcomputer resources can be managed efficiently as part of a network in which different, valuable devices and resources, such as printers, storage devices communication units, software packages, application programs, and data, are effectively shared by different users.

In a typical communication configuration, information is transmitted from a source computer. A receiving unit receives the data, while communication protocols regulate information transmission. Finally, a transmission medium channels information from device to device. Some of the best-known transmission media are twisted-pair wires, coaxial cable, and fiber optics. Each medium has certain advantages and disadvantages; the choice of transmission medium will have a great impact on the overall communication process.

In the past several years, many microcomputers dispersed throughout an office or limited area have been interconnected. This concept is known as a local area network (LAN). Different LAN options have been developd for achieving communication between microcomputers and other electronic devices. The term topology is used to describe the structure of a network. Among many available topologies are star, bus, and ring. Each topology has certain constraints and advantages that must be carefully assessed before you construct an appropriate microcomputer network.

Managing a communication network—regardless of its size—requires considerable planning, ongoing coordination, and monitoring. A network is an entity that must be constantly assessed and evaluated to ensure that the users of the network are properly served and that resources are effectively managed.

■ Key Terms

source, or host, computer
The computer from which data is transmitted to other devices.

front-end processor
A programmable minicomputer that handles the data communication for a host mainframe computer.

port
A hardware component that connects the source computer to another computer or front-end processor.

host operating system
The main software that coordinates the data communication process.

telecommunication access method (TCAM) or virtual telecommunication access method (VTAM)
Allows the data management facilities of the host operating system to support data communication.

receiving computer
Either a dumb terminal or a micro converted into a dumb terminal for the purpose of communication; the means through which the user accesses the computing capability or information of the host computer.

emulate
A computer system imitating another computer.

modem
MOdulator/DEModulator.

communication protocol
A set of rules outlining how data should be exchanged within a communication network.

transmission components
These components used in data transmission include a communication channel, a modem, and a transmission mode.

communication channel
The communication link between two or more computers; provided by an ordinary telephone line, a microwave, or a satellite.

modulation
A conversion process that changes digital data into analog data and *vice versa*.

simplex modem
Offers unidirectional data transmission.

half-duplex modem
Offers two-way data transmission in one direction at a time.

full-duplex modem
Offers simultaneous two-way data transmission.

internal modem
Also known as a "smart modem," this modem has a dialing capacity.

external modem
A modem located outside a micro that requires a communication link between the modem and the interface board and must conform to a set of interface specifications to ensure compatibility.

RS-232 interface
An electrical circuit for inputting and outputting data to and from the microcomputer.

serial transmission	Communication requiring one channel, over which bits of a byte or character are transmitted one at a time.
bit and character synchronization	Ensures that both the receiver and transmitter are operating at the same rate of data transmission.
asynchronous data transmission	Serial data transmission that occurs when different signals are sent to represent the status of data transmission.
mark status	Indicates data transmission is beginning, represented by a '1'.
space	Represented by a '0'; indicates that data transmission is not occurring.
start bit	A single bit ('1') transmitted by the sender to the receiver indicating the start of the first bit of the first byte.
stop bit	Indicates the end of a group of bits being transmitted.
parity bit	Examines and validates the accuracy of previously transmitted bits.
synchronous data transmission	Serial data transmission which does not use start and stop bits for each byte/character. Bits are sent in block form.
synchronization bytes or characters	Certain bytes or characters prior to each block of data transmission.
parallel transmission	Communication in which all bits of a byte are transmitted simultaneously.
electronic mail (E-Mail)	Sending an electronic message from one computer user to another, allowing users to store information or messages temporarily or permanently.
computer conferencing	A method of communicating that requires the receiver to be logged-on at the time of message transmission since the message will be received and displayed on the screen as soon as it has been sent, unless the receiver has the message-receiving option turned off.
electronic bulletin board (EBB)	A message system similar to a newspaper that a reader can browse for items of interest.
networking	Connecting micros so that they can share data and programs.
local area network (LAN)	Private, high-speed communication network connecting micros and other devices dispersed within a limited geographic area.
wide area networks (WANs)	Communication network that involves connection to a distant mainframe.
transmission media	Components that provide the necessary connection between the devices of the LAN.
twisted-pair wire	Sometimes called copper wire, a popular transmission medium for LAN links.
coaxial cable	A popular transmission medium in use by many LANs and known for its traditional use in the cable television industry.
baseband coax	Coaxial cable that provides a single channel with data rates between 10 and 15 megabytes per second in the half-duplex mode.
broadband coax	Cable TV (CATV) cable that provides hundreds of low-speed channels and uses radio frequency transmission to divide a much broader frequency range into a number of different channels.
fiber optics	A transmission medium that uses laser technology for data transmission.

network topology	The geometric arrangement pattern in which the transmission media and devices of a LAN are linked together; also known as structure.
star topology	Topology in which a central unit, known as a server or controller, and all the individual units have direct point-to-point communication links with the server.
server or controller	The central unit in a star network.
total connectivity	The dependence of units on the server.
bus topology	Topology in which all devices are attached to a common transmission medium, called the bus, that allows software, application programs, and data to be transferred among the participating units of the network, independent of any central server or controlling unit.
bus	The transmission medium in a bus network.
tree topology	An extended version of a bus network.
ring topology	Same as bus topology except that the two ends of the bus are connected.
repeaters	Devices that form point-to-point links.
star-shaped ring topology	A combination of ring and star topologies.
wiring closet	The central wiring system of the star-shaped ring topology.
ether	A designation for a passive medium.
station	The point where a device, the controller, and the transceiver are connected to the ether.
micro-mainframe link	The hookup making mainframe files or data available to a micro.
downloading	Transferring data from the mainframe to the microcomputer.
uploading	Transferring data from the microcomputer to the mainframe.

■ REVIEW QUESTIONS

1. What coordinates the data communication process?
2. The main objective of communication software is to allow a micro to _____ a dumb terminal.
   (a) emulate
   (b) enhance
   (c) linkup
   (d) port
3. The most important element of a communication system is a
   (a) protocol.
   (b) modem.
   (c) data.
   (d) host.

4. A communication _____ is a set of rules outlining how data should be exchanged within a communication network.
   (a) emulation
   (b) operating system
   (c) protocol
   (d) interface
5. Which of the following is *not* one of the communication protocols?
   (a) device control
   (b) data link control
   (c) communication link control
   (d) data format control
6. How is the speed of data transmission measured?
7. In _____ transmission, all bits of a byte are transmitted simultaneously.
   (a) serial
   (b) parallel
   (c) simplex
   (d) duplex
8. One computer user can send another computer user a message by
   (a) asychonus transmission.
   (b) electronic mail.
   (c) a database.
   (d) serial transmission.
9. Which of the following is similar to a newspaper that the user can browse through for items of interest?
   (a) computer conferencing
   (b) electronic mail
   (c) an electronic bulletin board
   (d) a database
10. A _____ is a privately owned communication network that connects micros and other supporting electronic equipment dispersed within a limited geographic area.
    (a) local area network
    (b) database
    (c) bulletin board
    (d) host
11. The main hardware component of a LAN is the _____ that allows communication between a micro and other devices of the network.
    (a) host
    (b) interface board
    (c) twisted pair
    (d) coaxial cable
12. Which of the following is a transmission medium in use in LANs?
    (a) coaxial cable
    (b) fiber optics
    (c) twisted-pair wiring
    (d) all of the above

13. The geometric arrangement pattern in which the transmission media and devices of a LAN are linked together is referred to as the network
    (a) grouping.
    (b) topology.
    (c) order.
    (d) controller.
14. _____ topology is characterized by a central unit known as the server, and individual units that have direct point-to-point communication links with the server.
    (a) Ring
    (b) Star
    (c) Bus
    (d) Tree
15. In _____ topology, all devices are attached to a common transmission medium, and data transmission is performed in one direction only, making a complete circuit.
    (a) bus
    (b) tree
    (c) star
    (d) ring
16. In Ethernet, the _____ is an integrated circuit chip that allows different types of devices to be connected to the ether, regardless of manufacture.
    (a) transceiver
    (b) controller
    (c) station
    (d) gateway
17. The process of transferring data from a mainframe to a microcomputer is known as
    (a) uploading.
    (b) linking.
    (c) downloading.
    (d) connectivity.
18. Once a LAN is installed and in operation, what is required in the way of maintenance or management?
19. What are the five components of a data communication system?
20. What is the difference between digital and analog data transmission?
21. Name the three components for transmitting information.
22. What is bit and character synchronization?
23. What is the major difference between synchronous and asynchronous transmission?
24. Name the three major areas of LAN components.
25. What are the two parts of LAN software components?
26. What is the difference between baseband and broadband coaxial cable?
27. What are the basic network topologies?
28. What are some major LAN applications?

Case One:
SUPERBRAND PLASTICS, INC.

Leroy Stevenson has been the data processing manager for Superbrand Plastics, Inc., for several years. During that time his department has concentrated on updating archaic systems, most noticeably the manufacturing control and warehousing systems, with the focus on terminal-based real-time systems as a replacement for outmoded batch processed systems. For as long as there has been a Data Processing Department, the company has relied entirely on IBM mainframe solutions to satisfy its business computing needs. There are some Hewlett-Packard minicomputers that support computer aided design/computer aided manufacturing (CAD/CAM) activities, but they belong to the Engineering Department. The recent influx of personal computers throughout the company has caught upper management's attention, and Leroy must quickly compose a long-term strategy for computing resources at Superbrand Plastics.

Superbrand Plastics manufactures a broad line of molded plastic products and serves a variety of industries, including automotive, electronics, food and beverage, military, and consumer markets. Last year's sales were slightly more than $125 million, the company employs about 1,200 people, and growth has averaged almost ten percent per year for the last five years. Corporate headquarters are located in Harrisburg, Pennsylvania, several manufacturing facilities are located in the greater Harrisburg area, and distribution outlets are located in nearby Mechanicsburg, as well as St. Louis and Los Angeles.

The organization is structured in a traditional pyramid shape (see Figure 16.17), with vice presidents in charge of manufacturing, marketing, engineering, and finance/accounting. Leroy reports to the vice president of finance/accounting, reflecting the department's roots as an automator of accounting functions. The four vice presidents report to the president and CEO, Bill McNally, who founded the company nearly twenty-five years ago in his garage with two employees and one molding press. Bill is a mechanical engineer whose attitude toward computing is one of reluctant acceptance.

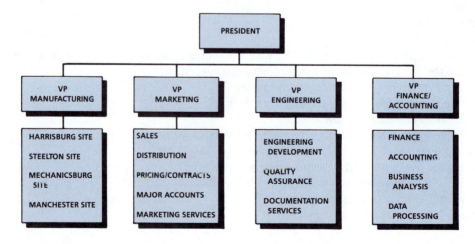

Figure 16.17
Superbrand Plastics' Organizational Structure

Almost two years ago, the Business Analysis section purchased a Hewlett-Packard HP-150 personal computer with a color plotter. The system was an overnight success within the group because of the volumes of charts and graphs that they had to prepare, often on short notice. These improvements did not go unnoticed by other department managers, who wasted little time purchasing their own systems. Within the year there was a virtual microcomputer explosion, with Apples, IBMs and compatibles, HPs, and a few other odds and ends strewn about. The machines functioned as information islands that earned their keep performing isolated tasks.

Leroy's first real awareness of the limitations of the computer configuration at Superbrand Plastics came about in response to requests for help from several department managers, all of whom were concerned about the volume of data entry that had evolved. A great deal of time was spent extracting numbers from mainframe-generated reports, then entering that same data into micro applications. Immediate cost savings could be realized if a facility was available to electronically link the mainframe and all of the various micros together. One of the managers had recently attended a presentation on local area networks and suggested that the micros should be grouped into a few LANs, with each LAN having a central file server that could communicate with the IBM mainframe. The concept seemed sound, and Leroy accepted the challenge of defining how such a system could be constructed.

Communication among the micros presented an immediate problem. The various brands of equipment used different communication protocols, which prohibited simple, direct communication links. The same was true of the mainframe-to-PC links. Even linking an IBM-PC to the IBM mainframe was not a simple matter and required the purchase of additional software and hardware. Leroy's systems programmers expressed concern that the mainframe might not have enough excess capacity to handle the additional load from this new network. Eventually the plan came together, but it was quite expensive, calling for a sophisticated communication network with protocol conversion capabilities, and a front-end processor that would fit between the mainframe and the network.

Bill McNally was predictably unhappy when the plan hit his desk. He perceived that the computing costs for the company were out of control and demanded that Leroy prepare a comprehensive plan that addressed both mainframe computing and personal computing.

Questions

1. What are the problems?
2. Do they need a local area network?
3. What are the alternatives for solving the problem in this case?
4. Which alternative do you recommend?

Case Two:
VICTORIA DEPARTMENT OF NATURAL RESOURCES

The Victoria Department of Natural Resources is a large state agency charged with protecting and enhancing the air, land, and water resources of the Commonwealth. The Department is also responsible for managing the state park and forest systems, and for conducting various public health and safety programs. In order to fulfill these responsibilities, the Department must continually collect and evaluate data concerning its resource management, environmental protection, and public safety responsibilities. The Department also requires information to support the administrative and planning needs of one of the most diverse agencies within Victoria state government.

The present organizational structure places the Bureau of Data Processing in charge of directing and controlling all data processing activities, including operations, planning, and purchasing of data processing equipment. The Bureau of Office Systems, on the other hand, is responsible for all activities concerning the operation and acquisition of automated office systems, such as word processors, fax machines, laser printers, and some personal computer workstations. Both of these bureaus are headed by Bureau Directors who report directly to the Deputy Secretary of Administration. The Deputy Secretary reports to the Secretary of Natural Resources, who is in charge of the entire department. The Bureau Directors have civil service status with guaranteed lifetime employment. The Deputy Secretary and the Secretary, on the other hand, are political appointees who are replaced on the average of every four years.

Today, the Department's complement of data processing equipment includes two Burroughs mainframe computer systems. The larger mainframe supports a user terminal network throughout the central office, as well as field offices throughout the state. The second mainframe supports specialized processing applications, such as the automated laboratory equipment used in the department's Bureau of Laboratories. Administrative functions are also performed on Xerox, IBM, and Burroughs microcomputers linked through Ethernet to a file server configuration. Additionally, numerous Apple and Tandy microcomputers are available for stand-alone microcomputer processing.

Recently, an effort was undertaken to link all of the department's microcomputer, word processing, and mainframe systems together to enhance the data sharing capabilities of the existing systems. After an in-depth analysis of the situation, it was determined that a department-wide communication link serving all existing systems was not feasible due to severe hardware incompatibilities.

Upon hearing this news, the department Secretary was furious. He demanded an explanation from the two Bureau Directors as to why the department had such a large installation of information systems that were for the most part incompatible with one another. The directors responded by stating that the department lacked any kind of computer purchasing policy aimed at establishing system standards. Because of this, systems were purchased on an as-requested basis.

Further analysis by the Secretary revealed that, in the past, former secretaries tried to implement "standard purchase" policies; however, they met with little success. The major reason for these failures was that managers with civil service status knew that all they had to do to avoid implementing a policy they disagreed with was to delay a final decision until the present Secretary was replaced. This cycle continued for many years and was largely responsible for the installation of incompatible computers, as well as other problems with the department's information systems.

The current Secretary knows that, in order for the department to fulfill its public mandates, he must be able to enhance the information processing and data sharing capabilities. He knows the controversy concerning information system policy implementation. He also knows that spending large amounts of money to make the system compatible would be politically unpopular.

Questions

1. What are the problems in this case?
2. What could have been done in the past to have prevented the current situation?
3. Do you think the problems are managerial or technical?
4. What can the current Secretary do to deal with the problems?

SELECTED BIBLIOGRAPHY

Bowers, J., "Network Analysis on a Micro," *Journal of the Operational Research Society*, July 1985, pp. 609-11.

Cook, R., "Communication Takes a Back Seat," [background communication capabilities for sending or receiving data by microcomputer], *Computer Decisions*, June 3, 1986, p. 45+.

Emmett, A. and D. Gabel, "Cases in Direct Microcomputer Connections: Nuts and Bolts," *Data Communication*, July 1986, pp. 195-6+.

_____, "Modem Connections: Practical, Quick Check," *Data Communication*, August 1986, pp. 174-5.

Gold, J., "Move Over Mainframes," *Computer Decisions*, July 15, 1986, pp. 56-8+.

Gorgens, R.A., "The Non-Network Network," *Infosystems*, October 1986, pp. 59-60.

Green, J.H., "Microcomputer Programs Can be Adapted for Data Network Design," *Data Communication*, April 1986, pp. 116-20+.

_____, "Multiuser Micro Boom?" *Computer Decisions*, December 2, 1986, p. 13.

Patterson, W., "Power Links," *Industry Week*, August 4, 1986, pp. 44-5+.

Snyders, J., "Resolving the Chinks in Micro-to-Mainframe Links," *Infosystems*, May 1986, p. 50+.

Rowe, C.J., "Installing a Micro Network in a Small Firm: The Personal Touch," *Industrial Management and Data Systems*, July-August 1985, pp. 17-20.

Taube, E.V., "Proper Modem Selection Ensures Free-flowing PC Communication," *Data Management*. September 1986, pp. 30-2.

Walsh, M. and F. O'Neill, "Downloading: Data Center Mainframe to PCs in the Real World," *Journal of Systems Management*, August 1986, pp. 24-9.

chapter 17

MICROCOMPUTER CRIME AND FRAUD

After completing this chapter, you should be able to

- *discuss the changes over the past decade that have contributed to the sharp increase in computer crime.*
- *discuss the different types of computer crime and misuse.*
- *describe how each type of computer crime affects the company.*
- *discuss why preventive measures, as well as controlling measures, are a must in dealing with computer crime.*
- *describe the ten security measures for protecting a company's microcomputer resources against computer crime and misuse.*

INTRODUCTION

Modern computer information systems have helped businesses invent new products, improve the performance of old products, manage products and employees more effectively and efficiently, provide better management control, increase productivity, achieve cost savings, create new jobs, and improve customer services. Unfortunately, these management power tools also have created new problems. One of the problems accompanying the advances in computer information systems has been an increase in computer crime and fraud. Micro-based information systems are no exception to this trend.

This chapter focuses on the microcomputer security and crime issue, including types of microcomputer crime and preventive measures.

MICROCOMPUTER CRIME

Many experts believe that widespread use of new technologies has made every business and governmental agency that possesses computers a potential target for **microcomputer crime**. It has been estimated that annual losses to business and government due to computer-related crime total several billion dollars (Cheney, 1984). Even this estimate may be misleading, since there is general agreement that only a small portion of these crimes has been detected (Simpkin, 1984). To complicate the issue, an even smaller number of the cases that have been discovered have actually been reported to authorities. The main reason for the reluctance to report these cases is the fear that a firm will receive unfavorable publicity.

Let's examine a few of the many reasons for the dramatic rise in the incidence of computer crime. See Figure 17.1 on the following page.

Availability of Microcomputers. Perhaps the single most important contributing factor to increased computer crime lies in the dramatic growth in the popularity of microcomputers. Today, microcomputers are available to almost everyone in our society, particularly in the business world. With the low cost of microcomputers and their ease of operation, many users are now able to access the information resources of a firm as well as a world of information outside of the organization.

Improved Communication Capabilities. The proliferation of computer crime and misuse also is directly related to the improved communication capabilities of modern information systems. Today, a communication device (for example, a communication interface card and modem) worth a few hundred dollars can connect a stand-alone microcomputer to many other information systems.

More Knowledgeable Users. Generally speaking, the users of computer information systems—either systems designed around mainframe computers, minicomputers, or microcomputers—are more knowledgeable than their counterparts were a decade ago with regard to accessing these systems. Furthermore, the ease of operation of many micro-based information systems and the familiarity of many people with common applications of these systems have created a unique environment for computer crime.

However, business managers' awareness has not kept pace with the dramatic growth of this modern business crime. In many ways, perpetrators have benefitted from this lack of awareness. It is encouraging that, in recent years, many managers and business owners have begun to become more familiar with this problem. As a result, more preventive actions are being taken.

Much of the current concern about computer crime stems from the fact that, in many organizations, information is now being treated as one of the major resources of the organization, along with money, material, equipment, personnel, and management. The recognition given to information resources has created interest in securing and protecting this valuable company asset. In the same fashion that equipment, materials, and physical properties of an organization are carefully secured against theft and misuse, information resources of an organization require a well-defined security plan and procedures.

Contrary to the popular belief that computer crime is the work of outsiders, most cases of computer crime involve employees of the victimized companies, a fact that is substantiated by a recent survey of members of the Data Processing Management Association (DPMA). Furthermore, twenty-one percent of the managers surveyed said that one or more instances of crime or abuse had occurred in their organizations during the last three years, and that, of those cases, only two percent were committed by outsiders. Participants also stated that most of the abuses were detected by accident (*Journal of Accountancy,* 1985).

1. Increased availability of microcomputers
2. Improved communication capabilities
3. More knowledgeable users

Figure 17.1
Reasons for the Increase in Computer Crime

1. Theft of computer hardware
2. Theft of data
3. Destruction of secondary storage media
4. Illegal copying of software
5. Unauthorized program alteration
6. Unauthorized accessing of other systems

Figure 17.2
Types of Computer Crime

Types of Microcomputer Crimes

Computer crime and miuse ranges from unauthorized use of microcomputers for personal tasks to use of a system for monetary gain. Some well-known types of computer-related crimes are shown in Figure 17.2 and discussed in this section.

Theft of Computer Hardware. Targets of this type of computer crime include hardware components such as the keyboard, monitor, disk drive, printer, floppy diskettes, interface boards, microchips, and other peripherals. It has been estimated that the microcomputer chip black market is as hot as the illegal drug market, and that the demand for sophisticated integrated circuits in the United States and in foreign countries involves underworld networks dealing in billions of dollars worth of stolen hardware (Braxton, 1984).

Theft of Data. As discussed earlier, information now is recognized as a major organizational resource. It is a serious crime when data is stolen from a company's storage media (hard disks or floppy diskettes) and sold to competitors or others who are interested in private information about the firm's employees financial status, market research findings, customers, or clients. As more recognition is given to the importance of information in determining the destiny of organizations, more people—particularly dishonest employees—will be tempted by this lucrative modern white-collar crime.

Destruction of Secondary Storage Media. In this category of computer crime, a person deliberately destroys a secondary storage medium (e.g., floppy diskette, hard disk, cassette) or its contents. In general, this type of crime is committed as an act of revenge motivated by employee dissatisfaction.

Illegal Copying of Software. This type of crime, almost unique to microcomputers, is better known as **software piracy.** It involves the copying and use of microcomputer software packages or application programs without proper authorization from the software developer. One recent study concluded that seven out of ten copies of the most commonly used software packages were made illegally, a crime that is costing software companies more than a billion dollars in lost revenues annually (Smiddy, 1985). In many ways, this act is also costly to society. Many software developers are discouraged from developing new, sophisticated software because piracy forces them to price their products higher, making them less attractive to law-abiding consumers.

Many employees of organizations do not consider illegal copying of software a serious problem. In fact, many think that making a copy of a software package for personal use is the same as making a photocopy of an article published in a magazine or journal for the same purpose. The truth of the matter is that this analogy is not valid; a software package is a tool capable of performing certain tasks, while a magazine article is classified as information about facts, ideas, or opinions. We should mention here that, today, the act of illegal software copying is considered a felony punishable by up to several years of imprisonment in some states. Experts have predicted that, by the end of this decade, even stiffer penalties and stronger federal laws will enforce software copyrights. Major software companies have been taking a tougher legal stance to prevent both their customers and their competitors from making unauthorized copies of their software packages. Recently, the developers of Lotus 1-2-3 sued a Maryland-based company for $10 million for making a small number of unauthorized copies of their software. The company settled out of court for a substantial amount.

Unauthorized Program Alteration. This is perhaps the most common type of computer crime affecting the financial resources of a company. In this case, an employee falsifies company records, generally for one of two reasons: (1) to gain monetary reward, for some direct or indirect benefit; (2) as an act of sabotage or revenge. Falsification of records and associated embezzlement or fraud is sometimes much easier to accomplish in computerized systems than in manual systems due to the fact that computerized systems do not include many traditional controlling and auditing procedures.

Unauthorized Accessing of Other Computer Systems. Today, the majority of microcomputers are equipped with a modem for communicating with other computer systems, particularly mainframes. Since mainframe-based information systems range from a parent company's own system to government systems to private databases, crimes may involve anything from the unauthorized use of data, embezzlement of company funds, or the use of hundreds of thousands of dollars' worth of pirated computer time or computer services.

Other, less dramatic microcomputer crimes are also responsible for millions of dollars' worth of lost business resources. These include using microcomputers for personal tasks or playing games.

Fighting Microcomputer Crime

The need for organizations to combat microcomputer crime is becoming more and more urgent. In order to reduce the chances of an organization's victimization, security measures must be twofold: securing the integrity of the organization's microcomputer information system resources from both insiders and outsiders, and making employees aware of the risks and consequences of computer crime and misuse, through both preventive and controlling programs. Over the past decade, many firms have tried to solve the problem of microcomputer crime by relying solely on lock-out devices and techniques to block the actions of intruders. Unfortunately, most of these companies were disappointed in their efforts. The truth of the matter is that computers don't commit crimes—people do. Without proper emphasis on preventive measures and understanding of the human aspect of computer crime, security procedures will fail to yield positive results. On the other hand, any effective security measures must be a combination of both technical and managerial techniques.

Many security measures can be employed to safeguard microcomputer information systems from criminal activity. In this section, we discuss some of these measures, which can be summarized in the following ten rules (and in Figure 17.3 on page 493):

1. Lock up your microcomputer. This can be done by either locking the system to the desk or keeping the system in a "safe" room, accessible only to authorized personnel. Many experts believe that, for security reasons, a micro-based information system facility should be located in a separate room away from public access areas.

2. Keep a log of system users. There must be a log-on procedure for the system, preferably for each unit in the firm. This way, the organization can control access to the system and to all the software used on the system. Management must make sure that everyone who uses the system obeys this rule.

3. Keep an inventory of hardware and software. By the time a micro-based information system is established, there should be a complete inventory list of all hardware components—keyboard, monitor, disk drives, printer, expansion boards, and all other peripherals connected to the system. This list should contain the brand name of the part, model, serial number, and date of purchase. A similar inventory must be made for all the available software packages and application programs. These two lists must be periodically updated or checked against the resources of the system. Keep a duplicate copy of this list in a secure environment.

4. Safeguard passwords. For those software packages in which a password or secret code is used, maintain the codes in a safe place and make sure only authorized personnel are aware of them. Safeguard the passwords for accessing other information systems, such as mainframe-based systems, in the same fashion. Make sure that users do not tape codes or passwords to the keyboard, the monitor, or a desk. Also, make sure that the password is not obvious—for example, the user's month of birth, spouse's name, or child's name. Most intruders manage to break into other systems by simply trying various common or predictable passwords. Passwords should be uncommon names or words, and should be changed frequently.

5. Designate a single phone line to the system. If the micro-based information system is connected to a telephone for communicating with other systems, then a separate phone line should be dedicated to the use of the system. The phone should be equipped with a lock, and the monthly phone bill of that line should be periodically reviewed for any irregular activity or unusual phone calls.

6. Secure floppy diskettes. All diskettes containing data or programs should be properly stored in a safe place, preferably in a locker or safety box. Unfortunately, in many organizations, diskettes containing valuable information can be found sitting on top of a monitor or next to a keyboard, making it easy for those people interested in misusing the system to obtain whatever information they need. In addition to keeping all diskettes in a proper place, keep at least one backup copy of each diskette, particularly those containing data. The backup copies should be stored separately from the original disks. Also, only authorized personnel should be allowed to access program software or data diskettes.

7. Secure the hard disk. Many micro-based information systems are equipped with hard disks for data storage. In most cases, data and programs are left on the hard disk all the time. This practice makes it easy for an unauthorized person to access the data stored on the system. There are two ways of protecting data stored on a hard disk: first, the system may be equipped with a security program that will not allow unauthorized users to access the disk. The second technique involves copying everything from the hard disk onto cartridge tapes at the end of each day, then erasing the entire hard disk. At the beginning of the next working day, everything is copied from the tapes back onto the hard disk. The second technique has two advantages: it prevents anyone from using data or programs stored on the hard disk during non-working hours, unless the person has proper authorization. Second, it provides a backup copy of everything stored on the disk up to the end of the previous day. If for any reason the data returned to the hard disk is lost, the firm has a backup copy that could restore the lost information.

8. Educate the users. Many users of computer systems, particularly micro users, are not aware of the nature of computer crime and its consequences. Therefore, it is management's responsibility to educate employees about microcomputer crime and misuse, and the implications for the individual and for the company. Personnel must be made aware of the legal remedies for this type of crime and other potential consequences, such as job loss. They should be reminded that the illegal use of software or data is considered a felony, and that violators can be prosecuted in the same way as bank robbers or shoplifters.

9. Establish a clear-cut policy. A straightforward company policy toward software piracy and illegal system use must be developed. The firm's position on unauthorized system activity must be clearly communicated to the system's users. In addition to distributing the policy among employees, highlights of the policy should be posted anywhere information system stations are located. This practice has two benefits: first, it makes the users aware of the company's position with regard to computer crime and misuse; second, it is good protection in the case of lawsuits by software companies against an employee for software piracy or illegal use of a system.

10. Obtain a protection policy. The final security measure that a firm can take to protect its microcomputer resources is to obtain all-risk insurance. This insurance coverage might already be available through the firm's general insurance policy, if there is one. It is a good idea to examine an existing policy to make sure that financial losses related to computer crime or misuse are covered. We should mention that most ordinary comprehensive business insurance does not cover data or information against theft or misuse. If this is the case, make sure that the insurance company will add this coverage, or obtain a new policy. The annual cost of a separate policy that protects both equipment and stored data is low in comparison to other business insurance coverage.

■ **SUMMARY**

In the last decade, the proliferation of microcomputers, advances in telecommunication, and the increasing sophistication of the computer user have been accompanied by a dramatic growth in the number of computer crime and misuse cases, particularly microcomputer-related cases. Microcomputer crime ranges from theft of computer hardware to theft of data, destruction of secondary storage media, illegal copying of software, unauthorized program fixing, and unauthorized accessing of other computer systems.

In the same way that other resources of a firm are protected against crime and misuse, microcomputer resources—equipment, software, and data—must be protected and secured against crime and misuse. Security measures include locking up the systems hardware components, keeping a users log, keeping an inventory of hardware and

1. Lock up the system
2. Keep a log of system users
3. Keep an inventory of hardware and software
4. Safeguard passwords
5. Designate a single phone line to the system
6. Secure floppy diskettes
7. Secure the hard disk
8. Educate users
9. Establish a clear-cut policy
10. Obtain a protection policy

Figure 17.3
Ways to Control Computer Crime

software, safeguarding passwords, designating a single phone line to the system, securing floppy diskettes and hard disks, educating users, establishing a clear-cut policy with regard to the firm's position about computer crime, and obtaining a protection policy. Management must remember that preventive measures and various controlling techniques together will increase the security of a system.

■ Key Terms

microcomputer crime   Any misuse or abuse of microcomputer information, data, files, or programs.
software piracy   The illegal copying of software.

■ Review Questions

1. The widespread availability and use of microcomputers has led to the _____ of computer crime.
   (a) decline
   (b) growth
   (c) development
   (d) end
2. What is the level of awareness of business managers with regards to computer crime?
3. In many organizations today, _____ is considered a valuable major resource, along with money, equipment, and materials.
   (a) hardware
   (b) software
   (c) storage media
   (d) information
4. Who commits most computer crimes?
5. Which of the following would *not* be a target for someone who has set his or her sights on stealing a firm's hardware?
   (a) a microchip
   (b) a monitor
   (c) a file of employee records
   (d) floppy diskettes
6. The illegal copying of software is known as software.
   (a) backup.
   (b) piracy.
   (c) sharing.
   (d) duplication.

7. The act of illegally copying software is considered a
   (a) minor problem.
   (b) felony.
   (c) misdemeanor.
   (d) accepted practice.
8. Which of the following is perhaps the most common type of computer crime affecting a firm's financial resources?
   (a) Unauthorized access of other computer systems.
   (b) Theft of computer hardware.
   (c) Theft of data.
   (d) Unauthorized program fixing.
9. Passwords on a computer system should be
   (a) common words or names.
   (b) taped to the monitor.
   (c) changed frequently.
   (d) made available to all personnal.
10. Whose responsibility is it to educate employees about microcomputer crime?
11. State the reasons cited for the rise in incidents of computer crime.
12. A person deliberately destroys some of a firm's secondary storage media. What items are they likely to have destroyed?
13. List the types of computer crime.
14. How would a log-on procedure help control computer crime?
15. Name two ways of protecting data stored on a hard disk.
16. Why is it important for a company to have a straightforward policy on software piracy and illegal use of the system?
17. An employee in the data processing section of a large firm has been evaluated as a poor performer and has been placed on two weeks' notice. What should the company do during the employee's last two weeks of work?
18. Is there really any difference between software piracy and photocopying other copyrighted materials? Explain your reasoning.
19. What is the single, most important thing to keep in mind when developing security measures?
20. What is the primary factor to increased computer crime?

Case One:
ACE INSURANCE COMPANY

Ace Life Insurance Company is a small insurance company located in Montana. There are two office locations, one in Helena and one in Billings. Helena is the main office, employing approximately sixty-five people. The payroll, accounting, and finance functions are performed at the Helena office through the use of seven Wang microcomputers, which form a local area network. The microcomputers are also used for word processing.

Several months ago, management discovered that one of the employees was coming to the office in the evenings and using the word processing software for typing church bulletins. Upset over this misuse of the computer facilities, management decided to establish and enforce a policy against the misuse of microcomputers.

The next day, all employees were sent a copy of the company-wide policy, which read:

Microcomputers may not be used for the following:

1) entertainment purposes,
2) non-work-related activities,
3) personal gain or achievement.

Anyone violating the above policy is subject to disciplinary action or immediate dismissal.

Harry Hutchinson, an agent with Ace Life Insurance Company for five years, was attending an evening class at a local college. His employer provided 100 percent tuition refund upon successful completion of the class, because he was working towards a business degree. Since Harry did not work with microcomputers, he figured the class, called "Microcomputer Applications," would be a great way to learn some of the capabilities of microcomputers and possibly use them on the job.

One evening, Harry was assigned a class project that required him to become familiar with Lotus 1-2-3. The next day, Harry approached his supervisor, John Jones, and asked if Ace Life Insurance had Lotus 1-2-3. John informed Harry that there was a 1-2-3 tutorial available on the Wang but, if he wanted to use it, he would have to use it after working hours. He told Harry to explore practical applications for the software package in their department. John was pleased with the interest that Harry took in the microcomputers. Harry did not tell John that he was attending an evening class on microcomputers.

Harry signed up to take the tutorial that afternoon at 4:30, after working hours. When he arrived at the training site, he was greeted by Mary Williams, who, along with her other responsibilities, was the microcomputer trainer. She was very helpful in showing Harry how to operate the Wang micro. He told Mary that he was very interested in learning about microcomputers and that he was attending a course on micros at a local college.

Harry stayed that evening until 8:00 p.m. and went step-by-step through the tutorial. He thought of several practical applications for Lotus 1-2-3 in his department. One of his ideas was to store customer information and rating information using 1-2-3's data management capabilities. This way, when a customer called for information about his account, the information would be right at an agent's fingertips. 1-2-3 could also provide "what-if?" capabilities when calculating and quoting rates to customers. Harry could not wait to tell his supervisor about his ideas the next morning.

Harry arrived at work the next morning at 7:25. At 7:30 the telephone rang. It was Peter Smith, Mary Williams's supervisor. Peter asked Harry if he took the Lotus 1-2-3 tutorial the previous evening. Harry replied "Yes." Peter then told Harry that he was informed that Harry was attending an evening class on microcomputers at a local college. He also told Harry that he knew he had a class assignment on Lotus 1-2-3. Peter said, "According to our microcomputer policy implemented four months ago, microcomputer resources may not be used for personal gain or achievement. Since you used the Wang micro for a homework assignment, which was for personal gain, you have violated the microcomputer policy. Therefore, you are subject to disciplinary action or dismissal."

Questions

1. What is the problem here?
2. Should Harry be subject to disciplinary action or dismissal?
3. Should the policy be reworded or made more specific?
4. What do you recommend as a solution to this case?

Case Two:
ROCKWELL STATE COLLEGE

Rockwell College is a private engineering school in North Carolina with an enrollment of 4,200 students. Many of the students come from the Raleigh area. In an effort to solve an overcrowding problem at the college, a branch campus has been established in Asheville to provide a two-year program and to potentially "weed-out" some of the student population. This campus enrolls approximately 1,500 students, all of whom commute on a daily basis. Approximately forty faculty members are employed in the science, math, business, and humanities areas.

Rockwell College has a state-of-the-art computer facility consisting of a mainframe computer for most of the college's business functions (billings, faculty payroll, grade reports), stand-alone minicomputers for specific engineering applications (CAD-CAM, simulation), and a microcomputer LAN for faculty use in scheduling, student record updating (including grades), and general office use. The LAN consists of forty-five terminals in a star configuration, with several terminals located in each department, and is tied to the mainframe via a gateway to allow for upload and download of data. The MIS department is headed by the Director of College Computing, Dave Dayton. Reporting to him are two technical analysts, two programming analysts, and an operations supervisor. Reporting to the operations supervisor are twenty-eight student operators who work a variety of hours to aid in the daily computer operation.

Although it was felt that the Asheville campus did not need a mainframe computer, it did receive one stand-alone minicomputer for engineering applications and a star-configution LAN, similar to that at the main campus, for faculty use. The LAN consists of twelve terminals and is connected to the main campus via a gateway. It was determined that Jim Metz, head of the engineering department at Asheville, would be in charge of the computer facilities, and that all operational duties would be handled by student operators. All technical and development skills would be imported from the main campus.

Over the next few months, the technical people from the main campus spent several weeks at the Asheville campus. They worked closely with Metz and the student operators to set up equipment, install software, test the system, set up the security system (sign-on IDs, security screens, and user activity reports), and train the faculty. Although Metz was in charge of the computer area, he delegated most of his duties to the student operations staff in order to free his time for teaching. Any problems encountered were to be resolved by the operators via contact with the main campus. A report of each problem and its resolution was to be forwarded to Metz. It was believed this technique would allow the operators to gain a more thorough understanding of the system and would expedite resolution of problems, thus minimizing down-time.

Several problems were encountered over the next month: files were not created properly, reports were not produced, users were not correctly set up in the security system, sign-on IDs were mixed up or not properly entered, terminals were constantly disconnected from the system, and there were general hardware problems. All these problems were finally resolved, and things started running smoothly. As a matter of fact, things ran well enough that Metz found himself spending a minimum amount of time in the computer area. He only had to schedule the student operators, review the problem sheets, and handle any special concerns brought to him by the operators. He was relieved to know that the operation ran as smoothly as it did.

At the beginning of the next semester, the Dean from the main campus was standing in Metz's office. The following conversation took place:

Dean: "Jim, we've got a problem. Can you get your user authorization control report?"

Metz: "I'll have to get my operator to locate it. They have taken responsibility for these reports. I'll be back in a second."

Dean: "Wait...let me explain what we have found."

The Dean then told Metz what had happened. Several senior students from the Asheville campus had received excellent grades and, in turn, were allowed to be admitted to the main campus for their graduate work. But it had been determined these students' grades had been changed just before the grade reports were issued. Control reports indicated that sign-on ID #038 submitted the changes. The Dean wanted to know: Who is #038?

Upon locating the Asheville reports, Metz found no #038 on the list. The specific reports of daily on-line transactions submitted from the Asheville LAN were incomplete. The reports made no reference to #038. The question was raised as to how an unauthorized user could access the system, given the existence of security screens and user passwords. None of the faculty made any updates.

At this point, it was assumed that one of the student operators had accessed the system and executed the transactions. Reviewing the list of students with changed grades revealed the name of Ben Small, a student operator. Ben was approached about the situation but claimed he had no knowledge of it.

Nevertheless, it seemed apparent to Metz and the Dean that Ben, in fact, had made the unauthorized changes.

Questions

1. Can a case be created against the student operator?
2. What is the underlying problem? (Disregard the possibility of non-trustworthy employees.)
3. What can be done to avoid such situations?
4. What is the difference between security and control?

SELECTED BIBLIOGRAPHY

Allen B.,"Embezzler's Guide to the Computer," *Harvard Business Review*, July-August 1975, p. 81+.
_____, "Danger Ahead: Safeguard Your Computer," *Harvard Business Review*, November 1968, pp. 97-101.
Batt, R.,"White-Collar Crime," *Computer World Forecast 1984*, December 1983.
Bequai, A.,"What to do About Crime in the Electronic Office," *The Office*, January 1985, pp. 101-104.
Braxton, M.,"Symposium Examines Terrorism, Espionage, and Computer Fraud," *Risk Management*, October, 1984, p. 74+.
Brown, P.S. and T. J. Saltmarsh, "Now is the Time to Implement Communication Security," *ABA Banking Journal*, July 1981, pp. 54-57.
Bus, M. D. and L. M. Salerno, "Common Sense and Computer Security," *Harvard Business Review*, March-April 1984, p. 18+.
Cheney, R. S. and J. E. Cheney, "Cracking Down on Micro Crime," *Business Computer System*, October 1984, pp. 40-46.
_____, "Coping: Survival in a Computerized Society," New York, Petrocelli Books, Inc., 1984, pp. 130-136.
_____, "What Can Be Done?" *Business Week*, September 26, 1983, p. 126.
Cullen, K. M.,"Systems for Authorized Access to Information," *Adminstrative Management*, May 1982, pp. 35-38.
Gynes, S., M. G. Laney, and R. Zant, "Computer Security Practice," *Journal of Systems Management*, June 1983, pp. 22-27.
Hemphill, C. F. and J. M. Hemphill, "Security Procedures for Computer Systems," Homewood, Illinois: Dow Jones-Irwin, 1973.
Kockowski, L.,"Computer Crime-Are You Vulnerable?," *National Underwriter* February 1984, p. 3+.
Shapiro, S.,"Computer Security A Critical Issue," *Business Insurance*, November 1984, pp. 8-12.
Simpkin, M. G., "Computer Crime: Lessons and Directions," *CPA Journal*, December, 1981, p. 10+.
Smiddy, J. D. and L. O. Smiddy, "Caught in the Act," *Datamation*, June 1985, pp. 102-106.
Walden, J. D.,"A False Sense of Security," *Infosystems*, August 1983, pp. 100-103.
_____, "DP Managers' Survey Cites Insiders as Crime Suspects in Computer Crime," *Journal of Accountancy*, August 1985, p. 42+.
Wood, C. C.,"Countering Unauthorized Systems Access," *Journal of Systems Management*, April 1984, pp. 26-28.

chapter 18

DESKTOP PUBLISHING SYSTEMS

After completing this chapter, you should be able to

- describe the steps involved in the traditional method of preparing a publication.
- describe the streamlined method of preparing a publication utilizing desktop publishing.
- discuss three major business applications for desktop publishing.
- discuss the benefits of in-house publishing.
- define the specialized terminology associated with desktop publishing.
- describe the hardware requirements for desktop publishing.
- discuss six popular desktop publishing software packages.
- identify some future trends in desktop publishing.

INTRODUCTION

Businesses spend millions of dollars each year to prepare, design, produce, and distribute publications ranging from simple product fact sheets to annual reports and proposals for new projects or services. According to one publishing industry expert, the annual publication output of some of the top 10,000 American companies exceeds that of the commercial book publishing industry. Another expert claims that ten percent of a corporation's revenues are spent on publishing-related expenditures.

In recent years, a new microcomputer application, known as **desktop publishing (DTP)**, or **electronic publishing**, has provided many businesses with the ability to design and prepare various publications in-house. DTP can be a cost-effective response to the millions of dollars that businesses spend each year on outside designers and typesetters in the preparation of proposals, presentations, reports, brochures, forms, letterhead, business cards, manuals, sales and product pamphlets, promotional literature, and much more.

This chapter discusses the concepts, tasks, applications, benefits, terms, hardware and software requirements, and reviews the available software packages for desktop publishing applications.

■ THE PUBLISHING PROCESS

Preparing a publication, regardless of its size or type, is a lengthy process. The following sections compare the traditional process of publishing to that of desktop publishing.

Traditional Approach

Traditionally, preparing a publication requires many steps and many individuals to perform them. Figure 18.1 lists the steps involved in the preparation of a publication.

1. Developing the idea or concept
2. Writing the copy
3. Editing the copy
4. Preparing the graphics
5. Typesetting
6. Designing the layout
7. Printing the final document

Figure 18.1
Steps in the Traditional Publishing Process

The following example illustrates this process. Let's assume that Sunshine Window Inc., Suppliers' management has decided to prepare a promotional brochure for a new a French window recently added to their line of products.

Step 1: The process is initiated by an idea or concept—in this example, the idea of promoting a product. At this stage, the individual in charge will develop a mental picture of what is supposed to be communicated to the customer, employee, client or reader, from applications of the idea to persuasive reasons for purchasing the product. It might take an individual hours or even days to analyze what should be said about the new product.

Step 2: Upon completion of the conceptualization process, the writing process begins. At this stage, the idea or concept is converted into specific language for a potential publication. The writing process usually starts with a draft and proceeds through revisions to the final document. In this stage, the writer usually experiments with many ways or styles of presenting the different views, benefits, or applications of the product to be promoted.

Step 3: The editing process is the next step. Normally, the final draft is distributed among managers or others with the authority to give final approval. Changes and recommendations suggested by management are then incorporated into the final document. The document may go through several editing steps before the final copy is prepared.

Step 4: After editing, art or graphics are prepared for the document. These may include a photo of the product or an illustration demonstrating its use. Furthermore, design work, such as charts, boxes, or illustrations, are prepared in this step. Art or graphic design tasks are normally performed by graphic artists.

Step 5: Upon completion of the graphics, the process of typesetting begins. Typesetting involves the preparation of the actual text to be printed and includes such things as choice of typeface, line length, how or whether words are to be hyphenated, and other technical printing considerations. Traditionally, a professional typesetter assembles the text of the document by placing metal characters, or letters, side by side on a metal plate which would later be used to print the document. Today, most typesetting is done through a phototypesetting process.

Step 6: The next step is the design of the layout of individual pages for the entire document. In this step, decisions are made about how text, charts, graphs, boxes, and other materials should be placed on the printed page. The process of designing an appropriate layout often involves consideration of several different layouts to determine the best possible presentation of material. Also in this stage, the prepared text and graphics are actually placed on the final layout. The process of fixing the text and the graphics on pages, called **camera-ready copy**, to be used by the printer, is known as **paste-up**.

Step 7: Upon completion of the camera-ready copy, the document is ready for mass production via photocopying machines, offset printing, or other printing methods. Also in this stage, the tasks of binding or stapling and packaging the document are performed.

Desktop Publishing Approach

With the help of special microcomputer software packages known as desktop publishing systems, the whole process of designing, preparing, and professionally printing business publications can be handled very easily in one office by perhaps a single person. Desktop publishing software allows a user to bypass many of the steps in the traditional publishing approach.

The steps performed in preparing the SWIS promotional flyer with desktop publishing software are illustrated in Figure 18.2.

Figure 18.2
Steps in the Desktop Publishing Process

1. Developing the idea or concept
2. Writing and editing text
3. Preparing graphics
4. Designing the page layout
5. Printing the final document

Step 1: The process of conceptualizing an idea is the same regardless of the tools or techniques used to turn the idea into a product. Therefore, the advent of desktop publishing has not affected tasks performed in the first stage. On the other hand, one could argue that this new tool has encouraged many businesses to be more creative and imaginative due to the ease of preparing a publication.

Step 2: Text preparation—writing and editing text material before it is finalized and approved—can be accomplished by using a word processing package such as WordPerfect or WordStar, or, with the new generation of desktop publishing software packages, within the environment of the software package itself. The main advantage of using microcomputer software packages to prepare text is that changes can be incorporated easily within the text stored in the computer. The manager in charge of approving a text can view the document on the screen of the microcomputer and recommend changes, if needed, instead of obtaining a printout. In many desktop publishing cases, the individual in charge of preparing a document is also the one who may authorize or approve the text. Figure 18.3 shows a portion of text prepared for the SWIS product promotional flyers.

Figure 18.3
A Portion of the SWIS Promotional Piece

Step 3: The graphics for the document under development is performed with the help of a graphics software package, such as Harvard Graphics or Micro Graphics. Graphics might include line, bar, or pie charts demonstrating relationships among various components, factors, or entities. With the availability of many user-friendly, powerful microcomputer graphics software packages, a manager can easily prepare state-of-the-art illustrations in a short period of time. Figure 18.4 on the following page is a pie chart of sales performance of SWIS's new French Window compared with sales of other products in 1988.

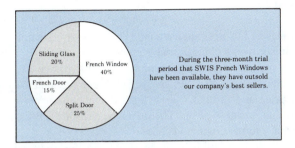

Figure 18.4
Adding Graphics

Step 4: The main task of desktop publishing software packages is to enable the user to do typesetting and layout on the microcomputer screen, including page layout, selection of type style, determining header and footer, page format and size, hyphenation, selection of vertical printing versus horizontal printing, and many other tasks. The user can do a layout of the camera-ready copy of the document on the screen, either by trying one of the various standard layout templates included in most software packages or by designing a new layout. Upon completion of this stage, a printed copy of the document can be obtained for use in duplication. Figure 18.5 shows the layout prepared for the SWIS product promotion, prepared with the help of a desktop publishing software.

Step 5: Finally, the camera-ready copy of the document prepared with the desktop publishing software package is mass-reproduced. The photocopying or printing can be performed either in-house or by professional printing shops.

The major difference between traditional document development and the desktop publishing approach is the fact that, in the latter, almost all the stages of preparing a publication except the photocopying can be performed by a user within an organization. With the traditional approach, many tasks, such as art, typesetting, and layout preparations, are performed outside of the organization or by individuals other than the user.

For some, the principal reasons for the popularity of desktop publishing are speed and economy. A publication that formerly took several weeks and cost several hundred dollars can now be prepared in-house in a few days, or even in a few hours, at a fraction of the traditional cost. By eliminating dependency on outside parties, desktop publishing has reduced some overhead costs significantly, so that now virtually anything can easily be given the appearance of a quality publication.

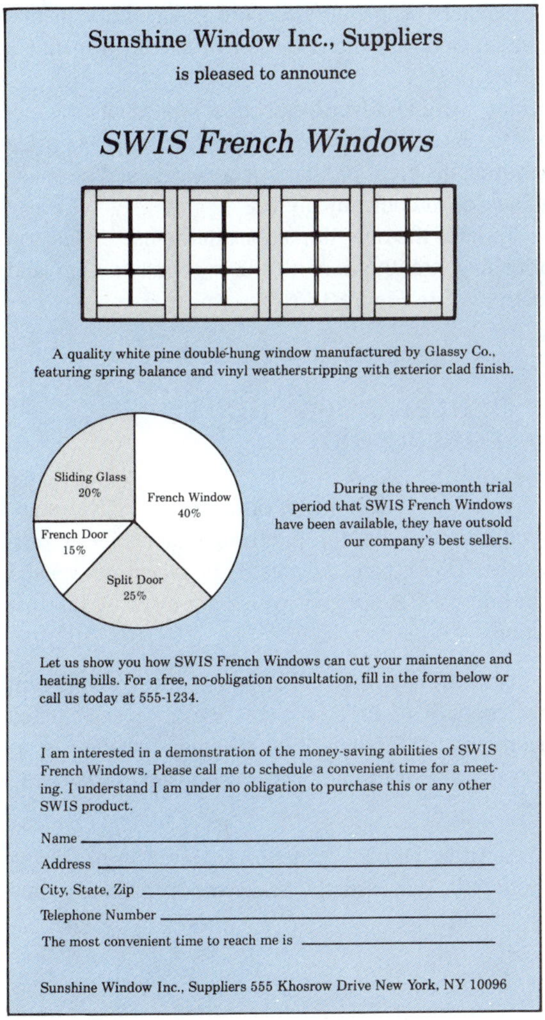

Figure 18.5
The Final SWIS Flyer

MAJOR USES OF DESKTOP PUBLISHING

Desktop publishing has a wide range of business applications. There are three major uses of desktop publishing: administrative, technical, and promotional.

Administrative applications include formal presentations, reports, proposals, correspondence, employee newsletters, telephone listings, special flyers to announce upcoming events to employees, price and inventory lists, legal documents or contracts, employee safety manuals, and business plans. The major benefit of DTP for administrative applications is better internal communications.

The **technical applications** of desktop publishing are mainly in the areas of specification sheets and manuals on training, product operation, and product safety. Until recently, the task of preparing a new product manual for a modified product, for example, would take weeks. Now, with the assistance of DTP, changes can be easily incorporated within existing manuals. The ability to store finished documents in an electronic database is a particular boon for the publisher of technical manuals or documents.

DTP's **promotional applications** include advertisements for products or services, logo preparation, brochures for business services or product listings, price sheets, fact sheets, posters for promoting different products or services, and newsletters or bulletins providing tips and advice to company clients.

Perhaps the only limitations in the use of desktop publishing are those of the user's imagination and creativity. See Figure 18.6.

Administrative

Presentations   Reports
Proposals   Newsletters
Lists   Legal documents

Technical

Training manuals   Operations manuals
Specification sheets   Safety manuals

Promotional

Advertisements   Brochures
Logo preparation   Price sheets
Fact sheets   Posters

Figure 18.6
Some Desktop Publishing Applications

BENEFITS OF IN-HOUSE PUBLISHING

In the past few years many organizations have established in-house desktop publishing divisions or procedures. There many advantages or incentives related to in-house DTP, some of which are discussed in this section.

Reduced time: This is the most significant direct benefit of DTP in preparing company-related documents. DTP has allowed many businesses to reduce lead times and develop faster turnaround times.

Less cost: Another direct benefit is the cost reduction achieved in preparing documents in-house. This comes both from consolidating tasks and from saving time in the various preparation stages.

Better control: Through DTP, the volume of printed documents can be significantly controlled. A company can print materials as needed instead of carrying a large inventory of printed material, which both costs more and requires greater space allocation.

Less waste: By maintaining less inventory, an organization wastes less on revisions of already printed materials.

Better security: Often, technical manuals and company documents are highly sensitive. In-house publishing provides better security procedures because fewer outsiders are involved in the preparation of the document.

Better communication: DTP applications have assisted many organizations to achieve better internal communications. For example, by publishing a weekly newsletter, a firm can provide an excellent channel of communication between management and employees about job opportunities, changes in policy, and so on.

Increased perceived value of services: With the assistance of a DTP system, services and products can be presented in a very professional manner. For example, a restaurant owner can easily update a menu, almost on a daily basis, at a fraction of the cost to revise a menu using traditional methods. Or an insurance agency could prepare flyers about new services provided for clients.

Improved company image: DTP now allows firms to prepare documents, such as proposals or reports, with the appearance of quality publications. This can help a firm to create a better image among current and prospective clients. In the past, the high cost of professionally published documents prevented many business from producing first-rate materials. No longer is cost a barrier. Now, almost anything can be given a quality presentation. Figure 18.7 summarizes the benefits related to use of desktop publishing systems.

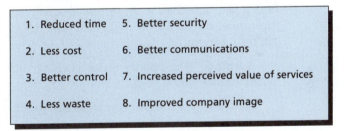

Figure 18.7
Benefits of Desktop Publishing

■ DESKTOP PUBLISHING TERMINOLOGY

Like many other microcomputer applications, desktop publishing uses certain terminology that may be unfamiliar to newcomers of this field. This section contains a mini-glossary of some of the most commonly used terms in desktop publishing.

Layout. The pattern in which text, graphs, charts, and boxes are placed on a single page.

Font. The style and size of a character within a type family. Each style (e.g., bold, or italic) and each size (e.g., 6-point, or 8-point) represents a different font.

Leading. The blank space between lines, measured from the base of one line of type to the base of the next line.

Pica. A standard typesetting measurement that represents approximately 1/6 of an inch. Many DTP software packages offer the user inch and line settings, then internally convert these into typesetting measurements.

Point. A standard typesetting measurement unit, representing 1/12 of a pica, most commonly used to measure leading and font sizes.

Crop. The ability to use only a portion of a graphic image. This is similar to using scissors to cut out a portion of a picture.

Hyphenation. Correctly breaking words at the end of a line so that a line does not have large gaps between characters or words.

Embedded codes. Information placed in various spots in a text or layout to specify treatment of the material.

Justification. The setting of lines according to a predetermined style. Hyphenation is an important factor in justification so as many words as possible can fit in a line. Justification can be *center* (a line of text is placed in the center of the page), *full* (straight left and right margins), *right* (ragged left margin), or *left* (ragged right margin).

Kerning. The ability to move character pairs farther apart or closer together to make them easier to read.

Header. The text that appears at the top of a document page, such as a title or page number.

Footer. The text that is placed on the bottom of a page, such as page number or totals.

Ruled lines. Lines of varying degrees of thickness that separate certain text, charts, or art work.

Vertical justification. The spacing of text lines in side-by-side columns to obtain alignment across the bottom of the page.

Style sheet. The standard use for typefaces, margins, fonts, and other settings for a document.

Laser printing. A new printing technology that allows characters or graphics to be transferred to a printed page in much the same way that photocopiers transfer images from one page to another.

Resolution. The number of *dots per inch* (dpi) used by a computer printer for forming characters. The more dpi, the greater the resolution and the better the quality of printing.

Landscape printing. Printing characters sideways or turning them ninety degrees, as compared to standard horizontal printing.

Double-sided. The ability to print on both sides of a sheet of paper in one pass through the printer, a feature of some laser printers.

Portrait printing. Printing across the narrower side of a page; considered the most common printing technique.

WYSIWYG. Acronym for "What You See Is What You Get," or what is shown on the computer screen is what a document will look like when it is printed on a sheet of a paper.

Greeking. A technique used by WYSIWYG DTP software to indicate how lines and white space mix on a page to create an image.

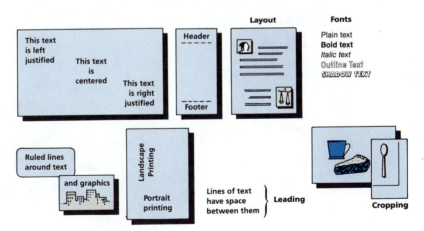

Figure 18.8
Examples of Some Publishing Terms

■ SYSTEM REQUIREMENTS

In order to achieve high-quality publishing results with the help of DTP software systems, certain hardware and software specifications must be met. The following sections discuss the necessary equipment and capabilities. Figure 18.9 illustrates a typical desktop publishing system.

Figure 18.9
A Desktop Publishing System

Hardware

Hardware components of a typical DTP microcomputer system include the system, storage media, a monitor, a mouse, a printer, and the scanner. See Figure 18.10 below.

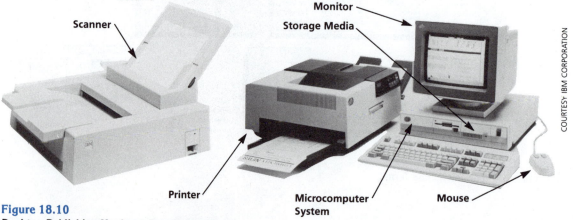

Figure 18.10
Desktop Publishing Hardware Requirements

The System. The microcomputer used in desktop publishing should have certain capabilities that facilitate the publishing process. Perhaps the most important characteristic of a system would be its speed of processing. Most DTP software packages will run slowly on the IBM PC-XT and compatibles because of the graphic display. Until a few years ago, almost all DTP software packages were designed for Apple Macintosh-based systems. Now, many DTP packages have been introduced for MS-DOS/PC-DOS-based systems.

The Storage. The storage capabilities of the system are also very important. Both RAM and secondary storage capacities must be adequate for the many applications of desktop publishing. Many DTP software packages require at least 640K of RAM and a hard disk for secondary storage.

Monitors. Standard monochrome monitors simply do not have the graphics range necessary to represent the printed page on the screen. Desktop publishing systems require a color graphic adapter (CGA), an enhanced graphic adapter (EGA), Hercules Graphics, or super-high-resolution controllers and compatible monitors.

Mouse. Many DTP software packages require a mouse, a device that allows the user to point at characters, objects, or menus on the screen. With the help of a mouse, the user can easily move blocks of text or graphics across a page or through the entire document.

Printer. Perhaps the most important hardware component of a desktop publishing system is the printer; two types of which are used in DTP: laser printers and dot-matrix printers, (see Chapter 2). Most DTP users assume they can use only a laser printer, but a dot-matrix printer with a large number of pins for creating higher resolution also can be used. On the other hand, laser printers provide much better resolution for quality printing. Printing quality is measured by the number of dots that form printed characters, known as **resolution**. Dot-matrix printers, while cost-effective, have limited graphics capabilities, with typical generated image densities of up to 150 dots per inch (dpi). By comparison, large, expensive typesetting machines start at 1,000 dpi, and laser printers now have resolutions of about 300 dpi.

Another factor is speed. Higher speeds of printing in laser printers are related to the size of the printer's internal memory. An increasing number of DTP software packages demand more internal printer memory. For instance, the new Hewlett-Packard laserjet printer is equipped with four million bytes of internal memory.

Scanner. Another useful hardware component for a DTP system is an image scanner. A **scanner** captures a text or a graphic image as a photocopier does, and stores it in a computer file. In the future, advanced scanners will eventually allow DTP users to scan a variety of text and graphics information that could be stored for further manipulation. See Figure 18.11 on the following page.

Figure 18.11
A Scanner

Software

Desktop publishing software packages integrate microcomputers into the publishing production process. Software allows users to select the layout, print fonts, and format of a publication. In the past few years, many DTP software packages have been introduced. The following sections discuss the characteristics of some of the most commonly used packages.

PageMaker. PageMaker, from Aldus Corporation of Seattle, Washington, is one of the pioneers in DTP software. It allows the user to insert images, boxes, or rules anywhere on the page, then reformat the text around it. This package allows up to 128 pages per file and 9,999 pages per document. However, PageMaker requires each page to be formatted and laid out separately. PageMaker does not offer style sheets, which makes it less desirable for long documents. This software package supports a variety of dot-matrix and laser printers.

Fontrix/Printrix. Fontrix/Printrix, from Data Transforms of Denver, Colorado, works with both dot-matrix and laser printers. Fontrix allows the user to develop simple art, technical symbols, foreign languages, and any number of fancy fonts. A mouse is highly recommended. On the other hand, Printrix commands control the page layout, including page size, margins, page numbering, headers and footers, and font selection. Both programs are menu-driven and have on-line help to make learning and use easy. Printrix can read text files prepared in WordStar, WordPerfect, Microsoft Word, or ASCII, without requiring additional formatting of text.

Harvard Professional Publisher. Harvard Professional Publisher, from Software Publishing of Mountain View, California, is a perfect package for both long and short documents. This software allows background gray scales or tints and reverse type, white on black. Furthermore, vertical justification, which aligns full columns on a page, is provided. This package accommodates a keyboard and function keys in place of a mouse to select menu options.

Ventura Publisher. Ventura Publisher, from Xerox Corporation of El Segundo, California, is a powerful DTP software package. This software supports layout control for headers and footers, justification, page and section numbering with Roman or Arabic numerals, and footnoting options. Ventura can read files directly from many word processing software packages, such as WordPerfect and WordStar, as well as ASCII files. This package supports almost a dozen dot-matrix and laser printers.

PagePerfect. PagePerfect, from IMSI of San Rafael, California, provides excellent word processing features, including a spelling checker and thesaurus. The software organizes graphic images through a software librarian, that makes the task of locating, selecting, and controlling images much easier. The package supports many layout options which can be implemented through PagePerfect's style sheet. It also supports different paragraph styles and makes background shades of gray and multiple background patterns available. There are many similarities between PagePerfect commands and those of the WordStar and MultiMate word processing packages.

FUTURE TRENDS AND ISSUES IN DESKTOP PUBLISHING

Electronic publishing covers a wide range, from the phenomenon of microcomputer-based desktop publishing to advanced photocomposition/computer work stations connected to mini- and mainframe computer systems. The latter is known as computer aided publishing.

The next trend in electronic publishing is to allow users who develop documents on their DTP systems to transfer these documents electronically to printing centers for mass duplication or for use in a larger document. With the recent telecommunications advances, it will not be long before DTP systems will be able to communicate with each other in order to share information and other resources.

Beyond desktop publishing, in the foreseeable future we will witness a new generation of desktop applications known as **desktop video production.** Within several years—at a cost of only a few thousand dollars—users will be able to edit video tape, perform sound mixing, generate low-end computer graphics such as titles and logos, experiment with special effects, and produce quality videos.

The primary reservation held regarding DTP is the possible erosion of high-quality procedures traditionally enforced in the publishing process. Many experts have voiced fears that lack of rigid quality control over what is published could hurt an organization utilizing DTP. To deal with this concern, many larger organizations using DTP have established new positions, including information designer, visual editor, and keeper of standards. The information designer establishes a working base for employees in other departments or positions. The main responsibility of the information designer is to organize content and design with company identity. The visual editor acts as a liaison between the writers and production artists. Finally, the keeper of standards' responsibility is to ensure that the image a company presents is consistent.

■ SUMMARY

Businesses invest a great deal of money and personnel in publishing a variety of documents such as letterhead, reports, proposals, training manuals, inventory lists, and brochures. In the past, the task of publishing was mainly handled by outside firms. In recent years, with the advent of a new publishing tool called desktop publishing (DTP), many organizations have managed to prepare high-quality publications. This new approach has eliminated some of the traditional stages of the publishing process. Today, one DTP user can design the format, layout, and other elements related to the appearance of a document in a few days or even a few hours, at a fraction of the cost of the traditional process.

Three major areas of desktop publishing discussed in this chapter are administrative, technical, and promotional. The benefits of desktop publishing include reduced time, cost savings, better control, less waste, better security, better communications, increased perceived value of services provided by the firm, and improved company image.

DTP system requirements include hardware and software. The necessary hardware components are a speedy microprocessor, a non-standard monochrome monitor (a color monitor or a standard monochrome monitor equipped with a graphics adapter), a mouse for command selection, a dot-matrix or laser printer, and possibly a scanner. In the area of software requirements, many DTP software packages are available that should be carefully examined before one is chosen. DTP software packages provide different features and require different hardware requirements.

■ KEY TERMS

desktop publishing (DTP) (electronic publishing) — A new microcomputer application that allows users to create high-quality publications, revolutionizing the traditional publishing process.

camera-ready copy — Text and graphics produced on ready-to-copy pages.

paste-up — The process of fixing the text and graphics on pages.

administrative applications of DTP — A company's formal internal documents, such as reports and employee safety manuals.

technical applications of DTP — A company's specification sheets and manuals.

promotional applications of DTP — A company's advertisements, logos, brochures, and the like.

resolution — The number of dots that form printed characters.

scanner — Hardware that captures a text or graphic image as a photocopier does and stores it in a computer file.

desktop video production A forthcoming generation of desktop applications that enables users to edit video tape, mix sound, generate computer graphics and special effects, and produce quality videos.

■ REVIEW QUESTIONS

1. In the traditional publishing method, _____ follows the conceptualization phase.
   (a) text preparation
   (b) writing
   (c) layout
   (d) editing
2. In the traditional approach, _____ involves the preparation of the actual text to be printed.
   (a) text preparation
   (b) layout
   (c) typesetting
   (d) editing
3. Which of the following is *not* a phase that is common to both the traditional and desktop publishing methods?
   (a) graphics
   (b) layout
   (c) publication
   (d) typesetting
4. The process of fixing the text and graphics on pages to be used by the printer is referred to as
   (a) layout.
   (b) paste-up.
   (c) preparation.
   (d) editing.
5. What is the main advantage of using software packages to prepare text?
6. What is the major difference between the traditional and desktop publishing approaches to publishing?
7. A principal reason for the popularity of desktop publishing is
   (a) economy.
   (b) effort.
   (c) graphics.
   (d) speed.
   (e) (a) and (d).
   (f) (b) and (c).
8. Which of the following is not an administrative application of desktop publishing?
   (a) proposals
   (b) correspondence
   (c) specifications
   (d) presentations
   (e) all are administrative applications

9. What are three major applications of desktop publishing?
10. Which of the following is *not* a benefit of desktop publishing?
    (a) less cost
    (b) less waste
    (c) better control
    (d) better quality
    (e) reduced time
11. Pica type is equivalent to _____ points.
    (a) 6
    (b) 12
    (c) 24
    (d) 18
12. The _____ is the style and size of a character within a type family.
    (a) point
    (b) layout
    (c) font
    (d) pica
13. Describe the four kinds of justification.
14. What does WYSIWYG stand for, and why is it important?
15. _____ components of a desktop publishing system include a monitor, a printer, and storage media.
    (a) CPU
    (b) Hardware
    (c) Software
    (d) PC
16. Until a few years ago, DTP software packages were designed for _____ systems.
    (a) IBM-PC
    (b) Apple Macintosh
    (c) mainframe
    (d) Apple II
17. What is the drawback in PageMaker that makes it undesirable for lengthy publications?
18. What is desktop video production?
19. Your company is a medium-sized manufacturing firm, employing about 1,000 individuals. Primary data processing requirements are handled by a small mainframe computer. However, report generation and word processing are accomplished using IBM-PCs and high-quality dot-matrix printers. Your position is Manager, Administrative Services. The company president has asked you to begin publishing a weekly newsletter for all employees; but he doesn't want to invest a large amount of money, just in case the newsletter is not popular. What combination of hardware and software would you purchase? Why?
20. With the advent of desktop publishing, many small companies have started producing newsletters and brochures in-house, whereas before they would have had much of the work done outside, or not at all. Comment on how you think this has affected other companies whose sole business is printing and publishing. What do you think will happen in the future?

Case One:
BCTA Enterprises

Bob, Carol, Ted, and Alice were all journalism majors at Central State. Upon graduation, the four decided to go into business together publishing brochures, pamphlets, newsletters, and the like for local small businesses.

BCTA Enterprises started off with eight clients; within three years, the list has grown to forty, and more firms want their services.

Initially, the firm had two IBM-PCs for word processing of their products and for the necessary business records and accounting data associated with BCTA. Now, with their client list growing, they are finding that this setup is not adequate. Since business has improved, BCTA has hired two associate editors and a part-time accountant.

Bob, President of BCTA, wants to modernize, but he is also concerned about the bottom line. He would like to expand their hardware to include facilities for the two associate editors and a dedicated system for accounting.

Carol, the business manager, also realizes that they need more facilities, wants to equip all editorial personnel with PCs, and thinks that the accountant could share one of the editorial computers. She feels that, this way, all of her existing (and potential) clients could be served in a timely manner and the firm would still have the computerized records available.

Alice has a different idea. She has been following the advent of desktop publishing systems and feels that BCTA needs to break into the '90s. She is proposing that they purchase two additional microcomputers (IBM-PS/2 Model 60) and the necessary support hardware and software for all four to run a desktop system. This way, she argues, they can maximize their return by keeping expenditures to a minimum and still service their customers because of the flexibility and power offered by desktop publishing.

The majority of BCTA's workload consists of multi-fold brochures, four- to eight-page pamphlets, and single-page, double-sided newsletters. Occasionally, a client requires a more lengthy document, but this is rare.

Questions

1. What is the problem?
2. What are BCTA's system requirements?
3. What are the alternative courses of action available to BCTA?
4. What do you recommend?

Case Two:
MULTI-FACTURE

Multi-Facture is a medium-sized manufacturing firm that fabricates custom assemblies for other industries. They employ about 1,000 workers and have an office and management staff of fifty. Since its founding in 1975, Multi-Facture has enjoyed reasonable growth and is planning a major capital expansion to improve production operations. This expansion will also mean the addition of about 300 workers and twenty staff members.

Multi-Facture has always attempted to keep its employees happy. Long before it became fashionable, Multi-Facture conducted regular meetings between management and hourly workers to improve operations and conditions. A secretary was made available for a weekly newsletter, which was written and distributed by the workers.

Recently, however, employee communications have become even more important. With the expansion project, the workers have generated numerous questions regarding seniority and new job availability. Also, a need has arisen to improve communication with the community, both to answer questions about the expansion and to advertise for additional business.

Multi-Facture's Manager of Employee Relations, Joe Blutarski, has been given the task of providing an internal and external communication system. Joe is a recent MBA graduate of Midtown State University, where he learned how to use microcomputers in several of his courses and was introduced to the concept of desktop publishing. He recommended that Multi-Facture invest in a desktop system, which would give them the capabilities that they need.

Joe's recommendation received glowing praise from Multi-Facture's president, and Joe was assigned to carry through with the idea. Encouraged, Joe went to the local business computer center, ComputerPlace, and told them what he wanted to do. The salesman at ComputerPlace was equally excited, and proceeded to put together a system.

Two months later Joe has a problem. The equipment from ComputerPlace arrived two weeks ago, and he spent most of a week getting everything connected. He and the secretary that had been typing the employee newsletter spent days working with the system and the software trying to get everything to work, but with little success. Finally, the secretary went back to her typewriter, which she knew how to operate, so that this week's newsletter could be printed.

Joe tried going back to ComputerPlace, but the salesman he had dealt with was no longer working there and no one at the store had any familiarity with any of the hardware or software that he had purchased. Joe's system includes an Apple Macintosh II, a laser printer, a dot-matrix printer, and Page-Maker software. Joe also purchased a 9,600 baud modem so that he could transmit data to his typesetter.

Questions

1. What is the main problem here?
2. What should Joe have done differently?
3. What are Joe's alternatives?
4. What do you recommend to Joe?

SELECTED BIBLIOGRAPHY

Allman, D. and E. Owens, "Confused? Use This Guide to Choose Your DTP Software," *Data Management*, May 1987, pp. 14–17.

Antonoff, M., "Setting Up For Desktop Publishing," *Personal Computing*, July 1987, pp. 75–82.

Hurst, R., "Desktop Publishing," *Computerworld*, March 4, 1987.

James, R., "Desktop Publishing: Boon or Boondoggle?," *Business Marketing*, March 1987, pp. 78–83.

Jarvis, P., "Desktop Publishing: Is It For Every Office?," *The Office*, June 1987, pp. 65–68.

Makley, W., "In-House Publishing: It Can Save Time and Money," *The Office*, June 1987, pp. 79–82.

Nolan, M., "The Communicator's Constitution," *Business Software Review*, August 1987, pp. 36–39.

Oefterling, A., "Everybody a Publisher," *MW*, February/March 1987, pp. 42–43.

Sheldon, G., "Desktop Publishing on Compaq Computers," *Compaq*, Fall/Winter 1986, pp. 54–63.

Wolff, B., "An Accountant's Guide to Desktop Publishing," *Computers In Accounting*, July/August 1987, pp. 71–96.

_____, "Putting The Finishing Touches On Electronic Publishing," *Modern Office Technology*, July 1987, pp. 60–66.

Part VIII

APPENDICES

Appendix A
INTRODUCTION TO THE SUNSHINE WINDOW INC., SUPPLIERS CASE

Appendix B
TEN SAMPLE CASES

Appendix C
ADVANCED DOS COMMANDS

Appendix D
ADVANCED FEATURES OF WORDPERFECT

Appendix E
ADVANCED FEATURES OF LOTUS 1-2-3

Appendix F
ADVANCED FEATURES OF dBASE III PLUS

Appendix G
ANSWERS TO REVIEW QUESTIONS

Appendix A

Introduction to the Sunshine Window Inc., Suppliers Case

Sunshine Window Inc., Suppliers (SWIS) is an emerging company in the window and door wholesale market. (A wholesaler is a middleman positioned between the manufacturer and the retailer.) SWIS sells finished window and door products to retailers, who then sell the products to the consumer.

SWIS began operations in July 1985. Martine A. Martinez and Chico A. Gonzales were the owners and sole employees at that time. Their major tasks included ordering products and selling them to the local home and building supply centers. SWIS's office and warehouse is located in an old building in Capitaltown, Pennsylvania. Originally, the company sold only to home centers in Dauphin County, but business has expanded to include four more central-Pennsylvania counties. Along with this growth in market territory has come an increase in the number of employees and the number of business problems. The company has experienced considerable growth since its incorporation in 1985 and is encountering problems handling its growing amount of business information.

SWIS has grown because of its excellent customer service. Because it serves a limited area, the company is closer to the retailer and therefore provides faster delivery and lower distribution costs than the manufacturers. In recent months, customers have complained that orders are late, the wrong products are being delivered, and response time to inquiries has lengthened. The owners, Martinez and Gonzales, do not have adequate sources of information for planning and decision making. Inventory planning is virtually nonexistent. Furthermore, productivity in clerical areas has been decreasing due to the volume of work. Files are lost or misplaced, and recorded data is inconsistent. Manual typing of repetitive work wastes valuable time. Martinez and Gonzales have been concerned over the increasing number of problems and decided to hire an office manager approximately two months ago.

Sandy Cofman, a secretary working toward a business administration degree from the local college, was selected for the position of office manager. Her duties included overseeing customer service, clerical responsibilities, and managing information. Because Sandy was new to SWIS, she wanted to understand the company's structure and the responsibilities of its employees. After working at SWIS for two months, Sandy was surprised by the success of the operation, given the procedures currently established for managing information.

At the time of her hiring, Sandy was enrolled in a microcomputer applications class. As she learned new concepts in class, she realized a micro-based information system would help solve many of SWIS's problems. Sandy discussed the idea of a micro-based information system at a status meeting with SWIS's owners.

Chico Gonzales and Martine Martinez did not respond favorably to the idea. Chico thought computers would only create more work for the already overworked office personnel. He was afraid the clerical staff would be angry if they were given additional responsibilities on fancy equipment. Martine was primarily concerned with the cost of a computer system; she did not feel a company of SWIS's size could afford a computer system. Martine said they could not afford high-priced computer programmers, either.

Sandy Cofman assured both of them that current technology in microcomputer applications is saving many companies a substantial amount of money. In the case of SWIS, she asserted, the appropriate microcomputer system and software applications would save the company valuable time and money. The clerical personnel could perform many of their duties more efficiently and also provide additional information resources to management. Sandy pointed out that microcomputers are reasonably priced, and that SWIS could afford a micro-based information system. A microcomputer's acquisition cost differs greatly from that of a large mainframe computer. She explained that SWIS would not have to hire special computer programmers for a micro-based system. Microcomputers and microcomputer software are designed with the user not a trained computer professional, in mind, she said.

Chico and Martine were still hesitant about the idea of computers in their business; however, they were willing to listen to Sandy's suggestions. To draw up an appropriate plan, Sandy evaluated SWIS's past and present needs. The following paragraphs provide background information about SWIS, specifically regarding the company's business operations and personnel.

■ BACKGROUND INFORMATION AND BUSINESS OPERATIONS

Manufacturers and Customers

SWIS started with one main product, storm windows, which they purchased form their largest manufacturer, Protect Company. SWIS still buys large quantities of these windows. Large orders mean a lower cost per unit; therefore, SWIS can offer a good price to retailers. Home & Building Outlet was their first retail customer and still is their largest customer today.

After their first year of operation, Chico and Martine decided to expand their product line to include patio windows and doors. Eventually, they offered a range of specialty products. They buy most of their products from medium-sized regional manufacturers. SWIS purchases only high-quality products. The manufacturers are not the best-known in the industry, but they do incorporate important features in their window products. SWIS emphasizes these quality features to its customers.

SWIS purchases items from five main manufacturers. From Protect Company, the firm buys the original product, storm windows. Most of its patio windows and doors come from Daylight Company. Glassy Company provides home products that include windows; the sliding glass doors and French doors SWIS sells usually come from Glassy Company. Bob & Son Company manufactures several specialty items; Chico feels Bob & Son offers the best value for the money when it comes to specialty items, such as bow windows and decorative windows. SWIS began buying products from Skylight Company, a new manufacturer, this year. Their side windows for bathroom skylights seem to be selling well.

SWIS's best customers are home and building supply centers. Home & Building Outlet and Handyman Supply are SWIS's largest customers. So far this year, SWIS has earned $300,000 in sales revenue, and projects $460,000 in revenue by year's end. In their first year of operation, SWIS totalled $380,000 in sales. Sales have been climbing at a steady rate of approximately ten percent since that time. Chico feels there are other potential customers in their market area, but SWIS is not prepared to handle an increased volume of orders at this time.

Personnel

To market all these products, SWIS has two sales representatives. SWIS added one representative, in addition to Chico and Martine, in the second year of operation, and one more in the third. The two sales representatives are paid a five percent commission on all sales. They sell SWIS window products to home and building centers in south-central Pennsylvania, where sales territories are divided geographically by salesperson (see Figure A.1).

The company has a staff of five support people in addition to the two sales representatives. Fred Hammak, the warehouse supervisor, oversees one stockroom person. Sandy Cofman

Figure A.1
SWIS Sales Territories

manages one inventory/order clerk and a part-time administrative clerk. Chico Gonzales, co-owner, serves as president, while Martine Martinez, the other co-owner, is vice president. Figure A.2 shows a diagram of the company's current organizational chart.

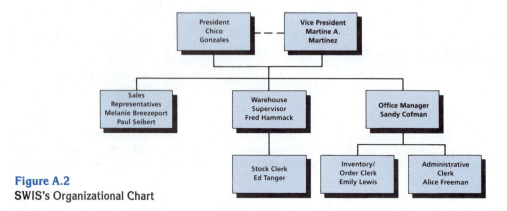

Figure A.2
SWIS's Organizational Chart

Warehouse Personnel. The warehouse personnel, Fred Hammak and Ed Tanger, fill orders and deliver them to customers by truck. When an order is received from the manufacturer, Fred sends a note to the inventory/order clerk, indicating the products received. The note lists product numbers, quantities, and manufacturing company information. Fred has been with the company since 1986, and he does not like the problems he has experienced recently with inventory stock. SWIS has always given the extra effort to make sure customers had the products they needed. Fred complains that, in recent months, the warehouse never seems to have the products customers need. SWIS has too many of the slow-moving items in stock, and not enough of the popular products. The warehouse has an increasing number of special inventory orders because normally stocked items are not available.

Inventory/Order Clerk. Emily Lewis, the inventory/order clerk, joined SWIS six months after Fred Hammak was hired. She keeps track of all inventory records on products ordered from manufacturers, as well as records on customer deliveries. Both Chico and Martine agree that Emily Lewis has been given too many responsibilities. Emily tracks the inventory, and assists in answering customer problems. Sandy Cofman has suggested Emily's workload could decrease if they changed the way she performs her duties.

Emily has her own method of organizing her work; only she knows where everything is. Both Chico and Martine have said that they waste a great deal of time trying to find inventory records when Emily is not available to locate files for them.

Emily keeps two separate filing systems for inventory. One file card box is organized alphabetically by product, and updated when Fred sends Emily a delivery notice. Sample product cards are illustrated in Figure A.3 on the following page. The product cards list the product number, description, cost, and price. The cards also indicate the current balance on hand, the reorder point, and the manufacturer's name. When Emily first tracked inventory, she had enough time to check the files weekly to determine if any products were needed. Emily is so busy now that she usually orders more products when Fred tells her the warehouse is running low. By the time Fred tells her supplies are low, it is usually too late to obtain products from the manufacturer in time for the next customer delivery.

Product #	Description	Cost	Price	Balance on Hand	Reorder	Mftg.
111	Bow Window	69.95	53.92	112	24	Bob & Son
Product #	Description	Cost	Price	Balance on Hand	Reorder	Mftg.
212	Patio Door #2	210.00	254.00	25	15	Daylight Co.

Figure A.3
SWIS's Product Inventory Cards

Emily keeps a second file card box for each manufacturer. She uses this file box for ordering. A company name and address are listed on each card, along with the product numbers of a particular item from that company, the quantity ordered, and the last order date. Figure A.4 represents Emily's manufacturer order cards. If products are not received from the manufacturer as expected, Emily must manually search through all the file cards to locate the most recent order request. This is a very tedious and time-consuming task. Sandy Cofman has recommended that this manufacturer order information be available in a format to which Chico Gonzales and Martine A. Martinez could also have access.

Product #	Manufacturer	Address	Qty Ordered	Date
213	Daylight Co.	K St. Buck, NY 11111	20	3/12/87
Product #	Manufacturer	Address	Qty Ordered	Date
114	Bob & Son Co.	L St. Mody, NY 12222	45	4/20/87

Figure A.4
SWIS's Manufacturer Order Cards

Administrative Clerk. When SWIS expanded their market in 1986 to include several more counties, they hired a part-time administrative clerk, Alice Freeman, to help Emily. However, Alice has never become involved in Emily's work. Once Alice suggested sending a mailing to potential customers when a new product was being sold by SWIS. The response was favorable, so SWIS has continued the practice of mass mailings when new products or special discounts are being offered. Alice spends most of her time typing these form letters on a manual typewriter. Alice also hand-sorts all the letters by zip code to save SWIS postage costs.

In order to prepare the mass mailings, Alice keeps a log of all customer information. Her log contains the customer number, name, and address. She also records the last time the customer ordered products from SWIS and the type of products purchased. This manual list undergoes frequent revisions. If a better method existed for preparing the mailings, Alice would have time available to help Emily.

In addition to these duties, Alice prepares and types all office correspondence for SWIS. She types all letters, memos, reports, and forms on her manual typewriter. If she prepares a draft for one of Martine's reports to a local bank, she must completely retype the draft to obtain a final copy for mailing. Frequently, Alice types form letters for distribution to employees, or standardized letters to manufacturers. These forms cause a highly repetitive and time-consuming process because Alice must individually type each document.

Management Personnel

Chico Gonzales, SWIS's President, works primarily on strategic planning for customer service and sales. He evaluates potential products and the sales of existing product lines to determine their profitability. For that task, Chico needs more information on orders by manufacturers. It currently takes Chico several days to determine the order levels of the different manufacturers because he has to search through all of Emily's file cards and individual manufacturer order transaction records.

Martine A. Martinez's contribution to the company is ensuring business solvency. SWIS usually has to pay for its products before the money for goods sold is collected from its customers. The cost of the goods sold represents fifty percent of SWIS's total sales. Martine makes arrangements with banks for financing inventory purchases. It is difficult to negotiate with the banks for money to buy new products when Martine cannot accurately identify the level of inventory on hand.

Martine also needs better information to project sales levels. She has great difficulty preparing an accurate sales analysis because she cannot figure out Emily's recordkeeping system. Reports on expected sales levels indicate SWIS's future profitability; if it looks as though future sales levels are not going to be high enough to cover expected future expenses, Martine could plan actions to ensure continued operations. The accounting firm that handles SWIS's bookkeeping provides adequate information on expenses, but Martine lacks the necessary sales information.

Martine and Chico agree that the main objective of SWIS is to provide high-quality products to its customers, while maintaining a high level of customer service. To further this goal, they have decided to explore new processes to increase the productivity and efficiency of their business practices. Martine and Chico have agreed that Sandy Cofman could start an investigation into the possibility of developing a micro-based information system to manage the company's information. For the next three months, Sandy Cofman followed the concepts and techniques, and applications of various microcomputer software packages that are discussed throughout this book.

Appendix B

Ten Sample Cases

Sample Case One:
INFORMATION PROCESSORS' ASSOCIATION

Information Processors' Association (IPA) is a student group organized to educate students about the field of computers and their operations. Any full-time student of a college or university who is not employed full-time is eligible to join IPA. IPA helps student members majoring in information processing and related fields of study broaden their knowledge and become more effective in their studies by offering an arena for the exchange of ideas and career development. As a management-oriented, nonprofit organization, the primary objective of IPA is to foster a better understanding of the vital relationship of information processing to management and society.

In 1975, IPA established its Education Foundation to provide leadership in identifying educational needs and opportunities for the information systems professional and, in particular, for IPA's members. The Foundation consists of people actively involved in information processing careers.

Regional IPA chapters meet once a month, offering educational programs that inform members of new developments in the field, new aspects of existing hardware, software, and techniques, and about IPA itself. Chapters also conduct seminars and technical sessions on specific topics. IPA's members, more than 50,000 worldwide, take part in these and other self-improvement programs to maintain and increase their skills in an occupation where information rapidly becomes obsolete.

The IPA chapter at Blue State University (BSU) was founded in 1968, and was originally designed for students planning a career in information processing and related fields. The chapter has an approximate annual budget of $5,000. Of this amount, members earn approximately $1,500 from selling subs and T-shirts. The balance comes from the SGA, the Student Government Association. The college administration allots the SGA a sum of money each year to help clubs and organizations when budgets run short (see Figure B.1).

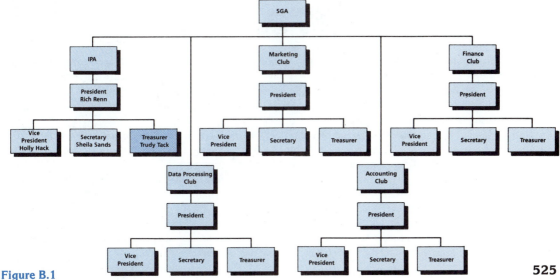

Figure B.1
The IPA Organizational Chart

The head of BSU's information systems program, Ben Brown, is also the college's IPA advisor. Ben has his Ph.D in Computer Applications from Plam University. He believes that every computer major should become a member of IPA because, he says, "Complete professional development requires knowledge that goes beyond the classroom." He feels this is especially true in a profession where the textbooks are, very often, obsolete before they are printed. Ben feels IPA complements classroom studies by providing students with opportunities to exchange information with members of the information processing community and to explore various career opportunities. The organization also gives regular IPA parent chapter members an opportunity to give insight and guidance to future generations of computer students.

The major problem confronting the IPA chapter at BSU is that all records of the organization's life cycle are still kept manually. This system is cumbersome and involves excess paper-shuffling. BSU does have available on its premises a mainframe computer system. However, the only students that utilize this mainframe system presently are students who take classes in which these units are used.

Ben Brown feels IPA should convert the present manual system to a computerized one. He has suggested to Rich, the IPA president, that this be done. Rich plans to suggest the idea to Sheila, the secretary of the organization, to see how she feels about it.

The IPA treasurer, Trudy Tack, has to keep track of all of money, receipts, vouchers, and reports to the president by means of the manual system. Since this is her first month as treasurer, she doesn't want to make "waves" by suggesting a more efficient way, but she knows the present system is cumbersome and a waste of time.

Aside from these problems, the parent IPA chapter, also located at BSU, would like to be able to access certain data resources used by the student chapter in full-screen format. This cannot be done using the mainframe computer system. Members of the parent chapter feel that this ability to access data resources will provide needed information to the parent organization, which keeps track of the student chapters' activities to make awards and guide their operations.

You have been chosen to make some recommendations to Ben Brown, the club advisor. What type of a system is needed for the IPA organization? The organization is in an awkward situation, being a computer organization and still using ancient methods of recordkeeping.

The IPA has no budget to use the university mainframe computer system, but if desired, they can get hooked into the system. There is also one room full of microcomputers that they could utilize, if needed. What would you suggest?

Sample Case Two:
ACCOUNTANTS ANONYMOUS, INC.

Diana and Amanda are both full-time accountants who work for private accounting firms. Since accounting is such a lucrative business—especially during the tax season—Diana and Amanda decided to open a part-time accounting agency of their own in their free time. These two bright accountants did not want their employers to know they were opening a business on the side—since it would undoubtedly take away some of their employers' business; hence, they named their business Accountants Anonymous, Inc.

Through word of mouth, this evenings-and-Saturdays-only business flourished. Tax accounting is a tedious, time-consuming task, so many people gladly pay to have their tax forms completed for them. This service industry is a growing one, and Diana and Amanda wanted to get in on the action.

Tax service is not the only accounting function that Accountants Anonymous performs. They do balance sheets, income statements, monthly, quarterly, and yearly financial statements, portfolio analysis, and any other accounting functions their clients need.

This accounting concern has grown significantly since it first began three years ago, to the point where Diana and Amanda find it difficult to meet their deadlines. At present, the main problem is preparing monthly statements on time. These monthly statements consist of both a balance sheet and an income statement.

The present system is a manual one. Data are received from a client once a month, in the form of checkbook stubs, pay stubs or other pay records, sales records such as a sales journal and sales receipts, and bank deposit statements.

Once the data are received, Diana or Amanda prepares a worksheet manually, with double entries entered for each transaction. Double-entry accounting consists of debiting and crediting an amount for each entry, whether the entry is for a check written, income received, or a miscellaneous adjustment.

After all entries—sometimes hundreds for one client during a single month—are made by hand, totals must be obtained. Diana and Amanda each own an adding machine, which helps to accurately add columns of numbers. These totals are then posted to a general ledger. The balance sheet is then prepared, showing the current balances in the appropriate accounts. The income statement is also prepared at this time. This is also a detailed statement consisting of income, expenses, and profit or loss figures for the current period, as well as year-to-date amounts. This laborious task is done monthly for certain clients.

This system has worked well in the past, but since business has continued to grow by word of mouth, it has become increasingly more difficult to prepare the statements in a timely manner. Another problem plagues the accountants. In order to attract more clients—preferably those with larger accounts— Accountants Anonymous would have to be able to deliver even longer, more detailed reports. This is not an easy task for accountants using manual systems. Also, some kind of a typing system would be needed for promotional activities because letters would need to be typed for advertisements in the local newspapers. The company would still be called Accountants Anonymous, Inc., but would advertise in order to increase business even more. Several types of form letters would be needed: one to advertise in newspapers, one for advertising in business magazines, and one each for advertising in legal and medical magazines.

Since they want to get into stocks and bonds servicing, Diana and Amanda would need to be able to contact Wall Street, Dow Jones, and Moody's, either by telephone or some other way, to keep up to date on prices and sales. With their present manual system, they are not able to access these highly developed areas of the business.

Diana and Amanda would also like to use graphs in their monthly reports for most of their clients and also for their own sales projections and forecasts. Manual graphs take hours to complete. Since most highly successful accounting firms and financial planners provide graphical presentations of items such as balance sheets and income statements, Diana and Amanda feel it would be in their best interests to purchase and utilize some type of a graphics instrument. Graphs are invaluable because of the large quantity of data they can display and because of the way they facilitate the interpretation and analysis of data.

Since its beginning, Accountants Anonymous, Inc., has increased its yearly earnings by twenty-five percent. This is a twelve to fourteen percent greater increase than they receive at their daytime accounting positions. Diana and Amanda do not particularly want to hire additional help; they would rather quit their full-time jobs. However, at the rate their business is growing, they may have to quit their jobs *and* hire five additional people to take care of the increase.

Still, accounting is a very tedious, time-consuming profession for two people to handle, especially since their clients are growing at a rate of five percent every year. The financial reports are long, and with larger accounts, more time will be required in preparing these statements and entering figures in the ledgers.

Although it is not needed immediately, a detailed monthly report of amounts posted to the general ledger will someday be required. Also, listings of the following journals will be needed in the very near future:

1. Cash Receipts Journal
2. Cash Disbursements Journal
3. Sales Journal
4. General Adjustment Journal

To keep accurate journals such as these, Diana and Amanda will have to put in sixty or more hours a week. Journal-keeping is an extremely tedious task, especially keeping each of these journals for every client.

Diana and Amanda want their business to prosper, but realize the need to have their tedious workloads cut down. They want to continue to accept new clients but need some advice on how to lessen the manual labor.

Diana has hired you as a consultant. She is the office manager, and she wants you to give her some suggestions to reduce the manual labor. Suggest ways to help her solve this problem.

Sample Case Three:
BETSY'S BASKETS, INC.

Bowman's Orchards, a family business, was established three decades ago. Originally, fruits were the only product line. The seasonal business began with strawberries in early summer, and progressed through the summer and into fall with cherries, peaches, and apples. The store remained open during the fruit season (the months of May through December).

Over the years, the orchard business became popular with the surrounding community. Seeing that the successful fruit business grossed $5,000 per month, the family expanded the product line to include poultry, vegetables, and canned goods. This profitable growth allowed the business to become a year-round operation rather than a seasonal one. Five years ago, Mr. and Mrs. Bowman's only daughter, Betsy—a talented, innovative woman—decided to perform an experiment to help increase sales.

Betsy decided to make fruit baskets during the Christmas season to increase business during this already busy time. This idea boosted sales by about a thousand dollars a week during the festive holiday season, and has gained appeal since then. Today, the greatest sales of fruit baskets still occur during the Christmas season but, with today's health-conscious Americans, fruit baskets are sold on a daily basis at Bowman Orchards. Buyers give fruit baskets as gifts for birthdays, to hospital patients, and at Easter-time. Fruit is enjoyed by just about everyone and can be eaten by dieters, diabetics, and people with various health problems. It is one of Nature's most perfect foods. It can be eaten in its natural form—no cooking or preparation is needed. In most cases, it can be just peeled and eaten. It's no wonder the fruit basket business is thriving.

The current fruit basket operation provides a wide range of selection for the customer. The display normally consists of thirty to forty baskets of ten different sizes, shapes, and styles. Special orders are also taken. Prices for the baskets range from $5 to $45, depending on what fruit is included.

The clerk enters all special orders into an order book according to the day the customer wishes to pick up the basket. The customer has the option of either picking up the basket himself or having it delivered—just as flowers are—to a specific address on a certain day. In either case, the basket must be paid for when ordered.

Bowman's fruit baskets are constructed in two stages. The first stage consists of placing the fruit into the basket and arranging it in an attractive fashion; an exact count is taken of the number and type of fruit placed in each basket. The next stage is adding the final touches: taping the fruit in place, adding nuts, candy, canned meat, or decorative items, covering the entire basket and fruit with colored cellophane, and then adding a small card and bows, if requested.

Special baskets normally take Betsy twenty minutes to construct. There is no additional cost for a special basket, but they do need to be ordered in advance. During a holiday season—particularly Christmas, Easter, or Mother's Day—Betsy has one assistant to help her make up these special fruit baskets, since this is the busiest season for special orders. Usually, a basket must be ordered one week in advance during the winter season and a day or two in advance during the off season.

The major problem with the current system is inefficiency, which has led to dissatisfied customers. Since Bowman's prides itself on customer satisfaction, even one unhappy customer is too many, especially in a specialty area such as fruit baskets, according to the owner, Mr. Bowman.

The main problems the Bowmans have encountered are in the areas of:

(1) *Customer information.* Sometimes certain customer information is not recorded. It is difficult, time-consuming, and sometimes impossible to retrieve this information.
(2) *Basket construction.* Since orders are entered under the appropriate order day on a first-come, first-served basis, it is difficult to manually sort the numerous orders by date of pick-up or delivery. This leads to mistakes, which in turn might cause an order to be late.
(3) *Completed baskets.* Once the baskets are completed, they are brought from the construction table and taken to a storage area until date of delivery or pick-up. In haste, sometimes the baskets are not labeled; then clerks must sort through the order book to identify which orders have been completed. Sometimes unlabeled orders are carried out onto the sales floor and sold as ordinary fruit baskets.
(4) *Inventory records.* There are no inventory records as to the number of baskets and the amount of paraphernalia needed to complete the baskets. This often causes shortages of the most popular basket styles, leading to modifications in basket orders and unhappy customers.

Besides the problems just listed, Betsy needs to be able to do a cost analysis of her business. How much do her supplies cost? She needs to know which is her best-selling basket. She also needs to be able to do an income projection.

In addition, Betsy needs a mechanism by which she can accurately keep track of her baskets in storage, without physically counting them. She wants to be able to prevent shortages on the best-selling baskets. She also needs to keep an accurate inventory of the baskets that do not move so that they are not reordered.

Betsy has consulted you to help her alleviate these problems. Suggest ways to make her fruit basket operation more efficient.

Sample Case Four:
PEONY AREA COMMUNITY COLLEGE

Peony Area Community College (PACC) is a two-year college designed to meet the varied needs of the residents of the south-central region of Iowa. As the state's first community college, established more than twenty years ago, PACC has been a leader in the nationwide movement to offer higher education to everyone in the community.

PACC is an open admissions college. A student need not have taken a college preparatory program in high school to gain admission. In fact, any student eighteen years of age or older may enroll in courses. However, the college may impose certain preparatory requirements and place other limitations on enrollment in particular programs.

PACC is prepared to help students pursue almost any academic or career interest. It offers certificate programs for thirty hours of work in career-related courses and Associate in Arts degrees for completion of at least sixty hours of work in courses leading to careers in more than thirty-five areas.

PACC's Allied Health Division, which is in the nursing curriculum, is one of the areas that has special admission procedures. Students in this particular program are being prepared for employment as nurses in hospitals, doctors' offices, and extended care facilities. The program is designed to lead directly to an occupation and is not intended as a transfer program. Students choosing to enter this program are subject to special admissions procedures, based on college placement scores and past academic performance, that are more stringent than general PACC admission requirements.

These special admittance requirements demand an inordinate amount of processing time. Data must be gathered from several sources, including high school grade transcripts and prior work experience, if any. Then the data must be collated, ranked, and evaluated in light of requirements.

The Allied Health Division is PACC's third largest division, the second largest being Police Science, and the largest, Business Administration (see Figure B.2). The Allied Health Division has Dr. Arthur Aldwin as its head and coordinator, and five professors serving as faculty members. There are three secretaries and two clerks. With this limited support staff, and with the possibility of personnel cuts in all departments within the coming year, the clerical tasks of processing applications have been falling more often upon Dr. Aldwin's shoulders. These added clerical tasks rob Dr. Aldwin of time he should use for more productive activities and more important counseling duties.

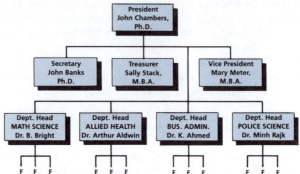

Figure B.2
Organizational Chart for Peony Area Community College

PACC's campus is equipped with computer facilities. There is no mainframe system, but there is one microcomputer lab with twenty-five microcomputers networked together, and a Data General MV 10000 (minicomputer) lab with twenty terminals located in Rocker Hall on the second floor. The Data General system is used for both learning classes and administrative tasks. The microcomputers are used mainly by professors and students for course-related activities.

Several PACC professors have access to micros located in some faculty offices. Other faculty members can use one of the micros in the computer lab between classes.

When a student first registers with the college, all pertinent information is entered into a terminal that is accessed by all staff who participate in or have anything to do with registration. Personal as well as grade information can then be obtained by anyone involved in the scheduling and registration process.

The only problem with this system is that the individual departments are not hooked into the Data General system that the registration people use. Therefore, there is tedious, time-consuming, repetitive questioning of the student and re-entering of this information by an advisor. Errors occur as some information is inadvertently forgotten or typed incorrectly into the computer. When a student registers, the nursing department has no way to tell if a particular class is full because they are not hooked up to the registrar's system.

There are also word processing, budgeting, and other information processing needs that are accomplished throughout the department by both faculty and staff. Letters are constantly being mailed out to students, school districts, and various other places. Currently, several microcomputers are used for word processing. There is a problem with software packages. One copy—two at the most—of each software package is purchased on the market. Since there are legal implications and high fines associated with copying software, staff heads think the micros should be linked together so everyone can share the software packages. This linkage would cut down on the costs of purchasing more than one copy of a software package. Most packages cost between $500 and $600, so this would save thousands of dollars in the long run.

There is another problem: not every micro is hooked to a printer. When this is the case, the person using a micro with no printer must finish typing, save the document to diskette, remove the diskette, and find an available micro that is hooked up to a printer. This can be time-consuming and frustrating, as there may be no available printer because every micro hooked to a printer is in use.

In such an intense program as nursing, with the numerous prerequisites for courses and all the additional information that is needed, students and faculty are becoming increasingly disgusted with the amount of time it takes to process the data. Clerks and secretaries do not have easy access to registration information; often, they have to physically walk across the campus grounds to other buildings to get this information.

It seems some type of a device needs to be added so that all of the computers can communicate with each other, thereby reducing much wasted time.

You have been chosen to help the Allied Health Division solve its problem. What can be done to cut down on wasted time?

Sample Case Five:
UNITED BRETHREN CHURCH

The United Brethren Church (UBC), founded in 1921, is located in a small community just outside of Middletown, Maine. Middletown is a city of about 35,000, and the UBC is one of only two Protestant churches serving the area. Currently, 1,000 residents of Middletown and surrounding communities make up the UBC's congregation.

The UBC has two Sunday worship services, one at 8:30 a.m. and the other at 11:00 a.m. It also has several Sunday School classes: one for adults, one for senior citizens, one for young adults, and one for children. The children's Sunday School class is broken down into several age groups. There is also a nursery provided for babies and children under two years of age.

Approximately 300 members attend one of the two worship services on a weekly basis. Church membership has remained relatively level since about 1941. Prior to that, membership had increased at a rate of eight percent per year for the first twenty years.

The mortgage on the church was paid in 1951. By 1971, there was enough money in the UBC escrow account to put a down payment on a parsonage for the paster and his family. There is a thirty-year mortgage on this property. The parsonage is a small, one-family dwelling.

The primary source of income for the church is offerings—donations from individual members of the congregation and occasionally, from non-members in the community. On average, about $600 is collected weekly at the Sunday worship services and Sunday School combined, with slightly more—a few hundred dollars—collected during the Christmas, Easter, and Lenten seasons. A secondary source of income is payments from trusts, which comes to about $50,000 per year. Income is also generated through fund raisers such as bingo, held weekly in the social hall located in the basement of the church, and a yearly bazaar to which members of the congregation donate their time and effort by making handcrafts, needlework and baked goods. These fundraisers taken together, generate about $10,000 per year.

The UBC pays the salaries of the pastor, office manager, groundskeeper, and maintenance person. The church's mortgage payment includes only the parsonage, since the church and land now belong to the members of UBC. Utilities include electricity, water, sewage, and telephone. A maintenance fund is also required for work not done by the groundskeeper, such as plumbing or other major repairs. Monthly disbursements are usually between $6,000 and $6,500. If major repairs or expenditures are needed, more money is disbursed.

Occasionally, improvements need to be made to the church, including repair to the pews, carpeting, pulpit, and other fixtures. Two years ago, an air-conditioning system was installed, for which the church owes another year of payments. Supplies and equipment must also be paid for out of the church funds.

Recordkeeping is provided by an office staff consisting of the office manager, two or three individuals from the congregation who volunteer their secretarial services, and two full-time secretaries. Both inventory and directory records are maintained. There are two typewriters at the church, one for the clerical volunteers—a portable electric that overheats when used for more than an hour at a time—and a manual, located in the pastor's office, which he uses for writing letters to shut-ins and hospitalized members.

Inventory is maintained for hymnals, Bibles, teaching materials for Sunday School classes, two movie projectors housed in the social hall, furniture, choir gowns, pastoral clothing, robes, baptismal equipment, and silverware and dishes located in the church kitchen.

Records are also kept of the church directory, including a membership roll kept in a three-ring binder. Names, addresses, and phone numbers are kept for each church member. When new members join, one of the volunteers writes in the new names and addresses. White correction fluid is used to make deletions or corrections. There are numerous scratch-outs and holes have been torn in the sheets from mistakes that have been made. Once a year, this roll is updated if the electric typewriter is not in the repair shop, which it frequently is. Therefore, the roll book is frequently in a state of disarray, with add-ins and scratch-outs.

Membership contribution logs are also kept, and once a year a statement of these contributions is sent to each member for use as tax deductions or just for general information about individual contributions. These statements also contain information about how each dollar contributed was allocated, whether it went toward maintenance, utilities, salaries, general upkeep, or the miscellaneous fund.

Recordkeeping at UBC is a tedious task. When contributions are made, the contribution envelopes must be opened, the currency counted, and the amount recorded in the log book. Some members write checks, which makes it one step easier—the money doesn't have to be counted. But even though the amount can be read off the check, the figures still must be entered in the log book. Sometimes the names are not easily located in the log book because they have not been entered yet, or have not been entered in proper alphabetical order.

Year-end statements are kept and compared to previous years' statements. This year, the church has an additional $2,000 compared to the same time last year. Statement preparation is also a tedious task due to the lack of availability of records. Records are kept everywhere in the office, in no logical order. The contents of various binders and notebooks are written on a piece of masking tape and stuck on the outside.

Lately, office help has been hard to get. In the last five to ten years, the only people who volunteered were non-working mothers of small children. When their children came of school age, these women usually joined the public workforce. UBC's present full-time employees are overburdened with work, especially when there are no volunteers to help with filing and recordkeeping. There has been a fifteen percent yearly increase in part-time help, which is too much for the church to afford.

The church does not want to hire full-time secretaries because there are certain slack times in the year when a few people could handle the work. Since the records are in such a poor state, it takes longer—sometimes three times longer—to do a simple task. With the increase in office work due to the mismanagement of the office filing system, improvements are needed immediately.

Assume you are the office manager. Suggest ways UBC's office problems could be alleviated.

Sample Case Six:
IRON STATE UNIVERSITY

Iron State University (ISU) was established in 1857 by Samuel Jones, a Ph.D in agriculture. His original idea was for ISU to be a school for agricultural engineering. There would be other courses available, but in the 1850s, most students attending college were primarily interested in agriculture. The college was situated in Iron City, Utah.

Over the next hundred years, the college expanded, adding seventeen branch campuses. ISU now offers a wide range of courses, including business, education, engineering, English, fine and performing arts, as well as math and science, philosophy, and the social sciences. The branch campuses are spread throughout Utah, with the main campus being the original college established in Iron City.

A branch of ISU—the Steel College, located near a major airport and the residential area of Steeltown—offers students the third and fourth years of baccalaureate programs, as well as graduate study. Approximately 3,500 students are served by this branch, which has various departments of study including English, math, engineering, business, and graduate studies. The Business Administration Division has its own special hierarchy, as shown in Figure B.3. The division is headed by Dr. Edward Edison, who has two assistants. Below the division head are the program heads, one for each of the five separate programs in the business division, and then twenty-five faculty members, five for each program, who report to the individual program heads. The division has five secretaries and two assistant division heads.

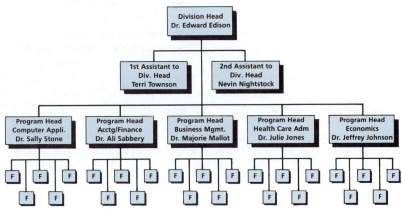

Figure B.3
Steel College's Organizational Chart

The university has a very sophisticated state-of-the-art mainframe computer system, located at the main campus, which is accessed by branch campuses through a communication line. Steel College has access to this mainframe, as do the other sixteen branch campuses.

Several years ago, the Business Administration Division installed a terminal, connected to the main system, which could be used by the faculty and staff. However, due to the complexity of the system, it has been under-utilized.

Since everyone had difficulty accessing and using the mainframe system, the university invested in IBM-PCs for faculty and staff. The Business Administration Division has ten IBM-PCs available for its use. There is one PC in each of nine different faculty offices, and one in a vacant office. Currently, there are thirty faculty members within the division, all of whom have access to the ten terminals. There are two printers, one letter-quality and one dot-matrix, located in the same vacant room. The division has a two-year plan that calls for each faculty member's office to be equipped with a PC.

Sometimes the faculty members complain that the printers are not available when they want to print. Often documentation or manuals explaining software packages are unavailable or missing, so certain helpful information cannot be found. The software packages in the department include two copies of Lotus 1-2-3, two copies of PC-DOS, two copies of WordPerfect, one copy of dBASE III PLUS, and one copy of Harvard Graphics. Often a particular software package cannot be located; either all copies are already in use or a copy was misfiled. This problem leads to disgruntled faculty members. One day, one of the secretaries overheard Edward Edison remark, "All this sophisticated and expensive equipment at our disposal, and there's never any software available to run in the computer."

There is another problem encountered by program heads often—sometimes daily. The program heads want to get together, which is often physically impossible, to schedule classes for an upcoming semester. They write memos back and forth to each other. The memos sometimes sit in their "in" baskets for several days before they get a chance to read them. Then they write a response memo. This process goes on and on.

Student advisors also face a problem. Students often go to see their advisors about which courses to take. The advisor then has to go to the student files and pull that particular student's file in order to be in a better position to advise a student. The advisor is continually going for student files, running back and forth.

Another problem the faculty members face is manuscript preparation. Each faculty member has, on average, five manuscripts to prepare each year. Some faculty members use the WordPerfect word processing package on the PCs for developing manuscripts, while other faculty members handwrite their manuscripts. The latter then give their handwritten material—often illegible notes—to a secretary for typing. The secretary then hands the complete typewritten manuscript back to its author for additions, corrections, and deletions; then the author passes the corrected version back to the secretary to incorporate changes. The secretary often has to retype the whole manuscript, as the changes often affect the line spacing on each page. Then the secretary returns the corrected copy of *this* manuscript. Often, the author makes additional changes yet again. Then it's back to the secretary, who makes the corrections, then it's sent back again to the author. Obviously, this method of manuscript preparation is extremely inefficient.

One month ago, Dr. Edward Edison attended a national conference held in Washington, where he ran into an old colleague, Dr. Ralph Cramden, head of the department of sociology at Quick State University. Dr. Cramden told Dr. Edison about a wonderful microcomputer network that he and his associates set up in the Department of Sociology. Since Dr. Edison's return, he has been wondering if his division can come up with ways to better utilize its microcomputer system.

The present computer system needs further development. You have been chosen to make recommendations to Dr. Edison as to what can be done to alleviate some of these problems within the Business Administration Division at Steel College.

Sample Case Seven:
ARCHITECTURAL DESIGN ASSOCIATES

Architectural Design Associates (ADA) is an emerging company of manufacturers' representatives for corrosion control, durable flooring, moisture protection, and structural repairs. The central headquarters is in Columbus, Ohio.

ADA officially began operations in August, 1986. Marvin M. McCormick and Martin A. McCoy were the owners and sole employees of the company at that time. Their major tasks included writing job specifications for architects, bidding on jobs for manufacturers, servicing customers, and making decisions about the future of the organization. Each controlled a specific geographic area. McCormick worked in Cincinnati, Ohio, while McCoy worked in Cleveland, (see Figure B.4). McCormick, acting president, also was in charge of the company's clients, sales, and order information. A microcomputer, along with database, spreadsheet, accounting, and word processing software, was purchased to help keep track of the data. So far, these software packages have been used to store data in separate files, with no special applications written for the company.

Figure B.4
ADA's Sales Territories

As sales ballooned and additional firms were represented it became necessary to hire a person to manage operations at the home office. Julia Jasmin was hired for the job on June 2, 1987. Her work included customer service, secretarial duties, and operation of the microcomputer.

A third manufacturers' representative, Mark Mason, was employed in July of 1987 to cover a new territory for the company in the state of Illinois. This increased the firm's client list to about 4,050 customers.

The objectives of ADA, as seen by McCormick, are to provide competent representation of manufacturers and solve the complex problems of customers while maintaining a high level of customer service and support. To further these goals, the company has decided to explore new methods of providing service while employing new processes to increase the productivity and practicality of their business practices.

ADA's main problem is the lack of an adequate management information system. At present, there is no structured system for retaining, processing, and utilizing client and sales information gathered by the company. Until recently, the firm had been able to manage its information resources with its computer and current personnel. Now, steady growth and an ever-increasing clientele have forced management to take steps toward expanding the company's data processing capabilities.

There are many negative consequences of this information management problem. First, management is not able to extract the strategic information it needs to create effective forecasts of the company's future. Historical sales figures and anticipated orders are vital to ADA's ability to forecast cash flow and expected sales. Currently, management must manually sift through a multitude of unorganized sales totals in order to obtain these figures. This wastes valuable planning time.

Also lacking in ADA's framework is the ability to efficiently create regional or special personalized mailings. The firm has on file eighty-five separate form letters, a number of which could be sent to any client, depending on the situation at hand. Currently, the clients to receive a certain mailing must be handpicked from an extremely large master customer list.

A third dilemma arises when the company attempts to gather information on new job leads and orders. When a new job is discovered, the data about the job is written on a sheet of paper and placed in a file. When it is time to call on clients, ADA employees must sift through the files to find all possible job leads in a specific area, or of a certain degree of importance. Once again, wasted time becomes an issue, and some customers are overlooked in the process. Furthermore, jobs are lost to other companies because inadequate data processing techniques prevent ADA from competing effectively. Finally, breakdown reports on leads and orders are nonexistent and, as a result, customer service suffers.

Another problem within the firm stems from storage of client data. At present, client information is contained in a computer database, as well as in filing cabinets. Redundant customer information may be found in other databases filed on the computer system. This is an inefficient use of space, which also increases the possibility of utilizing obsolete information.

Salespeople often call into the home office requesting customer information stored on the computer. Each time this happens, a secretary must stop working and look up the information on the computer. This often takes five or ten minutes. Sometimes a secretary is talking to a client on the telephone and cannot take the time to look up information for the rep. The reps find calling into the home office and waiting for a secretary to locate information to be extremely inefficient. This present method is also aggravating to the secretaries, who must interrupt their jobs to locate information on the computer for someone in the field.

ADA currently grosses about $80,000 a month in sales from its three territories. McCormick wants to hire three additional sales reps to help keep up with expanding sales in the Columbus, Cleveland, and Cincinnati areas.

He expects sales to reach as high as $100,000 per month by January of 1989, and as high as $150,000 per month by January of 1990, with the addition, in late 1989, of four additional manufacturers' reps.

With this expanding sales force and the increase in sales volume, the present information management must be improved. You have been hired by Mr. McCormick to conduct a study of the present ADA database system. What recommendations would you give for updating the present system? Can it be updated efficiently? Should a new system be implemented?

Sample Case Eight:
BORROWER'S UNLIMITED NATIONAL BANK

The Borrower's Unlimited National Bank (BUNB) was established in 1917 by Forest Brown, a lumberjack in the timberlands outside the city of Dakota Hills, North Dakota. He had scrimped and saved all his life; when he retired, he decided to open a bank with $800,000 in savings. His wife helped set up the office; she typed and filed and recruited customers. In the following ten years, the bank grew to almost 1,000 customers. When Brown and his wife died, they willed BUNB to their grandson, Franklin Brown.

Franklin had received his master's degree in banking and finance from a North Dakota school of business, hoping that someday he could help his grandfather run the bank. Now, Franklin is BUNB's owner and president.

The number of customers has continued to grow, and Frank Brown has opened two new branches: the North Street Branch and the South Street Branch. Assets have grown to well over $2 million. The bank currently has six departments: Finance, Loan, Personnel, Clerical, Marketing, and Administration. Each department is headed by an individual located at the main office. The chart in Figure B.5 illustrates BUNB's organizational structure.

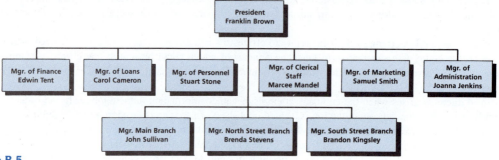

Figure B.5
BUNB's Organizational Structure

Seventy-five people are employed by BUNB and its branches. Some 5,000 customers are now using the bank's services: check cashing, IRAs, loans, free checking with a $200 minimum deposit, and even savings accounts, certificates of deposit, and savings bonds. The paperwork for all of these services keeps the banking personnel swamped with filing, locating various customer accounts, providing monthly financial statements in a timely manner, and producing monthly savings statements. Currently, all computing tasks, such as payroll, accounting, and checking and savings account statements, are handled through an outside firm, the computer service bureau.

Frank Brown believes in fast, efficient service for all customers. He also believes in high-quality customer service. He says that a satisfied customer is a permanent customer. Frank meets once a week with department and branch managers. At the last meeting, the subject of the Loan Department came up.

The Loan Department's main objective is to generate revenue from interest on loans. First, loan applicants must be drawn to the bank. At the same time, the promotion of checking, savings, and IRA accounts is paramount in order for the bank to have sufficient capital to make loans. There are two types of loans: commercial and consumer. Commercial loans are primarily for businesses, and consumer loans are primarily personal loans: mortgages, educational loans, automobile loans, and so on. There are also short-term loans such as cash advances for credit cards.

At the last departmental meeting, Frank discussed the amount of time it takes to thoroughly process a loan application. At present, this process takes between five and ten work days. Frank wants this time cut down to one or two days.

During that meeting, Frank also asked Carol Cameron, manager of the Loan Department, to explain the current procedure of loan processing. Carol explained that processing a loan involves various tasks. First, the client requests a loan. The client's name and address are recorded along with work history, length of time on the job, position, monthly salary, credit obligations, mortgage payments, car loans, and any amounts owed by the client to other parties. A list of assets is also recorded to ensure that the bank will be repaid in case of default by the customer. Employer references must also be acquired so that the customer's work history can be checked.

Next, a credit check is undertaken by a member of the Loan Department staff. This aspect of the credit check is the main holdup in loan approval. Creditors have to be telephoned and verifications made as to the amount the customer owes. After all the appropriate checks have been made, the client is called back into the bank to sign for the loan, and the transaction is completed.

What follows for the bank employees is not a pleasant task. The loan applications are filed in triplicate, one copy in each of three files: a customer file, a bank copy file, and a vault file, in case of accidental destruction of the other two copies. This is a safeguard the bank prides itself on, a sort of insurance policy. No copies have ever been destroyed or lost, but this is a practice Frank wants continued.

Another problem Carol Cameron brought up at the last departmental meeting was the amount of time it takes to get promotional loan letters sent to various customers. Promotional loan letters are letters that are written to current customers, past borrowers, and pre-qualified new customers, promoting loans with low interest rates, and longer financing terms. These letters entice borrowers to take out more loans.

Presently, 200 people receive these promotional letters on a bimonthly basis. The clerical staff spends an inordinate amount of valuable time manually typing these letters in triplicate, using carbon paper to make the copies, every two months. This is often a messy task. If a mistake is made, it must be erased three times, once on the original and once on each of the two copies. The carbons smear so badly that it is often better to throw the letter away and start over again.

The main reason carbons are used is that management believes it to be more cost efficient than photocopying each letter. The clerical staff believes it is more time-consuming to use carbon paper, but management has made the decision, so carbon paper is still an office staple.

Besides problems caused by carbon paper, it is time-consuming to type more than 200 letters and envelopes every two months. Carol Cameron believes more clerical help will expedite turnaround time for the promotional letters. She indicated to Frank at the last meeting the need for more help.

Frank is considering hiring an outside consultant to study the problems of the Loan Department. Assume that you are the consultant Frank hired. Analyze the situation and make the necessary recommendations.

Sample Case Nine:
J & E CONCESSION STAND

In 1977, Jim and Evie Jones decided to start their own business in Thomasville, a small town in a rural area. Jim and Evie both had full-time jobs, so they decided that this would be a part-time venture, preferably during the summer months.

Jim and Evie had been married for five years and had been saving every extra cent they could during those five years for something special. They each had always dreamed of owning their own business, but knew it was expensive to get started, especially with the legal fees, start-up costs, and equipment costs. After five years, Jim and Evie had accumulated $25,000 in their special fund and decided to open a concession stand.

Jim and Evie started out by purchasing one portable concession stand for $5,000. They decided to sell various food items at their stand, so they also purchased the equipment to handle these food items. The concession stand operated during the summer months only at events such as picnics, carnivals, fairs, sporting events, and other special outdoor gatherings.

The J&E Concession Stand was a big hit, generating $1,000 a week during the first summer. Evie's two sisters manned the stand whenever Jim and Evie were working their other jobs, but usually the stand was only open on weekends or evenings so that Jim and Evie could tend it themselves.

In the following two summers, the business grew. Jim and Evie added two concession stands to the thriving business, necessitating the hiring of more part-time help. These new stands each contributed an additional $1,000 a week.

Jim and Evie had so much business that they decided to work the concession business during the winter months at football games, ice skating parties, and hockey games. Income generated during the winter was not as great as in the summer months—only about $100 per week, on the average. The largest amount of revenue came during football season (from September through November), when income generated was $5,000.

Over the next eight years, the business continued to be successful. Jim and Evie opened three additional concession stands during the summer months, and income has averaged $2,000 per week per stand. During the winter months, only three stands are in operation, with income at about $10,000 during football season. These three stands are now operated only from September through November because there is not enough business to warrant their use later than mid-November.

Employees are hired on a part-time basis. Evie handles all job application processing and payroll functions. She writes employee checks by hand, but when all six stands are in operation, payroll checks become a tedious task. Five people work in each stand, so that a total of thirty checks are written on a weekly basis. Because employee scheduling often takes longer than Evie feels it should, Evie wants to devise a special system so she can make better use of her time.

Evie and Jim have a small office in their home where, until last year, everything was running smoothly. Since their business has grown, Evie and Jim are swamped with paperwork. Evie has to type letters periodically to several banks, many suppliers, and each of the employees. She does this typing on an antiquated portable manual typewriter she has owned since her college days. She is not an efficient typist and has to hunt and peck her way around the keyboard. Her typewriter is approximately twenty-five years old, and it squeaks when the manual return lever is used. She has no copying device, but must use carbon paper for each copy of a letter kept on file. This is a time-consuming method for making copies; therefore, few copies are made and kept. She also has to type many form letters, also a time-consuming process on her manual typewriter.

An inventory must be kept of all supplies ordered and used by each stand. Evie found this task easy when there were three stands, but with six it is nearly impossible. One person can hardly count every piece of physical inventory. Receipts for supplies purchased are stored in shoe boxes. At year's end, when Evie and Jim consult their accountant, it is a nightmare shuffling through shoe boxes, trying to get the receipts into some logical order. Jim and Evie desperately need a financial planning mechanism.

Ordering and maintaining proper food quantities is another problem faced by Jim and Evie. Since most of the ingredients used in their products are perishable items, inventory control is important to reduce spoilage and waste. Most food supplies are purchased a few days before use, and the amount purchased is determined by the previous years' sales records. Due to the limited storage space for supplies at each stand, it is impossible to store large quantities of nonperishable items in advance.

Since the operation has grown in both the number of units and total sales, more controls are needed to effectively manage sales revenue. Because Jim and Evie have a cash business, control of daily sales is difficult. A large number of transactions take place in a short span of time, and there is no cash register to record sales.

Data concerning bookings for each season is important, since the success of the business is determined by scheduling and confirming bookings at a specific time each year. The method of payment for the privilege of sales at each event is also confirmed at this time.

Keeping an accurate record of cash sales receipts, supply costs, operational costs, equipment costs, and employee salaries is imperative for the smooth operation and success of the business. This information is the basis for planning, coordinating, and controlling operations in the future.

Inventory control records need to be improved because sales revenue is lost when supplies purchased are below the demand level or perishable items are lost because of lack of sales. Sales revenues need to be monitored for effective profit control. Employee scheduling helps determine sales revenue, and important data need to be centralized for quick and easy access. The business has experienced a loss of revenue due to a lack of confirmation on bookings; therefore, information concerning bookings needs to be organized.

Jim and Evie are very happy with the way their business has grown in the past ten years. They are planning to open three more stands in the next three years. They are not very pleased, however, with the way their inventory control mechanisms seem to be getting away from them. It is a task that seems to be compounding year after year. Evie can barely keep up with the recordkeeping, and with the addition of three more stands, it really will be impossible. Evie and Jim would like some suggestions on how to handle this important task.

You have been hired as a consultant to clean up the present recordkeeping system and to streamline it, if possible. Suggest ways to improve the present system.

Sample Case Ten:
SHANGHAI SURPRISE, INC.

Chin Chang came to the United States in the mid-1970s to pursue his studies in medicine as a student at the Greenberg School of Medicine in Longstown, Texas. A stranger in a foreign land, Chin missed his native cooking. He soon became a frequent visitor of the local Chinese restaurants. To his surprise, not every dish he enjoyed in his native country was served in the American-Chinese restaurants. He could not understand this since most, if not all, of the Chinese restaurants were operated by native Chinese.

Some of the ingredients were missing in these Chinese meals, which disappointed him. Through talking with several of the Chinese restaurant owners, Chin learned that certain ingredients necessary for the preparation of some Chinese dishes were not available in smaller cities such as Longstown. Wholesale dealers in larger cities, such as New York and Houston, were not interested in shipping their products to Longstown because of the limited market demand and high transportation costs.

Chin saw a potentially lucrative opportunity in the shipping of Oriental groceries from Houston to Longstown for local Chinese restaurants. In 1982, Chin, now a pediatric physician, took the opportunity and started his own grocery business as a hobby. Chin's business was conducted mainly during the weekends. Operating a typical family business, he used the spare room of his home as an office and half of his two-car garage for storage. The purchase of a station wagon in 1983 gave him greater mobility and shipping convenience.

Chin would drive to Houston, and sometimes New York, on weekends to pick up a carload full of Oriental spices, vegetables, and herbs that were not available in the Longstown area. He would then transport them to Longstown in his station wagon and distribute them to the twenty-five Chinese restaurants in the area.

Restaurant owners were thrilled. Now they, too, could make all the dishes of their native land. Chin was thrilled, too, because what started out as a hobby had turned into a full-fledged business. He was able to sell about $500 worth of Oriental groceries each week.

The business grew to the point where Chin no longer could handle it in his spare time, and there was no more storage space in his garage. Chin asked his son, Minh, to take over the business for him. Since storage was a big problem, Minh moved the growing business into a one-story building. Minh no longer only sold to restaurants, but to the public, as well.

The Oriental food craze hit America several years later. Since everyone wanted to try his hand at preparing Oriental meals, and since the recipes called for certain items that only Minh's store could provide, he sold even more herbs, spices and groceries to the public. Minh was now operating a wholesale as well as retail business. The number of Chinese restaurants in the immediate area was now up to about fifty, and just about all of them purchased products from Minh's store.

In the past four years of operation, Minh has grossed a monthly income of $2,500. The number of Chinese and other Asian restaurants in the area has increased considerably during the past few years, adding to Minh's revenue. He has no competition in this line of business. Minh's business expenditures are very low—only the monthly $200 rent for the building plus the gas for the trip to Houston and back once a month. Also, an increasing number of local people have begun to appreciate ethnic food, mainly because it is lower in calories and cholesterol.

Shanghai Surprise, Inc., as the business is now called, has one major problem: inventory control. In the early stages of operation, Chin used a manual system of inventory control that was overseen by his wife on a monthly basis. This was a relatively easy task because of the limited number of items ordered and the small quantity carried in stock. As the business grew and moved from Chin's garage to the one-story building where Minh operates, inventory control has become increasingly difficult and costly.

Checking the level of reserve stock and reordering items manually is quite a chore for Minh. Sometimes he has to approximate the items to be reordered. Inaccurate estimates often result in overstocking or understocking of items. Ordering the right quantity is paramount to balancing the costs related to number of orders against the cost related to size of orders. It is extremely time-consuming for Minh to check the reserve stock, item by item, and to know exactly how much should be ordered. Miscalculations often result in reduced marginal profit.

It is also difficult for Minh to check the unit cost for each item ordered, an important piece of information in determining the proper price structure. As a result, the prices of many items are hastily set on the basis of experience or guesswork. This faulty pricing practice stems from Minh's lack of a systematic approach to inventory planning.

Inventory control contributes to the effective overall operation and profitability of an organization. With this fact in mind, decisions about inventory cannot be left to chance or guesswork. Minh needs a system whereby he can reorder appropriate numbers of stock items. He needs to know how much will sell or how to estimate how much will sell. He does not know how to determine his reorder point without physically going through and counting every spice bottle, every herb container, and every packet of vegetables.

Minh also needs a new billing system. Currently, he just pencils the sales into an old notebook. This is not very accurate or efficient because sometimes he forgets where his pencil is and then forgets entirely about making an entry in his notebook. His billing system also needs to keep track of the items sold, not just the amount of each sale, and provide a way to invoice customers.

Minh would like to start advertising in the local daily newspapers to help stimulate more business. He should have a typewriter or some other mechanism; otherwise, he would have to print each letter by hand to send along with his advertisements. Also, the ads need to be produced on a machine that will make them presentable. He wants one full-page ad in each newspaper and would like to list the items available to customers on either a daily or weekly basis. He would have to do this manually, which would take a lot of time.

This Oriental vegetable, spice, and herb business is a money-maker but it will not remain so if items are out of stock when needed, if spoilage occurs due to overstocks, or if customers are improperly billed. Minh is counting on you to help him out. What advice or suggestions can you give him to help make his business a more profitable one?

Appendix C

Advanced DOS Commands

After completing this appendix, you should be able to

- discuss the purpose of each advanced DOS command and the procedure for executing each one.
- create a new file or edit an existing file using the EDLIN text editor.
- describe the difference between regular batch files and the AUTOEXEC.BAT file.
- describe the procedure to format and prepare a hard disk for use.
- describe how to create, manage, and navigate through directories and subdirectories using directory-oriented commands.
- describe the purpose of the CONFIG.SYS file.
- describe how to create files directly from the keyboard using the COPY CONSOLE command.

INTRODUCTION

PC-DOS provides many advanced commands designed for tasks that are not as routine as those discussed in Chapter 5. The DOS commands in this appendix are not normally used by infrequent DOS users; rather, they tend to appeal to experienced users. It is assumed that the reader is thoroughly familiar with the commands discussed in Chapter 5 before attempting the commands in this appendix.

The Sort Command

Purpose: This command can either read a file from a directory, sort it, and write the sorted version to another file, or read files from a directory, sort them according to name, size, or date, and write them back onto an output device, possibly the original diskette.

How to enter the command: To sort a file called UNSORT.TXT stored on a diskette in Drive A and store the sorted version under SORT.TXT, at the DOS prompt, type

    A>sort <unsort.text >sort.txt

The following sort command causes the directory of the default drive (Drive A) to be displayed on the screen, sorted in ascending order by file name:

    A>DIR¦SORT [ENTER]

Figure C.1 on the following page illustrates an example of a sorted directory on the screen.

```
         40 files  58368 bytes free
       Directory of A:\
       Volume in drive a has no label
       ANSI     SYS   1651 3-07-85 1:43p
       ASSIGN   COM   1509 3-07-85 1:43p
       ATTRIB   EXE  15091 3-07-85 1:43p
              .
              .
              .
```

Figure C.1
A Sorted Directory by File Names

The system uses the standard ASCII collating sequence to determine the order of the sort. (Refer to the ASCII Table in Chapter 2.) Unless otherwise specified, the output will be sent to the screen.

Modifications: The following are variations of the SORT command.

    A>DIR¦SORT/R [ENTER]

causes the directory to be sorted in reverse order by file names, as shown in Figure C.2.

```
         40 files  58368 bytes free
       Directory of A:\
       Volume in drive a has no label
       VDISK    SYS    986 3-27-85 6:50a
       TREE     COM   2456 3-27-85 2:50p
       CONFIG   COM     22 9-27-85 6:00a
              .
              .
              .
```

Figure C.2
A Sorted Directory in Reverse Order

    A>DIR¦SORT/+10 [ENTER]

causes the directory to be sorted by extensions, such as in Figure C.3.

```
         40 files  58368 bytes free
       Directory of A:\
       Volume in drive a has no label
       MORE     COM    282 3-07-85 1:43p
       ASSIGN   SYS   1509 3-07-85 1:43p
       LABELB   SYS   1826 3-07-85 1:43p
              .
              .
              .
```

Figure C.3
A Sorted Directory by File Extensions

```
A>DIR¦SORT/+14 [ENTER]
```

causes the directory to be sorted by file size, as shown in Figure C.4.

```
      40 files   58368 bytes free
Directory of A:\
Volume in drive a has no label
CONFIG   SYS      22  9-27-85  6:00a
CONFIG2  SYS     128  9-27-85  6:00a
MORE     COM     282  3-07-85  1:43p
   .
   .
   .
```

Figure C.4
A Sorted Directory by File Size

```
A>DIR¦SORT/+24 [ENTER]
```

causes the directory to be sorted by date, as shown in Figure C.5.

```
      40 files   58368 bytes free
Directory of A:\
Volume in drive a has no label
ANSI    SYS    1651  3-07-85  1:43p
ASSIGN  COM    1509  3-15-85  1:43p
ATTRIB  EXE   15091  4-02-85  1:43p
   .
   .
   .
```

Figure C.5
A Sorted Directory by File Date

Note: DIR ¦ SORT sorts the directory only *once* and does not store the sorted directory for later reference.

■ THE DOS EDITOR

The following section describes DOS text editor functions, which allow users to create and modify files and programs. Many word processing software packages perform this same function. The main disadvantage of the DOS editor lies in the fact that editing is performed on a line-by-line basis (a line-mode editor as opposed to a full-screen editor). For this reason, it is referred to as line editor, or EDLIN.

The EDLIN program is a set of commands known as a line text editor, allowing the user to create and save new source files, update existing files by deleting, inserting, or editing lines, and save either the updated or the original file, or both.

The EDLIN Command

Purpose: The main purpose of this command is to enter the EDLIN environment. By issuing this command, the user begins the editing session.

How to enter the command: This command either edits an existing file or creates a new one, and is issued by specifying the file name. If the file specified already exists, it will be brought into main memory for editing. Otherwise, DOS will assume that you are creating a new file.

    A > EDLIN *filename.ext*

For example, to access the AUTOEXEC.BAT file with the line editor, you would enter

    A > EDLIN AUTOEXEC.BAT [ENTER]

If the file currently exists, it will become available for editing, as evidenced by the screen prompt in Figure C.6, signifying that the file's contents have been loaded into memory. In order to exit, type Q (for Quit) and [ENTER]. In response to the message "Abort edit (Y/N)?", type Y.

Figure C.6
EDLIN Command Used with Currently Existing Files

If the file name entered calls for a new file to be created, for example,

    A > EDLIN B:TEXTFILE.TXT [ENTER]

then the following screen will be displayed as in Figure C.7.

Figure C.7
EDLIN Command and Creation of a New File

```
A>DIR¦SORT/+14 [ENTER]
```

causes the directory to be sorted by file size, as shown in Figure C.4.

```
    40 files  58368 bytes free
Directory of A:\
Volume in drive a has no label
CONFIG   SYS     22 9-27-85 6:00a
CONFIG2  SYS    128 9-27-85 6:00a
MORE     COM    282 3-07-85 1:43p
    .
    .
    .
```

Figure C.4
A Sorted Directory by File Size

```
A>DIR¦SORT/+24 [ENTER]
```

causes the directory to be sorted by date, as shown in Figure C.5.

```
    40 files  58368 bytes free
Directory of A:\
Volume in drive a has no label
ANSI     SYS   1651 3-07-85 1:43p
ASSIGN   COM   1509 3-15-85 1:43p
ATTRIB   EXE  15091 4-02-85 1:43p
    .
    .
    .
```

Figure C.5
A Sorted Directory by File Date

Note: DIR ¦ SORT sorts the directory only *once* and does not store the sorted directory for later reference.

■ THE DOS EDITOR

The following section describes DOS text editor functions, which allow users to create and modify files and programs. Many word processing software packages perform this same function. The main disadvantage of the DOS editor lies in the fact that editing is performed on a line-by-line basis (a line-mode editor as opposed to a full-screen editor). For this reason, it is referred to as line editor, or EDLIN.

The EDLIN program is a set of commands known as a line text editor, allowing the user to create and save new source files, update existing files by deleting, inserting, or editing lines, and save either the updated or the original file, or both.

The EDLIN Command

Purpose: The main purpose of this command is to enter the EDLIN environment. By issuing this command, the user begins the editing session.

How to enter the command: This command either edits an existing file or creates a new one, and is issued by specifying the file name. If the file specified already exists, it will be brought into main memory for editing. Otherwise, DOS will assume that you are creating a new file.

    A > EDLIN *filename.ext*

For example, to access the AUTOEXEC.BAT file with the line editor, you would enter

    A > EDLIN AUTOEXEC.BAT [ENTER]

If the file currently exists, it will become available for editing, as evidenced by the screen prompt in Figure C.6, signifying that the file's contents have been loaded into memory. In order to exit, type Q (for Quit) and [ENTER]. In response to the message "Abort edit (Y/N)?", type Y.

Figure C.6
EDLIN Command Used with Currently Existing Files

If the file name entered calls for a new file to be created, for example,

    A > EDLIN B:TEXTFILE.TXT [ENTER]

then the following screen will be displayed as in Figure C.7.

Figure C.7
EDLIN Command and Creation of a New File

Now, let's assume that you want to enter a few lines of text into this file. To do so, you would use the INSERT (I) command, explained next.

The INSERT (I) Command

Purpose: This command allows new line(s) to be inserted in the specified file.

How to enter the command: In order to enter new lines in the file TEXTFILE.TXT, at the * prompt, type

  *i [ENTER]

Upon receiving this command, DOS will display the screen shown in Figure C.8.

Figure C.8
Initial Screen of EDLIN for New File

Start typing the following lines. (Make sure that you press the ENTER key after each line is typed.)

1:*This is line number one [ENTER]
2:*This is line number two [ENTER]
3:*This is line number three [ENTER]
4:*This is line number four [ENTER]

Once you have typed the last line and you are prompted with "5:*," press F6, then press ENTER. You now have exited the insert mode (notice that "^Z" appears after the asterisk of the last line as shown in Figure C.9).

```
A> edlin b:textfile.txt
New File
*i
   1:*This is line number one
   2:*This is line number two
   3:*This is line number three
   4:*This is line number four
   5:*
```

Figure C.9
Typed Lines to be Inserted into the New File

Now you must save what you created in the TEXTFILE.TXT file. To do so, at the "*" position, type E (for End)

    *E [ENTER]

which saves the file under the specified name TEXTFILE.TXT and exits the EDLIN environment. At this stage, use the DIR command to check the directory of your diskette in Drive B. You should see TEXTFILE.TXT.

Now let's bring TEXTFILE.TXT back into the memory. To do so, at the DOS prompt, type

    A>edlin b:textfile.txt [ENTER]

Since this file exists on the diskette in Drive B, EDLIN assumes that this is the file you want to work on. Once the file is in memory, you should be able to see its contents by using the LIST command.

The LIST LINES (L) Command

Purpose: This command displays the contents of the files loaded through EDLIN.

How to enter the command: At the * position of the EDLIN prompt, type

    *L [ENTER]

The screen will then display the contents of the entire file in a line format, with each line numbered consecutively. Figure C.10 illustrates the case of TEXTFILE.TXT.

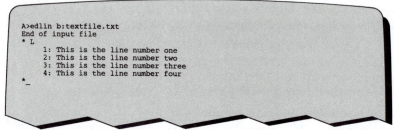

Figure C.10
A List of Lines in the Files

Modifications: The L command can be modified to display only a range of lines within a file (handy if the file is very long) by entering the command

    *RANGE L [ENTER]

For example,

    *1,3 L [ENTER]

will only display the first three lines as shown in Figure C.11 on the following page.

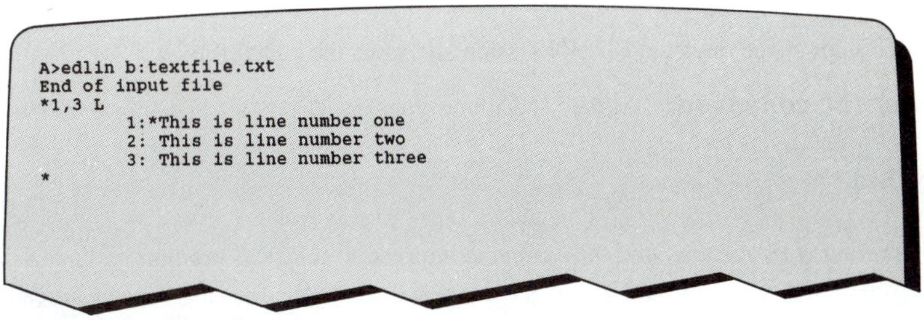

```
A>edlin b:textfile.txt
End of input file
*1,3 L
        1:*This is line number one
        2: This is line number two
        3: This is line number three
*
```

Figure C.11
A List of the First Lines in the File

If only lines two through four are desired, type

    `*2,4 L [ENTER]`

Let's now add a new line at the end of this file. To do so, at the * position, type

    `*5i [ENTER]`

This will put you back in the insert mode and give you a blank line. Type

    `5:*This is the line number five [ENTER]`

In order to cancel the insert mode at any time, press F6 followed by ENTER.

The DELETE (D) Command

Purpose: This command is similar to the INSERT command, but deletes, rather than inserts, lines in EDLIN files.

How to enter the command: DELETE is used by specifying the line to be deleted, followed by the letter D. For example, to delete *This is the line number one* (line #1), at the * position, type

    `*1D [ENTER]`

A range of lines can also be specified by using the following format:

    `*2,3D [ENTER]`

which deletes lines two and three.

Once the specified lines have been deleted, the remaining lines are automatically renumbered. To view the remaining lines, type

    `*L [ENTER]`

The END EDIT (E) Command

Purpose: This command ends the EDLIN session and saves the edited file.

How to enter the command: At the * position, type

    *E [ENTER]

The EDLIN program is terminated, and the system is returned to the DOS prompt.

If at any time you do not want to save the changes that you made to the file, just type Q instead of E. This means you want to exit the session without saving either a new text or changes to an old text.

Applications of EDLIN

One useful application of EDLIN is in creating batch files. Batch files are files that contain certain DOS commands and that can be created by the computer user with EDLIN. Upon execution of a batch file, a series of DOS commands will be executed in sequence. The file extension assigned to batch files must be *BAT*. There are two types of batch files: regular batch files, which require the user to request that its contents be executed, and the automatically executed batch file known as AUTOEXEC, the contents of which are executed during the booting process.

Regular Batch Files

Purpose: Batch files can be created to execute any number of DOS commands upon instruction.

How to establish the file: Like the text files discussed previously, regular batch files can be created using EDLIN. For example, to create a batch file that would format a diskette in Drive B, copy files from Drive A onto Drive B, and then compare the files on Drives A and B to ensure that both diskettes contain the same files, you could use the following batch file lines.

At the DOS prompt, type

    A> EDLIN B:FC.BAT [ENTER]

Type i and press ENTER to begin entering the following lines.

    CLS   [ENTER]
    FORMAT B: [ENTER]
    COPY A:*.* B: [ENTER]
    DISKCOMP B: A: [ENTER]
    CHKDSK A: [ENTER]
    CHKDSK B: [ENTER]

Upon completion of the last line, press the F6 key and press ENTER, then type E, and press ENTER. The screen shown in Figure C.12 on the following page will be illustrated.

Then, each time the user wants to execute this procedure, he or she just types FC (for Fast Copy) at the DOS prompt, which would save many keystrokes.

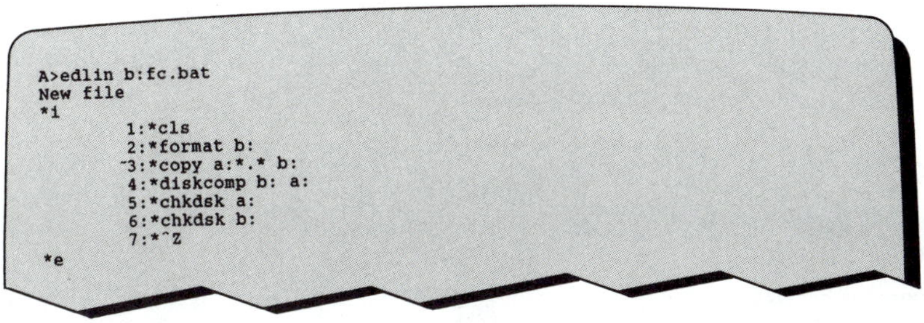

```
A>edlin b:fc.bat
New file
*i
        1:*cls
        2:*format b:
       -3:*copy a:*.* b:
        4:*diskcomp b: a:
        5:*chkdsk a:
        6:*chkdsk b:
        7:*^Z
*e
```

Figure C.12
Lines of a Regular Batch File

Autoexecute Batch (AUTOEXEC.BAT) File

Purpose: Each time DOS is started, the DOS command processor component searches for a file named AUTOEXEC.BAT in the root directory of the DOS diskette. The AUTOEXEC.BAT file is a batch file that stores and automatically executes a series of DOS commands. This file is useful because it enables the user to "program" the execution of a sequence of commands to perform predetermined tasks each time the computer is booted. DOS allows only one AUTOEXEC to be stored on a diskette.

How to establish the file: AUTOEXEC.BAT files can be created in the same manner as the regular batch files by using DOS EDLIN or a word processing software package. The only difference between an AUTOEXEC file and a regular batch file is the fact that the AUTOEXEC batch file is executed automatically at the time of booting.

- At the DOS prompt, type `AUTOEXEC.BAT` and press ENTER.
- Type I and press ENTER.
- Type the following lines:

CLS	[ENTER]
ECHO OFF	[ENTER]
REM Good Morning	[ENTER]
PAUSE Insert WordPerfect in drive A	[ENTER]
WP	[ENTER]

- Press the F6 key and press ENTER.
- At the * prompt, type E and press ENTER.

The screen should look like the one shown in Figure C.13.

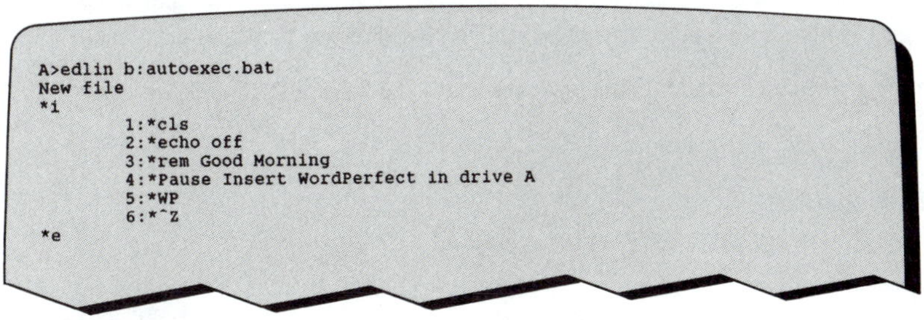

```
A>edlin b:autoexec.bat
New file
*i
        1:*cls
        2:*echo off
        3:*rem Good Morning
        4:*Pause Insert WordPerfect in drive A
        5:*WP
        6:*^Z
*e
```

Figure C.13
An Example of AUTOEXEC.BAT File

For frequent users of the WordPerfect word processing package, this AUTOEXEC would be very handy. With this batch file, part of the booting process would be to ask the user to insert the WordPerfect diskette in Drive A and then to have WordPerfect's main program executed automatically.

■ HARD DISK DOS COMMANDS

The following paragraphs discuss the various DOS commands related to hard disk data and program management. The hard disk, generally referred to as Drive C, can be partitioned into two or more logical disks, which would then be called "C", "D", "E", and so on. (See the FDISK section in this appendix.)

Formatting a Hard Disk

Purpose: As with diskette formatting, the format procedure for a hard drive checks the entire drive to sequester "bad" sectors from use and sets up the initial directory and file allocation table for the hard diskette.

WARNING: Any data contained on the hard disk will be lost as a result of the format procedure. It is suggested that the data first be "backed up" or otherwise copied as a precautionary measure.

How to enter the command: The FORMAT command is entered with the DOS diskette in default Drive A as

```
A>FORMAT C:/S [ENTER]
```

This command instructs DOS to format Drive C and to copy onto the hard diskette the system files that are required to make the system bootable from the hard drive alone. If for some reason the hard disk is not intended to be bootable, the /S parameter is omitted.

Note: The remainder of the files on the DOS diskette can now be copied onto Drive C using the COPY command previously discussed and specifying C as the target drive. Before doing so, read the information in the following sections for methods of placing these files in subdirectories, if desired.

The FDISK PROGRAM

Purpose: The FDISK program prepares your hard disk for use by dividing it into from one to four partitions, or individual disk space areas. Generally, the entire hard disk is prepared as one partition unless it is larger than 32MB. If more than one operating system will be used, each requires a separate partition.

Note: Only one partition can be bootable, even if there are four logical disks (partitions) on your hard disk. To change to another disk, you simply type d: and press ENTER, where d is the drive designator.

How to enter the command: This program is entered from a DOS diskette located in Drive A by typing, at the DOS prompt,

```
A>FDISK [ENTER]
```

The program that is started by the above command is menu-driven and will offer the following options on the start-up screen shown in Figure C.14.

Figure C.14
The Options of the FDISK Program

If the fixed disk is being initially set up, you will want to choose Option 1 and follow the menu-driven system prompts.

■ DIRECTORY COMMANDS

Unlike files on a floppy diskette, which are limited in number, the number of files that can accumulate on a hard disk can quickly become unmanageable unless they are organized in some logical fashion. A branching, tree-structure, hierarchical directory system can effectively solve this problem. Under this type of system, a series of directories at different levels are created under the main root directory for storage of logically-related data or programs.

This concept is illustrated graphically in the following directory structure.

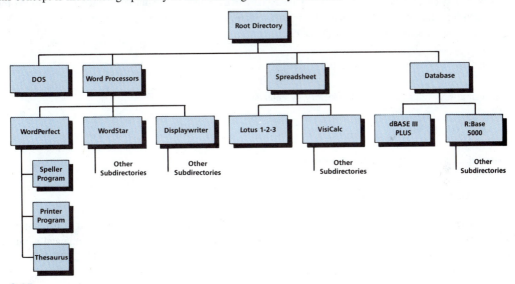

Figure C.15
A Sample Directory Structure

To create and navigate through these directories, you can use several directory-oriented commands.

The MAKE DIRECTORY (MD) Command

Purpose: The MAKE DIRECTORY command creates a new directory or subdirectory.

How to enter the command: Use this command to create a directory branching off of another. To create a WP (for word processing) directory beneath the root directory in the above example, you would enter the following command at the C prompt.

    C>MD\WP [ENTER]

Another directory could then be established under the WP branch called WORDP (for WordPerfect) by typing from the root level:

    C>MD\WP\WORDP [ENTER]

However, if the current directory were changed from the root directory to the WP directory, only MD \WORDP would be required to create the WORDP subdirectory.

The CHANGE DIRECTORY (CD) Command

Purpose: This command changes from the current directory to different directory path levels in the branching tree structure.

How to enter the command: The CHANGE DIRECTORY command is executed by specifying the path to be followed from the current directory to the desired directory level. To change from the root directory in the above example, enter the following command at the DOS prompt.

    C>CD\WP\WORDP [ENTER]

You can always return to the root directory by entering

    C>CD\ [ENTER]

where the backslash (\) signifies the root directory.

Set Search Directory – The PATH Command

Purpose: This command specifies the directories which DOS will search for command or batch file requests not found in the current directory. By specifying multiple directories in this way, the PATH command eliminates the need for multiple directory changes. It is often useful to include this command within an AUTOEXEC.BAT file so that the search path is automatically set upon booting.

How to enter the command: The search path is set from the DOS prompt by typing the specifications of each drive (assumed to be limited to Drive C) and path name to be searched, separated by semicolons, in the following manner.

C>PATH C:*subdirectory**subdirectory*;C:*subdirectory*

For example, if Drive C were organized into a root directory, with two subdirectories, SALES and SYSTEM, and with a subdirectory of DOS files entitled DOS under SYSTEM, the path to search each of these directories could be set by entering.

C>PATH C:\SALES;C:\SYSTEM\DOS [ENTER]

A DOS command to delete a file could then be issued from any level of the directory. The PATH command would search each of the indicated directories until the DOS delete command was found.

Note: The current directory is not changed when the PATH command is used in a search.

If the path includes a file that no longer exists, the file will be ignored. Furthermore, PATH only locates files that can be executed—those ending in the extensions COM, EXE, or BAT.

The REMOVE DIRECTORY (RD) Command

Purpose: The REMOVE DIRECTORY command enables you to remove directories that have become obsolete due to reorganization of the directory structure.

How to enter the command: A directory can be removed from the root directory level by specifying the path to the directory to be removed. To remove the WORDP directory in the previous example, you would type the following command at the DOS prompt at the root directory level.

A>RD \WP\WORDP [ENTER]

Another method of accomplishing the same objective would be to change to the WP directory just above WORDP and issue the following command.

C>RD WORDP [ENTER]

Since the directory to be removed is contained in the current directory listing, there is no need to specify the path.

Note: Before a directory can be removed, all files contained within it must be deleted. This can easily be accomplished using the DEL *.* technique discussed in the DELETE COMMAND section in Chapter 5. Be sure, however, that the DEL *.* is issued *only* from within the directory to be removed; otherwise, you may delete other files unintentionally.

The TREE Command

Purpose: The TREE command displays all of the directory paths on the specified drive.

How to enter the command: At the DOS prompt, type

C>TREE [ENTER]

The following screen (Figure C.16) represents a sample of the type of listing that will appear upon execution of the TREE command.

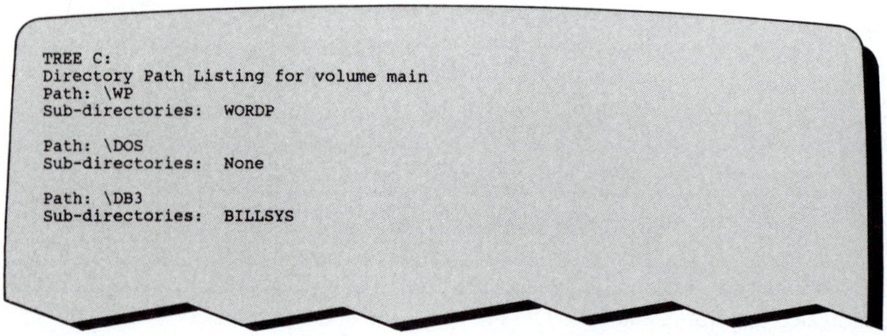

```
TREE C:
Directory Path Listing for volume main
Path: \WP
Sub-directories:   WORDP

Path: \DOS
Sub-directories:   None

Path: \DB3
Sub-directories:   BILLSYS
```

Figure C.16
A Sample Tree Directory

Modifications: By adding the /F modifier, the names of the files within the directories will also be displayed.

The PROMPT Command

Purpose: The PROMPT command can be embedded within the AUTOEXEC.BAT file to configure the DOS prompt to display the name of the current directory. This is useful to help keep track of where you are within multiple-branched directories.

How to use the command: The PROMPT command is included within the AUTOEXEC.BAT file as the line.

    PROMPT = PG

This will cause the DOS prompt to display the full path for the current directory.

■ MISCELLANEOUS DOS COMMANDS

The CONFIGURE SYSTEM (CONFIG.SYS) File

Purpose: The CONFIG.SYS file contains a series of commands that set up the system. When DOS is started, it searches the directory to see if the CONFIG.SYS file is present. If it is found, the system executes the commands. If it does not find the CONFIG.SYS file, the system uses default values in place of the CONFIG.SYS file. The file is "programmed" using EDLIN, and is automatically executed each time DOS is started.

How to establish the file: You are not required to start the CONFIG.SYS file; it is started each time DOS is executed. Many commands can be included in the CONFIG.SYS file through the use of the EDLIN program previously discussed. For example, the line *FILES* = *X* will instruct the system to allow a maximum of *x* files that can be opened concurrently during operation.

The line *DEVICE = VDISK.SYS* will partition a portion of the computer's RAM memory to act as though it were a separate disk drive (RAMDISK). Files can then be copied into the VDISK and used during operation, making access to RAM much quicker than through physical reading of disk drives.

Many options can be exercised in setting up the CONFIG.SYS file, largely dependent on hardware specifications.

The COPY CONSOLE (COPY CON) Command

Purpose: The COPY CONSOLE command is a useful method of creating batch files by instructing DOS to copy a file as typed from the console (the keyboard).

How to enter the command: To create a batch file using the COPY CONSOLE command, type

A>COPY CON b:FC.BAT [ENTER]

You would now type in each command line that is to be included in the FC.BAT file, pressing ENTER after each line. Enter the following lines.

```
ECHO OFF
CLS
FORMAT B:
COPY A:*.* B:
DISKCOMP B: A:
CHKDSK A:
CHKDSK B:
```

When all lines have been entered, press F6 and then press ENTER to exit the COPY CONSOLE routine.

Note: Make sure each line is correctly entered before pressing ENTER. If you make a mistake while entering the lines, you can correct it later by using the EDLIN program.

The BACKUP Command

Purpose: The BACKUP command makes backup copies of a file or files from one hard disk or diskette to another. This command should be used frequently to avoid data loss due to accidental erasure or diskette damage.

The BACKUP command is different from the COPY command. The COPY command makes an exact duplicate of the files being copied, whereas the BACKUP command copies not only the data within the specified file, but also the control data that the RESTORE command uses. Thus, a file that was backed up can only be used when it has been restored using the RESTORE command.

How to enter the command: The command is issued at the default drive (e.g., Drive A) and must specify the drive that will contain the backup copy. At the DOS prompt, enter

A>BACKUP *filename.ext x*:

where *x:* is the drive that the copy is to be written to. For example,

    A>backup file1.txt b: [ENTER]

will backup the file named FILE1.TXT, located on the default drive, onto the diskette in Drive B.

Modifications: The flexibility of BACKUP can be increased by specifying additional parameters in the command, such as BACKUP/S ENTER, which will backup all files, including those in the subdirectories of the default drive. If this parameter is not specified, only files that are in the current directory of the default drive will be backed up. For example,

    A>backup *.* b:/s [ENTER]

will backup all files on the default drive (including those in subdirectories) onto the diskette in Drive B.

The RESTORE Command

Purpose: The RESTORE command restores files that have been backed up using the BACKUP command. Files that have been backed up are not usable until they are restored.

How to enter the command: The RESTORE command must be issued in the default drive that contained the original backed up files. In addition, the drive containing the backup copy of the files must be specified. For example, if certain files were backed up from Drive A onto a diskette in Drive B, and the original Drive A files were later accidentally destroyed, the command to RESTORE the files onto Drive A from the backup diskette in Drive B (with Drive A again serving as the default drive) would be

    A>restore b: a:*.* [ENTER]

■ SUMMARY OF DOS COMMANDS

SORT	Sorts input data in ascending or descending order and writes them to a specified output device.
EDLIN	Enters EDLIN text editor environment.
I	Inserts new line(s) in EDLIN file.
L	Displays file loaded with EDLIN.
D	Deletes line(s) in an EDLIN file.
E	Ends EDLIN session.
FORMAT C:	Prepares hard disk for data storage.
FDISK	Prepares hard disk for use by dividing it initially into from one to four partitions.
MD (Make Directory)	Creates a new directory or subdirectory.
CD (Change Directory)	Changes from one directory to another.
PATH	Specifies directory for DOS to search for command or batch file requests not found in current directory.

RD (Remove Directory)	Removes directories that have become obsolete.
TREE	Displays all directory paths on specified hard disk.
PROMPT	Imbedded in AUTOEXEC.BAT file to allow DOS prompt to display name of current directory or other desired information.
COPY CONsole	Creates batch files by copying the file as typed from the console (keyboard).
BACKUP	Makes backup copies of file(s) from one disk or hard disk to another.
RESTORE	Restores files that have been backed up using the BACKUP command.

■ REVIEW QUESTIONS

1. Do the BACKUP and COPY commands perform the same function? Can they be used interchangeably?
2. The RESTORE command restores files that have been backed up using the _____ command.
    (a) COPY
    (b) FDISK
    (c) SORT
    (d) BACKUP
    (e) none of the above
3. The system uses the standard _____ collating sequence to determine the order for the SORT command.
    (a) ASCII
    (b) EBCDIC
    (c) ascending
    (d) descending
    (e) none of the above
4. Which of the following is *not* one of the EDLIN commands?
    (a) INSERT
    (b) FINISH
    (c) DELETE
    (d) LIST
5. The EDLIN command has been issued for the existing file AUTOEXEC.BAT, and the ENTER key has been pressed. The next thing to appear on the screen is
    (a) the DOS Prompt (>).
    (b) a listing of the AUTOEXEC.BAT file.
    (c) the EDLIN prompt (*).
    (d) a "New File" message.
6. What occurs when EDLIN's END EDIT (E) command is issued?
7. How many DOS commands can be executed by a batch file?
8. The _____ program prepares a hard disk for use by initially dividing it into from one to four different "partitions."
    (a) FORMAT C:
    (b) RESTORE
    (c) BACKUP
    (d) FDISK

9. The _____ command creates a new directory or subdirectory.
   (a) BACKUP RESTORE
   (b) CHANGE DIRECTORY
   (c) MAKE DIRECTORY
   (d) EDIT LINE
10. Which of the following characters signifies the root directory?
    (a) /
    (b) :
    (c) \
    (d) ^
    (e) none of the above
11. What types of files can be found with the PATH command?
12. The _____ command displays all the directory paths on the specified drive.
    (a) TREE
    (b) PATH
    (c) DIRECTORY
    (d) SORT
13. The DOS prompt can be configured to display the name of the current directory by imbedding the _____ command within the AUTOEXEC.BAT file.
    (a) PATH
    (b) DIRECTORY
    (c) PROMPT
    (d) TREE
14. What will occur if the system does not find the CONFIG.SYS file at the time of booting?
15. What does COPY CON mean? What is the command used for?
16. What parameter would be added to the SORT command to cause the directory to be sorted by extensions?
17. What keys must be pressed to exit the EDLIN INSERT mode?
18. What is the difference between a regular batch file and an AUTOEXEC.BAT file?
19. What are some methods of creating an AUTOEXEC.BAT file?
20. What task must be performed before a directory can be removed with the REMOVE DIRECTORY (RD) command?

☐ Appendix C

HANDS-ON EXERCISES

For these exercises, insert the DOS diskette in Drive A and a blank formatted diskette in Drive B. The default drive is Drive A.

1. Produce a sorted listing of the directory in Drive A.
2. Sort the directory again, this time by file extensions.
3. a. Using the EDLIN program, create a regular batch file called B:KWIKSTRT.BAT that will accomplish the following tasks when executed.
   1) Format the diskette in Drive B.
   2) Copy the entire contents of the diskette in Drive A to the diskette in Drive B.
   3) Compare the two diskettes.
   4) Do a directory on the diskette in Drive B.
   b. Do a DIRectory of the B drive to prove the existence of the newly created B:KWIKSTRT.BAT file.
4. Perform the following directory operations on the diskette in Drive B.
   a. Make a new directory called DATA.
   b. Change the current directory to the newly created DATA directory.
   c. Use the COPY CON command to create a file called B:TESTDATA.TXT in the DATA directory with the following information:
      Sue Wilson   DP
      Marilyn Winters   Sales
      Jim Ryan   Marketing
      Gregory Glenn   Finance
   d. Do a DIRectory of the B drive to prove the existence of the newly created B:TESTDATA.TXT file.
5. Change back to the root directory.
6. Use the EDLIN program to edit the B:TESTDATA.TXT file.
   a. List all employees.
   b. Delete Marilyn Winters from the employee file.
   c. Insert Marcy Davidson from Engineering in Marilyn Winter's old spot.
   d. List the contents of the new file to make sure that the insert and delete steps worked.
   e. End the EDLIN session.
7. Use the TYPE command to verify the contents of the file B:TESTDATA.TXT.
8. Use the TREE command to display the directory paths.

Appendix D

■ ADVANCED FEATURES OF WORDPERFECT

After completing this appendix, you should be able to

- *describe how to use the features of the WordPerfect Speller to check documents for misspellings.*
- *describe how to use the WordPerfect Thesaurus to vary the vocabulary of documents.*
- *describe the process of file merging to combine two documents or files.*
- *describe the process of file merging to have one file "feed" another file.*
- *describe the process of creating mailing labels.*
- *describe how to create and use a WordPerfect macro to simplify frequently performed tasks.*

■ INTRODUCTION

In this appendix you will become familiar with many advanced features of WordPerfect that are not normally utilized by the first-time user of this word processing package. As you become better acquainted with this package, you will want to take advantage of some of its other features. The material in this appendix is based primarily on material covered in Chapter 7. The user is advised to make sure that lessons covered in that chapter have been mastered. In order to exercise the advanced features of WordPerfect, you must boot the system and enter the WordPerfect environment.

This appendix covers the speller, thesaurus, document merging, and mailing label preparation features of WordPerfect through a series of examples developed around Sunshine Window Inc., Suppliers (SWIS). Before you start the exercises of this appendix, make sure you have the speller and thesaurus diskettes available.

Back to the Case of SWIS

As was mentioned in the case, SWIS informs their customers about any new items added to their product line. Recently, they added the French Window, a new product manufactured by the Glassy Co. Now, a letter is being sent to SWIS customers about this new product. With a clean WordPerfect screen, type the following letter exactly the way it is shown here. (*Note*: Do not correct the spelling mistakes; they are purposely placed in the letter to be corrected later with the WordPerfect Speller.)

```
                    Sunshine Window Inc., Suppliers
client-name
company-name
company-address

    I am writting to you on behalf of Sunshine Window Inc.
Suppliers, a Pennsylvania-based firm specielizing in providing
quality window and door products.
    We are pleased to anouncee the addition of a French Window,
another fine product of the Glassy Co., to our product line. Due
to the unique design of this window, we are certain that this
window will become one of our popular products. The Glassy Co.
has already experienced a great deal of success with this
product.
    I invitte you to call me for more information about this new
type of window. You can reach me at either 717-000-1111 or 717-000-1112.

Sincerely,


Martine W. Martinez
Vice President
```

Make sure that you did not make any mistakes of your own. Save the document as PROM.LTR on your diskette in Drive B.

■ WORDPERFECT SPELLER

The **Speller** is a useful tool for checking your WordPerfect documents after they have been completed, or for checking a single word or page while the document is being created. Let's correct the spelling mistakes in the PROM.LTR we just created. To do so, follow the instructions below. *Caution*: When using the WordPerfect Speller, you must remember three things: (1) don't remove the Speller disk from the drive while spell-checking is in progress, (2) don't type anything until you see the blinking cursor at the bottom of the screen, and (3) your default drive should be the Drive B.
Note: If your default drive is not already B, follow the steps below:

- Press F5.
- In response to "Directory A:*.*", type =B:.
- Press ESC.

Take the diskette that your files are stored on out of Drive B and replace it with the Speller diskette. Keep the Speller diskette in the B drive until the entire checking process is complete.
Follow these steps to start the Speller.

- Hold down the CTRL key and press F2.
- The speller's main menu will appear on the bottom of the screen, as shown in Figure D.1.

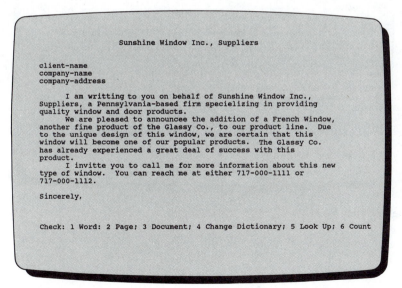

Figure D.1
WordPerfect's Speller Main Menu

Table D.1 describes the functions of the menu options.

1	Word	One word
2	Page	One page
3	Document	Entire document
4	Change Dictionary	Change to another dictionary
5	Look up	Search for words having certain patterns by using wildcards—e.g., s?t to match with sit, sat, etc.
6	Count	Total words in document

Table D.1 **Speller Main Menu Options**

- Select option 3 to check the entire letter by typing the number 3.

After a few seconds of searching, the Speller finds the first spelling error in this document, which happens to be *writting*. The screen shown in Figure D.2 will appear.

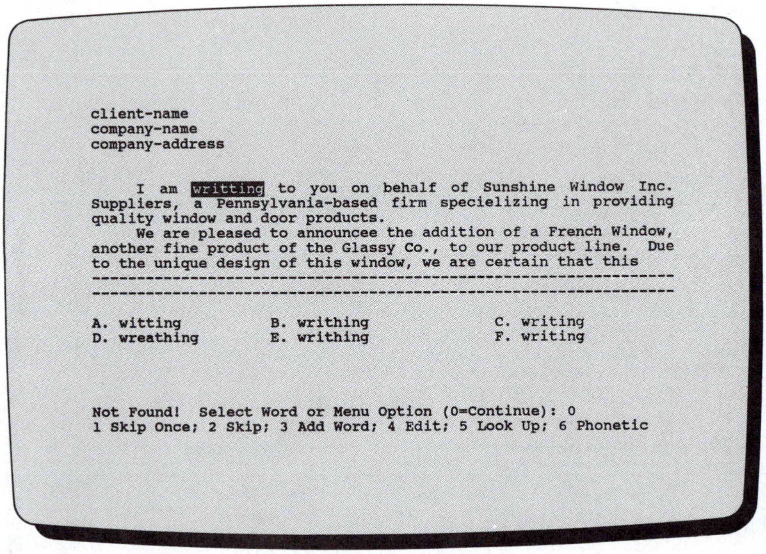

```
client-name
company-name
company-address

    I am writting to you on behalf of Sunshine Window Inc.
Suppliers, a Pennsylvania-based firm specializing in providing
quality window and door products.
    We are pleased to announcee the addition of a French Window,
another fine product of the Glassy Co., to our product line.  Due
to the unique design of this window, we are certain that this
_____
_____

A. witting         B. writhing          C. writing
D. wreathing       E. writhing          F. writing


Not Found!  Select Word or Menu Option (0=Continue): 0
1 Skip Once; 2 Skip; 3 Add Word; 4 Edit; 5 Look Up; 6 Phonetic
```

Figure D.2
WordPerfect's Speller Option Menu

Table D.2 describes the functions of the options listed at the bottom of the screen.

1	Skip once	Ignore just that occurrence of the word
2	Skip	Ignore all occurrences of the this word for the rest of the document
3	Add word	Add this word to the speller dictionary
4	Edit	Correct spelling manually
5	Look up	Search for word with certain pattern
6	Phonetic	List words that sound like word not found

Table D.2 *Speller Options*

In this case, the correct word is *writing*, shown on the screen as Selection C. Press the letter C.

The old word *writting* is now changed to the correct spelling *writing*. At this time, your screen should look the same as the one in Figure D.3, with the word *specielizing* highlighted.

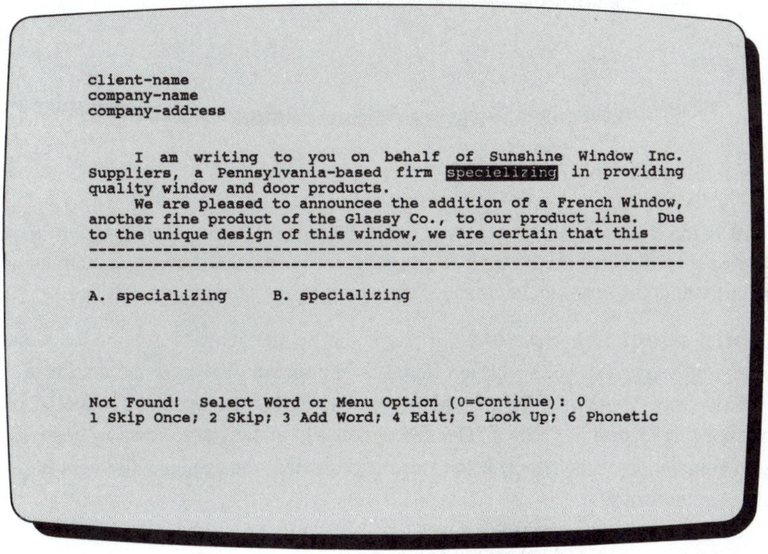

```
client-name
company-name
company-address

    I am writing to you on behalf of Sunshine Window Inc.
Suppliers, a Pennsylvania-based firm specielizing in providing
quality window and door products.
    We are pleased to announcee the addition of a French Window,
another fine product of the Glassy Co., to our product line.  Due
to the unique design of this window, we are certain that this
------------------------------------------------------------------
------------------------------------------------------------------

A. specializing    B. specializing



Not Found! Select Word or Menu Option (0=Continue): 0
1 Skip Once; 2 Skip; 3 Add Word; 4 Edit; 5 Look Up; 6 Phonetic
```

Figure D.3
Correcting the Word *Specializing*

In this case, the correct word is listed as B, *specializing*. Press the letter B to correct this mistake.

The next misspelling is the word *announcee*. When the Speller gives the correct version on the screen, press the letter that represents the correct version, *announce*.

The next error is *invitte*. The correct word is *invite*. Choose the appropriate letter to correct this word.

Finally, the last error should be the name *Martine*. In this case, since this is the way we want to spell this name, press 1 ("Skip Once") to indicate that you are accepting the spelling, or press 3 (for "Add Word") to add this name to the dictionary of the speller, if you plan to use this name again.

Upon completion of the last correction, the Speller will show you the screen in Figure D.4.

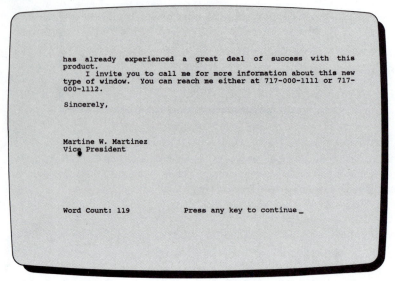

Figure D.4
The Screen after Correcting Spelling

The number 119 is the total number of words in your document. Press any key to terminate the spell-checking session. Remove the Speller diskette from Drive B and replace it with the diskette containing your files to save the corrected document. If you don't save the document, your changes and corrections will be lost.

Two final notes about the Speller: First, if the Speller reaches a word for which it does not find a match in its dictionary, no suggested word will be offered on the screen. You have the choice of ignoring the word by pressing 1 for the "Skip Once" option, 2 for the "Skip" option, adding the word to the Speller dictionary by pressing 3, "Add Word", or choosing Option 4, "Edit". The last option will allow you to rewrite the word, then press ENTER when finished. Upon completion of rewriting, if the word is corrected, the speller will begin the search process again. Otherwise, it would skip the word.

Second, if the Speller encounters a word that was typed twice in a row, the "Double Word" menu will appear on the screen with the following choices:

Option		Explanation
1 or 2	Skip	Continue without correcting
3	Delete 2nd	Delete second occurrence of the double word
4	Edit	Correct as you wish
5	Disable double word checking	Ignore any double occurrences found in the document

In this case, if you were interested in deleting the second occurrence, you would select option 3, "Delete 2nd," to erase the second occurrence of the word.

■ WORDPERFECT THESAURUS

The **Thesaurus** is another useful tool when creating a WordPerfect document. It offers synonyms and other related words to help vary the vocabulary in your text. To begin using the Thesaurus, remove the diskette on which your files are stored from Drive B and replace it with the Thesaurus diskette.

Let's suppose you decide that you would like to find an alternate word for the word *certain* in the second sentence of the second paragraph. Follow the steps below to activate the Thesaurus.

- Position the cursor to the word *certain*; the cursor can be positioned at any point on the word or just after it.
- Hold down the ALT key, and press F1 to start the Thesaurus; the screen will apepar as in Figure D.5.

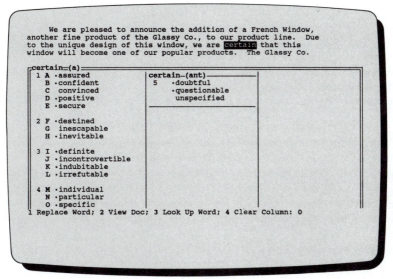

Figure D.5
Thesaurus Screen

Now suppose you decide you want to replace the word *certain* with the word *confident*.

- Press 1 to replace word.
- In response to the message "Press letter for word," type B for *confident*; you will be returned to the screen of text, and *certain* will have been replaced by *confident*.

Note: When you are in the WordPerfect Thesaurus, and you want to terminate the session without making any changes, just press F7 (Exit Function) to get out of the Thesaurus environment. Now that you have finished, remove the Thesaurus diskette from Drive B and replace it with your file diskette. Save your document before exiting WordPerfect.

■ FILE MERGING

File merging ranges from simply combining two files or documents to having a file "feed" another file, a function commonly seen in personalized form letters. In order to understand the file merging function of WordPerfect, let's use the promotional business letter PROM.LTR that we created for Sunshine Window Inc., Suppliers.

Combining Files

After you prepare the promotional letter, you realize that there is a paragraph at the beginning of another letter that you sent to the Pennsylvania Finest National Bank, LOAN.LTR, saved on your disk, that you would like to place at the beginning of this promotional letter. To do so, follow the instructions below.

- Press F7 to exit.
- In response to "Save Document? (Y/N)Y", type N.
- In response to "Exit WP? (Y/N)N," press ENTER.
- Press F5 followed by pressing ENTER to list your files.
- Move the highlighted line over the file LOAN.LTR.
- Press 1 to retrieve the file. You should see the loan letter on the screen.
- Position the cursor at the beginning of the first paragraph, which reads *Sunshine Window Inc., Suppliers is committed...* .
- Hold down the ALT key and press F4 to activate the BLOCK option.
- Use the DOWN and RIGHT ARROW keys to highlight the paragraph.
- Hold the CTRL key down and press F4 to copy the paragraph into memory.
- Select Option 2, "Copy block", from the menu at the bottom of the screen by typing the number 2.

You have just copied the desired paragraph into a temporary WordPerfect file. Now let's go back to the PROM.LTR document and insert the copied paragraph where we want it to be.

- Press F7 to exit the loan letter.
- In response to "Save Document? (Y/N)Y", type N.
- In response to "Exit WP? (Y/N)N", press ENTER.
- Press F5 for a file listing.
- Press ENTER once to see the directory.
- Move the highlighted line over PROM.LTR.
- Press 1 to retrieve the file.
- Move the cursor to the beginning of the line above the first paragraph, *I am writing to you...* .
- Hold the CTRL key down and press F4 to retrieve the paragraph that you copied from the previous file.
- Select text by pressing 5.

You see that the paragraph is copied right before the paragraph beginning *I am writing...* . If you have extra lines in between the paragraphs, use the DEL key to eliminate them. The screen in Figure D.6 on the following page illustrates what you should have on your screen.

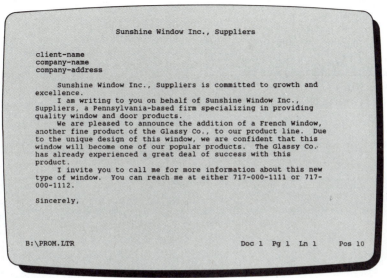

Figure D.6
Your Letter after Combining a Paragraph

With this feature of WordPerfect, you can copy an entire file or document to another one by highlighting the entire document when you activate the BLOCK option.

Merging Primary and Secondary Files

The merge feature can also combine the text of one file (called the **primary file**) with that of a second file (called the **secondary file**). The primary file normally contains the form or body of the document (i.e., the information that will remain constant in each document). The secondary file contains variable information—for example, a list of records, such as names and addresses, that change according to the recipient of the document. The MERGE function (CTRL-F9) is often used to personalize various form letters, memos, and reports that have the same text but are sent to different recipients. The result is a document that seems to have been individually prepared. To create this kind of document, a record is made for each specific recipient. Each item of that record (name, address, and so on) is considered a field.

In this section, you will perform a simple merge of the body of the PROM.LTR that you have created with a list of names and addresses. To perform this exercise, it is assumed that you have completed the previous sections and have a copy of the PROM.LTR stored on your diskette in Drive B. If you are just starting out, remember that you must first boot the system and enter the WordPerfect environment.

Let's assume that you have created the PROM.LTR, and are ready to send it to prospective clients.

Creating the Secondary File. The first step in this task is to create the secondary file, which consists of individual records made up of individual fields. In the steps to follow, the individual name, company name, and address constitute one record. Within that record, the person's name is one field, the company name is one field, and the address is one field.

To create a record, bring up a clear screen in WordPerfect and proceed as follows.

- Start in the upper left-hand corner at the cursor and type `Mrs. Joanne Chambers, President`.

- Press F9 to end the field. WordPerfect will place a ^R to mark the end of the field and move the cursor to the beginning of the next line.
- Type Stratford Window Fashions.
- Press F9 to end the company name field with ^R.
- Type Mahanoy City, Pennsylvania 18564.
- Press F9 to end the address field with ^R.
- Hold down the SHIFT key, and press F9 to end the record with ^E.
- Press ENTER to insert a blank line between this record and the next one.

The screen display will look like Figure D.7.

Figure D.7
The First Screen of the Secondary File

Now repeat those same steps for the following records.

```
Mrs. Linda Wagner, President
Capital Lumber Co.
New Cumberland, Pennsylvania 17000

Mr. William Shaw, Vice President
S & G Home Improvements
Bethlehem, Pennsylvania 18011

Ms. Betsy Rupport, Partner
Rupport General Contracting
Carlisle, Pennsylvania 17017

Mr. Harold Kleinpour, Owner
Universal Aluminum & Window Co.
Wilkes Barre, Pennsylvania 18032
```

After you have entered the five records, save the records under the file name B:ADDRESS.SEC. Exit this file (but do not exit WordPerfect).

Creating the Primary File. For this merge exercise, you will use the PROM.LTR as your primary file. You should now have a clean screen to work with after saving the secondary file. Retrieve the PROM.LTR file. Use the BLOCK option to delete the name, company, and address as follows.

- Position the cursor at the beginning of *client-name*.
- Hold down the ALT key, then press F4 to activate the BLOCK option.
- Use DOWN and RIGHT ARROWS to highlight the name, company, and address.
- Press the DEL key.
- In response to "Delete Block? (Y/N)", type Y.

Now you are ready to insert the merge codes into the primary file. Use the UP ARROW key to position the cursor at a point two lines above the first paragraph, which begins *Sunshine Window Inc., Suppliers is committed...* and execute the following steps.

- Hold the ALT key down, and press F9 to display the merge code menu. Your screen will look like Figure D.8.

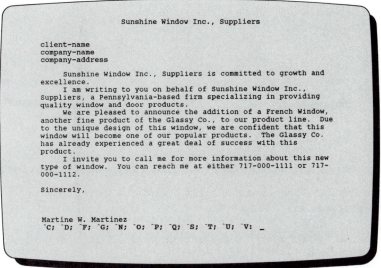

Figure D.8
Merge Code Menu

- Type F. In response to "Field Number?" press 1, then press ENTER. An ^F1^ will be inserted into the letter; the name field will be merged into this location.
- Press ENTER to move the cursor to the next line.
- Hold down the ALT key, and press F9 to display the merge code menu.
- Type F, then press 2, then press ENTER. The company name will be merged into this location.
- Press ENTER to move the cursor to the next line.
- Hold down the ALT key, and press F9 to display the merge code menu.
- Type F, then press 3, and then press ENTER. The address will be merged into this location.

You have now finished entering the merge codes into the primary file. Your screen should look like Figure D.9.

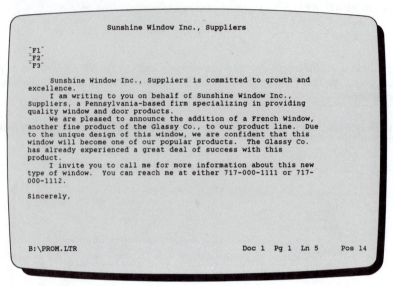

Figure D.9
The Primary File with Merge Codes

Save (F10) the primary file under the name B:LETTER.PRM. Exit this file, but do not exit WordPerfect.

Activating the Merge. The next step is to actually activate the merging of the two files. Start with a clear screen and follow the procedures below.

- Hold down the CTRL key, and press F9 to start the merge process. A menu with three options will be displayed at the bottom of the screen.
- Type the number 1 to display the "Primary file:" message.
- Type the primary file name B:LETTER.PRM and press ENTER.
- Type the secondary file name B:ADDRESS.SEC and press ENTER. You will see the message *merging* at the bottom of the screen.

The primary file has now merged with the secondary file. The letter from the primary file is merged with each of the records from the secondary file, creating a file of five letters. Now save the combined letters under the file name B:LETTER.MRG by pressing F10. Then print the combined letters as described below.

- Hold down the SHIFT key, and press F7.
- Select the option "Full Text" by typing the number 1.

The first letter merged with the first record of client information is shown in Figure D.10.

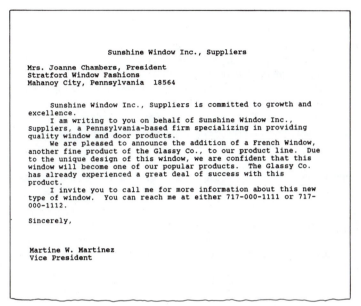

Figure D.10
The Promotional Letter for the First Record of the Secondary File

■ MAILING LABELS

Once all the personalized form letters are created, it would be very useful to be able to create mailing labels. The same secondary file of names and addresses that you created in the MERGE section above can be used to create a file for mailing labels, such as those shown in Figure D.11.

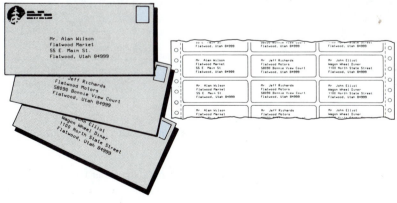

Figure D.11
Mailing Labels and Envelopes

In order to prepare mailing labels, a new file will be created and will be considered the primary file. **Start with a blank screen.**

- Hold down the ALT key and press F9 to display the merge code menu.
- Type F, then press 1, then press ENTER. ^F1^ will be inserted into the file.
- Press ENTER to go to the beginning of the next line.
- Hold down the ALT key and press F9 to display the merge code menu.
- Type F, then press 2, then press ENTER. ^F2^ will be inserted as the second line.
- Press ENTER to go to the beginning of the next line.
- Hold down the ALT key and press F9 to display the merge code menu.
- Type F, then press 3, then press ENTER. ^F3^ will be inserted as the third line.
- Press ENTER once.

The file is now complete. Save (F10) under the name B:LABEL.PRM, then use F7 to clear the screen. Do not exit the WordPerfect environment.

Activating the Merge

Now that the primary file has been completed, it must be merged with the secondary file to create a file of names and addresses suitable for mailing labels.

- Hold down the CTRL key, and press F9 to start the merge process.
- Type the number 1.
- Type the file name B:LABEL.PRM when prompted for the primary file, and press ENTER.
- Type the file name B:ADDRESS.SEC when prompted for the secondary file, and press ENTER.

The two files have now been merged. Before you save this new mailing label file follow the steps below to change the page length to print your labels:

- Hold down the ALT key and press F8 to get into the PAGE FORMAT menu.
- Press 4 to choose the page length option.
- Press 3 to select the option "other".
- Type 4 and press ENTER.
- Type 9 and press ENTER.
- Press ENTER once more to get back to your document.

```
Mrs. Joanne Chambers, President
Stratford Window Fashions
Mahanoy City, Pennsylvania  18564
-----------------------------------
Mrs. Linda Wagner, President
Capital Lumber Co.
New Cumberland, Pennsylvania  17000
-----------------------------------
Mr. William Shaw, Vice President
S & G Home Improvements
Bethlehem, Pennsylvania  18011
-----------------------------------
Mrs. Betsy Rupport, Partner
Rupport General Contracting
Carlisle, Pennsylvania  17017
-----------------------------------
Mr. Harold Kleinpour, Owner
Universal Aluminum & Window Co.
Wilkes Barre, Pennsylvania  18032
```

Figure D.12
Our Mailing Labels

Save this file under the name of B:MAIL.LBL. Now obtain a printout of your mailing labels from the printer. Your output should look similar to the one shown in Figure D.12. The mailing labels can be formatted for use with several types of continuous-feed labels.

■ MACROS

Often you'll find yourself using tasks or functions that frequently require more than one keystroke to accomplish. With the use of **macros** in WordPerfect, you can condense that series of keystrokes into one keystroke. Any series of keystrokes that can be performed in WordPerfect can be saved as a macro for later execution.

For example, during the course of this tutorial, you have had to retrieve the file B:LOAN.LTR a number of times. Let's set up a macro to perform this task. Start with a blank screen.

- Hold down the CTRL key, and press F10 to activate the definition of a macro.
- In response to the message "Define Macro:" shown at the bottom of the screen requesting the name of the macro, type R (for retrieve; any other word could have been used) followed by ENTER.
- The message "Macro Def" is now blinking at the bottom of the screen; every keystroke from now until the time you press CTRL-F10 to end the macro will be included in the macro stored as R.
- Hold down the SHIFT key, and press F10 to retrieve the file.
- In response to the message "Document to be retrieved:", type B:LOAN.LTR and press ENTER. Upon entering the name of the file, the document will appear on the screen.
- Hold down the CTRL key, and press F10 to end the definition of the macro, which stops the blinking "Macro" message at the bottom of the screen.

The macro, now stored in a file called R.MAC, is always automatically stored with the extension MAC.

Activating the Macro

Begin with a clear screen. Try the following steps to activate the macro R.MAC.

- Hold down the ALT key, and press F10 to activate the macro option.
- In response to the message "Macro:," type R (for retrieve) and press ENTER to retrieve the file.

■ KEY TERMS

Speller	Tool for checking misspellings in a document. Allows checking of a single word, a page, or an entire document.
Thesaurus	Tool to help vary the vocabulary in your text. Offers synonyms and related words.
file merging	Combining two files or documents.
primary file	In WordPerfect, this file usually contains the constant data (e.g., the body of a letter).
secondary file	In WordPerfect, this file usually contains the variable data (e.g., list of addresses).
macro	WordPerfect feature that allows the combining of numerous keystrokes into one keystroke that can be saved for later execution.

■ Review Questions

1. The WordPerfect _____ is a useful tool for checking misspellings in a document.
   (a) Thesaurus
   (b) Tutor
   (c) Speller
   (d) Dictionary
2. How is the Speller Diskette used?
3. Which of the following options of the Speller's "error" menu will allow you to ignore all occurrences of the current word for the rest of the document?
   (a) Add Word
   (b) Skip Once
   (c) Edit
   (d) Skip
4. Which of the following options of the Speller's "Double Word" menu will instruct the Speller to ignore double word occurrences for the entire document?
   (a) Skip
   (b) Delete 2nd
   (c) Disable double word checking
   (d) Edit
5. The WordPerfect _____ offers synonyms and related words to help vary the vocabulary in your text.
   (a) Speller
   (b) Dictionary
   (c) Program
   (d) Thesaurus
6. The WordPerfect function of combining two files is referred to as
   (a) mail merging.
   (b) file merging.
   (c) file retrieval.
   (d) primary merging.
7. A _____ file contains variable information.
   (a) primary
   (b) secondary
   (c) merge
   (d) document
8. Which of the following allows the combining of any series of keystrokes into one keystroke?
   (a) a primary file
   (b) macros
   (c) a secondary file
   (d) Thesaurus
9. How is a macro formulated?
10. A macro is stored with the _____ extension.
    (a) .MAC
    (b) .FIL
    (c) .MACR
    (d) >BAs

11. What are your alternatives if the Speller reaches a word that it does not find in its dictionary, offering no suggested words for you to choose from?
12. When would you use the WordPerfect Thesaurus?
13. What is the difference between a primary file and a secondary file when merging two files?
14. What is a WordPerfect macro?
15. What is a simple way of activating a macro?
16. When would you use a macro?
17. Why would you use the merge function?
18. You are just starting out in business as a micro-based systems consultant. Since you have a PC, you are using WordPerfect to prepare all of your correspondence. What features would be most helpful to you in getting word out to local businesses that you are available?
19. How is a secondary file created?
20. How can a business form letter be personalized?

HANDS-ON EXERCISES

1. Type the following paragraph as it appears with all the errors. Type continuously without pressing the ENTER key. You will correct the paragraph in the following steps.

        The efficiency of the present acounting department at
    our Tower City branch is among thebest we have ever seen.
    Concidering the the complexity of this operation, the
    accurasy is commendable.

   a. Use the WordPerfect Speller to correct the misspellings. Use the "Edit" option to correct the error *thebest*. Delete the second occurrence of the word *the* in the last sentence.
   b. Use the WordPerfect Thesaurus to select an alternate word for *complexity*. Choose any word that improves the meaning of the sentence while keeping it grammatically correct.
2. Begin with a clear WordPerfect screen, and type the following business letter as it appears in Figure D.13 on the following page, including any spelling mistakes. The letter will be edited and saved for use in Exercise 3.
   a. Use the WordPerfect Speller to correct the misspellings in the letter. Delete the second occurrence of the word *in* in the second paragraph.
   b. Use the WordPerfect Thesaurus to select an alternate word for *aim* in the second paragraph. Choose any word that improves the meaning of the sentence while keeping it grammatically correct.
   c. Save the letter under the file name B:PRIMARY.EX2.
   d. Exit this document, but do not exit WordPerfect.

```
                    BECKS APPLIANCE CENTER

    Mrs. Sherri Pattison
    711 Shard Court
    Hopkins, S.C.  34125

    Dear Customer:

         Thank you for the privillege of serving you.  We trust that
    your microwave oven is once again operating to your satisfaction.
         Because it is our aim to maintain the highest standards of
    customer satisfaction, we kindly ask your cooperaton in in
    helping us accomplish this objective.  Please fill out the
    enclosed card and drop it in the mail.  Any aditional comments
    and suggestions are welcomed.
         Thank you again for the opportunity of serving you.  Please
    call on us again when you need service.

                                        The Service Manager
```

Figure D.13
Business Letter

3. This exercise is designed to practice the concept of file merging. A secondary file of customer addresses will be created and merged with the customer service letter (primary file) you created in Exercise 2.
   a. Create a secondary file of customer names and addresses similar to B:ADDRESS.SEC using the data records below.

Mrs. Louise Smith	Mrs. Becky Hooven	Mr. John Lowden
406 Canter Lane	1155 Wilder Rd.	R.D. 1 Box 42
Columbia, S. C. 34111	Sumpter, S. C. 34112	Hopkins, S. C. 34120

Mrs. Linda Zubler	Mr. Doug Heineman	
4 Winding Hill Rd.	598 S. 4th St.	
Capital View, S. C. 34120	Columbia, S. C. 34111	

   b. Save the records under the file name B:SECOND.EX3.
   c. Exit this file, but do not exit WordPerfect. You will now have a clean screen to work with.
   d. Retrieve the B:PRIMARY.EX2 file created in Exercise 2.
   e. Use the block feature to delete the customer's name and address.
   f. Insert the merge codes into the primary file above the salutation, *Dear Customer:*.
   g. Save the primary file under the file name B:MERGE.EX3.
   h. Exit the document but do not exit WordPerfect.
   i. With a clear screen, activate the merge.
   j. Save the document under the name B:MERGE.LTR.
   k. Print the five letters that have been created.
   l. Exit WordPerfect.
4. The object of this exercise is to create and execute a WordPerfect macro. You are to define a macro that you can use to save any existing file that you have stored on your data diskette in Drive B.
   a. You will be using the letter you created in Exercise 2. With a clean WordPerfect screen, retrieve the B:PRIMARY.EX2 file.
   b. Define the macro as ALT-S. Enter the keystrokes to save the B:PRIMARY.EX2 file.
   c. Activate the macro.
   d. Exit the file and WordPerfect.

Appendix E

ADVANCED FEATURES OF LOTUS 1-2-3

After completing this appendix, you should be able to

- discuss the /GRAPH command and its sublevel commands.
- describe the procedure to create each of the five types of available graphs.
- describe the procedure to save, view, and print a graph.
- discuss the /DATA command and its sublevel commands.
- describe the procedure to create a 1-2-3 database.
- describe the procedure to sort and perform queries on the database.
- describe the procedure to define and execute a 1-2-3 macro.

INTRODUCTION

In this appendix, we discuss other features of Lotus 1-2-3, such as its graphics, database management, and macro capabilities. As mentioned in Chapter 8, Lotus 1-2-3 is considered part of the second generation of integrated software packages designed mainly around electronic spreadsheet applications. Lotus 1-2-3 provides three distinct applications; spreadsheet, graphics, and database management. We already experimented with the spreadsheet part of the software package; now it is time to utilize its graphics capabilities to enhance the spreadsheets we create.

Graphics are a very common, effective tool for business document preparations and presentations. Graphs often provide an excellent overview of a subject, whether it is a two-year income projection, the sales performance of various divisions, salespersons, or departments, or any other matter that requires comparison of data from the past, current, and future. Graphics applications have assisted many businesses in planning and forecasting.

LOTUS 1-2-3 GRAPHICS

This appendix thoroughly covers the various applications of Lotus 1-2-3 Graphics, known for its ease of operation and its capabilities. Graphs in 1-2-3 are created as part of a spreadsheet. In other words, without a worksheet or spreadsheet, one cannot use 1-2-3 graphics. Therefore, it is necessary to first create a spreadsheet before getting into graphics.

The /GRAPH Command

Lotus 1-2-3 allows you to graphically represent numeric information stored in a worksheet by means of the /GRAPH command (see Figure E.1 on the following page). You can create a graph and save it to be printed, or you can view it directly on your screen, provided your computer system has graphics capabilities. Five types of graphs are available under the /GRAPH option:

    1. Line   2. Bar   3. XY   4. Stacked-Bar   5. Pie

577

578 APPENDIX E ADVANCED FEATURES OF LOTUS 1-2-3

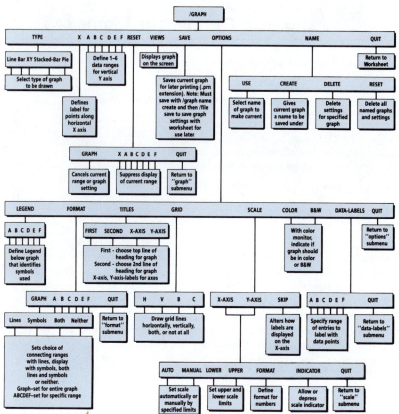

Figure E.1
Lotus 1-2-3's /GRAPH Command

To create the graphs in this section, you use the sales analysis data from the Sunshine Window Inc., Suppliers (SWIS) worksheet that you created in Chapter 9 (EXAMPLE1 on your diskette). If you are not presently in the Lotus 1-2-3 environment, perform the following steps.

- Boot up your computer system and start 1-2-3 by typing LOTUS.
- At the access system command menu, select the 1-2-3 option by typing 1.

For more complete instructions, see *Booting the System* at the beginning of Chapter 9.

Once you are in the 1-2-3 environment and a blank screen is displayed, execute the following instructions to retrieve the EXAMPLE1 worksheet.

Let's first change the default drive from A to B for the rest of this session.

- Type /FD to change the current directory from A: to B:.
- Type B: and press ENTER.

Now let's retrieve the EXAMPLE1 worksheet.

- Type /F and press ENTER to retrieve the worksheet file.
- Move the pointer to highlight the worksheet file EXAMPLE1.WK1 (if it is not already on the EXAMPLE1.WK1) and press ENTER.

The SWIS worksheet should now be displayed on your screen as shown in Figure E.2.

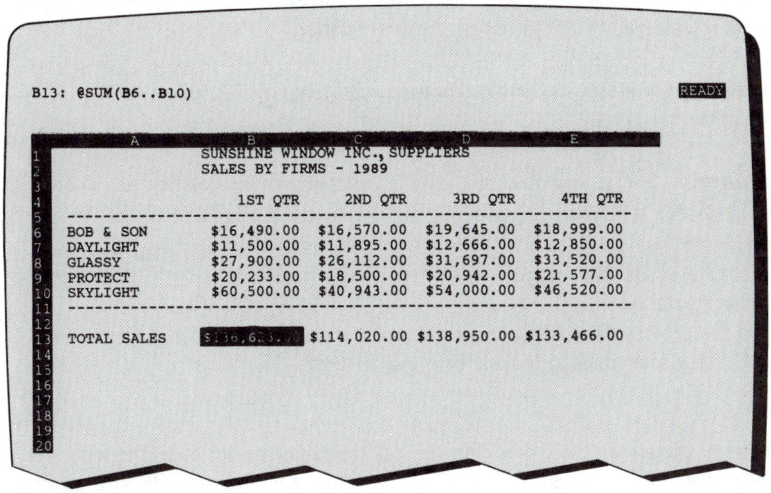

Figure E.2
SWIS Sales by Firm Worksheet

To begin the graphing procedure:

- Type /G to invoke the main menu and choose the GRAPH option. The following submenu is displayed as shown in Figure E.3.

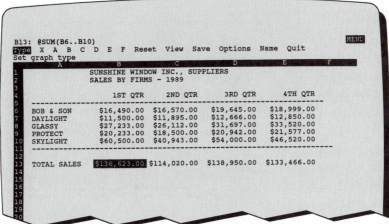

Figure E.3
Submenu of the /GRAPH Command

Back to the Case of SWIS

We will begin with a simple bar graph. SWIS owners need to see a graphic representation of sales analysis for the manufacturers' products during the past four quarters. You will create the desired graph.

Bar Graph. Bar graphs are the simplest form of graph. Ranges of data are illustrated in the form of bars, arranged side by side under different headings. The following instructions will allow you to prepare a bar graph for sales by manufacturers represented by SWIS during the first quarter.

- First, choose the type of graph you would like to create by typing T to select the TYPE option.
- Type B to select the bar graph.

Selecting Ranges. Next, you must specify the cell range or ranges that are to be graphed. The X option defines the range of labels that will be displayed along the x-axis (the horizontal axis) of the graph.

- Type X to select the x-axis label range.
- Move the pointer to cell A6.
- In response to the prompt "Enter X axis range: A6", press the period (.) to anchor cell A6, and press the DOWN ARROW key four times to include cells A6 through A10.
- Press ENTER.

Now the ranges to be plotted on the y-axis (the vertical axis) must be defined. The letters A B C D E F represent from one to six ranges that can be plotted on the y-axis. For this example, we will only concern ourselves with one data range, so the A range will be defined.

- Type A to select the y-axis data range.
- Move the pointer to cell B6 and press the period (.) key to anchor that cell.
- In response to the prompt "Enter first data range: B6..B6", press the DOWN ARROW key four times to highlight cells B6 through B10.
- Press ENTER.

View. Now you are ready to view the graph on the screen.

- Type V to select the VIEW option. Your graph should look like the one in Figure E.4.

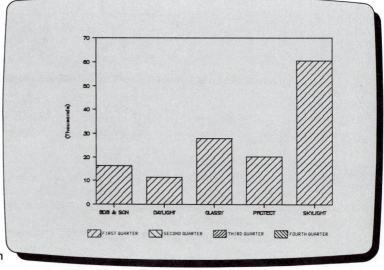

Figure E.4
Bar Graph of SWIS's Sales by Firm

- Press any key to return to the submenu.

Note: pressing the VIEW option at any time while in the /GRAPH submenu will cause the current graph to be displayed. Also, while working in the worksheet, you can press the F10 (GRAPH) function key, and the current graph will be displayed without having to go through the /GRAPH menu.

Title. A graph without some kind of description is very difficult to understand. Lotus 1-2-3 Graphics allows you to explain the various components of a graph through the use of the TITLE option. To understand how it works, let's assign different titles to our bar graph.

- Type O to select options.
- Type T to select the TITLE option.
- Type F to select the first line title.
- Type Sunshine Window Inc., Suppliers and press ENTER.
- Type T to select the TITLE option again.
- Type S to select the second line title.
- Type Sales Analysis - First Quarter and press ENTER.
- Type T to select the TITLE option again.
- Type Y to select the y-axis line title.
- Type Sales Amount (Dollars) and press ENTER.
- Type Q to quit the option submenu.
- Type V to view the graph. Your graph should look like the one in Figure E.5.
- Press any key to return to the worksheet.

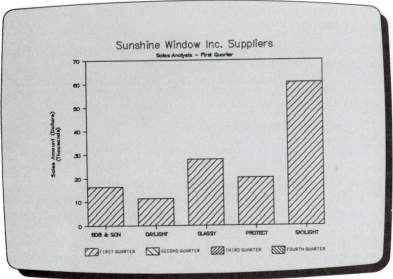

Figure E.5
SWIS Graph with Titles – First Quarter Results

Name. You will be creating other graphs from the same worksheet data. Therefore, it is necessary to give the graph you have just created a name so that the settings will not be lost.

- In the /GRAPH submenu, type N to choose the option Name.
- Type C to select the CREATE option.
- In response to the prompt "ENTER graph name:", type 1stQTR and press ENTER. This action will attach this bar graph to your worksheet, but it does not mean that you have saved this graph on your diskette. The graph's settings will be saved on your diskette along with the worksheet data when you issue the /FILE SAVE command discussed below.

Save. Whenever a graph is intended to be printed, either immediately or in the future, it must be saved with the extension .PIC. To do this, after you issue the /GRAPH NAME CREATE command, give the /GRAPH SAVE command as follows.

- In the /GRAPH submenu, type S to invoke the Save command.
- Type 1stQTR and press ENTER. 1-2-3 will automatically save the file with the .PIC extension. The same file name can be used in both naming and saving the graph file.
- Type Q to quit the GRAPH submenu.

Reset. If at any time you decide that you would like to change the settings of your graph, you can accomplish this by using the RESET option. The RESET option allows you to cancel all of the graph settings by selecting the GRAPH option in its submenu, or to change one or more of the graph settings by choosing the appropriate option: X A B C D E F.

Back to the Case of SWIS

SWIS's Martinez and Gonzales are satisfied with the graphic display for sales analysis and wonder if the same type of graph could be generated for the second-quarter sales. The two graphs are very similar in design, so this should not be a problem. In this case, the Type X settings can remain the same, but the A range should be changed from *1st QTR* to *2nd QTR*.

- In the /GRAPH submenu, type R to select RESET.
- Type A to reset the A range.
- Type Q to quit the RESET submenu.
- Type A to define the A range.
- Move the pointer to cell C6, and press the period (.) key to anchor cell C6.
- Press the DOWN ARROW key four times to include cells C6 through C10, and press ENTER.
- Type O to select the options.
- Type T to select titles.
- Type S for second to change the second title.
- Use the backspace key to erase the words *First Quarter*, type Second Quarter and press ENTER.
- Press ESC once.
- Type V to view the graph. Your graph will appear as shown in Figure E.6 on the following page.

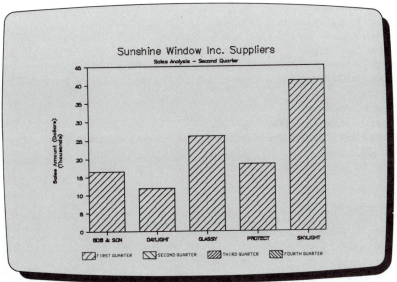

Figure E.6
SWIS Bar Graph with Titles – Second Quarter Results

Now, let's name and then save the second graph under the name 2ndQTR.

- Press any key to get back to the /GRAPH submenu.
- Type N for the NAME option.
- Type C for CREATE option.
- Type 2ndQTR and press ENTER.
- Type S for the SAVE option.
- Type 2ndQTR and press ENTER.
- Type Q to quit the GRAPH submenu.

Side-by-Side Bar Graph. At this point, the management of SWIS is interested in comparing the overall sales performance of the five companies they represented during the last four quarters. Lotus 1-2-3 Graphics offers a version of the bar graph it calls side-by-side bar graphs. In this case, the x-axis would remain the same as in the previous two graphs (*Firm Name*), the A range would be *First Quarter*, the B range *Second Quarter*, the C range *Third Quarter*, and the D range *Fourth Quarter*. Now, let's try to prepare a side-by-side graph for SWIS.

- In the /GRAPH submenu, type R to select RESET.
- Type A and press ENTER to reset the A range.
- Type Q to quit the RESET submenu.
- Type A to define the A range.
- Move the pointer to cell B6, and press the period (.) key to anchor cell B6.
- Press the DOWN ARROW key four times to include cell B6 through B10, and press ENTER.
- Type B to define the B range.
- Move the pointer to cell C6 and press the period (.) key to anchor cell C6.
- Press the DOWN ARROW key four times to include cell C6 through C10, and press ENTER.

- Type C to define the C range.
- Move the pointer to cell D6 and press the period (.) key to anchor cell D6.
- Press the DOWN ARROW key four times to include cell D6 through D10, and press ENTER.
- Type D to define the D range.
- Move the pointer to cell E6, and press the period (.) key to anchor cell E6.
- Press the DOWN ARROW key four times to include cell E6 through E10, and press ENTER.
- Type O to retrieve option menu.
- Type T to access Titles menu.
- Type S to go to the second line of the Graph Title.
- Use BACKSPACE key to change *Second Quarter* to *All Quarters* and press ENTER.
- Type Q to quit Titles menu.
- Type V to view the graph. Your screen should like the one in Figure E.7.

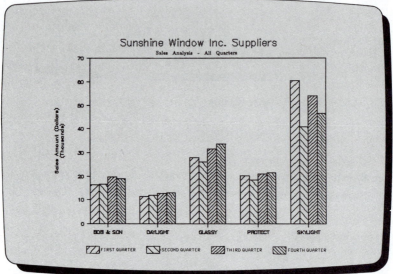

Figure E.7
Side-by-Side Bar Graph for All Quarters

Legend. Lotus 1-2-3 Graphics allows you to add to the bottom of the graph a description or legend of the different shadings used in a graph. This task is performed by using the LEGEND option. Let's try this option for the side-by-side graph we just created. First, we need to assign titles to the graph.

- Type any key to return to the submenu.
- Type O to select the options.
- Type L to select the LEGEND option.
- Type A to name the A range.
- Type First Quarter and press ENTER.
- Type L to select the LEGEND option again.

- Type B to name the B range.
- Type `Second Quarter` and press ENTER.
- Type L to select the LEGEND option again.
- Type C to name the C range.
- Type `Third Quarter` and press ENTER.
- Type L to select the LEGEND option again.
- Type D to name the D range.
- Type `Fourth Quarter` and press ENTER.
- Type Q to quit the option submenu.
- Type V to view the graph, which should look like the one in Figure E.8.

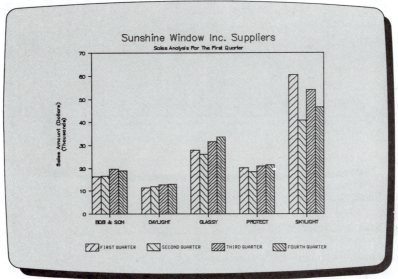

Figure E.8
SWIS Side-by-Side Bar Graph with LEGEND

Let's give this graph a name and save it as ALLQTR.

- Press any key to get back to the submenu.
- Type N to select the NAME option.
- Type C to select the CREATE option.
- Type `ALLQTR` and press ENTER.
- Type S to select the SAVE option.
- Type `ALLQTR` and press ENTER.

Stacked-Bar Graphs. Now let's create a stacked-bar graph, which stacks multiple data ranges on top of each other instead of placing them side by side as in vertical bar charts. Let's use the side-by-side graph that has just been created to create a stacked-bar graph.

- In the /GRAPH submenu, type T to select the TYPE option.
- Type S to select the STACKED-BAR option.
- Type V to view the graph, which should look like the one in Figure E.9.

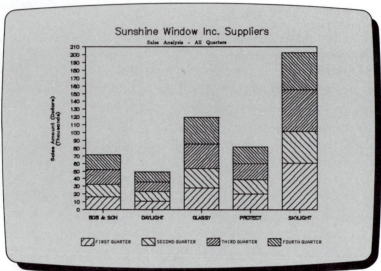

Figure E.9
SWIS Stacked-Bar Graph

Now, let's name and save this graph.

- Press any key to get back to the /GRAPH submenu.
- Type N to select the NAME option.
- Type C to select the CREATE option.
- Type ALLSTACK and press ENTER.
- Type S to select the SAVE option.
- Type ALLSTACK and press ENTER.

Line Graph. Line graphs present data on the vertical y-axis and item or data names and labels on the horizontal x-axis. Line graphs can depict a single set of data, such as the sales figures in SWIS's first quarter, or use different lines to represent different sets of data on a single graph. The latter case serves the same function as the 1-2-3 side-by-side bar graph. Let's try to create a line graph for SWIS's first quarter sales. In this case, since we have already created a bar graph from the same data, we will try to modify that earlier graph. This technique will also introduce you to the USE command.

- In the /GRAPH submenu, type N to select the NAME option.
- Type U to select the USE option.
- Move the pointer to *1STQTR* and press ENTER. Upon completion of this action, the original bar graph will be displayed on the screen.
- Press any key to get back to the /GRAPH submenu.

- Type T to select the TYPE option.
- Type L to select the LINE GRAPH option.
- Type V to view the newly created line graph shown in Figure E.10.

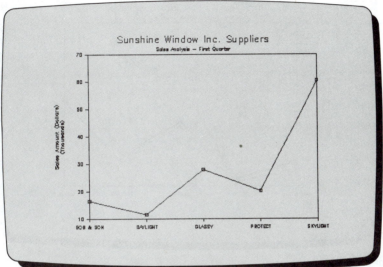

Figure E.10
SWIS Line Graph for First Quarter

Let's give this graph a name.

- Press any key to get back to the /GRAPH submenu.
- Type N to select the NAME option.
- Type C to select the CREATE option.
- Type 1stline and press ENTER.
- Type S to select the SAVE option.
- Type 1stline and press ENTER.

Multi-Line Charts. Lotus 1-2-3 Graphics also provides a multi-line charts option. This is similar to the side-by-side bar chart, except that lines are used instead of bars to illustrate the performance of different data sets. Let's try to use this Graphics option for the case of SWIS. We'll begin by bringing back the side-by-side bar chart that we created earlier.

- In the /GRAPH submenu, type N to select the NAME option.
- Type U to select the USE option.
- Move the pointer to *ALLQTR* and press ENTER. Upon completion of this action, the side-by-side graph will appear on the screen.
- Press any key to get back to the /GRAPH submenu.
- Type T to select the TYPE option.

- Type L to select the LINE option.
- Type V to view the graph shown in Figure E.11.

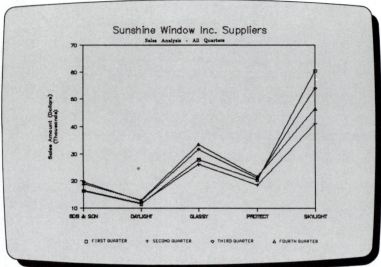

Figure E.11
Multi-Line Graph for All Quarters

Let's give this graph a name and save it.

- Press any key to get back to the /GRAPH submenu.
- Type N to select the NAME option.
- Type C to select the CREATE option.
- Type Multline and press ENTER.
- Type S to select the SAVE option.
- Type Multline and press ENTER.

Pie Charts. Lotus 1-2-3 pie charts divide a single data set into segments of a pie-shaped circle and labels each segment according to its percentage of the overall data "pie." Pie charts cannot be used for multiple data ranges. To see how pie charts work in 1-2-3, let's try to depict the first-quarter sales performance of the five companies that SWIS represents. We have already displayed this data in the form of a bar graph. Therefore, we will first access that information, which has been stored under the name 1stQTR. Follow the instructions below.

- In the /GRAPH submenu, type N to select the NAME option.
- Type U to select the USE option.
- Move the pointer to *1stQTR* and press ENTER.
- Press any key to get back to the /GRAPH submenu.
- Type T to select the TYPE option.
- Type P to select the PIE option.
- Type V to view the graph, which will look like the one in Figure E.12 on the following page.

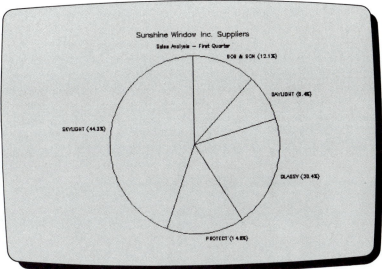

Figure E.12
A Pie Chart for the SWIS Worksheet

Let's name and save this pie chart.

- Press any key to get back to the /GRAPH submenu.
- Type N to select the NAME option.
- Type C to select the CREATE option.
- Type 1stPIE and press ENTER.
- Type S to select the SAVE option.
- Type 1stPIE and press ENTER.

■ PRINTING THE GRAPH

At this stage, you may want to obtain a hard copy of the graphs that you have created so far. *Remember that you must save your worksheet, with all the graphs that you have assigned to it, before proceeding with the printing function.* The graphs that you have saved are stored on your diskette separate from the worksheet file; these graph files will be used for obtaining the hard copy. However, in order to use the worksheet and related graphs later on, you must save the worksheet with all its graphs. To save your worksheet and graphs:

- In the GRAPHIC submenu, type Q to quit.
- Invoke the main menu and type F to select the FILE option.
- Type S to select the SAVE option.
- Press ENTER to confirm that you want to save the worksheet under the name EXAMPLE1.WK1.
- Type R to select the REPLACE option.

You cannot print your graph directly from the Lotus 1-2-3 program; you must exit 1-2-3 and enter the PrintGraph program from the access system command menu. To do so, follow these instructions.

- Type / to get the main menu.
- Type Q to select the QUIT option and exit 1-2-3.
- Type Y (for Yes) to end the 1-2-3 session.
- From the access system command menu, type P to select the PrintGraph program.
- You will be prompted to insert the PrintGraph Diskette in Drive A. Press ENTER after you have done so.

Once you are in the PrintGraph program, the menu shown in Figure E.13 will be presented.

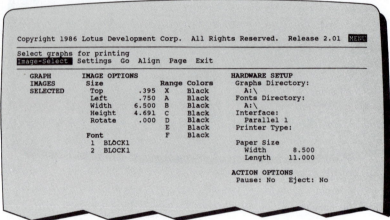

Figure E.13
PrintGraph Main Menu

Table E.1 illustrates the available menu options of the PrintGraph and their functions.

PRINT OPTION	DESCRIPTION
Image-Selection	Select the graph to print.
Settings	Allows the hardware and graph settings to be defined.
Go	Execute the print process to generate the graph.
Align	Inform printer that it is at the top of the page.
Page	Advance the paper to the top of the next page.
Exit	End the PrintGraph session.

Table E.1   A Brief Summary of the Print Options

To print some of the graph files that you saved previously, follow the steps below.

First let's change the default directory from A to B. PrintGraph initially assumes all graph files are stored on the diskette in Drive A.

- Type S to select the SETTINGS option.
- Type H to select the HARDWARE option.
- Type G to select the GRAPH-DIRECTORY option.
- Type B: and press ENTER.

- Type Q to quit the hardware menu.
- Type Q again to quit the settings menu.

Note: Make sure your printer is identified to the Lotus PrintGraph. To see what type of printer is defined, use the Printer option in the hardware menu. Now let's choose Graph files.

- Type I to select the IMAGE-SELECT option for printing. Upon completion of this action, the screen in Figure E.14 will appear.

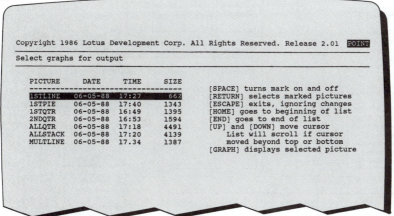

Figure E.14
PrintGraph Screen with All Graph Files

- Move the highlighted pointer to the *1STQTR* (if it is not already highlighting this graph file), and press ENTER.
- Type P to advance the printer to the top of a new page.
- Type G (for Go) to start the printing process.

During the printing process, there will be a blinking wait message at the top right of the screen.

You can repeat the same process for any of the other graphs that you have created. You can choose Multigraph files to be printed continuously. To do so, move the highlighted line over to the desired graph files and press ENTER. PrintGraph will place a pound sign (#) at the front of the file, marking it for printing. To remove the printing mark, press the spacebar while the file is highlighted.

Note: If you choose to print one graph file at a time, make sure you remove the printing mark from the front of the file that is already printed. Otherwise, regardless of your new selection, PrintGraph will print the first file that was marked for printing.

Upon completion of the printing process, choose E from the PrintGraph main menu to Quit. This will take you back to the Lotus 1-2-3 main menu. There, you can choose either E to exit or 1-2-3 to get back to the 1-2-3 environment.

■ LOTUS 1-2-3 DATABASE MANAGEMENT

The third subsystem of Lotus 1-2-3 is the database management system, which can be used to store and manipulate data. The database management system is part of the 1-2-3 program, and the user can easily access this subsystem from the main menu of 1-2-3.

The /DATA Command

The chart in Figure E.15 provides an overview of the /DATA command option and all of its associated submenus.

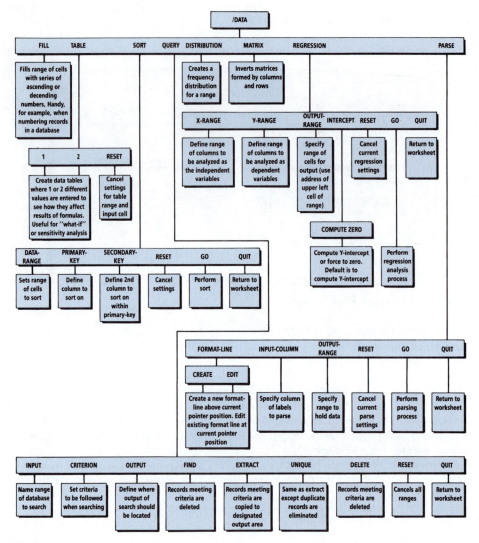

Figure E.15
Lotus 1-2-3's /DATA Command

The purpose of 1-2-3's database management system is to store, access, and manipulate data that have been stored—not in a database file as in other software packages—but in the worksheet format.

A 1-2-3 database is a table of rows and columns. The top row contains the names of the fields; in Figure E.16, for example, the field names are ACCOUNT, REPRESENTATIVE, PHONE, and SALES. Each subsequent row contains a record, or group of related data. For example, all the data in Row 3 constitute one record of descriptive information about Stratford Window Fashions.

Figure E.16 illustrates a portion of SWIS's database of clients, including the name of the account, the representative of the company who serves as SWIS's contact, the last four digits of the phone number (they are all in the 555 exchange), and the total amount of business done with each company this year to date.

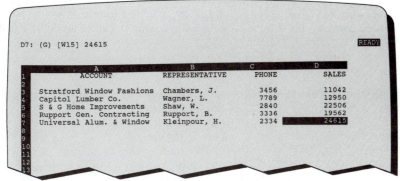

Figure E.16
SWIS's Database of Clients

You should begin this exercise with a clean worksheet. The settings for the column widths should be as follows:

- Move the pointer to cell A1, if it is not already there.
- Type /WEY to start a new worksheet area.
- Type /W to invoke the WORKSHEET submenu.
- Type C to invoke the COLUMN submenu.
- Type S to select the SET-WIDTH option.
- Type 26, and press ENTER to change the column width from nine to twenty-six.
- Move the pointer to cell B1.
- Type /WCS to change the column width.
- Type 15 and press ENTER.
- Move the pointer to cell C1.
- Type /WCS to change the column width.
- Type 12 and press ENTER.
- Move the pointer to cell D1.
- Type /WCS to change the column width.
- Type 15 and press ENTER.

Let's type labels in the first row as follows.

In cell:	Type label as:
A1	^ACCOUNT
B1	REPRESENTATIVE
C1	"PHONE
D1	SALES

Now, format column D.

- Move the pointer to cell D3.
- Type /RFG.
- In response to the prompt "Enter range to format:", press the DOWN ARROW four times to highlight the entire column.
- Press ENTER.

Enter the remaining data into the database as listed below (refer to Figure E.16 on the previous page for an illustration of the finished database). ENTER the sales figures in column D without the dollar sign or commas; they will be formatted for you.

In cell:	Type:	In cell:	Type:
A3	Stratford Window Fashions	A6	Rupport Gen. Contracting
B3	Chambers, J.	B6	Rupport, B.
C3	3456	C6	3336
D3	11042	D6	19562
A4	Capital Lumber Co.	A7	Universal Alum. & Window
B4	Wagner, L.	B7	Kleinpour, H.
C4	7789	C7	2334
D4	12950	D7	24615
A5	S & G Home Improvements		
B5	Shaw, W.		
C5	2840		
D5	22506		

Now let's save this database.

- Type /FS to select the SAVE option.
- In response to "A:*.WK1" press ESC two times.
- Type B:Client and press ENTER.

The /DATA SORT Command

Now let's use a couple of /DATA subcommands to work with our SWIS data. The /DATA SORT command sorts information in the database, and the /DATA QUERY command searches the database for records that meet certain criteria and extracts those records. Once all the data are entered into our database, the records can be sorted alphabetically by account name.

- Move the cursor to cell A3.
- Type /D to select the /DATA option.
- Type S to select the SORT option.
- Type D to select the DATA-RANGE option.
- Press the period (.) and then press the RIGHT ARROW three times to highlight the cells A3 to D3.
- Press the DOWN ARROW four times. All five records are now highlighted.

- Press ENTER.
- While in any row in column A, press P and press ENTER to select Primary-Key to determine the column that the data should be sorted on.
- Type A to specify that column A should be sorted in ascending order, and press ENTER.
- Type G to select Go. The data is now sorted alphabetically according to account name, as shown in Figure E.17.

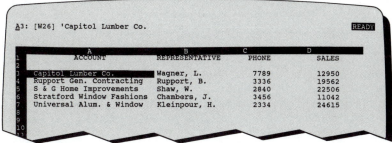

Figure E.17
Sorted SWIS Clients Database

The /DATA QUERY Command

SWIS's owners would like to know which clients have given them more than $20,000 in business so far this year. To produce an output report of clients meeting this criteria, three pieces of information must be defined: the input range, the criterion range, and the output range.

The input range. You must tell 1-2-3 the range of data you would like to search. In this example, cells A1 through D7 become the input range. The input range must include the first line of the database containing the field names and all of the records that follow. Let's define the input range for our example:

- Press HOME.
- Type /DQI.
- In response to the message "Enter Input range: A1", Press period (.) to anchor the upper left corner of the range.
- Press END followed by the RIGHT ARROW key.
- Press the DOWN ARROW six times until the entire worksheet of data is highlighted.
- Press ENTER.

The criterion range. Defining the criterion range tells 1-2-3 which records you would like to single out of the database. You can specify criteria that refer to one or more fields of the database.

First, you must select a blank area of your worksheet in which to set up the criterion range. Row 12 has been chosen at random for this example. The field names will be copied to the criterion range. Although the only fields that must be copied are the ones that will be checked by the criteria, it is a good practice to copy all of the field names to the criterion range. This allows you to add additional criteria more easily in the future, if the need arises. Using the /COPY command, copy the row of field names to the criterion range.

- Use the ESC key to back out of the DATA submenu until the main menu is displayed.
- Type C to select the COPY command.
- With the pointer in cell A1, press the period (.) followed by the RIGHT ARROW three time to define the range to copy *from*. Press ENTER.
- In response to "Enter this range to copy to", type A12.D12.
- Press ENTER.

Now, the criteria are entered on the second line of the criterion range.

- Move the pointer to cell D13.
- Type the formula +D2>20000 and press ENTER. A zero will be placed in this cell. Because it is typed under the field name of SALES, this criterion tells 1-2-3 to look for all records that contain a figure under SALES of more than $20,000.
- To format cell D13 so you can see the actual formula, type /RFT and press ENTER.

Now to actually define the criterion range:

- Type /DQC.
- Type A12.D13 and press ENTER. This defines both the row of field names and the row containing the criteria in the criterion range.

The database worksheet will look like the one in Figure E.18.

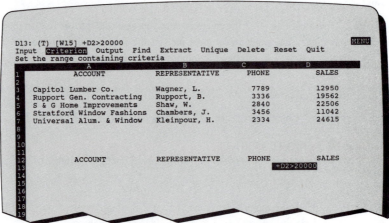

Figure E.18
SWIS's Client Database with the Selected Criteria

The FIND option moves the pointer to the first row that meets the criteria that you have defined. Use of the UP and DOWN ARROW keys will reveal any other rows that also meet the criteria. The computer will beep when there are no more records meeting the criteria in either direction.

- Type F to select the FIND option.

The third record (shown in Figure E.19) in the database will be highlighted since the sales figure exceeds $20,000.

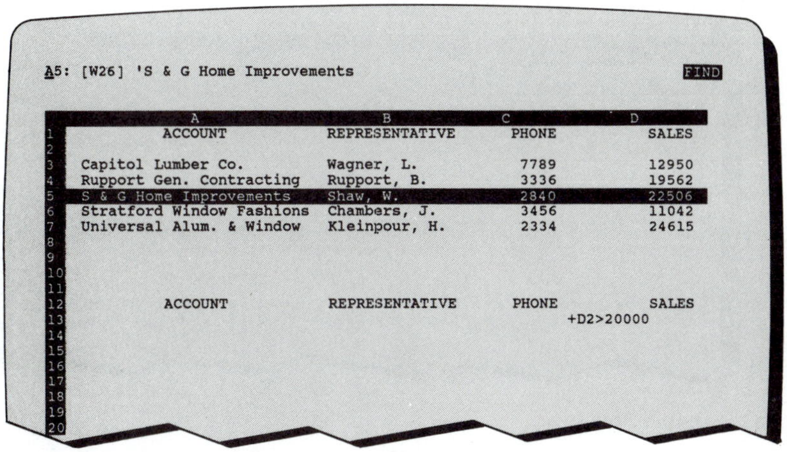

```
A5: [W26] 'S & G Home Improvements                              FIND

         A                    B                C           D
1      ACCOUNT          REPRESENTATIVE       PHONE       SALES
2
3    Capitol Lumber Co.      Wagner, L.       7789       12950
4    Rupport Gen. Contracting Rupport, B.     3336       19562
5    S & G Home Improvements  Shaw, W.        2840       22506
6    Stratford Window Fashions Chambers, J.   3456       11042
7    Universal Alum. & Window  Kleinpour, H.  2334       24615
8
...
12     ACCOUNT          REPRESENTATIVE       PHONE       SALES
13                                                    +D2>20000
```

Figure E.19
The First Record with the Sales Amount > $20,000

- Press the DOWN and UP arrow keys. Two records meet the criteria defined.
- Press ENTER (the ESC key can also be used) to return to the FIND submenu.

The output range. If a report of the FIND information is required, then an output area must be defined to display the data.

You must once again copy the row of field names to a blank area of the worksheet. Row 16 has been chosen at random to hold the output.

- Press the ESC key three times to back out of the menus.
- Move the pointer to cell A1.
- Type /C to select the COPY command.
- With the pointer in cell A1, press the period (.) followed by pressing the RIGHT ARROW three times. Press ENTER.
- Type A16.D16 as the range to copy *to*.

To define the output range,

- Type /DQO.
- Type A16.D16 to define the output range.
- Press ENTER.

The EXTRACT option retrieves the records meeting the specified criteria and displays the records in the output range.

- Type E to select the EXTRACT option. The two records meeting the criteria are displayed in the output area and should look like Figure E.20 on the following page.

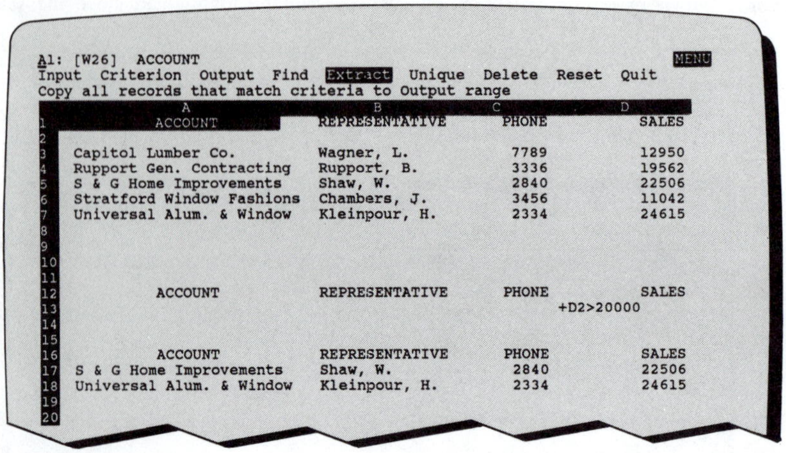

598 APPENDIX E ADVANCED FEATURES OF LOTUS 1-2-3

```
A1: [W26] ACCOUNT                                                    MENU
Input  Criterion  Output  Find  Extract  Unique  Delete  Reset  Quit
Copy all records that match criteria to Output range
            A                    B                  C             D
   1    ACCOUNT              REPRESENTATIVE       PHONE         SALES
   2
   3    Capitol Lumber Co.    Wagner, L.           7789         12950
   4    Rupport Gen. Contracting Rupport, B.       3336         19562
   5    S & G Home Improvements  Shaw, W.          2840         22506
   6    Stratford Window Fashions Chambers, J.     3456         11042
   7    Universal Alum. & Window Kleinpour, H.     2334         24615
   8
   9
  10
  11
  12    ACCOUNT              REPRESENTATIVE       PHONE         SALES
  13                                                        +D2>20000
  14
  15
  16    ACCOUNT              REPRESENTATIVE       PHONE         SALES
  17    S & G Home Improvements  Shaw, W.          2840         22506
  18    Universal Alum. & Window Kleinpour, H.     2334         24615
  19
  20
```

Figure E.20
Selected Records in the Output Area

■ LOTUS 1-2-3 MACROS

A macro is a time-saving tool that is useful when working on a Lotus 1-2-3 worksheet. Often, you will find yourself performing the same series of commands, for example, to save a file, copy a range of cells, or format a range. A macro allows you to combine a series of keystrokes, enter them in a blank cell in the worksheet, give the series a name, and execute them as one task simply by entering the name of the macro.

To learn about macros and apply them in a practical situation, we will use the EXAMPLE2 worksheet that you created in Chapter 9. If you have not worked through Chapter 9 and do not have the EXAMPLE2 worksheet stored on your diskette, you will still be able to work through this example using any existing 1-2-3 worksheet.

Defining a Macro

The first thing you must do is to decide on a task—a series of keystrokes—that you perform often and would like to be able to accomplish in one step. For example, each time you were finished working on the worksheet for Sunshine Window Inc., Suppliers, you had to go through a number of keystrokes to save the file. The task of saving the file, therefore, could be done using a macro.

At this time, enter the 1-2-3 environment and retrieve the EXAMPLE2.WK1 worksheet (or any existing file that you would like to use). ENTER the keystrokes to save the file; as you perform each keystroke, write it down on a sheet of paper. This is an important step in defining the macro. The time you take now to write the keystrokes down on paper can save you a great deal of time in editing later. The keystrokes you should have written down are:

Keystroke	Action Performed
/	Invokes the main menu
F	Selects the FILE option
S	Selects the SAVE option
[ENTER]	Accepts the file to save as EXAMPLE2.WK1
R	Selects REPLACE

The ENTER key is used extensively when working with macros, and is represented by the tilde (~) character.

Entering the Macro

The first step is to decide where in your worksheet to enter the macro. A blank area well away from current or any future worksheet data is necessary. It is advisable to choose an easily remembered area for your macros, such as cell AB1 or BB1. For this example,

- Press F5 and GOTO cell AB1.
- Press ENTER.

Macro keystrokes must be entered as labels, using one of the following label prefixes as the first character: ' " ^.

- Type '/FS~R and press ENTER. Your worksheet will look like the one in Figure E.21.

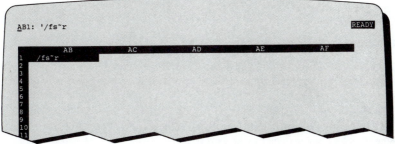

Figure E.21
The Initial Screen of the Lotus Macro

Naming the Macro

Now that the macro has been created, it must be given a name, using the /RANGE NAME CREATE command, so that it can be executed when needed. A macro name consists of the backslash (\) and any one letter of the alphabet. With the pointer in cell AB1, do the following:

- Type /R to select the RANGE option.
- Type N to select the NAME option.
- Type C to select the CREATE option.
- In response to the prompt "Enter name:", type \S and press ENTER to name your macro S for Save. (Remember, the first character is a backslash and the second character could have been any other letter.)
- In response to the prompt "Enter range: AB1..AB1", press ENTER to accept.

Note: If the macro had occupied more than one cell, the range would still have been AB1. 1-2-3 only needs to know the first cell of a macro.

Documenting the Macro

It is advisable to document your macro so that you, or anyone else that wants to use it in the future, know exactly what name will invoke the macro and the task it performs. Comments concerning a macro can be entered in the cells to the right of the macro, and the macro name should be entered in the cell to the left.

- In cell AA1, type the macro name, `'\S` and press ENTER.
- In cell AC1, type the description of the macro, `Save and update the worksheet` and press ENTER.

The macro and any documentation will be saved with the worksheet when the /FILE SAVE command is issued. The worksheet with the completed macro should look like the one in Figure E.22.

Figure E.22
Complete Macro Screen

Invoking the Macro

Now that the macro has been created, named, and documented, it is time to try it out. A macro is invoked by pressing the ALT key and the letter that you used to name the macro. Just press the letter; it is not necessary to press the backslash (\) key.

- Press the HOME key so your worksheet is displayed on the screen. (This step is for viewing purposes only; the macro can be invoked from any point in the worksheet.)
- Press the ALT and S keys simultaneously.

The mode indicator changes to WAIT, and the red light on Drive B is lighted. When the mode indicator changes to READY, your file has been saved. Your macro has accomplished the SAVE task in one step.

Special Keys

The keystrokes you used in the above macro example were entered by typing the appropriate keys. Some keys or commands that are to be used in a macro have to be entered with braces ({ }) around them. The {?} Command. The {?} macro key instructs 1-2-3 to pause so that the user can enter instructions manually. Any number of {?} commands can be entered in a macro, allowing data or instructions to be entered interactively. Each time, after the data or instruction is entered, the ENTER key must be pressed to resume execution of the current macro.

A Macro Example

Quit the EXAMPLE2.WK1 worksheet and begin with a new blank worksheet. We will work through a simple macro example using special keys, a formula, and the {?} interactive macro keystroke.

Type the six numbers in the new worksheet as shown in Figure E.23 on the following page. This example will take the sum of the numbers in column A and place the result in cell A5. The formula in cell A5 will be copied to cell B5, resulting in the sum of the numbers in column B being placed in cell B5. The entire worksheet will then be formatted as currency, the worksheet will be saved—pausing for the user to enter the file name—and the pointer returned to cell A1.

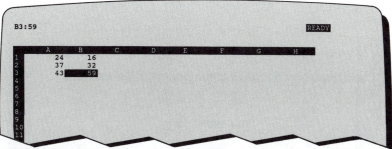

Figure E.23
A Sample Worksheet

Use function key F5 to GOTO cell AB1 to enter the macro. The following macro instructions are typed on six different lines. They could have been entered as one long string of instructions; however, splitting them into smaller sections makes them easier to edit, if necessary. The only spacing requirement for entering a macro is that the cell directly beneath the last instruction be left blank to tell 1-2-3 when it has reached the final instruction of the macro.

- In cell AB1, type the first line of the macro: {goto}a5~.
- In cell AB2, type '+a1+a2+a3~.
- In cell AB3, type '/c~b5~.
- In cell AB4, type '/wgfc~.
- In cell AB5, type '/fs{?}~.
- In cell AB6, type {home}.

The macro area of your worksheet will look like Figure E.24.

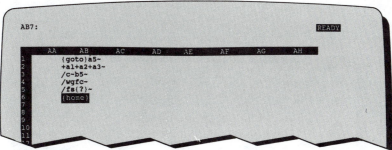

Figure E.24
A Macro Screen with a Set of Commands

To name this newly created macro,

- Press F5 (GOTO) cell AB1 and type /RNC.
- Enter the name as \A and press ENTER.
- Press ENTER to accept AB1 as the range.

To document the macro,

- In cell AA1, type '\a.

- Enter comments in column AD, as shown in Figure E.25.

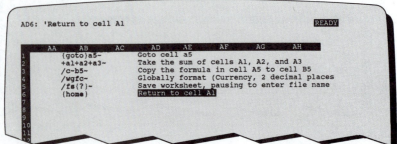

Figure E.25
Comments for the Macro Example

To execute the macro,

- Press the HOME key to be able to watch the changes in the worksheet as the macro is executed.
- Press ALT and the letter A simultaneously.

After the columns are totalled and formatted, the system will pause until you enter the file name under which to save the worksheet.

- Type the file name MACROEX and press ENTER.

The formatted figures in the worksheet will appear as in Figure E.26.

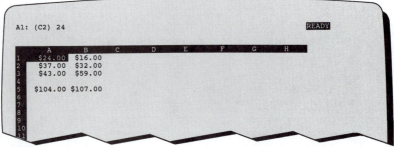

Figure E.26
Results of Macro Execution

■ Summary of Lotus 1-2-3 Commands and Terms

/GRAPH   Specify settings for 1-2-3's graphics capabilities.
/DATA   Subcommands perform operations such as sorting and querying on a 1-2-3 database.
macro   Allows you to combine a series of keystrokes and execute them as one task.

■ Review Questions

1. Which of the following submenu options causes the current graph to be displayed on the screen?
   (a) TYPE
   (b) RESET
   (c) VIEW
   (d) NAME
2. Which of the following submenu options allows you to choose a desired kind of graph?
   (a) TYPE
   (b) RESET
   (c) VIEW
   (d) NAME
3. If you have used the /GRAPH NAME CREATE sequence, will you be certain that your graph will be saved? Explain.
4. A graph is automatically saved with the _____ extension.
   (a) .PIC
   (b) .GRA
   (c) .WKS
   (d) .COM
5. The _____ option will allow you to add a descriptive key at the bottom of the graph labeling the different shadings used in a graph.
   (a) LEGEND
   (b) KEY
   (c) COLOR
   (d) TITLE
6. How many graphs can be defined for the same worksheet?
7. The _____ program must be used to print graphs in Lotus 1-2-3.
   (a) GraphicPrint
   (b) PrintColor
   (c) Print
   (d) PrintGraph
8. A 1-2-3 database is a _____ of rows and columns.
   (a) field
   (b) block
   (c) table
   (d) group
9. The /DATA _____ command allows the records in the database to be arranged in alphabetical order.
   (a) QUERY
   (b) SORT
   (c) PARSE
   (d) FILL
   (e) None of the above
10. When defining the criterion range, how many fields must be included?

11. Which of the following /DATA QUERY options retrieves the records meeting specified criteria and displays those records in the output range?
    (a) FIND
    (b) UNIQUE
    (c) DELETE
    (d) EXTRACT
12. When defining a 1-2-3 macro, which of the following characters represents the ENTER key?
    (a) '
    (b) ~
    (c) "
    (d) ^
13. When would a macro be used?
14. Which of the following is *not* a type graph?
    (a) Pie
    (b) Bar
    (c) Line
    (d) Stacked Pie
15. The _____ macro key instructs 1-2-3 to pause so the user can enter instructions manually.
    (a) { ~ }
    (b) { ? }
    (c) { | }
    (d) { * }
    (e) { ^ }
16. Name the five types of graphs available in 1-2-3.
17. What titles are you able to add to a graph with the /GRAPH OPTIONS TITLES option?
18. Explain the procedure for obtaining a hard copy of a 1-2-3 graph.
19. To produce an output report of database records meeting certain criteria, what three pieces of information must be defined?
20. What is the function of the FIND option when performing a database query?
21. How is a macro name defined?
22. You are working with a 1-2-3 worksheet developed last year by an accountant who has since left your company. The accountant was an advanced 1-2-3 user and used macro's extensively. You have several problems with the worksheet and are not sure what some of the macros are doing. What is the problem?
23. Which of the following is *not* a subsystem of 1-2-3?
    (a) graph
    (b) spreadsheet
    (c) macro
    (d) database
    (e) all are subsystems
24. Which of the following /DATA QUERY options determines the range of data to be searched?
    (a) EXTRACT
    (b) RANGE
    (c) FIND
    (d) INPUT
    (e) CRITERION

25. The /DATA _____ command finds all data records satisfying given criteria.
    (a) PARSE
    (b) SORT
    (c) TABLE
    (d) QUERY
    (e) DISTRIBUTION
26. Which of the following is a graph type in Lotus?
    (a) line graph.
    (b) side-by-side bar graph.
    (c) pie chart.
    (d) stacked bar graph.
    (e) all of the above

HANDS-ON EXERCISES

1. The owner of the chain of Glenn's Sporting Goods stores was pleased with the quarterly sales report (Chapter 9 Hands-on Exercises) and is now interested in seeing a graphic representation of the stores' performances. Using the B:STOREEX3.WK1 worksheet that you created in Chapter 9, create a bar graph using the data in that worksheet. Begin with a clean worksheet.
   a. Retrieve the B:STOREEX3.WK1 worksheet from your disk.
   b. Create a bar graph by defining the range of the x-axis to be the four quarters and the four y-axis to be plotted as four stores.
   c. Use the TITLE option to assign titles to the graph as follows.
      First line: GLENN'S SPORTING GOODS
      Second line: QUARTERLY SALES - 1989
      y-axis: SALES (DOLLARS)
   d. Use the LEGEND option to assign descriptive labels to the shaded areas on the graph:
      Range A   STORE 1
      Range B   STORE 2
      Range C   STORE 3
      Range D   STORE 4
   e. View the graph.
   f. Name the graph BARGR.
   g. Save the graph as B:BARGR. 1-2-3 will automatically save the file with the .PIC extension.
   h. Save the worksheet.
   i. Obtain a printout of the graph using the PrintGraph program.
   j. Exit 1-2-3 PrintGraph and return to DOS.

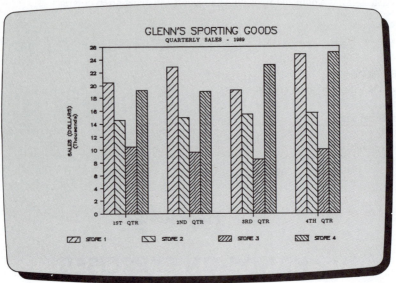

Figure E.27
Side-by-Side Graph of Glenn's Sporting Goods

2. Using the STOREEX3.WK1 worksheet, you are to create a line graph by modifying the bar graph (BARGR.PIC) settings you created in Exercise 1. Begin with a clean 1-2-3 worksheet.
   a. Retrieve the STOREEX3.WK1 worksheet.
   b. Create a line graph using the same titles and legend created in Exercise 1.
   c. View the graph.
   d. Name the graph LINEGR.
   e. Save the graph as B:LINEGR.
   f. Save the worksheet.
   g. Obtain a printout of the graph using the PrintGraph program.
   h. Exit PrintGraph and return to DOS.

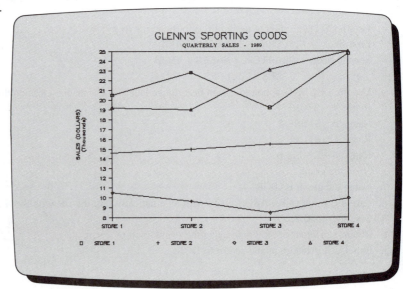

Figure E.28
Multi-Line Graph for Glenn's Sporting Goods

3. Using the STOREEX3.WK1 worksheet, create a pie chart of the fourth quarter sales for Glenn's Sporting Goods stores. Begin with a clean 1-2-3 worksheet.
   a. Retrieve the B:STOREEX3.WK1 worksheet.
   b. Create a pie chart for the fourth quarter. Change the A range to include only the fourth quarter sales. Change the X range to be Stores 1, 2, 3, and 4. Change the second line title to read 4TH QUARTER SALES - 1989.
   c. View the graph.
   d. Name the graph PIECHART.
   e. Save the graph as B:PIECHART.
   f. Save the worksheet.
   g. Obtain a printout of the graph using the PrintGraph program.
   h. Exit PrintGraph and return to DOS.

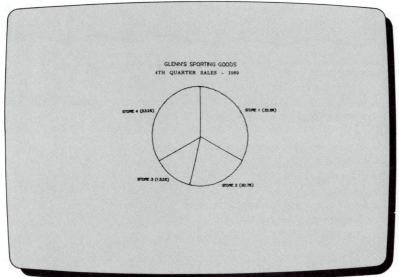

Figure E.29
Pie Chart for the Fourth Quarter

4. Glenn's Sporting Goods (Store 1) has been utilizing the database management capabilities of Lotus 1-2-3 to keep track of inventory. The following is an excerpt from that database, shown in Figure E.30 on the following page. Begin with a clean worksheet and enter the following data into the worksheet with these specifications:
   Global column width = 13
   Column width column B = 15
   Left-justify column B labels; right-justify all other labels in Row 4
   Format column D as currency

```
A1: [W13]                                                    READY

     A          B          C          D          E
1                 GLENN'S SPORTING GOODS (STORE 1)
2                 INVENTORY ANALYSIS
3
4    PROD. NO. DESCRIPTION              QTY    UNIT COST
5   ----------------------------------------------------
6         6157 ALUMINUM BAT              60       $34.50
7         8111 CATCHERS MIT              50       $53.00
8         6125 GRAPHITE RACKET           80       $82.00
9         6135 HOCKEY STICK              40       $24.50
10        6384 KNEE PADS                 85        $6.98
11        8371 SHIN GUARD               100        $8.95
12        3004 SWIM GOGGLES             100        $5.75
13        4999 TENNIS BALLS             100        $1.95
14        4950 VOLLYBALL NET             34       $39.95
15        4211 #5 SOCCER BALL            50       $24.99
16
17
18
19
20
```

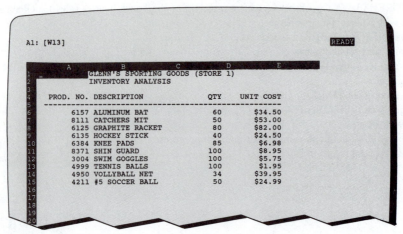

Figure E.30
Glenn's Sporting Goods Inventory

a. Add a fifth column to calculate the TOTAL COST of each product. Format column F as currency.
b. Sort the file by DESCRIPTION in ascending order.
c. Set up the following query:
   Find a list of products having a total cost of more than $2,000.
   1. Define the input range.
   2. Define the criterion range in Row 18.
   3. Define the output range.
   4. EXTRACT the records meeting the criteria set.
d. Get a printout of the entire database worksheet.
e. Save the worksheet as B:DBASEEX4.
f. Exit 1-2-3.

Your output should look like the one in Figure E.31.

```
               GLENN'S SPORTING GOODS (STORE 1)
               INVENTORY ANALYSIS

  PROD. NO. DESCRIPTION               QTY    UNIT COST   TOTAL COST
 ------------------------------------------------------------------
       6157 ALUMINUM BAT               60       $34.50    $2,070.00
       8111 CATCHERS MIT               50       $53.00    $2,650.00
       6125 GRAPHITE RACKET            80       $82.00    $6,560.00
       6135 HOCKEY STICK               40       $24.50      $980.00
       6384 KNEE PADS                  85        $6.98      $593.30
       8371 SHIN GUARD                100        $8.95      $895.00
       3004 SWIM GOGGLES              100        $5.75      $575.00
       4999 TENNIS BALLS              100        $1.95      $195.00
       4950 VOLLYBALL NET              34       $39.95    $1,358.30
       4211 #5 SOCCER BALL             50       $24.99    $1,249.50


  PROD. NO. DESCRIPTION               QTY    UNIT COST   TOTAL COST
                                                          +E5>2000


  PROD. NO. DESCRIPTION               QTY    UNIT COST   TOTAL COST
       6157 ALUMINUM BAT               60       $34.50    $2,070.00
       8111 CATCHERS MIT               50       $53.00    $2,650.00
       6125 GRAPHITE RACKET            80       $82.00    $6,560.00
```

Figure E.31
Completed Inventory Database with Selected Records Shown

5. Once more using the Glenn's Sporting Goods worksheet (STOREEX3.WK1), create a macro that will stamp the worksheet with the current date. Begin with a clean worksheet.
   a. Retrieve the B:STOREEX3.WK1 worksheet.
   b. Write the macro. Allow the user to execute the macro from any place in the worksheet, and enter the current date into cell A16. Format the cell as DATE type 1 (dd-mm-yy).
   c. Name the macro \D (for date).
   d. Document the macro. Your macro should look like the one in Figure E.32.

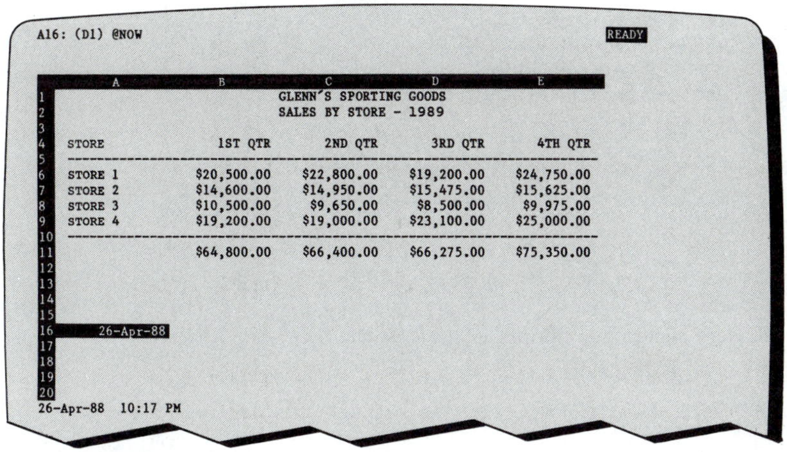

Figure E.32
The Output of Macro after Execution

   e. Execute the macro (try it by beginning in any cell other than A16). Your screen should be the same as Figure E.33.

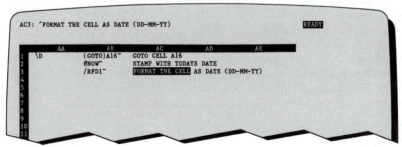

Figure E.33
Macro for STOREEX3.WK1

Note: You can execute the macro again at another time by moving the pointer to cell A16, pressing SPACEBAR once, and pressing ENTER to clear the cell. The cell is ready to be stamped with a new date.
   f. Save the worksheet as B:MACROEX5.
   g. Exit 1-2-3.

Appendix F

■ Advanced Features of dBASE III Plus

After completing this appendix, you should be able to

- define a dBASE III PLUS view.
- describe the procedure for creating a view using the SELECT and SET RELATION commands.
- describe the process of simultaneously querying the two databases joined by a view.
- describe the procedure for creating and printing mailing labels.
- describe the commands to copy the structure or contents of one database file into another.
- describe the command to permanently delete a file from a diskette.
- describe the command to list all or selected files on a diskette.
- describe the procedure to create a query file.

■ INTRODUCTION

This appendix discusses some of the more advanced features of the dBASE III PLUS software package. As you'll recall, Chapter 11 discussed the basics of the software and how a database can be created and later manipulated. In this appendix, you will learn about more dBASE applications and their use in business. The examples discussed in this appendix are related to the on-going case of the Sunshine Window Inc., Suppliers (SWIS).

■ VIEWS

A **view** is a method of linking two databases using a common key field to allow dBASE III PLUS to access data in two or more databases at the same time. To be able to view two databases, they must have a key field in common. The active database must contain the key field, and the second file must be indexed on the key field. We will look at two new commands in order to accomplish the view operation: the SELECT command and the SET RELATION command. But first let's establish a new data file for SWIS.

The data stored in this file represent information about the manufacturers from which SWIS buys goods. The file consists of a field for the manufacturer's name, address, quantity of last order, and date of last order. This file is constantly updated. Whenever a shipment for a particular item arrives, the warehouse notifies the clerk, Emily, and she deletes the order from the file. At the same time, as new orders are made, they are added to the database.

Creating the Database

- Type `set default to B:` and press ENTER.
- Type `create supplier`, and press ENTER. A field definition form will be presented.
- Enter the following fields.

Field name	Type	Width	Dec
PRODNUM	numeric	3	
MANUFACTUR	character	15	
MANUFADD	character	20	
QTYORD	numeric	5	
DATEORD	date	8	

- Press CTRL-END to save the structure when you have finished entering the five fields. The field definition screen will look like the one in Figure F.1.

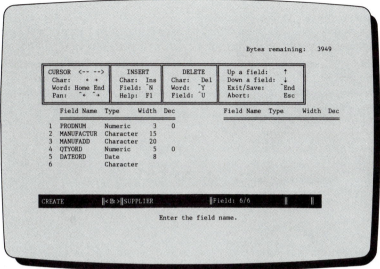

Figure F.1
Field Definition for the Supplier Database

- Press ENTER in response to the confirmation message and Y in response to the prompt "Input data records now? (Y/N)". The first data definition form will appear on the screen.

Inputting Records

- Input the following six records into the database.

Prodnum	Manufactur	Manufadd	Qtyord	Dateord
213	DayLight Co.	K St. Buck, NY 11111	20	03/12/88
114	Bob & Son Co.	L St. Mody, NY 12222	45	04/20/88
312	Glassy Co.	H St. Roof, PA 77777	15	05/13/88
411	Protect Co.	B St. Lony, PA 77772	35	06/12/88
314	Glassy Co.	H St. Roof, PA 77777	20	06/13/88
512	SkyLight Co.	D St. Penn, PA 77779	60	07/14/88

- Press CTRL-END to save the data records.

Listing the Database

To view the SUPPLIER database you have created

- Type `use supplier`, and press ENTER.
- Type `list` and press ENTER. The listing of the contents of the database file will look like Figure F.2.

Figure F.2
Listing of Supplier Database

Searching the Database

Let's assume that, after the data file has been created, you want to search the database for Item 312 to learn when this item was ordered and some information about the supplier.

- Type `list manufactur, manufadd, qtyord, dateord for prodnum = 312` and press ENTER. The screen will look like the one in Figure F.3.

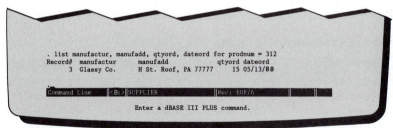

Figure F.3
Database Record for Product 312

Indexing

Index the INVENTORY file that was created in Chapter 11 on the PRODUCT NUMBER as follows.

- Type `use inventry` and press ENTER.
- Type `index on prodnum to numbers` and press ENTER.

To list the indexed file,

- Type `list` and press ENTER. The indexed file will appear as in Figure F.4.

```
Record#  PRODNUM  PRODDESC         COST    PRICE   BALANCE  LIMIT  MANUFACTUR
     1     111    Bow Window #12    69.95   83.94     112     24   Bob & Son Co.
     2     112    Octogon Window   220.00  264.00      54     35   Bob & Son Co.
     3     113    Double Window    180.00  216.00      75     50   Bob & Son Co.
     4     114    Single Window    120.00  144.00      35     45   Bob & Son Co.
     5     211    Patio Size #2    450.00  540.00      12     10   DayLight Co.
     6     212    Patio Door #2    210.00  254.00      25     15   DayLight Co.
     7     213    Patio Window     175.00  210.00      12     20   DayLight Co.
     8     214    Patio Shade      120.00  144.00      15     10   DayLight Co.
     9     311    Single Door      160.00  192.00      25     20   Glassy Co.
    10     312    Sliding Glass    285.00  342.00      10     15   Glassy Co.
    11     313    French Door      300.00  360.00      12     10   Glassy Co.
    12     314    Split Door       180.00  216.00      15     20   Glassy Co.
    13     411    Storm Door       350.00  420.00      25     35   Protect Co.
    14     412    Storm Door       350.00  420.00      12     10   Protect Co.
    15     413    Safe Window      220.00  264.00      19     15   Protect Co.
    16     414    Barn Window      250.00  300.00      14     12   Protect Co.
    17     511    Roof Window      175.00  210.00      25     20   SkyLight Co.
    18     512    Side Window      125.00  150.00      55     60   SkyLight Co.
    19     513    Sunshine Door    260.00  312.00      22     20   SkyLight Co.
    20     514    Sunshine Window  140.00  168.00      30     20   SkyLight Co.

Command Line     <B:> INVENTRY              Rec: EOF/20
                 Enter a dBASE III PLUS command.
```

Figure F.4
Indexed File Listing for Inventry Database

The SELECT Command

The SELECT command has the form

SELECT < *work area/alias* >

This command chooses a work area in which to open a database file. You can also use the SELECT command to change the active database file to one in a specified work area. The dBASE III PLUS program allows up to ten database files to be stored in selected areas, designated *1* through *10* or *A* through *J*. This means a user can bring up to ten files into the memory and use all ten database files simultaneously. It should be remembered that only one file is active, and the rest remain in their reserved areas. The user has the choice of making any of the files in the reserved areas the active file.

When the SELECT command brings a file in from a diskette and places it in a reserved area, dBASE expects the user to name the file in that select area. The dBASE term that refers to a file in a selected or reserved area is **alias**. If an alias is not specified when you open the file, the alias name defaults to the file name.

- Type `select` 1 and press ENTER to choose the first work area in which to load the first database file.

Next you must tell dBASE III PLUS which database file to open in work area one.

- Type `use supplier` and press ENTER.
- Type `select 2` and press ENTER to choose the second work area for the second database file.
- Type `use inventry index numbers` and press ENTER to tell dBASE which file to use for work area two.

Next, you must select the database file to be specified as the current file. All commands that relate to database files will act only on the active database in the current work area.

- Type `select 1` and press ENTER.

The SET RELATION Command

The form of the SET RELATION command is

SET RELATION TO <*key field*> INTO <*work area/alias*>

The SET RELATION command links the current work area database (in our example, INVENTRY) with the database in the second work area (SUPPLIER). The link is made over the common data field, the key field PRODNUM. Enter the command as follows:

- Type `set relation to prodnum into inventry` and press ENTER.

Searching Two Files

Now that a relationship has been established between the two files, SUPPLIER and INVENTRY, queries can be made against both databases at once.

To refer to a field in a related database other than the active database, use the form of:

alias-> field name

This means that the fields coming from the file that is in the current work area (the file name shown on the command line; in this case, SUPPLIER) can be referred to by their field names. However, any fields coming from the other file, INVENTRY, which has just been combined with SUPPLIER, must be referred to with the file name followed by "-" (the hyphen), ">" (greater than sign), and the name of the field. For example, BALANCE in the INVENTRY file would be referred to as INVENTRY->BALANCE.

Here are some demonstrations of ways you can access combined information through queries.

Query 1. List the product number, description, manufacturer's name, and address of the items that have been ordered.

Procedure:

- Type `list off prodnum, inventry->proddesc, manufactur, manufadd, qtyord, dateord` and press ENTER.

Display:

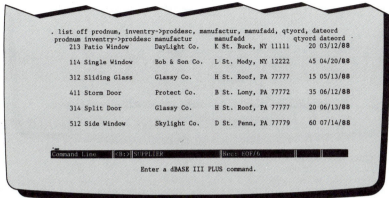

Figure F.5
A List of Combined Supplier and Inventry Database Records

Query 2. List the product number, description, price, quantity ordered, date ordered, and the manufacturer's name for product number 411.

Procedure:

- Type list prodnum, inventry->proddesc, inventry ->price, qtyord, dateord, manufactur for prodnum = 411 and press ENTER.

Display:

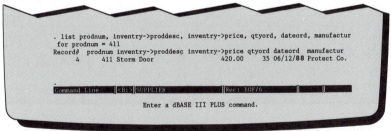

Figure F.6
Combined Supplier and Inventry Database for Prodnum 411

Query 3. List the product description, manufacturer's name and address, and price of those items costing more than $200.

Procedure:

- Type list off prodnum, inventry->proddesc, manufactur, inventry->price for inventry->price > 200.00 and press ENTER..

Display:

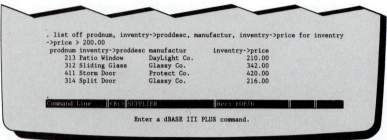

Figure F.7
Records with Price Greater than $200

Query 4. List product numbers, descriptions, prices, and manufacturers' names on the printer.

Procedure:

- Type `list off prodnum, inventry->proddesc, inventry->price, manufactur to print` and press ENTER.

Display:

```
       prodnum inventry->proddesc inventry->price manufactur
           213 Patio Window            210.00 DayLight Co.
           114 Single Window           144.00 Bob & Son Co.
           312 Sliding Glass           342.00 Glassy Co.
           411 Storm Door              420.00 Protect Co.
           314 Split Door              216.00 Glassy Co.
           512 Side Window             150.00 Skylight Co.
```

Figure F.8
A Printout of Records of Supplier and Inventry Database

Remember that you can switch back and forth between the files that you have stored in the selected areas. To do so, all you have to do is type SELECT and the storage area number. For example, to access the INVENTRY file,

- Type `select 2` and press ENTER.

Notice the name of the current file is changed from SUPPLIER to INVENTRY in the command line area.

- Now, type `select 1` and press ENTER to switch back to the SUPPLIER file.

The following queries utilize the two files that you have in the select areas, one at a time. But before you do so, let's talk about the logical operators.

■ LOGICAL OPERATORS

Along with the mathematical and relational operators that we discussed in Chapter 11, there are logical operators that can be used in conjunction with the other two types to build a compound condition.

The logical operators used in dBASE are

- .AND.   Logical and
- .OR.   Logical or
- .NOT.   Logical not
- ( )   Parentheses for grouping

The precedence of the logical operators is ( ), .NOT., .AND., and .OR..

The AND operator requires that both conditions must be true for the entire expression to be true. The OR operator requires that only one (or both) condition must be true for the expression to be evaluated as true.

Let's look at some examples of queries using the logical operators.

Query 1. (Use the INVENTRY database file) List any items with a price tag of more than $200 and balance (on hand) less than the limit (reordering point).

Procedure:

- Type `Select 2` and press ENTER to access the INVENTRY.
- Type `List proddesc, price, balance, limit for price > 200 .and. balance < limit` and press ENTER.

Display:

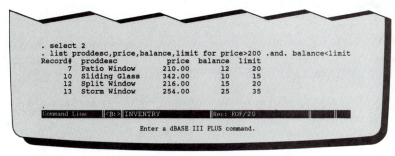

Figure F.9
List of Items with Price Greater than $200 and Balance Less than Limit

Query 2. (Use the SUPPLIER database file) List those products that either are manufactured by Glassy Co. or whose quantity ordered is greater than fifty.

Procedure:

- Type `Select 1` and press ENTER to access the SUPPLIER
- Type `list prodnum, manufactur, qtyord, dateord for manufactur = 'Glassy Co.' .or. qtyord > 50` and press ENTER.

Display:

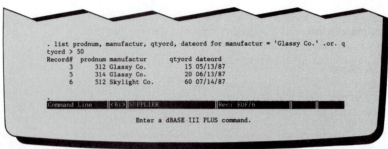

Figure F.10
A Listing of Items of Either Glassy Co. as the Manufacturer or Quantity Ordered is Greater than Fifty

■ CREATING MAILING LABELS

Another popular feature of the dBASE III PLUS is the label-generating option of the software package. This feature allows you to generate labels from a database file. The labels could be used, for example, to send a letter or correspondence to a group of people or companies. The dBASE program assumes that you already have a database from which to extract certain fields and place them in a label format.

To understand how the label feature works, let's assume that SWIS is sending a letter to all of its suppliers informing them about a change in policy regarding future payments to be made by SWIS to its creditors. In order to help accomplish this mailing, a user could easily obtain the suppliers' names and addresses from the SUPPLIER database created earlier in this appendix. The following steps will describe how the desired labels could be prepared in dBASE III PLUS.

Note: You have files in selected work areas. In order to close and remove them, type SELECT 1 [ENTER], then USE [ENTER]. Initiating a USE without specifying a file will remove the file from the selected area. Type SELECT 2 [ENTER], then USE [ENTER] to remove the second selected area.

- Type use supplier, and press ENTER.
- Type CREATE LABEL SUPLABEL and press ENTER to create a label file called SUPLABEL. The screen like the one in Figure F.11 on the following page will be displayed.

At the top of the screen, you see three choices: *Options,* which is highlighted, *Contents,* and *Exit.* Below the three selections is the list of default parameters for printing labels. To change any of the predefined parameters, simply move the highlighted line to the desired item by using the DOWN ARROW key. For example, you may want to print two labels across a page:

- Press DOWN ARROW six times to highlight the last option on the predefined parameters box, "Label across page:".
- Press ENTER once. A little arrow will be placed before the number "1".
- Type 2 and press ENTER.

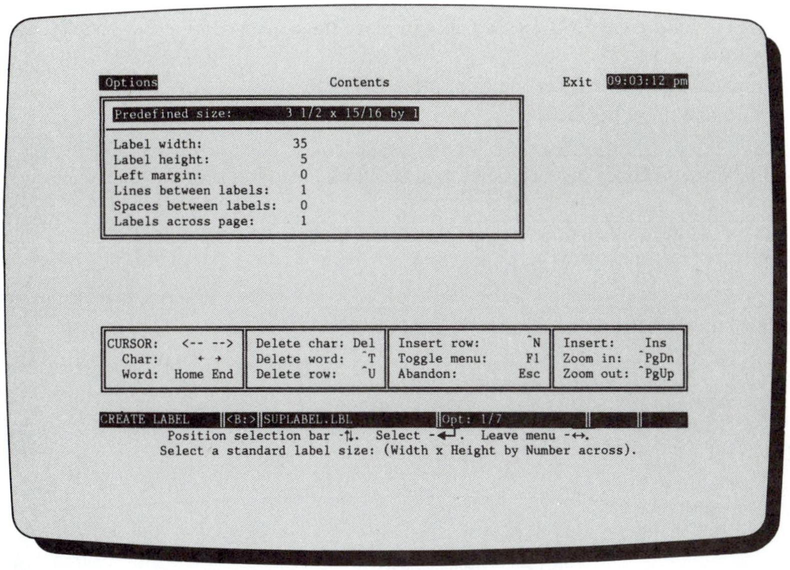

Figure F.11
Mailing Labels Initial Screen

Upon completion of any changes in the options parameters, you will move to the next step: identifying the fields that you want to be extracted from the SUPPLIER file and placed in the label file.

- **Press RIGHT ARROW** once to move from *Options* to *Contents* at the top of the screen. A screen will be displayed like the one in Figure F.12.

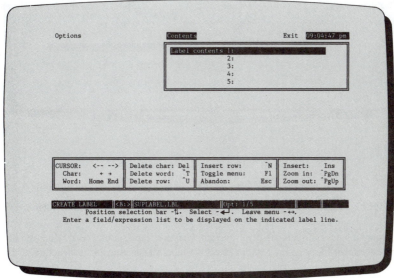

Figure F.12
The Contents Menu

- With the highlighted line over the "label Contents 1:", press ENTER.
- Type `manufactur` and press ENTER, which will place the contents of the field MANUFACTUR on the first line of the label.
- With the highlighted line over the second line, press ENTER.
- Type `manufadd` and press ENTER.

Since there will be only two lines on each label, you should be ready to save the label file.

- Press the RIGHT ARROW once to go to the last choice, *Exit,* on the top menu.
- With the highlighted line over Save, press ENTER.

To display the label on the screen,

- Type `label form suplabel` and press ENTER.

The following screen will appear.

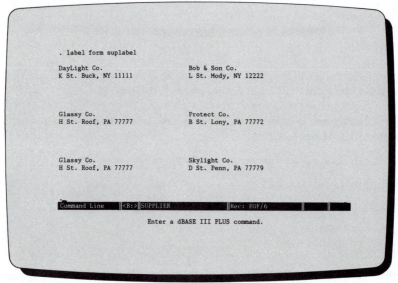

Figure F.13
Mailing Label Listing

In order to print the labels on the printer,

- Type `label form suplabel to print` and press ENTER. Make sure your printer is on.

Once you've created a label file, you can print it again whenever labels are needed. Changes in the contents of the original file on which the label file is based will not affect the label file as long as the structure of the original file stays the same.

■ FILE MANAGEMENT ACTIVITIES

As you create different database files in dBASE, you will want to delete files, list all files on the diskette, copy files, and copy file structures. In this part of the appendix, we discuss some of the dBASE commands frequently used for file management activities.

The COPY Command

The form of the COPY command is

COPY TO <newfile> [<scope>] [FIELDS <field list>] [FOR <condition>] [WHILE <condition>] [TYPE] <file type>]

This dBASE command allows a file to be copied into another file with a different name. The file type of the second file must be the same as that of the first. Now, in order to understand how the COPY command works, follow the instructions below.

- Type `clear` and press ENTER.
- Type `use inventry` and press ENTER.
- Type `copy to b:invtemp` and press ENTER. The message "20 records copied" will be shown.

To make sure the INVTEMP is on the diskette in Drive B

- Type `DIR` and press ENTER.

Another use for the COPY command arises in copying only those records that satisfy certain conditions specified in the copy statement. Let's try the following:

- Type `copy to b:invorder for balance < limit` and press ENTER. This will result in six records being copied into the new inventry file, called INVORDER.

The COPY FIELD Command

It is also possible to copy certain fields of a database file into a new database file under a different name. The structure of this command is the same as the COPY command, except that a list of fields is specified in the command statement.

- Type `use inventry` and press ENTER.
- Type `list next 10` and press ENTER.
- Type `copy field prodnum, cost, price to invshort` and press ENTER.

Now let's display the contents of this new file.

- Type `clear` and press ENTER.
- Type `use invshort` and press ENTER.
- Type `list next 15` and press ENTER.

A screen will appear like the one in Figure F.14.

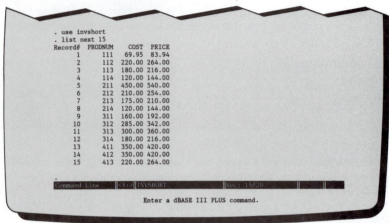

Figure F.14
The First Fifteen Records of Invshort

The COPY STRUCTURE Command

The COPY STRUCTURE command takes the form

COPY STRUCTURE [EXTENDED] TO <*new file*> [FIELDS <*field list*>]

This command creates a duplicate of the structure of the database file that is in the active work file area. This command could be very useful when creating a new database, some of the fields and their structures of which happen to be similar to those of the database already created.

- Type clear and press ENTER.
- Type use inventry and press ENTER.
- Type copy structure to tempry and press ENTER.
- Now, type dir and press ENTER to list all the files on your diskette. The file TEMPRY will be listed with 0 records in it.
- Type use tempry and press ENTER.

If you are interested in modifying this structure for a new database file,

- Type modify structure and press ENTER to list the structure of the new file. Make the necessary corrections; at the end, press CTRL-END.

The DELETE FILE Command

The form of the DELETE FILE command is

DELETE FILE <*file.extension*>

Files can be permanently deleted from the surface of the diskette with the DELETE FILE command. Let's try to delete the file called INVTEMP that we just created.

- Type `delete file invtemp.dbf` and press ENTER. The message "File has been deleted" will be shown.

The LIST FILES Command

The LIST FILES command takes the form

LIST FILES [LIKE <*skeleton*>] [TO PRINT]

This command displays all or selected files on the directory of a diskette. The following example shows how this dBASE command works.

- Type `list files` and press ENTER to list all the database files.
- Now type `list files like *.ndx` and press ENTER to list all the files with extension ndx.
- Now type `list files like *.*` and press ENTER to list all the files on the diskette, regardless of their names and extensions.

Query Files

The task of issuing query commands for a frequently performed search can become a tedious task. The dBASE program allows the user to store the statements or conditions, known as query files, used for searching a file. A query file contains all the conditions set up for searching a database.

In order to understand query files, let's try a simple example. Assume that the clerk in charge of inventory records at SWIS often needs to know whether the balance on hand of particular items is less then their reordering points (limits). We can simply store this query in a query file that can be used when needed.

- Type `use inventry` and press ENTER.
- Type `create query lookup` and press ENTER.

A screen like the one in Figure F.15 will be shown.

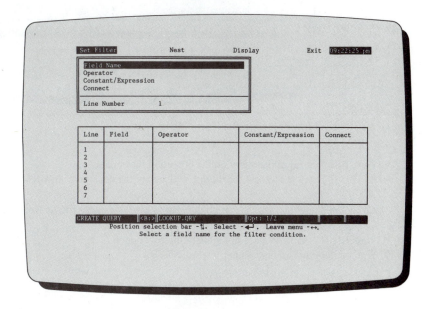

Figure F.15
The Query Lookup Screen

At the top of the screen are four options: *Set Filter,* used to define fields, the conditional operators, constant/expression to be compared to, and connect for possible use of logical operators; *Nest,* used to define any orders used for established conditions; *Display,* used to perform the search based on the established conditions; and *Exit,* which allows the user to save or abandon the query file. Let's now complete the query file.

- With the highlighted line over *Field Name,* press ENTER. A little menu will appear on the right-hand side of the screen with a list of all the field names in the INVENTRY database file.
- Press DOWN ARROW four times to bring the highlighted line over BALANCE, and press ENTER.
- With the highlighted line over *Operator,* press ENTER.
- Press DOWN ARROW three times to bring the highlighted line over < (*less than*), and press ENTER.
- With the highlighted line over *Constant/Expression,* press ENTER, type limit and press ENTER.
- Press RIGHT ARROW twice to go to the *Display* option, and press ENTER to start searching.

The following screen will be shown, with the first record found in the database that satisfies the condition. The screen will look like the one in Figure F.16.

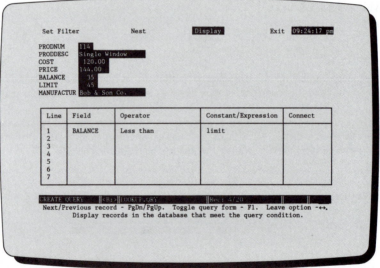

Figure F.16
The Screen for the First Record on the Query Menu

- Press F1 to get rid of the query on the bottom of the screen.
- Press PGDN to see the next record that will satisfy the condition. PGUP will show you the previous record.

Upon completion of the search, you might want to save this query file for later use. To do so,

- Press RIGHT ARROW once to highlight the *Exit* option.
- With the *Save* option highlighted, press ENTER.

To use the query file later on,

- Type `use inventry` and press ENTER.
- Type `create query lookup` and press ENTER.
- Move the highlighted line over the *Display* option, and press ENTER to begin the search again.

Query files can be very helpful when multiple or complex conditions are used to search a large database.

■ Summary of Advanced dBASE III Plus Commands

SELECT — Chooses a work area in which to open a database file, or changes the active database file to one in a specified work area.
SET RELATION — Links the databases to two different work areas.
COPY — Allows a file to be copied into another file with a different name; also used to copy specified fields instead of an entire file.
COPY STRUCTURE — Duplicates the structure of the database in the active work area.
DELETE FILE — Permanently erases the file form the diskette.
LIST FILES — Lists all or specified files on the directory of a diskette.

■ Key Terms

view   A method of linking two databases using a common key field.
alias   A dBASE file in a selected or reserved area.

■ Review Questions

1. A _____ is a method of linking two databases using a common key field to allow dBASE III PLUS to access data in both databases at the same time.
   (a) display
   (b) view
   (c) select
   (d) link
2. When using select, up to _____ database files can be brought into memory and used simultaneously.
   (a) two
   (b) six
   (c) ten
   (d) unlimited

3. The _____ command retrieves a file from a diskette and places it in a reserved area.
   (a) SELECT
   (b) LOAD
   (c) SET RELATION
   (d) LINK
4. A file stored in a reserved area is referred to as a
   (a) object.
   (b) alias.
   (c) view.
   (d) unnamed.
5. When the _____ command is issued, the active database file is linked with a database file in a second specified work area.
   (a) SELECT
   (b) SET RELATION
   (c) LINK
   (d) LOAD
6. When referring to any fields of the database stored in a selected work area, the file name and the field name must both be specified, separated by which of the following signs?
   (a) = >
   (b) - >
   (c) >
   (d) < -
7. Which of the following is *not* a logical operator?
   (a) .AND.
   (b) .BUT.
   (c) .NOT.
   (d) .OR.
8. What does the AND operator signify?
9. Which of the following statements would have the effect of listing the NAME field from a file called STUDENT where the student's GPA is greater than or equal to 3.0 and the STATUS is equal to the sixth semester?
   (a) list name for GPA > = 3.0 and status = 6
   (b) list name for status = 6 .or. GPA > = 3.0
   (c) list student for GPA > = 3.0 .and. status = 6
   (d) list name for GPA > = 3.0 .and. status = 6
10. What is the order of procedure for logical operators?
11. The _____ feature allows you to generate labels from the database file.
    (a) genlab
    (b) lab
    (c) label
    (d) print
12. Under what circumstances would you need to use a database file to generate labels?
13. A _____ command issued without specifying a file will remove the file from the selected area.
    (a) DELETE
    (b) ABANDON
    (c) USE
    (d) ELIMINATE
14. Once a label file has been created, what effect will changes to the original data file have on the label file?

15. Commands that delete, copy, and list files are referred to as _____ commands.
    (a) file management
    (b) DOS
    (c) query
    (d) filing
16. The COPY command in dBASE III PLUS can be used to copy both _____ and _____ .
    (a) files, diskettes
    (b) files, file structures
    (c) fields, files
    (d) files, field structures
17. The _____ command creates a duplicate of the structure of the file in the active area.
    (a) COPY FIELDS
    (b) COPY STRUCTURE
    (c) COPY
    (d) COPY FILE
18. What is the difference between the LIST and QUERY commands?
19. What is the difference between the SELECT and SET RELATION commands?
20. _____ operators can be used with mathamatical and relational operators to build a compound condition.
    (a) Arithmetic
    (b) Logical
    (c) Compound
    (d) Complex

Appendix F

HANDS-ON EXERCISES

1. Create a small database called STORES to store information for each of four Rachel's Fashions boutiques, using the data structure shown below.

Field name	Type	Width	Dec
STORENUM	Numeric	1	
ADDRESS	Character	30	
YTDSALES	Numeric	10	2

    a. Set the default to Drive B.
    b. Create the database called STORES.
    c. Define the three fields.
    d. Save the structure.

2. The following records will be entered into the STORES database.

Storenum	Address	Ytdsales
1	415 Green St, Tampa, FL 11111	279000.00
2	612 F St, Brandon, FL 11222	326000.00
3	45 Sun Plaza, Tampa, Fl 11110	198500.00

   a. Enter the three records into the database file.
   b. Save the data entered.

The completed database will appear as shown in Figure F.17.

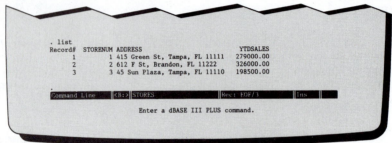

Figure F.17
Completed STORES Database

3. Create a view using the EMPSORT database file (created in Chapter 11) and the STORES database file created in Exercises 1 and 2.
   a. Store the indexed version (EMPSORT) of the EMPLOYEE file in the first work area (Select 1).
   b. Store the STORES file in the second work area (Select 2).
   c. Make the EMPLOYEE file the active file.
   d. Link the two database files on the key field **STORENUM** using the SET RELATION command.
4. Perform the following queries using the EMPLOYEE file created in Exercise 1 of Chapter 11.
   a. List the store number, store address, last name, first name, and date hired for employee number 8.
   b. List the store number, store address, last name, first name, and employee ID for the employee named Nancy Mobley (use a compound condition—there could be more than one employee named Mobley).
   c. List the last name, first name, and salary of the employees who work at store number 2 and who earn at least $20,000 per year.
   d. List the store number, last name, first name, salary, and date hired for those employees who earn more than $21,000 per year or who were hired before December 31, 1983.

Appendix G

Answers to Review Questions

CHAPTER 1

1. C
2. E
3. E
4. C
5. B
6. E
7. D
8. A
9. E
10. C
11. C

12. Operational/technical decisions deal with enforcing policies, procedures and standards which can be defined and stored on a computer. In some cases the computer can perform as a useful tool for the person making the operational/technical decision. For instance, a loan officer can enter variables such as income, debt-service, and loan amount requested into the computer and the computer can reject or deny the applicant based on a predefined model selected by the bank.
13. The decision maker must first identify the problem and analyze the situation. He must then identfy and assess alternative solutions. Finally, he must select the most appropriate solution or course of action.
14. Informal information is also important to a decision maker because at times, formal information is not readily available.
15. The time cards consist of data which will be manipulated by the computer and result in formal information.
16. No. Information is a major requirement of the decision-making process regardless of the size of the organization.
17. Manual systems are considered the most common and least expensive way of generating information.
18. No. A database can be housed in a file cabinet, a library, an index card file, or a checkbook, etc.
19. An information system is utilized when applying for a mortgage/loan; Money Access Machines are common computer systems; paychecks are most likely generated by a computer system; availability of classes are determined by a computer system during registration.
20. Banking, financial, accounting, manufacturing, insurance, medical, educational, etc.
21. Many users can use data stored in common files.
    Marked the beginning of the movement from Data Processing to Database Processing.
22. The "Ultimate Weapon" for most organizations is Information and Information Processing. Information is mandatory in order to maintain a competitive edge and is necessary for the survival of some organizations in the business world.
23. A centralized computer system consists of a mainframe with all components directly attached to it. Components include terminals, printers, and communications units.
24. High-level languages allow computer programmers to write instructions using English-like words.
25. A distributed computer system allows computing operations to be performed at different locations, and the opportunity to share information and resources with each other.
26. 1950 – Computers were used mainly for scientific applications.
    – Computers were large and expensive.
    – Computers were difficult to program.
    1960 – Financial and accounting applications were developed.
    – Data Processing (DP) systems evolved.
    – Computers were viewed as number-crunching devices. Domination of centralized computer systems.
    – Introduction of high-level programming languages.

1970 – Introduction of mini-computers.
  – Introduction of Management Information Systems (MIS).
  – Introduction of Database Management Systems.
  – Development of Distributed Processing Systems.
  – Introduction of microcomputers.
  – Introduction of Decision Support Systems (DSS).
1980 – Recognition of information as a corporate resource.
  – Acceptance of microcomputers as a business tool.
  – Powerful software packages for microcomputers.

27. More accurate and timely information is available through the use of an automated information system.
28. A computer would be helpful to the decision maker after he has identified the alternatives. For instance, let's assume that John is going to build a deck. Once he identifies several plans for his deck, the amount of each type of lumber needed for each plan, and the prices of each type of lumber, he can then enter this data into the computer (assuming he had the appropriate software). The computer would process this data and supply him with the information needed to assess the different plans and select the most appropriate one.

■ CHAPTER 2

1. F
2. E
3. D
4. A
5. Read Only Memory
   Random Access Memory
6. A
7. D
8. D
9. B
10. A
11. A
12. B
13. B
14. D

15. Apple Computer Corp. developed the first microcomputer.
16. The U.S. Space Program performed a great deal of research during the 1960s to develop smaller electronic circuitry that could be installed in spaceship computers.
17. The first generation of microcomputers was used extensively in education. In 1979, VISICALC was released enabling microcomputers to be used for numerous business applications.
18. Software packages designed for the IBM-PC can be used on compatible machines. Compatibility is very important because most software is designed around the IBM-PC.
19. They are equally important. Hardware is useless without software and vice versa. However, it is a good idea to identify the software you need before purchasing hardware.
20. CPU is the microprocessor in the microcomputer. It consists of the Control Unit which makes the "brain" of the microcomputer functional, the ALU which handles all decision making and arithmetic functions, and the Memory Unit, RAM and ROM.
21. The Read Only Memory (ROM) is available only to the processing unit and its components, not to the user. It holds instructions permanently.
22. The contents of Random Access Memory (RAM) are completely erased when the power is turned off. RAM is considered "volatile memory."
23. ROM is not available to the user while RAM is used as a scratch pad area for the user. ROM holds instructions permanently while RAM does not.
24. The microprocessor's computing power is measured by the number of bits that are accessed during processing.
25. Binary coding system represents characters in the form of 0s and 1s. 0 = off, 1 = on.

26. The math coprocessor assists the ALU with data manipulation so the microprocessor is free to perform other tasks.
27. Connectivity allows microcomputers to communicate with each other and other systems. They are considered part of an organization's information system.
28. Printer performance is measured by quality and speed.
29. The read/write head moves vertically as the diskette spins around the middle shaft.
30. One advantage of a hard disk is that large amounts of data can be stored. A disadvantage of a hard disk is that the entire contents of a disk can be wiped out due to a system failure.
31. Without the interface board, data cannot be exchanged between two devices.
32. To handle large amounts of data, the firm would need a hard disk and at least one floppy disk drive to accompany it. In order to produce top-quality documents, the firm should use a laser printer.
33. Yes. By using the concept of connectivity, the branches could send data to the head office via the PC. A program could then be written that would consolidate this data.

■ CHAPTER 3

1. C
2. D
3. E
4. A
5. B
6. D
7. C
8. B
9. Integrated

10. Six categories of microcomputer software include: Word Processing, Spreadsheet, Database Management, Graphics, Communications, and Desktop Publishing.
11. Basic Command Programs and Utility Programs are the two groups of programs in the operating system.
12. CP/M (earliest), MS-DOS (standard operating system), PC-DOS, APPLE DOS, TRS-DOS, UNIX, XENIX, OS/2 (newest).
13. Menu driven software packages are called user friendly because the user can move easily through the system by selecting options on menus rather than remembering hundreds of technical commands.
14. Word processing increases productivity by eliminating some of the time-consuming and tedious tasks of text processing with traditional typewriters.
15. A Local Area Network (LAN) is a system in which microcomputers are linked together to share computing power, information and hardware resources.
16. Five common programming languages include: COBOL, FORTRAN, BASIC, C, and Pascal.
17. An interpreter is a set of programs that accept programming instructions, examine the syntax of these instructions and if acceptable, translates them into machine language so the computer can carry out the intended tasks.
18. Spreadsheet software packages allow a user to create a table of figures and relationships in the form of equations. Once the figures/relationships are defined, different alternatives/projections can be evaluated by simply changing the assumption(s) in the appropriate cell(s). Database software is a collection of programs that allow users to store data in electronic files and retrieve and/or update data when needed. The data stored in these files is independent of the application programs that use them.
19. A Spreadsheet software package can be used as a tool for decision makers in financial analysis. Word processing can be used in report generation, and preparation of presentations can be performed with the help of a Desktop Publishing software package.
20. Graphics software packages can be useful tools in analyzing data and trends through graphs and charts. For example, a salesman can demonstrate the benefits of their products, engineers can visualize and experiment with a variety of designs, and manufacturers can determine schedules and priorities.

21. One advantage of an integrated software package is that a user can easily share data and information among different applications without leaving the software environment. A disadvantage is in the limited capability of each component (spreadsheet, database management) in comparison to each of the stand-alone versions of these packages.
22. Publishing can be a major expense for many businesses. The process of designing, preparing, and professionally printing documents, reports, and forms can be done with the help of Desktop Publishing software packages. This is beneficial to both large and small businesses. For example, a small computer consulting firm could use Desktop Publishing when submitting proposals for new business. A large business may want to use Desktop Publishing for various types of presentation material.
23. A laser printer would be the most suitable type of printer for Desktop Publishing due to the fine quality of printing.
24. Communication software packages allow a microcomputer to communicate and share its processing power with other systems. Microcomputers can now be connected to other computers to obtain or exchange information within or outside the same location.
25. Utility programs are retrieved from the operating system disk and brought into memory for execution when needed. They are designed to perform less-routine tasks such as formatting a blank disk or copying contents of one disk to another.
26. Control programs manage the entire computer system. These programs are executed automatically before the user can use the system. They examine various components of the hardware, such as memory, keyboard, and secondary storage units. Control programs also maintain control over various components of the system while the microcomputer is in use.
27. A fully integrated package would be the most beneficial since it is capable of providing word processing for correspondence, database management for data, and spreadsheet and graphics for budget forecasts, financial reports and distribution schedules. An integrated package will enable them to share data/information between all subsystems.
28. The microcomputer network would probably be more efficient since it would allow each department to access data as needed. The network would also be less expensive, allow more control over hardware, and require less maintenance since only one database would have to be maintained.

■ CHAPTER 4

1. A
2. D
3. C
4. B
5. D
6. C
7. D

8. An operating system provides the linkage between the application software and the microcomputer hardware.
9. An operating system is a collection of programs designed to handle selected micro tasks, manage I/O devices to enter/display information, manage data files, store/retrieve information on secondary storage units, and work with software packages to carry out specific functions.
10. A single-task operating system can only work on one task at a time, whereas a multi-tasking operating system can work on many tasks at the same time.
11. The Macintosh operating system facilitates the use of a mouse and is one of the most friendly packages.
12. MS-DOS, PC-DOS, Apple DOS, Macintosh, OS/2.
13. The degree of difficulty and understanding of the system prevented the CP/M from maintaining its popularity.
14. The term "multi-user" means that many users can communicate with the system at one time
15. IBMBIO.COM–IBM Binary Input/Output
    IBMDOS.COM–Disk Operating System

CHAPTER 5

1. The DOS diskette is inserted in Drive A. The system will go through a system check that takes from 3 to 45 seconds, depending on the memory in the microcomputer you are working on. When the red light on the front of the disk drive is turned off, the loading process has ended. The user is then prompted to enter a date and time. Upon completion of the date and time settings, the system has been succesfully booted. That is, all I/O Handler and Command Processor files have been read from the DOS diskette and are now stored in memory.
2. D
3. B
4. D
5. The CLS command clears the screen.
6. The DIR/W command would be used when you need to view large directories.
7. B
8. C
9. A
10. D
11. The function of the RENAME command is to assign a new name to a file that already exists.
12. DOS looks in the drive specified for the file to be deleted.
13. C
14. B
15. The screen contents can be sent to the printer by pressing the SHIFT and PRTSC keys.
16. A diskette should be handled very carefully because a damaged diskette could result in a loss of data.
17. The difference between a warm boot and a cold boot is that in a warm boot, the computer is already on.
18. /S is added to the format command to make the disk bootable.
19. /P is used when a directory is long and you wish to see one screen at a time.
20. /F is added to the CHKDSK command to instruct DOS to repair errors found in the file allocation table or directory.
21. The primary difference between the COPY command and the DISKCOPY command is that the COPY command can not format a disk whereas the DISKCOPY does, and the COPY command eliminates fragmentation.
22. The difference between the DISKCOMP command and the COMP command is that the DISKCOMP command compares the status of two disks while the COMP command compares the contents of two specified files.
23. The SYSTEM command allows the user to transfer a copy of the system files to a formatted disk or an applications program diskette.
24. When the DEL/ERASE command is used on a file, DOS denies future access to that file. The command does not actually erase the data. It just marks it as available to be written onver on the diskette.
25. Fragmentation is unused space on a diskette due to deletion and addition of files over time. The COPY *.* command will copy all the files on the disk to another disk without fragmentation.

CHAPTER 6

1. C
2. B
3. A
4. A

5. The basic functions of a word processing package are:
   a. Allows a user to easily create a document (input).
   b. Allows the document to be stored on a secondary medium for future use (save).
   c. Allows the user to correct and modify the document as needed (edit).
   d. Enables the user to obtain a hard copy of the document (print).
6. A
7. B
8. A
9. C
10. A
11. Word processing has improved the timeliness of information since it allows deletions, additions, and modifications to be made easily to a document rather than retyping the entire document.
12. Electronic word processing has gained acceptance quickly because of the low cost of microcomputers and the ease of operation.
13. The six disks in a Word Perfect word processing package include WordPerfect Diskette, two Printer Diskettes, Speller Diskette, Thesaurus Diskette, and the Learning diskette.
14. The WordPerfect Printer Diskettes are necessary when you need to change the specifications and definitions of the printer used by the PC.
15. The task of searching words similar in meaning can be done very easily with the Thesaurus Diskette.
16. Although WordStar has entered the market in 1979, a new version had been later introduced to run on PC-DOS and MS-DOS. This software package provided a variety of features and it utilizes the menu option to its fullest capacity, thus making it easy to operate.
17. Microsoft Word allows a user to communicate with the system through the use of a mouse to select menu options.
18. She could benefit greatly by applying various features of word processing packages. She could create the basic business letters and modify them as it becomes necessary.
19. The steps include: inputting the text into the computer, saving it on the secondary storage medium, and obtaining a hardcopy of the text.
20. Bob could benefit by using a word processing package, despite his claim that his reports are short. The package allows him to create well-organized reports for his classes, and be able to share information from report to report. Furthermore, knowledge of the package will become beneficial to him when he graduates.

■ CHAPTER 7

1. B
2. B
3. C
4. C
5. The LIST FILES command displays a menu in which the user must move the cursor to the selected file and press the retrieve option. The RETRIEVE command requires the user to know the exact name of the file after pressing SHIFT-F10.
6. A
7. The SAVE command (F10) is used to save a document. It is recommended that your documents be saved at regular intervals while working on them.
8. D
9. C
10. C

11. A document is saved by pressing F10 (SAVE) or F7 (EXIT) and entering the name of the document.
12. A
13. A
14. The term "Pitch" represents the number of characters per inch when printing a document.
15. B
16. When you reach the end of a line while typing a document using WordPerfect, the cursor is automatically wrapped around to the beginning of the next line. You do not need to press the ENTER key until you get to the end of the paragraph or choose to end a short line.
17. The cursor can be repositioned to the beginning of the document by pressing the HOME key twice followed by the up arrow key.
18. A Hard Return Code is inserted into the text when you press the ENTER key. A Soft Return Code is automatically inserted into the text at the end of a line when WordPerfect wraps the line to the beginning of the next line.
19. A block of text can be one or more sentences, a paragraph, or all pages of the document.
20. The cut option removes the block of text from the screen and saves it temporarily in RAM. The copy option saves the block of text temporarily in RAM but leaves it on the screen.
21. No. A file can be given a name of up to eight characters, which can be followed by a period and a file extension of up to three characters, if desired.
22. A combination keystroke is when you use a function key in conjunction with the CTRL, ALT, and SHIFT keys. For example, CTRL-F2 activates the Speller Diskette, SHIFT-F6 centers the current line of text, and ALT-F4 activates the block function.
23. A command can be cancled by pressing the F1 function key.
24. ALT-F3 displays the format codes which are embedded in the text.
25. The steps involved in saving a document include:
    a. Press F10 to activate the save document function.
    b. Enter the name of the document to be saved.
    c. If the document had already been saved under the file name entered, respond appropriately to the message of whether you wish to replace the document.
26. A line of text can be deleted by pressing the CTRL-END keys.
27. D
28. You can send a document to the printer by holding the SHIFT key down and pressing F7. Type "1" to select the full text option in order to print the entire document.
29. The Page Format (ALT-F8) sets the page size and controls page numbering. The Print Format (CTRL-F8) allows you to adjust the appearance of the printed document by changing the pitch, lines per inch, right justification, underline, style, etc.
30. If a file is currently in memory and another file is retrieved, WordPerfect brings the new file into memory and adds it to the existing document in memory.

■ CHAPTER 8

1. A   5. A   9. C
2. C   6. C   10. D
3. C   7. B   11. B
4. B   8. A   12. C

13. Framework is capable of handling word processing, spreadsheet, graphics, database management, and communications.
14. The applications of LOTUS include spreadsheets, graphics, and database management.

15. The LOTUS 1-2-3 Software Package includes the 1-2-3 System Disk, Printgraph, Utility Disk, Install Library Disk, and View of 1-2-3.
16. "What-if" questions are semi-structured problems, where not all of the parameters or assumptions are predefined.
17. The five components of a Decision Support System include the Decision Maker, Microcomputer, LOTUS 1-2-3 Software Package, Decision Model, and Data.
18. A second generation software package includes three different groups of programs in which one software package is used for spreadsheet analysis, graphics and database management. The various applications communicate easily with each other without requiring the user to leave the software environment.
19. It could be possible that the quick popularity of IBM-PCs came when LOTUS was introduced to the market, however, the IBM-PC and LOTUS together have been major factors in making microcomputers useful for business applications.
20. The first generation spreadsheet packages were limited to spreadsheet analysis. Second and third generation packages include graphics and database management. Third generation also includes word processing and communications.
21. A
22. The use of spreadsheets is not a new concept. Accountants and financial analysts have been using worksheets/spreadsheets for many years. The figures on these worksheets were constantly changing, resulting in recalculations. This process became very tedious and time-consuming. Once the microcomputer was introduced, the entire process was soon found to be performed more easily.
23. Some common business applications of electronic spreadsheets include payroll calculations, accounts receivable/payable, and investment analysis.
24. B
25. He can use the spreadsheet software package such as LOTUS 1-2-3. He should develop an inventory model which could utilize the stored data, interact with the users through "What-If" questions, and finally provide inventory reports.

■ CHAPTER 9

1. A	6. C	11. B
2. C	7. B	12. C
3. B	8. A	13. D
4. D	9. D	
5. C	10. B	

14. Yes. The /PRINT RANGE command allows you to select specific rows and columns to be printed.
15. C
16. D
17. A cell can be changed by typing over it and if the cell entry is long, the Edit Mode (F2) can be used.
18. Absolute, or permanent addressing, is used when you want a variable to remain constant when copying. For example, a tax rate would remain constant. Relative, or variable addressing, is when the variables are relative to the cells they are copied into. The copying is thought of as a relationship between the cells.
19. A formula can be entered in a cell by: (1) typing it in using a leading character of + − (@ or $, and (2) using the "Pointing" method where the arrow keys are moved to each cell location involved in the operation.
20. The /COPY command transfers an exact copy of the range to the receiving area, leaving the sending area intact. The /MOVE command transfers a range of cells to another part of the worksheet, removing the contents of the original sending area.

21. The /WORKSHEET GLOBAL FORMAT option allows you to format the entire worksheet. The /RANGE FORMAT option allows you to format a particular part of the worksheet. The /RANGE FORMAT option has precedence over the /WORKSHEET GLOBAL FORMAT option.
22. The "Pointing" method uses arrow keys to move the pointer to the cell locations that are involved in an operation.
23. The /RANGE FORMAT would be used when you only want to format a particular range of cells on the worksheet. For example, you may want to format a particular range of cells to identify currency (dollars and cents), a percentage (%), or specific date format (day-month-year).
24. A
25. C
26. B
27. 240 characters
28. Yes. If you want to start the label with a number, precede the number with " or '.
29. Enter the formulas in the appropriate cells for Year 1. Using the/COPY command, copy the cells from Year 1 to the appropriate cells for the remaining years.
30. When the SHIFT and PRTSC keys are pressed simultaneously, a copy of what you are currently viewing on the screen will be sent to the printer.

■ CHAPTER 10

1. B
2. B
3. B
4. B
5. C
6. The number of databases required for an organization depend on the needs of the organization and volume of data.
7. Microcomputers were considered inadequate for database processing during the 1970s due to their limited storage capacity and low-speed processing.

8. D	11. A	14. D
9. D	12. B	15. C
10. B	13. B	16. D

17. Data can be entered/inserted into any part of the database or it can be appended, added to the end of the database.
18. B
19. C
20. D
21. Two major problems with having multiple files containing information about different entities of the organization and at the same time having different programs use this data include: (1) the data files are not independent, rather they are considered part of the computer programs, and (2) duplication and inconsistency of data arises because data representing the same entity is located in different files.
22. The following factors led to the development of database concepts: (1) large volume of data, (2) availability and low cost of magnetic disks, and (3) data was recognized as a major corporate resource.
23. The components of a micro-based database system include: (1) data, (2) database structure, (3) DBMS, and (4) application programs.
24. The two types of data structures within a database include: (1) Logical structure–the relationship between files, records, and fields, and (2) Physical structure–how the records are actually stored/organized on the computer media or within internal memory.

25. The four types of logical structures include: (1) Network, (2) Hierarchical, (3) Relational, and (4) Link List.
26. The main objectives of a DBMS are to: (1) increase data independence, (2) reduce data redundancy, and (3) allow users to communicate with the database.
27. The two ways of accessing a database are by query access or application programs.
28. The diskettes that comprise the dBASE III PLUS database software package include: (1) System Disk 1, (2) System Disk 2, (3) Sample Programs and Utilities, (4) On-Disk Tutorial, (5) dBASE Administrator 1, (6) dBASE Administrator 2, and (7) Application Generator.

■ CHAPTER 11

1. B	6. C	10. A	14. A
2. E	7. B	11. C	15. C
3. C	8. B	12. B	16. C
4. C	9. E	13. D	17. C
5. A			

18. The List command displays all records in the active file. The Display command displays the record the pointer is currently pointing to.
19. The Modify Structure command is used to alter the record structure of an existing database file.
20. The Append command allows the addition of records at the end of the database and the Insert command allows records to be added at any specified position in an existing database.
21. The Pack command permanently erases records that have been marked for deletion.
22. The Index command allows you to organize the file by a key field while maintaining the original record sequence. The Sort command requires that another file be created.
23. D
24. The Delete command only marks the record for deletion and the Pack command actually deletes the record.
25. D

■ CHAPTER 12

1. D	6. F	11. A
2. F	7. F	12. E
3. C	8. A	13. C
4. C	9. F	
5. E	10. F	

14. Six major corporate resources are material, people, equipment, financial, management, and information resources. Information is perhaps the most important organizational resource.
15. The steps of the systems investigation are: (1) collecting background information, (2) defining the problem, (3) assessing information requirements, (4) costs and benefit analysis, and (5) documenting investigation results.
16. A systems investigation may need to be carried out further because (1) investigator did not have sufficient time to gather all the necessary information, (2) investigator did not have access to certain information, (3) investigator did not have full cooperation from the staff who are affected by the system, and (4) new development may have occurred within the area of investigation after the information was collected.

17. For both small and large firms, potential benefits for a micro-based information system include: reduction in staff requirements, increase in productivity of staff, increase in accuracy and precision of information generated, increase in quality of services provided, increase in assistance to decision makers, improvement in security procedures of firm's data, and reduction in the amount of time needed to generate information.
18. An organization may need to change procedures due to functional changes, environmental factors, or changes in tax laws and government regulations.
19. A major factor in the increase of productivity is the timeliness and accuracy of information provided by formal information systems to information users.
20. Better services can be provided with a micro-based information system by providing timely information. For example, a doctor's office could quickly identify appointments or any outstanding financial obligations, an educational institution can quickly identify available classes during registration, and an insurance agent could quickly provide information about a customer's policy status or different alternatives/options.
21. There are advantages and disadvantages to having an inside or outside investigator. If an insider does the assessment, collecting the information will be much easier than it would be for an outsider. However, the insider may tend to rely primarily or even exclusively on personal experience, whereas the outsider would tend to be less biased.
22. The critical characteristics of required information during the assessing process are: How much data will be handled? What type of data will be handled? How often is the information needed? How large are the output documents? What is the output format? and, How repetitive is the processing?
23. Some indirect costs of developing a micro-based information system, which could be overlooked, include: system's maintenance, system's designer and developer, training of personnel, systems conversion and expansion, and supplies.
24. An investigator may want to postpone the development of a computer system because funds are not available, the problem is low priority, lack of technology, or lack of management support.
25. If a micro-based information system is used properly, resources can be managed more efficiently, productivity levels will increase, and services provided will improve.
26. The end user is: (1) informed of status of different functions, (2) assisted in the decision making process, and (3) can participate in the development of the system.
27. One of the reasons that require an investigator to conduct a further study is lack of information gathered. This may be due to lack of time or cooperation, or even security reasons. Another reason would be because of new developments that occurred after the initial investigation began, thus, the investigator may not feel confident recommending a solution based on old data.

■ CHAPTER 13

1. B
2. C
3. D
4. A
5. A
6. A
7. C
8. E
9. C
10. D
11. C
12. D

13. Both software and hardware evaluation are very important. However, software should be evaluated first, in order to best satisfy the needs of the firm, before selecting hardware.
14. The most important factor in reflecting the quality of documentation is the simplicity of the language for explanations. Use of computer jargon, technical terms, or buzzwords are indicators of poor quality software.
15. Yes. During the System Selection and Design process, the user's future requirements must be considered as well as their immediate needs.

16. The activities that constitute the Design Phase are: (1) identifying the systems security and maintenance requirements, (2) consultation with the users, (3) software evaluation, (4) hardware evaluation, (5) identifying different alternatives/options, (6) preparing a system selection and design report, and (7) selecting the most appropriate system.
17. The three types of security concerns in a typical micro-based information system are (1) availability of the system, (2) accuracy of information, and (3) confidentiality of information.
18. The three types of system maintenance include: (1) hardware maintenance, (2) software maintenance, and (3) programming maintenance.
19. Other considerations concerning the volume of data to be processed include: (1) What are the future requirements concerning data? (2) How often will the data be processed? (3) What is the average size of each document? (4) How often will the data be accessed? (5) Does the system need to interface with other information systems?
20. A Request for Proposal (RFP) is a report summarizing the objectives of the system, user requirements, system requirements, and other relevant information about the company's needs. This report is usually distributed to different system vendors for recommendation of a suitable software package.
21. During the Software Maintenance Evaluation process, the following issues should be addressed: Is the vendor willing to correct errors discovered during the use of the software? If so, how long will it take to correct the problem? If the software disk is damaged, will the vendor provide another copy? What is the additional cost? How long will this take?
22. The main advantage of buying hardware that is designed around the industry PC standard is the availability of software, expansion options, and services by vendors other than the manufacturer.
23. Each proposed alternative should include descriptions of software and hardware, possible benefits, additional comments, and the overall cost of the particular alternative. There may be many alternatives, however, the developer should limit the choices to a few.
24. The System Selection and Design Report contains the overall status of the system evaluation and alternatives for consideration by other people involved in the selection process.
25. Although the controller feels there is a need for a micro-based system, she should first consider whether the benefits of a microcomputer will substantiate its cost and whether a microcomputer will solve her requirements. If the answer to these two questions is yes, then there are several other areas to be addressed before purchasing a system. For example, what are the maintenance and security requirements? Did she consult the end user's on their particular needs of a micro-based system? What are the organization's future data requirements? Who will perform the task of program maintenance when the organization grows or user requirements change? These are just a few of the issues to be considered before actually buying a system.

■ CHAPTER 14

1. C
2. B
3. B
4. During the implementation stage, software packages should be thoroughly tested to ensure the basic functions and features are working properly.
5. D
6. D
7. E
8. A
9. C
10. The key elements of a useful operating manual are the simplicity of explanation and validity of assumptions.

11. No. The best approach to developing a user's manual is to have it written by an average user of the system. An average user will use language related to the actual use of the system, rather than to an analysis of the system as a whole.
12. C
13. The activities of the system implementation phase are:
    a. Installation and testing
    b. Applications program development
    c. Data file creation
    d. System conversion
    e. Development of the user's manual
    f. Development of the user's training program
14. The formatting program of the operating system can be used to format blank floppy disks or a hard disk to make sure the disk drives are working properly. The copying program can be used to make backup copies, with the operating system disk in one drive and a blank disk in the second drive, to make sure the two disk drives can interact with each other.
15. Three tools that a programmer can use to develop the logical structure of a program are: (1) flowcharts, (2) psuedocode, and (3) hierarchy charts.
16. The amount of program testing depends on the following factors: (1) the sensitivity of the information generated by the system, (2) cost of applications testing which is dependent on the availability of financial and human resources, and (3) complexity of applications.
17. Unplanned conversion procedures can create an interruption in the work flow, user dissatisfaction, and damage to the credibility of the system.
18. The three common techniques of conversion are: (1) Cold Conversion–where you stop the old system and start the new one, (2) Parallel Conversion–where the old system is changed over to the new system with some overlap, and (3) Phased Conversion–where the conversion process is done in phases or modules.
19. A user's manual or operation's manual must be developed in order to assist users who do not know how to operate the system. In addition, appropriate training programs should be developed for users of the system. Other alternatives include bringing in an outside instructor for staff training, encouraging users to attend software courses offered by local educational institutions or by the vendor, and the use of videos.
20. The cold conversion method is the cheapest and simplest conversion method available.
21. With a phased conversion, the success of a subsequent phase is completely dependent upon the success of the previous phase.
22. For a small company in business for only six months, a cold conversion would probably be the best approach due to its simplicity and low cost. A large company formed 25 years ago should use a parallel conversion since it is considered almost risk-free. With this method, the organization would have ample time to monitor the performance of the new system and correct errors and deficiencies.

CHAPTER 15

1. D
2. B
3. B
4. B
5. C
6. C
7. C

8. New security concerns may be discovered during the post implementation review that were non-existent in the initial security planning process.
9. B

10. The activities of the maintenance and management phase include: (1) development of a maintenance and security procedure manual, (2) post-implementation review, and (3) documentation of post-implementation results.
11. The maintenance manual should cover hardware maintenance, software maintenance, and programming maintenance.
12. Misuse of an information system can be reduced by properly locking system components in a safe place or posting the organization's policy regarding unauthorized system use. For example, confidential data stored on a diskette should be locked up.
13. Software maintenance preventative measures include informing users on the proper procedures for handling diskettes, and the importance of making backup copies of the contents of a diskette and any hard disks in case of loss or damage to the original.
14. Areas of the post-implementation review process include cost analysis, availability of information, accuracy of information, personnel requirements, volume of transactions, satisfaction with vendor, and security and maintenance measurements.
15. The hardware maintenance manual should clearly identify the procedures for keeping hardware components in working order. It should contain the source to be contacted for repair or routine maintenance on the system, and some possible steps to be taken in order to solve unexpected problems. The hardware maintenance manual should also specify the terms of each maintenance contract. The software maintenance manual should identify procedures to prevent losses or disasters and the importance of backup copies of diskettes and hard disks. The software maintenance manual should also list procedures in order to develop these backup copies.
16. If a software program is lost or damaged, the user can either use the backup copy or, if no backup copy exists, the user can contact the software vendor.
17. Some problems that can result from lack of programming maintenance are: (1) additions or updates to a data file may not have occurred and user is not aware of the problem, (2) a field may not be large enough to hold data/figures, and (3) programs may not be able to handle additional volume of data.
18. No. Like other organizational assets, information is a valuable asset and the micro-based system must be protected against theft and misuse.
19. Documenting the original installation process could save time when such a situation occurs. The documentation allows the firm to go back and review the steps involved in the installation process and compare results with other installations performed.

■ CHAPTER 16

1. The host operating system is the main software that coordinates the data communications process.
2. A
3. C
4. C
5. C
6. The speed of data transmission is measured in number of bits transmitted per second (BPS).
7. B
8. B
9. C
10. A
11. B
12. D
13. B
14. B
15. D
16. B
17. C
18. Management of a LAN should provide reliable and effective service to its users. Overall performance of the system should be constantly monitored and the growth rate of the LAN should be continually assessed to anticipate the need for rearrangement and expansion.

19. A typical data communications configuration includes:
    a. Source/Host Computer
    b. Receiving Computer
    c. Data/Information
    d. Communication Protocols
    e. Transmission Components
20. Digital data is represented as a combination of 0s and 1s. Analog data is represented by a continuous flow with different frequencies.
21. Communication components used for transmitting data include: (1) communication channel, (2) modulator/demodulator, and (3) transmission mode.
22. Bit and character synchronization is a process of translating a bit stream into bytes/characters upon arrival of data at a receiver site.
23. Asynchronous data transmission requires start and stop bits for each character and synchronization data transmission does not.
24. The three major areas of a LAN are: (1) hardware, (2) software, and (3) transmission media.
25. The first part of a LAN software component is a communications program that controls the overall functions of networking. The second part consists of communication programs used on individual PCs in order to make the initial connections and prepare the PCs for communication.
26. Baseband coax provides a single channel with data rates typically between 10 and 15 megabits per second in the half-duplex mode. Broadband coax provides hundreds of low-speed channels, and uses radio frequency transmission to divide a much broader frequency range into a number of different channels.
27. The basic network topologies are Star, Bus, and Ring.
28. Some major LAN applications include computing applications, office automation, and industrial and laboratory automation.

■ CHAPTER 17

1. B
2. The awareness of business managers has not kept pace with the dramatic growth of modern business crime. However, many managers and business owners are becoming more familiar with the problem and, as a result, more preventive actions are being taken since information is now treated as a major resource of an organization.
3. D
4. Most cases of computer crimes/misuse involve employees of the company.
5. C
6. B
7. B
8. D
9. C
10. It is management's responsibility to educate employees about microcomputer crime/misuse and the implications involved for the individual and for the company.
11. Some reasons cited for the rise in incidents of computer crime are: (1) increased availability of microcomputers, (2) improved communications capabilities of modern information systems, and (3) more knowledgeable users.

12. Floppy diskettes, the hard disk, or cassette are common secondary storage media that a person may deliberately destroy.
13. Types of computer crime include: (1) theft of computer hardware, (2) theft of data/information, (3) destruction of secondary storage media, (3) illegal copying of software, (4) unauthorized program fixing, (5) unauthorized access to other systems.
14. A log-on procedure for a computer system can control access to the system and to all the software used on the system.
15. Two ways of protecting data stored on a hard disk are: (1) install a security program which will not allow unauthorized users to access the disk, and (2) copy everything from the hard disk onto tapes at the end of each day as a backup.
16. Two benefits can be provided when a company has a straightforward policy on software piracy and illegal use of the system: (1) the users are made aware of the company's position with regard to crime/misuse, and (2) it is good protection in the case of lawsuits by software companies against an employee for software piracy or illegal use of the system.
17. The company could take the following steps when terminating an employee and the employee has been given a two week notice: (1) backup contents of hard disk and secure backup, (2) emphasize to the employee the firm's position about computer crime or misuse of the system, (3) restrict access to certain data, (4) take an inventory of software and/or hardware, and (5) lock up hardware components.
18. Both software piracy and photocopying copyrighted material are considered felonies and are punishable by law.
19. The most important thing to keep in mind when developing security measures is making the employees aware of the risks and consequences of computer crime/misuse through preventive and controlling programs. Security measures must be a combination of technical and managerial techniques.
20. The primary factor for increased computer crime is the dramatic growth in the use of microcomputers.

■ CHAPTER 18

1. B
2. C
3. D
4. B
5. The main advantage of using microcomputer software to prepare text is the fact that changes can be incorporated easily within the text stored in the computer.
6. The major difference between the traditional document development and the Desktop Publishing approach is the fact that with Desktop Publishing, almost all the stages of preparing a document/publication can be performed by the user, while with the traditional approach, many of the tasks such as art, typesetting, and layout preparations are performed outside of the organization or by individuals other than the user.
7. E
8. C
9. The three major uses of Desktop Publishing are technical, administrative, and promotional.
10. D
11. B
12. C
13. The four types of justification are:
    a. Center (a line of text is placed in the center of page)
    b. Full (straight left and right margins)

c. Right (ragged left margin)
d. Left (ragged right margin)
14. WYSIWYG is an acronym for "What You See Is What You Get," or what is shown on the computer screen is what a document will look like when it is printed on a sheet of paper.
15. B
16. B
17. Pagemaker does not offer style sheets, which makes it less desirable for long documents.
18. Desktop Video Production allows users to edit video tapes, perform sound mixing, generate low-end computer graphics such as titles and logos, experiment with special effects, and produce quality videos.
19. The hardware requirements for a Desktop Publishing System include the system, storage, monitor, mouse, and printer. The company currently owns an IBM-PC and a high-quality dot matrix printer. Therefore, the hardware that needs to be purchased is probably a monitor, since standard monitors don't have the graphics range necessary to represent the printed page on the screen, and a mouse. As for software, FONTRIX/PRINTIX enables the user to develop simple art, technical symbols, and fancy fonts which seem appropriate for publishing a weekly newsletter. In addition, Printix commands control page layout, margins, page numbering, header/footers, and font selection. Printix also reads text files prepared from many word processing software packages such as Wordstar/WordPerfect, which the organization most likely uses on the PC. On the other hand, Ventura Publisher is also a powerful software package and can also read files directly from word processing software packages. Both Desktop Publishing software support a dot matrix printer and are likely candidates to purchase.
20. The overall business of companies whose primary business is printing and publishing has probably decreased due to the popularity of Desktop Publishing software used in many organizations. However, some new foreseeable trends in desktop publishing allow organizations to develop documents using their own system and transferring those documents electronically to printing/publishing companies for mass duplication. This is beneficial for an organization as long as policies and procedures are enforced throughout the generation of the documents and the image of the company remains consistent.

APPENDIX C

1. The Backup and Copy commands are both used for copying files. However, the Copy command will make an exact duplicate of files being copied, whereas the Backup command copies the control data the Restore command uses, in addition to the data in the specified file. Therefore, a file that was "backed up" can only be used once it has been restored.
2. D
3. A
4. B
5. C
6. The EDLIN program is terminated and the system is returned to the DOS prompt.
7. Any number of DOS commands can be executed by a batch file.
8. D
9. C
10. C
11. The PATH command only locates files that can be executed, that is, those ending in the extensions COM, EXE, or BAT.
12. A
13. C

14. If the CONFIG.SYS file is not found when booting the system, default values are used in place of the CONFIG.SYS File.
15. The COPY CON, or Copy Console command, is a useful method of creating batch files by instructing DOS to copy a file as typed from the console/keyboard.
16. The "/+10" parameter causes the directory to be sorted by extension.
17. Press F6 followed by ENTER to exit the EDLIN insert mode.
18. The only difference between an AUTOEXEC.BAT file and a regular batch file is the fact that the AUTOEXEC.BAT file is executed automatically at the time of booting.
19. AUTOEXEC.BAT files can be created by using the DOS EDLIN command or a word processing software package.
20. Before a directory can be removed, all files contained within it must be deleted.

■ APPENDIX D

1. C
2. Remove your disk in Drive B and replace it with the Speller Diskette. Hold down the CTRL key and press F2 to activate the Speller.
3. D   5. D   7. B
4. C   6. B   8. B
9. CTRL-F10 activates the definition of a macro.
10. A
11. If the Speller reaches a word that it does not find in its dictionary, offering no suggested words for you to choose from, you have a choice of ignoring the word, adding the word to the Speller Dictionary, or editing the word.
12. You can use the WordPerfect Thesaurus when you need help with the vocabulary in your text.
13. The primary file contains information that will remain constant in each document. The secondary file contains variable information.
14. A WordPerfect macro is a combination of keystrokes condensed into one keystroke.
15. Macros can be activated by pressing ALT-F10 and entering the macro name.
16. You would use a macro when there are a series of tasks you find yourself using frequently.
17. The merge function is often used to personalize various form letters, memos and reports that have the same text but different recipients.
18. The file merging function could be used to personalize each letter and to create mailing labels. The Speller Diskette would also be beneficial to check all correspondence for accuracy.
19. Create a record by typing in a line of text and ending the line by pressing F9. Repeat this procedure until each field has been defined. Once the record is complete, hold down the SHIFT key and press F9 to end the record.
20. By merging a primary and secondary file. The primary file would contain the business letter and the secondary file would contain the recipients.

■ APPENDIX E

1. C
2. A
3. No. /GRAPH NAME CREATE will save the settings. /GRAPH SAVE will save the graph with the .PIC extension.
4. A

5. A
6. Six graphs can be defined for the same worksheet.
7. D
8. D
9. B
10. One or more fields must be included when defining the criterion range.
11. D
12. B
13. A macro is used when you use the same series of commands frequently for the same worksheet.
14. D
15. B
16. The five types of graphs available in 1-2-3 are Line, Bar, XY, Stacked-Bar, and Pie.
17. The following titles can be added to a graph with the /GRAPH OPTIONS TITLES option: First, Second, X-Axis, Y-Axis.
18. The procedure for obtaining a hardcopy of a 1-2-3 graph is as follows: (1) save worksheet graphs, (2) /S Q Y P, (3) insert PrintGraph Disk, press ENTER, (4) I, select graph to print, and (5) go.
19. The input range, criterion range, and output range must be defined in order to produce an output report of database records meeting certain criteria.
20. The Find command highlights records meeting the criteria.
21. /R N C, enter the name and press ENTER.
22. The primary problem is that the accountant did not document the macros.
23. C
24. D
25. D
26. E

■ APPENDIX F

1. B   3. A   5. B   7. B
2. C   4. B   6. B

8. The AND operator identifies that both conditions must be true for the expression to be true.
9. D
10. The order of procedure for logical operators are ( ), .NOT., .AND., .OR..
11. C
12. A database file is always needed to generate labels.
13. C
14. Changes made to an original data file will not have any affect on a label file previously created as long as the structure of the original file stays the same.
15. A
16. B
17. B
18. The List command lists all or specified files on the directory of a diskette and the Query command contains conditions set up for searching a database.
19. The Select command chooses a work area in which to open a database file and Set Relation command links the databases in two different areas.
20. B

Glossary

absolute addressing The variable in a formula stays constant.
active file area A temporary file area in RAM.
adaptor An expansion board that helps establish a communication link between one CPU and other devices.
administrative applications of desktop publishing A company's formal internal documents, such as reports and employee safety manuals.
alias A dBASE file in a selected or reserved area.
Alternate (ALT) key The key, marked Alt, located immediately beneath the CTRL key.
appending Adding data to the end of a database file.
AppleDOS Operating system developed by Apple Corporation around the Motorola 6502 microprocessor.
application program Collection of programs designed to make the computer's performance of specific tasks faster, easier, and more efficient.
arithmetic logic unit (ALU) The unit responsible for all arithmetic operations and decision-making processes.
ascending order A sorting method based on increasing sequential factors.
ASCII Acronym for American Standard Code for Information Interchange.
assistance menu A tool that allows the user to create data files, routines, menus, and reports without writing one single line of a computer program.
assist menu (the Assistant) The menu-driven mode of the dBASE III Plus software package.
asynchronous data transmission Serial data transmission that occurs when different signals are sent to represent the status of data transmission.
auxiliary storage units Devices or media that give users a way to store data on a permanent basis.
baseband coax Coaxial cable that provides a single channel with data rates between 10 and 15 megabytes per second in the half-duplex mode.
basic command programs Programs loaded during the booting process and designed to perform specific tasks essential to the easy operation of the computer.
baud Baud rate or bits per second (bps); speed of data transmission.
Beginner's All-Purpose Symbolic Instruction Code (BASIC) The programming language used most frequently on microcomputers.
binary code A code system consisting of zeros and ones, zero being the "off" stage of a circuit and one the "on" stage.
bit A single, basic unit of information to be stored; the smallest pieces of information that can be recorded in the memory of the system.
bit and character synchronization Ensures that both the receiver and transmitter are operating at the same rate of data transmission.
block of text One or more consecutive sentences, paragraphs, or pages of a document.
booting the system Loading the operating system into the primary system storage area to start the computer.
broadband coax Cable TV (CATV) cable that provides hundreds of low-speed channels and uses radio frequency transmission to divide a much broader frequency range into a number of different channels.
buffer The availability of memory within the printer.
bus The transmission medium of a bus network.
bus topology Topology in which all devices are attached to a common transmission medium, called the bus, that allows software, application programs, and data to be transferred among the participating units of the network, independent of any central server or controlling unit.
byte A collection of bits.
camera-ready copy Text and graphics produced on ready-to-copy pages.

cell Unique address that distinguishes each location in the worksheet from all others; found by the intersection of a worksheet column and worksheet row.

cell pointer Rectangular highlighted area in the worksheet—the cursor.

centering hole The large circular hole in the middle of the diskette used by the disk drive for rotating the disk in its protective jacket.

centralized system A mainframe-based computer network, with central computing location for operations of various computing tasks.

central processing unit (CPU) The heart of the microcomputer; also referred to as the microprocessor.

coaxial cable A popular transmission medium in use by many LANs and known for its traditional use in the cable television industry.

cold boot Starting the system by turning on the power source.

cold conversion Simply stopping the old system and starting the new one.

COMMAND.COM The command processor program of PC-DOS, responsible for performing many fundamental tasks. This program is loaded into the main memory of the microcomputer at the time of booting.

command-driven A program that reacts to specific instructions given by the user.

command processor On PC-DOS, the interpreter of data entered.

communication channel The communication link between two or more computers provided by an ordinary telephone line, a microwave, or a satellite.

communication protocol A set of rules outlining how data should be exchanged within a communication network.

communication software A program that allows users of a microcomputer to communicate with other computer systems by establishing the initial connection, transmitting data, receiving data, and monitoring the communication process.

compiler A more advanced version of the interpreter.

computer-based information system (CIS) A collection of electronic devices that operate through various instructions provided in a well-defined structure to capture raw data, and process, store, and generate information.

computer conferencing A method of communicating that requires the receiver to be logged-on at the time of message transmission since the message will be received and displayed on the screen as soon as it has been sent, unless the receiver has the message-receiving option turned off.

computer program A set of instructions that direct a computer to perform a certain task.

computer software Programs used in conjunction with hardware components.

connectivity Sharing data, programs, and hardware resources, both within and outside an organization.

Control (CTRL) key The key, marked "Ctrl," located next to the "A" key.

controller The central unit in a star network.

Control Program for Microcomputers (CP/M) An early operating system designed around the 8-bit microprocessor.

control programs Programs that manage the entire system; part of ROM.

control unit Comprises all of the instructions for performing computer functions.

coprocessor A component that assists with data manipulation, often referred to as a math coprocessor.

current record The last record created or accessed.

current record pointer An unseen pointer to mark the current records.

cursor The small blinking underline that indicates your current position on the screen.

customizing The task of modifying a software package to suit the needs of an organization.

database A collection of interrelated data files stored to serve the community of users in an optimal fashion.

database management A concept of managing data files by using information stored in common files.

database management software A collection of programs that allow users to keep data in electronic files, and provide the capability for retrieving, updating, data-manipulating, and report-generating.

database management system A software package that is a collection of programs that manage database-related activities.

database structure or organization The way that record are organized and related to each other in a database.
DataEase A relational DBMS software package designed by Software Solutions, Incorporated.
data file A collection of records, each of which contains information about an item, person, or situation, organized into a form of specified fields.
data processing The profession that evolved to carry out the task of managing files and other computer functions.
data processing (DP) system Early computer system development for financial and business applications.
dBASE III Plus The most commonly used microcomputer relational database management system, developed by Ashton-Tate, Incorporated.
debugging The task of correcting errors in a computer program.
decision maker Person who makes decisions based on decision models and information.
decision making Selecting the most appropriate or optimum alternative to resolve a problem or achieve a goal.
decision making process A set of systematic steps consciously worked through by a decision maker.
decision model A set of instructions or procedures necessary to solve a problem.
decision support system (DSS) Computer systems designed to assist decision makers in dealing with "what-if?" questions.
Delete (DEL) key The key, marked Del, located beneath the "2" and "3" keys.
descending order A sorting method based on decreasing sequential factors.
desktop publishing (DTP) A new microcomputer application that allows users to create high-quality publications, revolutionizing the traditional publishing process.
desktop publishing software Integrates personal computers into the publishing production process by allowing users to choose the layout, print fonts, format, and graphical presentations.
desktop video production A forthcoming generation of desktop applications that enables users to edit video tape, mix sound, generate computer graphics and special effects, and produce quality videos.
disk drive Hardware component that holds the diskette in place.
diskette Storage device of circular mylar plastic.
DisplayWrite A software package that does just about everything that can be done with electronic word processing.
distributed processing system A new concept in which computing operations can be performed at different locations while, at the same time, sharing computing ability and information with each other.
documentation Consists of a tutorial guide or training manual, a reference manual, and programming manual.
DOS prompt The signal that appears on the screen when the system is ready to process commands or applications.
dot matrix printer Most commonly used printer; uses dots to form characters.
dot prompt command mode The command-driven portion of the dBASE III Plus software package.
double-density (DD) diskette A diskette on which 512 bytes can be stored on each sector.
double-sided diskette A diskette capable of storing data on both its top and bottom surfaces.
downloading Transferring data from the mainframe to the microcomputer.
EBCDIC Acronym for Extended Binary-Coded Decimal Interchange Code.
editing The process of making additions, deletions, and corrections to the input data.
electronic bulletin board (EBB) A message system similar to a newspaper that a reader can browse for items of interest.
electronic mail (E-Mail) Sending an electronic message from one computer user to another, allowing users to store information or messages temporarily or permanently.
electronic publishing A new microcomputer application that allows users to create high-quality publications, revolutionizing the traditional publishing process.
electronic spreadsheets Software packages developed for spreadsheet analysis on microcomputers.
emulation A computer system imitating another computer.
encryption Converting data/information to an unrecognized format.
end users Those who apply information systems to the real world.
Enter The key marked "Enter" or noted by a bent arrow.

ergonomics The field of study that examines the physical aspects of the workplace and their effect on productivity.
ether A designation for a passive medium.
expansion slots Slots that allow for the addition of extra memory cards or boards into the CPU.
expert system A computer-based system with the ability to think rather than simply compute.
extension name Accompanies the file name; describes the type of data or instructions stored in the file. Separated from the file name by a period (.).
external modem A modem located outside a micro that requires a communication link between the modem and the interface board and must conform to a set of interface specifications to ensure compatibility.
fiber optics A transmission medium that uses laser technology for data transmission.
field Information related to one characteristic of a record; a collection of characters.
file merging Adding input data, or parts of it, to another group of data previously stored on your disk; combining two files or documents.
file name An identification for each program or file.
file size The number of bytes or characters in a file.
first-generation spreadsheet packages Spreadsheet packages limited to spreadsheet analysis (VisiCalc and PC-Calc).
fixed hard disk A hard disk permanently mounted in a microcomputer.
flat files Data stored in a form such that each row represents a record.
floppy disks Storage device of circular mylar plastic.
formal channels Company files, documents, and so on generated by the existing system.
formal information The primary product of a well-conceived and organized information system.
formatting Magnetically marking tracks and sectors on a diskette.
fourth-generation language Language that simplified writing of computer programs.
fragmentation Scattering of data over non-contiguous sectors of a diskette.
Framework One of the best-known third-generation, or full-skilled, integrated software packages.
front-end processor A programmable minicomputer that handles the data communication for a host mainframe computer.
full-duplex Data transmission in two directions simultaneously.
full-duplex modem Offers simultaneous two-way data transmission.
full-skilled software packages Software packages that can be used for word processing, spreadsheets, graphics, database management and communications.
function keys (F1-F10) Perform predefined tasks (HELP feature, EDIT, etc.).
graphics software A collection of programs that help users analyze data via creation of graphs and charts.
half-duplex Data transmission that is bi-directional but not simultaneous.
half-duplex modem Offers two-way data transmission in one direction at a time.
hardcopy A paper printout.
hard disk A storage device consisting of a platter on which data are recorded, sealed inside an enclosure.
hard return (HRt) A return the user inserts into the text by pressing ENTER.
hard-sectored diskette A diskette with tracks and sectors added during manufacture.
hardware The part of a computer that consists of all its mechanical and electronic devices.
hardware maintenance The procedures required to keep the hardware components of the system in working order.
hierarchical structure A type of organization, very similar to many business organizational structures, defining the position of various elements, which assumes each subordinate reports to one superior.
high-density diskette A diskette with storage capacity of up to 1.2 megabytes.
high-level language Computer programming language, such as BASIC or COBOL, that allows a user to create instructions in an English-like language.
host computer The computer from which data is transmitted to other devices.
host operating system The main software that coordinates the data communication process.
icon Small representative images the user selects with a pointing device.

index A limited version of a table, which contains only one or a small number of key fields.
informal channels Employee interviews, needs analysis-surveys, personal judgment and intuition.
informal information Information that is mainly the product of the human mind.
information Knowledge about an object, phenomenon, environment, issue, or subject.
information resources One of the six major corporate resources, along with money, materials, equipment, personnel, and management.
information system A system designed to manage, process, and produce information for an organization's decision makers.
ink-jet printer A printer that uses a cartridge to shoot ink onto a page.
input/output (I/O) devices Units that allow the user to communicate with the computer.
input/output (I/O) handler A group of "hidden files" that manage data programs on the PC-DOS operating system.
inputting Entering data through the keyboard and placing it into the computer's RAM.
insert mode Characters are inserted at the current cursor position. In WordPerfect, insert is the fault mode.
integrated software A collection of several subsystems capable of providing word processing, spreadsheet, database management, and graphics, all in one software environment.
interface board An expansion board that helps establish a communication link between one CPU and other devices.
internal modem Also known as a "smart modem;" this modem has a dialing capacity.
interpreter A set of programs that translate instructions from non-machine languages (e.g., BASIC) into machine language.
investigation report A report made after the systems investigation and analysis, which states the main problem, gives information requirements, states the costs and benefits, and provides recommendations.
keyboard The most common input device for entering data or instructions into the computer.
laser printer A printer in which a laser positions dots of magnetically charged ink-like toner on a rotating drum, then transfers the image onto paper by a xerographic process.
learning diskette An on-line tutorial for teaching a program to a new user.
letter-quality printer An impact printer that uses a wheel-shaped element on which the characters are placed.
linked list structure One of the four major types of logical structure that uses files known as primary and secondary keys to logically connect records.
local area networks (LANs) A system in which microcomputers can be linked together to share computing power and information.
logical structure The way files, records, and fields within the database are related to each other; the overall relationship environment of the database and its data components.
Lotus @ functions Preprogrammed sets of instructions that perform mathematical tasks.
Lotus 1-2-3 A second-generation spreadsheet software package; the most popular of all microcomputer software packages.
machine language A computer's native language, usually expressed as a system of zeroes and ones.
Macintosh Operating system developed by Apple Corporation, which uses a mouse in addition to a keyboard for selecting options and issuing commands.
macro Feature that allows the combining of numerous keystrokes into one keystroke that can be saved for later execution.
mainframes Large-scale "number-crunching" computers.
main memory unit Part of the CPU where data or programs are stored while being processed.
maintenance and security procedure manual The manual that covers hardware maintenance, software maintenance, programming maintenance, and system security.
manual system A structured accumulation of information developed around manual devices.
mark status Indicates data transmission is beginning, presented by a "1".
master files The permanent data files in a microcomputer information system.
memory unit Unit where data and instructions are stored; divided into two parts (ROM and RAM).

menu-driven program A program that presents menus for selection of options.
merge To combine files.
micro-based information systems Scaled-down computer systems that put computing power in the hands of the individual via microcomputers and software application packages; also known as microcomputer information systems.
microcomputer crime Any misuse or abuse of microcomputer information, data, files, or programs.
microcomputers Compact, affordable, easy-to-use computers.
micro-mainframe link The hookup making mainframe files or data available to a microcomputer.
microprocessor A single semiconductor chip containing the circuitry to perform computing tasks.
MicroSoft Corporation Disk Operating System (MS-DOS) Today's standard operating system, designed around the Intel 8088/8086 16-bit microprocessor.
MicroSoft Word A word processing software package that is menu-driven but also uses keyboard-entered commands.
minicomputers Smaller versions of mainframes; used mainly in distributed processing systems.
mode indicator area Displays the present status of the worksheet.
modem MOdulator/DEModulator. The device that performs the modulation and demodulation of transmitted data.
modulation A conversion process that changes digital data into analog data and vice versa.
monitor Also called a screen; a primary output device.
monochrome A non-color monitor which uses many dot matrices to display characters.
mother board A large board to which the CPU and all its components are connected.
multiple-field index An index based on more than one key field.
network Computers linked by communication programs to share information and computer power.
networking capability The ability of a microcomputer to communicate with other systems in which a microcomputer is linked to a mainframe, a minicomputer, or other microcomputer through the use of communication devices.
network topology The geometric arrangement pattern in which the transmission media and devices of a LAN are linked together; also known as structure.
non-procedural language Language that simplified writing of computer programs.
one-step conversion Simply stopping the old system and starting the new one.
operating system A collection of programs designed to manage the resources of the microcomputer system.
Operating System 2 (OS/2) A multi-task operating system designed jointly by IBM and Microsoft Corporation, capable of running several programs simultaneously.
operational decisions Enforcing organizational procedures for various tasks.
optical disk A storage that uses a laser to record data.
parallel conversion Both old and new systems operate side by side for a specified period.
parallel mode Data transmission (of all the bits contained in a byte) simultaneously through at least eight wires, one for each bit.
parallel printer Printer that uses multiple channels to receive data.
parallel transmission Communication in which all bits of a byte are transmitted simultaneously.
parity bit Examines and validates the accuracy of previously transmitted bits.
paste-up The process of producing camera-ready copy.
PC clones, PC look-alikes, or PC compatibles Microcomputers built around IBM-PC architectures.
PC standard An industry standard in which IBM-PC look-alikes use architecture and design similar to IBM-PCs.
permanent addressing The variable in a formula stays constant.
phased conversion Converting to a new computer system in phases.
physical structure The way records are organized on the computer media or within the internal memory of the computer.
pixel One of the many dots in a screen that form an image when lit.
plotter An output device for preparing graphics and pictures.
pointing method Method of entering a formula by using the ARROW keys to move the pointer to the cell locations involved in the operation.

port A hardware component that connects the source computer to another computer or front-end processor.
post-implememtation review The process of assessing the current status of the system and comparing it to past performance and future needs.
primary file In WordPerfect, this file usually contains the constant data (e.g., the body of a letter).
primary key A field within a record that contains a unique type of data used as identification for that record.
primary memory unit Part of the CPU where data or programs are stored while being processed.
printer An output device that provides a hard copy.
ProDos The more advanced version of AppleDOS.
programmer Person who develops computer programs.
programming maintenance The task of modifying and expanding programs developed as a part of an information system.
PROM Acronym for Programmable Read Only Memory.
promotional applications of desktop publishing A company's advertisements, logos, brochures, and the like.
protected mode Allows a user to operate other programs while one is running.
query access The process of accessing files performed either by a menu-driven mechanism or through a sequence of user-issued commands.
Random Access Memory (RAM) The memory available to the user of the microcomputer.
range A rectangular grouping of cells.
R:Base 5000 A relational DBMS designed by Microrim, Incorporated.
Read Only Memory (ROM) The part of the microcomputer memory that stores system instructions.
read/write access hole An oval-shaped hole under the centering hole through which data is recorded on the surface of the disk or read from the disk.
read/write head A device mounted on a mobile arm inside the disk drive that writes data on or retrieves data from the diskette.
real mode Standard mode used by most current operating systems.
receiving computer Either a dumb terminal or a microcomputer converted into a dumb terminal for the purpose of communication; the means through which the user accesses the computing capability or information of the host computer.
record Information related to one member of a file; a collection of fields.
record pointers The connectors between records in a linked list system that allow the user to go from one record to the next.
relational structure A structure that stores data in the form of tables, referred to as "flat files," in which each row represents a record.
relative addressing Variables in a formula are relative to the cells into which they are copied.
removable hard disk A hard disk that can be moved from one microcomputer to another.
repeaters Devices that form point-to-point links.
Request for Proposal (RFP) A request provided to various vendors specifying requirements of the system under development.
resolution The number of dots that form printed characters.
ring topology Same as bus topology except that the two ends of the bus are connected.
RS-232 interface An electrical circuit for inputting and outputting data to and from the microcomputer.
saving Storing data on a diskette as a text file to which you assign a name.
scanner Hardware that captures a text or graphic image as a photocopier does, and stores it in a computer field.
search The process of finding a particular record, field, or piece of data.
secondary file In WordPerfect, this file usually contains the variable data (e.g. list of addresses).
secondary key Fields which contain either unique or non-unique data that identify a record or assist in searching the records.
secondary storage units Devices or media that give users a way to store data on a permanent basis.

second-generation software packages Integrated software packages capable of performing three different groups of programs in one software package (spreadsheet analysis, graphics, and database management).
sectors Sections of a track.
semiconductor chip A collection of thousands of transistors placed on a square of silicon the size of a postage stamp.
semi-integrated software packages Integrated software packages capable of performing three different groups of programs in one software package (spreadsheet analysis, graphics, and database management).
semi-manual system A collection of manual and semi-manual devices.
semi-structured decision A decision in which the variables are a combination of probabilistic and deterministic.
semi-structured process A procedure in which all parameters or assumptions are not predefined; answers "what-if?" questions.
serial mode Data transmission of the bits of a byte, one at a time.
serial printer Printer that uses a single channel to receive data.
serial transmission Communication requiring one channel, over which bits of a byte or character are transmitted one at a time.
server The central unit in a star network.
simplex Data transmission in which signals move in a single direction.
simplex modem Offers unidirectional data transmission.
single-density (SD) diskette A diskette on which 256 bytes can be stored on each sector.
single-field index An index based on one key field.
soft return (SRt) A return the program inserts into the text at the end of a line when wrapping the text around.
soft-sectored diskette A diskette that needs tracks and sectors added through the formatting process.
software The part of the computer that consists of all the programs and instructions for performing various tasks.
software maintenance The procedures for maintaining software and information kept on secondary storage media; includes modifications to software packages either in having the packages perform additional tasks or perform tasks differently.
software package Collection of programs designed to make the computer's performance of specific tasks faster, easier, and more efficient.
software piracy The illegal copying of software.
sorting The task of rearranging data within a file.
source computer The computer from which data is transmitted to other devices.
space Represented by a "0"; indicates that data transmission is not occurring.
speller diskette Word processing diskette which provides a tool for checking misspellings in a document. Allows checking of a single word, a page, or an entire document.
spreadsheet A sheet of paper divided into columns of figures representing different entities.
spreadsheet software A collection of programs that allow the user to create a spreadsheet, perform arithmetic calculations, recalculate, save, and prepare analysis reports.
stand-alone device A computer used as a single entity.
star-shaped ring topology A combination of ring and star topologies.
start bit A single bit ("1") transmitted by the sender to the receiver indicating the start of the first bit of the first byte.
star topology Topology in which a central unit, known as a server or controller, and all the individual units have direct point-to-point communication links with the server.
station The point where a device, the controller, and the transceiver are connected to the ether.
status indicator Displays when special keys have been pressed (CAPS LOCK, NUM LOCK, etc.).
status line Indicates your current location in the document.
stop bit Indicates the end of a group of bits being transmitted.
strategic decision Involves planning and formulating objectives for the long and short term.
stress notches Cut-outs on a diskette that allow the jacket to bend without breaking.
structured decision A decision involving a great deal of certainty.

structured process A procedure in which all steps are well-defined.
synchronization bytes or characters Certain bytes or characters prior to each block of data transmission.
synchronous data transmission Serial data transmission which does not use start and stop bits for each byte/character. Bits are sent in block form.
syntax The structure of a command.
system bus An electronic pathway that allows different components of the CPU to communicate with each other.
system clock A clock of crystal that vibrates at a frequency of several million times per second and measures the internal operations of the processing unit.
system conversion Transferring the tasks performed by the old system to the new system.
system developer The person who carries out the tasks of the systems selection and design phase.
system development cycle The process of developing a system, which includes system investigation and analysis, selection and design, implementation, and maintenance and management.
system diagnostics programs Microcomputer systems that conduct status tests on each component of the system.
system disk The disk that contains the operating system.
system implementation phase The process of bringing the selected system into operational use and turning it over to the user.
system implementor The person who conducts the activities of system implementation.
system investigation and analysis First phase of the systems development cycle.
system security Availability of the entire system, accuracy of information generated by the system, and the confidentiality of certain information stored in the system; protecting information and data against theft and misuse.
system selection and design phase The tasks of identifying necessary features of the computer system, identifying different alternatives, and choosing and obtaining actual system components.
system selection and design report A report on the possible alternatives of software and hardware options.
systems files DOS programs needed for booting and basic input/output operations.
systems software Programs that manage the microcomputer's resources.
systems staff Responsible for developing and maintaining an organization's computer systems.
tables Data stored in a form such that each row represents a record.
tactical decisions Allocation of resources to accomplish goals or objectives established at the strategic level.
tape cartridge A storage device often used to back up the data stored on a hard disk.
technical applications of desktop publishing A company's specification sheets and manuals.
technical decisions Enforcing organizational procedures for various tasks.
telecommunication access method (TCAM) Allows the data management facilities of the host operating system to support data communication.
template A guide that fits over the function keys on the keyboard; feature key combinations are color-coded on it.
text formatting The process of adjusting your input on the computer until it appears as you want it.
thermal printer A printer that uses a dot matrix to form characters by burning dots into the paper.
thesaurus diskette Word processing diskette which acts as an ordinary thesaurus, suggesting other words or expressions for a particular word or expression.
third-generation software packages Software packages that can be used for word processing, spreadsheets, graphics, database management and communications.
timing hole Smaller hole to the right of the centering hole on floppy diskettes.
total connectivity The dependence of units on the server.
tracks Circular rings on a diskette's surface on which data are stored.
transaction files Files created on a periodic basis and then run against the master file.
transmission components Those components used in data transmission including a communication channel, a modem, and a transmission mode.
transmission media Components that provide the necessary connection between the devices of the local area network (LAN).

tree structure A type of organization, very similar to many business organizational structures, defining the position of various elements, which assumes each subordinate reports to one superior.
tree topology An extended version of a bus network.
twisted-pair wire Sometimes called copper wire; a popular transmission medium for local area network (LAN) links.
typeover mode Activated by pressing the INSERT key; characters typed replace existing characters.
Unix An operating system developed by AT&T Corporation initially for use on Digital Equipment Corporation's PDP-7 and PDP-11 minicomputers.
unstructured decisions A decision in which the variables are probabilistic.
updating a file Process of applying transaction files to the master file.
uploading Transferring data from the microcomputer to the mainframe.
user-friendly Software which allows a user to interact with its programs in the simplest possible way.
utility programs Programs stored on the DOS disk for special tasks, such as sorting.
variable addressing Variables in a formula are relative to the cells into which they are copied.
view A method of linking two databases using a common key field.
virtual telecommunication access method (VTAM) Allows the data management facilities of the host operating system to support data communication.
VisiCalc The first electronic spreadsheet software package; the first microcomputer business application.
volatile memory Random Access Memory (RAM).
volume label The name or number assigned to a formatted disk.
warm boot Starting the system without turning the power off, then on.
wide area networks (WANs) Communication networks that involves connection to a distant mainframe.
Winchester disk A storage device consisting of a platter on which data are recorded, sealed inside an enclosure.
wiring closet The central wiring system of the star-shaped ring topology.
WordPerfect A software package that is considered easy to use and offers many helpful features. All the programs of WordPerfect come on six diskettes: WordPerfect, Learning, Speller, Thesaurus, Printer 1, Printer 2.
word processing software A collection of programs that allow the user to create, delete, insert, modify, save, merge, and print text.
WordStar A microcomputer word processing software package that comes in four distinct programs: WordStar, Spellstar, MailMerge, and IndexStar.
word wrap When the end of a line of text is reached, WordPerfect automatically "wraps" the next word around to the beginning of the next line.
worksheet A sheet of paper divided into columns of figures representing different entities.
write-protect notch A rectangular-shaped hole on the upper right edge of a diskette, which allows material to be recorded on the diskette.

Index

-A-

Absolute Addressing 235-236, 257
Active File Area 315, 348
Adaptor 47, 52
Administrative Applications 506, 514
Alias 614, 625
Appending 278, 285
AppleDOS 93, 96, 98
Application Programs 62-63, 79, 280, 285
Application Software 58
Arithmetic Logic Unit (ALU) 30, 50
Ascending 278, 285
ASCII 31-32, 50, 459-460, 463
Assist Menu 295, 348
Assistance Menu 417, 429
Assistant 295, 348
Asynchronous Transmission 462-463, 478
Automated Information Systems (AIS) 11
Auxiliary Storage 41, 51

-B-

Baseband Coax 468, 478
BASIC 60-61, 397, 406
Basic Command Programs 59
Baud 48, 52
Binary Code 31, 50
Bit 31, 50
Bit Synchronization 462, 478
BITNET 464
Booting 59, 105-108, 128
 Cold Boot 105-107, 128
 Warm Boot 107-108, 128
Bricklin, Dan 202
Broadband Coax 468, 478
Buffer 40, 51
Bus 470, 479
Bus Topology 470-471, 479
Business Decisions 4-5, 7-8
Business Information Systems (BIS) 11
Byte 31, 50, 419, 429

-C-

Camera-ready Copy 503, 514
Cell pointer 218, 257
Cells 202, 208, 218, 257
Centering Hole 43, 51
Central Processing Unit (CPU) 29, 50
Centralized Systems 12, 19
Character Synchronization 462, 478
Coaxial Cable 468, 478
COBOL 62
Cold Boot 105-107, 128
Cold Conversion 421, 430

Command Processor 96-97, 98
Command-driven Software Packages 63, 79
Communication Channel 460, 477
Communication Protocol 460, 477
Communications Devices 46, 29
Communications Software 64, 72-74
Compatibility 27
Compiler 60-61, 79
Computer Conferencing 465, 478
Computer Program 57
Computer Software 57, 78
Computer Technology 12-15
Computer-based Information Systems (CBIS) 11, 19
Connectivity 35, 50
Control Programs 58-59
Control Unit 30, 50
Controller 469, 479
Controller Board 34
Coprocessor 34, 50
CP/M 59, 79, 92, 96, 98
Crop 508
Current Record Pointer 313, 348
Cursor 107, 128, 153, 190, 218, 257
Customizing 387, 406

-D-

Data 13, 459-460
Data Communication Components 458-460
 Communication Protocol 460, 477
 Host 458-459, 477
 Receiving Computer 459, 477
 Source Computer 458-459, 477
 Transmission Components 460-462, 477
Data File 270, 284
Data Processing (DP) 12, 19, 270-271, 284
Database 13, 271-272, 284, 465-466
Database Management 13, 19, 269-284
Database Management Software 64, 69-71
 DataEase 71, 282-283, 285
 dBASE III PLUS 63, 71, 282-283, 285, 293-348, 417, 610-625
 R:BASE 5000 71, 281, 285
Database Management System (DBMS) 278-280, 285
Database Organization 273-278, 284
Database Structure 273-278, 284-285
 Hierarchical 275, 284
 Linked List 273-274, 284
 Logical 273, 284
 Network 275, 285
 Physical 273, 284
 Relational 276-277, 285
 Tree 275, 284
DataEase 71, 282-283, 285

INDEX

dBASE III PLUS 63, 71, 282–283, 285, 293–348, 417, 610–625
  Assist Menu 295, 296, 348
  Assistant 295, 348
  Booting the System 294–295
  Creating a Database 303–309, 610–611
  Dot Prompt Command Mode 295, 348
  Entering Commands 301–302
  Entering Data 309–310
  Exiting 301
  File Management 621–625
  Function Keys 299
  Indexing 339–342, 612–613
  Inputting 611
  Keyboard Arrangement 298
  Labels 618–620
  Learning 303–346
  Listing 312–319, 612
  Menu Options 297
  Modifying 320–326
  Querying 342–346
  Relations 614–616
  Reporting 329–335
  Searching 342–346, 612, 614
  Selecting 613–614
  Sorting 329–339
dBASE III PLUS Diskettes
  Applications Generator 283
  On-disk Tutorial 283
  Sample Programs 283
  System Disks #1 and #2 283
  Utilities 283
Debugging 61, 79
Decision Maker 206, 208
Decision Making 3, 6–8, 18
Decision Model 206–208
Decision Support System (DSS) 13, 19, 206–208
Decisions
  Business 4–5, 7–8
  Operational 4–5, 8, 18
  Semi-structured 5–6, 18
  Strategic 4–5, 8, 18
  Structured 5–6, 18
  Tactical 4–5, 8, 18
  Technical 4–5, 8, 18
  Unstructured 5–6, 18
Descending 278, 285
Desktop Publishing (DTP) 64, 76–77, 79, 501–514
Desktop Publishing (DTP) Software
  Fontrix/Printrix 512
  Harvard Professional Publisher 512
  Lasersoft 77
  PageMaker 77, 512
  PagePerfect 513
  Powerform 77
  The Newsroom 77
  Ventura Publisher 513

Desktop Video Production 513, 515
Disk Drive Arrangement 104
Disk Drives 42, 51
Diskettes
  Double-density 44, 52
  Double-sided 44, 52
  Hard-sectored 43, 51
  High-density 44, 52
  Single-density 44, 51
  Soft-sectored 43, 51
Disks
  Fixed 45, 52
  Floppy 42–44, 51
  Hard 45, 52
  Optical 46, 52
  Removable 45, 52
  Winchester 45, 52
DisplayWrite 67, 141–144
Distributed Processing Systems 13–14, 19
Documentation 391, 406
DOS 89, 96–98, 103–128, 541–556
  Backup 555-556
  Booting the System 105–108
  Command Processor 96–97, 98
  Directories 551–554
  Editing 543–550
  Formatting 550–551
  Input/Output Handler 96–97, 98
  Keyboard Arrangement 108–109
  Learning 103–128, 541–556
  Restore 556
  Sorting 541–543
  System Files 97
  Utility Programs 96–97
DOS prompt 107, 128
Dot Matrix Printers 39, 51
Dot Prompt Command Mode 295, 348
Double-density Diskettes 44, 52
Double-sided 509
Double-sided Diskettes 44, 52
Downloading 474, 479

        –E–

EBCDIC 31–32, 50, 459–460
Editing 138, 144
Electronic Bulletin Board (EBB) 465, 478
Electronic Mail 464–465, 478
Electronic Publishing 501, 514
Electronic Spreadsheet 68, 199, 202–203
Embedded Codes 508
Emulate 459, 477
Encryption 390, 406
End user 17, 19
Ergonomics 416, 429
Ether 473, 479
Expansion Board 34, 50

Expansion Slots   34–35, 50
Expert Systems   15, 19
Extension Name   110, 129
External Modem   461, 477
External Programs   97
E-mail   464–465, 478

–F–

Fiber Optics   468–469, 478
Field   419, 429
File Merging   138, 144
File Names   110, 129
File Size   111, 129
First-generation Spreadsheet Packages   203, 208
Fixed Disks   45, 52
Flat Files   276, 285
Floppy Disks   42–44, 51
Font   508
Fontrix/Printrix   512
Footer   508
Formal Channels   366, 376
Formal Information   9, 19
Formal Information Systems   13–14
Formatting   43, 51, 138, 144
FORTRAN   62
Fourth-generation Programming Language   13, 19
Fragmentation   127–128, 129
Framework   76, 203–204, 208
Front-end Processor   459, 477
Full-duplex   49, 52
Full-duplex Modem   461, 477
Full-skilled Spreadsheet Packages   203, 208

–G–

Graphics Software   64, 71–72, 79
  Harvard Graphics   72
  Lotus 1-2-3   27, 63, 69, 72, 75–77, 203–208, 215–257, 577–602
  Micro Graphics   72
Greeking   509

–H–

Half-duplex   49, 52
Half-duplex Modem   461, 477
Hard Copy   39, 51
Hard Disks   45, 52
Hard Return   160, 190
Hardware   11, 16, 19
Hardware Evaluation   394–399
Hardware Maintenance   387, 406, 439, 449
Hard-sectored Diskettes   43, 51
Harvard Graphics   72
Harvard Professional Publisher   512
Header   508
Hierarchical Database Structure   275, 284
High-level Programming Language   13, 19
High-density Diskettes   44, 52

Host Computer   458–459, 477
Host Operating System   459, 477
Hyphenation   508

–I–

IBM PC-DOS   89, 96–98, 103–128, 541–556
  Backup   555–556
  Booting the System   105–108
  Command Processor   96–97, 98
  Directories   551–554
  Editing   543–550
  Formatting   550–551
  Input/Output Handler   96–97, 98
  Keyboard Arrangement   108–109
  Learning   103–128, 541–556
  Restore   556
  Sorting   541–543
  System Files   97
  Utility Programs   96–97
Icon   93, 98
Index   276–277, 285, 339, 341, 348
  Multiple-field   341, 348
  Single-field   339, 348
Informal Channels   366, 376
Informal Information   9, 19
Information   8–9, 11, 18–19
  Formal   9, 19
  Informal   9, 19
Information Processing   9
Information Resource Management   11–12
Information Resources   359
Information Systems   10–11, 13–14, 17, 19, 359–360, 376
  Automated (AIS)   11
  Business (BIS)   11
  Computer-Based (CBIS)   11, 19
  Formal   13–14
  Management (MIS)   11
  Manual   10, 19
  Microcomputer   360, 376
  Micro-based   17, 19, 360
  Semi-manual   10, 19
Ink-jet Printers   40, 51
Input/Output Devices   29, 36, 51
Input/Output Handler   96–97, 98
Inputting   137, 144
Insert Mode   155, 190
Integrated Software   74–76
  Framework   76, 203–204, 208
  Lotus 1-2-3   27, 63, 69, 72, 75–77, 203–208, 215–257, 577–602
  Open Access   76
  Smart Software System   76
  Symphony   76, 203
Integrated Spreadsheet Packages   203–204, 208
Interface Board   47, 52
Internal Modem   461, 477
Interpreter   60–61, 79

In-house Publishing 506–507

–J–

Jobs, Steve 25
Justification 508

–K–

Kerning 508
Keyboard 36–37, 51, 108–109

–L–

Landscape Printing 509
Laser Printer 39, 51
Laser Printing 509
Lasersoft 77
Layout 508
Leading 508
Letter-quality Printers 39, 51
Linked List Database Structure 273–274, 284
Local Area Network (LAN) 15, 19, 73–74, 467–468, 472–474, 478
  Bus 470–471, 479
  Ethernet 473
  Hardware 467
  IBM PC-Network 474
  Ring 471–472, 479
  Software 467
  Star 469, 478
  Starlan 474
  Star-shaped Ring 472, 479
  Transmission Media 467–468, 478
  Tree 471, 479
Logical Database Structure 273, 284
Lotus 1-2-3 27, 63, 69, 72, 75–77, 203–208, 215–257, 577–602
  @ Functions 241–243, 257
  Booting the System 216–217
  Command Menu 223
  Copying 234–237
  Database Management 591–598
  Entering Data 228–229
  Exiting 249
  Formatting 238–240
  Function Keys 221–222, 257
  Graphics 577–591
  Keyboard Arrangement 220–222
  Learning 224–256
  Macros 598–602
  Menu Options 222, 232, 241, 246, 248, 578, 592
  Mode Indicators 219, 257
  Moving 244–245
  Printing 245–247
  Ranges 234–236, 240, 257
  Saving 247–249
  Status Indicators 220, 257
Lotus 1-2-3 Diskettes 204–205
  1-2-3 System 205
  Install Library 205
  PrintGraph 205
  Utility 205
  View of 1-2-3 205

–M–

Machine Programming Language 12, 19
Macintosh 93–94, 96, 98
Main Memory Unit 41, 51
Mainframe 18, 28
Maintenance and Security Procedure Manual 439, 445, 449
Management
  Database 13, 19, 269–285
  Information Resources 11–12, 359
Management Information Systems (MIS) 11
Manual Information Systems 10, 19
Mark Status 462, 478
Master Files 420, 429
MegaHertz (MHz) 34
Memory Unit 30, 41, 50
Menu-driven 63, 79, 391, 406
Merging 279, 285
Micro Graphics 72
Microcomputer Communication 457–477
Microcomputer Crime 487–494
Microcomputer Hardware Components 29
Microcomputer History 26–28
Microcomputer Information Systems 360, 376
Microcomputer Networking 466–467, 478
Microcomputer Software
  Application Software 58
  Command-driven 63
  Communications 64, 72–74
  Database Management 64, 69–71
  Desktop Publishing 64, 76–77
  Graphics 64, 71–72
  Integrated 74–76
  Menu-driven 63
  Spreadsheet 64, 67–69
  Programming Languages 58, 60
  Systems Software 58
  Word Processing 64–67
Microcomputers 13, 15–16, 19
Microplan 203
Microprocessor 29, 30–33, 50
Microsoft Word 67, 139–140, 143–144
Micro-based Information Systems 17, 19, 360
Micro-to-mainframe Link 474–475, 479
Minicomputers 13, 19
Modem 48, 52, 459, 461, 477
  External 461, 477
  Full-duplex 461, 477
  Half-duplex 461, 477
  Internal 461, 477
  Simplex 461, 477
Modulation 461, 477
Modulation Techniques 461

Monitors 38–39, 51
Mother Board 35, 51
MS-DOS 60, 79, 92–93, 96, 98
Multiplan 69, 72
Multiple-field Index 341, 348

–N–

Network 17, 19
Network Management 475–476
Network Planning 475–476
Network Database Structure 275, 285
Network Topology 469, 478
Networking 467, 478
Networking Capability 397–398, 406
Non-procedural Programming Language 13, 19

–O–

One-step Conversion 421, 430
Open Access 76
Operating System 58–59, 89–98
  AppleDOS 93, 96, 98
  Basic Command Programs 59
  CP/M 92, 96, 98
  IBM PC-DOS 89, 96–98, 103–128, 541–556
  Macintosh 93–94, 96, 98
  MS-DOS 92–93, 96, 98
  OS/2 94–96, 98
  Unix 94, 96, 98
  Utility Programs 59–60
  Xenix 94, 96
Operational Decisions 4–5, 8, 18
Optical Disks 46, 52
OS/2 94–96, 98

–P–

PageMaker 77, 512
PagePerfect 513
Parallel Conversion 421, 430
Parallel Mode 47, 52
Parallel Printers 40, 51
Parallel Transmission 463–464, 478
Parity Bit 463, 478
Paste-up 503, 514
PC Clones 27, 50
PC Compatibles 27, 50
PC Look-alikes 27, 50
PC Standard 396, 406
PC-Calc 203
Permanent Addressing 235–236, 257
Phased Conversion 421–422, 430
Physical Database Structure 273, 284
Pica 508
Pixel 38, 51
Plotters 39–40, 51
Point 508
Pointers 274, 284
Pointing Method 226, 257
Portrait Printing 509

Ports 459
Post-implementation Review 441–445, 449
Powerform 77
Primary File 567, 573
Primary Key 273, 284
Primary Memory Unit 41, 51
Printers
  Dot Matrix 39, 51
  Ink-jet 40, 51
  Laser 39, 51
  Letter-quality 39, 51
  Parallel 40, 51
  Serial 40, 51
  Thermal 40, 51
Procedural Programming Language 13, 19
ProDOS 93, 98
Program Development Process 62, 417–418
Programmable ROM (PROM) 30, 50
Programmer 57
Programming 13
Programming Languages 58, 60
  Fourth-generation 13, 19
  High-level 13, 19
  Machine 12, 19
  Non-procedural 13, 19
  Procedural 13, 19
Programming Maintenance 386, 406, 440–441, 449
Promotional Applications 506, 514
Protected Mode 95, 98
Publishing Process 502–505

–Q–

Query Access 280, 285

–R–

R:BASE 5000 71, 281, 285
Random Access Memory (RAM) 29–30, 50
Read Only Memory (ROM) 30, 50, 91
Read/Write Access Hole 43, 51
Read/Write Head 44, 52
Real Mode 95, 98
Receiving Computer 459, 477
Record 272, 284, 419, 429
Relational Database Structure 276–277, 285
Relative Addressing 235–236, 257
Removable Disks 45, 52
Repeaters 471, 479
Request for Proposal (RFP) 388, 406
Resolution 509, 511, 514
Ring Topology 471–472, 479
RS-232 Interface 461–462, 477
Ruled Lines 508

–S–

Sample Cases 525–540
Saving 137, 144
Scanner 511, 514
Screen Adjustments 109–110

Screens 38–39
Search 279, 285
Secondary File 567, 573
Secondary Key 274, 284
Secondary Storage 41–42, 51
Second-generation Spreadsheet Packages 203, 208
Sectors 43, 51
Semiconductor Chip 26, 50
Semi-integrated Spreadsheet Packages 203, 208
Semi-manual Information Systems 10, 19
Semi-structured Decisions 5–6, 18
Semi-structured Process 206, 208
Serial Mode 47, 52
Serial Printers 40, 51
Serial Transmission 462, 477
Server 469, 479
Simplex 49, 52
Simplex Modem 461, 477
Single-density Diskettes 44, 51
Single-field Index 339, 348
Smart Software System 76
Soft Return 160, 190
Software 11, 16, 19
Software Evaluation 389–394
Software Maintenance 387, 390–391, 406, 439–440, 449
Software Packages 58, 60, 62–63
　Command-driven 63
　Communications 64, 72–74
　Database Management 64, 69–71
　Desktop Publishing 64, 76–77
　Graphics 64, 71–72
　Integrated 74–76
　Menu-driven 63
　Spreadsheet 64, 67–69
　Word Processing 64–67
Software Piracy 490, 494
Soft-sectored Diskettes 43, 51
Sorting 278, 285
Source Computer 458–459, 477
Space Status 462, 478
Spreadsheet 199–202, 208
Spreadsheet Software 64, 67–69, 79, 199–207
　First-generation 203, 208
　Framework 203–204, 208
　Full-skilled Spreadsheet 203, 208
　Integrated Spreadsheet 203, 208
　Lotus 1-2-3 27, 63, 69, 72, 75–77, 203–208, 215–257, 577–602
　Microplan 203
　Multiplan 69, 72, 203
　PC-Calc 203
　Second-generation 203, 208
　Semi-integrated 203, 208
　SuperCalc 69, 203
　Supercalc-3 203
　Third-generation 203, 208

VisiCalc 27, 69, 202–204
Stand-alone Devices 17, 19
Star Topology 469, 478
Start Bit 462, 478
Star-shaped Ring Topology 472, 479
Station 473, 479
Status Line 153, 190
Stop Bit 462, 478
Storage Unit 29, 41
Strategic Decisions 4–5, 8, 18
Stress Notches 43, 51
Structured Decisions 5–6, 18
Structured Process 206, 208
Style Sheet 509
Sunshine Window Incorporated, Suppliers Case 520–524
SuperCalc 69
Supercalc-3 203
Symphony 76, 203
Synchronization Bytes 463, 478
Synchronization Characters 462, 478
Synchronous Transmission 463, 478
Syntax 301, 348
System Bus 34, 50
System Clock 34, 50
System Conversion 420–421, 430
　Cold 421, 430
　One-step 421, 430
　Parallel 421, 430
　Phased 421–422, 430
System Developer 384, 405
System Diagnostics Programs 416, 429
System Disk 59
System Documentation 423–424
System Files 97, 98
System Implementation Report 424–428
System Implementor 414, 429
System Installation 415–416
System Investigation Report 370, 372–376
System Maintenance 386–387
System Security 384–386, 405, 411, 449
System Selection and Design 383–405
System Selection and Design Report 399–404, 406
System Testing 415–416
Systems
　Centralized 12, 19
　Data Processing 12, 19
　Decision Support 13, 19
　Distributed Processing 13–14, 19
　Expert 15, 19
Systems Development Cycle 360, 376
Systems Implementation 413–429
Systems Implementation Activities 414–424
Systems Investigation Activities 364–372
Systems Investigation and Analysis 359–376
Systems Maintenance and Management 437–449
Systems Maintenance and Management Activities 438–445

Systems Software 58
 Control Programs 58
 Operating System 58-59
Systems Staff 17, 19

-T-

Tables 276, 285
Tactical Decisions 4-5, 8, 18
Tape Cartridges 45, 52
Technical Applications 506, 514
Technical Decisions 4-5, 8, 18
Technological Advances 12-15
Telecommunication Access Method (TCAM) 459, 477
Template 156, 190
The Newsroom 77
Thermal Printers 40, 51
Third-generation Spreadsheet Packages 203, 208
Timing Hole 43, 51
Total Connectivity 470, 479
Tracks 43, 51
Transaction Files 420, 429
Transmission Components 460-462, 477
 Communication Channel 460, 477
 Modulation Techniques 461
 Transmission Modes 462
Transmission Modes 462
 Asynchronous 462-463, 478
 Parallel 463-464, 478
 Serial 462, 477
 Synchronous 463, 478
Tree Database Structure 275, 284
Tree Topology 471, 479
Twisted-pair Wire 468, 478
Typeover Mode 155, 190

-U-

Unix 94, 96, 98
Unstructured Decisions 5-6, 8, 18
Updating Files 420, 429
Uploading 474, 479
User Manual 422
User Training 423
User-friendly 391, 406
Utility Programs 59-60, 96-98

-V-

Variable Addressing 235-236, 257
Ventura Publisher 513
Vertical Justification 508
View 610, 625
Virtual Telecommunication Access Method (VTAM) 459, 477

VisiCalc 27, 69, 202-204
Volatile Memory 30, 50
Volume Label 115-116, 129

-W-

Warm Boot 107-108, 128
What You See Is What You Get (WYSIWYG) 509
Wide Area Network (WAN) 467, 478
Wildcards 126-127
Winchester Disks 45, 52
Wiring Closet 472, 479
Word Processing 135-144
Word Processing Concepts 136-138
Word Processing Software 64-67, 79
 DisplayWrite 67, 141-144
 Microsoft Word 67, 139-140, 143-144
 WordPerfect 67, 135, 142-144, 151-190, 560-573
 WordStar 67, 138-139, 143-144
Word Processing Steps 137-138
Word Wrap 155, 190
WordPerfect 67, 135, 142-144, 151-190, 560-573
 Block Commands 182-188
 Booting the System 151-153
 Document Creation 158-167
 Editing 167-172
 Exiting 167, 172, 182, 189
 File Handling 173-177
 Formatting 177-182
 Function Keys 156-157
 Keyboard Functions 153-154
 Labels 571-572
 Learning 158-189, 560-573
 Macros 573
 Merging 566-571, 573
 Printing 172
 Saving 166, 170, 182
 Spelling 561-564, 573
 Status Line 153, 190
 Thesaurus 565, 573
WordPerfect Diskettes
 Learning 143-144
 Printer 142
 Speller 142, 144
 Thesaurus 142-144
 WordPerfect 142
WordStar 67, 138-139, 143-144
Worksheet 199, 208
Wozniak, Steve 25
Write-protect notch 43, 51

-X-

Xenix 94, 96

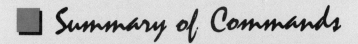

Summary of Commands

SUMMARY OF DOS COMMANDS

Command	Function
BACKUP	Makes backup copies of file(s) from one diskette or hard disk to another.
CD (Change Directory)	Changes from one directory to another.
CHKDSK	Produce report on status of files on diskette to assure their integrity.
CLS	Clear the screen.
COMP	Compares specified files of one diskette to those of another diskette.
COPY	Copy one or more files from one diskette to another.
COPY CONsole	Creates batch files by copying the file as typed from the console (keyboard).
DATE	Change current date.
DEL or ERASE	Remove one or more files from a diskette.
DIR	Lists the contents of a specified diskette.
DISKCOMP	Compares the contents of two diskettes.
DISKCOPY	Copies the contents of an entire diskette to another diskette.
EDLIN	Enters EDLIN text editor environment.
I	Inserts new line(s) in EDLIN file.
L	Displays file loaded with EDLIN.
D	Deletes line(s) in an EDLIN file.
E	Ends EDLIN session.
FDISK	Prepares hard disk for use by dividing it initially into from one to four partitions.
FORMAT	Prepare new diskettes for data storage.
FORMAT C:	Prepares hard disk for data storage.
MD (Make Directory)	Creates a new directory or subdirectory.
PATH	Specifies directory for DOS to search for command or batch file requests not found in current directory.
PROMPT	Imbedded in AUTOEXEC.BAT file to allow DOS prompt to display name of current directory or other desired information.
RD (Remove Directory)	Removes directories that have become obsolete.
REN	Assign a new name to a specified file.
RESTORE	Restores files that have been backed up using the BACKUP command.
SORT	Sorts input data in ascending or descending order and writes them to a specified output device.
SYS	Transfer system files to formatted diskette.
TIME	Change current time.
TREE	Displays all directory paths on specified hard disk.
TYPE	Display contents of any file on a diskette.
VER	Determine current DOS version being used.
VOL	Display volume number of specified diskette.

SUMMARY OF WORDPERFECT COMMANDS

Command	Function
BLOCK FORMAT	Changes the format of a specified block of text.
BLOCK DELETE	Erases a specified block of text.
BLOCK MOVE	Moves a specified block of text.
BLOCK COPY	Makes a copy of a specified block of text in a specified location.
DELETE	Deletes a file from a diskette.
EXIT	Leaves a file or WordPerfect.
INSERT	Inserts text within the existing text.
LIST FILES: CHANGE DIR	Changes the default directory or makes a new directory.
LIST FILES: COPY	Copy contents of the current file to another file, drive, or directory.
LIST FILES: DELETE	Erases a file from your diskette.
LIST FILES: EXIT	Leaves the LIST FILES menu.
LIST FILES: LOOK	Scrolls through a document without allowing changes.
LIST FILES: PRINT	Sends a file to a designated printer.
LIST FILES: RENAME	Changes a file name.
LIST FILES: RETRIEVE	Obtains a copy of a file from a diskette.
LIST FILES: TEXT IN	Brings a DOS (ASCII) file to the screen.
LIST FILES: WORD SEARCH	Selects all files that contain one or more specific words.
LIST FILES	Handles file management in WordPerfect by pressing F5.
PRINT	Provides a hardcopy of a document.
RETRIEVE	Retrieves a file from a diskette.
RIGHT-JUSTIFY	Aligns the right-end of lines in a document.
SAVE	Stores a file on a diskette.

SUMMARY OF LOTUS 1-2-3 COMMANDS

Command	Function
/COPY	Copies a cell or range of cells to another location in the worksheet.
/DATA	Subcommands perform operations such as sorting and querying on a 1-2-3 database.
/FILE	Subcommands perform file handling functions such as retrieving, saving, listing, or combining files.
/GRAPH	Specify settings for 1-2-3's graphics capabilities.
/MOVE	Allows you to move the contents of a cell or range of cells to another area of the worksheet.
/PRINT	Allows you to get a hardcopy of your worksheet or send your worksheet to an ASCII file.
/QUIT	Used to exit the 1-2-3 environment at the end of a session.
/RANGE	Subcommands perform functions such as the formatting, naming, or protecting of a specified portion of the worksheet.
/SYSTEM	Allows you to switch back and forth from your 1-2-3 worksheet to DOS.
/WORKSHEET	Subcommands perform functions such as formatting, set column width, add or delete rows and columns, or erase the worksheet.

SUMMARY OF dBASE III PLUS COMMANDS

Command	Function
APPEND	Allows the addition of records to the end of an existing database file.
BROWSE	Used to scan, edit, and append records to the active database file.
COPY	Allows a file to be copied into another file with a different name; also used to copy specified fields instead of an entire file.
COPY STRUCTURE	Duplicates the structure of the database in the active work area.
CREATE	Creates a new data file.
CREATE REPORT	Creates a report file (.frm).
DELETE	Marks a record in the active database for deletion but does not actually remove it from the file.
DELETE FILE	Permanently erases the file from the diskette.
DIR	Lists all database files on the diskette in the current disk dirve.
DISPLAY	Displays the record to which the pointer is currently pointing.
EDIT	Alters the contents of a record(s) in an active database file.
INDEX	Sets up an index file (.ndx).
INSERT	Allows the addition of records at any position in an existing database.
LIST	Displays all records in the active file.
LIST FILES	Lists all or specified files on the directory of a diskette.
LIST OFF	Displays specified records from the active file without their record numbers.
LIST STRUCTURE	Displays the file structure of the active .dbf file.
MODIFY REPORT	Used to make changes to an existing report form.
MODIFY STRUCTURE	Used to alter the record structure of an existing database file.
PACK	Permanently erases records that have been marked for deletion.
RECALL	Reinstates all records that have been marked for deletion.
REPORT	Takes data from the active database file and uses a specified report form file (.frm) to print a report.
SELECT	Chooses a work area in which to open a database file, or changes the active database file to one in a specified work area.
SET DEFAULT	Used to change the current disk drive setting.
SET HEADINGS	Allows the setting of field or column headings on or off.
SET RELATION	Links the databases to two different work areas.
SORT	Allows the active database to be arranged in a specified order and stored under a new file name.
USE	Signals dBASE to activate a specified file.